Media Law

Media Law

RALPH L. HOLSINGER
Indiana University, Bloomington

Consulting Editor
PETER SANDMAN
Rutgers University

Random House New York

First Edition
987654321
Copyright © 1987 by Random House

Library of Congress Cataloging in Publication Data

Holsinger, Ralph L.
  Media law.

  Includes indexes.
  1. Mass media—law and legislation—United States.
2. Press law—United States. I. Title.
KF2750.H65   1986   343.73′0998   86-26148
                         347.303998
ISBN 0-394-32953-8

Manufactured in the United States of America

Cover Design: Fred Charles
Book Design: Glen M. Edelstein

PREFACE

Media Law is written for today's journalism students—in the broad meaning that term has assumed in the 1980s. Thus, while major chapters are designed to help future reporters and editors recognize and avoid the many legal pitfalls that await the unwary, there is essential information here, too, for students planning careers in broadcasting, advertising, public relations, and corporate communications.

I began this book because my students made it clear to me that they wanted a text written in the language of journalists, and they wanted it to be interesting. Because I had worked as a newspaper reporter and editor for eighteen years before I became a teacher, I thought I could meet their demands. During my newspaper career, I had covered state and federal courts, the Ohio Legislature, Congress, and federal administrative agencies, which gave me a good grounding in how laws are made and applied. As a reporter, I had to meet the daily challenge of gathering news, frequently from reluctant sources, and writing for a mass audience. This gave me experience in translating the complexities of government and law into language readers could understand.

Later, as managing editor of a metropolitan daily newspaper, my horizons were broadened. I learned to consult lawyers to avoid legal problems that had not seemed very important to me as a reporter. I also became much more aware of those gray boundaries of the law where ethical considerations come into play, which not only made me appreciate the many points at which journalists risk collision with the legal system, but aroused my interest in learning more about what we mean when we talk about the First Amendment guarantee of freedom of speech and press.

Thus, when I joined the journalism faculty at Indiana University, Bloomington, more than twenty years ago, I began a systematic reading of First Amendment and media law cases. I am forever indebted to the late Austin Clifford, professor of torts at the Indiana University School of Law, who taught me at an early stage that the meaning of the law is found in the cases and cannot be understood without them. Thus, *Media Law* is based firmly on the cases. Some of these have defined the constitutional limits of the freedom of the press clause of the First Amendment. Others have interpreted the many statutes applying to journalists and the mass media. The major Supreme Court cases—most notably *New York Times* v. *Sullivan*, *Gertz* v. *Robert Welch, Inc.*, and *Branzburg* v. *Hayes*—are given extensive treatment. Students need to become familiar with these cases, above all others, because courts look to them for guidance in the important areas of libel and the right of journalists to protect their confidential sources.

While I place great reliance on the cases, I recognize that decisions usually are written by judges for lawyers. This means that students, and even journalism professors, can find them hard to understand. Thus, I have used verbatim excerpts only where I thought the judges wrote more clearly than I could. Where they did not, I have tried to translate their legal language into words students can understand. In this I have been guided by my students who have been kind enough to evaluate my lectures as usually clear and interesting. As a teacher, I have always acted in the belief that to be boring is to commit a cardinal sin. I have tried to apply that belief to my writing.

Media Law is written on three levels. At its heart, it is a practical guide to the legal problems likely to confront professional journalists. At this level, I have given a great deal of emphasis to libel, invasion of privacy, and the clash between lawyers and journalists over the right of accused persons to a fair trial and the right of journalists to protect their confidential sources and information. But there also is practical guidance for students who plan careers in broadcast news, advertising, and public relations. The chapter on copyright law should be of interest to students thinking of a career in the creative arts. A final chapter covers the business aspects of the media, including the right to distribute news and opinion in public places.

At a second level, *Media Law* is a guide to the meaning of the speech and press clauses of the First Amendment. I have written these parts of the book in the belief that the right to speak and write without hindrance from government is absolutely essential to a free society. The First Amendment says flatly, "Congress shall make no law . . . abridging the freedom of speech, or of the press." And yet the Congress has passed laws restricting both freedoms, and the Supreme Court has upheld them. I think it is important that students get some idea of why we have a First Amendment and of why limits have been imposed on it. Freedom can not be taken for granted—in today's world, the freedoms of speech and press are endangered species. Each generation must care enough about freedom of expression to protect it, or it will be lost here, too. Therefore, I have written about the development of the idea of freedom, the philosophy underlying the First Amendment, the various theories as to its meaning, and the major cases interpreting the speech and press clauses.

At the third level, I have gone beyond the law into the realm of ethics. I think this dimension makes *Media Law* unique among communications law texts. Each chapter ends with a section, "In the Professional World," that discusses the ethical aspects of its subject matter. These sections are not exhaustive, but they are written to suggest that the question, "Is it right?" is sometimes as important as the question, "Is it legal?"

Shortly after I became a teacher, the late Richard G. Gray became chairman of Indiana University's then Department of Journalism. He entrusted me with organizing our first senior seminar on the philosophy and ethics of the media. That has developed into a course all seniors are required to take. I still teach it occasionally. In the early 1970s, I was cochairman, along with George Gill of the *Louisville Courier-Journal* and Paul Poorman of the *Detroit News*, of the first Professional Standards Committee of the Associated Press Managing Editors Association. In effect, it was a committee on ethics and later under other leadership drafted the association's code of ethics. Over the years, its studies have contributed significantly to raising the level of ethical performance among newspaper professionals and to the growing body of literature on journalism ethics. I hope that "In the Professional World" will stimulate students to think about the ethical dimension of whatever branch of journalism they enter.

A major problem in writing a textbook on media law is deciding what to leave out. State and federal courts decide hundreds of cases each year in which the media or media professionals are involved as plaintiffs, defendants, or interested parties. Fortunately, most of these simply apply settled principles and therefore plow no new legal ground. Other court decisions may seem to change the law, but do so at such a low level that the decision can be put on hold until a higher court either reverses or affirms. Still other decisions change the law, but in esoteric detail of interest only to lawyers specializing in the field. Then there are those decisions, frequently by the Supreme Court of the United States, that make significant changes in principle. In this book, I have tried to focus on the latter. To do otherwise would result in clutter more likely to confuse than to inform students. Therefore, I have given major treatment to two kinds of case. First, of course, are the landmark decisions that have established essential principles of media law. Second are the cases that illustrate how other courts have applied the essential principles.

Part I deals with the origins and development of the idea that freedom of expression serves the public interest. Chapter 1 begins with a survey of the idea's historical origins, leading up to the adoption of the First Amendment as part of the Bill of Rights of the Constitution. The second part of the chapter examines the meaning of the First Amendment, first through the works of legal scholars, and then through the theories applied by the Supreme Court.

Chapter 2 is devoted exclusively to the various ways in which government officials at all levels have sought, and continue to seek, to prevent publications considered harmful to society or national security. When government acts directly to prevent publication, as it has in time of war, it is called censorship. When, as is more common, a court is asked to prevent publication, it is called prior restraint. Although some scholars believe that the purpose of the First Amendment was to prevent prior restraint, the Supreme Court has held that publication can be prevented if the government can demonstrate a compelling need for it.

Chapter 3 deals with the power of government to punish persons whose speech or writing threatens to harm national security. This is a power that was widely used during World War I, and again during the so-called Cold War with the Soviet Union after World War II, but has lain dormant since. However, at this writing, the Reagan administration has warned several newspapers, a news magazine, and a television network that they may be subject to punishment if they disclose too much detail about the CIA's intelligence gathering methods.

Part II covers libel, invasion of privacy, fair trial, the right of journalists to protect their confidential sources, and access to government information. Few months pass without a major confrontation between professional reporters and editors and the courts in one or more of these areas of media law.

Chapter 4 surveys the complex and volatile law of libel. Important Supreme Court decisions, two of them handed down in the 1985–1986 session, have made this one of the most important areas of First Amendment law. The keys to understanding this chapter are found in the sections devoted to *New York Times* v. *Sullivan* and *Gertz* v. *Robert Welch, Inc.*

Chapter 5 deals with invasion of privacy. While polls show that it is a major concern of many persons, courts have been reluctant thus far to return privacy judgments against the media primarily because newsworthiness is a strong defense, and the Supreme Court has held that facts found in the public records of a court are not actionable. Certain aspects of privacy law that apply to advertisers and public relations practitioners are also discussed in Chapter 5.

Chapter 6 begins with a survey of criminal justice procedures and moves to an examination of the meaning of a fair trial. At the heart of this chapter is a conflict between two guarantees found in the Bill of Rights. Journalists believe that the freedom of the press clause gives them the sole right to decide what news they can publish about the criminal justice system. Lawyers and judges believe that on occasion news can be of such a nature as to prevent a fair trial, thus violating a defendant's rights as defined by the Sixth Amendment.

Chapter 7 deals with another major source of conflict between the courts and the media: the right of journalists to protect their confidential informants. The chapter is based on *Branzburg* v. *Hayes*, a Supreme Court decision widely seen at the time as a defeat for the news media. However, the Court was so badly divided that lower courts, particularly in the federal system, have found in it a limited First Amendment privilege for journalists.

Chapter 8 is devoted in large part to the Freedom of Information Act, a federal statute prescribing the terms under which the media and others can obtain data from federal agencies. The Act contains nine exceptions, seven of which have resulted in a considerable body of case law. The chapter ends with a unique feature—the answers to six commonly asked questions about access to information at state and local levels.

Part III brings together the media and aspects of the media that are regulated by government. Here First Amendment guarantees have been held subordinate to more compelling public interests. Part III has chapters on obscenity, which the Supreme Court has held to be so lacking in ideas that it can be banned outright; broadcasting, which is the only news medium licensed by the government; advertising, which only recently was held to be protected by the First Amendment, but to a lesser degree than news and opinion; copyright, which permits creators of original works in any medium to protect them from unauthorized copying, and the business aspects of the media, which are subject to the same degree of regulation as any other kind of business.

The key to Chapter 9 is *Miller* v. *California*, the Supreme Court's most recent attempt to define obscenity. In that decision, the Court gave local juries broad discretion in determining whether sexually explicit materials violate community standards. The topic is of interest mainly because it helps define the limits of First Amendment protection for materials some find objectionable.

Chapter 10 focuses on those aspects of broadcasting law that have survived a movement toward deregulation that began with President Carter. At this writing, broadcasting stations still must offer equal opportunities for air time to political candidates and they must abide by the fairness doctrine, which requires stations to present all sides of controversial public issues. The closing section focuses on cable television, which has cast doubt on the scarce frequency theory, which for more than fifty years has supported government regulation of broadcasting.

Chapter 11 surveys the Supreme Court decisions which established First Amendment protection for commercial advertising. This protection is limited to truthful advertising for legal goods and services, and may be overridden if government can establish a compelling reason for regulating or even prohibiting advertising. This chapter also explains the media's right to refuse advertising and examines the largely discredited argument that the public should have a mandatory right to present its views in the media. It includes a 1986 Supreme Court decision holding that public utilities can not be compelled to include special interest messages with their bills.

Chapter 12, on copyright, is largely concerned with the distinction between fair use and infringement. It includes the Supreme Court's 1985 decision in *Harper & Row* v. *Nation*, rejecting the argument that highly newsworthy infringements should be protected by the First Amendment. This chapter also contains an explanation of plagiarism that my students found useful.

The final chapter focuses on the business aspects of the media. Much of it deals with the application of antitrust law to the media, including President Kennedy's ill-fated attempt to preserve competitive newspapers. It also presents the leading cases dealing with the right to place newsracks in public places and with the taxation of the media.

I have tried to avoid making one chapter dependent upon another. I have done this in recognition of the fact that some instructors elect not to cover all that comes under the broad topic of media law. However, I also have learned from the many instructors who have read all or part of this manuscript that there is little agreement as to what can be left out. Therefore, I have decided to offer it all and trust those who adopt the book to decide what they need and what can be ignored.

While it was student reaction to the textbooks I chose that spurred me to think about a book of my own, nothing would have happened had it not been for two persons, Richard G. Gray and Roth Wilkofsky. Dick not only was my chairman, director, and dean for fifteen years, he was my friend. He believed that I had a book in me and he let me know during our annual review chats that I ought to write it. When I decided to give it a try, Roth, as a senior editor at Random House, was willing to consider a proposal. From the beginning, he has given me strong support, and showed the utmost patience when time proved that writing a book is not as easy as I once naively thought it was. He has gone many extra miles with me to bring the work to fruition. For that, I wish there were stronger words than "thank you." I deeply regret that Dick Gray died before I finished this book.

At a critical moment in the project, Dr. Peter Sandman, professor of journalism at Rutgers University, agreed with Roth's request to read the manuscript. His helpful advice resulted in major restructuring designed to make the book a better teaching instrument, and I am grateful for his help.

I also wish to thank the following reviewers of various drafts of the manuscript for their helpful suggestions: Douglas Anderson, Arizona State University; Edmund Blinn, Iowa State University; John J. Breen, University of Connecticut; James K. Buckalew, San Diego State University; T. Barton Carter, Boston University; Bill Chamberlin, University of North Carolina, Chapel Hill; Carolyn Stewart Dyer, University of Iowa; Marian Huttenstine, University of Alabama; Paul Jess, University of Kansas; Kelly Leiter, University of Tennessee; Kent R. Middleton, University of Georgia; John Murray, Michigan State University; James M. Neal, University of Nebraska, Lincoln; Mack Palmer, University of Oklahoma; P. E. Paulin, Oklahoma State University; David Protess, Northwestern University; J. D. Rayburn, University of Kentucky; Jack Schnedler, Northwestern University; Todd Simon, Michigan State University; Don Smith, Pennsylvania State University; William Steng, Oklahoma State University; and John D. Stevens, University of Michigan.

I also want to acknowledge support from two lawyers, my long-time friend Francis T. Martin of Cincinnati and Ralph Fuchs, emeritus professor of law at the Indiana University

School of Law. Both were formidable advocates who were willing to tolerate a journalist's attempts to talk law and offer constructive advice. I regret that neither lived to judge his pupil's work.

I have been helped, too, by my students who have been willing, semester after semester for more than fifteen years, to enroll in my communications law classes despite my reputation as a tough grader. They have taught me what sells and what does not when your audience is made up of twenty-year-olds trying to learn enough law to pass a required course on the way to a degree. A goodly number of my students have thought enough of my wares to desert journalism and go on to law school.

Dr. Herbert Terry of the Telecommunications faculty at Indiana University offered helpful advice, and more documents than I could use, for the chapter on broadcasting.

Keith A. Buckley and Linda K. Fariss, research librarians at the I.U. School of Law, have been most helpful in finding obscure citations and essential reference materials.

Finally, I acknowledge the support of Elizabeth, my wife. It has not been easy for her to share me with a project that has demanded a goodly part of my time on more days than I care to count.

Despite their involvement in the work, none of the above should be held responsible for any errors or omissions that have made their way into print. The buck stopped at the point where my fingers met the keyboard of my typewriter.

Ralph L. Holsinger

CONTENTS

xi

PART 1

FREEDOM OF SPEECH AND FREEDOM OF THE PRESS

CHAPTER *1*

FREEDOM OF SPEECH AND PRESS: HISTORY AND PHILOSOPHY

For more than two thousand years, people have struggled to win the right to speak freely and critically about political, economic, religious, and social issues. And for most of that time, in most places, they did so at the risk of severe punishment, including death. Even today, many governments consider critics of official policies enemies of the state, to be tortured, imprisoned, or exiled. The Soviet Union and the Union of South Africa are but two examples.

Those who believe in freedom of speech and press argue that such freedom ensures government that is responsive to the needs of the people. Only if men and women are free to talk about their problems can they arrive at mutually acceptable solutions. The Supreme Court of the United States has endorsed that view, holding in several cases that debate on public issues should be robust, uninhibited, and wide open.

There are also those who believe that the news media should serve government by helping it win public approval for policies designed by government officials to meet the people's needs. In this view, uninformed criticism merely creates dissatisfaction and interferes with the ability of government to perform.

The debate between those who advocate freedom of expression and those who argue for restraint continues today. Every recent American president has complained that a "negative press" has made it difficult to carry out his policies. Nor are critics of freedom of speech and press confined to government. When American Nazis have demonstrated in Jewish neighborhoods, or when Ku Klux Klansmen have burned crosses in cities with a large black population, riots have resulted. At another level, people have sought to censor or ban MTV, the lyrics of popular rock songs, and movies featuring sex and violence because they believe such things contribute to the decay of our culture. So the question of how far freedom of speech and press should be permitted to go remains important as we approach the end of the twentieth century.

This chapter presents a brief history of the development of the idea that people ought to be free to criticize their rulers. The first part is designed to highlight the forces that led to the American Declaration of Independence and the Constitution, particularly the First Amendment guarantees of freedom of speech and press. The second part examines the philosophy supporting and limiting freedom of speech and press.

Major Cases

American Communications Association v. *Douds*, 339 U.S. 382, 70 S.Ct. 674, 94 L.Ed. 925 (1950).

Schenck v. *United States*, 249 U.S. 47, 39 S.Ct. 247, 63 L.Ed. 470 (1919).

THE HISTORY OF FREEDOM OF SPEECH AND PRESS

The Idea of Freedom

In the fifth century B.C., the city-state of Athens adopted a form of democracy. The experiment proved short-lived, but the idea that people should be able to govern themselves survived. So did the companion idea that people should be free to talk about the policies of government and decide for themselves which are good and which are bad. Socrates and, later, Plato based their philosophy on the belief that truth is best reached through a process called *dialectic*—rigorous discussion from which no fact or argument is withheld. Plato believed that such discussion is essential if a government is to serve its people well. He wrote a book, the *Republic*, describing an ideal form of government in which the good, the beautiful, and the true would prevail.

However, Plato was realistic enough to recognize that those who achieve power in government are not always willing to submit their policies to rigorous discussion. A notable passage from the *Republic* illustrates the dilemma faced not only by Plato but by other advocates of freewheeling discussion of government policies:

> Till philosophers become kings, or those now named kings and rulers give themselves to philosophy truly and rightly, and these two things—political power and philosophic thought—come together, and the commoner minds, which at present seek only the one or the other, are kept out by force, states will have no rest from their troubles . . . and, if I am right, man will have none.[1]

Plato put those words in the mouth of Socrates, who had been executed by order of the Athenian rulers before the *Republic* was written. Socrates had fought bravely for Athens against its enemies, but when he was not serving as a soldier he wandered the streets questioning authority, particularly that based on religious belief. He acquired followers, Plato among them, and at the age of thirty-one was deemed such a threat to Athens that he was charged with corrupting the morals of the young and sentenced to death by drinking hemlock.

The Athenian flirtation with government by the people, and with the freedom of speech that accompanied it, did not last long. But the writings of Plato gave birth to an idea that has lived ever since—Truth can best be reached through free discussion.

Divine Right versus the Rights of the People

Ancient Rome also experimented with a form of popular rule. During the Roman Republic, 509–265 B.C., the people elected two chief executives, and nobles and plebeians elected members of a senate, which enacted laws. But as Rome gobbled up more and more of what is now Italy, the fruits of conquest enriched relatively few of its citizens. In time, the Republic foundered on internal dissension between wealthy aristocrats and the masses of the poor. Some of the forms remained, but rule henceforth was by the rich and the powerful.

For more than fifteen centuries thereafter, most of the peoples of the Western world lived under various forms of autocracy, a system in which a few persons at the top impose their will on the masses at the bottom. Such rulers drew their power from three

---

1. Benjamin Jowett, trans., *Republic of Plato* (Oxford: Clarendon Press, 1908), V: 473.

sources: (1) They were in active command of the nation's armed forces. (2) They either controlled the nation's economic wealth or were closely allied with those who did. And in most states, especially from the fourth century on, (3) they invoked the spiritual power of the church to preach the doctrine of obedience, reinforced by the promise of a better life in the world hereafter. In time, this alliance between church and state became formalized in the political system known as *divine right:* Kings ruled because they were ordained by God to do so. Therefore, to question their authority was not only a crime, known as **sedition,** but **blasphemy** as well. Critics of a king's decisions might lose their livelihoods or their property, or they might be tortured or killed by the king's soldiers. And, as blasphemers, they might be condemned to eternal damnation.

In the fifteenth century, the triple ramparts of autocratic power came under siege. The development of printing, the Protestant Reformation, and the Renaissance set in motion forces that even the cruelest tyrants could not put down forever. Printing, generally attributed to Johann Gutenberg in Germany, took from the clergy its power to control the dissemination of knowledge. For centuries, books had been copied by hand, generally in the monasteries, which meant that the ability to read, and to transfer written information, was in large part the domain of the clergy. When printing made books more readily available, many more people had an incentive to learn to read. From the mid-sixteenth century on, what they read, among other things, were tracts written by various religious dissenters, starting with Martin Luther. Luther, also a German, was a

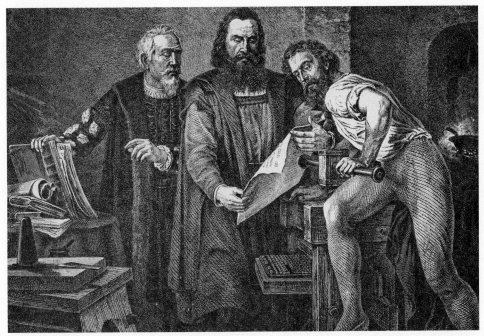

By developing the art of printing, Johann Gutenberg (center) offered an incentive for people in all walks of life to learn to read. This fifteenth-century development was one of the forces that created that remarkable explosion of knowledge known as the Renaissance. With knowledge came the questioning of authority that ultimately made possible both religious and political freedom. (Culver Pictures)

member of the Roman Catholic clergy who became appalled by what he saw as that body's corruption. He and his followers, who came to be known as Protestants, took the position that anyone who could read the Bible could figure out what it meant without having to rely on the official doctrine imposed by the pope and his bishops.

Authority was being questioned in other areas, too. Throughout Western Europe, writers, painters, sculptors, artisans, musicians, natural scientists, and others demonstrated that one did not have to look backward to ancient authority to find truth or beauty. Explorers demonstrated that the earth was not flat, as the Church had said it was. In Italy, Galileo peered at the planets through a crude telescope and concluded that, despite passages in Scripture, the earth was not the center of the universe. Such heresy did not go unchallenged by the Inquisition, the Church's tribunal, and in his old age, Galileo was forced to recant.

The forces of knowledge, once set in motion, could not be stayed. By the seventeenth century, dissenters in England were questioning not only the authority of the Church, but that of the Crown. One king, Charles I, was beheaded in 1649, leading the English monarchy to agree to share its power with an elected Parliament. Today, in royal ritual, Queen Elizabeth II is referred to as the Protector of the Faith, meaning the Church of England, but that is about all that remains of the divine right of kings.

The transfer of power from monarchs to people required drastic changes in political theory. When kings ruled because they were ordained by God to do so, the people were their subjects. Kings gave orders; underlings were expected to obey those orders without question. Those rash enough to question the wisdom of a king's policies might find themselves charged with **seditious libel,** a crime punishable with death. But when most of a king's power had been transferred to an elected parliament, the old rules came under question. Members of Parliament represented the people, in whom the authority of the state ultimately resided. Did this not mean that the people had a right to inform themselves about government policies? And did it not mean that they could criticize those policies without being charged with seditious libel?

One who raised these questions was John Milton, who is remembered today mainly for such enduring classics as *Paradise Lost*. However, during the Civil War that followed Charles's beheading, Milton served as an official of, and apologist for, the parliamentary government of Oliver Cromwell. During that period, Milton came under attack from some of the Puritan members of Parliament because he had written a tract arguing that partners to an unhappy marriage should have the right to get a divorce. Puritans disapproved of divorce. To compound Milton's crime, he had managed to get his tract published without first obtaining approval from a government censor. According to the law in effect at that time, nothing could be published until it had received a license from the government. The purpose was to nip any seditious libel in the bud.

As Milton's experience suggests, the licensing system had begun to break down in the seventeenth century as printing presses became more common. Milton responded to the attack on his works by proposing that the system be abolished. In 1644, he composed "A Speech for the Liberty of UNLICENC'D PRINTING," which, published in essay form, bears the title *Areopagitica*. It is a passionate yet well-reasoned argument against government censorship of written works dealing with political policy.

It is illogical to assume, Milton wrote, that any government can satisfy all its people. It is equally illogical to assume that everything a government does will be done justly.

But if the people are free to talk and write about government policies, and if those who govern are willing to pay attention, the result should be an improvement in the quality of government and the well-being of the people.

Milton, like Plato, had reservations about how far freedom of expression ought to go and who could be trusted with it. Note the conflicting currents running through this passage from *Areopagitica:*

> I deny not, but that it is of greatest concernment in the Church and Commonwealth, to have a vigilant eye how Bookes demeane themselves, as well as men; and thereafter to confine, imprison, and do sharpest justice on them as malefactors; for Bookes are not absolutely dead things, but do contain a potencie of life in them to be as áctive as that soule was whose progeny they are; nay they do preserve as in a violl the purest efficacie and extraction of that living intellect that bred them.[2]

Milton's contribution to the advancement of freedom of expression lies in his recognition that such freedom is in the public interest. He summarized his message in a notable passage:

> And though all the windes of doctrin were let loose to play upon the earth, so Truth be in the field, we do injuriously by licencing and prohibiting to misdoubt her strength. Let her and Falshood grapple; who ever knew Truth put to the wors, in a free and open encounter.[3]

Milton's optimism about the ability of truth to prevail did not take into account the cruel refinements of repression and propaganda used by twentieth-century dictatorships. Nor could he anticipate the unyielding positions taken by both sides in the debate over a woman's right to have an abortion. Despite the light of reason emitted by *Areopagitica*, Milton himself was willing to **censor** the works of Catholic writers. But then he was a Protestant at a time when differences between the two faiths were taken as seriously in London as they now are in Northern Ireland.

Old ideas die hard. After 1660, when the English Parliament restored Charles II to the throne, but with less power than his father had had, Englishmen continued to suffer cruel deaths for the crime of seditious libel. One of the more interesting of the many cases reported in *Howell's State Trials*[4] involved a printer, John Twyn, whose shop was raided by constables in the early hours of the morning. They found smudged page proofs of a book arguing that a king whose decrees violated the "law of God" should be called to account by the people. Twyn and his helpers were thrown into jail and denied contact with even their wives until they were brought out months later to stand trial. Accused of "imagining and intending the death" of the king, they were tried without counsel. After thirty minutes of testimony, dominated by the judge, a jury found them guilty and condemned Twyn to a horrible death.

The trial had overtones that are at issue today. The author of the book was not known, and much of the judge's questioning was directed at persuading Twyn to name

---

2. *Complete Poetry and Works of John Milton* (New York: Modern Library, 1950), pp. 681–82.
3. Ibid., p. 719.
4. 15 Charles II 1663, p. 513.

the author. Such questions followed Twyn to the scaffold, where he was told that his soul might rest more easily in the hereafter if he were to identify the source of the offending work. It is not clear from Twyn's answers whether he remained silent because he did not know who had written the draft, or because he was protecting the author. But the terms of the sentence were carried out. He was forced to straddle a triangular wooden beam on which he was carried at shoulder height to the place of execution. There he was hanged, but not in such a way as to kill him. He was cut down, revived, and then forced to watch while his "privy-members" were cut off and burned. Finally, he was beheaded, and his body was hacked into four pieces. Each part was nailed above a different gate to the city to stand as a warning to others who might dare urge the overthrow of the king.

Twyn was a victim of a final Royalist backlash surrounding the king's return to England and the throne after exile in France. Milton, too, was a victim of it, but only to the extent of being driven out of public life. He died in 1674, twenty-one years before Parliament let the Printing Act expire; thus, he did not live to see licensed printing abolished in England.

There is a striking similarity between the ideas for which Twyn was executed and those that survive in John Locke's *Treatises on Government*, published in 1690. Locke designed these *Treatises* to rationalize the transfer of power from a king, who ruled by divine right, to a parliament that represented the people. This was a serious matter, as is evidenced by the fact that the shift of power was marked by nearly a century of turmoil, including a bloody civil war. In writing his *Treatises*, Locke borrowed the social-compact theory of the origins of government from Thomas Hobbes, an earlier political philosopher. This theory rests on the assumption that at some time in the past people recognized that they would be better off working together than they were in a "state of nature," where every family had to provide for all its needs. In that state, the only law was the "law of the jungle," which meant, in effect, that only the strongest or the most clever survived. Hobbes theorized that at some point people had become tired of fending for themselves and had agreed to surrender some of their independence in return for security. These agreements, or compacts, signaled the beginning of organized society and of rudimentary governments.

Locke expanded on Hobbes's social-compact theory and sought to formalize it. He wrote as one who had escaped Twyn's fate, although he, too, believed that those who govern should be held accountable to the people. Locke recognized that tyranny is not the sole province of absolute monarchs; majorities can also oppress minorities. To counter that possibility in newly created democracies, Locke advocated two safeguards:

1. People creating new governments should reduce the compact to writing in the form of a constitution. That document should clearly establish the limits of the government's power.

2. The people should make clear that they are not giving up all of the personal rights that were theirs in the state of nature. Life in the jungle may have been hard, but, Locke argued, some aspects of the freedom that went with it ought not be surrendered to any government.

As further barrier against oppression by majority vote, Locke argued that the powers of government ought to be divided three ways: An elected legislature should have the power to adopt laws; an independent executive branch should have the power to carry the laws into effect; and a court system should have the power to "dispense justice and decide the rights of the subject." Finally, all three branches of government should be constrained by a duty to the law of nature, which, in Locke's view, guaranteed the personal, or natural, rights retained by the people.

Under Locke's system, then, there would be a check on the will of the majority. People who believed a law violated their **natural rights** could appeal to the courts for justice. If the judges decided that the law did indeed infringe those rights, they had the duty to hold that the law was void. Further, Locke argued, the people have a right to resist officials who exceed the powers given them by the compact.

Locke's views gradually prevailed in England and, later, in the American colonies. In the eighteenth century, the rights of the people came to the fore in Anglo-Saxon countries and, at the end of the century, in France. Political thought literally was turned upside down. No longer was the power to govern seen as flowing from the top down. No longer were the common people required to obey without question whatever order a monarch might give them. Authority had shifted, in some parts of the world, to the people. With that authority came the right to choose their rulers, and to oust them if they abused their powers. This implied, at the least, the people's right to criticize those they had elevated to public office. Divine right had given way in some places to the rights of the people.

Speech in Colonial America ═══════════════════════════════════

When Locke wrote his *Treatises on Government*, the English colonies in America had been in existence for nearly a century. Already, some colonists were beginning to object to the idea of being ruled from London. Although each colony had a legislative body of some kind, the governors were appointed in London, and colonial laws were subject to veto by the British Parliament. In addition, laws enacted by Parliament were to be obeyed by the colonists as they were in the homeland. One of these was the law of seditious libel.

In 1734, that law was challenged in an action in the New York courts. John Peter Zenger, publisher of the *New York Weekly Journal*, had published articles accusing Governor William Cosby of dishonesty and oppression.[5] Cosby reacted by charging Zenger with seditious libel. Zenger spent nine months in jail awaiting trial, while his wife continued to publish the paper. When Zenger came to trial, he faced a rule of law that made it almost impossible for him to win. Under that rule, any words, whether they were true or false, that tended to undermine the people's faith in their government were punishable. During the trial, the judge instructed the jury that the truth of Zenger's articles was not at issue. Zenger's lawyer, Andrew Hamilton, invoked English precedent to argue that the jury could disregard the judge's instruction without fear of punishment. He also argued so eloquently that truth ought never to be libelous that the jury found Zenger not guilty. The verdict did not change the law of seditious libel—truth was still

---

5. Frederic Breakspear Farrar, "A Printer, a Lawyer, and the Free Press," *Editor & Publisher*, 3 August 1985. The article includes a facsimile of the *New York Weekly Journal* for 2 December 1734 reporting the order to burn several issues of the *Journal* because they had been declared seditious.

A SERIOUS

ADDRESS

TO. THE

INHABITANTS

OF THE COLONY OF

NEW-YORK,

Containing a full and minute SURVEY of the
BOSTON-PORT ACT, calculated to
excite our Inhabitants to confpire, with the other
Colonies on this Continent, in extricating that
unhappy Town from its unparalleled Diftreffes,
and for the actual Redemption, and Security of
our general Rights and Liberties.

NEW-YORK
Printed by JOHN HOLT, in Dock-STREET, near the COFFEE-HOUSE.
M,DCC,LXXIV.

Words become weapons in times of political crisis. This pamphlet, written by John Jay, was one of many used to stir up opposition to British policies prior to the American Revolution of 1776. Note the linking of the "Security of our general Rights" with liberty. The belief that people have natural rights that governments should respect was a common theme in the revolutionary literature of the time. (The Bettmann Archive)

not officially recognized as a defense for harmful criticism of government. However, the case is generally regarded as the beginning of press freedom in America because it was the first recorded victory in a Colonial court for the principle that people ought to be able to write and speak freely about their government.

The belief in such freedom was by no means universal. In the years leading up to the Revolution of 1776, editors who favored English rule were the victims of mob violence. However, persons who believed that the colonists were victims of oppressive laws enacted by a Parliament in which they had no representation found a ready outlet for their protests in newspapers, in pamphlets, and in the pulpits of many churches. Historian Lawrence Henry Gipson, in his definitive thirteen-volume study *The British Empire Before the American Revolution*,[6] lists freedom of discussion as one of the factors responsible for the break with Great Britain.

In his concluding volume, he says many Americans were familiar with the writings used to justify England's earlier rebellion against its monarchs:

> Thus armed, the colonial leaders seized their pens. The ideas they expressed were widely disseminated from the pulpit and other public rostrums and especially by the American press in innumerable letters to the editors of the forty-three colonial newspapers (published for brief or extended periods between 1763 and 1775), as well as in broadsides, pamphlets,

---

6. New York: Knopf, 1958–1967.

and books. Some of the writings were mere emotional outpourings, but others of a much higher order were addressed to the intellect and sought to rationalize the rights that all mankind should demand of any government. Taken together these expressions of intense opposition to the policies of the mother country by their very volume could have had only one effect—the implanting in the minds of Americans of a sense of urgency for the establishment of a new political order.[7]

That urgency took tangible form in 1776 in the Declaration of Independence, which touched off more than five years of war, leading to the creation of the United States of America. Both the Declaration and the Constitution, which established our present form of government in 1789, draw heavily from Locke's *Treatises on Government*. The first paragraph of the Declaration invokes the authority of "the Laws of Nature and of Nature's God" to justify separation from English authority. The Constitution, enacted in the name of "[w]e, the people of the United States," is a social compact of the kind Locke recommended.

The Constitution and the Bill of Rights

It is impossible at this distance to imagine what it must have been like to establish a new government stretching from Maine to Georgia along the Atlantic coast two hundred years ago. Having experienced what they regarded as tyranny under English rule, the founders seemed to have been clear about several things. They did not want a monarch, or an executive who could assume the powers of one. They believed that the people were the source of the government's power. They thought the primary responsibility for day-to-day governing should rest with the states. But they needed a central government to conduct relations with foreign countries, to protect them from foreign enemies, to create a monetary system, and to ensure the flow of commerce among the states and with other countries. However, they did not want that government to become strong enough to take away the powers of the states or certain basic liberties of the people.

After the colonists had won their freedom at Yorktown, with help from the French army and navy, they tried to get along with an almost powerless central government operating under the Articles of Confederation. When it became evident that such a government was not going to work, the states elected delegates who met in secret in Philadelphia for four months in 1787 and produced a brief document of seven articles. Including the names of its forty signers, the Constitution takes up about four pages of the *World Almanac*. Amendments added since it went into effect in 1789 take up another three and a half pages.

In simplest terms, the Constitution is a plan of government. It established the institutions of government—Congress, the Executive, headed by the president, and the Judiciary, headed by the Supreme Court of the United States. Numbered sections and subsections define the powers of each. Other articles define the relationship between the federal and state governments. Another prescribes the slow, deliberate procedure by which the Constitution can be amended.

As presented to the states for adoption, the Constitution said nothing about the rights of the people, including the right to speak and write freely about the actions of the

---

7. Gipson, vol. 13, *The Triumphant Empire*, 1967, pp. 193–94.

central government. The drafters had acted on the theory that they were creating a central government of carefully defined, limited powers. In their view, they had given that government no authority to meddle with the rights of its citizens. The Constitution's silence on the people's rights raised suspicions in some states. They made a point of conditioning their approval of the new union on the promise that the Constitution would be amended to protect the rights of individuals.

Within two years after the federal government began functioning in 1789, Congress proposed, and the states quickly ratified, ten amendments now known as the Bill of Rights. They were designed as barriers to prevent the new central government from trampling on the people's natural or personal rights. In large part, the subject matter of the amendments reflects specific injustices experienced by Americans during the latter days of British colonial rule. First among them is a concern with religion. Congress is neither to tax the people to support a state church nor to interfere with the right to worship as one pleases. Next is what appears to be a flat prohibition on any attempt by Congress to limit freedom of speech or of the press. Then there is a guarantee of the right of the people to assemble peacefully and to ask government "for a redress of grievances." Three of the amendments are designed to protect the privacy of the home and to prevent seizure of property. Five, with some overlapping, detail the rights of persons accused of crime.

Our focus is on the First Amendment, which reads:

> Congress shall make no law respecting an establishment of religion, or prohibiting the free exercise thereof; or abridging the freedom of speech, or of the press; or the right of the people peaceably to assemble, and to petition the Government for a redress of grievances.

Strangely, there is little in the debates of the time to show what the drafters meant when they wrote and adopted that amendment. Read literally, it seems to say that Congress has no authority to limit freedom of speech or of the press. The realities of the time suggest otherwise.

According to one view, the founders were influenced by Sir William Blackstone, whose *Commentaries on the Laws of England* was considered the definitive discussion of the meaning of the common law here as well as in England. He wrote that punishment of "blasphemous, immoral, treasonable, schismatical, seditious, or scandalous libels" did not infringe on freedom of the press:

> The liberty of the press is indeed essential to the nature of a free state; but this consists in laying no previous restraints upon publications, and not in freedom from censure for criminal matter when published. Every freeman has an undoubted right to lay what sentiments he pleases before the public: to forbid this is to destroy the freedom of the press: but if he publishes what is improper, mischievous, or illegal, he must take the consequences of his own temerity.[8]

In this view, England had enjoyed liberty of the press since the Printing Act had expired in 1695, and the American colonies since 1725 when the licensing act was

---

8. William Blackstone, *Commentaries on the Laws of England*, facsimile ed. (Chicago: University of Chicago Press, 1979), vol. 4, pp. 151–52.

permitted to expire on this side of the Atlantic. But if writers knew they might suffer Twyn's fate or languish in jail like Zenger, how likely were they to share their views with the public?

Clearly, Blackstone's view of liberty of the press was a limited one. People could say or write what they pleased as long as they were prepared to take the consequences. If words violated a law, or were even considered "improper [or] mischievous," the writer might well end up in prison, if not on the scaffold.

Only scanty written evidence remains as to what the founders meant when they sought to protect freedom of speech and of the press. Thomas Jefferson, who wrote the Declaration of Independence, and James Madison, who wrote the First Amendment, seem to have rejected the English common law of seditious libel.[9] Benjamin Franklin, a member of the committee that drafted the Declaration and a delegate to the convention that drafted the Constitution, said in 1789 during a discussion of the freedom of speech clause in the Pennsylvania constitution: "[I]f by the liberty of the press were to be understood merely the liberty of discussing the propriety of public measures and political opinions, let us have as much of it as you please. On the other hand, if it means liberty to calumniate another, there ought to be some limit."[10] That he would put some limits on liberty of speech is notable in light of the fact that he made his living as a successful printer and publisher until he became caught up in public life in 1748.

The first ten amendments to the Constitution—the Bill of Rights—took effect in 1791. At that point, the United States not only had a form of government based squarely on John Locke's *Treatises on Government*, it also had taken steps to guarantee the rights of the people, an idea borrowed from Thomas Hobbes. In a sense, the Bill of Rights created a law above the law to which people could appeal, through the courts, when they believed their freedom was being violated. The Supreme Court has held on numerous occasions that laws, or acts of public officials, which violate rights guaranteed by the first ten amendments are void.

The Sedition Act of 1798

Within a decade after the adoption of the First Amendment, freedom of speech was put to the test and lost. Reacting to the possibility that inflamed passions might draw the United States into a renewed war between England and France, Congress adopted the Sedition Act of 1798, which was plainly a seditious libel law. The Act made it a crime, punishable by fine and imprisonment, to engage in harmful criticism of President John Adams and his policies.

The Sedition Act had its origins in the highly charged partisan politics of the time. President Adams headed the Federalist party, which was sympathetic to England while it wanted to keep the United States out of the war. The Federalists also believed in a strongly centralized government in which the president played a dominant role. Ranged

---

9. Zechariah Chafee, Jr., *Free Speech in the United States* (Cambridge: Harvard University Press, 1941), and Leonard W. Levy, *Legacy of Suppression* (Cambridge: Belknap Press of Harvard University Press, 1960).

10. Chafee, *Free Speech in the United States*, Atheneum ed. (New York, 1969), p. 17.

in opposition were the Republicans, headed by Vice-President Thomas Jefferson. Theirs was a party of small farmers and artisans who mistrusted a strong central government. Party members leaned toward the French, remembering their help in the Revolution. It soon became apparent that the Sedition Act was aimed primarily at the editors of Republican newspapers.

Viewed from the vantage point of today, there is no doubt that the Sedition Act was a serious abridgment of freedom of speech and of the press. And yet, judging from the records of the time, there were few who believed in 1798 that it violated the First Amendment guarantees. The debate in Congress preceding passage of the Act indicates that the amendment was seen only as a protection against direct **censorship.** One speaker said that the First Amendment could not prevent punishment of an editor who published material that "offends against the law."[11] Alexander Hamilton, who had been President Washington's secretary of state and remained one of the leaders of the Federalist party, defended the Sedition Act, partly because it contained at his insistence a clause making truth a defense. In a 1799 letter, Hamilton argued that officers of government could serve effectively only if law protected "their reputations from malicious and unfounded slanders."[12]

This view was shared by Justice Samuel Chase of the Supreme Court of the United States. As was the practice in those days, he also sat as a trial judge assigned to a "circuit" comprised of one or more states. In his decision finding Dr. Thomas Cooper, editor of the *Sunbury and Northumberland Gazette*, guilty of sedition, Justice Chase noted that "all governments which I ever heard of" have laws to protect themselves and their officials from harmful criticism. In a passage that might have been written by some present-day politicians, he said:

> A Republican government can only be destroyed in two ways; the introduction of luxury or the licentiousness of the Press. The latter is the more slow, but more sure and certain, means of bringing about the destruction of the government. The legislature of this country, knowing this maxim, has thought proper to check the licentiousness of the press.[13]

Cooper's crime was the writing of an editorial taking issue with President Adams's trade policies. He wrote that when Adams had taken office, "he was hardly in the infancy of political mistake." That was enough to put him among the approximately twenty-five persons arrested on charges of sedition in 1798 and 1799. Fifteen were indicted, eleven tried, and ten were found guilty.[14] The crime was a **misdemeanor** punishable by a fine or a jail term, or both. Almost all of those who were tried were editors of Republican newspapers.

The Act aroused opposition. Two states, Kentucky and Virginia, passed resolutions condemning it; the former written by Thomas Jefferson, the latter by James Madison. The resolutions took the position that in passing the Sedition Act, Congress had usurped

---

11. Robert Harper, a representative from South Carolina, 8 *Annals of Congress*, 5th Cong. 1797–1799, p. 2101.
12. *The Papers of Alexander Hamilton*, vol. 23, April–October 1799 (New York: Columbia University Press, 1976), p. 604.
13. United States v. Cooper, 25 Fed. Cas. 631, 635 (1800).
14. Clifton O. Lawhorne, *Defamation and Public Officials: The Evolving Law of Libel* (Carbondale: Southern Illinois University Press, 1971), p. 51.

powers expressly denied it by the Constitution. This left the inference that a similar act might be legal if it was drafted and adopted by the various state legislatures.

The Act expired, by its own terms, in March 1801 with the expiration of Adams's term. Historians differ as to the role public resentment over its enforcement played in the election of Thomas Jefferson as president in 1800. One of the first things he did was to pardon all who had been convicted under the Act. Because all of the victims were members of his Republican party, it is impossible to know whether he acted on a firm belief in freedom of speech or out of political motives. During his first term he took no action to prevent the trial of one of his critics, Harry Croswell, who was charged with violating New York's seditious libel law.[15]

Justice Chase was **impeached** by the House and tried by the Senate in 1805, largely for his role in the trials of Dr. Cooper and of James Callender, author of a book written with Jefferson's encouragement attacking the Adams administration. Evidence indicates that Chase read the book, instigated the prosecution, presided during the trial, and charged the jury in terms that left no doubt he believed Callender guilty. More than half the Senate voted to remove Chase from the Supreme Court, but the total did not reach the required two-thirds majority.[16] In 1840, Congress voted to refund the fines imposed on the victims of the Act. In the process, the House Committee on the Judiciary declared the law "unconstitutional, null and void, passed under a mistaken notion of delegated power." This was simply an opinion, with no force as legal precedent.

The episode lies embedded deep within American history, but its lessons remain valid. Even in a nation with a Constitution that guarantees freedom of speech and press, the urge to suppress unpopular speakers and writers lies just beneath the surface. When foreign enemies threaten, or economic hardship creates unrest, that urge may well be translated into action, official or unofficial. Experience with the Sedition Act did nothing to demonstrate how much protection the First Amendment offers to critics of government because none of the cases reached the Supreme Court.

THE PHILOSOPHY OF FREEDOM OF SPEECH AND PRESS

For more than a century after the Sedition Act expired in 1801, the First Amendment lay dormant. Censorship of news dispatches from the war zones was accepted without legal challenge during the Civil War. Without a sedition law in the statutes, criticism of government and of government officials was accepted as part of the game of party politics. When individuals in and out of government felt that they had been defamed by an overly abusive editor, they might sue for **libel** in the state courts. But not until well into this century was the Supreme Court ever asked to decide how far the First Amendment goes in protecting freedom of speech and of the press.

---

15. People v. Croswell, 3 Johns. Cas. 337 (1804).
16. Samuel Eliot Morison and Henry Steele Commager, *The Growth of the American Republic* (New York: Oxford University Press, 1937), vol 1, p. 293.

The limits of the guarantees were tested first in World War I when Congress enacted the **Espionage Act** of 1917, followed quickly by the Sedition Act of 1918. Since then, and especially since 1945, courts at all levels have decided thousands of First Amendment cases. These cases have dealt not only with the right to criticize government and government officials, but with the right to picket in labor disputes, the right to demonstrate against racial and other forms of discrimination, the right to protect one's privacy, the right to protect one's reputation, the right to see sexually explicit movies, the right to insist that broadcasters present a wide spectrum of opinion, and the right to advertise. Few aspects of our lives have not been touched by the expanding definition of First Amendment freedoms.

Court decisions, especially those of the Supreme Court of the United States, tell us what is legal with respect to speech and the media at any given time. Much of the subject matter of this book is devoted to the major cases defining the rights of the media. But there is also the question of how far freedom of speech and of the press ought to go. This is the realm of philosophy and ethics. Several respected scholars have attempted to develop a rational theory of the meaning of the First Amendment. In doing so, they have sought to offer guidance to those who would use speech for the maximum benefit of society. At a personal level, we know from experience that we sometimes feel better when we have "let off steam" or given someone "a piece of our mind." The First Amendment theorists have sought to demonstrate, in the tradition of John Milton, that unfettered debate is the best means of arriving at the truth about important public issues. In the process, most have discerned limits beyond which words can become harmful. Ethics is concerned with the moral aspects of freedom of speech and of the press. In some areas both law and theory permit speech that some might believe to be harmful. In some instances, media professionals must draw on their own sense of ethics in deciding what to do.

The rest of this chapter presents a sampling of the theories about freedom of speech and of the press. It also outlines the Supreme Court's application of various theories to speech and press cases. A knowledge of First Amendment theory can help us understand why the Supreme Court decided a case as it did. Within limits, it might permit us to anticipate the outcome of a case. However, the Court is made up of nine justices, each of whom looks at any given case in his or her own way. Prediction is therefore best treated as a game of chance rather than a certainty.

The most important reason for studying First Amendment theory is to build a foundation on which to decide for ourselves how important it is to insist that others be permitted to speak their minds. In a society such as ours, no person's right to speak and write freely is any more secure than that of the least rational and most repulsive member of society. If any person is to be punished for his or her views, or forced to be silent, we need a clear understanding of why it is done. Because public opinion does prevail in a rough way in American society, each of us ought to have a theory of the meaning of the First Amendment.

The Meaning of Freedom of Speech and Press

The belief that free discussion offers society the best hope for peaceful resolution of its differences has advanced haltingly and still is held by only a minority of the world's peoples. Such belief assumes that the participants in the debate are rational and willing to compromise on something short of each side's view of absolute truth. The alternative is suppression of one side or the other, or the kind of "debate" that has torn Northern Ireland and Lebanon.

This section summarizes the work of three First Amendment scholars: Zechariah Chafee, Jr., for many years a professor of law at Harvard; Alexander Meiklejohn, a professor of philosophy at Brown, Amherst, and the University of Wisconsin; and Thomas I. Emerson, professor of law at Yale. It also includes the views of Walter Lippmann, for many years a respected newspaper columnist and author of books on public affairs. Each came to firm conclusions about the meaning of the First Amendment.

Zechariah Chafee, Jr.

Chafee's masterwork is *Free Speech in the United States*, published in 1941 just prior to this country's entry into World War II. It was completed at a time when freedom was the exception, not the rule, for a majority of the world's people. Chafee was by no means an absolutist in his view of the First Amendment. He saw freedom of speech as only one interest, but a very important one, which government must protect for its own good and that of society. When debate focuses on government policies, it must be "absolutely unlimited," because only through the free play of ideas is truth likely to be found. If the government uses its power to suppress a point of view, "it becomes a matter of chance whether it is thrown on the false side or the true, and truth loses all the natural advantages of the contest."[17]

But government, Chafee noted, also has other interests to protect, "such as order, the training of the young, protection against external aggression." If speech threatens to interfere with these other interests, courts must balance one against the other. In such instances, Chafee said, speech "ought to weigh very heavily in the scale." It should be punished "only when the interest in public safety is really impaired." The line between acceptable speech and unacceptable speech should be drawn, he argued, "close to the point where words will give rise to unlawful acts."[18]

Chafee's theory of the First Amendment is important because it embodies the approach—the balancing test—that the Supreme Court has commended to lower courts in freedom of speech cases. Each attempt at suppression is treated as a balancing of interests: the speaker's right to participate in the search for truth, for example, versus the government's right to raise an army in time of war. The same test also is applied to cases in which it is alleged that the news media have harmed a person's reputation, or have interfered with the right to a fair trial.

Walter Lippmann

At about the time Chafee was writing his book, Lippmann was writing in a different style but to the same end in his newspaper columns and in an article, "The Indispensable Opposition," published in the *Atlantic Monthly* in 1939.[19]

---

17. Chafee, Atheneum ed., pp. 31–32.
18. Ibid., p. 35.
19. Reprinted in Henry Steele Commager, ed., *Living Ideas in America* (New York: Harper & Row 1951), pp. 400–03.

Lippmann started from the assumption that government is not the only enemy of freedom of speech. He noted that while most persons say they believe in such freedom, they have no strong commitment to it. They may tolerate an unpopular speaker, as they might tolerate a baby howling in an adjoining apartment, but tolerance is not enough. Freedom of speech cannot survive in any society, Lippmann wrote, unless people realize that "because freedom of discussion improves our own opinions, the liberties of other men are our own vital necessity."

He illustrated his point by describing what happens when a person with a severe stomachache goes to a doctor. The doctor may ask embarrassing questions, and diagnostic procedures may be unpleasant. But if the physician is less than thorough, if the patient is less than candid, and if, in the end, the physician does not speak freely and frankly, the patient may die. The process does not always reach the truth, but Lippmann concluded that no other "will normally and habitually find so much truth."

The process should be no different when the patient is a government beset with grave problems, even those of peace or war. Under such circumstances, Lippmann argued, freedom of speech is indispensable. A leader surrounded by advisers who never contradict him may well take his nation to disaster. He must turn to his opponents to learn where the hazards or the follies of his policy lie.

Lippmann's pessimistic assessment of the public's attitude toward freedom of speech is supported by public opinion polls. A survey taken by the Gallup organization in 1979 showed that more than a third of the sample believed that the press is not strictly enough controlled by government.[20] The precise figure was 37 percent, compared to 32 percent who believed such controls as exist are about right, 17 percent who believed controls are too strict, and 14 percent who had no opinion. Those in the first group supported their opinion by saying they believed newspapers sometimes print information that is not in the best interest of the nation and should be kept confidential, that newspapers distort and exaggerate the news in the interest of making headlines and selling newspapers, and that they rush into print without making sure all the facts are straight.

Thus Lippmann's insistence that freedom of speech is indispensable in a free society is not something to be shrugged off as good advice for government officials. The urge to censor, intimidate, or join a noisy mob lies more or less dormant in most people. It is one thing to take part in a noisy debate or even to heckle a speaker. That is part of the political process. So are sign-waving demonstrators. But it is a much more serious matter to use physical coercion to prevent a person from speaking at all, or to set fire to an abortion clinic. In his later years Lippmann, too, yielded to the temptation to suppress offensive speech. His biographer, Ronald Steel, reports that Lippmann became revolted by the excesses of the Nazis on the right and the Communists on the left, each of whom took extreme positions and showed no willingness to tolerate any other views.[21] He then argued that access to the public forum should be reserved for those who believe in freedom of speech, not only for themselves, but for others, and are willing to abide by the rules of civilized debate. Thus, Lippmann cannot be counted among those who believe in absolute freedom of speech. His position at the end was that such freedom is

---

20. George Gallup, Jr., "Americans Favor Tougher Controls on the Press," *Editor & Publisher*, 19 January 1980, p. 7.
21. Ronald Steel, *Walter Lippmann and the American Century* (Boston: Little, Brown, 1980), p. 315.

good for society up to the point where the speaker will not tolerate those with opposing points of view.

Alexander Meiklejohn

After World War II, Alexander Meiklejohn addressed the same streak of oppression Lippmann had observed. In a series of lectures later expanded into a book, this long-time commentator on the meaning of freedom in the university focused on the meaning of freedom of expression guaranteed by the First Amendment. He argued that there are two layers of freedom: at the higher level, speech devoted to public affairs; at a lower level, actions that distort debate on public matters, speech that directly provokes illegal acts, and speech that brings harm to other individuals.

Speech devoted to public affairs, Meiklejohn continued, should receive a very high degree of protection from the First Amendment. Such speech is in the public interest and should therefore be encouraged. Starting from the belief that the Constitution not only makes the public at large, which he called "the electorate," a branch of the government, but the most important one, he wrote:

> The First Amendment seems to me to be a very uncompromising statement. It admits of no exceptions. It tells us that the Congress and, by implication, all other agencies of government are denied any authority whatever to limit the political freedom of the citizens of the United States. It declares that with respect to political belief, political discussion, political advocacy, political planning, our citizens are sovereign, and the Congress is their subordinate agent.[22]

Meiklejohn's repeated use of the word "political" to describe the kind of speech worthy of absolute protection under the First Amendment should not be misconstrued. He was not limiting himself to the kind of oratory that takes place during political campaigns. Taken in connection with his references to public policy, it is clear that his theory would extend full First Amendment protection to economic and social issues—to arguments over factory closings, air pollution, abortion, and racial or sexual discrimination—because all involve government intervention at some point.

Building on his belief that the First Amendment should give absolute protection to the debate over public policy, Meiklejohn argued that the government should do more than merely tolerate all shades of opinion. Nor is it enough to extend the protection of the courts to the participants in this debate. Government should open public buildings and other public places to those who want to debate public policy. Such places should be as open to those who attack the government's policies as they are to those who support them. Today this may sound tame, but in 1948, when Meiklejohn wrote, public platforms at even the most liberal state universities were seldom open to speakers considered un-American. It would be another decade before the Supreme Court would hold that they must be.

However, Meiklejohn relegated speech-related action and some forms of pure speech

---

22. Alexander Meiklejohn, *Political Freedom* (New York: Harper & Row, 1960), pp. 107–08.

to a lower level where they were protected, not by the First Amendment, but by the due process clause of the Fifth Amendment. While he expressly rejected the application of Chafee's balancing test to speech having to do with public policy,[23] he was willing to apply it to lower-level speech. Some such speech grows out of personal relationships: one person, for instance, does not have an absolute right to speak ill of another. Other such speech is a product of commercial relationships: A merchant does not have a right to make false advertising claims for his wares, or to misrepresent the terms of a contract. Meiklejohn also put on his lower level some speech directed at government. Once the debate on policy has ended and has been formalized into statute law, the people are required to obey the law until it has been changed. Speech or speech-related action, in defiance of law, may be punished if the punishment is carried out in accord with the due process guarantees of the Fifth Amendment.

"The First Amendment . . . is not the guardian of unregulated talkativeness," Meiklejohn wrote.[24] Thus, to ensure orderly debate of the issues, noisy obstructionists can be removed from the forum. Or if twenty persons are of the same mind, it is time-wasting to insist that each should have time to say the same thing. "What is essential is not that everyone shall speak, but that everything worth saying shall be said." Nor does the First Amendment mean that an individual should be permitted to use a sound truck in a residential neighborhood in the middle of the night to argue a point of view. Nor does it mean that demonstrators should be permitted to stop traffic in rush hour to make a point. In short, Meiklejohn was saying, as the Supreme Court has said consistently, that the state may regulate the *process* of debate—the time, place, and manner of speaking. But, in doing so, it must be neutral as to the *content* of the speech.

Meiklejohn differs from Chafee and Lippmann in two respects: He would give absolute protection to debate over public policy and he injected a positive element into First Amendment theory. As he saw it, the amendment imposes a mandate on government to encourage debate. The Supreme Court has not yet gone all the way with Meiklejohn on either premise, but it has come close to doing so. However, Meiklejohn, like Chafee and Lippmann, was not willing to interpret "Congress shall make no law" as an absolute protection for all kinds of speech.

Thomas I. Emerson

Emerson wrote *The System of Freedom of Expression* in the late 1960s.[25] Turmoil boiled around him as he wrote. A law professor at Yale, he was able to observe firsthand the demonstrations fueled in the 1960s by opposition to the war in Vietnam and the struggle of blacks for a greater degree of equity in society. What he saw obviously disquieted him. In an epilogue he expresses doubt that freedom of expression could survive an assault on one side from a New Left that equated freedom of speech with lack of conviction, and on the other from a Right determined to preserve the status quo.

Emerson went beyond the others in arguing that all "expression" which bears on government policy ought to have the full protection of the First Amendment. Further, he went beyond Meiklejohn and included some kinds of speech-related action in his

---

23. Ibid., pp. 58–59.
24. Ibid., p. 26.
25. New York: Random House, 1970.

definition of "expression." He would protect peaceful picketing, demonstrations, the carrying of signs, and symbolic speech, such as burning an American flag. He also sought to answer a question Chafee and Meiklejohn left unanswered, except in general terms: At what point does speech-related action become a criminal act that can be punished?

Emerson found no room in a system of free expression for application of the balancing test advocated by Chafee. In his view, courts considering First Amendment cases would be limited to defining the "key elements" of that Amendment, which he listed as "expression," "abridge," and "law." Any form of speech or action that met his definition of "expression" would be protected absolutely against any act of government that sought to limit it.

Like Lippmann, Emerson recognized that private individuals and institutions, as well as organized groups, can discourage freedom of speech. Under current interpretations of First Amendment law, the courts can do little to prevent such abridgments unless a criminal act, such as vandalism, is involved. Emerson argued that the courts ought to be able to deal directly with nongovernmental acts intended to silence unpopular speakers.

Like Meiklejohn, he found a positive element in the First Amendment. Not only should government offer its facilities to those who would debate public policy, but it should attempt, through education, to expand the understanding of such policy. Further, he argued that the First Amendment imposes a mandate on government to release information essential to proper appraisal of its actions. Finally, he saw an expanded role for radio and television in the discussion of public affairs. As the only media licensed by government, they should be required to seek out and present all sides of controversial public issues. Emerson considered the extension of that mandatory role to the privately owned print media and then concluded that any attempt to do so would raise insurmountable constitutional barriers. The Supreme Court has since endorsed that position. Through the fairness doctrine, broadcasting stations can be required to carry balanced programming on controversial public issues. But the Court has held that any attempt by government to mandate the content of newspapers and magazines is a form of **prior restraint.**[26]

A major portion of Emerson's work is devoted to exploring the boundary between speech and action that Chafee saw as the test of how free any society is. Emerson would push that line far into territory usually perceived as the domain of action. In his view, a peaceful strike is expression, not action. So are street gatherings and marching. Where, then, is the line between the permissible and the impermissible?

Emerson saw no problems with the discussion of violence as a means of solving a political impasse. Speakers could point out that certain kinds of oppression had led to violence in the past. They could warn that if oppressive policies were not changed, they might lead to violence. Speakers could advise their followers that they might have to use force at some point to protect themselves from acts of violence. While some of these would come close to the line between the permissible and the impermissible, they ought to be protected as acceptable expression, Emerson argued. But there was a limit:

---

26. The Supreme Court upheld the fairness doctrine in Red Lion Broadcasting Co., Inc., v. Federal Communications Commission, 395 U.S. 367, 89 S.Ct. 1794, 23 L.Ed.2d 371 (1969). In Miami Herald Publishing Co., v. Tornillo, 418 U.S. 241, 94 S.Ct. 2831, 41 L.Ed.2d 730 (1974), the Court declared unconstitutional a Florida law requiring newspapers to publish statements from persons who believed they had been treated unfairly in a news story or an editorial.

On the other hand, the urging of immediate, specific acts of violence would, under circumstances where violence was possible and likely, fall within the category of "action." Such communication would be so interlocked with violent conduct as to constitute for all practical purposes part of the action; it would be in effect the beginning of the action itself. In short the basic effort would be to formulate the definition of "expression" in terms of the difference between the ideational preparation for subsequent conduct and actual participation in it.[27]

By way of illustration, there would be nothing wrong, in Emerson's view, with a speaker's urging an audience in Peoria "to evict that rotten president from his Oval Office." But if the same speaker were to say the same thing to an angry crowd in Lafayette Square in Washington, D.C., and that crowd seemed on the point of crossing Pennsylvania Avenue to assault the White House, he could be punished for his words. "Expression" would have become a strong likelihood of harmful "action."

Chafee, Lippmann, Meiklejohn, and Emerson's differing views of the First Amendment can be made clearer by applying them to the announcement that the Ku Klux Klan plans a rally in a city park in a community where racial tensions are near the flash point. In Chafee's view, persons opposed to the rally could go to court and argue that it was likely to cause violence. If a reasonable case could be made, the court would be required to balance it against the probable message of the Klan speakers. If the court concluded that the possibility of violence outweighed the speakers' likely contribution to the debate on racial policy, it could issue an **injunction** forbidding the rally.

The Lippmann who wrote "The Indispensable Opposition" might take the position that while the Klan's message was likely to be distasteful to some, the speakers should be permitted to deliver it because they might make some contribution to the debate over race relations. He would argue that some worthwhile speech, like some medicine, leaves a bitter taste. But the later Lippmann might well have argued that the Klan, if given power, would repress all speech except that supporting its position. Therefore, because it would not tolerate free and open debate on racial policy, it ought not to be allowed to participate in the debate. Thus, he too might have favored an injunction.

Meiklejohn would have looked at the rally in two ways. He would regard the speechmaking in one way, but the surrounding elements—the robes, the hoods, the possibility of a march through the streets, the number of participants, and the likelihood of a cross being burned—in another. Whatever the speakers might have to say about race relations ought to be given the utmost protection, in Meiklejohn's view, because it would be a contribution to the debate on the public policy. If police were required to protect the speakers from violence originating among opponents of the Klan, then it ought to be provided. Further, Meiklejohn would see the park as an appropriate forum for the speakers. Its use would be in conformity with the government's obligation to encourage debate on public policy. But if the Klan members were to wear hoods, or march through a black neighborhood, or burn a cross, that would be another matter. Such actions might well be intimidating rather that persuasive. They might provoke violence. In Meiklejohn's view, they could be challenged in the courts. If, after a hearing with both sides represented, the court concluded that any speech-related action was likely to cause violence, such action could be forbidden.

---

27. Emerson, pp.17–18.

Emerson's theory of the First Amendment would protect not only the speeches, but any peaceful action Klan members might take to draw attention to their cause. They could march, as long as they did not block traffic, they could wear robes and hoods, and they could burn a cross if they wanted to. What they could not do is create a situation in which it appeared likely that they might resort to violence against others. But the likelihood that the speeches would spur members to action would have to be clear. By the same token, Emerson would expect the police to intervene if others should attempt violence against the Klan. But their actions would be directed at those who were threatening violence, not at the participants in the rally.

Thus, all the theories start with the assumption that members of the Ku Klux Klan are entitled to participate in the debate over public policy. So are those who hold other points of view. All the theories further assume that those who do not participate in the debate, and even the debaters themselves, will weigh the various arguments and decide for themselves what the policy ought to be. Finally, First Amendment theorists assume that most people are rational. Therefore, they will reject extreme positions and reach an accommodation that will be acceptable to a majority. This is the process through which public opinion is formed and shapes public policy.

The Supreme Court's Interpretation of Freedom of Speech and Press

The Supreme Court of the United States is made up of lawyers, many of whom have had experience as judges of lower courts. A few have been professors of law. Most come to think of themselves as legal philosophers. Nevertheless, critics, including some members of the present Court, have complained that the Court has not been able to settle on any consistent theory of First Amendment law. Whether any one theory can be applied to the great variety of cases that reach the Court is an open question. In any case, in the more than sixty years in which it has dealt with First Amendment cases, the Court has applied several theories, or tests.

One theory can be rejected at the start: the Court has never agreed with Meiklejohn or Emerson that some kinds of speech should be given absolute protection. Between 1939 and 1971, two members of the Court, Hugo L. Black and William O. Douglas, argued on occasion that the First Amendment means precisely what it says—Congress shall make no law abridging freedom of speech, press, religion, and assembly. But Black drew back from that position in the late 1960s and told an interviewer he could not support the right of demonstrators to gather outside the homes of public officials.

A majority has come close on occasion to granting absolute protection to speech, but has always left an exception which could be applied as a check in an extreme case. The Court's actions have rested on the following grounds: the bad tendency theory, the clear and present danger test, the theory of the balancing of interests, the preferred position theory, and a positive theory of the First Amendment. Each will be discussed in order.

The Bad Tendency Theory

This theory came out of the kind of English common law that was used against poor Twyn and that justified the convictions of the Republican editors caught up in the

Sedition Act of 1798. If words had a tendency to undermine the authority of government or to corrupt the morals of some members of society, the writer or speaker could be punished. Under this theory, there was no need to show that any harm had been done. The mere likelihood of harm was enough to support a conviction.

The Clear and Present Danger Test

This test was formulated by Justice Oliver Wendell Holmes in *Schenck* v. *United States* in 1919. Charles Schenck was general secretary of the Socialist party. During World War I, he and an associate printed and distributed fifteen thousand leaflets urging resistance to the draft. The two were charged with violating the Espionage Act, found guilty, and sentenced to prison. They appealed to the Supreme Court, arguing that their right to free speech had been violated. The case was not decided until four months after the war had ended in victory for the United States and its allies. Nevertheless, the Court found, with Holmes writing a unanimous decision, that the leaflets presented a "clear and present danger" to the draft system, and thus to the nation's efforts to win the war. In time, the decision was seen as giving speech greater protection than that offered by the bad tendency test, but in its early applications, in the 1920s, the distinction was hard to see.

Schenck v. *United States,*
249 U.S. 47, 39 S.Ct. 247,
63 L.Ed. 470 (1919).

In the *Schenck* decision, Holmes made the following points:

1. Government must, under mandate from the Constitution, protect certain vital interests—the lives and properties of its citizens, peace and good order, and the security of the nation against threats from foreign enemies. Anything that would prevent government from carrying out its required functions is a "substantive evil that Congress has a right to prevent."

2. In protecting vital interests, there are times when government must override First Amendment interests and punish persons whose words might bring harm to the state. This is especially true in time of war. Another such time might be a period of turmoil brought on by economic depression. At such times, government is particularly vulnerable to agitators seeking to capitalize on heightened emotion.

3. Speech may also lose its protection because of the place in which it is uttered or the audience to which it is addressed. A disgruntled speaker who chooses to shout his discontent into the wind blowing across an empty beach is no threat to anyone. But those same words spoken to a mob outside the White House would be another matter.

4. The circumstances surrounding the speech must also be taken into account. Holmes illustrated with a sentence which has been more frequently quoted than fully understood, even by some judges: "The most stringent protection of free speech would not protect a man in falsely shouting fire in a theater and causing a panic." If this sentence is examined closely, its meaning is found to be much closer to Meiklejohn and Emerson than the

decision in *Schenck* put it. First, Holmes was saying that the content of the speech must be a lie. Not a mistaken opinion; not an illegal appeal based on emotion: only a deliberate misstatement of fact can be punished. Clearly, his choice of words means that there could be no punishment for the person who found a fire in a theater and whose warning saved the lives of the audience. Nor could the law punish an actor whose lines required him to shout "Fire!" The speaker must have resorted to falsehood in order to cause trouble. Second, Holmes was saying that there must be a direct connection between the false speech and a harmful act—in this instance, panic, the kind of action that leads to people getting trampled or piled up against the doors, causing injury or death.

In later cases, Holmes and Justice Brandeis were to say that the meaning of the clear and present danger test was wrapped up in that one sentence about "shouting fire." Speech creates a clear and present danger only when it is obvious that it will immediately produce actions harmful to a vital interest Congress has the authority to protect. If the test is properly applied, it puts the line between speech and action very close to the latter, as Chafee, Meiklejohn, and Emerson advocated.

The Theory of the Balancing of Interests

Under this theory, the First Amendment interest in free discussion is seen merely as one of many interests safeguarded by the Constitution. When one comes into conflict with another, it is the duty of the courts to weigh the competing interests against each other and decide which has the greater value to society under the circumstances. Obviously, the outcome of the contest is as subject to the personal leanings of the individual judges involved as under any other theory.

Balancing in speech cases had its formal origins in *American Communications Association* v. *Douds*. The case involved the refusal of an officer of a labor union to sign an **affidavit** stating that he was not a member of the Communist party or of any

American Communications Association v. Douds, 339 U.S. 382, 70 S.Ct. 674, 94 L.Ed. 925 (1950).

other organization advocating violent overthrow of the government, and that he did not believe in violent overthrow. A union could not take advantage of the National Labor Relations Act unless all its officers signed such affidavits. Lower courts upheld the requirement. A majority of the Supreme Court agreed that labor union officers should be required to forswear affiliation with subversive organizations, but the justices split evenly on whether they should be required to take an oath as to what they believed, thus upholding the right to require union officers to sign the affidavits.

Chief Justice Fred M. Vinson, who wrote the prevailing opinion, explained the balancing concept applied by the Court. He reasoned that the oath did not prevent anyone from believing what he or she pleased. All it did was deny certain federal benefits to persons who believed in overthrowing the source of those benefits. Vinson saw this as a limited restriction on freedom of expression, both in terms of the numbers of persons affected and in the degree of restriction on speech.

On the other hand, there is considerable societal interest in preventing those who believe in violent overthrow from achieving positions of power. Communist leaders of labor unions might well call for strikes for political purposes rather than to achieve economic goals. Further, if the Court held the oath invalid for labor union leaders, for whom else might a similar oath be invalid? Could the government be denied the right to ask a prospective member of the Secret Service if he believed in assassinating presidents? Vinson wrote, "An affirmative answer hardly commends itself to reason," and he concluded that the oath "does not unduly infringe freedoms protected by the First Amendment."

The balancing theory is still the most common method used by the courts in determining when expression can be punished. However, in recent years, the Supreme Court usually has given First Amendment rights a greater weight in the scale of justice than did the Vinson court in *Douds*.

The Preferred Position Theory

A series of recent Court decisions has held that First Amendment rights, and some others guaranteed by the Bill of Rights, occupy a **"preferred position."** The Court also has held that these guarantees stand, through the Fourteenth Amendment, in a preferred position as a barrier against state interference. Preferred position theory is used in all instances in which government is seen as trying to prevent allegedly harmful speech. Thus it is a weapon against censorship, also called prior, or **previous, restraint.** The theory begins with the assumption that the people enjoyed freedom of speech before they entered into the compact that resulted in the Constitution. Therefore, while the Constitution specifically protects that right, it did not grant it. Because freedom of speech lies at the heart of a free society, it must be guarded diligently. Any encroachment by government is a serious matter, so serious that the courts assume that any restriction on freedom of speech is unconstitutional until proved otherwise. In such cases, the burden of proof is on the government. It must show (1) that the restriction has been imposed to protect an interest it is entitled to protect under the Constitution, (2) that the law has been drafted in such specific terms that it will do what it is supposed to do with a minimum of harm to freedom of speech, and (3) that the government's vital interest cannot be protected without some restriction on speech. If there is more than one way to protect the government's basic interest, it must use the method that does the least harm to speech.

The government must show in such cases that its need to act is "compelling." The courts assume that government has acted improperly until it proves otherwise. If speech is the subject of an attempted restraint, the Court has said there is both a "heavy presumption" that the restraint is unconstitutional[28] and a "heavy burden of showing justification for such a restraint."[29]

The effect of the preferred position theory has been to grant pure speech—that is, speech untainted by action—a high degree of freedom. At times the Supreme Court has come very close to the positions advocated by Meiklejohn and Emerson, especially when speech concerns the actions of government and government officials.

---

28. Bantam Books, Inc., v. Sullivan, 372 U.S. 58, 83 S.Ct. 631, 9 L.Ed.2d 584 (1963).
29. Organization for a Better Austin v. Keefe, 402 U.S. 415, 91 S.Ct. 1575, 29 L.Ed.2d 1 (1971).

A Positive Theory of the First Amendment

Until 1980, the Court had flirted with, but generally rejected, the idea advanced by Meiklejohn and made more specific by Emerson that the First Amendment requires positive steps by government to ensure free and informed debate on its policies. The Court has had few problems with cases involving the right to present ideas in public places. As far back as the 1930s, it held that the streets are proper places for the peaceful dissemination of ideas. The Court stretched that definition in the 1960s to include demonstrations. However, it has upheld the right of the state to regulate the time, place, and manner of such use.

The Court also has held that radio and television, as licensed media, occupy a special place as forums of debate on controversial public issues. They have an obligation to present all sides of such issues in a balanced manner. But, except for candidates for public office, the Court has rejected the suggestions that the First Amendment can be used to force a broadcasting station to carry the views of any particular individual or group. This is true even if the person or group is willing to pay for time on the air.

Nor has the Court found in the First Amendment any levers that can be used to pry information out of the government. It has held that the Amendment protects a reporter's right to share information with the public, but offers no help in getting information. In 1966, Congress moved into that breach by passing the Freedom of Information Act, establishing by law a right of access to a great deal, but not all, of the information generated by government agencies. The Supreme Court has upheld that Act in numerous decisions, but has construed it rather narrowly.

In 1980, the Court handed down its first First Amendment access decision in *Richmond Newspapers* v. *Virginia*.[30] The case grew out of an order by a judge who ejected journalists and other spectators from his courtroom while he conducted a murder trial. On appeal, a majority of the Court held that the First Amendment protects the right to be present in a courtroom while a trial is being conducted. Chief Justice Warren E. Burger reasoned that courtrooms historically have been public assemblies and therefore come within the First Amendment's guarantee of the right to assemble. That right, he said, is not absolute, but can be restricted only for the most compelling reasons. Justice John Paul Stevens noted the potentially far-reaching aspects of that ruling. The Court, he said, had for the first time found in the First Amendment a right of access to the news. How far that right goes cannot be known until the Court decides future cases, but it stands as a step toward the positive role for the First Amendment postulated by Meiklejohn and Emerson.

In the Professional World

Reporters and editors act on the belief that the First Amendment gives them the right to publish or broadcast any information they are able to obtain. They are correct in that belief, or nearly so. Examples of outright government censorship are extremely rare and have been confined to time of war or to instances that were perceived at the time to present grave threats to national security.

---

30. 448 U.S. 555, 100 S.Ct. 2814, 65 L.Ed.2d 973 (1980).

Editorial writers, political cartoonists, producers of documentaries, and others who offer their opinions to the public operate on the theory that they can be as harsh as they please in commenting on government policy or the actions of government officials. So far as censorship or punishment by government is concerned, that is true. The law of seditious libel does not exist in the United States.

However, despite its wording, the First Amendment is not absolute. The Supreme Court has reserved the right to impose censorship if national security is clearly endangered, to protect the right to a fair trial if all other measures fail, and to suppress obscenity. Also, the First Amendment does not prevent punishment of those who deal in **obscenity.**

Nor does the First Amendment offer journalists, public relations specialists, advertisers, photographers, and authors in general freedom from liability in civil actions. Professionals who get their facts wrong, and as a consequence harm the reputation of an identifiable individual, may have to defend themselves against a libel action. If the individual is in the public eye, the First Amendment gives the professional a strong defense, but it is not absolute. Nor does it take away the cost of hiring a lawyer to prepare the defense. Professionals who pry too deeply into the private lives of others, or who use intrusive measures to gather information, may also invite a lawsuit.

Despite these and other limitations, the First Amendment still offers all who work with words, pictures, and graphics a greater degree of freedom that can be found almost anywhere else. Except for libel, which offers journalists one of their most serious problems, professional communicators need give little thought to the legality of their work. Thus, the question of what to share with the public and what not to share is more a matter of ethics than of law. Cartoonists and commentators are free to present the president as a sleepy near-moron who can read an actor's lines well, but who cannot be trusted to perform without a script. Such criticism goes with the territory. But what does a steady diet of such portrayals do to the president's power to negotiate at the summit with other heads of state? The news media are free to dig up and present all the facts—and even the rumors and gossip—they can find about a suspected mass murderer. But what happens if the publicity is so prejudicial and so pervasive that the suspect cannot get a fair trial, and therefore cannot be legally convicted? Advertisers are free to portray men as macho and women as their willing victims. But should they do so if such advertising seems to encourage violence against women? Such questions cannot readily be answered by resort to the courts. Indeed, attempts to do so would invite censorship. But they are questions professional communicators need to ask themselves and questions they must answer.

FOR REVIEW

1. Plato portrayed political power and philosophic thought as antagonists. Are they? Need they be?

2. Think about living in a land where a monarch rules by divine right. If you were a student there instead of here, what differences might you expect in your day-to-day life?

3. What is the difference between a natural right and a legal right? What is the importance of the difference?

4. "Congress shall make no law . . . abridging the freedom of speech, or of the press." Is that indeed the case?

5. Does the Sedition Act of 1798 tell us anything that is of value today?

6. Of the First Amendment philosophers whose views are summarized in this chapter, which has the greatest appeal to you? Why? Now think of the position on public policy that irritates you the most. How would your favored philosophy apply to those who argue that position?

7. If you were a justice of the Supreme Court, what philosophy of the First Amendment would guide you? How would you apply it if a group of twenty self-proclaimed Nazis applied for a permit to speak in a predominantly Jewish neighborhood with the avowed purpose of arguing that the Holocaust is a figment of Jewish propaganda and that Hitler was right when he put Jews in concentration camps?

8. Explain what is meant by "balancing." How does it work? Are there any interests that should outweigh freedom of speech? Why or why not?

9. What is meant by "preferred position"? Give an example to show how it might be applied.

CHAPTER 2

GOVERNMENT CENSORSHIP

The Supreme Court and Prior Restraint

Barriers against Prior Restraint

The Protection of Unpopular Opinions

The Protection of National Security
  The Pentagon Papers / The H-Bomb Secret

Prior Restraint by Contract

A government trying to win a war, keep vital secrets, or ensure what the Preamble to the Constitution calls "domestic tranquility" can take one of three courses with those whose words might cause trouble:

1. It can adopt the First Amendment theories of Emerson and Meiklejohn and take its chances that the people will reject advocates of harmful action and do what is best for the nation.

2. It can adopt laws providing for punishment of those whose words might help the enemy, or who would disclose vital secrets, or try to stir up trouble.

3. It can impose censorship, thus cutting off at the source any words that might help the enemy, disclose vital secrets, or provoke harmful action. Obviously, if censorship can be made effective, it offers the most certain way of preventing speech the government considers harmful. On the other hand, it is also the most stringent possible abridgment of the freedom of speech and press guaranteed by the First Amendment.

As this book will demonstrate, the first course has been the one usually taken in the United States. On numerous occasions, the Supreme Court has held that free debate is the preferred method of resolving differences in our society. The Court has so held even when the debaters have played fast and loose with the truth, or have used language that others have found offensive. However, the Court also has upheld laws designed to punish persons whose speech is considered harmful to national security, to an orderly society, or to the rights of others. If such laws are carefully drafted to protect governmental interests, and if they do not restrict speech unduly, they can be enforced. For instance, as we will see in chapter 3, people have been sent to prison for long terms because it was believed that their speech might help an enemy in time of war or might have led to overthrow of the government in time of peace. The third course, censorship, has rarely been imposed. In modern times, the Supreme Court has held in several notable instances that censorship violated the First Amendment guarantees of freedom of speech and press, but the Court also has refused to hold that it can never be imposed. The Court has always left open the possibility that at some time, under certain extreme circumstances, government could use its power to suppress speech that posed a direct threat to a vital interest.

At this point, it might be well to reflect on the difference between punishing someone for speech considered harmful and suppressing that speech altogether. People who know they might go to prison or be fined heavily if they criticize government officials too severely will think twice before they do so. But as we saw in chapter 1, in the discussion of the Sedition Act of 1798, there are people who will go ahead and criticize anyway. They do so for several reasons. They know that their comments will reach the public and may even have an influence on policy in the long run. They may also reason that a possible arrest will lead more people to pay attention to their comments. And it is possible, as is Zenger's case, also described in chapter 1, that a jury may find the critics not guilty. Thus, laws designed to punish some participants in the debate on public policy may have a deterrent effect, but they do not prevent determined speakers from being heard at all. That is what censorship attempts to do. Thus, the difference can be quite significant. The Supreme Court once expressed the difference this way: it said laws punishing speakers can be said to chill speech; censorship freezes it.

This chapter examines several cases in which the government sought to freeze speech by imposing a prior restraint, as government censorship is also called. We will start where the Court started, in 1931, when the state of Minnesota ordered a weekly newspaper to stop publishing. In that case, and in two more recent cases, the Court erected the high barriers that must be overcome before a prior restraint can be imposed. The remainder of the chapter will examine attempts to suppress unpopular religious and economic views, to prevent publications considered harmful to national security, and to prevent disclosure of nuclear secrets. We also will find that the Central Intelligence Agency has been able to use contracts to impose censorship on works written by its former employees. Later in the book, we will see that prior restraint has been imposed to protect privacy (chapter 4), suppress obscenity (chapter 9), and prevent infringement of **copyright** (chapter 12).

Major Cases

Alfred A. Knopf v. *Colby*, 509 F.2d 1362 (4th Cir. 1975).

Bantam Books v. *Sullivan*, 372 U.S. 58, 83 S.Ct. 631, 9 L.Ed.2d 584 (1963).

Carroll v. *President and Commissioners of Princess Anne*, 393 U.S. 175, 89 S.Ct. 347, 21 L.Ed.2d 325 (1968).

Lovell v. *Griffin*, 303 U.S. 444, 58 S.Ct. 666, 82 L.Ed. 949 (1938).

Near v. *Minnesota*, 283 U.S. 697, 51 S.Ct. 625, 75 L.Ed. 1357 (1931).

New York Times Co. v. *United States*, 403 U.S. 713, 91 S.Ct. 2140, 29 L.Ed.2d 822 (1971).

Organization for a Better Austin v. *Keefe*, 402 U.S. 415, 91 S.Ct. 1575, 29 L.Ed.2d 1 (1971).

Snepp v. *United States*, 444 U.S. 507, 100 S.Ct. 763, 62 L.Ed.2d 704 (1980).

Thornhill v. *Alabama*, 310 U.S. 88, 60 S.Ct. 736, 84 L.Ed. 1093 (1940).

United States v. *Marchetti*, 466 F.2d 1309 (4th Cir. 1972).

United States v. *The Progressive*, 467 F.Supp. 990 (W.D.Wis. 1979).

The Supreme Court and Prior Restraint

Censorship has rarely been imposed in the United States, even in time of war. During the Civil War, the army sometimes used its control of the telegraph system to prevent newspapers from receiving dispatches describing Union defeats. However, such steps served only to delay publication of the bad news.[1] In reaction to news and comment considered harmful to the Union cause, the army ordered the *Chicago Times*, the *New York World*, and the *Journal of Commerce* to cease publication, but President Lincoln quickly countermanded the orders.[2] During World War I, censorship was imposed through the postal system and was directed mainly at Socialist party newspapers.[3] In neither war was the Supreme Court asked to rule whether censorship violated the First Amendment guarantees of freedom of speech and press.

Indeed it was not until 1931, when the nation was at peace, that the Court had its first opportunity to decide whether the First Amendment forbids censorship. When the test did come, it had nothing to do with national security. The question was: could a newspaper be shut down because it was considered scandalous?

---

1. An interesting account of how Northern newspapers covered the Civil War and bypassed the army censors is found in J. Cutler Andrews, *The North Reports the Civil War* (Pittsburgh: University of Pittsburgh Press, 1955).
2. Carl Sandburg, *Abraham Lincoln: The War Years*, vol. 3 (New York: Harcourt, 1939), pp. 53–55.
3. For a discussion of the actions taken by the Post Office to bar allegedly subversive publications from the mails, see Zechariah Chafee, Jr., *Free Speech in the United States* (New York: Atheneum, 1969).

Authorities in Minnesota, acting under powers given them by a state law, had obtained a court order forbidding J. M. Near and Howard Guilford to publish further issues of the weekly *Saturday Press* until they promised to print only the truth, and that "with good motives and for justifiable ends."[4] The Supreme Court ruled, five to four, that Near and Guilford could resume publication without making such a promise. The decision in *Near v. Minnesota*, written by Chief Justice Charles Evans Hughes, has become a **landmark case** quoted frequently by lower courts. While the majority held that prior restraint usually violates the First Amendment guarantee of freedom of speech and press, it also suggested several specific instances in which restraint might be justified. Thus, *Near* has proved to be both a victory and a defeat for those who believe that whatever else it does, the First Amendment ought to stand as a barrier against censorship.

Near v. Minnesota, 283 U.S. 697, 51 S.Ct. 625, 75 L.Ed. 1357 (1931).

The *Saturday Press* was one of many unexpected by-products of a constitutional amendment, adopted in 1919, that prohibited the manufacture and sale of alcoholic beverages. It soon became evident that while the amendment cut off the legal sale of beer, wine, and spirits, it did not end the people's thirst for such beverages. To satisfy that thirst, an illegal network of distillers, brewers, distributors, and sellers came into existence. This illegal network was able to exist in part because police chose to ignore it, or because they were bribed to do so. Because laws in some states made mere possession of alcoholic beverages a crime, one of the effects of the prohibition amendment was to make lawbreakers out of everyone who wanted to drink something stronger than soda pop. Near and Guilford sought to capitalize on the situation by publishing a weekly newspaper devoted to exposing wrongdoers, of whom there obviously were many.

At one level, the *Saturday Press* served a public purpose by pointing to public officials who were taking bribes to ignore the illegal traffic in liquor. But their critics alleged that at another level Near and Guilford used their paper for a form of blackmail. The critics charged that some people were given a chance to keep their names out of the paper if they agreed to buy advertising or make a direct payment to the publishers. Additionally, the *Saturday Press* published derogatory comments about Jews and others. Its content and the tactics of its publishers made many people angry. As a result, Guilford was shot and wounded by unknown assailants shortly after publication began, and there were threats of further violence. After the ninth issue of the paper appeared, a county attorney went to court and, without notice to either Near or Guilford, obtained an order shutting the paper down. In this court order, the *Saturday Press* was condemned as a nuisance devoted to fomenting violence. The publishers, with help from the *Chicago Tribune*, the American Civil Liberties Union, and the American Newspaper Publishers Association, were able to take their case to the Supreme Court of the United States.

That Court overturned the state court's order. Chief Justice Hughes, writing for the majority, saw the case as a conflict between two important interests. On one side was the First Amendment interest in freedom of speech and press, which lies at the heart of a free society. On the other side was another vitally important interest—the preservation of an orderly society. Hughes noted that states inherently have the authority to protect

---

4. "Scandal and Defamation! The Right of Newspapers to Defame," American Civil Liberties Union, 1931. See also Fred W. Friendly, *Minnesota Rag* (New York: Random House, 1981).

the health, safety, morals, and general welfare of their residents. This authority, called the **"police power,"** is exercised in many ways. Some courts have held that it is of equal importance with freedom of speech and press, reasoning that if society cannot maintain itself in an orderly manner, freedom of speech and press will have little meaning. Hughes noted that the Minnesota law used to shut down the *Saturday Press* was designed to promote public safety, and therefore was an exercise of the police power. Under it, a judge could suppress any publication which, in his opinion, might provoke violence. However, and this was critical to the judgment in *Near*, the law made no distinction between truthful and untruthful articles. Nor did it establish any clear guidelines for determining when a publication might provoke violence. In short, the law's language was so broad that the decision was entirely up to the judge's discretion. That, Hughes concluded, was "the very essence of censorship."

The chief justice then examined what Blackstone and other legal commentators have said about previous restraint. His conclusion was that where libel is concerned, the generally approved remedy is a suit for damages, not suppression of the libelous publication. However, Hughes continued, some commentators have argued that the First Amendment, despite its seemingly absolute terms, does not prohibit all previous restraints. He agreed that it does not:

> No one would question but that a government might prevent actual obstruction to its recruiting service or to the publication of the sailing dates of transports or the number and location of troops. On similar grounds, the primary requirements of decency may be enforced against obscene publications. The security of community life may be protected against incitements to acts of violence and the overthrow of orderly government. The constitutional guaranty of free speech does not "protect a man from an injunction against uttering words that may have all the effect of force."

The majority of the Court concluded that the *Saturday Press* did not come under any of these categories and therefore had been shut down in violation of the First Amendment. The Court also held that the Minnesota law was unconstitutional because it did not define with precision when a paper might be suppressed, and because it permitted suppression of truth as well as falsehood.

It should be emphasized that decisions written by five justices are as strong in establishing **precedent** as decisions written by all nine. But it is also worth noting that the first time the Court was confronted by a prior restraint of a newspaper, four of the nine justices acted on the belief that abuse of First Amendment freedoms could justify prior restraint. In the opinion of the minority, Near and Guilford were engaged in the publishing business for purposes of blackmail and extortion. Such businesses, the minority reasoned, could be shut down by court order.

The decision illustrates the dilemma that lies at the heart of many First Amendment cases. Beyond question, by the standards of most publishers of the era, the *Saturday Press* was a product of bad journalism. Some of its contents were highly offensive; other parts of it were false. In short, in the eyes of many people, it was garbage, and the Minnesota court treated it as such. So did the minority in the Supreme Court. It took the position that a rag like the *Saturday Press* was not entitled to First Amendment protection. But the majority took the position that the First Amendment was designed to protect speech that some people condemn as garbage. In fact, that is the point of having constitutional protection for freedom of speech and press. No one makes an issue of speech everyone agrees with. Nor is there likely to be a problem with publications reflecting the opinions of a majority. It is only when speakers begin making someone uncomfortable that they run into problems. In *Near*, the majority held that the state could not use its power to put shabby journalists out of business, even when much of what they published was considered trash.

The *Near* decision is of continuing importance for two reasons:

1. A majority of the Court condemned prior restraint of a newspaper on First Amendment grounds. Its reasons for doing so were not particularly strong, but the precedent was established and would be followed by other courts.

2. However, a majority of the Court also suggested that under certain specified circumstances, listed in the passage quoted above, prior restraint might be proper. Thus, in striking down a restraint imposed to prevent libelous assertions deemed likely to provoke violence, the Court opened the way for attempts to impose censorship for other purposes. Indeed, this is what has happened, as the remainder of this chapter will illustrate. *Near*, then, must be seen in perspective as a paradox. It extended the meaning of the First Amendment in a specific case, but also seemed to approve some limits to its scope.

Barriers against Prior Restraint

For thirty years, *Near* was the Supreme Court's only authority to which lower courts could refer in prior restraint cases. Not until 1963 did it have any more to say about the matter. Then in 1971 came a second decision further defining procedures that must be followed if a prior restraint is to be upheld. These two cases, taken with *Near*, have erected high barriers that must be surmounted if censorship is to survive appeal to the courts.

The first of these cases, *Bantam Books v. Sullivan*, grew out of an attempt by the state of Rhode Island to prevent allegedly obscene publications from reaching young people. In the 1950s, the state's legislature was persuaded that there was a link between juvenile delinquency and the kinds of sexually provocative books and magazines found on many newsstands. It created a commission with power to alert the public to the tendency of such materials to corrupt the morals of youth. As part of their duties, members of the commission examined books and magazines being sold in the state, came to their own conclusions as to which were fit for the young and which were not, and notified distributors of their findings. If the notice did not lead to withdrawal of the offending publications, police officers called on the distributors, most of whom quickly got the message. Such a widely read novel as *Peyton Place* was among the 106 titles on the list in January 1960. *Playboy* was there, too.

Bantam Books, a paperback publisher, decided to challenge the listing procedure and

Bantam Books v. Sullivan,
372 U.S. 58, 83 S.Ct. 631,
9 L.Ed.2d 584 (1963).

the law that made it possible. It asked a Rhode Island **superior court** to declare the law unconstitutional and issue an injunction against further listings. Rebuffed by the Rhode Island courts, Bantam won a decision from the Supreme Court holding the law unconstitutional. Writing for the majority, Justice William J. Brennan, Jr., drafted a standard that since has been applied to most prior restraint cases.

The state took the position that it was doing nothing wrong—that there was nothing compulsory in the commission's procedures. Booksellers could continue to offer books and magazines it had found objectionable. The police officers who came calling to find out whether the sellers had taken the commission's advice took care to tell them they had a right to appeal the findings. In any event, the state argued, the Supreme Court itself had said in *Near* that obscene works are not protected by the First Amendment. In the commission's opinion, the listed works were obscene.

But Bantam offered testimony from retailers and wholesalers who said they had felt intimidated and had taken the listed works off their shelves. This, Bantam argued, demonstrated that the law had resulted in effective prior restraint without benefit of a formal hearing, thus violating the Constitution.

Brennan agreed, holding that the state's position was untenable:

> [T]he record amply demonstrates that the commission deliberately set about to achieve the suppression of publications deemed "objectionable" and succeeded in its aim. . . . [I]nformal censorship may sufficiently inhibit the circulation of publications to warrant injunctive relief.
> What Rhode Island has done, in fact, has been to subject the distribution of publications to a system of prior administrative restraints. . . . Any system of prior restraints of expression comes to this Court bearing a heavy presumption against its constitutional validity. . . . We have tolerated such a system only where it has operated under judicial superintendence and assured an almost immediate judicial determination of the validity of the restraint. . . . The system at bar includes no such saving features.

At minimum, Brennan suggested, a proper system for determining obscenity would include notice that action was contemplated, an **adversary hearing** before a judge, a precise definition of the standard applied by the court, and a statement of the reasons why the material was found objectionable. Because none of these safeguards had been applied to the banning of books in Rhode Island, the Court held that the commission's actions were an unconstitutional prior restraint.

In later decisions, courts have focused on the Court's holding that there is a "heavy presumption against" the "constitutional validity" of "any system of prior restraint." This means that a trial court judge considering a request to prevent circulation of printed matter, or to keep a program off the air, must assume that the attempt violates the First Amendment. The burden is on the government to prove that it is trying to protect some vital interest, and that it can do so only by imposing a restraint.

Eight years later, the Supreme Court reinforced those procedures in a case involving an attempt to prevent distribution of handbills in a Chicago suburb. The case, *Organization for a Better Austin* v. *Keefe*, originated with Jerome M. Keefe, owner of a real estate agency. The Organization for a Better Austin, a group of home-owners formed to protect the racially mixed nature of their community, accused Keefe of trying

Organization for a Better Austin v. *Keefe,* 402 U.S. 415, 91 S.Ct. 1575, 29 L.Ed.2d 1 (1971).

to upset that mixture by promoting "block-busting" and "panic peddling" designed to induce white owners to sell and move out. They prepared leaflets denouncing Keefe's sales tactics and distributed them widely in the community where he lived. Contending that the organization's tactics were coercive and invaded his privacy, Keefe went to court and obtained an injunction forbidding further distribution of the leaflets. The organization appealed through the state courts, arguing that it was the victim of an impermissible prior restraint, and in 1971 the Supreme Court held that it was. In a brief decision, the Court said that in any such restraint the government "carries a heavy burden of showing justification" for its enforcement. In this case that had not been done.

The key points of *Near, Bantam Books,* and *Organization for a Better Austin* may be put together and summarized thus: Despite its seemingly absolute wording, the speech and press clause of the First Amendment does not stand as a barrier against all forms of censorship. If words have "all the effect of force," or if they obstruct the recruiting service in time of war or give away vital military secrets, if they are obscene, or incite violent overthrow of the government, they may be restrained. But this cannot be done casually or arbitrarily. There is a "heavy presumption" that any restraint of speech or press is unconstitutional. The government can prevail only if it "carries [the] heavy burden of showing justification" for restraint. It must show that it is trying to protect a vital interest, such as national security, that the Constitution gives it a right to protect. The government must show that the restraint will accomplish its intended purpose without also restraining speech that offers no threat to the vital interest. The victim of the intended restraint must be given an opportunity to counter the government's evidence. In short, prior restraint can be imposed only after an adversary hearing before a judge.

The Protection of Unpopular Opinions

Starting in the 1930s when a small religious movement, Jehovah's Witnesses, was the victim of widespread persecution in the United States,[5] the Supreme Court wrote a remarkable series of decisions banning the use of prior restraint to suppress the spread of unpopular opinions.

Members of Jehovah's Witnesses made themselves highly visible during the 1930s because of the nature of their doctrine and their methods of disseminating it. Each member is considered a minister and is under obligation to propagate the faith by preaching or, more commonly, by selling or giving away religious tracts door to door or on public streets and sidewalks. Witnesses see themselves as citizens of the Kingdom of Jesus Christ, which was reestablished on earth in 1914. Hence, true believers refuse to salute any flag, vote, perform military service, or otherwise show allegiance to any established government. Further, Witnesses' doctrine in the 1940s portrayed the Roman

---

5. For a sampling of the more than a thousand recorded instances of persecution of Jehovah's Witnesses, see Leonard A. Stevens, *Salute! The Case of the Bible vs. the Flag* (New York: Coward, 1973).

The First Amendment gives peaceful pickets, whatever their cause, the right to use public property to appeal for support. The Supreme Court has held in numerous instances that no matter how unpopular the message, the streets and other public places are proper forums for the dissemination of ideas. (Bohdan Hrynewych/Stock, Boston)

Catholic Church as the creation of the devil, with the pope as his vicar. Obviously, such beliefs are likely to offend persons who are strongly patriotic or strongly committed to other religious faiths.

To curb Witnesses' efforts to spread their doctrine, many communities enacted ordinances requiring door-to-door distributors of printed material to obtain a license from a city official. A 1938 Supreme Court decision in *Lovell* v. *Griffin*, in which one of those ordinances was struck down, established the principle that people have a right to take their message to others without seeking official approval.

Lovell v. *Griffin,* 303 U.S. 444, 58 S.Ct. 666, 82 L.Ed. 949 (1938).

The *Lovell* case began under circumstances that made it an unlikely candidate for a landmark decision of the Supreme Court. The Griffin (Ga.) city council, responding to complaints from residents who considered Witnesses a nuisance, adopted an ordinance designed to control distribution of their publications. It forbade anyone to distribute pamphlets or leaflets without getting written permission from the city manager, who could deny, grant, or revoke such permission at will. Alma Lovell ignored the requirement. As she went door to door, trying to sell or give away Witnesses' tracts, she was arrested and fined $50 for refusing to obtain a permit. When she refused to pay the fine, she was ordered to spend thirty days in jail.

Georgia courts affirmed the order. With help from Witnesses' national headquarters, the case was taken to the Supreme Court, which reversed unanimously, holding the ordinance unconstitutional. Chief Justice Hughes wrote:

> Whatever the motive which induced its adoption, its character is such that it strikes at the very foundation of the freedom of the press by subjecting it to license and censorship. . . . The ordinance would restore . . . license and censorship in its baldest form.
>
> The liberty of the press is not confined to newspapers and periodicals. It necessarily embraces pamphlets and leaflets . . . historic weapons in the defense of liberty. . . . The press in its historic connotation comprehends every sort of publication which affords a vehicle of information and opinion.
>
> Nor does it save the ordinance that it is directed only at distribution. Liberty of circulating is as essential to that freedom as liberty of publishing; without the circulation, the publication would be of little value.

This case did not end attempts to prevent distribution of unpopular views. But the principle established in *Lovell* prevailed and was enlarged upon. Any law that makes the right to disseminate a point of view dependent on the judgment of a public official is a form of prior restraint made intolerable by the First Amendment.

Two years later, in 1940, the Court reiterated and expanded that principle in *Thornhill* v. *Alabama*. In its decision, the Court held that ideas need not be put on paper to qualify for First Amendment protection. The freedom of speech clause also protects picketing designed to call attention to a labor dispute.

Thornhill v. **Alabama, 310 U.S. 88, 60 S.Ct. 736, 84 L.Ed. 1093 (1940).** In expanding on the meaning of the speech clause, the Court struck down an Alabama law that forbade loitering or picketing "without just cause or legal excuse." The law's real target was labor unions, which had become increasingly militant in the state in response to the Depression. Thornhill was one of several pickets arrested and fined during a strike against a wood preserving plant.

In holding that the arrests and the law itself violated the Constitution, the Court said that picketing is a form of speech protected by the First Amendment. The effect of the Alabama law, it added, was to set up a licensing system similar to that condemned in *Lovell*. Under its terms, state officials had the power to decide when picketing was for "just cause." Thus, the statute lent itself "to harsh and discriminatory enforcement by local prosecuting officials against particular groups deemed to merit their displeasure." It resulted "in a continuous and pervasive restraint on all freedom of discussion that might reasonably be regarded as within" its reach. Applying the clear and present danger test, the Court said it could not find in Thornhill's peaceful picketing any threat to public safety that would justify the prosecutions.

In a real sense, the victories won by Jehovah's Witnesses in *Lovell* and in several other cases during the six years after 1938, and by labor in *Thornhill*, made possible the victories of the black civil rights movement in the 1950s and 1960s. Courts cited those cases in striking down attempts to prevent or suppress the protest marches and demonstrations that brought the movement to public attention. Some of these cases reached the Supreme Court.[6] In its decisions, it reiterated principles in the Witnesses'

---

6. See, for instance, Shuttlesworth v. City of Birmingham, 394 U.S. 147, 89 S.Ct. 935, 22 L.Ed.2d 162 (1969).

and labor cases: government cannot prevent the use of streets and other public places for the dissemination of ideas, no matter how unpopular. Government can require that demonstrations be peaceful, and it can limit the time, place, and manner of dissemination, but such regulation must be reasonable.

Two more recent cases illustrate how far local officials must go to protect the rights of individuals to express unpopular—and even repugnant—points of view. In each, the Supreme Court held that prior restraint cannot be used to silence the most obnoxious speakers unless the threat of violence is so imminent, and so beyond the control of local officials, that no other remedy will work.

The leading case, *Carroll v. President and Commissioners of Princess Anne*, grew out of an ugly series of events on Maryland's Eastern Shore. In August 1966, members of

Carroll v. President and Commissioners of Princess Anne, 393 U.S. 175, 89 S.Ct. 347, 21 L.Ed.2d 325 (1968).

the National States' Rights Party conducted a rally in Princess Anne, a community of less than a thousand. About a quarter of the 150 persons present were black. The audience was subjected to a series of antiblack and anti-Semitic tirades. Feelings were running high, and state police were on hand to prevent a riot. There was no trouble that night, but one of the speakers promised that even stronger speeches would be made at a similar rally the next night.

That rally was not held. Early in the day, local officials went to Somerset County Circuit Court and, without notice to any member of the States' Rights Party or even a hearing, obtained a **restraining order** forbidding any further rallies in the county during the next ten days. After a trial at the end of that time, the court extended its order to cover the next ten months.

The Maryland **Court of Appeals** endorsed the ten-day order, but reversed the ten-month order on the ground that a restraint of that length was unreasonable. On further appeal, the Supreme Court of the United States held that even a ten-day order was unconstitutional. The Court's decision, written by Justice Abe Fortas, stuck to the narrow ground offered by the arbitrary nature of the original proceeding. Speech should never be restrained, even briefly, except as the result of an **adversary proceeding** where all sides can be heard.

But at the same time the Court endorsed the view that if the threat of violence is great enough, a prior restraint can be imposed. Fortas wrote:

> We do not here challenge the principle that there are special, limited circumstances in which speech is so interlaced with burgeoning violence that it is not protected. . . . "No one would have the hardihood to suggest that the principle of freedom of speech sanctions incitement to riot."[7]

A decade later, both state and federal courts held that the Village of Skokie, Illinois,

---

7. Quoting from Cantwell v. Connecticut, 310 U.S. 396, 60 S.Ct. 900, 84 L.Ed. 1213 (1940), a Jehovah's Witnesses case in which the Court found that the threat of violence was not so imminent as to justify the arrest of a Witness who was playing an anti-Catholic recording on a public street in a Catholic neighborhood.

could not prevent a rally that did promise to incite a riot. At issue was the right of a small group of self-proclaimed American Nazis who espoused virulent anti-Semitism to meet on the streets of a city with a predominantly Jewish population, some of them survivors of Germany's death camps of World War II. Members of the group wore uniforms patterned on those worn by Hitler's infamous SS squads, who enforced his attempt to exterminate Jews. When they asked to conduct a rally on the steps of the Skokie Village Hall, residents reacted with fear and indignation. Militant Jewish groups threatened violence. Caught in the middle, the Skokie Village Council adopted three **ordinances** designed to make it difficult if not impossible for the meeting to be held. This set off a series of lawsuits in both state and federal courts, which held that the ordinances were unconstitutional attempts at prior restraint. The Supreme Court refused pleas that the decisions should be overturned because they would lead to violence.[8]

The Nazi group's right to freedom of speech and assembly was upheld. But as Justice Harry A. Blackmun noted, every court that considered the case felt a need to apologize for its verdict. Blackmun argued that the Supreme Court should have taken the case in order to determine how far a community must go to protect inflammatory and provocative speakers. It is interesting to compare his view with that of Thomas I. Emerson, the First Amendment scholar whose views were summarized in chapter 1. Emerson argued that the First Amendment imposes a duty on government to provide a forum for all shades of opinion. Blackmun, confronted with an extreme application of that argument, wrote:

> I . . . feel that the present case affords the Court an opportunity to consider whether . . . there is no limit whatsoever to the exercise of free speech. There indeed may be no such limit, but when citizens assert, not casually but with deep conviction, that the proposed demonstration is scheduled at a place and in a manner that is taunting and overwhelmingly offensive to the citizens of that place, that assertion, uncomfortable though it may be for the judges, deserves to be examined. It just might fall into the same category as one's "right" to cry "fire" in a crowded theater, for "the character of every act depends upon the circumstances in which it is done." [Quoting Holmes in *Schenck.*]

Blackmun's concern raises serious questions. How far must society go to provide a forum for those whose only purpose seems to be to stir up racial, religious, or political hatred? How much exposure should the news media give to persons whose arguments are based on deliberate misstatement of fact, or are devoid of both reason and logic? In short, should all speech be equally free? Is there an obligation under the First Amendment to provide a forum for any kind of expression uttered in the name of a cause? It is a question that vexes not only judges, but all journalists as well.

The Protection of National Security

Twice in recent times, the federal government has asked the courts to prevent publication of information believed harmful to national security. In the first instance,

---

8. Smith v. Collin, 439 U.S. 916, 99 S.Ct. 291, 58 L.Ed.2d 264 (1978). See also 447 F.Supp 676 (N.D.Ill. 1978), 578 F.2d 1197 (7th Cir. 1978), and Village of Skokie v. National Socialist Party, 373 N.E.2d 21 (Ill. 1978).

the *New York Times*, the *Washington Post*, and other newspapers were prevented for about two weeks from publishing secret documents dealing with the Vietnam War. The Supreme Court ruled that the government had not met the heavy burden of proving that the restraint was essential to the nation's security. In the second instance, a **United States district court** prevented a magazine from publishing an article purporting to describe how a hydrogen bomb is made. That episode ended indecisively when the information was disclosed in other media.

The Pentagon Papers

Serious-minded readers of the *New York Times* on Sunday, June 13, 1971, were offered an unusual opportunity. They could read the first installment of the top-secret story of how the United States came to be mired in the war in Vietnam, which was at its height. The *Times* had obtained a copy of a 7,000-page study prepared by the federal government for official use only and said that it would publish those parts *Times* editors believed to be of public interest. Henry Kissinger, then President Nixon's national security adviser, said in his memoirs that the disclosure of the documents "came as a profound shock to the Administration."[9] That shock very quickly was converted into action of an unprecedented nature. Within three days, the attorney general of the United States managed to obtain court orders that stopped first the *Times* and then the *Washington Post* from publishing further installments of the documents.

The material at issue bore the prosaic title of *History of U.S. Decision-Making Process on Vietnam Policy.* Because it had been prepared for the Defense Department, the study quickly became known as the "Pentagon Papers." None of the information in the History was less than three years old. It described events that had taken place during the administrations of John F. Kennedy and Lyndon B. Johnson, some of which had already become common knowledge. However, the documents also contained still-secret information about the conduct of the war and diplomatic maneuvering, some of which did not reflect favorably on the United States. For instance, the documents confirmed speculation that officials in Washington had conspired in the overthrow and murder of Ngo Dinh Diem, president of South Vietnam.

At the time it was impossible to predict the effect of the publication of the papers. On the very weekend that the first installment appeared, Kissinger was preparing to leave on a secret mission to China that would lead to the opening of relations with that previously hostile nation. He wrote later that there were real fears that unauthorized disclosure of so many secret papers would convince the Chinese that the United States could not be trusted to keep diplomatic secrets. Thus, they might not be willing to open relations. Further, the United States also was engaged in secret peace talks with North Vietnam, and was at a sensitive point in nuclear arms talks with the Soviet Union. Although the negotiations with the Vietnamese did fail, Kissinger concluded later that publication of the Pentagon Papers had nothing to do with it. However, he wrote, "neither those who stole the documents nor the government could know that at the time."[10] Kissinger was referring to the fact that when the *Times* began its publication of

---

9. Henry Kissinger, *White House Years* (Boston: Little, Brown, 1979), p. 729.
10. Ibid., p. 1021.

Dr. Daniel Ellsberg (right) receives a huge "declassified" stamp in recognition of his role in publication of the "Pentagon Papers" by the *New York Times* and other newspapers in 1971. Ellsberg helped write the papers, a top secret history of American involvement in Vietnam, and gave a copy of them to the *Times*. The Justice Department's short-lived attempt to prevent publication led to a decision by the Supreme Court condemning prior restraint. (UPI/Bettmann Newsphotos)

the Papers, the United States was at war in Vietnam. No one could predict the effect disclosure of some of the sensitive information might have on the course of the war. He also was referring to the fact that the Papers were, in effect, stolen property. Dr. Daniel Ellsberg, one of the thirty-six authors of the Papers, had become disillusioned with the government's war policies and, with the help of Anthony J. Russo, Jr., had copied the entire body of the report and delivered it to the *Times*. The government's attempt to prosecute the pair ended in a mistrial in 1972.

After the first three installments of the Pentagon Papers had been published by the *Times*, Justice Department attorneys went to Murray I. Gurfein, then in his first month as a judge of the United States District Court in New York City, and asked for an order restraining further publication. They offered witnesses from the Defense and State Departments who argued, without going into specifics, that further disclosures would permit the enemy in Vietnam to gain insights into American methods and further endanger the lives of soldiers in combat. Witnesses also testified that the disclosures would embarrass the United States in peace negotiations then underway. Gurfein restrained publication until he could hear and consider the arguments at greater length, but refused the government's request for a **permanent injunction.** He conceded that the government might be embarrassed by publication of what he called "historical documents," but he was not convinced that it would be harmed. He wrote:

> The security of the nation is not at the ramparts alone. Security also lies in the value of our free institutions. A cantankerous press, an obstinate press, a ubiquitous press must be suffered by those in authority in order to preserve the even greater values of freedom of expression and the right of the people to know. In this case there has been no attempt to stifle criticism. Yet in the last analysis, it is not merely the opinion of the editorial writer or of the columnist which is protected by the First Amendment. It is the free flow of information so that the public will be informed about the Government and its actions.[11]

Judge Gurfein based his decision on the language of the Espionage Act of 1917.[12] The Act, he wrote, provides only for punishment of those who illegally acquire **classified** (secret) **materials** for the purpose of passing them along to foreign powers with the intent to harm the United States. Thus, he held, the Department of Justice was trying to act against the wrong party for the wrong reasons. Although he was overruled immediately by the Court of Appeals for the Second Circuit, which continued his restraining order in effect, he was ultimately to have the satisfaction of knowing that the Supreme Court endorsed his reasoning.

Meanwhile, the *Washington Post* began publishing the same set of documents. Again, the government went to court. This time, both the district court and the court of appeals denied it even a temporary restraining order. But it did get a stay, a court order preventing publication pending an immediate appeal to the Supreme Court. That Court acted with unusual speed, reflecting the utmost seriousness with which a prior restraint is regarded. Both federal appeals courts acted on June 23.

The next day, the *New York Times* asked the Supreme Court for review. Although the Court was approaching the end of its term—it usually recesses for the summer about July 1—it agreed to hear the case, scheduling oral argument for June 26. It issued its decision in *New York Times Co. v. United States* on June 30. Seldom has the Court acted with such speed. Normally two to four months will elapse between argument and the Court's decision, and it is not at all unusual for a year to pass between the time the Court agrees to take a case and its decision.

New York Times Co. v. United States, 403 U.S. 713, 91 S.Ct. 2140, 29 L.Ed.2d 822 (1971).

In the Supreme Court, as in the lower courts, the government argued that the executive branch, meaning the president, had authority to protect the nation against publication of information that would endanger its security. While it could not point to any law that would authorize the government to act against the newspapers, the Justice Department argued that such authority was inherent in the president's constitutional power to conduct foreign affairs and in his role as commander-in-chief of the armed forces.

Not a single member of the Supreme Court accepted that argument. While no more than two of the justices could agree on any one rationale, the Court agreed, six to three,

---

11. United States v. New York Times Co., 328 F.Supp. 324 (S.D.N.Y. 1971).
12. 18 U.S. Code, §793(e). It is still in effect.

that the prior restraint should be lifted immediately. Quoting directly from *Near, Bantam Books,* and *Organization for a Better Austin,* the Court said in a brief **per curiam decision** that it agreed with Judge Gurfein and the District of Columbia courts: the government had not carried the "heavy burden" required to justify its request for a restraint. Thus, it had not overcome "the heavy presumption against" the restraint's constitutional validity. Even the three dissenters took pains to say that they opposed prior restraints in general, but thought this case had moved through the courts too quickly to develop a factual basis on which to judge whether national security was indeed in danger.

The case was of great importance to the news media because it was the first time the Department of Justice had asked the courts to restrain publication of information. As with Judge Gurfein, that request raised grave concern among the judges who considered it. Judge J. Skelly Wright of the United States Court of Appeals for the District of Columbia Circuit said of the stay imposed pending appeal to the Supreme Court:

> This is a sad day for America. Today, for the first time in the 200 years of our history, the executive department has succeeded in stopping the presses. It has enlisted the judiciary in the suppression of our most precious freedom.[13]

The individual opinions written by each of the nine justices of the Supreme Court reflect similar concern for the gravity of the action. While the Court wrote no new precedents, the justices' opinions are of some interest because they demonstrate the strong differences of opinion, even among leading legal authorities, over prior restraint. The differences serve as reminders to journalists that even something as basic as the right to publish without censorship cannot be taken for granted.

The opinions ranged through a spectrum beginning with William O. Douglas and Hugo L. Black, who were alone in taking the position that *any* prior restraint violates the First Amendment. Neither is still living, and no other member of the Court has adopted their view. Justice Brennan has come closest. But in this instance, he was content to quote approvingly from the majority's decision in *Near.* He concluded that publication of the Pentagon Papers did not present a danger to the lives of troops then in combat in Vietnam and therefore should not be restrained further.

Justices Potter Stewart and Byron R. White took a legalistic position. They conceded that the government has a right to prevent its vital secrets from reaching the public. They also suggested that the government has a problem because it tries to keep too many secrets. But they were troubled by the nature of the action the Justice Department took in this case. The Espionage Act makes it a crime for persons in government to disclose secret information to unauthorized persons, but it was not clear that the statute authorizes punishment of newspapers for publishing classified information. White argued that the Senate debate in 1917, when the Espionage Act was adopted, seemed to indicate that Congress intended such authority. Stewart joined White in writing that they "would have no difficulty in sustaining convictions" of crime under circumstances that would not justify prior restraint. Because nothing in the Espionage Act authorized restraint, the justices voted to let the *Times* resume publication.

Justice Thurgood Marshall also avoided the First Amendment issue by referring to

---

13. United States v. Washington Post Co., 446 F.2d 1322 (D.C.Cir. 1971).

the doctrine of **separation of powers.** Under that doctrine, Congress makes law, the executive carries it into effect, and the judiciary stands apart from both, prepared to settle disputes arising from the process. In this instance, Congress had made no law giving the executive branch authority to prevent newspapers from publishing secret government documents. Marshall took the position that the Supreme Court could not do what Congress had not done—that is, create authority under which the government could restrain publication.

The three dissenters—Chief Justice Warren E. Burger and Justices John Marshall Harlan and Blackmun—cited *Near* in taking the position that government can use prior restraint to protect itself against harmful disclosure of vital secrets. But in this instance, each took the position that he did not know whether such secrets were being disclosed. As they saw it, the case had progressed so rapidly through the lower courts that the record was incomplete. There was not enough evidence to prove or disprove the government's claim that it would suffer irreparable harm if the *New York Times*, the *Washington Post*, and other newspapers published the remainder of the documents. Thus, the dissenters would have sent the case back to the district courts for trial and a full development of the issues. Meanwhile, they would have continued the restraint.

In his dissenting opinion, Chief Justice Burger raised two questions that continue to plague relations between the news media and the government. Lawyers for the *Times* had asserted in argument to the Court that the paper was serving the public's **"right to know"** when it began publication of the documents. Burger said he could not find that right in the First Amendment. Even if it were there, as the *Times* lawyer seemed to argue, it would not be absolute, Burger wrote, but might have to yield in some instances to other important interests. If the Court were to recognize such a right, and ground it in the Constitution, Burger asked, who would be responsible for fulfilling it? The news media? Or the government, which is the main repository of information on its own activities? Burger could not resist pointing out that the editors of the *Times* had held up publication of the papers for three months while they decided what parts of them would be published. Why, in the fulfillment of a "right to know," should the courts be required to act in a few days?

Burger's questions are good ones. They will arise in different contexts later in this book. "The right to know" is a phrase that slips easily off the tongue, especially when a journalist is denied access to information that seems important. Usually it is asserted in a context that suggests the journalist is acting on behalf of the people, who are the ultimate possessors of "right to know." That people who govern themselves have a right to know everything their various governments are doing is an appealing concept in a free society. If that indeed is the ultimate nature of the right, it has awesome implications, as Burger suggests. If such a right were to be found in the First Amendment, would it not compel journalists to transmit in unedited form every last word they found in public government documents and in the utterances of government officials? Would not any abridgment of that flow by an editor become a violation of the public's "right to know"? This may sound far-fetched, but a **constitutional right,** once defined, holds a preeminent position in the legal hierarchy.

Burger also taunted the *Times* for its willingness to accept and publish documents he saw as stolen property. *Times* editors, he wrote, should have known something was wrong when they were handed such a vast quantity of documents, clearly marked "top secret" and clearly the property of the United States government. It should have occurred to them to notify the proper government departments of their windfall and to seek **declassification** of the materials through proper channels. "With such an approach—one that great newspapers have in the past practiced and stated editorially to be the duty of an honorable press—the newspapers and Government might well have narrowed the area of disagreement" and settled it through litigation.

Burger let fly a final arrow:

> To me it is hardly believable that a newspaper long regarded as a great institution in American life would fail to perform one of the basic and simple duties of every citizen with respect to the discovery or possession of stolen property or secret Government documents. That duty, I had thought—perhaps naively—was to report forthwith to responsible public officers. This duty rests on taxi drivers, justices and the *New York Times.*

Chief Justice Burger's belief that documents, or even copies of them, are property and therefore subject to criminal law defining theft was to surface in each succeeding session of Congress through 1977. Proposals were made to make unauthorized possession of such documents a crime. But each time, representatives of the news media and civil libertarians raised enough objections to defeat the attempt.[14]

What harmful consequences, if any, flowed from the subsequent publication of the Pentagon Papers remains for historians to discover. Ten years later Floyd Abrams, co-counsel for the *Times* in the case, interviewed those who had testified for the government. He concluded, "[I]t now seems unlikely that there was any damage at all."[15] As noted earlier, Henry Kissinger concluded that the publication was not responsible for the collapse of the peace negotiations with North Vietnam. His mission to China did proceed, and it led to the establishment of diplomatic relations with that country. Still, questions persist.

Should information that is so sensitive to national security that it is classified "top secret" be subject to disclosure by any reporter who can lay hands on it? Or should disclosure be permitted only by "responsible" reporters, such as those employed by the *New York Times* and the *Washington Post?* If reporters may tell the world about matters the government deems secret, who else may do so?

Or does the problem lie, as Justice Stewart suggested, in the government's trying to keep too many secrets? When the secrecy stamp is applied, as it has been, to clippings from newspapers and magazines, doesn't this make a mockery of the classification system? And isn't the system further mocked when government officials, including presidents, selectively disclose classified information that will help them score a political point? In its brief in this case the *New York Times* pointed to many instances of such disclosure in memoirs, in press conferences, and in "don't quote me" leaks to favored reporters.

If Congress should try to enact a law, as some members of the Court suggested, providing for punishment of the publisher of classified information, what is to be done in those instances in which a knowledgeable reporter, working with readily available

---

14. *Congressional Quarterly Almanac* (Washington, D.C.: Congressional Quarterly), ed. from 1971 through 1980.
15. Floyd Abrams, "The Pentagon Papers a Decade Later," *New York Times Magazine,* 7 June 1981, p. 22.

information, reaches conclusions that have also been reached in a classified document? Would shrewd analysis of a broad range of sensitive information thus become a crime?

Despite the troubling questions raised by publication of the Pentagon Papers, the fact remains that a majority of the Supreme Court again struck down a prior restraint. In doing so, the Court did not write any new law, placing its reliance on *Near, Bantam Books,* and *Organization for a Better Austin,* but it reinforced the principle that censorship is a weapon of last resort, to be used only when the danger is so serious that nothing less stringent will work.

The H-Bomb Secret

Early in 1979, the editors of *The Progressive* magazine announced that they would publish an article entitled "The H-Bomb Secret: How We Got It, Why We're Telling It." The author, Howard Morland, said the article would tell how to make a hydrogen bomb—the most powerful force under the control of human beings. He said he had put the story together entirely out of information in the public realm, that he had culled his basic data from books and documents in various public libraries and from interviews with government officials and researchers who were or had been involved in nuclear development. His purpose, he said, was to show that the so-called secrets of the atom were already general knowledge and that anyone with the necessary technology could build a hydrogen weapon. It was his expressed hope and that of his editors that their publication of such a message would lead to more diligent efforts to abolish nuclear weapons.

The Department of Justice reacted to the announcement by asking Judge Robert W. Warren of the United States District Court in Milwaukee for an injunction. The action was brought in the federal district court in Madison, where the magazine was published,

United States v. *The Progressive,* 467 F. Supp. 990 (W.D.Wis. 1979).

with Judge Warren serving by assignment after the judge at Madison had excused himself. This time, government lawyers could find support for their request in a federal statute. The Atomic Energy Act of 1954[16] contains language forbidding all disclosure of nuclear secrets. The government argued that under terms of the law, all information dealing with nuclear weapons technology is "classified at birth"; that is, it must be treated as a secret as soon as it takes tangible form.

After hearing the evidence in a proceeding closed to the public, Judge Warren issued a **temporary restraining order.** He concluded that "few things, save grave national security concerns, are sufficient to override First Amendment interests." Despite claims by Morland and his editors that all technical information in the article had previously been made public, the judge was not convinced. He concluded that it did indeed reveal secrets "vital to the operation of the hydrogen bomb." While the article was not a "do-it-yourself" guide for the home tinkerer, "it could possibly provide sufficient information to allow a medium size nation to move faster in developing a hydrogen weapon. It could provide a ticket to by-pass blind alleys."

---

16. Atomic Energy Act, 42 U.S. Code, §§2274, 2280.

Judge Warren wished Morland and his editors well in their laudable goal of persuading the peoples of the world to insist that their leaders keep nuclear weapons under control. But he said he could find "no plausible reason why the public needs to know the technical details about hydrogen bomb construction to carry on an informed debate."

He balanced the public interest in knowing how a hydrogen bomb works, against national security, with a predictable result:

> A mistake in ruling against *The Progressive* will seriously infringe cherished First Amendment rights. . . . A mistake in ruling against the United States could pave the way for thermonuclear annihilation for us all. In that event, our right to life is extinguished and the right to publish becomes moot.

Under court order, the article did not appear in the next issue of *The Progressive*.

An appeal was taken to the Court of Appeals for the Seventh Circuit in Chicago. Before it could reach its decision, the case blew up in the government's face. On September 15, 1979, the *Madison* (Wis.) *Press Connection*, a newspaper published by striking employees of that city's two newspapers, ran a letter from Charles Hansen, a thirty-two-year-old computer programmer, containing most of the technical information at issue in the Morland article. Hansen had sent his letter originally to Charles Percy, a Republican senator from Illinois. Then he had sent copies to eight newspapers. He explained that his information had been obtained entirely from materials in the public domain, although he conceded that some of it had been put there by three scientists who allegedly had violated their security clearances. However, no one was ever punished.[17]

Journalists and First Amendment lawyers viewed the episode with mixed feelings. Morland and editors of *The Progressive*, along with some other journalists, hailed the outcome as a victory for freedom of the press. *The Progressive* published the original version of the article in the November 1979 issue under the title "The H-Bomb Secret: To Know How Is to Ask Why." The *Chicago Tribune*, one of the seven recipients of Hansen's letter, published it. Stanton Cook, the newspaper's publisher, said he and his editors concluded the letter did not contain any secret information that would endanger national security. The *Palo Alto* (Calif.) *Peninsula Times-Tribune*, owned by the *Chicago Tribune*, received the letter but did not publish it because a Department of Energy official told the paper's editor it might violate the law by doing so. It did, however, publish an accompanying diagram purporting to show how a hydrogen bomb works. The *Daily Californian*, the student newspaper at the University of California at Berkeley, announced its intention to print the Hansen letter, but was served with a federal court injunction before it could do so.[18]

Editors of the *Milwaukee Journal*, *Oakland Tribune*, *San Jose Mercury News*, and *Wall Street Journal* decided not to publish the letter. The editors of the *Wall Street Journal* published on the editorial page an article by the newspaper's specialist on nuclear matters, John R. Emshwiller.[19] He did not see the outcome of *The Progressive* case as a

---

17. John Consoli, "The Progressive Triumphs in H-Bomb Case," *Editor & Publisher*, 22 September 1979, pp. 9, 36.
18. "Judge Bars Newspaper on Coast from Using Letter about H-Bomb," *New York Times*, 16 September 1979.
19. "Progressive Case: Did the Press Win or Lose?" *Wall Street Journal*, 28 September 1979.

victory for freedom of the press. He wrote that in the eyes of many persons, the magazine and its friends in other media had fought and won a battle to print nuclear secrets. The end result, he predicted, would be further erosion of the press's credibility. Jack Landau, director of the Reporters' Committee for Freedom of the Press and a stalwart battler for freedom of the press, commented, "The First Amendment is in worse shape than when [*the Progressive* episode] started."

Such comments reflect, in part, the belief that the Morland article may indeed have contained secrets that could help other nations join the H-bomb club. At the start of its case, the government told editors of *The Progressive* that if they would delete about 10 percent of the article it would have no objections to publication of the rest. By standing on First Amendment principle, the editors became the subjects of prior restraint, imposed on the grounds of protecting national security. The appeal to the Seventh Circuit Court never was resolved because publication of the Hansen letter, which largely duplicated the subject matter of the Morland article, took away any reason for the court to reach a decision.

At the time of the district court's decision, the *Progressive* case seemed to put the First Amendment issue squarely—a serious risk to the nation's security was countered by imposition of prior restraint, the most serious infringement of freedom of the press. Had it gone up through the appeals process, the case might well have resulted in a decision defining the point at which harmful disclosures can be prevented. However, the multiple publications that brought the case to an end suggest that the editors of *The Progressive* may have been right when they argued that as of 1979 there no longer was any secret to protect. Thus, the Supreme Court has still to confront a case in which censorship in the name of national security and the First Amendment meet head-on.

Prior Restraint by Contract

In the Pentagon Papers and *Progressive* cases, the government managed to delay publication of secrets whose release it believed would be harmful to national security. In 1974, in an instance in which national security was not directly at issue, the government succeeded in forcing deletion of secret information from a book, *The CIA and the Cult of Intelligence*,[20] written by Victor L. Marchetti, a former official of the CIA, and John Marks, a former employee of the State Department. This was censorship in the classic meaning of the term. The book can be found in many libraries, where it serves as a reminder that despite the First Amendment and the heavy presumption against prior restraints, there are circumstances under which the federal government can say, "You can't print that." It should be noted that as recently as 1983, President Reagan proposed expanding the scope of the government's power to issue such orders.

The government was able to censor *The CIA and the Cult of Intelligence* because Marchetti was its coauthor. As one might expect, persons who go to work for the CIA must agree not to disclose any information learned during their employment that would disclose "intelligence sources or methods." Some of the agency's employees occupy such sensitive positions that they cannot even tell outsiders whom they work for. This insistence

---

20. New York: Knopf, 1974.

on secrecy continues when employees leave the CIA for whatever reason. The employment agreement has been construed to require such persons to submit to the agency for security clearance any article, book, or speech based on their previous work. The purpose is to prevent disclosure of information learned during the course of employment that still might be classified.

Marchetti had spent fourteen years with the CIA, rising to the position of special assistant to the executive director. He left because he had become disenchanted with the agency's covert actions directed at undermining governments considered unfriendly to the United States.[21] He wrote a novel and an article, both casting the CIA in an unfavorable light, neither of which he submitted for clearance. Marchetti wrote a second article and an outline for a nonfiction book designed to call public attention to what Marchetti saw as the excesses of his former employer. He sent both manuscripts to several publishers, but submitted neither to the CIA for clearance.

When the CIA found out what Marchetti was doing, government lawyers went to a United States District Court judge in Alexandria, Virginia, and obtained an order forbidding the author from "disclosing in any manner (1) any information relating to intelligence activities, (2) any information concerning intelligence sources, or (3) any intelligence information." He was the first writer in the United States to be subjected to such a censorship order.[22] An appeal was taken to the Fourth Circuit court, where Marchetti argued that the lower court's order violated his First Amendment right to expose what he believed to be mistaken government policy. In its decision in *United States v. Marchetti*, the court conceded that Marchetti had the same right as any other person to criticize government policy. But, it held, the government also has a right to protect vital secrets. Then, shifting its ground, the court focused on Marchetti's employment agreement with the CIA, seeing it as a contract, which the government could enforce. Therefore, the author would have to submit his manuscripts to the agency for review before they could be sent to any publisher.

United States v. *Marchetti,* **466 F.2d 1309 (4th Cir. 1972).**

But the court also recognized that the CIA might abuse its right to review. Therefore, it ordered that the review must be completed within thirty days. To guard against capricious deletions, or censorship solely for the purpose of muting Marchetti's criticism, the court told the former agent he could ask a judge to review the CIA's editing decisions.

Marchetti had no choice but to do as the court ordered. Alfred A. Knopf, Inc., had agreed to publish the book, and could not do so until the CIA had reviewed the manuscript. The CIA ordered deletion of 339 passages, or nearly 20 percent of the book. Knopf asked a federal district court to review the deletions. While that action was pending, the CIA agreed, in negotiations, to insist on only 168 of its original deletions. When these were reviewed by the district court, it concluded that the CIA could prove that only 27 contained still-classified, sensitive information not previously published by others.

However, the court delayed putting its decision into effect pending the outcome of an appeal to the Fourth Circuit Court. That court's decision, in *Alfred A. Knopf* v.

---

21. From Marchetti's Introduction to the book.
22. From the Introduction by Melvin L. Wulf, legal director, American Civil Liberties Union, who was Marchetti's counsel, p. xix.

Colby, was devoted largely to establishing the rules a trial judge should follow in deciding whether the CIA is entitled to delete material from a manuscript. The court also held that the district court judge had not followed these rules in restoring most of the CIA's deletions, remanding the case to him for further action. To avoid deletion of disputed material, the court held, the author must show (1) that the item was not classified by a person authorized to do so, or (2) that it was not classified when the author came into possession of it, or (3) that it had been declassified. The court said Marchetti could not be permitted to publish still-classified information merely because the gist of it had been published by someone else. The court reasoned that a foreign agent who read a story written by an ordinary reporter might have doubts about its truth. But if he were to read the same information in an article written by a former CIA agent, his doubts would be resolved. The fourth circuit's guidelines remain in effect for disputed items in any manuscript prepared for publication by former employees of the CIA.

Alfred A. Knopf v. Colby, 509 F.2d 1362 (4th Cir. 1975).

However, they were not applied to *The CIA and the Cult of Intelligence*. Perhaps to capitalize on the publicity surrounding the case, Knopf decided to publish the book before the litigation was resolved. A Publisher's Note calls attention to the court action and the negotiations with the CIA that preceded it. Passages the CIA ordered deleted and then agreed to restore are printed in boldface type. Passages the agency refused to clear are indicated by blank spaces of varying length that are given emphasis by the word DELETED, printed in boldface capital letters. There are 168 such blank spaces in the book, varying in length from a single word to more than two pages. Judging from the restored material, the author's theses, and the context in which the deletions occur, the reader can get some indication of their nature. The second chapter, for instance, opens with the authors' version of the CIA's covert intervention in Chile in 1970 to try to prevent the election as president of Salvador Allende, an avowed Marxist. The account starts with the deletion of a quotation attributed to Henry Kissinger, then adviser to President Nixon for national security affairs, during a secret meeting at the White House. The account was heavily censored, apparently to remove details of the decision to intervene and how it was to be carried out. In any event, Allende won the election, only to become the victim of a military putsch in 1973 in which he was killed. Heavy deletions were also made in chapters discussing the Bay of Pigs operation against Castro's Cuba, the war in Vietnam, and attempts to stir up opposition against the Communist government of China. Some of the shorter deletions appear to be of the names of CIA agents or of persons cooperating with them.

The Supreme Court refused to become involved in the Marchetti-Marks censorship, but in 1980 it left no doubt that a majority endorsed the rationale for it. Another former agent of the CIA, Frank Snepp, wrote a book, *Decent Interval*,[23] about the United States's pell-mell withdrawal from Vietnam in 1975. He, too, had not submitted his manuscript for review. Although the government conceded that there was no still-classified material in the book, it filed suit in a federal district court to compel Snepp to surrender his profits from the work. The court granted the request, but the Court of

Snepp v. United States, 444 U.S. 507, 100 S.Ct. 763, 62 L.Ed.2d 704 (1980).

---

23. Frank W. Snepp, *Decent Interval* (New York: Random House, 1977).

Appeals for the Fourth Circuit reversed. The Supreme Court agreed to review the decision and restored the district court's verdict. In a brusque *per curiam* decision, it held that a former agent's judgment as to what may be disclosed safely is not to be substituted for that of the CIA. In its decision in *Snepp* v. *United States*, the Court wrote:

> Undisputed evidence in this case shows that a CIA agent's violation of his obligation to submit writings about the agency for prepublication review impairs the CIA's ability to perform its statutory duties. Admiral Turner, director of the CIA, testified without contradiction that Snepp's book and others like it have seriously impaired the effectiveness of American intelligence operations.

As a consequence, the Court required that all of Snepp's earnings from the book, estimated at $125,000 or more,[24] be placed in trust for the benefit of the government. The Court said its order "simply requires him to disgorge the benefits of his faithlessness."

Within two years, the government demonstrated that it would not limit the *Snepp* rationale to small fry. In December 1981, William Colby, who was director of the CIA when it censored Marchetti's book, ran into trouble with the publication of the French version of his memoirs, *Honorable Men*.[25] He had received the agency's clearance for the version printed in the United States, but the French edition contained material that had been deleted from the former. Colby agreed to pay the government $10,000 for the oversight, which he blamed on the French publisher.[26]

To protect its intelligence secrets, and particularly to guard the identity of its agents, the CIA took action of another sort against Philip Agee, another disenchanted former employee. Agee's publications were used to identify CIA agents in foreign countries in the expectation that they would then be driven out by anti-American groups. To avoid the kind of legal action that had ensnared Marchetti and Snepp, he lived and worked abroad. The State Department revoked his passport in order to force his return to the United States. That action ultimately was upheld by the Supreme Court on the ground that the government could forbid travel abroad by persons whose intent was to harm national security.[27]

In the wake of the *Agee* case, President Reagan sought and obtained legislation making it a federal crime for anyone to publish information with knowledge that it would disclose the identity of United States intelligence agents.[28] The news media protested in vain, arguing that fear of prosecution might hamper legitimate newsgathering in the intelligence area.

There were even stronger protests in March 1983 when President Reagan, upset over what he believed to be breaches of security, issued a directive that would have greatly expanded the reach of the principle upheld in *Snepp*.[29] Under its terms, anyone in government who had access to secret or top-secret documents that included information about intelligence operations or methods would have to sign the same kind of agreement

---

24. "Top Court Rules CIA Has Power to Screen Writings by Past and Current Employees," *Wall Street Journal*, 20 February 1980.
25. New York: Simon & Schuster, 1978.
26. *New York Times*, 21 and 24 September 1981, 2 October 1981, 1 January 1982.
27. Haig v. Agee, 453 U.S. 280, 101 S.Ct. 2766, 69 L.Ed.2d 640 (1981).
28. Intelligence Identities Protection Act, P.L. 97–200, 96 Stat. 122, 50 U.S.C.A. §§421–26.
29. Directive Safeguarding National Security Information, 11 March 1983, 9 Med.L.Rptr. 1759.

required of CIA agents. The House Government Operations Committee estimated that as many as 128,000 persons, including some employed by contractors doing business with the government, would be affected. In effect, anyone who worked for or with sensitive government agencies, even briefly, and who was cleared for access to intelligence reports, would be required for the rest of his or her life to submit any public statements to the government for clearance. Persuaded by the argument that such a sweeping order could be used for political ends, Congress attached a rider to the State Department funding authorization bill late in 1983, postponing the effect of the directive until April 1984.[30] When members of the president's administration also advised against the directive, Reagan delayed its effect indefinitely, explaining that he was "talking to Congress about ways to improve security without interfering with the people's rights."[31]

As the court decisions presented in this section clearly show, the federal government can require certain of its employees to sign contracts subjecting themselves to lifetime censorship. The courts have held that as long as such contracts forbid publication only of classified information obtained by the employees in the course of their employment, they do not run afoul of the First Amendment. But in *Marchetti*, the first of the CIA censorship cases, the Court of Appeals for the Fourth Circuit clearly warned that the government's right of review should not be used to restrict the right of former employees to criticize the government and its policies. Nor, the court said, can the right of review be used to restrain publication of unclassified information. However, the decision in *Knopf*, if followed by other circuits, puts on former employees the burden of proving that sensitive information either was not acquired in the course of their duties or is no longer classified. Finally, the Supreme Court's decision in *Snepp* stands as a powerful warning to all federal employees or former employees who have signed a review agreement. Failure to abide by that agreement can result in forfeiture of all proceeds from the offending publication.

To some, with the benefit of hindsight, the cases in this chapter may seem like much ado about nothing. In all instances except those involving CIA contracts, an attempt was made to halt publication or dissemination of material considered harmful to the government, to public order, or to the sensitivities of some segment of society. In all instances but one, the restraint was lifted sooner or later by a court decision holding that that particular restraint violated the First Amendment's guarantee of freedom of speech and of the press. In the one exception, the *Progressive* case, the government's imposition of censorship was made a mockery when essentially the same information surfaced in other media. And yet the fact remains that despite the seemingly absolute language of the First Amendment—"Congress shall make no law . . . abridging the freedom of speech, or of the press . . ."—censorship can be imposed. The Supreme Court has overturned specific restraints, but it has refused to hold that censorship cannot be imposed under any circumstances. If the government can carry the heavy burden of proving that the threat to national security, to public order, or even to a decent society, is great enough, it can overcome the heavy presumption against the constitutional validity of a

---

30. James E. Roper, "Congress Acts to Curb Censorship Bill," *Editor & Publisher*, 24 December 1983, pp. 9, 19.

31. "President Delays Polygraph Order Aimed at Leaks," *Wall Street Journal*, 17 February 1984.

prior restraint. Further, we will see in future chapters that some kinds of language—obscenity, misleading advertising, works infringing copyright, or falsifying an individual's life story—can be restrained successfully. Thus, if this chapter says nothing else, it says that the First Amendment is not absolute, even against prior restraint.

In the Professional World

It is unlikely that any journalist will be confronted with a direct attempt to impose a prior restraint. And yet what cannot be achieved directly may sometimes be achieved indirectly. Any time a public official offers information "off the record," the intent is to bind the reporter to an agreement not to share that information with the public. Sometimes reporters make such promises in the belief that temporary withholding of some information will lead to disclosure of more important information. However, such agreements can also keep the public in ignorance of planned government actions at a time when discussion is most needed. For this reason, the best reporters do not lightly promise to go off the record.

Advertising professionals are somewhat more likely to encounter formal prior restraint, but only if the Federal Trade Commission or a court holds that an advertisement is misleading. Both the FTC and the courts have ruled that misleading ads must either be corrected or taken out of circulation. This form of prior restraint will be discussed in chapter 11.

Obviously, government is not likely to try to suppress speech except for the most serious of reasons. In the Pentagon Papers case, it reacted to wholesale disclosure of documents classified as "secret" or even "top secret." If such classifications are used properly, the material so marked is considered vital to the nation's security. The editors of *The Progressive* announced they were going to tell one of the nation's most closely guarded secrets—how to make a hydrogen bomb. While neither disclosure seems to have caused any harm, the episodes raised interesting questions.

The *New York Times* assigned a team of editors and reporters to go through the Pentagon Papers not only to select the most newsworthy portions for publication, but to take out material believed harmful to national security. In a sense, the editors substituted their judgment of what was safe for the public to know for that of the officials responsible for document classification. Presumably, the editors did their work well. But what might have happened if the Papers contained material that was damaging only in light of other information unknown to the editors of the *Times?* Or what happens if other secret government information is obtained, not by the *Times* or some other "reputable" news organization, but by persons who would very much like to cause trouble? At what point do we distinguish between publishing government secrets and delivering them to a foreign agent?

As we saw, editors themselves were split down the middle over publication of the alleged secrets of the hydrogen bomb. Most who had the information chose not to use it. Some took the position that they did not know enough about nuclear weaponry to make certain they would not be giving away harmful secrets. These differences among editors point up more than anything else the dilemma presented by government secrets. It is easy to understand why government officials want to keep some information secret. It is even easy to understand why they may at times confuse the important interest in protecting national security with the lesser interest in protecting their own political security. But when editors, whose normal instincts call for publication of any information deemed of public interest, see an arguable case for suppression, they raise questions that demand serious attention. A decision to publish government secrets is not likely to be made lightly.

FOR REVIEW

1. What courses are open to a government confronted with the likelihood of possible harmful disclosure of information or inflammatory rhetoric designed to stir up trouble? Discuss the advantages and disadvantages of each.

2. Distinguish between prior restraint and punishment of persons whose speech violates a law. Illustrate with examples.

3. The Supreme Court's decision in *Near* v. *Minnesota* has been characterized as a weak defense of First Amendment rights. Why might it be so considered? On what rationale was the *Saturday Press* permitted to resume publication?

4. Under what circumstances might a prior restraint be upheld? Outline the procedures that would have to be followed to impose such a restraint.

5. What elements link the Supreme Court's decision in *Lovell* v. *Griffin* with Milton's *Areopagitica?*

6. What elements distinguish the Wisconsin district court's decision in the *Progressive* case from the Supreme Court's decision in the Pentagon Papers case? What questions do the cases raise?

7. Discuss the implications of treating classified government information as a form of private property owned by the government.

8. On what grounds could the government censor the Marchetti-Marks book, *The CIA and the Cult of Intelligence?*

CHAPTER 3

SEDITION

The Prosecution of Sedition

The Smith Act of 1940

The Prosecution of American Communists

The Political Climate Changes

The End of State Sedition Laws

The Vietnam War: Advocacy and Action

Punishable Speech

As we saw in chapter 2, the government of the United States has rarely used direct censorship to protect national security, but in several periods of stress, it has punished its critics for sedition: Chapter 1 discussed the enforcement of the Sedition Act of 1798. And during World War I, in 1917 and 1918, nearly two thousand persons were prosecuted because their statements were considered harmful to the government. The Depression of the 1930s, and strained relations with the Soviet Union in the aftermath of World War II, also resulted in prosecutions for sedition.

With governments, as with individuals, the instinct for self-preservation is a powerful force. Thus, all nations have laws providing for punishment of those who would attempt to destroy them. Persons who take up arms against their own government had better be prepared to win or face imprisonment, exile, or death. In all nations, laws designed to prevent violent overthrow also make it a crime to advocate such overthrow. The United States is no exception.[1] The problem with such laws, of course, lies in drawing the line between words advocating a change in government policies or the form of government, and words designed to provoke rebellion. Advocacy of peaceful change is politics. Advocacy of violent change can be punished as sedition.

This chapter examines the use of sedition law in the United States. Because there was no federal sedition law between 1801, when the Sedition Act of 1798 was permitted to lapse, and 1917, when the United States entered World War I, the focus will be on the twentieth century. This is not to say that people were not punished for harmful

---

1. U.S.C. §2385.

speech during the nineteenth century. They were, but advocates of radical change were punished under state laws or under laws punishing criminal conspiracies. A federal sedition act was adopted by Congress in 1917 during Word War I. The victims were in large part persons of German descent, Socialists, and pacifists whose words were believed to undermine the will to fight.

In the 1920s, the focus changed. The Communist Revolution in Russia that established the Soviet Union in 1917 sent shock waves around the world. The United States reacted by prosecuting American Communists and others who sought to end what they saw as capitalist oppression. By 1940, the fear of Communism became so great that Congress enacted the Smith Act, making it a crime to advocate violent overthrow of government. The Japanese attack on Pearl Harbor in December 1941 drew the United States into World War II, but so united the American people that few people were accused of sedition. However, after the war ended in 1945, prosecution of Communists was renewed during the period of mutual suspicion between the United States and the Soviet Union that was known as the Cold War. During that time, the entire leadership of the U.S. Communist party was sent to prison. In the late 1950s, when relations between the two powers entered the period known as détente, prosecutions dwindled and ended. The Supreme Court held that people could not be punished for advocating violent overthrow of the government unless they clearly intended to incite immediate harmful action. During the Vietnam War, when hundreds of thousands of people converged on Washington, D.C., to demonstrate their opposition to it, sedition law was not brought into play. When police arrested thousands of the demonstrators and charged them with committing various illegal acts, the courts held that the procedures used violated the demonstrators' rights.

Thus, Americans can say pretty much what they please about the president, Congress, and government at any level. Those who advocate a violent change in the system may find themselves watched by the FBI, but unless they plant bombs in public buildings, as a few have, they are not likely to be arrested. The line is drawn, however, at death threats, particularly those directed at the president. Persons who talk openly about killing the president are likely to be arrested.

MAJOR CASES

Brandenburg v. *Ohio*, 395 U.S. 444, 89 S.Ct. 1827, 23 L.Ed.2d 430 (1969).

Dellums v. *Powell*, 566 F.2d 167 (D.C.Cir. 1977); cert. den., 438 U.S. 916 (1978).

Dennis v. *United States*, 341 U.S. 494, 71 S.Ct. 857, 95 L.Ed. 1137 (1951).

Scales v. *United States*, 367 U.S. 203, 81 S.Ct. 1469, 6 L.Ed.2d 782 (1961).

Yates v. *United States*, 354 U.S. 298, 77S. Ct. 1064, 1 L.Ed.2d 1356 (1957).

The Prosecution of Sedition

When Congress declared war on Germany and its allies in April 1917, many Americans doubted that it had acted wisely. To many, Europe was far away, and its wars no concern of ours. Consequently, there was a belief in Congress that the people's doubts would undermine the will to fight. Two groups were viewed with particular suspicion:

— The large numbers of Germans who had come to this country in the 1890s. Many had settled in midwestern cities like Cincinnati, St. Louis, and Milwaukee, where they continued to speak German in their homes and attended churches where services were conducted in German.

— Socialists, who were numerous enough to have elected mayors in Milwaukee, Hartford, and other cities. The Socialists were pacifists and saw the war as an effort to shore up declining capitalist systems.

To cope with anticipated antiwar talk from these and other suspect groups, Congress quickly followed up its declaration of war by adopting the Espionage Act of 1917.[2] The third section of Title I established three new crimes:

1. making false reports with the intent to harm the United States military forces or aid the enemy

2. attempting to cause "insubordination, disloyalty, mutiny, or refusal of duty" in the military forces

3. obstructing the recruiting of troops

Conviction could be punished by a fine of not more than $10,000 or imprisonment of not more than twenty years, or both.

The Act was enforced with vigor. Attorney General Thomas W. Gregory soon concluded it did not go far enough. He asked Congress to strengthen the law by adding sections dealing with attempts to obstruct recruiting and to discourage the sale of the bonds sold to finance the war. The Senate Judiciary Committee, prodded by its sense of public opinion, went even further.

It became a crime not only to obstruct the draft and the sale of bonds, but to use words designed to cause contempt, scorn, contumely, or disrepute directed at the government, the Constitution, the flag, the uniform of the army or navy, or any of the

---

2. Zechariah Chafee, Jr., *Free Speech in the United States*, Atheneum ed. (New York: Atheneum, 1969), pp. 37–39.

nations with which the United States was allied. It became a crime to do anything that might curtail production of materiel needed in the war effort. A catchall section made it a crime to advocate, teach, defend, or suggest the doing of any acts forbidden by the **statute.**

Nearly two thousand espionage and sedition arrests were made in less than eighteen months. The attorney general reported that 877 resulted in convictions. Other cases were dismissed after the war ended in November 1918. Sentences were **commuted** in other instances, and some, but not all, of the victims were **pardoned.**[3]

The cases were decided on the theory that the right of the government to preserve itself from conquest by foreign enemies and from violent overthrow by domestic enemies is paramount. Under this theory, words that have a tendency to help either kind of enemy may be punished. Convictions were based on the belief that forces which might be set in motion by seditious words must be checked at the start before they grow to the point of actual harm. In this view, liberty of speech protects reasoned discourse in which truth is used for good purposes. But when speech becomes "license" in the old sense of "licentiousness," it becomes destructive of orderly discourse and therefore punishable. Obviously, reasonable persons can disagree widely as to when liberty becomes license. Under the pressures of fear generated by the war, the field of license expanded. It was seen by juries and judges to cover words that in ordinary times would have been dismissed as the spoutings of harmless hotheads or pondered as valid debate on public policy.

The Supreme Court recognized that very point in the first World War I sedition case to reach it, *Schenck* v. *United States,*[4] in 1919. Chapter 1 presented the facts of this case and an analysis of it, which we will not repeat here. In holding that Schenck's pamphlets urging resistance to the draft violated the law, Justice Oliver Wendell Holmes, writing for a unanimous Court, said, "We admit that in many places and in ordinary times the defendants in saying all that was said in the circular would have been within their constitutional rights." But the times were not ordinary. The nation was at war, and it was widely believed that Socialists of German heritage represented a threat to national security. In the opinion of the Supreme Court, that threat was real. It held that Schenck and his fellow Socialist, Baer, would have to go to prison.

In reaching that conclusion, the Court formulated the clear and present danger test as a means of determining when words urging resistance to government policy could be punished as sedition. Holmes wrote:

> The question in every case is whether the words used are used in such circumstances and are of such a nature as to create a clear and present danger that they will bring about the substantive evils that Congress has a right to prevent.

In this instance, the Court held that Congress had a right to punish those who urged resistance to the draft when the nation was at war. The Court was saying that in time of war a nation's right to protect itself must at some point override its citizens' First Amendment rights.

With the benefit of hindsight, one may wonder whether Schenck presented *any*

---

3. Ibid., p. 52.
4. 249 U.S. 47, 39 S.Ct. 247, 63 L.Ed. 470 (1919).

danger to national security, let alone a "clear and present" danger. By the time the Supreme Court acted on his appeal, the war was over, and there was no doubt that the United States and its allies had defeated Germany and its allies. Also with the benefit of hindsight, one can question the degree of danger presented by other critics of the war, who also were sent to prison. Some of these did no more than question the reasons President Wilson gave Congress when he asked for a declaration of war, or curse the president in the hearing of an informant. But these reservations merely reinforce the point: When a nation is under stress, it is likely to punish those who oppose its policies. That happened in World War I, and the Supreme Court held that despite the First Amendment's guarantee of freedom of speech and of the press, the government can punish its critics.

The Smith Act of 1940

The World War I Sedition Act was permitted to lapse during the 1920s. The nation was at peace and was enjoying prosperity, fueled by speculation in a stock market that seemed destined to go no way but up. The bubble burst in 1929, when stock prices literally collapsed in a matter of days, and the 1930s brought severe economic depression to the United States and Europe. At the Depression's depth in 1933, about one-quarter of the work force in this country was jobless. The impact of the near collapse of the economic system cannot be understood without recalling some additional facts. There were few two-income families in the United States of the 1930s. Woman's place was seen as in the home. According to statistics compiled by the Bureau of the Census in 1975, only 3 million of the 26 million married women counted by the census of 1930 had outside employment. Prior to July 1932, when the Emergency Relief Act became law, there were no federal welfare programs. Unemployment compensation and Social Security were not begun until the mid-1930s. Therefore, being unemployed in the early part of the Depression meant relying on more fortunate friends and relatives for help, making do with what you had, or, as a last resort, relying on private charity. Thus, the Depression put American society under great stress—a stress that was compounded by events elsewhere in the world.

In a Europe not yet recovered from the World War, the Depression bred political instability, most notably in Germany, where Adolf Hitler quickly rose from an anti-Semitic beer hall brawler to Reichschancellor. Once elected to that office, he embarked on a plan to restore German prosperity through conquest of weaker nations to the south and east. He had sympathizers in the United States who thought America could profit from some of his methods. During this same period, Joseph Stalin emerged as the leader in the Soviet Union and by means of bloody purges and state trials made that nation his personal instrument of power. Although Stalin made the Soviet Union virtually a closed state, his propaganda, like that of Hitler, made it look as if the two dictators had discovered the road to economic security.

The decade of the 1930s was the decade of Mussolini's war against Ethiopia, of the Spanish Civil War, of Japan's conquest of Manchuria, and of Hitler's annexation of Austria. It was a period of searching for economic panaceas and of choosing up sides, a period of political zealotry when ideology was taken seriously. Those who were university students at the end of that decade found themselves courted by one group or another playing on the uneasy knowledge that commencement might lead only to military service or unemployment.

This ferment was made to order for those who saw traditional institutions of government crumbling under siege from alien creeds. Thus, Congress in 1940 undertook enactment of a statute designed to make deportation of aliens easier. On its way to passage, the bill became a vehicle for an amendment offered by Howard W. Smith, a Democratic representative from Virginia. His amendment became America's first peacetime sedition law since the Alien and Sedition Acts had expired in 1801. The central language of what quickly became known as the Smith Act was aimed at those who might seek quick and radical changes in the form of government. The Act made it a crime to

> knowingly or willfully advocate, abet, advise or teach the duty, necessity, desirability, or propriety of overthrowing or destroying the government of the United States, or the government of any State . . . or . . . any political subdivision therein, by force or violence, or by the assassination of any officer of any such government.

Oddly, Representative Smith's law received little use until well after World War II had ended. The one prosecution that began before the United States entered the war carried political overtones that illustrate how a law designed to protect national security can be used for other purposes. In 1941, Daniel Tobin, president of the International Teamsters Union and one of President Franklin D. Roosevelt's staunch supporters, was faced with revolt by a Minneapolis local union. Its leaders wanted to leave the Teamsters and affiliate with the Congress of Industrial Organizations. Tobin asked the Department of Justice to act against the insurgent leadership on grounds that as members of the Socialist Workers party they represented a threat not only to the Teamsters but to the nation's security.

A federal grand jury in Minneapolis indicted eighteen of the union's leaders on charges of advocating violent overthrow of government in violation of the Smith Act. On December 1, 1941, six days before the Japanese attack on Pearl Harbor, a jury in a federal district court found them guilty. One of the defendants, Grant Dunne, whose name survives in the title of the case, *Dunne v. United States*,[5] was so mortified that he committed suicide. Eventually, a unanimous court of appeals for the Eighth Circuit upheld the prison terms imposed on the surviving defendants.

The Smith Act was adopted to give the Department of Justice a weapon against those who were advocating changes in our form of government to cope with economic depression and those who were trying to get us involved in the war in Europe that began in 1939. When we did enter the war, in 1941, sedition was not a problem for a number of reasons. Foremost among them was the manner in which the United States entered the war. The Japanese attack on Pearl Harbor not only provoked an immediate declaration of war but united the nation in a determination to win it. A second factor was the Soviet Union's role in the war. In 1939, Stalin's nonaggression pact with Hitler made it possible for the latter to conquer Poland and, by the end of 1940, most of the rest of Europe.

---

5. 138 F.2d 137 (8th Cir. 1943). The origins of the case and its political implications are treated in "First Conviction under Federal Sedition Act," *International Judicial Association Monthly Bulletin*, December 1941, pp. 60–61.

During that period, Communists in the United States vigorously opposed this country's efforts to help Great Britain. But when Hitler sent his armies into the Soviet Union in June 1941, the Communists changed their tune. When the United States entered the war, it became an ally of the Soviet Union, and American Communists became ardent supporters of the war effort. Finally, a strict immigration law enacted in 1921 had greatly reduced the flow of immigrants to this country. Only persons of Japanese descent were seen as a problem, and most of them were interned for the duration of the war. Thus, there were few prosecutions for sedition in World War II, and no significant court decisions interpreting the Smith Act.

The Prosecution of American Communists

With the war's end in 1945, America's longstanding fear of communism quickly revived. The United States and the Soviet Union, uneasy allies in defeating Germany, entered into a period that became known as the Cold War, an era of mutual suspicion between the Soviet Union on one side and the United States and Great Britain on the other. This suspicion was fanned by Stalin's use of Soviet troops to impose Communist governments on the occupied nations of Eastern Europe. Because at that time American Communists were seen as taking orders from Moscow, they, too, became subjects of suspicion and distrust.

Thus, the officers and Central Committee of the U.S. Communist party, headed by Eugene Dennis, were among the first victims of the Cold War. The Department of Justice, through the Federal Bureau of Investigation and a squad of undercover informants,

Dennis v. United States, 341 U.S. 494, 71 S.Ct. 1064, 95 L.Ed. 1137 (1951).

began to gather information on the party shortly after the war ended. In July 1948 a federal **grand jury** in New York City was persuaded that the party's officers were in violation of the Smith Act. It **indicted** twelve members of the national board, charging them with organizing a political party with the intent of over-throwing the government, and of teaching and advising others to join them in the project. At the time, the Communist party had a known membership of about 74,000 in the United States, but such was the political climate that it was widely believed to have hundreds of thousands of sympathizers.

The trial in the United States District Court for the Southern District of New York lasted nine months, six of them devoted to the taking of testimony. The party officers argued that they were using means protected by the First Amendment to operate like any other political party. They differed only in offering voters a genuine alternative. In their eyes, a choice between a Democrat and a Republican was not a choice because, no matter who won, capitalist oppression of the working class would continue.

Government witnesses, all of them informants, painted a different picture. In their inner councils, the informants testified, party leaders conceded they could never win an election. If they did manage to do so, the capitalist oppressors would never surrender power without a fight. Therefore, the path to power lay through disciplined use of force. Any member who did not believe this was denounced as an enemy of Marxist-Leninist principles. All that was needed to carry the party's plan into effect was another sharp crisis that would paralyze the will of the elite to act. If there were any doubts, jurors were reminded that no Communist government had come into being anywhere except as a result of revolution or, as in Eastern Europe, through occupation by the Soviet Army.

The jury's verdict was "guilty." All the defendants were sentenced to prison. They appealed to the United States Court of Appeals, Second Circuit, which affirmed.[6] When the Supreme Court reviewed the case, six of the justices agreed that the party's officers should go to prison, but no more than four of them could agree on any one reason why they should. Thus, the decision of the Court in *Dennis* v. *United States* did not establish a firm precedent, but for a decade lower courts looked to it for guidance in Smith Act cases.

Chief Justice Fred M. Vinson wrote the judgment of the Court. He was joined by Justices Stanley F. Reed, Harold H. Burton, and Sherman Minton. Vinson started with a firm premise: Congress has the power to draft laws designed to protect the nation from armed rebellion. Theoretically, as recognized by the Declaration of Independence, there is a right to rebel against a dictatorial government. But that right has no meaning, Vinson wrote, when "the existing structure of government provides for peaceful and orderly change." This was a reminder that in the United States, the route to power runs through the ballot box.

As the **plurality** saw it, the question facing the Court was not whether Congress had the power to enact the Smith Act, but whether it swept too far by making it a crime to advocate violent overthrow. Much of the government's case against the Communist party's leaders rested on articles appearing in the party's newspaper, the *Daily Worker*; on other party publications, and on speeches made by the leaders. Dennis and his associates argued that they were protected by the First Amendment in speaking and writing as they had. They argued further that the language of the Act was so broad that it could be used to punish classroom discussion of Communist party doctrine. The plurality rejected those arguments.

It said the law was directed at advocacy, not discussion. Indeed, the trial judge had told the jury it could not convict the party leaders if it concluded they were engaged only in peaceful discussion of ideas. He had also told the jury the Smith Act did not make it a crime to study the principles of communism in colleges and universities. The plurality concluded that when Congress wrote the law, it was concerned with speech and writing used to plan and set in motion illegal acts against the government.

In this part of its opinion, the plurality was attempting to do two things, both crucial to the outcome of the case. It was attempting to distinguish between "advocacy" and "discussion" in a way that would bring the former within the scope of the Smith Act. And it was attempting to move the activities of the Communist party leadership out from under the protective umbrella the First Amendment gives to speech. If those activities, even though they involved speech, could be portrayed as harmful action, they could be punished.

At what point do words become so intermingled with action that their users can be punished? Vinson answered that question by adopting the clear and present danger test

---

6. United States v. Dennis, 183 F.2d 201 (2d Cir. 1950).

as it had been refined by a series of cases interpreting the World War I Sedition Act and various state sedition laws. That test, he wrote, comes into play when the government is seeking to protect an important state interest. In this instance, the United States was trying to protect itself against violent overthrow, which is certainly an interest substantial enough to support a government limitation on speech:

> Indeed, this is the ultimate value in any society, for if a society cannot protect its very structure from armed internal attack, it must follow that no subordinate value can be protected. If, then, this interest may be protected, the literal problem which is presented is what has been meant by the use of the phrase "clear and present danger" of the utterance bringing about the evil within the power of Congress to punish.
>
> Obviously, the words cannot mean that before the Government may act, it must wait until the *putsch* is about to be executed, the plans have been laid and the signal is awaited. If Government is aware that a group aiming at its overthrow is attempting to indoctrinate its members and to commit them to a course whereby they will strike when the leaders feel the circumstances permit, action by the Government is required. The argument that there is no need for Government to concern itself, for Government is strong, it possesses ample powers to put down a rebellion, it may defeat the revolution with ease needs no answer. For that is not the question. Certainly an attempt to overthrow the Government by force, even though doomed from the outset because of inadequate numbers or power of the revolutionists, is a sufficient evil for Congress to prevent. The damage which such attempts create both physically and politically to a nation makes it impossible to measure the validity in terms of the probability of success, or the immediacy of a successful attempt. In the instant case the trial judge charged the jury that they could not convict unless they found that petitioners intended to overthrow the Government "as speedily as circumstances would permit." This does not mean, and could not properly mean, that they would not strike until there was a certainty of success. What this meant was that the revolutionists would strike when they thought the time was ripe. We must therefore reject the contention that success or probability of success is the criterion.

The plurality concluded that the threat in this instance lay in the nature of the organization. The Communist party was a tightly disciplined group whose members were taught to strike at vital services when their leaders gave the signal. Vinson said in the strongest possible language that the government not only could act against such groups, but was required to act. The Court's decision thus was seen as a mandate to the Department of Justice to proceed with the prosecution of any Communist party cell, wherever it might be found.

Justice Felix Frankfurter concurred in the Court's judgment but not in the plurality's reasoning. He clearly was bothered by Vinson's attempt to distinguish between "advocacy" and "discussion." The plurality seemed to have said that the party leaders' crime was advocacy of violent overthrow of the government. Frankfurter was not willing to concede that all advocacy is illegal. He wrote at length about his unease in confirming five-year prison terms and $10,000 fines for the defendants.

Frankfurter conceded that there must be some limits on speech. And he conceded, too, that the courts have the duty of determining in each case what these limits are. He also recognized that "not every type of speech occupies the same position on the scale of values." For instance, courts traditionally have held that one who uses words to persuade another to commit a crime is as guilty as the person who does the act. That is one kind of advocacy. But advocacy also "shades into legitimate discussion of ideas," and there is a difference of opinion over the point at which it does. Thus, courts ought to be cautious about proscribing all advocacy, Frankfurter concluded.

Despite his fears that the plurality might be defining "advocacy" too broadly, Frankfurter was swayed by the conspiratorial nature of the Communist party and its seemingly blind adherence to policies dictated by Stalin. He noted that the party rejected the usual political methods of persuasion and compromise and that it had relied on spies to obtain the military secrets of other nations. (While the Court was considering the *Dennis* case, a trial court had found Julius and Ethel Rosenberg and Morton Sobell guilty of giving Soviet agents secret information about the development of the atomic bomb.)

Justice Robert H. Jackson did not share Frankfurter's doubts. He saw no room for the clear and present danger test in the *Dennis* case. Nor did he see the case as a test of First Amendment protection. To his mind, the defendants were engaged in an illegal conspiracy to commit a crime. Their words were not part of a discussion of ideas, but means to a criminal end. He chided the other justices for making more of it than that.

Justices Hugo L. Black and William O. Douglas were the only dissenters. They took the position that while the Communist leaders might make a lot of noise about overthrowing the government, there were few who would follow them. They were "merchants of unwanted ideas." The ninth member of the Court, Tom C. Clark, took no part in the decision because, as attorney general, he had approved the prosecution.

At the time, the Court's decision seemed clear. Congress was within its authority in making it a crime to "advocate" violent overthrow of government. Because the Communist party was seen as a tightly disciplined organization, whose members were being "steeled" to strike when their leaders gave the signal, its advocacy of violent overthrow represented a clear and present danger to the security of the United States. Therefore, the party's leaders would have to go to prison.

The Court's decision in *Dennis* cleared the way for 141 additional prosecutions under the Smith Act.[7] In 1951, the nation also was well along into a period of freewheeling congressional investigations of alleged subversives. Some of these were products of accusations made by Joseph McCarthy, a Republican senator from Wisconsin. He had leaped into prominence in February 1950 by asserting during a speech broadcast on radio that he had a list of fifty-seven employees of the State Department who were members of the Communist party. He expanded on that list during the next three years and then, as chairman of a Senate subcommittee, conducted wide-ranging investigations of government agencies alleged to harbor subversive employees. The House Committee on Un-American Activities conducted similar investigations of labor unions and the film industry, which were alleged to be infiltrated by Communist sympathizers. The hearings became showcases for a variety of persons who said they had worked within allegedly subversive groups as informants for the FBI. Each accusation created a widening circle of suspicion, which was spread by a largely uncritical press. That period in American history has become known as the McCarthy era. It was a period when many Americans strongly believed that other Americans, whose views today would be described as only moderately liberal, were part of a secret subversive conspiracy. Such suspicions were at their height when the Court decided *Dennis*.

---

7. Victor S. Navasky, *Naming Names* (New York: Viking, 1980), p. 33.

Joseph McCarthy (right) used his position as chairman of a U.S. Senate subcommittee to spread the belief that communists were widely dispersed in American institutions and represented a threat to national security. At this hearing in 1954 he ran into a determined foe in Army counsel Joseph N. Welch (left), who exposed McCarthy as a blustering bully. This led to the latter's censure by his fellow senators and the end of the era of fear caused by what was known as "McCarthyism." (AP/Wide World Photos)

The Political Climate Changes

Oleta O'Connor Yates and thirteen other officers of the Communist party in California were among those prosecuted on the strength of the *Dennis* decision. They were tried in a federal district court in Los Angeles. Seeking guidance, the judge read *Dennis* and told the jury it could find the defendants guilty if it believed they had advocated violent overthrow of the government "unrelated to [the] tendency [of their words] to produce forcible actions." The jury found Yates and her associates guilty. The judge ordered each to spend five years in prison and pay a fine of $10,000. The Court of Appeals for the Ninth Circuit affirmed, holding that the judge's instruction to the jury was based correctly on the Supreme Court's **plurality opinion** in *Dennis*. On appeal, the Supreme Court agreed to take the case.

Yates v. *United States*, 354 U.S. 298, 77 S.Ct. 1064, 1 L.Ed.2d 1356 (1957).

Its decision in *Yates* v. *United States* surprised many. The Court focused on the trial judge's instructions to the jury on the meaning of advocacy, holding that he had misread *Dennis*. That decision had not condemned all advocacy, not even that directed at violent overthrow of the government, the Court said. The advocacy in *Dennis* could be punished because it involved a rigidly disciplined organization that was being prepared for action. Justice John Marshall Harlan expanded on that theme:

> This is quite a different thing from the view of the District Court here that mere doctrinal justification of violent overthrow, if engaged in with the intent to accomplish overthrow, is punishable per se under the Smith Act. That sort of advocacy, even though uttered with the hope that it may ultimately lead to violent revolution, is too remote from concrete action to be regarded as the kind of preparatory indoctrination [to action] which was condemned in *Dennis*.

The trial judge's instructions were held to be inadequate because

> the jury was never told that the Smith Act does not denounce advocacy in the sense of preaching abstractly the forcible overthrow of the Government. . . . The essential distinction is that those to whom the advocacy is addressed must be urged to *do* something, now or in the future, rather than merely believe in something.

The Court said that in its review of the testimony it found very few examples of speech that could be considered "advocacy to action." Indeed, the Court said the evidence was so lacking for five of the defendants that they should be **acquitted** at once. These included two editors of the *Daily People's World* who had been prosecuted on the basis of articles appearing in that newspaper. The Court said it found nothing in the publication that would support a conviction. The other nine were remanded for retrial under proper instructions to the jury. Government attorneys, concluding that they faced an impossible burden of proof under the Court's definition of "advocacy," dropped the charges.[8]

What happened? Was it all as simple as Harlan made it seem? Was it merely a matter of misreading *Dennis?* If so, an attorney general of the United States, who authorized the *Yates* prosecution, and his staff of lawyers had all misread it. So had a trial judge and the members of a circuit court of appeals. And so had other judges in other cases, including members of the Supreme Court itself in 1952 in a decision upholding the deportation of aliens who had maintained their membership in the Communist party.[9]

The *Dennis* and *Yates* cases offer the student a classic example of the truth embedded in the words Finley Peter Dunne put in the mouth of his mythical Irish immigrant, Mr. Dooley, at the turn of the century: "No mather whether th' constitution follows th' flag or not, th' Supreme Coort follows th' iliction returns." It is not quite that bald, of course. But inevitably, Supreme Court justices, being human, are affected by their perceptions of events outside the courtroom. The *Dennis* opinions have many references to such events. What had changed between 1951 and *Dennis* and 1957 and *Yates?*

The membership of the Court itself had changed. Three of the four members who joined in the plurality opinion in *Dennis* no longer were on the Court. Chief Justice Vinson, who wrote it, had died in 1953. Minton had retired from the Court in 1956, and Reed at the beginning of 1957. Thus only Burton remained. Jackson, who had seen *Dennis* as a simple conspiracy case, had died in 1954. The three, other than Burton,

---

8. "U.S. Court Clears 9 California Reds," *New York Times*, 3 December 1957.
9. Harisades v. Shaughnessy, 342 U.S. 580, 72 S.Ct. 512, 96 L.Ed. 1356 (1952).

who participated in both decisions were Black and Douglas, the only dissenters in *Dennis*, and Frankfurter, who had joined in the decision of the Court in that case despite his doubts about the plurality's definition of "advocacy."

Of the carry-overs, Frankfurter and Burton joined Harlan's opinion for the Court in *Yates*. Douglas and Black agreed with the result, but would have gone further than Harlan and acquitted all the defendants. Of the new members of the Court, Chief Justice Earl Warren joined Harlan's opinion. William J. Brennan, Jr., and Charles E. Whittaker had joined the Court too recently to take part in the *Yates* decision. Tom C. Clark, who had taken no part in *Dennis*, was the only dissenter in *Yates*. He wrote that he could see no difference between the two cases.

The world outside the Supreme Court building had changed, too. By 1957, Dwight Eisenhower, who had led the Allied forces to victory in Europe in World War II, had served one term as president and was starting his second. While it was possible for some to believe that Harry Truman, his predecessor, might be "soft on communism," as the phrase went in those days, few could see any Communist leanings in "Ike," who was not only a Republican but looked like a benign grandfather.

Leadership had changed in the Soviet Union, too. Joseph Stalin had died in 1953. His death was followed closely by the dismissal of Lavrenti P. Beria, chief of the KGB and Stalin's enforcer. Beria was executed late in 1953 as an enemy of the people. Nikita Khrushchev had emerged as the new Soviet leader in 1955. In a secret speech to the Twentieth Congress of the Soviet Communist party he had denounced Stalin, repudiated his cruelties, and announced a policy of peaceful coexistence with the West. The speech created a sensation when it was leaked to Western correspondents. There was to be an even greater sensation in 1959 when Khrushchev would step out of a gigantic Soviet Tupolev 114 airliner onto a red carpet at Andrews Air Force Base near Washington to be embraced by President Eisenhower. So at the time the Court acted on *Yates* in 1957, the Cold War had begun to thaw.

In this country, McCarthyism had foundered on its leader's excesses. He had stubbed his toe badly in 1954 by conducting long hearings into his charges that even the army had become infiltrated by Communists. McCarthy ran into a dogged seeker of fact and an advocate of fair play in the person of the army counsel, an aging Boston lawyer named Joseph N. Welch, who picked persistently at the senator's assertions, exposing him finally as a blustering bully. The drama was played out on television for all to see. At the end, McCarthy's own Permanent Subcommittee on Investigations, which conducted the hearings, could not agree on a verdict. But the public, according to polls conducted at the time, sided with the army. In December 1954, the Senate voted, 67 to 22, to condemn McCarthy for contempt in his treatment of subcommittee members and for insults to the Senate itself. By 1956, he was living out his days in an alcoholic fog, shunned by his former colleagues. According to one senator, he was given to calling some of them in the middle of the night to ask, "What have I done? Why don't people like me any more?"[10] He died at the age of forty-seven in the same year the *Yates* decision was handed down.

The fever of fear brought on by Communist advances into Eastern Europe and China after World War II, by the disclosure that there had been Soviet spies in the United

---

10. As told to the author, then a Washington correspondent, by a senator who received such a call.

States, by the war in Korea, and by McCarthy's ability to play on the suspicions of many had run its course. The danger that had seemed so clear and present in 1951 had become the subject of embarrassed laughter in 1957. The era of détente had begun. And now it could be seen by all that Communists had not been able to sell their doctrine to many of the American people. It was clear at last that they could not persuade others to join them in a revolution. But the Court had held in *Yates* that they could not be prosecuted for trying. Advocacy, even of violent overthrow of government, is protected by the First Amendment as long as it is not linked directly with plans for action.

This is not to say that there were no further prosecutions for sedition after 1957. There were, and a few of them survived appeal, reflecting the fact that legal precedents, even those set by the Supreme Court of the United States, are not applied with mathematical precision. A different factual base can lead to a different result. In 1961, for instance, the Supreme Court itself upheld a Smith Act case that had been in the courts for seven years. Junius Irving Scales, the former chairman of the Communist party in North Carolina, was one of those prosecuted on the strength of the *Dennis* decision. Scales was a sixth-generation white Anglo-Saxon Protestant whose family had both wealth and social position. His great-uncle had been a governor of North Carolina. Scales had become a member of the Communist party during the Depression and had remained in it during World War II. When the Justice Department moved against Dennis and the national leadership of the party after the war, Scales, like some other Communists, "went underground"; that is, he adopted a new identity in order to escape arrest and continue his work.

Scales v. *United States,* 367 U.S. 203, 81 S.Ct. 1469, 6 L.Ed.2d 782 (1961).

When Scales was discovered and arrested, he steadfastly refused to identify his associates in the party. He also refused an offer from the FBI to serve as a double agent in return for immunity from prosecution. A federal district court found him guilty of violating the Smith Act and sentenced him to six years in prison, one year longer than the terms imposed on any of the others convicted in that era.[11]

The Supreme Court's five-to-four decision upholding Scales's conviction was based more on what the plurality wrote in *Dennis* than on what the majority wrote in *Yates*. In this instance, Harlan, who had written for the Court in *Yates*, reasoned that the Communist party actively was engaged in attempting to overthrow the government and intended to do so when the time was ripe. Scales, as one of the dedicated leaders of the party and a recruiter of members, knew full well what the intent was and yet persisted in his membership. Thus, as the Court saw it, he was a party to an illegal conspiracy designed to violate the law. The Court concluded that this was not advocacy, but action of a kind not protected by the First Amendment.

The End of State Sedition Laws

Standard legal reference works show no reported federal sedition cases after 1961. However, state sedition laws, most of them enacted during the early part of this century,

---

11. Laurent B. Frantz, "Junius Scales," *The Nation*, 30 December 1961, pp. 528–30.

were brought into play during a new period of tension starting in the 1950s. For many years, black citizens of the United States had been victims of segregation imposed under the "separate but equal" doctrine forged by the Supreme Court in the 1890s. This gave approval to a system in many parts of the country, particularly in the South, that consigned blacks to separate schools, eating places, railroad coaches, and restrooms. In 1955, in Birmingham, Alabama, that system came under challenge when Rosa Parks refused to give up her bus seat to a white man, as the local law required. Her act started a movement toward integration that grew into a major confrontation between militant blacks and white officialdom through boycotts, lunch counter sit-ins, demonstrations, and forced integration of public schools. State sedition laws were among the legal devices invoked in a vain attempt to preserve segregation.

For instance, when William Ware and other members of the Council of Federated Organizations sought to help blacks register to vote in Mississippi in 1964, they were arrested and charged with violating the state's **Criminal Syndicalism Act.** Such laws were designed to punish anarchists and others advocating violent changes in the form of government. Ware and his associates asked a federal district court to prevent the state from prosecuting them. It did so, holding the Act in violation of the First Amendment. The court held, in *Ware* v. *Nichols*,[12] that the law was written so broadly that it could punish mere advocacy or teaching of violent overthrow as an abstract theory.

Brandenburg v. Ohio, 395 U.S. 444, 89 S.Ct. 1827, 23 L.Ed.2d 430 (1969).

Ironically, it was the arrest of a Ku Klux Klan leader in southwestern Ohio that gave the Supreme Court an opportunity to nullify all state sedition laws aimed at advocacy divorced from the direct likelihood of action.

In politics as in physics, every action produces a reaction, and one by-product of the civil rights movement was a resurgence of the Klan. Clarence Brandenburg, owner of a television repair shop in a Cincinnati suburb, was an officer in a Klan. In the mid-1960s, he telephoned a reporter-announcer for a Cincinnati television station and invited him to cover a Klan rally and cross burning. The reporter accepted and brought along a camera crew. On the basis of what authorities saw and heard in the telecast, Brandenburg was arrested and charged with violating Ohio's Criminal Syndicalism Act. Like Mississippi's, it was written in broad terms. A Hamilton County **common pleas court** found him guilty, sentenced him to one to ten years in prison, and fined him $1,000. Ohio's appeals courts affirmed, holding that his arrest raised no constitutional questions. The Supreme Court took the case and disagreed.

The Court took the position that it was writing no new law, merely reiterating established principles. Therefore, it disposed of the case with a *per curiam* decision, with only one justice dissenting and another writing to elaborate on his views. The Ohio law had been adopted in 1919 in response to the Red scare of that era. Nineteen other states had enacted similar laws, some of which had been upheld by the Supreme Court in the 1920s.

In this instance, the Court focused on the law's broad language. It began by reviewing Brandenburg's rambling speech, in which he talked about seeking "revengeance" if the president, Congress, and the Supreme Court continued "to suppress the white, Caucasian

---

12. 266 F.Supp. 564 (S.D.Miss. 1967).

race." The talk was laced with antiblack and anti-Semitic vulgarities. The Court concluded that for all his bluster, there was no likely link between Brandenburg's words and imminent lawless action. Nor would the Ohio statute itself pass muster. It was invalid on its face because, as it was written, speakers could be punished for doing no more than talk about resorting to violence. The Court said that the law could survive only if it were aimed at speech directly linked to "imminent lawless action" or likely to "incite or produce such action."

With that decision, the Court seems to have brought to an end the line of cases starting with *Schenck* in 1919. It has said that governments, federal and state, have a right to protect themselves against those who would resort to violence to change the system. Governments can also protect themselves against those who would advocate such violence. However, with *Yates* and *Brandenburg*, the Court said that "advocacy" cannot be punished unless its purpose is to incite direct and immediate violence. Any law that fails to make that clear violates the First Amendment.

The Vietnam War: Advocacy and Action

The Vietnam War divided the American people as have few events since the Civil War. And yet, despite violent demonstrations against our involvement in Vietnam, sedition law was not brought into play. Instead, events that once might have been considered seditious led to three significant civil lawsuits, in all of which the government was the loser. The courts held that government could not violate the basic rights of individuals in order to put down demonstrations against its policies.

Much of the strongest opposition to the war was centered on college campuses, but as the war dragged on from 1960 to 1975, violence spilled onto the streets of many cities. Chicago was racked by riots for four days during the Democratic National Convention in August 1968. In November 1969, about 250,000 persons gathered around the Washington Monument to declare their opposition to the war. In May 1970, Ohio National Guard troops opened fire on student demonstrators at Kent State University, killing four. The following April, tens of thousands of demonstrators began gathering in Washington. The avowed purpose of their leaders was to force President Nixon to end the war, even if they had to "bring the government to a halt" to do so. The administration, which had been trying for more than a year to negotiate terms with North Vietnam, refused to yield.[13] Leaders urged the demonstrators to block the major highways leading into Washington during the morning rush hour on Monday, May 3.

Chief of Police Jerry V. Wilson feared that his force would be overwhelmed. He sought help from Attorney General John N. Mitchell. The Defense Department assigned four thousand troops to duty in the District and called up the District's National Guard units for training. Key federal employees were asked to report for work on Sunday evening. Sanitation trucks were moved into position to cope with roadblocks.

Early Monday morning, Chief Wilson ordered police to move in and arrest demonstrators at the first sign of any attempt to block traffic. That day, nearly eight

13. Henry Kissinger, *White House Years*, (Boston: Little, Brown, 1979), pp. 1012–1013.

During the Vietnam War, the courts protected opponents of government policy even when they conducted demonstrations in the shadow of the Capitol in Washington, D.C. Such demonstrations were held to be a form of symbolic speech fully protected by the First Amendment even when they bordered on violence. (J. Berndt/ Stock, Boston)

thousand persons were herded into buses and trucks and taken to all kinds of improvised detention centers, including Robert F. Kennedy Stadium. Almost all were charged with disorderly conduct and were required to post bail or remain in custody. So quickly did the police act that no attempt was made to record each individual arrest with the name of the arresting officer. Thus, there was no way of proving in court that any of the suspects had committed a specific wrongful act. It was this suspension of normal arrest procedures that led to two of the civil suits, *Sullivan* v. *Murphy*[14] and *Apton* v. *Wilson*.[15]

In *Sullivan*, the United States Court of Appeals for the District of Columbia held that all persons against whom a valid case could not be made were entitled to refund of bail, which had ranged up to $250, and to have the arrest expunged from their records. About five thousand of the demonstrators were affected by this suit. Of the 2,878 others who elected to go to trial, the prosecutor dismissed about 2,600 for lack of evidence.

The *Apton* suit was brought by thirty-four individuals who contended they had been arrested even though they had done nothing wrong. The District appeals court held that they were entitled to sue Wilson, Mitchell, and other officials for damages. However,

14. 478 F.2d 938 (D.C.Cir. 1973). Statistics in this section, as well as much of the narrative, are taken from a comprehensive report on what came to be known as the "May Day Demonstrations," which is a part of this case.
15. 506 F.2d 83 (D.C.Cir. 1974).

it said they would have to prove that the officials had exceeded their authority and had acted unreasonably in response to circumstances as they knew them at the time.

The third lawsuit, *Dellums* v. *Powell*, grew out of events on the Capitol Plaza on May 4. About 2,000 persons had moved from the *Dellums* v. *Powell,* **566** Mall to the Plaza in order to impress their views on **F.2d 167 (D.C.Cir. 1977).** members of Congress. Ronald V. Dellums, a representative from California, tried to speak to the crowd from the Capitol steps. While he was doing so, Capitol and District police moved in and began making arrests of the demonstrators.

Dellums later joined nine members of the group in suing James M. Powell, chief of the Capitol Police, in behalf of all who were arrested. The United States District Court for the District of Columbia held that the arrests were wrongfully made and amounted to a denial of First Amendment rights. It awarded the plaintiffs varying sums, depending on how long each was detained, but starting with $7,500 each for the First Amendment violation.

The court of appeals held that that was too much. But it did not quarrel with the principle. The court's decision, written by Judge J. Skelly Wright, is grounded solidly on the premise advanced by Thomas I. Emerson that some kinds of action convey a message that should be protected by the First Amendment:

> Basically, what is at stake here is the loss of an opportunity to express to Congress one's dissatisfaction with the laws and policies of the United States. Staged demonstrations—capable of attracting national and regional attention in the press and broadcast media—are for better or worse a major vehicle by which those who wish to express dissent can create a forum in which their views may be brought to the attention of a mass audience and, in turn, to the attention of a national legislature. It is facile to suggest that no damage is done when a demonstration is broken up by unlawful arrests simply because one could write an individual letter to a congressman or because the demonstration might be held another day or time. Few letters to congressmen command a national or regional audience. And often it is the staging and theatrics—if you will, the time, place, and manner of the demonstration—which expresses the passion and emotion with which a point of view is held. The demonstration, the picket line, and the myriad other forms of protest which abound in our society each offer peculiarly important opportunities in which speakers may at once persuade, accuse, and seek sympathy or political support, all in a manner likely to be noticed. Loss of such opportunity is surely not insignificant.

However, the court drew the line at letting a jury, "informed only by platitudes about priceless rights," set the worth of that loss. This was a task for a judge. The court let stand awards of from $120 to $1,800 each, depending on the length of detention, and of $500 each for malicious prosecution. The court also let stand an award of $3,000 to each of the named plaintiffs for the latter. (This was a **class action suit** in which nine of those who were arrested filed an action in behalf of all others who had been. Payments to other members of the class were not automatic. Thus, there is nothing in the court's decision to indicate how many actually collected these sums.) The case was remanded so that the district court judge could decide how much, short of $7,500, the loss of First Amendment freedoms was worth.

On remand, the district court judge fixed damages, at the request of the parties to the lawsuit, at $750 for each of the persons whose freedom to demonstrate had been violated.[16]

These decisions represent the latest step in a march that began with the Republican editors who violated the Alien and Sedition Act and has continued through enforcement of the World War I Sedition Act into modern times. At the start of that march, and for more than a century thereafter, writers and speakers could be punished if their words had a tendency to undermine the authority of government leaders. The *Schenck* decision began to change that. Dissenters could be punished only if their words seemed likely to provoke illegal acts. With the benefit of hindsight, it can be said that that likelihood probably was remote in the cases decided prior to World War II. Even in *Dennis*, the danger probably was not clear and imminent, although the Supreme Court found it so. Since *Yates*, vocal critics of government have had little to fear. With the advent of television in the 1950s, those who espouse unpopular causes have learned that action—demonstrations, marches, symbolic speech, guerrilla theater, all summed up as "media events"—makes news. As Judge Wright pointed out in *Dellums*, when action has a First Amendment purpose, it can give a relatively few dedicated persons a powerful voice in the making of public policy. Such action, the court emphasized in *Dellums*, is protected up to the point at which it becomes illegal violence. If, as Chafee, Emerson, and others have argued, the line between freedom and repression is drawn at the point where government begins to punish its critics by putting them in jail, Americans enjoy a high degree of freedom.

Punishable Speech

While the courts seemingly will tolerate speech advocating almost every kind of action aimed at demonstrating opposition to government policies, there is one kind of speech that can lead to a prison term. Law enforcement officers and the courts have taken a serious view of threats to the lives of public figures, particularly the president. That this is so reflects a disturbing fact of political life in the latter part of the twentieth century: There are some who make targets of presidents and other prominent persons. The recent victims of assassins include President John F. Kennedy; his brother, Robert, a candidate for president; and Rev. Martin Luther King, Jr., a giant among civil rights advocates. Others have survived, among them former President Gerald Ford; President Ronald Reagan; former presidential candidate and Alabama Governor George Wallace, paralyzed for life from the waist down; and Vernon Jordan, another civil rights leader.

It should be no surprise, then, that courts have not been disposed to interfere with punishment of those who threaten to kill the president. Presidents can be and have been portrayed in words and cartoons as inept, as liars, and as robbers of the poor. This has come to be expected as part of the political game. But individuals have been sent to prison for threatening to kill a president, even when the threat was made by a person who was many miles distant from his target. The statute defining the crime is at 18 U.S.C. §871, adopted in 1948.

---

16. Hobson v. Wilson, 566 F.Supp. 1157, 1190 and 1191 (D.D.C. 1982). The information is footnoted to Dellums v. Powell, Civil Action No. 2271-71 (D.D.C. Dec. 13, 1979).

One case illustrates its use. Bill B. Moorefield, who was employed as a security guard in Newport News, Virginia, was twice sentenced to prison for threatening to kill former President Nixon in conversations with a fellow guard many miles from Washington. Years later, when Moorefield filed a civil suit against the government seeking access to information about him in its files, he learned that the Secret Service had compiled a 225-page dossier.[17] He also learned that the Service considered him such a threat that it "wanted to know where he was any time the president ventured into public."

The *Moorefield* case is one of the few of its nature reaching the appellate court level and hence included in the case reports. Other people who are indiscreet enough to talk openly of killing the president, or who send threatening letters to the White House, become known only through scattered reports in the news media. It is assumed, judging from Moorefield's experience, they also become entries in the Secret Service's check list. However few the cases, they serve as a reminder that the First Amendment right to criticize government, and even to advocate its overthrow, does not protect speech threatening harm to the president.

The Sedition Act has lain dormant for more than twenty years. However, its continued presence in the U.S. Code serves as a reminder that governments have a right, if not a duty, to protect themselves from those who would use violence to change the system. The cases in this chapter make a further point: In times of great national stress, sedition law can be used to punish those who advocate violent change.

In *Yates*, the Supreme Court held that speakers and writers can condemn the system, and even talk about overthrowing it, as long as they do not urge others to take immediate violent action against it. Even then, the connection between speech and action would have to pose an imminent and plausible threat to public safety. No police officer is likely to arrest a farmer who tells a mass meeting he sees no hope of saving farms from foreclosure unless the president and the bankers who support him are driven from power. Such language is accepted as part of the political process. And, as we have seen, the Sedition Act was not brought into play during the Vietnam War, when speech brought thousands of demonstrators to the streets near the White House and to the Capitol Plaza.

However, the *Schenck*, *Dunne*, *Dennis*, and *Scales* cases indicate that if this nation again should teeter on the brink of war, or if economic depression should reduce millions to despair, sedition prosecutions could be renewed and convictions upheld on appeal. Advocacy now perceived as political rhetoric could be seen as presenting a clear and present danger to the nation's security. When the nation's existence seems to be at stake, the First Amendment does not prevent punishment of those who advocate its destruction.

In the Professional World

For most journalists, advertising copywriters, and public relations practitioners, "sedition" is a word found in history books or in the news from a country with a government that permits no opposition. Professionals in the conventional media,

---

17. Moorefield v. United States Secret Service, 611 F.2d 1021 (D.C.Cir. 1980).

like the overwhelming majority of the American people, take the U.S. political and economic systems as givens.

However, there are a few Americans who take a different view of society. They see the conventional political process as a sham. Politicians seeking to hold or win office make a big fuss every two years, but they offer voters a choice between Tweedledum and Tweedledee. Whether the Democrats or Republicans win, they believe the government will continue to shore up an economic system that oppresses the poor, pollutes the environment, rapes the world's natural resources, and keeps the Third World in bondage. Such believers are few in number in this country, but they argue there can be no change for the better until the people rise up and take control of the land, the factories, the transportation system, and all other private businesses. Only then can the nation's resources be used to give everyone a comfortable living, rather than to enrich the few.

There are enough such opponents of the establishment to organize political parties and qualify for a place on the ballot in most states. In most presidential elections in recent times, candidates have represented the Communist, Socialist Workers, Workers World, and Socialist parties. Along with candidates of other unconventional political parties, they have campaigned with little or no attention from television, the wire services, newspapers, and magazines. Most people aren't even aware of the existence of minor party candidates until they enter the voting booth and see the names on the ballots. Thus, candidates who argue that the existing political and economic structure should be scrapped so that a better one can replace it must resort to their own party publications. In one sense, they are talking to themselves, because the usual readers of such publications have already been converted to the cause. Few outsiders are aware of the existence of the *Revolutionary Worker* or other organs published more or less regularly by anti-establishment parties.

This situation raises questions not of law, but of ethics: If the mass media give time and space only to those who work within and support the system, is there a true marketplace of ideas? Milton complained that truth and falsehood could not truly grapple if government used its power to keep some ideas out of the arena. Is the contest any less rigged when media indifference keeps them out? When Eugene McCarthy, a former United States senator and by no stretch of the imagination a radical opponent of the system, ran for president as an independent in 1976, he complained with elegance and wit that he was ignored by the major media. Editors responded that they were merely reflecting the perceived interests of their audience. Everyone knew McCarthy's cause was doomed from the start, so why give it any attention? The circular logic of such a position is evident.

There are those who believe that mainstream journalism has become subversive. This is not a new idea. In chapter 1, we saw that advocates of the Sedition Act of 1798 believed it necessary to curb a "licentious" press in order to preserve the government. Today, questions are being raised about the adversary stance adopted by most journalists in their reporting of government. While there has always been a tension between journalists and politicians, there was also a longstanding symbiotic relation between them. Since the Republic began, politicians have relied on journalists to publicize their views, and journalists have courted politicians as sources of news. For decades, both sides were comfortable with the relationship. If the occasional result was the cover-up of a president's sexual adventures, or a committee chairman's excessive drinking, that was accepted as part of the game.

The relationship between journalists and officials changed markedly during the Vietnam War when Presidents Johnson and Nixon felt compelled to withhold information from the news media, or even to lie about events. The crowning blow came from the Watergate episode, which began with a bungled burglary of Democratic party headquarters in 1972 and ended with Nixon's resignation in disgrace two years later. Since then, many journalists have tended to treat all officeholders as liars, as dealers in half-truths, or, at best, as withholders of vital information. A generation of journalists has grown up hoping to achieve the fame of Carl Bernstein and Bob Woodward, whose Watergate stories for the *Washington Post* helped bring down a president. This new generation works in the knowledge that reporters who succeed in exposing an official's flaws, or who point up the shortcomings of his policies, win the lead spot on the evening news or on page 1. Reporters who are content to cover the news of government as it happens may get thirty seconds at the end of the newscast or a brief item on the inside pages. The result, in the eyes of some critics, is a badly skewed picture of government in which officials always appear incompetent or worse.

What effect does adversary journalism have on the government's ability to function? The truth is, no one knows. Beyond question, it is news when a president lies to the people. Nor is there any question that policy should be debated. Few proposals for dealing with problems as persistent and complex as poverty, racial relations, farm debt, and the arms race with the Soviet Union are likely to offer perfect solutions. It is precisely because such problems, and others, are persistent and complex that their every aspect needs to be studied critically and attacked logically. The question is, what happens to any administration's ability to deal with such problems when its proposals are overwhelmed by instant reaction, much of it originating with those who have a vested interest in seeing that the status quo is maintained or whose purpose is to hold, or even increase, their share of government expenditures? One effect may be a form of paralysis that rules out any significant change. Another may be a loss of faith in the ability of the system to meet the people's needs. This is indicated by the steady decline over the last two decades of the percentage of eligible voters who go to the polls, especially in nonpresidential years. In recent off-year elections, fewer than half the eligible voters have cast ballots for members of Congress.

In the legal sense, there is nothing seditious in proclaiming that our emperors aren't wearing clothes. The First Amendment does not require that journalists be cheerleaders for government. One of the most important purposes of that amendment is to prevent government from punishing journalists and others who expose its mistakes and hoot at its follies. For more than twenty-five years, the courts have protected this purpose with zeal. The freedom to criticize government is near or at that absolute level advocated by Meiklejohn and Emerson.

It is this freedom from government control that raises serious ethical questions for professional journalists. Few would deny that some form of government is necessary. Realists know that no government is going to rule perfectly, human nature and human limitations being what they are. To expect otherwise is to expect the impossible. What happens to government's ability to function, even imperfectly, if only its faults are newsworthy? Or if complex issues are simplified to fit the public's assumed 90-second attention span? Or if high officials are lampooned as bumbling, uninformed ignoramuses? Or if the measure of government, to paraphrase John F. Kennedy's inaugural address, becomes how much we can get from government rather than how much we can do to serve our own little corner of society? There are no easy answers to such questions. They are asked to raise the larger questions: Are the media completely without blame for the near-paralysis that afflicts the federal government? Would the media serve us better by finding a role somewhere between cheerleader and adversary? In short, if the media have power, as is generally assumed, how should that power be used?

FOR REVIEW

1. What is the rationale for a sedition law in time of peace? Need there be such law? Why or why not?

2. What was the rationale for the Supreme Court's decision in *Dennis* v. *United States?* How did it define "advocacy," and why did the Court find it harmful in this instance?

3. Contrast the Supreme Court's decision in *Dennis* with its decision six years later in *Yates* v. *United States.* How do you account for the difference?

4. What is the significance of the Supreme Court's decision in *Brandenburg* v. *Ohio?*

5. What conclusion with respect to First Amendment theory can be drawn from the lower court decisions in cases brought by persons arrested for demonstrating against the Vietnam War?

PART 2

NEWS MEDIA AND THE LAW

CHAPTER 4

LIBEL

For more than six centuries, courts in England and the United States have recognized the value of reputation—what others think of us. The have also recognized that reputation can be harmed by words—such things as <u>accusations of crime, of immorality, or of lying.</u> Therefore, courts have permitted victims of harmful words to sue their detractors and recover sums of money calculated to make good the harm to reputation. The great body of law that has grown out of such actions is called the law of defamation, commonly known as the law of libel.

In the last quarter of the twentieth century, libel law has become of greater concern to journalists and other communicators than any other kind of law. Libel actions are being brought against the media in record numbers. The Supreme Court, in several significant decisions that will be emphasized in this chapter, has held that the First Amendment protects the media in libel actions, but not absolutely. Because of this protection, plaintiffs who sue the media win only one case in ten.[1] However, in the cases that have gone against the media, judgments in six figures are common, and some of the awards have run into the millions of dollars. Many of these have been reduced or wiped out on appeal, but libel suits, win or lose, are expensive. Floyd Abrams, a lawyer with extensive experience in defending libel cases, estimated in 1985 that legal costs average $150,000 in those lawsuits that go to trial.[2] Professional communicators can and do buy libel insurance to guard against such costs, but that, too, is expensive. Abrams and others argue that fear of the cost of litigation has led some publishers and broadcasters to avoid the kind of reporting that might expose official wrongdoing.

If this is indeed the case, the expense of libel litigation is not the only reason for caution. Another lies in the many uncertainties that surround the resolution of a libel action in the courts. Ironically, these uncertainties are products of the Supreme Court decisions that extended First Amendment protection to the media in libel actions. In the two most significant of those decisions, *New York Times* v. *Sullivan*[3] and *Gertz* v. *Robert Welch, Inc.*,[4] the Court held that persons who sue the news media for libel must prove some degree of fault. This has meant that media performance—such things as reporting and editing methods, news judgment, and other factors shaping the story—has become subject to searching examination in the courts. The Court has held that libel **plaintiffs** may even inquire into the state of mind that led a media professional to believe one source and disbelieve another. In close cases, this means that a jury lacking media experience is asked to pass judgment on media performance. In doing so, the jurors are

---

1. Randall P. Bezanson, Gilbert Cranberg, and John Soloski, "Libel and the Press, Setting the Record Straight," the 1985 Silha Lecture, University of Minnesota, 15 May 1985.
2. Floyd Abrams, "Why We Should Change Libel Law," *New York Times Magazine*, 29 September 1985, p. 34+.
3. 376 U.S. 254, 84 S.Ct. 710, 11 L.Ed.2d 686 (1964).
4. 418 U.S. 323, 94 S.Ct. 2997, 41 L.Ed.2d 789 (1974).

asked to apply complex legal principles they may not fully understand. For whatever reasons, in the cases that go to trial, juries tend to rule against media defendants.

This chapter attempts to sort out and clarify the legal principles that are applied in libel actions involving media professionals. The chapter begins with a brief survey of the common law of libel prior to 1964, when the Supreme Court decided *New York Times* v. *Sullivan*. For centuries, libel was strictly a matter of state **common** or statute **law.** Therefore, it varied in detail from state to state. However, certain general legal principles evolved from the decisions of the courts. It became well established that anyone who was the target of harmful words had a right to sue for damages. The victim had only to prove that the offending language was disseminated to the public in some way, that he or she was its target, and that its nature lowered the victim in the esteem of others. From that point on, all the assumptions were in the plaintiff's favor. Courts assumed that the offending language was false, and that if it made certain particularly serious charges, such as accusation of crime, the plaintiff had suffered harm. The defendant could win the case only by proving one of three things: that the charge made by the offending language was true, that it was a fair and accurate report of the public proceedings or records of a court or some other agency of government, or that it was fair comment on the plaintiff's public activities. The latter defense was used for comment directed at public officials, authors, entertainers, and others who invited public attention. Such comment had to be based on facts either stated as part of the article or generally known to the audience. The rules of proof were quite strict. For instance, the defendant who chose truth as a defense had to be able to convince a jury that every detail of the offending statement was true.

In 1964, the *New York Times* decision stood the common law of libel on its head. Because that decision was based on the First Amendment, it brought libel into the realm of federal **constitutional law.** This meant that media **defendants** were given much greater protection against successful libel actions than they previously had known. In deciding *New York Times*, the Court held that one purpose of the First Amendment is to ensure that debate on the performance of public officials is "uninhibited, robust, and wide-open." When that debate involves issues of great public importance, people sometimes speak before they have time to check all the facts. Consequently, some comment directed at public officials may be both defamatory and false. Ordinarily that would give the public official grounds for a successful libel action. But in *New York Times*, the Court said that a public official ought not be permitted to recover damages unless he could prove with "clear and convincing evidence" that the defamatory falsehood was a product of "**actual malice.**" The Court defined that term as publishing with knowledge of falsity, or in reckless disregard of the truth. A major consequence of this decision was to shift most of the **burden of proof** from the defendant to the plaintiff, if the latter was a public official. Unless such plaintiffs could establish at the start that they had been victims of a knowing or reckless defamatory falsehood, they were not likely to get their case to a jury.

Because the *New York Times* decision was so at odds with the long-established common law of libel, lower courts varied widely in their application of it and further decisions of the Supreme Court were required to clarify its meaning. In 1967, the Court held that public figures also must prove actual malice if they begin a libel action. Persons become public figures, the Court said, by thrusting themselves into the vortex of the discussion of a controversial public issue. This decision recognized the fact that people do not need to seek or win public office in order to influence public policy. Public figures, like public officials, are able to win media attention for their views.

In 1971, a badly divided Court seemed to extend the First Amendment's protection of media libel defendants still further. Ruling in *Rosenbloom* v. *Metromedia*,[5] a plurality of the Court reasoned that the purpose of the First Amendment is to protect the discussion of public issues. Therefore, it argued that any person who is defamed by news or comment directed at such issues should have to prove actual malice. That view has been adopted by the courts in a few states, but the majority of the states now look elsewhere for guidance, most of them to *Gertz* v. *Robert Welch, Inc.*

In *Gertz*, decided in 1974, a majority of the Supreme Court reinforced the Court's earlier decisions holding that public officials and public figures must prove actual malice if they are to bring libel actions. But it said that the states might, if they wished, permit private individuals to prevail against the media on a lower level of proof. The only condition imposed by the Court was that private plaintiffs be required to show harm and some degree of fault on the part of the media. Most states have accepted that invitation, permitting private individuals to win libel suits if they can prove **negligence** or some other fault short of actual malice, on the part of the media. Negligence is a departure from the standard of care a prudent person would follow in the factual circumstances of a particular case. Also in *Gertz*, the Court sought to define public figures more precisely, dividing them into two groups: public figures for all purposes and public figures only with respect to a particular controversial public issue.

Gertz further changed libel law in two respects. The Court said private individuals should not be permitted to recover damages unless they could prove that had been harmed. However, it defined harm to include not only a showing of loss of standing in the community but personal humiliation and embarrassment, which are hard to value with precision. The Court also said that libel actions should be grounded only on false and defamatory assertions of fact. This has led lower courts generally to hold that libel plaintiffs must prove that the offending language was false as well as defamatory. Courts in a few states, Pennsylvania foremost among them, took the position that the language in *Gertz* permitted them to assume falsity in libel suits brought against the media by private individuals. The Supreme Court overruled that position in 1986, holding that the First Amendment requires anyone who sues the news media for libel in connection with a matter of public interest to prove with clear and convincing evidence that the alleged defamation is false.[6] Also as a result of their reading of *Gertz*, courts are generally holding that libel actions cannot be based on opinion, no matter how harsh. Therefore, as of this writing, a libel action directed at the media cannot get very far unless the plaintiff can prove he or she was the victim of a false and defamatory assertion of fact.

New York Times and *Gertz* are by far the most influential cases shaping the modern law of libel. The latter part of this chapter will present subsequent decisions further defining public officials, public figures, and private individuals; actual malice; negligence; the role of truth and the burden of proving falsehood; the distinction between fact and opinion; and the journalist's right to report and comment on public affairs.

---

5. 403 U.S. 29, 91 S.Ct. 1811, 29 L.Ed.2d 296 (1971).
6. Philadelphia Newspapers, Inc., v. Hepps, ___U.S. ___, 106 S.Ct. 1558, 89 L.Ed.2d 783 (1986).

MAJOR CASES

Akins v. *Altus Newspapers, Inc.*, 609 P.2d 1263 (Okla. 1977).

Bose Corp. v. *Consumers Union*, 466 U.S. 485, 104 S.Ct. 1949, 80 L.Ed.2d 502 (1984).

Bufalino v. *Associated Press*, 692 F.2d 266 (2d Cir. 1982).

Cole v. *Westinghouse Broadcasting*, 435 N.E.2d 1021 (Mass. 1982).

Dun & Bradstreet, Inc., v. *Greenmoss Builders, Inc.*, __U.S. __, 105 S.Ct. 2939, 86 L.Ed.2d. 593 (1985).

Edwards v. *National Audubon Society*, 556 F.2d 113 (2d Cir. 1977).

Fitzgerald v. *Penthouse International*, 525 F.Supp. 585 (D.Md. 1981).

Garrison v. *Louisiana*, 379 U.S. 64, 85 S.Ct. 209, 12 L.Ed.2d 1042 (1964).

Gertz v. *Robert Welch, Inc.*, 418 U.S. 323, 94 S.Ct. 2997, 41 L.Ed.2d 789 (1974).

Greenbelt Cooperative Publishing Co. v. *Bresler*, 398 U.S. 6, 90 S.Ct. 1537, 26 L.Ed.2d 6 (1970).

Herbert v. *Lando*, 441 U.S. 153, 99 S.Ct. 1635, 60 L.Ed.2d 115 (1979).

Hutchinson v. *Proxmire*, 443 U.S. 111, 99 S.Ct. 2675, 61 L.Ed.2d 411 (1979).

McCall v. *Courier-Journal and Louisville Times*, 623 S.W.2d 882 (Ky. 1981).

McHale v. *Lake Charles American Press*, 390 So.2d 556 (La.Ap. 1980).

New York Times v. *Sullivan*, 376 U.S. 254, 84 S.Ct. 710, 11 L.Ed.2d 686 (1964).

Newell v. *Field Enterprises, Inc.*, 415 N.E.2d 434 (Ill.Ap. 1980).

Old Dominion Branch No. 496, National Association of Letter Carriers, AFL-CIO, v. *Austin*, 418, U.S. 264, 94 S.Ct. 2770, 41 L.Ed.2d 745 (1974).

Ollman v. *Evans*, 750 F.2d 970 (D.C.Cir. 1984).

Raymer v. *Doubleday and Co., Inc.* 615 F.2d 241 (5th Cir. 1980).

Rinaldi v. *Holt, Rinehart & Winston*, 42 N.Y.2d 369 (N.Y.Ap. 1977).

Rosenblatt v. *Baer*, 383 U.S. 75, 86 S.Ct. 669, 15 L.Ed.2d 597 (1966).

Rosenbloom v. *Metromedia, Inc.*, 403 U.S. 29, 91 S.Ct. 1811, 29 L.Ed.2d 296 (1971).

Ryder v. *Time, Inc.*, 557 F.2d 824 (4th Cir. 1976); 3 Med.L.Rptr. 1170 (1977).

St. Amant v. *Thompson*, 390 U.S. 727, 88 S.Ct. 1323, 20 L.Ed.2d 262 (1968).

Sharon v. *Time, Inc.*, 575 F.Supp. 1162 (D.N.Y. 1983).

Stone v. *Essex County Newspapers, Inc.*, 330 N.E.2d 161 (Mass. 1975).

Time, Inc., v. *Firestone*, 424 U.S. 448, 96 S.Ct. 958, 47 L.Ed.2d 154 (1976).

Wolston v. *Reader's Digest Association*, 443 U.S. 157, 99 S.Ct. 2701, 61 L.Ed.2d 450 (1979).

THE COMMON LAW OF LIBEL BEFORE 1964

The Law of Defamation: An Overview

In general terms, the law of defamation is concerned with protection of reputation. One dictionary defines the root word, *defame*, thus: "to attack the good name of an individual by **slander** or libel." A usage note goes on to explain that defamation implies the open circulation of an evil report calculated to harm the reputation of an identifiable person. Legal reference works, reflecting decisions of the courts, attempt to be more precise. *Restatement of Torts*, which is prepared by lawyers specializing in **tort law** and published by the American Law Institute,[7] says:

> A communication is defamatory if it tends to so harm the reputation of another as to lower him in the estimation of the community or to deter third persons from associating or dealing with him.

The problem with any definition is that it cannot anticipate the variety of ways in which allegedly defamatory words will confront the unsuspecting journalist. The *Restatement's* definition is followed by five paragraphs of elaboration that can be boiled down to another principle: Any time the journalist is required to write a story that suggests a person may be involved in illegal, unethical, immoral, or dishonest activity, there is a risk of being sued for defamation. This does not mean the story should not be written. At times the public needs to know that individuals, particularly those in government or in other influential positions, seem to be doing wrong. The courts have recognized that fact and have established defenses that can be used by the news media, and others, as protection against successful defamation suits.

Common law recognized two kinds of defamation, *libel* and *slander*. Libel is defamation stated in a tangible medium—in print, or in a photograph, or in some other form with a capacity to endure—slander rises out of spoken words. Because libel usually exists in a medium capable of being widely circulated, courts applying common-law principles treated it seriously. Victims of a libel were assumed to have been injured by it. In contrast, slander was taken much more lightly by the courts. Slanderous words usually were heard by relatively few persons, and the defamatory sting of the statement might soon be dissipated. Therefore, slander victims were required to prove that they had suffered some harm before they could collect damages.

---

7. *Restatement of the Law, Second, Torts 2d*, as adopted and promulgated by the American Law Institute, Washington, D.C., 19 May 1976 (St. Paul, Minn.: American Law Institute Publishers, 1977), vol. 3, §559, p. 156.

With the advent of radio in the 1920s, and its capacity to carry slanderous words to a large audience, the legal distinctions between libel and slander began to blur. Television has all but eliminated them when the news media are defendants. Today, most courts treat an action in defamation directed at a radio or television station as they would a libel suit directed at a newspaper, magazine, or book publisher.

Common law divided libel suits into two kinds, **libel *per se*** and **libel *per quod.*** Once there was a significant difference in the way courts treated each kind of libel. Certain classes of words were considered so harmful on their face—that is, *per se*—that courts did not require the persons at whom they were directed to prove they had suffered harm. Further, courts assumed such accusations were false until proved otherwise. For instance, if a newspaper reported that a person had committed a crime, and if it was unable to prove that its report was true or that it had been obtained from an official source, the only task left for the jury was to set the amount of damages to be awarded. Some degree of harm was assumed without any need for the plaintiff to offer proof of financial loss or loss of standing in the community. In practice, some persons whose reputations had in no way suffered from publication of the libel were awarded sizable sums in damages.

In addition to accusations of crime, other kinds of allegations considered libelous *per se* included accusations that a person, especially a woman, was immoral; that a person had a mental illness, or was the victim of a "loathsome" disease; that a physician, lawyer, or other professional was generally incompetent, or that a business firm was engaging in dishonest practices. Such allegations still carry a high degree of risk and should be used with care.

A libel *per quod* was not evident on its face. Indeed, the language might seem to be harmless, and to many persons it would be. But to those who knew what the unstated facts were, the language would be defamatory. In an era when moral standards were much stricter than they are now, newspapers found themselves involved in libel suits because of names listed in birth announcements. If a newspaper mistakenly listed a single woman, or a recently married couple, as having a baby, the item was defamatory in the eyes of those who knew the announcement was untrue, although in most circumstances giving birth is a cause for celebration. Under the common-law rules of libel *per quod*, the woman victimized by a false birth announcement would have to prove that others knew her circumstances and that she had suffered loss of reputation as a consequence.

Courts still use the terms *libel per se* and *libel per quod* in their decisions. The distinctions still have some meaning in the method used by a jury to assess damages against a losing defendant. They also retain some meaning for journalists. Reporters and editors handling stories that raise questions about an individual's conduct need to be aware of the thrust of other news stories dealing with the same person, or even with other persons involved in the same kind of event. Libel cases have been lost because headlines used over stories about one official evoked a false association with another who had been convicted of wrongdoing.[8]

Courts consider libel a *tort*—that is, "an injury or wrong committed, either with or without force, against the person or property of another."[9] The usual remedy is a lawsuit

---

8. Sprouse v. Clay Communication, Inc., 211 S.E.2d 674 (W.Va. 1974).
9. "The Reporter's Guide to Legalese and the Courts," Indiana State Bar Association, Indianapolis (1982).

for damages. Thus, libel is a private matter, to be resolved through the courts by the parties involved. Unless the injured party is willing to hire a lawyer and go to court, he is without formal remedy.

Under common law, a person who had been defamed by a news medium could sue anyone who had any connection with the offending item. Invariably, the owner of the medium was named as defendant because the owner bore ultimate responsibility for the product, and, more importantly, because the owner is most likely to have the resources to pay a judgment. However, the plaintiff could also sue the reporter who prepared the offending item, the copy editor who put it in final form, the printer who set it in type, or any of their supervisors. Courts acted on the theory that everyone who was involved in disseminating a libel, or who had authority over those involved, shared responsibility for it. The law still holds the media responsible for their entire content, including letters to the editor, statements made in interviews or talk shows, and the comments made on call-in programs. However, individual employees can be sued successfully only if they were at fault in the preparation and dissemination of a libel.

To begin a libel action at common law, the victim of the allegedly harmful words filed a petition with a court alleging three things: (1) The offending language was published or broadcast; (2) it identified the plaintiff, either by name or by implication; and (3) it defamed him or her. The court assumed that the offending language was false and that the victim had been harmed. The legal meaning of these three elements will be explained later in the chapter.

Once a libel action began, the defendant carried the entire burden of proof and could prevail only if one of three defenses were proven to the satisfaction of a jury: (1) The offending words were true; or (2) they were a fair and accurate report of an official proceeding, or the public record, of an agency of government; or (3) they were fair comment based on an accurate statement of the underlying facts. The comment had to be directed at someone whose public acts had invited comment. The legal meaning of the defenses will be explained later in the chapter. If the target of a libel action was unable to prove one or more of the defenses, the only task left for the jury was to set the amount of the damages.

In about half the states, the defendant might reduce the amount of the potential award by publishing a **retraction.** If this was an honest confession of mistake, coupled with an apology, the judge would instruct the jury to take it into account in fixing the amount of **compensatory** or **actual damages.** The victim of the libel was supposed to be awarded a sum of money sufficient only to make good any monetary loss he may have suffered, or to compensate him for demonstrated loss of standing in the community. An honest retraction stood as a bar against an award of **punitive damages,** which are levied to punish the publisher of a libel and deter others from publishing libels.

At common law in most states, all plaintiffs stood on the same legal footing. It made no difference in most states whether the victim of the libel was a public official, a person trying to mold public opinion, or a carpenter working for hire. Thus, it was not uncommon for holders of public office, or for candidates for election, to use a libel suit, or the threat of one, to silence their media critics. Such suits eventually might be dropped or forgotten, but they sometimes did dampen debate.

Thus, under the common law in effect until 1964, the balance was tipped in favor of libel plaintiffs. Prudent publishers and broadcasters were unlikely to disseminate allegations they could not prove to the satisfaction of a jury. Investigative reporting was engaged in before 1964, but findings were treated with caution. The Supreme Court's decision in *New York Times* v. *Sullivan* changed the rules dramatically, tipping the balance to favor the media by putting most of the burden of proof on libel plaintiffs who sue the media. As we have seen, the new rules have neither ended successful libel actions against the media nor even reduced the number of actions begun, but they have greatly lessened the chances for success against professionals who use care in their investigation of the misdeeds of people in the public eye.

The Elements of a Libel Case

As we have seen, libel actions begin with the filing of a **legal petition** with a court. Under common law, the plaintiff had to offer plausible evidence of three elements: publication, identification, and defamation. These elements continue to be basic to any libel action.

Publication

In virtually all libel actions, *publication* is proved by a copy of the offending item. This can be a certified copy of a newspaper article or editorial, the transcript of a broadcast, or a photograph, if the alleged libel was pictorial in nature. It is assumed from the fact of publication that someone read, heard, or saw the offending words or image. The case reports contain a few instances in which publishers tried to argue that, owing to the paper's poor circulation, no one probably saw the story. Such arguments are rejected. At law, publication is proved if the circumstances suggest that anyone other than the author of the libel and its target saw the offending words. Cases have been based on letters typed by a secretary and seen otherwise only by the person who dictated the letter and its recipient, who was the subject of the libel. At the minimum, it takes only three people to lay the groundwork for a libel case: the libeler, the target of the libel, and a third person who read the libel or heard it broadcast by a radio or television station. Therefore, the fact of publication is not likely to be at issue in a case involving the news media.

Identification

Sometimes the element of *identification* may be at issue. Occasionally, a reporter will write a story in the belief that there can be no libel if no names are mentioned. And, on occasion, reporters have found the hard way that they were wrong. A Hearst newspaper columnist lost a suit based on an item reporting gossip in Palm Beach of an affair between the wife of a wealthy pillar of society and a former FBI agent who had become a lawyer. No names were mentioned, but there was only one lawyer in Palm Beach who had been an FBI agent and who mixed with the upper levels of society. He won a judgment for $60,000.[10]

---

10. Hope v. Hearst Consolidated Publications, 294 F.2d 681 (2d Cir. 1961).

Libel cases sometimes can result from too little identification. For instance, at the time of Watergate, when several lawyers on the White House staff were found guilty of misconduct, *Time* magazine published an article on unprofessional conduct by lawyers in general. One lawyer whose conduct was described by the article was Richard R. Ryder, who practiced in Virginia. He had been accused of hiding evidence for a client suspected of dealing in narcotics. Following its usual editorial style, *Time* omitted the middle initial and did not name the town in which Richard R. Ryder practiced.

Ryder v. *Time, Inc.*, 557 F.2d 824 (4th Cir. 1976); 3 Med.L. Rptr. 1170 (1977).

Richard J. Ryder, who also practiced law in Virginia, sued *Time* for libel, asserting that he had suffered embarrassment because some persons thought he was the subject of the article. Eventually, *Time* won the case, but the magazine was put to the expense of defending itself in more than three years of litigation that reached the federal appeals level. The action ended when a federal magistrate held that *Time* could not reasonably be expected to check the roster of lawyers in Virginia to make certain there was only one Richard Ryder.

Thus, win or lose, mistakes in identification in connection with libelous assertions can be costly. To avoid them, reporters should obtain precise identification of anyone mentioned in a story involving wrongdoing. This should include exact spelling of first and last names—some Smiths spell it Smythe—middle initials, age, address, and occupation. This is especially important if the last name is common in the community. The telephone directory in even a medium-sized city may show two or three Ralph Johnsons, Raymond Johnsons, or Robert Johnsons. Under such circumstances, to report simply that Ralph Johnson was arrested for assault is to invite, at the least, an outraged telephone call from the Ralph Johnsons who weren't arrested and their families.

Defamation

In many libel cases, the decisive question is whether the language at issue is defamatory; that is, whether it is of such a nature as to lower the plaintiff in the estimation of others. At an early stage of the proceedings, a judge must look at the evidence and decide as a **matter of law** whether defamation is present.

As we have seen, at common law, certain kinds of allegations were considered libelous *per se*—so damaging that they were held to be defamatory on their face. Therefore, if the item in question accused the plaintiff of committing a serious crime, the judge's decision was easy to make. Defamation was present. The case could proceed, and its outcome would depend on the proofs the defendant could muster.

The judge's decision is also easy if the item in question clearly is not defamatory. There are occasions in which people feel highly insulted by accusations that strike others as reasonable. For instance, the case reports include instances in which persons sued because they were identified as police informants. Courts have held that such accusations are not defamatory because it is the duty of every person who has knowledge of crime to report it to the police.

The problems come with statements that do not make clearly defamatory assertions but are not clearly harmless. Suppose, for instance, that an officeholder has been accused of neglecting his duties. How is "neglect" defined? At what point does an observer's "neglect" become the officeholder's wise discretion? Do the facts point to a failure to perform duties required by law, or simply to a difference of opinion as to what the officeholder should have done? In such instances, the judge may decline to rule on whether defamation is present. That question would be reserved for trial where it would be decided by the "**trier of fact**," usually a jury, in the light of the evidence presented and argued by both sides. If the trial were by jury, the judge would instruct the jurors to consider the words at issue in their ordinary meanings and determine for themselves whether they would lower the plaintiff in the esteem of the community.

One state, Illinois, follows what is called the "innocent construction" rule.[11] If a statement is capable of two meanings, one of them defamatory and the other not, the rule requires that the innocent meaning prevail. In making a decision, the judge must consider a statement as a whole, give the words their natural and obvious meanings, and reach a conclusion that will withstand the test of reasonableness.

To clarify the way the principles above are applied, the remainder of this section presents excerpts from cases in which a key issue was the presence or absence of defamation.

A decision of the U.S. Court of Appeals, 5th Circuit, in *Raymer* v. *Doubleday and Co., Inc.*, illustrates the type of analysis courts use in determining whether passages are defamatory. Doubleday published a nonfiction book, *Blood and Money*, describing a series of murders in Houston. Part of the story focused on John Raymer, a Longview, Texas, police sergeant who shot one of the murder suspects to death in a poolroom. Raymer sued the publisher for libel, alleging that six passages in the book defamed him. A federal district court judge ruled that only one of the six disputed passages was capable of a defamatory meaning and submitted it to a jury. The jury held that the passage was not defamatory, thus ruling in Doubleday's favor. On appeal, the court of appeals affirmed. Its reasoning follows:

Raymer v. **Doubleday and Co., Inc.**, 615 F.2d 241 (5th Cir. 1980).

Raymer said the first of the six disputed passages violated a Texas statute that defined libel, in part, as treating a person's "natural defects" in a way designed to ridicule him. The passage read:

> John Raymer's round face, with a disappearing fringe of hair at the crown, resembled a hard-boiled egg. A few more pounds and he would be roly-poly, like a rubber beach toy that bounces every time it is knocked to the sand.

The appeals court held that neither baldness nor pudginess qualified as "natural defects" within the meaning of the law. Nor was it libelous to say that Raymer resembled a hard-boiled egg. That was "merely a literary description of the author's impression designed to create for the reader an immediate mental picture of the character."

Nor was there any libel in the second disputed passage. It was no more than a summary of the author's opinion of Raymer's feelings about himself and therefore not subject to proof. It read:

> [H]e was . . . well accommodated to the fact that he had made but slight scratches on the face of the earth. . . . He did not expect to light historic fires at the age of 49 . . . John

---

11. Chapski v. Copley Press, 442 N.E.2d 195 (Ill. 1982).

Raymer was relentlessly small town in fashion and horizon, and he knew it and would have it no other way.

In any event, the court added, there is nothing defamatory about being content with one's lot in life or in being the kind of person who is at home in a small town.

Raymer argued that the third disputed passage impeached his virtue and was therefore libelous on its face. It read:

> [A waitress who was the murder suspect's girlfriend] struck Raymer as a sexless, vacant girl. "Well, she won't last long with him," Raymer thought to himself. "These old boys swap these girls back and forth like used cars."

Raymer argued that the passage implied that he looked at the waitress "in a sexual manner," thus defaming him. The court said it could not find a harmful inference in it.

Raymer contended that a fourth passage, the book's highly graphic and colorful account of the suspect's death in the poolroom, suggested he had not acted in self-defense. The court found that contention "singularly unpersuasive." The account made clear that when Raymer tried to arrest the suspect, the suspect grabbed the barrel of Raymer's pistol and pulled a weapon of his own. The court ruled that the passage left no doubt that the subsequent shooting was in self-defense. Therefore, it could not be defamatory.

The fifth disputed passage explored the theory that Raymer had been hired to kill the suspect. The author made clear that he believed there was no truth in that theory. In arguing that the passage defamed him, Raymer selected only those parts of it that portrayed him as a hired killer. The court ruled that he could not avoid summary rejection of his argument "by taking statements out of context to force a libelous meaning where none exists."

The sixth passage, the one submitted to the jury, suggested that Raymer used his reputation as a "tough cop" to run possible thieves and prostitutes out of Longview. Taken in one sense, that could mean that he used intimidation to deprive suspected wrongdoers of their civil rights. If so, the passage accused him of committing a crime and was defamatory. But the passage also was capable of an innocent meaning—that his reputation was such that potential wrongdoers left town of their own accord to avoid trouble. Where such ambiguity existed, the judge acted properly in letting a jury determine how ordinary persons would understand the passage. The jury had heard the evidence as the law required it to do and had ruled in favor of the innocent construction.

In the *Raymer* case, all the rulings were in favor of the book publisher. No defamation was found. In two other instances, the news media were on the losing end. Courts ruled that defamation was present.

Time magazine reported the findings of the Kahan Commission, which was appointed by the Israeli government to investigate the murders of several hundred Palestinians at two refugee camps in Lebanon. The killings occurred at a time when the Israeli army was in control of much of Lebanon as a result of its invasion of that country in 1982.

Sharon v. Time, Inc., 575 F.Supp. 1162 (D.N.Y. 1983).

The commission found that Israeli troops had permitted members of the Christian Phalangist militia to enter the camps, knowing that there was ill will between them and the Palestinians. In its article on the Kahan Commission's report, *Time* said a secret appendix found that Ariel Sharon, the Israeli defense minister, "reportedly discussed with the Gemayels the need for the Phalangists to take revenge for the assassination of Bashir, but the details of the conversation are not known." (Bashir Gemayel was the president-elect of Lebanon when he was assassinated shortly before the killings that were the subject of the Kahan investigation.)

When Sharon sued Time, Inc., for libel, a federal district court judge in New York City ruled that the quotation above was reasonably susceptible of a defamatory connotation. He said that when it was read in the context of the entire article it could be understood as showing that Sharon encouraged the Phalangists to take revenge, thus portraying him as an accessory to murder. The judge's ruling was borne out when the case came to trial two years later. A jury found that the passage in question did indeed portray Sharon as an accessory to murder. However, *Time* won the case for reasons that will be examined later.

The U.S. Court of Appeals, Seventh Circuit, ruled in *Brown & Williamson Tobacco Co. v. Jacobson*[12] that a television newscast dealing with the company's advertising campaign was libelous on its face. The court said the news item led viewers to believe that the company had adopted an advertising policy designed to get children to smoke cigarettes. The court also held that the newscast associated cigarette smoking "with slightly illicit activity." Thus, the tobacco company was portrayed as violating the law because most states have laws forbidding sale of cigarettes to minors. The case was remanded for trial. In 1985, a federal district court jury in Chicago found that the station's commentator not only had libeled the tobacco company, but had done so with knowledge that the company had not adopted the advertising campaign he attacked on the air. The jury awarded Brown & Williamson $5 million from CBS Inc., owner of the station, and $50,000 from the commentator.[13]

Such examples could be multiplied endlessly. They make the point that at an early stage in any libel suit, the judge to whom the case is assigned must, as a matter of law, rule on the presence of defamation. The statements at issue must directly portray the plaintiff in a way that would lower him in the esteem of others, or, when taken in context, tend to do so. Otherwise, there is no cause for action, and the lawsuit will be dismissed. If the passage is capable of both defamatory and innocent meanings, the question is for a jury to decide. Any story that imputes commission of a crime, immorality, or dishonesty, or that attacks the competence or ethics of a professional person or the reputation of a business firm, should raise a red flag of caution in the minds of reporters and editors who are preparing it.

The Traditional Defenses

Under common law, a plaintiff's burden ended with the showing of the three elements dicussed above: publication, identification, and defamation. It was not necessary for the plaintiff to prove that the allegedly defamatory statement was false. The court assumed it was false until the defendant could prove otherwise. Once the plaintiff had established the three basic elements, the burden of proving some justification for the libel rested on

---

12. 713 F.2d 262 (7th Cir. 1983).
13. "Cigarette Maker Wins $5 Million in TV Libel Case," *New York Times*, 6 December 1985.

the defendant. If they were to win, defendants had to prove to the satisfaction of the trier of fact, usually a jury, one or more of the available defenses:

— The defamatory statement was true. This was not a defense of choice because truth can be difficult to prove.

— The defamatory statement was protected by **privilege.** This could be done by proving that it was a fair and accurate account of the acts or proceedings of some agency of government, a court, or a government official.

— The defamatory statement was fair comment on the public performance of a government official or some other individual whose work had invited public comment, such as an author, actor, or musician. Comment was considered fair if it rested on an accurate statement of the facts or if it rested on facts generally known.

Truth

"But what if it is true?" is a question that comes easily to those who first confront the law of libel. The simple answer is that truth may be defamatory in nature, but, if proved, cannot support a successful libel action. At common law, truth was reconized in all states as a defense against libel actions, although a few required that even the truth had to be used with good motives for a justifiable end. In such states, if someone dredged up a long-past arrest for a minor infraction and published it for no other reason than to embarrass a pillar of the community, truth might not prevail as a defense if a libel suit resulted.

In all states, the problem with the defense of truth at common law lay in proving it to the satisfaction of a jury. It is one thing to know that something is true, but another to marshal the evidence that will prove it to the satisfaction of twelve strangers. A reporter and her editors might be convinced that the mayor used city equipment and employees to improve his private property. They might have informants who told them all about it. But if the editors used the story, and the mayor sued for libel, the news medium would have had to prove, prior to 1964, that the equipment and employees had been used in violation of law.

Courts required that truth be proved with strict precision. There are cases on record in which the news media lost libel cases for reporting that a person was charged with one crime when, in fact, he had been charged with another.

Because of the difficulties with proof, truth was not a defense of choice in the common-law era. However, the defense survives in an altered and much stronger form under *New York Times* v. *Sullivan.* Today, truth has become an absolute defense against a libel action, no matter what its motives. The burden of proof has been shifted to the plaintiff, who must prove that an allegedly defamatory statement is a false assertion of fact. The effect of this change will be explained later in the chapter.

Absolute and Qualified Privilege ═══════════════════════

Privilege, in the legal sense, has a special meaning. As used here, the word is closely related to "immunity." A defamatory statement is protected by privilege if it serves a public purpose that makes it immune to a successful libel action. The law recognizes two degrees of privilege, *absolute* and *qualified*. The theory underlying both is the same: When the public's business is being conducted, the need for complete candor is so great that participants should have absolute protection from successful libel actions. Only with such protection will persons who have knowledge of wrongdoing feel free to talk about it. Generally then, agencies of government, the courts, and government officials are protected by absolute privilege when they are conducting official business. The common law also recognized that under a system of self-government, the people have a right to be informed fully about the activities of government. Therefore, it gave the news media a privilege to report those activities, qualified only by the requirement that the reports be fair and accurate. Thus, in their coverage of public affairs, the media are protected by a qualified privilege.

At common law, privilege was the strongest defense available to a media libel defendant. It owed its strength to the fact that governments keep voluminous records of their activities. Thus, a newspaper, magazine, or broadcaster confronted with a libel action growing out of coverage of government usually could point to documentary evidence to support its case. The only question to be decided by the court was whether the report was fair and accurate.

Other questions arose when journalists reported the oral statements of government officials. Were such statements made in line of duty? Was the official commenting on matters within the scope of his duties? Were they part of an official proceeding? Such questions still arise today. How they are resolved is illustrated by the decision of an Indiana court of appeals in *Henderson* v. *Evansville Press*,[14] in 1957.

A **circuit court** judge lost his temper when a lawyer representing a burglary suspect appeared before him at the start of the trial and asked that the case be assigned to another judge. That provoked an outburst in open court in which the judge accused the lawyer of "one of the lowest forms of shysterism." A reporter from the *Evansville Press* was present and thought the outburst worth a story. The quotation was in the lead, with the added information that the rebuke was "one of the strongest court attachés could recall."

The lawyer sued the newspaper for libel, which argued that it was protected by a qualified privilege. The appeals court held that it was not. Had the reporter merely quoted the judge, the story would have been a fair and accurate account of the proceeding. But when the reporter went outside the courtroom to seek comment on the judge's statement, his article accentuated the shyster label, thus destroying any claim of impartiality.

The case points up the limits of common-law privilege. Journalists can rely on qualified privilege as a defense in libel actions only when they are covering the business of government. When officials speak or act in line of duty, they are in a protected forum. The news media can cover all that happens in that forum, no matter how defamatory, as long as they tell the story straight. If they go outside the protected forum to get additional information, and in the process tilt the story against the victim of a defamatory statement, they may have to pay for their zeal.

Privilege continues to be a strong and frequently used defense against libel actions. Indeed, it has been made stronger by the Supreme Court's holding in *New York Times* v. *Sullivan*. The modern applications of qualified privilege will be examined later in the chapter.

---

14. 142 N.E.2d 920 (Ind. App. 1957).

Fair Comment

President Harry S Truman, who guided the nation through troubled times after World War II, was subjected to considerable critical abuse. During the Cold War period, he was called "soft on communism" and worse. When he was asked if he had any advice to offer those who might be tempted to seek public office, he said, "If you can't stand the heat, stay out of the kitchen." His answer reflected his knowledge, learned during thirty years in government service, that people who seek the public's favor must expect criticism.

The common law recognized that fact by establishing fair comment as a defense in libel actions. Because no one is perfect, nor is it possible to please everyone, some of the comment about those in the public eye is bound to be unfavorable. The defense of fair comment was grounded firmly in the Miltonian concept of the marketplace of ideas. It protected unfavorable comment in the belief that persons who perform for the public can benefit from criticism. Because fair comment was a broad defense that applied generally to people who seek the public's favor, it was widely used, limited only by the qualifications that the comment must be an honest expression of the critic's views, and that it must have some factual basis for support.

The defense of fair comment no longer exists as such. In *New York Times* in 1964, and in *Gertz* ten years later, the Supreme Court held that the First Amendment protects even unfair comment on the activities of people in public life. In *New York Times*, the Court held that public officials who are the victims of defamatory falsehoods cannot recover damages for libel unless they can prove actual malice. This means that they must offer "clear and convincing" evidence that the publisher knew the words in question were false or showed a "reckless disregard" for the truth. The Court later extended that same requirement to people outside government who try to influence public opinion. And, as we will see later, since 1974 courts have been reading *Gertz* to mean that statements of opinion—no matter how harsh or even unfair—cannot be the basis for a libel action unless they contain or imply a defamatory falsehood. Because this new First Amendment defense has proved to be much broader and stronger than the common-law defense of fair comment, the latter has been deleted from *Restatement of Torts*.

THE FIRST AMENDMENT AND THE LAW OF LIBEL

The Constitutional Defense: *New York Times* v. *Sullivan*

In 1908, Kansas was the first state to apply the *public principle* to libel actions.[15] Under this principle, which was adopted by a few other states, public officeholders were required to carry a heavier burden of proof than that carried by other libel plaintiffs. The public principle was grounded in the belief that persons who seek and hold public office ought to expect searching examination of their public actions. Such people enjoy

---

15. Coleman v. MacLennan, 98 P. 281 (Kans. 1908).

advantages that private citizens do not, including access to the media, where they can respond to criticism. Courts in the public principle states reasoned, therefore, that it ought to be more difficult for public persons to win libel actions.

In 1964, the Supreme Court of the United States accepted an appeal by the *New York Times* and ruled that the First Amendment requires all state and federal courts to apply the public principle to libel suits brought by public officials. With its decision in

New York Times v. Sullivan, 376 U.S. 254, 84 S.Ct. 710, 11 L.Ed.2d 686 (1964).

New York Times v. *Sullivan*, it federalized much of libel law, moving it out of the realm of common law and state statute and into the realm of constitutional law. At the same time, the Supreme Court literally revolutionized libel law, shifting most of the burden of proof from the defendant onto the plaintiff, at least in actions involving the news media. The importance of the case cannot be overstated. An understanding of the present status of libel law must begin with mastery of *New York Times* v. *Sullivan*.

The case was one of the byproducts of the civil rights movement that swept the South in the late 1950s. Racial segregation was the rule in all parts of the United States at that time, but it reached its extremes in the former slave states stretching from Virginia to Louisiana. In those states, law as well as custom forced blacks to live separated from whites.

About 1955, this segregated system came under challenge from blacks seeking the right to do such things as sit where they pleased in city buses, or eat at lunch counters in downtown department stores. In 1960, whites used violence against demonstrations by black students at Alabama State College in Montgomery who were seeking to integrate such public facilities. In March of that year, an advertisement appeared in the *New York Times* appealing for financial support for the embattled students of Alabama State. The ad was signed by sixty-four persons, white and black, many of them prominent in public affairs, religion, trade unions, and the performing arts. Headed "Heed Their Rising Voices," the ad said in part:

> In Montgomery, Ala., after students sang "My Country, 'tis of Thee" on the State Capitol steps, their leaders were expelled from school, and truckloads of police armed with shotguns and tear gas ringed the Alabama State College campus. When the entire student body protested to state authorities by refusing to register, their dining hall was padlocked in an attempt to starve them into submission. . . .
>
> Again and again, the Southern violators have answered Dr. [Martin Luther] King's peaceful protests with intimidation and violence. They have bombed his home almost killing his wife and child. They have assaulted his person. They have arrested him seven times—for "speeding," "loitering," and similar "offenses." And now they have charged him with "perjury"—a felony under which they could imprison him for *10 years*.

Attorneys representing Police Commissioner L. B. Sullivan, one of three elected commissioners of the city of Montgomery, wrote the *Times* asserting that those two paragraphs libeled their client. In accordance with Alabama law, they asked for a retraction, a published admission from the *Times* that it had published untruths. The *Times* responded by asking the attorneys to point to specific libelous passages in the advertisement. Sullivan's response was to file a lawsuit in a Montgomery court.

At trial, Sullivan argued that the ad's general references to "police" pointed a finger at him because he supervised the police force. Therefore, he reasoned, the ad accused him of being responsible for padlocking the dining hall in order to starve the students into submission. And, since arrests ordinarily are made by police, it accused him of arresting Dr. King seven times, perhaps illegally, thus making Sullivan one of the "Southern violators." Further, he said, the ad made it look as though he encouraged the violence directed at Dr. King and his family. Six witnesses testified that they had read the ad and concluded it was referring to Sullivan in a derogatory way.

Other witnesses testified that much of the detail in the offending paragraphs was false. The students had not sung "America"; they had sung "The Star-Spangled Banner." Only nine students were expelled, but not for leading the demonstration at the Capitol. Only part of the student body had protested the expulsions, not by refusing to register, but by boycotting classes for a single day. The campus dining hall was not padlocked at any time. The only students who may have been refused service were those who did not have meal tickets, and there were few of them. Police were deployed near the campus in large numbers, but at no time did they ring the campus.

Nor were those the only errors. Dr. King had been arrested four times, not seven. Although he claimed he had been assaulted when he was arrested for loitering outside a courtroom, one of the officers involved denied at the libel trial that there had been an assault. Dr. King's house had indeed been bombed, but that had happened before Sullivan became police commissioner. No evidence ever implicated police in the bombing. Three of Dr. King's four arrests also took place before Sullivan's election. Dr. King was indicted on two counts of perjury, for which the maximum term was five years, not ten, but he had been acquitted on both. Sullivan testified that he had had nothing to do with either charge.

Clippings in the *Times*'s own files showed that some of the allegations made in the ad were false. The manager of the newspaper's Advertising Acceptability department testified that he had not checked the files because the ad had been prepared by a reputable agency. It was accompanied by a letter from A. Philip Randolph, president of the Brotherhood of Sleeping Car Porters and a New York City resident, certifying that all the persons whose names appeared in the ad had given their permission. The manager said he knew and respected Randolph. He said he had approved the ad for publication becaue he knew nothing to cause him to believe it was false, and because it bore the endorsement of "a number of people who are well known and whose reputations [he] had no reason to question."

The jury found that Sullivan had been libeled and awarded him a judgment for $500,000. The Alabama Supreme Court affirmed. In light of the facts as presented in court it had no other course. The decision was in accord with the law of libel as it was at that time. Sullivan and his witnesses had proved the only issue in doubt—identification. Once that was established, he stood accused of condoning, if not participating in, a series of felonies. Such accusations were libelous on their face. Nor, according to the law of the time, did the *Times* have any workable defenses. The proven errors in fact undercut any attempt to establish truth, privilege, or fair comment. The only question left for the jury was to establish the degree of harm to Sullivan's reputation and, hence, the size of the award.

The outcome of the suit in the state courts struck not only at the *Times*, but at other news media. The *Times* faced eleven other libel suits in Alabama courts in which plaintiffs were seeking more than $5 million. The Columbia Broadcasting System was defending five libel suits in Southern states in which plaintiffs were asking for nearly $2 million. Most of these suits were based on news coverage of the racial integration movement. Against that background the Supreme Court agreed to review the case and reversed unanimously.

Justice William J. Brennan, Jr., wrote the Court's opinion. He was joined by four others. From the outset, he took the position that comment on the public conduct of public officials is protected by the First Amendment. His clear intent was to take the case out of the realm of Alabama's common and statute law, where the *Times* could not win, onto the higher ground of constitutional law, where, the decision would prove, it could. In the process, the Court made four fundamental changes in legal principles.

The Protection of Editorial Advertising

The first change in traditional law was made to counter Sullivan's contention that "Heed Their Rising Voices" was not protected by the First Amendment because it was a paid advertisement. In making this point, Sullivan's lawyers relied on the Supreme Court's decision in *Valentine* v. *Chrestensen* in 1942.[16] In that case, in which the Court held that the owner of a submarine had no right to distribute commercial advertising handbills on the streets of New York city, the majority had seemed to say that advertising was not protected by the Constitution. In response to Sullivan's argument, Brennan wrote:

> The publication here . . . communicated information, expressed opinion, recited grievances, protested claimed abuses, and sought financial support on behalf of a movement whose existence and objectives are matters of the highest public concern. That the *Times* was paid for publishing the advertisement is as immaterial in this connection as the fact that newspapers and books are sold. Any other conclusion would discourage newspapers from carrying "editorial advertisements" of this type, and so might shut off an important outlet for the promulgation of information and ideas by persons who do not themselves have access to publishing facilities—who wish to exercise their freedom of speech even though they are not members of the press. The effect would be to shackle the First Amendment in its attempt to secure "the widest possible dissemination of information from diverse and antagonistic sources."[17] To avoid placing such a handicap upon the freedom of expression, we hold that if the allegedly libelous statements would otherwise be constitutionally protected from the present judgment, they do not forfeit that protection because they were published in the form of a paid advertisement.

With those words, the Court established its first new principle. Editorial advertising stands on higher constitutional ground than does ordinary commercial advertising. Editorial advertising gives people an opportunity to plead their cause in the news media. It is concerned with ideas. In contrast, commercial advertising simply offers a product

---

16. 316 U.S. 52, 62 S.Ct. 920, 86 L.Ed. 1262 (1942).
17. Quoting the Court's 1945 decision in Associated Press v. United States, an antitrust case, 326 U.S. 1, 65 S.Ct. 1416, 89 L.Ed. 2013 (1945).

or a service at a price. By bringing editorial advertising under the protection of the First Amendment, the Court was raising a barrier against successful libel suits, thus encouraging publishers to accept such appeals. Ten years later, the Court would extend limited First Amendment protection to commercial advertising, too (See chapter 11).

The First Amendment and Libel *Per Se*

Sullivan's next argument went to the heart of the common law of libel, the concept of libel *per se*. Under Alabama law, a statement was libelous on its face if it imputed misconduct to a public official. If a jury found that the complained-of words applied to the official, it was assumed that he had suffered harm to reputation. The defendant could escape an award of damages only by proving that the allegedly defamatory allegations were true in all respects or that they were fair comment based on a solid bed of fact. If either defense was tried and failed, the law further assumed that publication of a libel *per se* was a product of malice, in the sense of ill will. This meant that a jury could require the defendant to pay not only compensatory damages, a sum designed to make good the plaintiff's harm, but punitive damages, an additional sum levied as punishment.

The question thus became, could the First Amendment be invoked to interrupt this march to a costly conclusion once a publication had been found to be libelous on its face? Sullivan's lawyers quoted from numerous decisions in which Supreme Court majorities had seemed to say that libel *per se*, like obscenity, fighting words, and other language devoid of idea content, was outside the scope of First Amendment protection. But, responded Brennan, none of those cases involved criticism of the public conduct of public officials:

> [W]e are compelled neither by precedent nor policy to give any more weight to the epithet "libel" than we have to other "mere labels" of state law. Like insurrection, contempt, advocacy of unlawful acts, breach of the peace, obscenity, solicitation of illegal business, and the other various formulae for the repression of expression that have been challenged in this court, libel can claim no talismanic immunity from constitutional limitations. It must be measured by standards that satisfy the First Amendment.
>
> The general proposition that freedom of expression upon public questions is secured by the First Amendment has long been settled by our decisions.

Brennan thus forged the second link in the progression required to reverse the Alabama courts. Even statements libelous on their face must be examined in the light of First Amendment guarantees if they arise out of the discussion of public issues. With this platform built, the Court proceeded to the heart of its decision:

> Thus we consider this case against the background of a profound national commitment to the principle that debate on public issues should be uninhibited, robust, and wide-open, and that it may well include vehement, caustic, and sometimes unpleasantly sharp attacks on government and public officials. The present advertisement, as an expression of grievance and protest on one of the major public issues of our time, would seem clearly to qualify for the constitutional protection.

The Partial Protection of False Statements

Having established that "Heed Their Rising Voices" was protected by the First Amendment even though it had appeared as a paid advertisement and was libelous on its face, the Court had an even higher hurdle to jump. Beyond question, the ad contained false assertions of fact, and some of these were libelous. Does the First Amendment also condone falsehood?

Brennan examined the "public principle" cases and found that courts in a minority of the states had tolerated some error in the criticism of public officials. He concluded, quoting James Madison, who wrote much of the Constitution, that "some degree of abuse is inseparable from the proper use of everything; and in no instance is this more true than in that of the press." Brennan also noted that in some areas of law, the Supreme Court already had rejected the suggestion that the First Amendment protects only those statements that can be proved to be true. He added, again quoting Madison:

> [E]rroneous statement is inevitable in free debate, and . . . it must be protected if the freedoms of expression are to have the "breathing space" that they "need . . . to survive."

With those words, Brennan, writing for a majority of the Court, established a third legal principle, and a most significant one: The First Amendment excuses some falsehoods uttered in the heat of debate over the public conduct of public officials.

Brennan expanded on the reasons for the Court's new approach. The *Times* had already been ordered to pay a $500,000 judgment, which Brennan likened to a fine, and faced other civil suits for comparable sums. Newspapers confronted with such prospects might well succumb to a "pall of fear and timidity" and mute their criticisms of public officials, Brennan said. In such an atmosphere, he noted, "First Amendment freedoms cannot survive." Nor can state libel laws be saved, Brennan added, by permitting publishers to win libel suits by proving the truth of their statements. He wrote:

> A rule compelling the critic of official conduct to guarantee the truth of all his factual assertions—and to do so on pain of libel judgments virtually unlimited in amount—leads to . . . "self-censorship." Allowance of the defense of truth, with the burden of proving it on the defendant, does not mean that only false speech will be deterred. Even courts accepting this defense as an adequate safeguard have recognized the difficulties in adducing legal proofs that the alleged libel was true in all its factual particulars. . . . Under such a rule, would-be critics of official conduct may be deterred from voicing their criticism, even though it is believed to be true and even though it is in fact true, because of doubt whether it can be proved in court or fear of the expense of having to so do. . . . The rule thus dampens the vigor and limits the variety of public debate. It is inconsistent with the First and Fourteenth Amendments.

Proving Actual Malice

Brennan saved the Court's most explosive change for last:

> The constitutional guarantees require, we think, a federal rule that prohibits a public official from recovering damages for a defamatory falsehood relating to his official conduct unless he proves that the statement was made with "actual malice"—that is, with knowledge that it was false or with reckless disregard of whether it was false or not.

The term "actual malice" was not new in court decisions, as is evidenced by the fact that Brennan put it in quotation marks. But it must be emphasized that his definition of the term was new. The dictionary defines "malice" in terms of "evil intent or motive"—the desire to cause harm to another. But, as used in libel decisions, "actual malice" means precisely what the Supreme Court said it means in *New York Times*, no more and no less. It means that the publisher of the libel either acted in the knowledge that his assertion was false or in reckless disregard of whether it was true or not.

Seldom has a single paragraph in a Supreme Court decision brought about such a revolutionary change in the law. With that paragraph, the Court shifted most of the burden of proof in libel suits brought by public officials against the news media. Not only would public official plaintiffs have to prove publication, identification, and defamation, but they would have to prove that the defamatory passage was false, and that the publisher either knew it was false or acted in reckless disregard of the truth. Further, Brennan wrote, for a majority of the Court, public official plaintiffs would have to prove actual malice with "convincing clarity." This, he made clear, would require a higher level of proof than the **"preponderance of the evidence"** test required in other civil actions.

To avoid the expense of returning the case to an Alabama court for possible retrial under the new rules, the Court proceeded to hold that Sullivan could not prove that the *Times* acted in actual malice. At the most, Brennan wrote, Sullivan might be able to prove that the *Times's* advertising department was negligent in not checking the assertions in the advertisement against clippings in the newspaper's own files. But, Brennan added, a mere failure to investigate is not reckless disregard. Such failure must be coupled with a showing that the publisher doubted the truth of the statement in question. In this instance, there was no doubt. The advertisement bore the signatures of respected persons of substance. There was no reason why anyone at the *Times* should doubt them.

The Supreme Court's decision in *New York Times* v. *Sullivan* sent lower courts everywhere a clear signal: Public officials should not be permitted to collect libel judgments from the news media except for a knowing or reckless lie. Further, the burden was on the public official plaintiff to prove knowledge of falsity or reckless disregard of truth on the part of the publisher.

It quickly became apparent that the Supreme Court's decision in *New York Times* raised significant questions:

— Sullivan was an elected public official with responsibility for overseeing a police department. The Court's decision was written with frequent reference to a "public official," and therefore seemed limited in its application. But who else on the public payroll might be classed as a public official?

— Some persons in public life have considerable influence even though they hold no public office. Others seek influence by becoming candidates for election to public offices. Shouldn't such persons be subject to robust and uninhibited debate?

— The Court defined "actual malice" in terms that looked deceptively easy. It is the knowing lie, or the assertion that is a product of a reckless disregard for the truth. But how might a public official prove either one with "convincing clarity"? Brennan had written that doubt on the part of the publisher is an element in reckless disregard, but how much doubt? And how can it be proved? Did the decision mean that libel plaintiffs could examine the editorial process? Could they pry into the state of mind of the reporter who gathered the facts and wrote the story, and of the editors who approved it?

There were also more subtle questions. Does the First Amendment protect discussion of persons or discussion of ideas? Could the same statement libel one person because he did not hold public office and not libel another because she did? If a public official plaintiff must prove actual malice, would he also have the burden of proving that the statement at issue was false? In view of the Court's robust commitment to freewheeling debate, even to the point of tolerating some degree of falsehood, were judges expected to dispose of more cases through **summary judgment**?

Cases seeking answers to some of these questions reached the Supreme Court during the decade after 1964. In its decision in three of the cases, the Court extended the scope of the *New York Times* rule, as the constitutional defense quickly came to be known. In 1966, in *Rosenblatt* v. *Baer*,[18] the Court defined "public official" to include "those among the hierarchy of government employees who have, or appear to the public to have, substantial responsibility for or control over the conduct of government affairs." A public official, then, is not just anyone on a government payroll, but only those employees who make policy or who have considerable discretion in how they carry out their duties.

In 1967, in *Curtis Publishing Co.* v. *Butts*,[19] the Court extended the application of the *New York Times* rule to "public figures." These it defined in part as persons who thrust themselves "into the 'vortex' of an important public controversy." That definition would prove to be too vague. Subsequent decisions refining and narrowing the definition of public figures will be treated later in this chapter.

The Constitutional Defense Further Defined

The *New York Times* decision was a product of a Supreme Court led by Chief Justice Earl Warren. Warren had been appointed by President Dwight D. Eisenhower in 1953 and presided for sixteen years over one of the most liberal eras in the history of the Supreme Court. Particularly during the 1960s, the Court greatly expanded the protections afforded by the Bill of Rights, including freedom of speech and press. The *Rosenblatt* and *Butts* decisions were also products of the Warren Court.

In 1969, Warren retired as chief justice, giving Richard M. Nixon, a Republican who was elected president the previous year, an opportunity to make his first appointment to the Court. Nixon chose Warren E. Burger, then a judge of the United States Court of Appeals for the District of Columbia Circuit, to replace Warren. Burger was known to believe that the Warren Court had gone too far in applying federal constitutional law

---

18. 383 U.S. 75, 86 S.Ct. 669, 15 L.Ed.2d 597 (1966).
19. 388 U.S. 130, 87 S.Ct. 1975, 18 L.Ed.2d 1094 (1967).

to cases that he thought best left to state courts for decision. A year later, Burger was joined on the Court by the second Nixon appointee, Harry A. Blackmun, who had been a judge of the Court of Appeals for the Eighth Circuit in Minnesota. He replaced Abe Fortas, who had been appointed to the Court by President Lyndon B. Johnson, a Democrat. With Nixon's first two appointments, the Court's membership began to move in a conservative direction.

Rosenbloom v. Metromedia

During its 1970–1971 term, the Court accepted for review a libel case growing out of the arrest of a book and magazine distributor in Philadelphia on obscenity charges.

Rosenbloom v. Metromedia, Inc., 403 U.S. 29, 91 S.Ct. 1811, 29 L.Ed.2d 296 (1971).

In reporting the arrest, a Philadelphia radio station owned by Metromedia had referred to the distributor as a "smut peddler." It did so even after the distributor had called the station and told its news staff the magazines in question had been held not to be obscene by courts elsewhere. The epithet was also used to describe the distributor, Rosenbloom, after the charges against him had been dismissed. Rosenbloom sued the station for libel and won a six-figure judgment. The Supreme Court reversed, but was so badly divided that a majority could not agree on a rationale.

At issue was whether Rosenbloom should have to prove actual malice. He was not a public official, and the Court was in disagreement as to whether he was a public figure. Justice Brennan's view was decisive, although he could not get a majority of the Court to accept his position as he had in *New York Times*. Arguing that the purpose of the First Amendment is to protect the discussion of ideas and to protect the news media in the reporting of public affairs, he and three other justices concluded that Rosenbloom's status was immaterial. At its heart was the bigger issue of obscenity and the attempt to control its distribution in the public interest. Rosenbloom was caught up in the attempt to resolve that issue. Therefore, he should be required to prove actual malice.

At that point, the Supreme Court had gone as far as it was going to go in extending First Amendment protection to libel defendants. Had Brennan been able to muster a majority behind his opinion, all libel plaintiffs suing the news media would have had to prove actual malice. The *Rosenbloom* decision continues to be of importance because courts in a few states have adopted its rationale. However, within three years, the Supreme Court was to accept another libel case and hold that states could permit private individuals to sue the news media for libel on a lesser showing of fault than actual malice.

Gertz v. Robert Welch, Inc.

In the same year that *Rosenbloom* was decided, Justices Hugo L. Black and John Marshall Harlan died. Black had taken the position that the First Amendment gives absolute protection to pure speech, including libel. Harlan, an Eisenhower appointee, was more conservative. After a long fight with the Senate, Nixon replaced them in 1972 with Lewis F. Powell, Jr., and William H. Rehnquist, both of whom took the position at the time that the Constitution should be construed in strict terms. Rehnquist, perhaps even more than Burger, has taken the position that many issues, including libel, should be resolved at the state level, without resort to federal constitutional law. Powell has become more flexible on First Amendment issues.

Thus there were four Nixon appointees on the Court when it decided its next significant libel case in 1974. The plaintiff was a Chicago lawyer, Elmer Gertz, who had been criticized severely by an article in *American Opinion*, the magazine of the ultraconservative John Birch Society. Gertz drew the magazine's fire when he agreed to represent the parents of a youth who had been shot to death by a Chicago police officer. When police officials ruled that the shooting was unjustified, the parents sued their son's

Gertz v. *Robert Welch, Inc.*, 418 U.S. 323, 94 S.Ct. 2997, 41 L.Ed.2d 789 (1974).

killer for damages. The magazine took the position that Gertz's role as the family's lawyer made him part of a plot to discredit the police. The writer referred to the lawyer as "Leninist Elmer Gertz" and "Communist-fronter Gertz." A photo caption referred to Gertz as a member of the "Red Guild," a reference to the fact that some years earlier he had been active in the National Lawyers Guild. Its membership was made up largely of lawyers opposed to the dominant and somewhat conservative American Bar Association. Some Guild members had attracted attention in the McCarthy era by defending persons identified as Communists by congressional investigating committees. There was little doubt that the article made false statements about Gertz. For instance, it said the police file on the lawyer was so voluminous that only "a big Irish cop" could lift it. Gertz had no police record.

When Gertz sued the magazine's publisher, Robert Welch, Inc., for libel, the district court judge who heard the case was somewhat confused as to the meaning of the *New York Times* rule. He had decided at the start of the trial that it did not apply. After the jury had returned a $50,000 judgment in Gertz's favor, he held otherwise on grounds that the article in *American Opinion* discussed an issue of public importance. The United States Court of Appeals for the Seventh Circuit affirmed the judge's ruling. Gertz, who had seen his $50,000 award wiped out, asked the Supreme Court to accept the case for review, which it did.

Justice Powell, writing for a five-member majority that included Blackmun and Rehnquist, specifically repudiated the plurality ruling in *Rosenbloom.* The majority held that the nature of the plaintiff is the crucial element in deciding whether the *New York Times* rule protects a media libel defendant. Justice Powell's decision for the Court is not a model of judicial writing because he chose to discuss elements of libel law that were not properly a part of the case brought to the Court by Gertz. When judges write, as Powell did here, on issues that are not essential to a resolution of the case, such passages are called *dicta.* Strictly speaking, they are viewed as extraneous comment and are not considered as precedents that lower courts are expected to follow. However, Powell's dicta in *Gertz* have been looked to for guidance by most lower courts. Thus, the Court's decision has established important new guidelines for libel law, both supplementing and limiting *New York Times.*

LIBEL IS LIMITED TO FALSE AND DEFAMATORY ASSERTIONS OF FACT   Powell began by writing about the nature of defamation:

> We begin with the common ground. Under the First Amendment there is no such thing
> as a false idea. However pernicious an opinion may seem, we depend for its correction not

on the conscience of judges and juries, but on the competition of other ideas. But there is no constitutional value in false statements of fact. Neither the intentional lie nor the careless error materially advances society's interest in "uninhibited, robust, and wide-open debate" on public issues. . . . They belong to that category of utterances which "are no essential part of any exposition of ideas, and are of such slight social value as a step to truth that any benefit that may be derived from them is clearly outweighed by the social interest in order and morality."[20]

With the second and third sentences of the above paragraph, the Court said that statements of opinion are not actionable as libel. Defamatory statements, the Court seemed to be saying, are actionable only if they make a false assertion of fact. Because Gertz's suit against Robert Welch, Inc., involved false assertions of fact, this part of the decision can be considered dicta. However, by 1986, as we will see later, it was clear that courts in most jurisdictions were ruling that opinion is not actionable.

In *Gertz*, Powell wrote that expressions of opinion are a legitimate part of public debate. Because they are not subject to being proved or disproved, courts should let debate in the public forum correct opinions believed to be harmful.

THE STATES MAY MAKE IT EASIER FOR PRIVATE INDIVIDUALS TO WIN LIBEL ACTIONS AGAINST THE MEDIA   Powell next reviewed the Court's decision in *New York Times*, focusing on the protection it gave to falsehoods uttered in the heat of debate. To retreat from that holding, he said, would run the risk of restricting debate through "intolerable self-censorship." Some error must be protected, Powell added, "to protect speech that matters."

However, Powell noted for the majority, freedom of speech and press do not stand alone. Other interests must also be protected. For instance, the justice wrote, states have a legitimate interest in providing "compensation of individuals for harm inflicted on them by defamatory falsehoods." Therefore, the Supreme Court would not foreclose the right of any state to protect an individual's reputation. Here Powell was addressing an issue raised by the case and no longer was writing dicta.

However, without directly saying so, Powell was responding to the criticism that the Supreme Court, in writing the *New York Times* decision, had sought to bring all libel law within the scope of the First Amendment, thus federalizing it. The words above signaled the Court's intention to pull back somewhat from the extreme reading of *New York Times*. Powell made clear that the Court did not intend to weaken the actual malice rule as it applies to public persons. He wrote:

> Those who, by reason of the notoriety of their achievements or the vigor and success with which they seek the public's attention, are properly classed as public figures and those who hold governmental office may recover for injury to reputation only on clear and convincing proof that the defamatory falsehood was made with knowledge of its falsity or with reckless disregard of the truth.

The majority recognized that some deserving plaintiffs might not be able to surmount that barrier. But, on the other hand, its presence serves as "an extremely powerful

---

20. Quoting Chaplinsky v. New Hampshire, 315 U.S. 568, 62 S.Ct. 766, 86 L.Ed. 1031 (1942), in which the Court held that "fighting words," in this instance insulting epithets, are devoid of idea content, hence not protected by the First Amendment.

antidote" for the tendency toward self-censorship induced by the old common law of libel. For that reason, Powell wrote, "the Court has concluded that the protection of the *New York Times* privilege should be available to publishers and broadcasters of defamatory falsehood concerning public officials and public figures." But, he added, the Court also had concluded that states should have the right to apply a less stringent rule to private individuals who might be defamed by the news media.

The majority offered a simple justification for its conclusion. Public officials and public figures are newsworthy. If they are subjected to criticism, they can fight back in print and on the air. Private individuals are less likely to reach the public with their views, even when they have been the subject of a defamatory story. Therefore, the Court concluded, they are "more vulnerable to injury, and the state interest in protecting them is correspondingly greater." On the other hand, persons who hold public office, or who try to influence public affairs, should do so in full knowledge of the likely consequences. They run "the risk of closer public scrutiny than might otherwise be the case."

At this point in its decision, the Court had made it possible for the states to again apply common-law principles to some part of the law of libel. It had said that public officials and public figures who sued the news media for libel would continue to have to prove actual malice by "clear and convincing evidence." But if states so chose, they could establish a lighter burden of proof for private individuals.

PUBLIC FIGURES ARE DEFINED AND CATEGORIZED   Powell turned next to a discussion of the criteria that would help lower courts classify libel plaintiffs. He wrote that there are three kinds of public figures:

> Hypothetically, it may be possible for someone to become a public figure through no purposeful action of his own, but the instances of truly involuntary public figures must be exceedingly rare. For the most part those who attain this status have assumed roles of especial prominence in the affairs of society. Some occupy positions of such persuasive power and influence that they are deemed public figures for all purposes. More commonly, those classed as public figures have thrust themselves to the forefront of particular public controversies in order to influence the resolution of the issues involved. In either event, they invite attention and comment.
>
> Even if the foregoing generalities do not obtain in every instance, the communications media are entitled to act on the assumption that public officials and public figures have voluntarily exposed themselves to increased risk of defamatory falsehoods concerning them. No such assumption is justified with respect to a private individual. He has not accepted a public office or assumed an "influential role in ordering society." He has relinquished no part of his interest in the protection of his own good name, and consequently he has a more compelling call on the courts for redress of injury inflicted by defamatory falsehood. Thus, private individuals are not only more vulnerable to injury than public officials and public figures; they are more deserving of recovery.
>
> For these reasons we conclude that the States should retain substantial latitude in their efforts to enforce a legal remedy for defamatory falsehood injurious to the reputation of a private individual.

PRIVATE INDIVIDUALS MUST PROVE SOME DEGREE OF FAULT ON THE PART OF THE MEDIA   The phrase "substantial latitude" was used for a purpose. The Supreme Court was willing to let the states apply their own rules to libel suits directed at the news media by private individuals, but it was not willing to let them restore the old rule of common law in its entirety. There were limits, which the Court sought to define as follows:

> We hold that, so long as they do not impose liability without fault, the States may define for themselves the appropriate standard of liability for a publisher or a broadcaster of defamatory falsehood injurious to a private individual. This approach provides a more equitable boundary between the competing concerns involved here. It recognizes the strength of the legitimate state interest in compensating private individuals for wrongful injury to reputation, yet shields the press and broadcast media from the rigors of strict liability for defamation. At least this conclusion obtains where, as here, the substance of the defamatory statement "makes substantial danger to reputation apparent."

While Powell did not define what he meant by "liability without fault," Chief Justice Burger, writing in dissent, did. He said the majority had established a "new negligence standard," as indeed it had. In most states that have chosen the option offered by *Gertz*, private individuals who sue the news media for libel need show only that reporters or editors have fallen short of a recognized standard of care. State courts have varied in defining that standard. Some have applied the well-established principles of ordinary negligence, in which persons are at fault if they have failed to do what a "prudent person" would have done under the circumstances. What such a person would do is a matter for a jury to determine after listening to witnesses for both sides. Other courts have held that the performance of journalists should be measured against the standard of care that would be followed by professional reporters and editors caught up in similar circumstances. Again, the determination is one to be made by the jury after listening to the testimony of witnesses deemed to have knowledge of professional practices.[21] In either event, *Gertz* has given courts responsibility for doing what journalists themselves have not done in a systematic fashion: that is, establish professional standards for performance. A few states have set other standards, varying from "gross negligence" in New York to California's holding that its state constitution confers a qualified privilege on the reporting of newsworthy events.

In this section of its decision, the Court sought to protect the news media from libel judgments based on inadvertent mistakes, such things as typographical errors, confusion in addresses, or mistaken information accepted in good faith from usually reliable sources. The Court held that even private individuals should not be permitted to succeed in a libel suit against the media unless they could prove some kind of fault.

PRIVATE INDIVIDUALS MUST ALSO SHOW THAT THEY HAVE BEEN HARMED UNLESS THEY CAN PROVE ACTUAL MALICE   The Court moved next to the question of damages. If states were permitted to apply their old common-law standards in libel suits brought by private individuals, the sky might be the limit. Under those standards, juries could award damages to persons who had suffered no injury, such as loss of income or standing in the community. At common law, injury was assumed from the fact of publication. Powell noted that common law gave juries "largely uncontrolled discretion" to "award

---

21. John B. McCrory, "Development of the Defense of Constitutional Privilege in Libel Law," *Communications Law 1983* (New York: Practicing Law Institute, 1983), vol. 1, pp. 167–71.

substantial sums as compensation for supposed damages to reputation without any proof that such harm actually occurred." If states were to revert to common law in assessing damages, they would invite "juries to punish unpopular opinion rather than to compensate individuals for injury." The prospect of such awards might "inhibit the vigorous exercise of First Amendment freedoms by inviting self-censorship." To prevent that, Powell wrote for the Court, states could go no further in protecting the reputation of private individuals "than compensation for **actual injury**. . . . [W]e hold that States may not permit recovery of presumed or punitive damages, at least when liability is not based on a showing of knowledge of falsity or reckless disregard of the truth."

After saying that it need not attempt to define "actual injury," the Court seemed to do just that. Powell wrote:

> Suffice it to say that actual injury is not limited to out-of-pocket loss. Indeed, the more customary types of actual harm inflicted by defamatory falsehood include impairment of reputation and standing in the community, personal humiliation, and mental anguish and suffering. Of course, juries must be limited by appropriate instructions, and all awards must be supported by competent evidence concerning the injury, although there need be no evidence which assigns an actual dollar value to the injury."

The Court turned next to a strong criticism of awards of punitive damages in libel suits, but it stopped short of outlawing them. Punitive damages are designed to punish a defendant for alleged wrongdoing, and to deter others who might be tempted to commit a similar offense. The Court said:

> We also find no justification for allowing awards of punitive damages against publishers and broadcasters held liable under state-defined standards of liability for defamation. In most jurisdictions jury discretion over the amounts awarded is limited only by the gentle rule that they not be excessive. Consequently, juries assess punitive damages in wholly unpredictable amounts bearing no necessary relation to the actual harm caused. And they remain free to use their discretion selectively to punish expressions of unpopular views. Like the doctrine of presumed damages, jury discretion to award punitive damages unnecessarily exacerbates the danger of media self-censorship, but unlike the former rule, punitive damages are wholly irrelevant to the state interest that justifies a negligence standard for private defamation actions. They are not compensation for injury. Instead, they are private fines levied by civil juries to punish reprehensible conduct and to deter future occurrence. In short, the private defamation plaintiff who establishes liability under a less demanding standard than that stated in *New York Times* may recover only such damages as are sufficient to compensate him for actual injury.

With that part of its decision, the majority seemed to be trying to bring awards of damages in libel cases under control. Recovery by private individuals would be limited to compensation for actual injury, unless they could prove actual malice. Public officials and public figures could not recover anything unless they could prove actual malice. However, the Court could not define harm in such a way as to reduce it to a tangible measurement. Juries were left with considerable discretion. What, for instance, is the dollar value of "impairment of reputation and standing in the community?" Or of "personal humiliation, and mental anguish and suffering?" How does one prove the latter? Subsequent cases have proved that some juries are willing to put six- and seven-figure values on such intangibles despite Powell's condemnation of "private fines levied by civil juries."

The remainder of the decision was devoted to the Court's finding that Gertz was not a public figure, although he had had some minimal participation in public affairs in Chicago. In essence the Court concluded that he had attracted *American Opinion's* libelous lightning not because he was trying to influence public opinion against police in general, but because he had been hired to file suit against one police officer. He was simply a lawyer doing his job. That did not make him even a limited-purpose public figure. The case was sent back to the federal district court in Chicago.

There, seven years later in the spring of 1981, the case again reached trial. In the meantime, Gertz had achieved a sort of fame as the lawyer whose lawsuit had changed the law of libel. He was in demand as a lecturer. He had become a professor at the John Marshall Law School. Gertz commented in an interview with a reporter for the *Chicago Law Bulletin* that the case "may have made me a public figure."[22]

Nevertheless, the trial was conducted on the ground that he was a private individual, as the Supreme Court had held him to be at the time the libel was published in 1969. Gertz testified that when he saw the article he was shocked and that it "knocked me out emotionally for a long period of time." He also testified that he thought he had lost clients as a result of it.

This time, a six-member jury found that *American Opinion* not only was negligent in publishing the article, but had acted with actual malice. The jurors concluded that Gertz had suffered $100,000 in actual harm. They assessed an additional $300,000 in punitive damages against Robert Welch, Inc. Gertz was quoted as viewing the outcome as a "blow for responsible journalism."[23] More than a year later, an appeals court affirmed the award.[24] The Supreme Court refused to review the verdict.[25]

The Law of Libel since Gertz

As a result of the Supreme Court's decision in *New York Times* and *Gertz*, and of subsequent decisions by it and by lower courts, certain principles have become well established in libel law.

Libel Plaintiffs and the Burden of Proof

All persons who believe they have been defamed by the news media must establish three basic facts if they sue for libel. These basics are the same as they were under common law:

1. Publication. This is proved by offering a copy of the offending article or a transcript of the broadcast.

---

22. "Landmark Libel Case Being Quietly Retried," *Chicago Law Bulletin*, 17 April 1981.
23. "Gertz Case Finally Settled," *Newsletter*, Inland Daily Press Association, 30 April 1981.
24. Gertz v. Robert Welch, Inc., 680 F.2d 527 (7th Cir. 1982).
25. Robert Welch, Inc., v. Gertz, 103 S.Ct. 1233 (1983).

2. Identification. If the individual was named in the submitted material, there is no issue, provided the allegedly defamatory portions were directed at the plaintiff. If the identification is not direct, there must be evidence, as in *New York Times*, showing that others understood the defamatory language to be directed at the plaintiff.

3. Defamation. The language in question must be of such a nature as to lower the plaintiff in the esteem of others, or be reasonably susceptible of doing so. As in common law, the threshold decision is made by a judge. If the passage at issue makes an accusation of serious crime, or is otherwise libelous *per se*, the judge will so hold and the case will have to be resolved on other grounds. If the meaning of the passage is ambiguous, a jury will be permitted to decide whether it is defamatory. If the meaning clearly is not defamatory, the judge will dismiss the case if the plaintiff so moves.

From this point on, the nature of a libel proceeding has changed markedly as a result of the Supreme Court's decisions in *New York Times* and *Gertz*. Under common law, once the three basics had been established, the burden of proof moved to the defendant. Unless he could prove truth, qualified privilege, or fair comment, the only question left for a jury was to fix the size of the award to the plaintiff. Now, libel plaintiffs carry the burden of proving additional facts.

PUBLIC OFFICIALS AND PUBLIC FIGURES   In all state courts and in the federal courts, a public official or public figure who brings a libel action against the news media must establish proof of two additional facts:

1. *Falsehood*. It no longer is enough for public official/public figure plaintiffs to show that they have been victims of defamatory language. Nor do the courts assume that such language is false, as they did at common law. The plaintiff must offer as part of his pleadings some evidence pointing to a false assertion of fact. Courts are holding that a defamation is not actionable unless it is false.

2. *Actual malice*. The plaintiff must allege that someone who had responsibility for publishing or broadcasting the allegedly defamatory item either knew it was false or acted in reckless disregard for the truth. An element in the latter is evidence that someone in the chain of responsibility had serious doubts about the story or put too much reliance on sources of doubtful credibility. Assertions of actual malice must be supported by clear and convincing evidence.

If the plaintiff cannot make a convincing case for any of the points above, many courts will grant a defendant's motion for summary judgment. In June 1986, the Supreme Court encouraged judges to dispose of libel suits through summary judgments, holding that actions brought by public plaintiffs ought not go to trial unless there is "clear and convincing evidence" of both falsehood and actual malice (*Anderson* v. *Liberty Lobby, Inc.*, No. 84-1602, June 25, 1986). If the preliminary evidence as reflected in the affidavits and in the process of discovery leaves any of the points in doubt, the court will refuse a motion for summary judgment and reserve the disputed points for a jury to resolve at trial. However, in 1984, in a case that will be discussed later, the Supreme Court emphasized that the determination of actual malice ultimately is a question of law. The Court held that a jury's finding of actual malice can be reviewed and overruled by an appellate court.[26]

While the burden of proving the two points above rests squarely on the plaintiff, the defendant's attorneys will not be idle during the early stages of the case. They will be obtaining affidavits, depositions, and other evidence pointing to the truth of the allegedly defamatory facts and to the care with which the article or broadcast was prepared.

PRIVATE INDIVIDUALS   Most states have accepted the Supreme Court's invitation in *Gertz* and have established a lower standard of proof of fault for private individuals who sue the news media for libel. As Chief Justice Burger predicted in his dissent in *Gertz*, the great majority of these states require private plaintiffs to prove negligence. In the remaining states, the standard lies somewhere between negligence and actual malice. Under the new rules, private plaintiffs who bring libel actions against the media must prove three things in addition to the usual publication, identification, and defamation.

1. *Falsehood.* The Supreme Court held, five-to-four, in 1986 in *Philadelphia Newspapers, Inc.*, v. *Hepps*,[27] that private individuals who sue the news media for libel in a matter of "public concern" must prove that the alleged defamation is false. The Court held that the First Amendment interest in uninhibited debate does not permit state courts to hold to the common-law assumption of falsity in media libel cases. Courts in a few states had read *Gertz* as permitting them to do so. The decision seems to mean that no libel action directed at the mass media's treatment of a public issue can survive unless the plaintiff offers convincing evidence of a false and defamatory assertion of fact. However, the decision also seems to leave open the possibility that a private individual could prevail on some lesser standard of proof if the alleged libel concerned a private matter.

2. *Fault.* As a minimum, private libel plaintiffs must prove that media libel defendants were negligent. Depending upon the rule in effect in the state in which the action is brought, the plaintiff must show either that those who prepared the story did not follow a standard of ordinary care or did not follow the professional standards of qualified journalists. In general, courts have defined negligence as the failure to do what a prudent person would do under a given set of circumstances to avoid harm, or as doing something that caused harm that a prudent person would not have done under the circumstances. To use an illustration from the everyday world, a prudent motorist does not plow through a busy intersection at 50 miles an hour when the streets are covered with ice. Nor does a prudent pedestrian

---

26. Bose Corp. v. Consumer Union of the United States, Inc., 466 U.S. 485, 104 S.Ct. 1949, 80 L.Ed.2d 502 (1984).
27. ___ U.S. ___, 106 S.Ct. 1558, 89 L.Ed.2d 783 (1986).

cross a busy street in the middle of a block without looking both ways. Courts have held that prudent journalists must at least check such things as street addresses and names.

3. *Harm.* Private plaintiffs must show that they have been harmed in some way. Such harm can be monetary loss coming from the loss of a job, cancellation of a contract, or a decline in business. But harm need not be financial. The plaintiff has also proven harm if he can show he has been shunned by others, or has suffered humiliation and embarrassment. If the plaintiff can offer clear and convincing evidence of actual malice on the part of the defendant, he becomes eligible for an award of punitive damages as well as compensatory damages for the proven harm.

Private Individuals and the Burden of Proof

Since 1974, not all states have had occasion to decide libel actions brought by private individuals against the news media. In those that have, courts in twenty-eight states, the District of Columbia, and Puerto Rico had adopted a negligence standard as of mid-1985.[28] The states are Alabama, Arizona, Arkansas, California, Delaware, Florida, Georgia, Hawaii, Illinois, Kansas, Kentucky, Maryland, Massachusetts, Minnesota, Mississippi, New Jersey, New Mexico, North Carolina, Ohio, Oklahoma, Oregon, Pennsylvania, Tennessee, Texas, Utah, Virginia, Washington, and Wisconsin.

New York stands alone in requiring private libel plaintiffs to prove that the media acted with "gross negligence." This is something more than carelessness, but does not require a showing that the publisher had serious doubt.[29]

Courts in four states have looked either to *Rosenbloom* or their own state constitutions for guidance and require private plaintiffs caught up in media discussion of public issues to prove actual malice. The states are Alaska,[30] Colorado,[31] Indiana,[32] and Michigan.[33]

The remaining seventeen states either have had no libel cases in which private individuals sued the news media for libel, or have been able to resolve them without reaching the question as to the standard of fault. However, the trend is clear. Courts in most states that have confronted the issue have elected to permit private individuals to prevail on proof of negligence.

Proving Actual Malice or Gross Negligence

In *Gertz*, the Supreme Court gave states the option of making it easier for private individuals to sue the news media for libel, but it did not say they had to do so. As a result, a few states have elected to require private individuals to prove something other

---

28. John B. McCrory, Robert C. Bernius, and Andrew C. Rose, "Development of the Defense of Constitutional Privilege in Libel Law," *Communications Law 1985* (New York: Practising Law Institute, 1985), pp. 202–207.
29. Chapadeau v. Utica Observer-Dispatch, 341 N.E.2d 569 (N.Y. 1975).
30. Gay v. Williams, 486 F.Supp. 12 (D.Alaska 1979).
31. Diversified Management v. The Denver Post, 653 P.2d 1103 (Colo. 1982).
32. Aafco Heating & Air Conditioning Co. v. Northwest Publications, 321 N.E.2d 580 (Ind.App. 1974).
33. Peisner v. Detroit Free Press, 266 N.W.2d 693 (Mich.App. 1978).

than negligence in order to prevail against the media. Thus, in these states, the media enjoy a higher degree of protection against successful libel actions than they do in the states that permit private individuals to prevail on proof of negligence.

Courts in the minority states have looked either at their own state constitutions or at the Supreme Court's decision in *Rosenbloom* v. *Metromedia* for guidance. As a result, they have held that the media are protected in covering news generated by public issues, no matter who is involved. This means that news media in those states are protected against libel suits, not only by the *New York Times* rule, if public officials or public figures are the plaintiffs, but by the state's free press guarantee or common law, if private individuals are plaintiffs. The degree of fault required if private individuals are to overcome the qualified privilege must rise above the level of negligence. How high it must rise varies from state to state.

New York courts have held that private individuals who allege they have been libeled by the news media must prove "gross negligence." This has been defined as "grossly irresponsible" conduct by reporters and editors. The cases offer little guidance as to the meaning of those terms. However, the state's Court of Claims, in an opinion that is pure dicta, said that editors of the student newspaper at a state university were grossly negligent in running a letter to the editor without checking it.[34] The letter, which identified the signers as members of the gay community who were coming out of the closet, was signed with the names of two students who had not written it. When the two students whose names were on the letter sued for libel, the claims court said the newspaper editors' failure to verify the identity of the writers, coupled with the lack of consistent procedures for verifying letters to the editor, was "grossly irresponsible." However, the suit was dismissed because the students had sued the state. The court held that because state officials had no authority to censor the newspaper, the state could not be held responsible for what happened. But it said the student editors could.

Courts in Colorado and Indiana, looking to their constitutions and to the plurality decision in *Rosenbloom* for guidance, have held that private individuals who are libeled in connection with a public issue must prove actual malice if they are to prevail. However, the leading decision in Colorado, *Walker* v. *Colorado Springs Sun*,[35] permits private individuals some leeway in proving actual malice. The state's supreme court held that in accord with the state's common law, a private plaintiff can show reckless disregard on the part of a publisher without proving that the latter had "serious doubt" as to the truth. In the case in point, the court found reckless disregard in an editor's selection of letters to the editor and the captions he wrote for them. Assertions made in both were contradicted by stories in his own newspaper. Within weeks after *Gertz* was decided, an Indiana appeals court rejected its rationale, electing in *Aafco Heating & Air Conditioning Co.* v. *Northwest Publications*,[36] to follow *Rosenbloom*. It did so, the court said, because the Indiana constitution protects the reporting and discussion of public events. The court further said it believed trial courts could more easily identify public issues than attempt to determine whether plaintiffs were public figures or private individuals. Private plaintiffs must prove actual malice as defined in *New York Times*, with one variation. A divided

---

34. Mazart v. State, 441 N.Y.S.2d 600 (N.Y.C.C. 1981).
35. 538 P.2d 450 (Colo. 1975).
36. 321 N.E.2d 580 (Ind.App. 1974).

state supreme court has permitted plaintiffs to offer evidence of ill will toward them on the part of the reporter as an element in proving actual malice.[37]

Since 1887, Michigan courts have recognized a qualified privilege by the news media to publish matters in the public interest. In the post-*Gertz* libel suits decided in that state, courts acted on the theory that private individuals must prove actual malice if they were to overcome this privilege.[38] However, in 1983, a federal district court judge, ruling in a libel suit against the *Muskegon Chronicle*, held that private individuals might also overcome Michigan's common-law privilege by proving malice in the traditional sense— that is, ill will, spite, or a desire and intent to injure.[39] In the Michigan decisions, courts have taken pains to emphasize that mere newsworthiness does not equate with "in the public interest." The event at issue must be of consequence to the public. Further, the private individual allegedly libeled in connection with the discussion of the event must have had more than a peripheral role in it.

The position taken by the Michigan courts received reinforcement from the Supreme Court in 1985. Ruling in *Dun & Bradstreet, Inc.*, v. *Greenmoss Builders, Inc.*, the

Dun & Bradstreet, Inc., v. Greenmoss Builders, Inc., _ U.S. _, 105 S.Ct. 2939, 86 L.Ed.2d 593 (1985)

Court said it has held in its libel decisions that the First Amendment protects debate on "public questions" and "public issues"—a position like that of the plurality in *Rosenbloom* more than a decade earlier. However, the Court showed no disposition to adopt the plurality's argument that all libel plaintiffs caught up in the discussion of public issues should have to prove actual malice. On the contrary, in *Greenmoss* the Court seems intent on further restricting the reach of *Gertz*, if not of *New York Times*.

The case began when Dun & Bradstreet falsely reported to five of its clients that Greenmoss, a building contractor, had filed for bankruptcy. When Greenmoss sued for libel, the Vermont courts held that because Dun & Bradstreet is not a news medium, the state's common law should prevail. Under that law, the jury was permitted to presume damages. It awarded Greenmoss $50,000 in compensatory damages and $300,000 in punitive damages. The Supreme Court agreed to review the case and upheld the verdict, five-to-four.

However, the Supreme Court did not adopt the Vermont courts' rationale. The justices did not attempt to distinguish between media and nonmedia defendants in libel cases. Rather, they focused on the facts from which the case arose, reasoning that Greenmoss's credit rating was a private matter. It was of interest only to the contractor and those who did business with him. Justice Powell, writing for only two other members of the Court, reasoned that because the libel arose out of a private matter, *Gertz* did not apply. Therefore, Greenmoss did not have to prove any degree of fault on the part of Dun & Bradstreet, nor did it have to prove it had been harmed. Vermont's common law properly governed the case.

---

37. Cochran v. Indianapolis Newspapers, 372 N.E.2d 1211 (Ind.App. 1978).
38. Peisner v. Detroit Free Press, 266 N.W.2d 693 (Mich.App. 1978); Clark v. ABC, 684 F.2d 1208 (6th Cir. 1982); Bichler v. Union Bank, 9 Med.L.Rptr. 2033 (1983). However, in Rouch v. Enquirer & News, 357 N.W.2d 794 (Mich.App. 1984), an appellate court held that a negligence standard applies to private individuals who sue over a matter that does not truly promote the public interest.
39. Apostle v. Booth Newspapers, Inc., 572 F.Supp. 897 (W.D.Mich. 1983).

The two others who made up the majority, Chief Justice Warren Burger and Justice Byron R. White, would have gone further. They would have seized the occasion to overrule *Gertz*, which Burger called "ill-conceived." Both also questioned the wisdom of *New York Times*. White wrote at length to argue that neither case is serving the purposes their drafters intended. He said that taken together they have made it more difficult for victims of harmful falsehoods to clear their names and have made it more expensive for the media to protect themselves against libel actions. White said the Court "engaged in massive overkill" when it stretched the First Amendment to protect false assertions of fact.

However, the four justices in dissent reiterated their support for both *New York Times* and *Gertz*. In their view, there was sufficient public interest in a contractor's credit status to require Greenmoss to show both fault and harm. Nor did Powell and his associates question the *Gertz* rationale. They held only that it did not apply to Greenmoss because no public issue was involved. Thus, as of mid-1985, seven of the nine justices continued to support the right of states to classify libel plaintiffs as public or private and to permit the latter to prevail on a lesser showing of fault than actual malice if they choose to do so.

Proving Harm

In *Gertz*, the Supreme Court condemned the common-law doctrine of presumed damages. It held that libel plaintiffs, in cases involving public issues, are required to offer evidence showing that they have been harmed. The Court said its purpose was to prevent juries from making "gratuitous awards of money damages far in excess of any actual injury." It compared such awards to "private fines," imposed for no other reason than to punish unpopular media. In addition to requiring libel plaintiffs to prove that they had been hurt, the Court also held that the states could not award punitive damages in libel cases involving public questions unless the plaintiff could prove actual malice.

Thus, libel plaintiffs, public or private, are required as a matter of constitutional law to offer the court some evidence of injury. As the Supreme Court pointed out in *Gertz*, this need not be a showing of specific monetary loss, although it can be that if the plaintiff has lost income as a consequence of the libel. With respect to the required showing of harm, the Court said:

> We need not define "actual injury," as trial courts have wide experience in framing appropriate jury instructions in tort actions. . . . [T]he more customary types of actual harm inflicted by defamatory falsehood include impairment of reputation and standing in the community, personal humiliation, and mental anguish and suffering. Of course, juries must be limited by appropriate instructions, and all awards must be supported by competent evidence concerning the injury, although there need be no evidence which assigns an actual dollar value to the injury.

Since then, the Supreme Court has not accepted for review any libel case in which the amount of the award in damages was at issue. Therefore, it has offered lower courts no additional guidance for determining when an award becomes high enough to be considered a "private fine."

Entertainer Carol Burnett testified during a libel trial in 1981 that an article in the *National Enquirer* made her "very, very angry." It falsely reported that she had been tipsy and boisterous in a Washington, D.C., restaurant. A jury awarded Miss Burnett more than $1 million in damages, which was reduced to $200,000 on appeal. (AP/Wide World Photos)

One conclusion is clear: The Court's decision in *Gertz* has not stood in the way of libel judgments running in excess of $1 million. The Libel Defense Resource Council reported in 1984 that jury awards in libel cases have risen faster than awards in any other category.[40] The average during the period studied by the council was $2 million. This figure was distorted by an Ohio jury's $26 million award against *Hustler* magazine[41] and several others approaching that magnitude. But even when these exceptional awards were removed from the calculation, the average libel award was $850,000. By contrast, the average award in product liability cases over the same period was $750,000, and in medical malpractice cases, $665,000.

The comparison indicates that, for whatever reason, juries are inclined to place a high value on such intangibles as embarrassment, mental anguish, and social ostracism. Appeals courts have been less harsh in their treatment of the media, reversing about

40. "Media Lawyers Talk Shop at ANPA Clinic," *Editor & Publisher*, 5 May 1984, p. 44.
41. Guccione v. Hustler Magazine, 7 Med.L.Rptr. 2077 (1981). The award was held to be so grossly excessive as to be designed to put *Hustler* out of business. A new trial was ordered on the issue of damages.

seven of each ten libel judgments taken to them and reducing the award in others, but not all.

The experience of Carol Burnett is illustrative. In 1976, a gossip item in the *National Enquirer* reported that she was drunk and annoying other diners in an exclusive Washington restaurant. When she sued for libel, editors of the weekly tabloid were forced to concede that the item was based on the flimsiest of evidence. A jury in California awarded Burnett $300,000 in actual damages and $1.3 million in punitive damages. The trial judge held that both figures were excessive, reducing the former to $50,000 and the latter to $750,000. On appeal, a state appellate court upheld the $50,000 award, but reduced the punitive damages to $150,000. The court gave Miss Burnett the option of accepting the sum or seeking a new trial limited to the amount of punitive damages. She chose to settle with the *National Enquirer* for an undisclosed amount.[42]

A key issue in the *Burnett* case was whether the *National Enquirer* could limit its damages by making a retraction; that is, by admitting in its columns that it had been in error and apologizing. Under a California statute, a newspaper or broadcaster who makes a prompt, complete, and unqualified correction of a libelous assertion can be required to pay only "special damages" if it is sued and loses.[43] "Special damages," as defined by the statute, include only proven harm to property, business, trade, profession, or occupation. They do not include such intangibles as loss of reputation or hurt feelings. The California courts held that the *Enquirer* did not fit the statute's definition of a newspaper and thus did not qualify for the protection offered by the retraction law.

More than half the states have retraction laws. They cannot prevent libel actions, but they can help reduce an award of damages if a suit should result. Evidence suggests further that if professional journalists caught in a misstatement of fact were readily willing to admit it and issue a prompt retraction, they might head off legal action altogether. A comprehensive study of libel cases conducted by three University of Iowa faculty members found that most libel plaintiffs start by approaching the media to seek a correction.[44] It is only when they have been rebuffed, sometimes rudely, that they begin legal action.

The Status of Libel Plaintiffs

Clearly, as a result of the Supreme Court's decisions in *New York Times* and *Gertz*, the legal status of the plaintiff is an important factor in any libel action. If the suit is brought by a public official or public figure, the plaintiff must offer clear and convincing evidence of actual malice. In the twenty-eight states that have chosen the option offered by *Gertz*, and in New York, a plaintiff classified as a private individual may prevail on a lesser showing of fault. If the plaintiff is the mayor, a member of a legislative body, or a person deeply involved in trying to influence public opinion for or against a controversial issue, his status is determined without much question. But if the plaintiff

---

42. "Burnett Settles Libel Suit," *Editor & Publisher*, 26 January 1985, p. 33.
43. California Civil Code §48a.
44. Bezanson, Cranberg, and Soloski, "Libel and the Press."

is a welfare department case worker, a teacher, a lawyer, or a party to a legal preceeding, his status is more difficult to determine. This is especially so when the plaintiff also is newsworthy. The Supreme Court has offered lower courts guidance in making such determinations. These have been supplemented by appellate court decisions. The principles derived from these decisions are summarized below.

Public Officials

There is no doubt that L. B. Sullivan, whose libel suit resulted in the *New York Times* rule, was a public official. He held an elective office, and as supervisor of the police department in Montgomery, Alabama, made public policy and had considerable discretion in how he carried out his duties. Therefore, what he did and how he did it had an impact on a good many persons and were proper subjects for public debate.

However, only a minority of public officials is elected. Many are appointed to office, and still others are simply hired to do a job. Thus it is not surprising that within two years after it decided *New York Times* v. *Sullivan*, the Supreme Court sought, in *Rosenblatt* v. *Baer*, to define public officials. Baer had been manager of a county-owned ski slope in Laconia, New Hampshire. He was caught **Rosenblatt v. Baer, 383** in a political dispute and had to resign. During the **U.S. 75, 86 S.Ct. 669, 15** following ski season, Rosenblatt wrote a column for **L.Ed.2d 597 (1966).** the local newspaper commenting on how much more profitable the ski slope was under the new manager. Arguing that the column implied that he'd been skimming funds from the slope's till, Baer sued Rosenblatt for libel, winning a $31,500 judgment in the state courts. The Supreme Court took the case and reversed, holding that Baer was a public official who would have to prove actual malice, which he could not do. The Court's decision said:

> We remarked in *New York Times* that we had no occasion "to determine how far down into the lower ranks of government employees the 'public official' designation would extend for purposes of this rule, or otherwise specify categories of persons who would or would not be included." . . . No precise lines need to be drawn for this case. The motivating force for the decision in *New York Times* was twofold. . . . There is, first, a strong interest in debate on public issues, and, second, a strong interest in debate about those persons who are in a position significantly to influence resolution of those issues. . . . It is clear, therefore, that the "public official" designation applies at the very least to those among the hierarchy of government employees who have, or appear to the public to have, substantial responsibility for or control over the conduct of government affairs.

In this instance, Baer's testimony at the trial helped the Court classify him as a public official. He had said that the public regarded him as the man responsible for the success or failure of the ski slope's operation. Thus he had both "responsibility for" and "control over" a function of government that was important in a snow state like New Hampshire.

In recent decisions, courts have been asking two questions in deciding whether a person is a public official:

— Does he or she have policy-making authority?

— Does he or she ordinarily have access to the news media?

If the answer to both questions is yes, the person is a public official. In recent decisions, courts held the following to be public officials:

— A physician who was under contract at $125,000 a year to provide medical services to prisoners in Alaska state correctional facilities.[45] The Alaska Supreme Court quoted *Rosenblatt* in holding that the public had an interest in how he performed his duties.

— The building inspector in Ocean Beach, New York.[46] Building permits were issued or denied on the basis of his recommendations.

— A territorial detective in the Virgin Islands.[47] Courts generally have held that any law enforcement officer who has authority to make arrests is a public official. Police officers have broad discretion in deciding whether to take persons into custody. If they decide to make an arrest, the consequences are severe, resulting in at least temporary loss of freedom for the subject of the arrest.

— The executive director of the State Human Relations Commission in Georgia.[48] Although he was appointed, not elected, he exercised broad discretion in carrying out his duties.

— The director of financial aid at Weber State College in Utah.[49] As the official responsible for administering $2 million a year in student aid, he invited public scrutiny, especially because most of the money came from public funds.

Several recent decisions serve as a reminder that not everyone on the public payroll qualifies as a public official for purposes of a libel suit. Courts in California and New York held, for instance, that public school teachers do not become public officials by carrying out the duties assigned to them in the classroom.[50] The courts ruled that because teachers are expected to conform to policies set by school boards and administrators, they are employees.

The United States Court of Appeals, Fourth Circuit, ruled that an archeological firm hired as a consultant to a county government was not a public official.[51] The court said the firm was a "fact-finder . . . [with] no control over governmental affairs. It made no recommendations, participated in no policy determinations, and exercised no discretion."

Public officials, then, may be elected or appointed, but they must be able to exercise discretion. They must be able to make public policy or make decisions that have an effect on others. They must be involved in duties in which some segment of the public has an interest and which they can influence through discussion. This means that those persons on a public payroll who do no more than perform a job under the direction of a superior are not public officials for purpose of a libel suit.

---

45. Green v. Northern Publishing Co., 655 P.2d 736 (Alaska 1982).
46. Dattner v. Pokoik, 437 N.Y.S.2d 425 (N.Y.App. 1981).
47. Zurita v. Virgin Islands Daily News, 578 F.Supp. 306 (D.V.I. 1984).
48. Walker v. Southeastern Newspapers, 9 Med.L.Rptr. 1516 (1982).
49. VanDyke v. KUTV, 663 P.2d 52 (Utah 1983).
50. Franklin v. Lodge 1108, 97 Cal.App.3d 915 (1979); DeLuca v. New York News, 109 Misc.2d 341 (N.Y.Sup. 1981).
51. Arctic v. Loudoun Times Mirror Co., 624 F.2d 518 (4th Cir. 1980).

Public Figures

In its decision in *Gertz*, the Supreme Court recognized a class of persons known as public figures and held that they, like public officials, should be required to prove actual malice if they sue the news media for libel. Such persons, the Court said, invite public attention and, because they are newsworthy, have ready access to the news media to respond to their critics. The Court went on to define three kinds of public figures:

— All-purpose public figures. Such persons "have assumed roles of especial prominence in the affairs of society." They have "persuasive power and influence."

— Limited or "vortex" public figures. These are persons who "have thrust themselves to the forefront of particular public controversies in order to influence the resolution of the issues involved."

— Involuntary public figures. These are persons who do nothing to attract attention or influence public policy, yet find themselves in the middle of a controversy over a public issue. The Court has concluded that such persons are "exceedingly rare."

The Court was trying to define more precisely a category that had emerged casually seven years earlier in its decision in *Curtis Publishing Co. v. Butts*.[52] In that decision it had held that Edwin Walker, a retired army general who was active in trying to prevent blacks from entering southern universities, and Wally Butts, athletic director at the University of Georgia, were public figures. Therefore, they, like public officials, would have to prove actual malice if they were to prevail in a libel suit. The Court's decision offered few specific guidelines to judges seeking guidance in deciding whether a plaintiff was a public figure. That is what the Court tried to do in *Gertz*. However, the Court has had occasion three times since to refine the guidelines further. Those decisions, and the pertinent decisions in state and federal appeals courts, will be treated below.

ALL-PURPOSE   All-purpose public figures have continuing news value. Or they exercise "persuasive power and influence" in matters of public concern. They are celebrities whose names are recognized by the general public. The public follows their ideas and actions with great interest. Because they have so much influence, courts have held that the media have considerable leeway in commenting on their activities. Chief Judge Edward Allen Tamm of the United States Court of Appeals, District of Columbia Circuit, had this to say in *Waldbaum* v. *Fairchild Publications, Inc.*,[53] in 1980:

> The media serve as a check on the power of the famous and that check must be strongest when the subject's influence is strongest. Fame often brings power, money, respect, adulation, and self-gratification. It also may bring close scrutiny that can lead to adverse as well as favorable comment. When someone steps into the public spotlight, or when he remains there once cast into it, he must take the bad with the good.

---

52. 388 U.S. 130, 87 S.Ct. 1975, 18 L.Ed.2d 1094 (1967).
53. 627 F.2d 1287 (D.C. Cir. 1980).

Courts have held that Johnny Carson, for many years host of the "Tonight" show on NBC television, is an all-purpose public figure.[54] So is William F. Buckley, Jr., the nationally syndicated conservative columnist and novelist.[55]

Institutions have been held to be all-purpose public figures, among them the Church of Scientology,[56] which has five million members, the Reliance Insurance Co.,[57] a billion-dollar corporation, and Ithaca College,[58] a private liberal arts college that a New York court found to be pervasively involved in public affairs as an educational institution.

Several courts have held that individuals can be all-purpose public figures with respect to a limited geographic area. Kansas courts held that an attorney who had practiced in the same community for thirty-two years, during which time he had taken an active role in resolving many public issues, became an all-purpose public figure.[59] New York courts came to the same conclusion about an individual who for ten years had injected himself into the attempt to resolve public controversies in his community.[60] Montana courts held that a former state chairman of the Republican party, an author of books on stocks and commodities, and the subject of articles in several business magazines, was an all-purpose public figure within that state.[61]

Notoriety can also make an all-purpose public figure, as a federal court demonstrated by holding that James Earl Ray, the convicted assassin of Rev. Martin Luther King, Jr., has that status.[62]

A common theme runs through the cases. Persons or institutions become all-purpose public figures because they voluntarily seek public attention and support. They try to influence the outcome of controversial public issues, and do it on a grand scale. Thus, they become widely known.

LIMITED OR "VORTEX"   Some persons become limited public figures because of their involvement in an attempt to resolve a specific public controversy. Usually, a person becomes a limited public figure because he or she voluntarily entered the fray. However, courts have recognized that persons can become limited public figures because events have drawn them into the conflict over a public issue. But even here, there is a voluntary element. Once drawn into the conflict, the limited public figure has chosen to stay involved.

"Limited" must be understood in two ways. The individual's involvement in public affairs is limited to a particular controversy. And the media comment that becomes the subject of a libel suit must be limited to the individual's role in the particular controversy. If the comment is directed only at the individual's involvement in the controversy, it is privileged under the *New York Times* rule, requiring the limited public figure to prove actual malice.

Courts apply a two-step analysis in determining whether an individual is a limited

54. Carson v. Allied News Co., 529 F.2d 206 (7th Cir. 1976).
55. Buckley v. Littell, 539 F.2d 882 (2d Cir. 1976).
56. Church of Scientology v. Siegelman, 475 F.Supp. 950 (S.D.N.Y. 1979).
57. Reliance Insurance Co. v. Barron's, 442 F.Supp. 1341 (S.D.N.Y. 1977).
58. Ithaca College v. Yale Daily News Publishing Co., 105 Misc.2d 793 (N.Y.Sup. 1980).
59. Steere v. Cupp, 602 P.2d 1267 (Kans. 1979).
60. Clements v. Gannett Co., 5 Med.L.Rptr. 1657 (1979).
61. Williams v. Pasma, 656 P.2d 212 (Mont. 1982).
62. Ray v. Time, Inc., 452 F.Supp. 618 (W.D.Tenn. 1978).

public figure. First, a public controversy must exist. The outcome must affect some segment of the general public in an appreciable way. Second, the plaintiff must be trying to influence the outcome of the controversy, and must be in a position to have an effect on the outcome. Obviously, these are matters of judgment.

This two-step analysis was applied to an unusual case by Judge James R. Miller of the United States District Court, District of Maryland, in 1981. The action was brought by James W. Fitzgerald, a marine biologist, over an article, "The Pentagon's Deadly

Fitzgerald v. Penthouse International, 525 F.Supp. 585 (1981).

Pets," that appeared in *Penthouse* magazine. The article said Fitzgerald had trained dolphins for use by the navy and the Central Intelligence Agency to detect and even blow up submarines and frogmen. The biologist said the article defamed him by making it look as though he was involved in espionage. He sued Penthouse International for libel. Once the court had established that the article could be read in a defamatory way, the major question at issue was Fitzgerald's status: Was he a limited public figure or a private individual?

Judge Miller began his analysis by noting that Fitzgerald could not be a public figure unless he were involved in a public controversy. A public controversy, for libel purposes, he noted, has two principal aspects:

> First, the topic of the alleged defamation must concern matters of some significance for persons who are not direct participants in the dispute. Second, there must have been some level of awareness of, or participation in, the subject matter of the alleged defamation by persons other than the litigants.

Judge Miller had no trouble with the first aspect. There is no doubt, he wrote, "that the Government's use of dolphins and other marine animals for military and intelligence operations, such as those conducted during the Viet Nam war, are matters of legitimate, if not vital public concern." Fitzgerald argued that there was no general awareness of the use of dolphins for military purposes because much of the program was kept secret. But the evidence showed that more than one hundred technical articles had come out of the navy program. It also had been the subject of at least one book, newspaper and magazine articles, and a segment of "60 Minutes," on which Fitzgerald had been interviewed. This, Judge Miller concluded, pointed to enough interest to satisfy the second aspect and establish the topic of Penthouse's article as a public controversy.

The second inquiry required by *Gertz*, Judge Miller wrote, is aimed at finding out whether the plaintiff was deeply enough involved in the controversy to become a limited public figure. That determination has five aspects:

> (1) [W]hether the plaintiff had access to channels of effective communication; (2) whether the plaintiff voluntarily assumed a role of special prominence in a public controversy; (3) whether the plaintiff sought to influence the resolution or outcome of the controversy; (4) whether the controversy existed prior to the publication of defamatory statements; and (5) whether the plaintiff retained public figure status at the time of the alleged defamation.

Fitzgerald argued that he did not have effective access to the media as evidenced by the fact that no reporters had asked him for comment on the *Penthouse* article. Judge

Miller said that was beside the point. The record showed that he had published numerous articles and reports on the use of dolphins for intelligence work, that he had lectured publicly on the topic, that he had written and disseminated brochures seeking business for a laboratory he had established, that he had been on "60 Minutes," and had been the subject of an article in *Newsday*. All of this was evidence, Judge Miller concluded, that Fitzgerald had met the standard the Supreme Court set in *Gertz*: He had "significantly greater access to the channels of effective communication . . . than private individuals normally enjoy."

The court considered the next two aspects together: Had he entered into the controversy voluntarily? And had be tried to influence its outcome in a particular way? Judge Miller held that Fitzgerald's appearance on "60 Minutes" took care of both elements. He had freely discussed and sought to justify the military and intelligence uses of dolphins and other marine animals. Further, he had special prominence in the field. The program had identified him as one of the pioneers in dolphin research.

The fourth aspect—the existence of the controversy prior to publication of the allegedly defamatory article—also was met by the appearance on "60 Minutes." The program had been broadcast in 1973, four years before the *Penthouse* article was published.

Did he retain public figure status during the intervening four years? Here, Judge Miller found little in prior decisions to guide him. The justices of the Supreme Court seem divided on the topic, with some noting in dicta that public figure status can be lost with time, another noting that it depends on what the person has done in the interim, and still another noting, "The mere lapse of time is not decisive." At least one federal appeals court has taken the position that once a person becomes a limited public figure, he or she retains that status with respect to the particular public controversy. In this instance, Judge Miller pointed to the fact that within a year after the *Penthouse* article was published, the military and intelligence uses of dolphins were the subject of an article in *Parade* magazine and that Fitzgerald's work was mentioned. This was taken as evidence that the controversy, and Fitzgerald's role in it, endured at least through 1978. Therefore, Fitzgerald was a limited public figure and would have to prove actual malice if he were to win his lawsuit. On appeal, the United States Court of Appeals, Fourth Circuit, affirmed and adopted Judge Miller's analysis, finding that Fitzgerald is a limited public figure.[63]

A survey of the reported cases shows numerous examples of limited public figures. One way to achieve that status is to seek public office. Another is to attempt to influence the outcome of a referendum. Persons also have become limited public figures by writing letters to newspapers on controversial public issues.

A high school football coach became a limited public figure when he bawled out the officials handling one game and threatened to beat them up after it was over.[64] A law professor and former dean became a public figure by entering a fight to obtain accreditation for his school.[65] A college dean achieved that status by going public with his opposition to the proposed abolition of his job.[66]

At another level, a court held that the agent of a baseball player became a public

63. 691 F.2d 666 (4th Cir. 1982).
64. Winter v. Northern Tier Publishing Co., 4 Med.L.Rptr. 1348 (1978).
65. Avins v. White, 627 F.2d 637 (3d Cir. 1980).
66. Byers v. Southeastern Newspapers, 288 S.E.2d 698 (Ga.App. 1982).

figure because he used interviews in newspapers, magazines, and on television to put pressure on Ted Turner, owner of the Atlanta Braves, in an attempt to win better terms for his client.[67] A New York court held that a belly dancer became a public figure with respect to her professional activities when she agreed to be interviewed for a Sunday magazine feature.[68] In the interview she sought to dispel the notion that belly dancing connotes immorality. A Pennsylvania court held that a "Playmate of the Month" was a public figure for the purposes of *National Lampoon's* satirical comment on her title, but not for purposes of satirizing her political affiliations.[69]

The last case lends emphasis to a point made earlier. A limited public figure becomes one only for purposes of media comment on his or her role in attempting to influence the outcome of a specific public controversy. Limited public figures do not open all aspects of their lives to media comment. They must prove actual malice only when the allegedly defamatory media comment is directed at their voluntary participation in a public controversy.

INVOLUNTARY   In *Gertz*, the Supreme Court used the word "hypothetically" to introduce the suggestion that some persons might become public figures "through no purposeful action" of their own. It added that "instances of truly involuntary public figures must be exceedingly rare." That prediction has proved accurate. Decisions of lower courts have mentioned the category, but a survey prepared for the Practising Law Institute late in 1984 found no cases in which a person had been held to be an involuntary public figure. The report noted that later decisions of the Supreme Court, which will be examined in the section on private individuals, raise doubt about "the continued vitality of this category."[70]

Three concepts are the keys to understanding the public figure categories. Foremost is the term *voluntary*. Persons become public figures because they want to. They seek public attention. They try to influence events. They are the movers and shakers of society. The second key is *access to the media*. Public figures show up on television talk shows. Their opinions are sought by reporters. If they issue press releases or call a news conference, the media pay attention. Newspapers run their letters to the editor. The third concept is *public controversy*. Public figures are involved in issues that count. They have put themselves into the midst of disputes that will have an effect on persons who are not directly involved. Court after court has emphasized that the media cannot create a public figure simply by making an individual newsworthy. Public figures create themselves by attempting to influence opinion in matters of public interest.

In those states that have accepted the Supreme Court's invitation in *Gertz* and permitted private libel plaintiffs to prevail on a lesser showing of fault, a ruling on the plaintiff's status can be crucial. It is more difficult to prove actual malice than to prove negligence.

Public Personalities

Courts in a few jurisdictions have recognized a class of persons who do not precisely fit the public figure categories above but who nevertheless have ready access to the

67. Woy v. Turner, 573 F.Supp. 35 (N.D.Ga. 1983).
68. James v. Gannett Co., 353 N.E.2d 834 (N.Y. 1976).
69. Vitale v. National Lampoon, 449 F.Supp. 422 (E.D.Pa. 1979).
70. *Communications Law 1984*, Vol. 2, pp. 799–800.

media. New York courts have taken the lead in calling such persons *public personalities*.[71] The category is made up mainly of entertainers who do not rise to the level of a Johnny Carson, of professional athletes, magazine writers, and small businesspeople. These are people who seek publicity and who need it in some measure for their professional survival. Their names have not become household words. They are not trying to influence the outcome of public controversies. Therefore, they are not conventional public figures. However, because they do have ready access to the news media, and thus are able to respond to their critics, courts in a few places have been requiring them to prove actual malice if they bring libel actions.

Private Individuals

If the libel plaintiff does not meet the criteria required to attain public official or public figure status, he or she is a private individual. This means that in all but a few states, such persons can prevail in a libel action if they can prove that the defendant was negligent.

Four times since the Supreme Court decided the *Butts* case in 1967, the Court has agreed to review cases in which the status of the plaintiff was at issue. In each instance, the Court has held that the individual in question was a private individual. Taken together, these decisions have limited the public figure category.

The first of these limiting decisions was *Gertz* itself. In it, the Court held that a lawyer hired to represent a client does not, by that act alone, become a public figure. Even though the lawyer may be required to try a case that deals directly with a public controversy, that in itself does not make the lawyer a public figure. He could become one for purposes of comment on that case only by going beyond the normal bounds of his profesisoal duties. He would have to become an advocate of a cause rather than the agent of a client, and would have to try the case in the media rather than in the courts. In line with *Gertz*, lower courts have held that lawyers hired to represent various kinds of clients are not public figures. Nor are other professionals, including consultants, who are hired to perform duties for, or give advice to, clients.

The second limiting decision came in 1976 in *Time, Inc., v. Firestone*. *Time* magazine had reported falsely that Russell A. Firestone, Jr., heir to the tire fortune, had been granted a divorce from his wife, Mary Alice, on grounds of adultery. The couple had been divorced, but not on those grounds. The magazine also reported that the divorce

Time, Inc., v. Firestone, 424 U.S. 448, 96 S.Ct. 958, 47 L.Ed.2d 154 (1976).

trial had "produced enough testimony of extramarital adventures on both sides, said the judge, 'to make Dr. Freud's hair curl.' " The brief item did not report another, more crucial, fact. The court had ordered Russell to pay Mary Alice $3,000 a month in alimony.

The fact was crucial because, under Florida law, a court could not then award alimony to a person who had been found guilty of adultery. The divorce had been granted because the trial judge found "a gross lack of domestication" on both sides. An appeals court, finding no such grounds for divorce in Florida law, changed that to extreme cruelty. There was no finding of adultery.

---

71. James, note 67.

Pouncing on *Time*'s error in fact, Mrs. Firestone sued the magazine for libel. A trial court awarded her $100,000 in damages, which the Florida Supreme Court affirmed. The U.S. Supreme Court agreed to take the case to review *Time*'s argument that, in light of *Gertz*, Mrs. Firestone should have been considered a public figure and required to prove actual malice. *Time* pointed to the nationwide publicity the divorce proceeding had received, largely because of the prominence of Russell Firestone and the steamy nature of the evidence. *Time* called the case "*a cause célèbre*." It pointed to the fact that interest in it was so great that Mrs. Firestone had been the center of several televised news conferences.

Writing for the Court, Justice Rehnquist held that none of the above made her a public figure:

> [Mrs. Firestone] did not assume a role of especial prominence in the affairs of society, other than perhaps Palm Beach society, and she did not thrust herself to the forefront of any particular public controversy in order to influence the resolution of the issues involved.

Time argued that there was indeed a public controversy over who was right and who was wrong in the Firestones' tempestuous marriage and divorce. Rehnquist rejected that argument, holding that a divorce proceeding "is not the sort of 'public controversy' referred to in *Gertz*, even though marital difficulties of extremely wealthy individuals may be of interest to some portion of the reading public."

Mrs. Firestone had not sought attention. She got attention by going to court to protect her rights under the law. Mere involvement in a legal proceeding does not make one a public figure, Rehnquist said.

From the point of view of the judicial bench, the decision made sense. Courts are for the use of persons who think they have been wronged. One who is thinking about filing a lawsuit, a right guaranteed by the Constitution, should not also have to think about whether that act will open him or her to defamatory falsehood under a rule that would make recovery difficult. *Firestone* also can be seen as a logical extension of *Gertz*. Gertz did not become a public figure by representing a client in a lawsuit, even though that suit touched many nerves, bore on the performance of the police, and drew much public attention. Why, then, should participants in such a suit become fair game for libel solely because of their participation?

But from the point of view of the news media, the decision had an ominous note. If calling a news conference to air one's side in a civil suit does not make one a public figure, what will? If a civil suit of the kind the Firestones were involved in does not make its participants public figures, what other newsworthy events could hide the same trap? Is the defendant in a criminal case also a private individual for libel purposes?

Three years later, the Supreme Court sought to answer those questions by deciding two cases on the same day. The cases had separate origins, but both were brought by persons who found themselves in the news because of their association with public controversies. The Supreme Court held that neither person's newsworthiness had made him even a limited public figure.

The first of the cases, *Hutchinson* v. *Proxmire*, was unusual in two ways. The defendant, William Proxmire, was a United States senator, and the suit was based on a news release from his office. Dr. Ronald Hutchinson was drawn out of the obscurity of the laboratory and the pages of learned journals in 1975 when Senator Proxmire awarded him his "Golden Fleece," a satirical award given periodically to agencies the senator considers particularly wasteful of federal funds. In this instance, his targets were the

Hutchinson v. Proxmire,
443 U.S. 111, 99 S.Ct.
2675, 61 L.Ed.2d 411
(1979).

Defense Department and NASA, which had given Hutchinson $500,000 in grants to study stress. The researcher used monkeys as subjects and made thousands of feet of videotape of their facial expressions as they reacted to varying kinds of stress. In Proxmire's opinion, the whole project was monkey business of another kind, and he said so in a scathing press release. Hutchinson immediately was catapulted into the public spotlight. Arguing that Proxmire had falsely labeled his research as worthless, thus subjecting him to public ridicule, Hutchinson sued the senator for libel. A federal district court dismissed his lawsuit, holding, in part, that he was a public figure who would have to prove actual malice, which, it ruled, he could not do. An appeals court affirmed. The Supreme Court took the case and reversed, ruling that Hutchinson was a private individual.

Proxmire argued that Hutchinson was a public figure for two reasons:

— He had applied for and received federal grants, which had been reported in the newspapers.

— He had access to the media as demonstrated by the fact that he was sought out by newspapers and wire services for comment at the time of the Golden Fleece award.

Chief Justice Burger, writing for the Court, said neither point proved he was a public figure at the time of the award. His work under the grants was of interest only to a "relatively small category of professionals concerned with research in human behavior." It was not controversial until Proxmire made it so. Burger wrote, "Clearly those charged with defamation cannot, by their own conduct, create their own defense by making a claimant a public figure."

Nor did Hutchinson's newsworthiness at the time of the award make him a public figure. He was sought out by reporters only because Proxmire had called him to public attention. Burger wrote, "He did not have the regular and continuing access to the media that is one of the accouterments of having become a public figure."

Nor, said the chief justice, had Proxmire identified a particular controversy into which Hutchinson had thrust himself. His grants did not make him a participant in the general debate over federal spending. The Court, said Burger, had already rejected the suggestion that all who receive public funds are thereby made either public officials or public figures.

In the second case decided that day, *Wolston v. Reader's Digest Association,* the Supreme Court said flatly that mere involvement in criminal conduct does not make

Wolston v. Reader's Digest Association, 443 U.S. 157, 99 S.Ct. 2701, 61 L.Ed.2d 450 (1979).

one a public figure. Wolston had a brief brush with the law during the McCarthy era after World War II when he failed to appear before a grand jury for questioning about Soviet spying. He was summoned because he had emigrated to the United States from the Soviet Union and because he was a nephew of

Myra and Jack Soble, who pleaded guilty to espionage for the Russians in 1958. However,

Wolston had become an American citizen, had served in the Army during World War II, and had remained in government service after the war.

Wolston lived in Washington with his wife and child at the time of the grand jury investigation. The jury was in New York. On one occasion when Wolston was summoned to appear, he did not make the trip because he was ill. When he showed up the next day, he found that he had been cited for **contempt** for failing to appear. He was taken before a judge for a hearing on the contempt citation. His wife became hysterical. To save her further stress, Wolston pleaded guilty and was given a suspended sentence on condition that he cooperate with the grand jury. The incident attracted brief attention in the New York and Washington newspapers, largely because at the time other suspected Soviet sympathizers were refusing on principle to appear before grand juries. Wolston answered the grand jury's questions. He was not indicted and thereafter returned to the obscurity from which he had come.

In 1974, he found himself listed in a book *KGB: The Secret Work of Soviet Agents*, published by Reader's Digest Association. His name was among those, including his aunt and uncle, who either had been identified as Soviet agents or had been found guilty of perjury or contempt in connection with spying charges. Wolston sued the publisher for libel. A federal district court judge dismissed his suit, ruling that he was a public figure and that he could not prove actual malice. The Supreme Court agreed to take the case and reversed. Six members of the Court held that he was not now a public figure, nor had he been at the time he made news by failing to appear before the grand jury. Two others said he had been a public figure at that time, but was not one when the book appeared.

Justice Rehnquist, writing for the Court, said Wolston was not a public figure because he had done nothing voluntarily to thrust himself into the post–World War II controversy over Soviet espionage. He had been brought into the controversy by the FBI and the grand jury. His refusal to appear was not an act of defiance to call attention to a cause, but a result of his illness. His good faith was proved when he showed up the next day and offered to testify, only to be cited for contempt. None of that made him a public figure "for purposes of comment on the investigation of Soviet espionage." Nor did he become a public figure because he was the subject of news stories. Rehnquist wrote, "A private individual is not automatically transformed into a public figure just by becoming involved in or associated with a matter that attracts public attention."

Reader's Digest Association had argued in its brief that Wolston became a public figure when he pleaded guilty to criminal contempt and was put on **probation.** Justice Rehnquist replied:

> [W]e reject the further contention of respondents that any person who engages in criminal conduct automatically becomes a public figure for purposes of comment on a limited range of issues relating to his conviction.

That rejection was supported by reference to the Court's holding in *Firestone* that an individual's involvement in the judicial process does not make him a public figure. Rehnquist commented, "To hold otherwise would create an 'open season' for all who sought to defame persons convicted of crime."

Taken together, *Gertz, Firestone, Hutchinson,* and *Wolston* tell us that people do not become public figures simply because they have been in the news. The decisions also tell us that journalists cannot create public figures by writing about them in newspapers and magazines or talking about them on television programs. Individuals make the transition from private to public, for purposes of a libel suit, when they involve themselves in a public controversy and try to influence its outcome. Mere involvement in a court action, no matter how newsworthy, does not in itself make an otherwise private person a public figure.

That conclusion is borne out by numerous court decisions. The following have been held to be private individuals: a private trucking company whose notice of the sale of its assets because of the death of one of its partners was included in a story about bankrupt truckers,[72] a person falsely listed among those arrested in a series of drug raids,[73] a public school teacher charged with possession of drugs,[74] the owner of an advertising agency who was reported to have absconded with his clients' funds,[75] a driver accused of fixing harness horse races,[76] and a Turkish national who was described as a specialist in drug smuggling.[77]

Persons who are engaged in private business, or who are employed by business firms, are private individuals unless they enjoy unusual prominence or seek to influence the outcome of a public controversy. Courts have held the following to be private individuals: a pet store owner whose shop was the subject of a telecast alleging that the animals were poorly cared for,[78] a former vice president of an airline who was the subject of a magazine article a year and a half after he had been fired,[79] an automobile dealer who was said to be the subject of a record number of complaints to the Better Business Bureau,[80] the owner of a shopping center,[81] a resort whose owners were alleged to have connections with organized crime,[82] and a seller of Olympic souvenirs.[83]

It is also worth noting that courts have found the following to be private individuals: A former Miss Wyoming, who participated in the Miss America contest and who alleged that she was identified as the subject of a short story attributing amazing sexual powers to a "Miss Wyoming";[84] the author of novels on human sexuality, when her name was used in connection with the nude photo of another person;[85] a tennis professional who was the victim of a controversial dismissal,[86] and a woman who was photographed on the street during the filming of a televised documentary on prostitution.[87]

These decisions, which are only a sample of the reported cases, make clear that prominence in the community does not in itself make a person a public figure for purposes of a libel suit. Nor is a newsworthy dispute necessarily a public controversy. A

---

72. Drotzmann's, Inc., v. McGraw-Hill, Inc., 500 F.2d 830 (8th Cir. 1974).
73. Wilson v. Capital City Press, 315 So.2d 393 (La.App. 1975).
74. Chapadeau v. Utica Observer-Dispatch, 341 N.E.2d 569 (N.Y. 1975).
75. Taskett v. KING Broadcasting Co., 546 P.2d 81 (Wash. 1976).
76. Andreescu v. Lane, 5 Med.L.Rptr. 1290 (1979).
77. Karaduman v. Newsday, 51 N.Y.2d 531 (N.Y. 1980).
78. Martin v. Griffin Television, 549 P.2d 85 (Okla. 1976).
79. Dixson v. Newsweek, 562 F.2d 626 (10th Cir. 1977).
80. Peagler v. Phoenix Newspapers, Inc., 560 P.2d 1216 (Ariz. 1977).
81. Grobe v. Three Village Herald, 69 A.D.2d 175; affirmed, 49 N.Y.2d 932 (N.Y. 1980).
82. Rancho La Costa v. Superior Court, 106 Cal.App.3d 646 (Cal.App. 1980).
83. Zates v. Richman, 86 A.D.2d 746 (N.Y.App. 1982).
84. Pring v. Penthouse International, 695 F.2d 438 (10th Cir. 1982).
85. Lerman v. Chuckleberry Publishing, 521 F.Supp. 228 (D.C.N.Y. 1981).
86. From v. Tallahassee Democrat, 400 So.2d 52 (Fla.App. 1981).
87. Clark v. ABC, 684 F.2d 1208 (6th Cir. 1982).

public controversy for libel purposes is one that affects persons in the community who are not directly involved in the dispute. An argument over ownership of a building probably would not be a public controversy, even if it got into the courts and into the news, because the outcome would affect only the participants. However, a dispute over zoning of the building probably would be a public controversy because the outcome might affect the future of the neighborhood, or even of the city itself. Individuals become limited public figures only when they voluntarily enter public controversies with a reasonable prospect of affecting the outcome.

Defining the Standards of Fault

For more than twenty years, courts have been defining the standards by which fault is measured in libel cases. In the decade after the *New York Times* decision, the focus was on actual malice, which the Court defined as knowledge of falsity or reckless disregard for the truth. The second prong of that definition has caused the most difficulty. The Supreme Court itself has sought to define reckless disregard in a case to be discussed shortly.

Since 1974, when the Supreme Court in *Gertz* offered states the option of permitting private individuals to prevail on proof of some lesser degree of fault, the difficulties have multiplied. As noted above, most states that have had occasion to consider the matter have decided to adopt a negligence standard for private individuals. At law, negligence is a departure from a reasonable standard of performance. Courts have differed in applying that test to journalists. Some have held simply that journalists must do what any reasonable person would do under the circumstances. Others are holding that journalists must follow the procedures recognized professionals would use in preparing a news story or an editorial. We will see later that because journalists themselves have been unable to agree on standards for professional practice, juries have become involved in deciding what those standards should be.

Actual Malice

Public officials and public figures must offer clear and convincing evidence of actual malice if they are to have any chance of winning a libel suit directed at the news media. In *New York Times* the Supreme Court defined actual malice as publishing with knowledge of falsity or with reckless disregard for the truth. Knowledge of falsity is clear-cut. It means deliberately publishing a lie. There are some instances in which plaintiffs have been able to prove such publication.

More common have been cases in which plaintiffs have proved reckless disregard. In *New York Times*, the Supreme Court made only a general attempt to define the term. It noted that the advertisement was signed by a number of persons who were distinguished in various fields. The advertising staff of the *Times* would have no reason to doubt their version of the facts. It was true, the Court noted, that clippings in the *Times's* own library contradicted statements in the ad. But in the absence of a reasonable doubt, the advertising director's failure to check the files was not reckless disregard. At worst, the Court held, it was no more than negligence.

St. Amant v. Thompson, 390 U.S. 727, 88 S.Ct. 1323, 20 L.Ed.2d 262 (1968).

Four years later, in 1968, the Court took a Louisiana case and used it to define further the meaning of reckless disregard. That case, *St. Amant v. Thompson,* is the definitive guide to the meaning of that term. It was supplemented in 1979 by the court's decision in *Herbert v. Lando,*[88] and in 1984 by *Bose Corp. v. Consumers Union.*[89]

In these three decisions, the Court has emphasized several points, which may be stated briefly as follows:

— "Actual malice" means what the Supreme Court said it means. It is knowledge of falsity or reckless disregard of the truth. It does not embody the traditional meaning of "malice" as ill will or intent to harm.

— Public officials or public figures cannot prevail in a libel suit unless they prove actual malice with clear and convincing evidence. No plaintiff, public or private, can be awarded punitive damages in the absence of proof of actual malice.

— Actual malice is a subjective standard. This is particularly true of reckless disregard. Therefore, the Court has held in *Herbert* that libel plaintiffs must be permitted to inquire into the state of mind of the journalist defendants. In practical terms, this means that journalists can be required to justify the editorial decisions that went into preparation of allegedly libelous material. Journalists can be asked why they believed one source and not another; why they used some facts harmful to the plaintiff while ignoring others that were favorable.

— Key elements in reckless disregard are "serious doubts" about the truth of the publication or "a high degree of awareness of their probable falsity."[90] The existence of such doubt, or awareness, need not be proved directly. It may be inferred from the circumstances, such as the nature of the defendant's sources, ready access to information contradicting the libelous assertion, and deadline pressures.

— The determination of actual malice is a mixed question of law and fact. If a plaintiff can offer no evidence pointing to knowledge of falsity or reckless disregard, the court may grant a defendant's motion for summary judgment. If the facts are in doubt, the question is submitted to a jury. However, in 1984, in its *Bose* decision, the Supreme Court held that a jury's finding of actual malice can be reviewed by an appellate court, which is free to come to its own conclusions as to the meaning of the evidence.

The *St. Amant* case had its origins in a political appeal broadcast over a Baton Rouge television station. Phil St. Amant, a candidate for public office, accused his opponent

---

88. 441 U.S. 153, 99 S.Ct. 1635, 60 L.Ed.2d 115 (1979).
89. 466 U.S. 485, 104 S.Ct. 1949, 80 L.Ed.2d 502 (1984).
90. Garrison v. Louisiana, 379 U.S. 64, 85 S.Ct. 209, 13 L.Ed.2d 125 (1964).

of accepting bribes. In the process, he read a sworn statment from a Teamsters Union member which portrayed Herman Thompson, a deputy sheriff, as a middleman in the process. Thompson sued St. Amant for libel and won a $5,000 judgment before Louisiana courts became hopelessly bogged down in trying to define actual malice. The Supreme Court agreed to take the case, holding that Thompson was not entitled to damages because there was no reckless disregard on St. Amant's part. Justice Byron R. White wrote the decision, in which he was joined by seven other members of the Court.

He started by emphasizing that reckless disregard is a product of the factual situation of each case. But it begins with evidence of doubt:

> There must be sufficient evidence to permit the conclusion that the defendant in fact entertained serious doubts as to the truth of his publication. Publishing with such doubts shows reckless disregard for truth or falsity and demonstrates actual malice.
>
> It may be said that such a test puts a premium on ignorance, encourages the irresponsible publisher not to enquire, and permits the issue to be determined by the defendant's testimony that he published the statement in good faith and unaware of its probable falsity. Concededly the reckless disregard standard may permit recovery in fewer situations than would a rule that publishers must satisfy the standard of the reasonable man or the prudent publisher. . . .
>
> The defendant in a defamation action brought by a public official cannot, however, automatically insure a favorable verdict by testifying that he published with a belief that the statements were true. The finder of fact must determine whether the publication was indeed made in good faith. Professions of good faith will be unlikely to prove persuasive, for example, where a story is fabricated by the defendant, is the product of his imagination, or is based wholly on an unverified anonymous telephone call. Nor will they be likely to prevail when the publisher's allegations are so inherently improbable that only a reckless man would put them in circulation. Likewise, recklessness may be found where there are reasons to doubt the veracity of the informant or the accuracy of his reports.
>
> . . . Failure to investigate does not in itself establish bad faith.

With its decision in *St. Amant,* the Court did what it could to tell lower courts how to know actual malice when they see it. The standard does not require reporters and editors to check every conceivable loose end as a story is being developed, especially if it is "hot news" where time is of the essence.[91] Mere failure to check will not, of itself, prove reckless disregard. But if such failure is coupled with the publisher's doubt, or with evidence suggesting he should have had doubts, then there can be reckless disregard. At that point, courts look at the events leading to publication. Who were the sources of information? What was known of their reputation for honesty? How many sources were there? Why did the publisher accept information from one source and reject contradictory information from another? Were the published allegations "so inherently improbable that only a reckless man would put them in circulation?"

The answers to some of those questions lie in the editorial process—in the decisions reporters and editors make in gathering and presenting news and comment. That process requires judgment, which is a factor of the state of mind of the participants. Obviously, individuals can and do disagree over news values and over the truth or falsehood of allegedly defamatory statements. What seems obviously true to a person with one point of view may seem like an improbable falsehood to a person with another point of view.

---

91. Curtis Publishing Co. v. Butts, 388 U.S. 130, 87 S.Ct. 1975, 18 L.Ed.2d 1094 (1967).

Herbert v. *Lando* grew out of a libel plaintiff's efforts to obtain the answers to state-of-mind questions. Anthony Herbert, a retired army officer who had served in Vietnam, was the subject of a segment of "60 Minutes" produced by Barry Lando of CBS News and narrated by Mike Wallace. Herbert said the segment, which dealt with atrocities allegedly committed by American troops, made him appear to be a liar. He sued for libel and, because he conceded he was a public figure, sought to prove actual malice.

Herbert v. *Lando,* 441 U.S. 153, 99 S.Ct. 1635, 60 L.Ed.2d 115 (1979).

During the process of **discovery,** Herbert's lawyer questioned Lando at length about the news judgments that shaped the telecast. Discovery is a pretrial process that involves the questioning of potential witnesses under oath to narrow the issues that need to be resolved at trial. Lando was asked why he had believed some sources, but not others, and why he had used some information harmful to Herbert while rejecting information favorable to the officer. The lawyer also asked for details of the discussions between Lando and Wallace, and with others, that went into the shaping of the telecast. Lando refused to answer such questions, arguing that freedom of the press would be restricted if reporters and editors could be compelled to answer questions about their state of mind during the editorial process. A district court judge ordered Lando to answer the questions, but a federal appeals court reversed, holding that the First Amendment stood as a barrier against such questions. The Supreme Court agreed to review the decision. It held that the appeals court was wrong.

Justice White, joined by six others, wrote for the Court. He pointed out that *New York Times* had erected a strong safeguard for the media by requiring public official/public figure plaintiffs to prove acutal malice. To do so, they must show that the defendant acted either with knowledge that the alleged libel was false, or with serious doubts about its truth. Both knowledge and doubt are states of mind. White concluded that if the Court were to shut off all inquiry into the editorial decision-making process, including the state of mind of defendants, proving actual malice would become virtually impossible.[92]

The *Herbert* decision has been a factor contributing to the expense of taking a libel suit to trial. Plaintiffs now commonly ask during discovery for the names of all persons who played any role in preparing allegedly defamatory material. These persons can be asked about what they said to each other, with focus on whether any of them raised doubts about any element of the story. Further, reporters can be asked to identify their sources of information and even to produce transcripts of their notes or copies of any audio tapes of interviews. If the offending story was based on an investigation of any consequence, discovery can result in the preparation of thousands of pages of transcripts, all of which is quite expensive. Questions are likely to focus on such matters as why reporters believed some sources, but not others; why they followed up some leads, but ignored others; what state of mind with respect to the plaintiff shaped the story, and what the intent was in deciding to publish at all.

Thus, more than anything else, the *Herbert* decision makes clear that actual malice, particularly reckless disregard for the truth, is a subjective question likely to be submitted to a jury for resolution.

---

92. In 1986, the United States Court of Appeals for the Second Circuit held that Herbert was unable to prove actual malice. 781 F.2d 298.

The *Bose* decision also dealt with the process involved in proving actual malice. In it, the issue was how far appeals courts can go in reviewing the factual situation that led a trial court to conclude that a media defendant acted in actual malice. The case had its origins in the May 1970 issue of *Consumer Reports* magazine in an article evaluating the quality of stereo speakers. Included was the Bose 901 speaker system, which had only recently come into production. The magazine's engineers found that it had some virtues, but that it was incapable of allowing the listener to pinpoint the location of individual instruments in an orchestra:

Bose Corporation v. Consumers Union, 466 U.S. 485, 104 S.Ct. 1949, 80 L.Ed.2d 502 (1984).

> Worse, individual instruments heard through the Bose system seem to grow to gigantic proportions and tended to wander about the room. For instance, a violin appeared to be 10 feet wide and a piano stretched from wall to wall. With orchestral music, such effects seem inconsequential. But we think they might become annoying when listening to soloists.

Bose sued Consumers Union, the magazine's publisher, for libel, alleging that the statement about the instruments' tending "to wander about the room" was false and defamatory. Bose also offered evidence that sales of the 901 speaker system had gone down after the review appeared. After lengthy discovery, the facts were presented to a federal district court judge in Massachusetts. Consumers Union asked him to dismiss the suit. The judge refused, holding that sworn statments taken during discovery showed that the passage quoted above was false and defamatory and that it was a product of actual malice. The judge reasoned that the word "about" conveyed the meaning of free movement throughout the room. The engineer who tested the speakers, and who used the word "about" in his report to the magazine's editorial staff, testified that in reality the sound of a solo instrument seemed to move along, or near, the wall of the listening room, between the two speakers. He said the apparent location of a solo instrument seemed to vary with the pitch of the notes being played. Dr. Amar G. Bose, the inventor and manufacturer of the 901 system, testified that no other reviewers had noticed such a phenomenon, and that it had not occurred in his own tests. He also said that sales of the speakers had gone down. The court accepted the facts above as proof of the review's falsity and of harm.

The court found clear and convincing proof of actual malice in the engineer's choice of the word "about." The judge examined his testimony during discovery and excerpts from his writings, concluding that both showed the engineer's mastery of the English language. The judge wrote: "It is simply impossible for the Court to believe that he interprets a commonplace word such as 'about' to mean anything other than its plain, ordinary meaning." The judge concluded that the engineer had used the word deliberately, making it a knowing falsehood.

The only issue left for trial was the extent of Bose's harm. After a nineteen-day trial, another court concluded in 1981 that Bose had lost $106,296 in sales because of the review. Dr. Bose also had devoted $9,000 worth of his time to an attempt to counteract the review's effect, making for a total award of $115,296, which Consumers Union was ordered to pay.

It appealed to the federal appeals court in Boston, which reversed. That court assumed that the passage at issue was both false and defamatory. It also agreed that Bose had proved harm. But it did not agree that Bose had offered clear and convincing proof of actual malice. The offending review was edited at least five times. It had been approved by editors at several levels. The editor who gave it final approval testified that he had not given much thought to the use of "about" to describe the seeming movement of the instruments. The court concluded that the care taken by the editors did not exemplify "the very highest order of responsible journalism," but added, "CU does not have to meet such high standards in order to prevail." At worst, it stood convicted of falsely using imprecise language, perhaps to make the article more readable. But that does not rise to the level of actual malice, the court said.

This time, Bose appealed, arguing that the court in Boston had violated the Federal Rules of Civil Procedure when it reviewed the facts that had led the district court to conclude there was actual malice. Rule 52(a) provides:

> Findings of fact shall not be set aside [by an appeals court] unless clearly erroneous, and due regard shall be given to the opportunity of the trial court to judge the credibility of the witnesses.

The Supreme Court agreed to review the case, holding six-to-three that the appeals court had acted properly. Justice John Paul Stevens, writing for a majority of the court, held that the *New York Times* decision imposed a special obligation on appeals courts considering libel judgments against the media. In such instances, courts must " 'make an independent examination of the whole record' in order to make sure 'that the judgment does not constitute a forbidden intrusion on the field of free expression.' " This means, Stevens explained, that when an appellate court is reviewing a libel judgment against the news media, the judges have "a constitutional responsibility that cannot be delegated to the trier of fact, whether the factfinding function be performed in the particular case by a jury or by a trial judge."

Applying this rule to its own review of the *Bose* case, the Supreme Court majority concluded that the appeals court had made the correct interpretation of the facts. The engineer's attempt to defend his use of "about" showed nothing more than the human tendency to refuse to admit a mistake. That does not prove that the mistake was deliberate. Stevens added that if the district court's rationale were to be endorsed, "any individual using a malapropism might be liable, simply because an intelligent speaker would have to know that the term was inaccurate in context, even though he did not realize his folly at the time."

Although the *Bose* decision may strike nonlawyers as technical, media lawyers generally acclaimed it. Floyd Abrams, who has defended several major libel suits, said the decision was "the most significant libel ruling of the decade."[93] It means that media defendants who lose a libel trial because of a finding of actual malice can obtain an independent review of that finding by taking an appeal to a higher court. Because appeals courts review only the records from the court below, and do not hear testimony, this means that decisions will be made without the opportunity to evaluate the demeanor of the witnesses. Justice Rehnquist noted that in a vehement dissent. He said he doubted that appellate courts,

---

93. James E. Roper, "Supreme Court Rules on Libel," *Editor & Publisher*, 5 May 1984, p. 15.

with only bare records before them, are likely to be any more reliable than the findings reached by trial judges. . . . I believe that the primary result of the Court's holding today will not be greater protection for First Amendment values, but rather only lessened confidence in the judgments of lower courts and more entirely fact-bound appeals.

The effect of the decision remains to be seen. But at the time it was handed down, some media lawyers were looking to it for relief from the tendency of trial judges and juries to rule against media defendants in libel suits.

While the Supreme Court has had to deal with actual malice on only a few occasions, lower courts have had to do so many times. It cannot be said too strongly that a court's decision as to the presence or absence of actual malice is crucial to the outcome of most libel cases, even in states that permit private individuals to win on a lesser showing of fault. Public officials/figures must prove actual malice if they are to win anything, while private individuals who prove actual malice become eligible for an award of punitive damages in addition to compensatory or actual damages. Because a finding of actual malice is so important to both sides in a libel action, it should be helpful to look at several representative lower-court cases.

A Louisiana appeals court upheld a finding of actual malice in a libel action based on an editorial in the *Lake Charles American Press.* The editorial denounced the

McHale v. Lake Charles American Press, 390 So.2d 556 (1980).

reappointment of a city attorney who, as part of his duties, approved bond issues for the city and its harbor. Demanding an accounting of the fees the attorney had collected in connection with the bonds, the editorial said, "No bond buyer would buy a nickel's worth of securities on McHale's opinion." The lawyer sued the newspaper for libel, winning a $150,000 judgment.

On appeal, the appellate court held that the editorial was both false and written in actual malice. Legal advertisements published in the newspaper over a six-year period showed that buyers had purchased $2.5 million in bonds approved by McHale. The newspaper publisher, who had instigated the editorial, said he never read legal advertisements. But the court said that as a director and a member of the loan committee of a bank that had bought some of the bonds approved by McHale, he had to know that someone was buying the city's securities. On the basis of this and other facts, the court concluded, "Defendants were in possession of knowledge so completely at odds with the published statement that only a reckless disregard for the truth can account for its utterance."

The Oklahoma Supreme Court upheld a jury's decision that the *Altus Times-Democrat* and its staff acted in actual malice in reporting that a police officer had kidnapped a boy

Akins v. Altus Newspapers, Inc., 609 P.2d 1263 (1977).

at gunpoint. The story was written by a reporter who had spent most of the night in the sheriff's office working as a freelance photographer to cover a narcotics raid. At various times, he overheard deputies talking about an incident involving a police officer, his son, and another teenager.

The next morning, the reporter heard one end of a telephone call in which a deputy prosecutor was talking about the need to investigate the incident. The reporter did not talk to the police officer or to a deputy sheriff who had been sent to investigate. An editor of the paper showed enough doubt about the story to ask the reporter if he had checked it out. The reporter said he had. The editor showed the story to the publisher, who asked the editor if she could verify it. The editor, assuming that the reporter had talked to the prosecutor, who was quoted in the story, said she could. A jury concluded that the reporter, editor, and publisher had acted in reckless disregard for the truth. It awarded the police officer $20,000 in damages.

The state supreme court found the jury's conclusion reasonable. The whole episode had grown out of a fight between two boys, one of whom happened to be a police officer's son. The officer helped break up the fight. The other boy got into the officer's car, which took him away from the scene of the fight, but he got in at his mother's request, not at gunpoint. All of the witnesses, including the mother of the other boy, said they had not seen a gun. The reporter had relied solely on what he overheard. He had made no attempt to check with any of the persons on whose conversations he relied. He had read an incident report in the sheriff's office, and it had said nothing about a kidnapping at gunpoint. The court held that the official report's omission of a serious charge central to the point of the reporter's story should have alerted him to its probable falsity. The jury thus had concluded correctly that he had acted in actual malice.

However, if the facts do not point to a reasonable doubt as to the truth of a story or to an awareness of its likely falsehood, there is no actual malice. This is illustrated by a federal district court jury's finding in *Sharon* v. *Time, Inc.*, in 1985.[94] The case was based on *Time*'s report in 1983 that Ariel Sharon, then the Israeli defense minister, had encouraged Phalangist militiamen to kill hundreds of Palestinian civilians in a refugee camp in Lebanon.

Sharon viewed the article as a "blood libel" and sued *Time* for $50 million. Judge Abraham Sofaer of the United States District Court in New York City made legal history by submitting the case to the jury one step at a time. The first question was, "Was the article capable of a defamatory meaning?" The jury held that it was. It portrayed Sharon as a party to the killing of about seven hundred people. The second question was, "Was the story false with respect to Sharon's role?" *Time*'s item was based on the report of a blue-ribbon commission appointed by the Israeli government to investigate the massacre. That commission had held that Sharon was responsible only to the extent that he should have anticipated that the Phalangists would seek revenge and that he should have taken steps to prevent it. The *Time* article said that a secret appendix to the report showed that Sharon had confered with the Gemayels and encouraged their forces to act. There was indeed a secret appendix, which the Israelis refused to declassify for use at the trial. However, lawyers were permitted to examine it and report to the court. They said it did not say what the *Time* article said it did. At that point, *Time* conceded its report was false and apologized for its error. The article, therefore, was both defamatory and false.

That left the crucial question, "Did the reporter who gathered information for the story, and the editors who put the story in final form, have any reason to doubt what it said about Sharon's role?" The original version of the story was prepared in Israel by *Time*'s correspondent, David Halevy, who had lived in the country for forty-three years.

---

94. Andrew Randolf, "Hats Off to the Judge," *Editor & Publisher*, 2 February 1985, pp. 9,29; Paul Janensch, "Time's Costly 'Victory' in the Sharon Libel Case," *Louisville Courier-Journal*, 3 February 1985.

Ariel Sharon, former Israeli defense minister, was both a winner
and a loser when he sued *Time* magazine for libel. In 1985 a jury
held that the magazine defamed Sharon by reporting falsely that he
had encouraged Lebanese Christians to massacre Palestinians. But
because Sharon was unable to prove that the magazine's editors
knew the story was false, or had serious doubts about it, he lost his
suit for damages. (Tannenbaum/Sygma)

He did not see the appendix to the commission's report, but relied on "a highly reliable
source," who said Sharon had met with Phalangist leaders prior to the massacre. Halevy
also said he relied on hints from high-ranking Israeli army officers and his own analysis
to conclude that Sharon gave the Phalangists "the feeling" that he understood their need
for revenge. Editors in New York changed Halevy's language to make the story say
Sharon had discussed the need for revenge. Underlying the story was Sharon's reputation
as an advocate of strong measures against Palestinians suspected of acts of terrorism
against Israelis. The defense minister was highly controversial, and there were many in
his own country who believed him capable of doing what *Time*'s story said he did.
Indeed, the investigatory commission was appointed because of rumors to that effect.
Therefore, there was no reason for Halevy or his editors to doubt the story. The jury
found that there was no actual malice, but the jurors felt compelled to issue a statement
castigating *Time* for acting "negligently and carelessly." However, that was not enough
to keep *Time* from winning the lawsuit.

Courts have also held that there is no actual malice in relying on the accuracy of
news provided by a wire service, especially against a deadline.[95] Nor is there actual
malice in relying on the work of a highly respected journalist,[96] or on articles previously

---

95. "Suit v. 32 Papers Dropped," *Editor & Publisher*, 4 February 1984, p. 37.
96. Loeb v. Globe Newspaper Co., 489 F.Supp. 481 (D.Mass. 1980).

published without question as to their accuracy.[97] Reporters who obtain information from police reports, from reports of other government agencies, or in interviews with public officials will not be found in actual malice if the resulting article accurately reflects the source material.[98] Careful research, coupled with reliance on recognized authorities, has resulted in a finding that there was no actual malice.[99]

Courts have more difficulty with actual malice than with any other element of First Amendment libel law. This is illustrated in part by varying approaches to the admission of evidence of ill will as a part of the plaintiff's burden of proof. Some courts have held flatly that "actual malice simply does not mean ill-will or spite."[100] But in Indiana and some other states, courts accept evidence of ill will as part of the proof of actual malice. The leading case is *Cochran* v. *Indianapolis Newspapers*,[101] in which an appellate court held:

> While "ill-will" is not an element of the legal definition of "actual malice," . . . it is nevertheless relevant and admissible as evidence in the determination of whether defendant possessed a state of mind highly conducive to reckless disregard of falsity. Circumstantial evidence may also be relied upon to show a "high degree of awareness of probable falsity."

Thus, if a reporter has acted aggressively in investigating a story, to the point of leading the subject of it to feel threatened, that could be a factor in the jury's determination of actual malice—especially if the reporter also relied on sources with known biases against the subject of the story, or on sources whose own criminal activities raised questions about their honesty.

As the *Sharon* case, and indeed *New York Times* itself, illustrate, the heavy burden of proving actual malice with clear and convincing clarity permits the news media to publish harmful falsehoods about public persons and escape the consequences, except for the sometimes heavy costs of defending a libel action. Conversely, a plaintiff's estimate of the heavy expense of winning a suit may deter some from trying to clear their names. It is these considerations that have led critics to question the value of *New York Times* and *Gertz* as precedents. When the decisions are applied as the Supreme Court apparently intended, they give near absolute protection to reporters who research their stories carefully, completely, and conscientiously, and to editors who insist on fairness and on double-checking all harmful assertions. But the precedents also can protect journalists who cut corners. The *New York Times* rule permits the media to publish assertions because "everyone knows they're true," when some extra digging might disclose their falsity. As the Court has said, not only in *New York Times*, but in *St. Amant*, mere failure to check a story may prove negligence, but it does not prove actual malice unless other evidence points to reasons for serious doubt. Further factors that separate actual malice from negligence will be examined next.

Negligence

In response to *Gertz*, about half the states now permit private individuals to prevail in libel suits if they can prove negligence on the part of the news media. As suggested

---

97. Dupler v. Mansfield Journal Co., 64 Ohio St.2d 116 (Ohio 1980).
98. Catalano v. Pechous, 83 Ill.2d 146 (Ill. 1980).
99. Yiamouyiannis v. Consumers Union, 619 F.2d 932 (2d Cir. 1980).
100. Reliance Insurance Co. v. Barron's, 442 F.Supp. 1341 (S.D.N.Y. 1977).
101. 372 N.E.2d 1211 (Ind.App. 1978).

above, this is easier than proving actual malice, but it has by no means reestablished the old common-law standards. At common law, libel plaintiffs could win if they were the victim of a defamatory falsehood. They did not have to prove fault, nor did they have to prove that they had been harmed. Both elements were assumed. Thus, even where private individuals are the targets of defamatory falsehoods, the law still leans toward protecting journalists. Proof of negligence, like proof of actual malice, involves examining the editorial process, including state of mind. However, it is not necessary for private plaintiffs to show serious doubt on the part of the media defendant. All that is required is a showing of some departure from the standard of care ordinarily followed by journalists or by any prudent person under the circumstances.

Restatement of Torts 2d, which reflects the conclusions of lawyers who practice libel law, offers the following definition of negligence:

> Negligence is conduct that creates an unreasonable risk of harm. The standard of conduct is that of a reasonable person under like circumstances. . . .
>
> The defendant, if a professional disseminator of news, such as a newspaper, a magazine, or a broadcasting station, or an employee, such as a reporter, is held to the skill and experience normally possessed by members of that profession. Customs and practices within the profession are relevant in applying the negligence standard, which is, to a substantial degree, set by the profession itself, though a custom is not controlling.[102]

Restatement enlarges on these generalities by noting three factors that must be taken into consideration in determining whether a reporter or editor was negligent:

1. *Was time of the essence?* "Was the communication a matter of topical news requiring prompt publication to be useful, or was it one in which time and opportunity were freely available to investigate? In the latter situation, due care may require a more thorough investigation." This is a recognition of the "hot news" principle.

2. *What interest was being promoted by the publication?* Was the subject essential to an understanding of a public issue? Would it help people make up their minds about a candidate for public office? Or was it merely gossip? The latter has little public purpose, but great capacity for harm. Therefore, the publisher ought to go to great pains to ensure its accuracy. A lesser standard of care might prevail in the first two instances.

3. *How extensively would the private individual's reputation be damaged if the defamatory statement proved to be false?* This could involve considerations of whether the plaintiff had any reputation to lose, how widely the alleged libel was circulated, and its nature.

Obviously, negligence, like actual malice, must be determined in the light of the facts of each case. Courts trying libel cases brought by private individuals have shown willingness to seek guidance from expert witnesses. These include reporters and editors, journalism professors, consultants, and others who can demonstrate sufficient knowledge

---

102. *Restatement*, §580B(g), pp. 227, 228.

of reporting and editing practices to withstand challenge by counsel. Reflecting the lack of agreement on the standard of care expected by journalists, each side can usually produce experts who will support its position. In the end, then, the decision is one for the trier of fact, that is, a jury or a judge. Thus, the *Gertz* decision has put nonjournalists in the position of deciding the standard of care expected of reporters and editors.

Courts in Florida and Kansas expect reporters and editors to know enough law to cover legal proceedings accurately. In Florida, the supreme court said a *Time* magazine reporter was negligent in reporting the Firestone divorce, referred to earlier. He should have known, the court said, that Mrs. Firestone could not have been awarded alimony if she had been found guilty of adultery.[103] In Kansas, the supreme court held that a reporter and her editor were negligent in preparing a story on a farmer accused of starving his hogs.[104] The story said the farmer had pleaded guilty to the charge when, in fact, it had only been filed. Both the Florida and Kansas courts used strong language in condemning the reporters' ignorance of the law. Noting the great harm to reputation that can come from mistakenly reporting that a person is guilty of a crime, the Kansas court said the least a journalist can do is "use due care in gathering and reporting court proceedings."

The highest court of Massachusetts also found negligence in a cub reporter's coverage of a court proceeding. The case is of special interest because it illustrates the distinction between negligence and actual malice, which, in this instance, were found in the same case. The reporter's problem came, not from a lack of knowledge of the law, but from timidity. Not knowing that a table was reserved for *Stone* v. *Essex County* reporters at the front of the courtroom, the reporter *Newspapers, Inc.* 330 sat at the back of the spectators' section during a N.E.2d 161 (1975). narcotics trial. From there, he had difficulty in hearing the witnesses. One of the defendants was the twenty-year-old son of the operator of the public schools' lunchrooms. When the prosecutor asked the town marshal who possessed the drugs in question, the reporter thought he heard the marshal respond, "Mr. Stone." The reporter assumed the reference was to the father—the only Mr. Stone he knew. Without checking further with the marshal or the prosecutor, the reporter used the father's first name in his story.

When the reporter submitted the story to his editor, the latter expressed surprise. He had known the elder Stone for twenty years and had never known him to do wrong. He asked the reporter if he was sure. The reporter said the marshal had said on the witness stand that Mr. Stone possessed the drugs. The editor had also known the marshal for a long time and knew he could be trusted. With a deadline approaching, the editor cleared the story for publication.

Stone sued for libel. Eventually, the Massachusetts Supreme Judicial Court ruled that if Stone were held to be a public figure there could be no recovery from the reporter. His failure to sit where he could hear clearly, coupled with his failure to ask someone for Stone's first name was "gross carelessness," but it did not rise to the level of reckless disregard. He was new to the town and to his job. He did not know many people and had no reason to doubt that the Stone mentioned in court was the only Stone he knew.

---

103. Firestone v. Time, Inc., 405 So.2d 172 (Fla. 1974).
104. Gobin v. Globe Publishing Co., 531 P.2d 76 (Kans. 1975).

But the editor's reaction to the reporter's story was enough in itself to prove actual malice. He did have doubts, and they could have been removed by a telephone call. His failure to react to his doubts was enough to establish reckless disregard.

An Illinois appeals court held that a reporter was negligent in placing too much reliance on a complaint filed in connection with a civil suit. The reporter compounded his problem by omitting some of the detail in the complaint in order to make a better story. The resulting article was headlined: "SAVED PARROT, LET WOMAN DIE, SUIT SAYS." The defendant in the suit had indeed saved his parrot when he awakened to find his

Newell v. *Field Enterprises, Inc.,* 415 N.E.2d 434 (1980).

house on fire. But he had been unable to reach a woman who was asleep in an upstairs room, and he had tried in vain to awaken her. These facts were stated more clearly in the petition to the court than they were in the news story. When the man who rescued the parrot filed a libel suit, the appeals court ruled that the discrepancy between the story and the facts in the petition, which was the reporter's sole source, permitted "an inference of negligent reporting." The court said the facts chosen for the story portrayed such callous conduct that the reporter should have made "a reasonable investigation" to make sure they were true.

The decision serves as a reminder that **pleadings** filed in connection with civil suits should be handled with care. Allegations made in pleadings present only one side of the case, and that usually in absolute terms. One purpose of a civil suit is to let a jury or judge determine where, between the extremes, the truth lies.

An Arizona court found a reporter negligent in relying on a disgruntled employee for information harmful to her boss.[105] The reporter checked the information with other sources, but had stopped short of confirming the employee's assertion that the Better Business Bureau had received more complaints about her boss's firm than about anyone else. In the end, the finding of negligence made no difference. At trial, a jury found that the story was substantially true.[106]

Courts have found that reporters are not negligent if they rely on the word of a police officer[107] or an officer of the immigration service,[108] even if the information proves to be incorrect.

State courts vary in the standard of proof required to show negligence. However, a survey of the cases indicates that the majority are holding it need be shown only by the preponderance of the evidence. At law, this is a lesser burden than the "clear and convincing evidence" required of public officials and public figures. Thus, in most of the states that have adopted a negligence standard, private plaintiffs not only may win libel suits against the media on a lesser showing of fault, but the rules of evidence make it easier for them to prove.

Obviously, people can and do differ over what is "reasonable care." However, reporters who have been trained well, or who have worked for careful editors, are not likely to be found negligent. Nor are public relations practitioners and advertising copy writers who

---

105. Peagler v. Phoenix Newspapers, Inc., 560 P.2d 1216 (Ariz. 1977).
106. Peagler v. Phoenix Newspapers, Inc., 640 P.2d 1110 (Ariz. 1982).
107. Wilson v. Capital City Press, 315 So.2d 393 (La.App. 1975).
108. Karp v. Miami Herald Publishing Co., 359 So.2d 580 (Fla.App. 1978).

adhere to the standards of their professions. Prudent professional communicators rely on documentary evidence where it is available. They know that even the best of memories can falter, and that participants in a dispute usually make their side look good when they talk to outsiders. This means that potentially defamatory assertions are checked against other sources before they are passed along to the public. Courts have held on numerous occasions that negligence begins with a failure to check dubious assertions of fact.

THE COMMON-LAW DEFENSES REVISITED

Truth or Falsehood: the Plaintiff's Burden

As noted earlier, common law assumed that an allegedly defamatory statement was false. The defendant carried the entire burden of trying to prove truth, or of otherwise justifying the statement at issue. In *New York Times*, the Supreme Court did not address itself directly to this point. However, the Court said that a public official plaintiff must prove either knowledge of falsity or reckless disregard of probable falsity, and must offer convincing evidence of one or another. From this, lower courts began to infer that public officials could not prove knowledge of falsity without also proving falsity. One case, decided by the New York Court of Appeals in 1977, illustrates the point.

Jack Newfield wrote a series of articles for the *Village Voice* in which he strongly criticized a New York judge. Excerpts from the articles were used in an advertisement for a book published by Holt, Rinehart & Winston. The judge sued for libel, but lost because he could not prove falsity. In its decision in *Rinaldi* v. *Holt, Rinehart & Winston*, the appeals court said:

Rinaldi v. *Holt, Rinehart & Winston*, 42 N.Y.2d 369 (1977).

> [T]he burden is now on libel plaintiffs to establish the falsity of the libel. . . . This requirement follows naturally from the actual malice standard. Before knowing falsity or reckless disregard for truth can be established, the plaintiff must establish that the statement was, in fact, false.

With respect to private individuals, *Gertz* left doubt as to whether they, like public persons, must prove falsity. Courts in most jurisdictions took the position that they did, but a few continued to apply common law. In those jurisdictions, the courts assumed that defamatory statements directed at private individuals were false, thus placing on the defendant the burden of proving truth or some other defense. The doubts were resolved in 1986 by the Supreme Court's decision in *Philadelphia Newspapers, Inc.* v. *Hepps*, referred to earlier. The Court said that private persons who feel they were libeled by the mass media during the discussion of a matter of "public concern" must prove falsity. This means that in virtually all libel actions directed at the mass media, the plaintiffs carry the burden of proving the falsity of the alleged defamation and of fault. The ruling is important to journalists because the Supreme Court has also held that there can be no defamation in a true statement of fact. Thus, if a plaintiff is unable to establish falsity, he has no case.

Under common law, courts in some states had held that truth could be libelous if it were published with an intent to harm someone. The Supreme Court held in *Garrison* v. *Louisiana* in 1964 that such holdings violate the First Amendment.

Jim Garrison was district attorney in New Orleans. Displeased with the performance of eight judges, he called a press conference at which he accused them of neglecting their duties and favoring the operators of places offering prostitution and gambling. The judges charged Garrison with violating a state law defining some kinds of libel as a crime. A state court found him guilty. The Supreme Court reversed, holding the Louisiana law unconstitutional because under its terms a person could be prosecuted for making a true statement if his intent was to cause harm. The Court said:

Garrison v. *Louisiana,* 379 U.S. 64, 85 S.Ct. 209, 12 L.Ed.2d 1042 (1964).

> Truth may not be the subject of either civil or criminal sanctions where the discussion of public affairs is concerned. . . . [O]nly those false statements made with a high degree of awareness of their probable falsity demanded by *New York Times* may be the subject of either criminal or civil sanctions.

That should resolve any doubt. Actionable defamation can be found only in a false statement. The burden of proving falsity rests in all instances on public official/public figure plaintiffs and, in all except rare instances, on private plaintiffs as well. In *Philadelphia Newspapers*, the Court seems to have left open the possibility that a private individual who is defamed by the media in connection with a private matter can bring an action under the old common-law rule in which falsity is assumed.

Fair Comment

In *Gertz* a majority of the Supreme Court said that "there is no such thing as a false idea." Opinions, no matter how "pernicious," ought to be corrected through debate rather than in the courts. Eight years later, in a brief opinion rejecting a request for review, the Supreme Court itself said that its reference to opinion in *Gertz* was dicta.[109] The Court said it had not federalized libel law with respect to opinion. It was still up to each state to determine whether opinion can be defamatory. Nevertheless, a survey of recent cases shows that almost without exception, state courts and lower federal courts are citing *Gertz* and holding that opinion cannot be defamatory.

Even under common law, courts in most states had shown a willingness to protect opinion. Libel defendants could rely on the defense of "fair comment" if they could show that a statement of opinion was grounded in an accurate statement of fact, or based on facts commonly known, and was directed at the public performance of persons who had invited comment. Thus, it served as a protection for literary, drama, art, dance, and music critics, and for writers of editorials directed at persons in public office or

---

109. Miskovsky v. Oklahoma Publishing Co., 459 U.S. 923, 103 S.Ct. 235, 74 L.Ed.2d 186 (1982).

otherwise in the public eye. The burden of proving the truth of the underlying facts lay on the defendant, and usually it was left to a jury to determine whether the proof was adequate and the comment fair.

In the aftermath of *Gertz*, many courts are holding that under the First Amendment opinion enjoys an absolute immunity from libel actions.[110] As of late 1984, a majority of the federal circuit courts of appeal had adopted this position. These include the District of Columbia circuit and the first, second, third, fourth, fifth, sixth, ninth, and tenth circuits.[111] The Supreme Court itself quoted the *Gertz* dicta with approval in its *Bose* decision.

Problems arise when opinion and assertions of fact are mixed in the same article, when what is advanced as opinion is in reality an assertion of fact, or when an opinion implies fact. In such instances, if the assertion of fact is false and defamatory, a libel plaintiff may still be able to prevail. However, in the recent decisions, most courts are holding that the distinction between fact and opinion is a question of law to be resolved by the judge. Courts that have taken this position have done so on the theory that where First Amendment values are at stake, decisions should be made by application of fixed and predictable standards. However, as of 1985, courts still were groping toward a uniformly accepted definition of the standards to be used in separating opinion from fact.

The Supreme Court has offered only minimal guidance in *Gertz* and in two other decisions, *Greenbelt Cooperative Publishing Co.* v. *Bresler*,[112] decided in 1970, and *Old Dominion Branch No. 496, National Association of Letter Carriers, AFL-CIO,* v. *Austin*,[113] decided in 1974.

In *Gertz*, the Court said:

> Under the First Amendment there is no such thing as a false idea. However pernicious an opinion may seem, we depend for its correction not on the conscience of judges and juries but on the competition of other ideas. But there is no constitutional value in false statements of fact. Neither the intentional lie nor the careless error materially advances society's interest in "uninhibited, robust, and wide-open debate on the public issues."

While neither *Greenbelt* nor *Old Dominion* involved opinion directly, courts look to them for guidance in separating fact from opinion. *Greenbelt* grew out of a heated exchange during a hearing on a request for a zoning change in Greenbelt, Maryland. Bresler, a real estate developer, was seeking permission to rezone a tract of land so he could erect a high-rise apartment house. Residents of the community opposed him vigorously. He offered a deal: He would give the city land for a badly needed school if it would approve his zoning change. An opponent told the meeting the offer was a form of blackmail. This quotation was picked up by a reporter and used in the newspaper report of the meeting. The developer sued the paper for libel and won a judgment in the Maryland courts. The Supreme Court held that the

Greenbelt Cooperative Publishing Co. v. Bresler, 398 U.S. 6, 90 S.Ct. 1537, 26 L.Ed.2d 6 (1970).

---

110. Ollman v. Evans, 750 F.2d 970, 974 (D.C. Cir. 1984).
111. Ollman, p. 974, note 6.
112. 398 U.S. 6, 90 S.Ct. 1537, 26 L.Ed.2d 6 (1970).
113. 418 U.S. 264, 94 S.Ct. 2770, 41 L.Ed.2d 745 (1974).

word "blackmail" could not reasonably be understood as an accusation of crime, but was invective, uttered in the heat of debate. The Court reasoned that in the full context of the article, the ordinary reader would understand that "blackmail" was one person's view of Bresler's negotiating tactics, not an accusation of crime. It was, in short, "rhetorical hyperbole" and could be expected of participants in a debate that might affect the property values of the participants.

Old Dominion grew out of a labor dispute. Austin and several other post office employees in Richmond, Virginia, refused to join the Letter Carriers union. The union issued a leaflet denouncing them as "scabs." The epithet was reinforced by a quotation attributed to Jack London portraying scabs as traitors to their religion, their country,

Old Dominion Branch No. 496, National Association of Letter Carriers, AFL-CIO, v. Austin, 418 U.S. 264, 94 S.Ct. 2770, 41 L.Ed.2d 745 (1974).

their families, and their class. Austin and the others sued the union for libel, arguing that the leaflet falsely accused them of the crime of treason. The Supreme Court eventually held that the leaflet's language, strong as it was, was absolutely protected. In reaching that conclusion, the Court referred to *Gertz*, which was decided the same day. To show that the union's description of a "scab" was opinion, the Court looked at its specific linguistic context and its broader social setting. People who know anything about labor disputes would know that "traitor" was used in a "loose, figurative sense" and not as an accusation of crime. They also would know that in the larger social context, "exaggerated rhetoric was commonplace in labor disputes." Thus, the ordinary reader would understand that the leaflet was an expression of opinion, not fact.

Taken together, the three decisions tell us that opinion is protected absolutely by the First Amendment. Where there is doubt as to whether an assertion at issue in a libel action is fact or opinion, the court must look not only at its linguistic context, but at the issue which gave it birth. If the ordinary reader would understand that the offending language was opinion, not subject to being proved true or false, the language cannot sustain a libel action. The importance of a court's decision on the opinion issue cannot be overstated. If the matter at issue in a libel suit is held to be opinion as a matter of law, the court should also uphold a defendant's motion for summary judgment, thus saving the considerable expense of a trial.

In 1985, the Supreme Court rejected an opportunity to offer further guidance to courts seeking to separate fact from opinion. It did so by refusing to review *Ollman* v. *Evans*,[114] a libel case that had been in the courts for nearly seven years and on which the United States Court of Appeals for the District of Columbia Circuit had divided six-to-five, with the judges writing seven separate opinions. Justice Rehnquist and Chief Justice Burger wrote that they would have taken the case for the purpose of reconsidering the *Gertz* dicta on opinion. The two indicated that they would limit the First Amendment's protection of opinion to political ideas for which the test of truth "is indeed the market place and not the courtroom." They complained that "lower courts have seized upon the word 'opinion' [in *Gertz*] to solve with a meat axe a very subtle and difficult question. . . ." Because the District of Columbia circuit court attempted in *Ollman* to draft standards for separating fact from opinion, the case is worth more than passing attention.

---

114. ___ U.S. ___, 105 S.Ct. 2662, 86 L.Ed.2d 278 (1985).

In 1978, Bertell Ollman, a professor of political science at New York University, was nominated by a search committee as chairman of the Department of Government and Politics at the University of Maryland. The provost of the university and the chancellor of the College Park campus approved. Before Ollman's name was presented to the board of trustees, Rowland Evans and Robert Novak made him the subject of one of their nationally syndicated columns. It appeared in the *Washington Post* under the headline "The Marxist Professor's Intentions." The column noted that Ollman was a Marxist in political philosophy and said, "His candid writings avow his desire to use the classroom as an instrument for preparing what he calls 'the revolution.' " The column went on to say that Ollman "is widely viewed in his profession as a political activist" whose purpose in teaching was "to convert students to socialism." Near the end of the column, Evans and Novak quoted an unidentified political scientist as saying, "Ollman has no status within the profession, but is a pure and simple activist." The board of trustees did not approve the appointment.

Ollman v. Evans, 750 F.2d 970 (C.A.D.C. 1984).

Four days after the column appeared, the *Washington Post* published a letter from Ollman denying that he used his classroom to indoctrinate students and attempting to put in context the excerpts from his writings that the columnists had used against him. The professor's lawyer asked Evans and Novak to publish a retraction. When they refused to do so, Ollman sued for libel.

A United States district court judge granted the columnists' motion for summary judgment, holding that the article was opinion and thus absolutely protected by the First Amendment. On appeal, a three-judge panel considered the column paragraph by paragraph and concluded that false and defamatory assertions of fact were mixed with opinion. Therefore, they sent the case back to the district court for trial. That court again ruled for Evans and Novak. On further appeal, the circuit court agreed to consider the case *en banc*, that is, with all eleven judges considering the arguments. The court concluded, six-to-five, that the district court had reached the correct verdict, but no more than five members of the panel could agree on a rationale for the decision. The leading opinion was written by Judge Kenneth W. Starr, who sought to establish standards for separating fact from opinion.

Judge Starr began his search for standards by noting that "[e]xpressions of opinion are protected whether the subject of the comment is a private or public figure." He based that assertion on the Supreme Court's statement in *Gertz* that there is no such thing as a "false" opinion.

Judge Starr moved then to an analysis of the decisions in which courts have distinguished between fact and opinion. He concluded that courts have taken three approaches to the problem.

— "Some courts have . . . eschewed any effort to construct a theory and simply treated the distinction between fact and opinion as a judgment call."

— "Other courts have concentrated on a single factor, such as the verifiability . . . of the allegedly defamatory statement."

— "Still others have adopted a multi-factor test, attempting to assess the allegedly defamatory proposition in the totality of the circumstances in which it appeared."

In effect, Judge Starr rejected the first two approaches and chose to elaborate on the latter. In doing so, he wrote, "[W]e agree with the overwhelming weight of post-*Gertz* authority that the distinction between opinion and fact is a matter of law." He did so, he said, because the Supreme Court "has clearly ruled that questions as to other privileges derived from the First Amendment, such as the qualified privilege as to public officials and public figures, are to be decided as matters of law." Here, he referred to *Gertz*.

Judge Starr noted that fact and opinion frequently are so intertwined that it is difficult to determine where one ends and the other begins. Separating them is further complicated because assertions that might be factual in some contexts can be seen as opinion in others. He concluded that in such instances, "courts should analyze the totality of the circumstances in which the statements are made to decide whether they merit the absolute First Amendment protection enjoyed by opinion." He proposed that the analysis be based on four factors:

1. What is "the common usage or meaning of the specific language of the challenged statement itself"? The ordinary reader is less likely to infer fact from indefinite or ambiguous statements than from those that make a clear and positive assertion.

2. Can the statement be verified? Does it lend itself to objective proof of truth or falsehood?

3. If these questions do not lead to a conclusion, the disputed language must be looked at in the context of the statement as a whole. Does the unchallenged language around the disputed passage point to its being fact or opinion?

4. What is the broader context in which the statement appears? Public debate is accompanied by "widely varying social conventions which signal to the reader the likelihood of a statement's being fact or opinion." Those conventions were crucial factors in the *Old Dominion* and *Greenbelt* decisions noted above.

In *Ollman*, the court of appeals concluded that because Evans and Novak make their living writing columns that ordinarily appear on the editorial or op-ed page of newspapers, readers would believe they dealt in opinion. Readers would be

> fully aware that the statements found there are not "hard" news like those printed on the front page or elsewhere in the news sections of the newspaper. Readers expect that columnists will make strong statements, sometimes phrased in a polemical manner that would hardly be considered balanced or fair elsewhere in the newspaper. . . . That proposition is inherent in the very notion of an "Op-Ed page." Because of obvious space limitations, it is also manifest that columnists or commentators will express themselves in condensed fashion without providing what might be considered the full picture. . . . This broad understanding of the traditional function of a column like Evans and Novak will therefore predispose the average reader to regard what is found there to be opinion.

Applying his four-step analysis, Judge Starr concluded that the bulk of the column readily would be understood as opinion. He and his colleagues had the greatest difficulty with the assertion attributed to the anonymous professor: "Ollman has no status within the profession but is a pure and simple activist." To some of the judges that was a damning assertion of fact that could be proved or disproved. The minority suggested that it could be resolved by resort to a poll of political science professors. The majority rejected that suggestion. The column had noted that Ollman did have some stature in the profession. He was a member of the faculty of a respected university. He had been selected in competition with others as the chairman at Maryland. He had published. The article also made clear that as a Marxist he was highly controversial. It conceded that the Maryland search committee's choice was opposed by a minority of academics. Taken in the context of the dispute over the appointment, and in light of the nature of the Evans and Novak column, readers would see the unidentified professor's assertion as the kind of "rhetorical hyperbole" that the Supreme Court protected in *Greenbelt*. Therefore, Ollman had no cause of action against Evans and Novak because he was not the victim of a false and defamatory assertion of fact.

The Supreme Judicial Court of Massachusetts reached a similar conclusion in 1982 in a case brought by a television reporter who had been fired. As in *Ollman*, the Supreme Court of the United States refused to review the verdict. John D. Cole III, a reporter for WBZ-TV in Boston, had helped prepare a series of telecasts on the fund-raising activities of then mayor Kevin White. The telecasts generally were critical of the mayor.

Cole v. *Westinghouse Broadcasting*, 435 N.E.2d 1021 (1982).

Cole had interviewed White, but the latter's comments were in large part omitted from the series. Shortly thereafter, WBZ-TV discharged Cole, issuing a press release which said he had been guilty of "misconduct and insubordination." When a newspaper reporter pressed the station's spokeswoman for more detail, she said, stressing that she was speaking unofficially, that Cole also had a history of "bad reporting techniques . . . [and of] sloppy and irresponsible reporting." The quoted remarks appeared in the newspaper's story about Cole's firing. Cole sued his former employer for libel. Massachusetts courts held that he had no case because the spokeswoman's comments were statements of opinion.

The Supreme Judicial Court of Massachusetts, that state's highest court, discussed the difference between fact and opinion. The analysis begins, the court said, with an examination of the statement at issue in its entirety and in the context in which it appeared. In this analysis, words should be given their ordinary meaning and should be considered in connection with any cautionary terms included in the statement. The nature of the medium and the audience to which it is addressed also are factors to be considered. Thus, the court concluded, it is possible for a passage to be considered fact in some contexts and opinion in others. If, for instance, an employer were to say during heated contract negotiations with a labor union that the union's chief bargainer was a robber, no one would take it as a statement of fact. But if an article on street crime were to refer to a named individual as a robber, that might well be taken as a factual accusation. In the end, the Massachusetts court said, "The only test with ultimate merit is: whether a reasonable person would be likely to understand the remark as an expression of the source's opinion or as a statement of existing fact." With that, the court concluded that the remarks directed at Cole were opinion. Reasonable people can disagree on whether a reporter is sloppy and irresponsible without being able to offer conclusive proof either way.

In line with the rule of reason implicit in the cases above, courts in Ohio, Missouri, and Oregon have ruled that newspaper editorials were not libelous. An editorial in a Dayton, Ohio, newspaper said that the National Rifle Association murdered good sense in opposing one of President Carter's appointments. The resulting libel suit was dismissed.[115] The *South County Journal* in suburban St. Louis summed up a squabble over fire protection by characterizing a lawyer's role in the dispute as "sleazy sleight-of-hand." That suit, too, was dismissed with a state court's holding that in the context of the editorial, readers would recognize it as opinion.[116] An Oregon appeals court, upholding the dismissal of a lawsuit brought against the *Portland Oregonian* by a county prosecutor, simply held, "[I]t is not for the courts to pass on the validity of, or the basis for, an editorial opinion."[117]

However, one exception should be noted. Accusations of criminal conduct, asserted as opinion, get careful scrutiny from the courts. If the factual support for the accusations is ambiguous, or suggests that the accusations were meant to be taken seriously, courts have held them to be actionable. *Braig* v. *Field Communications*,[118] decided by the Superior Court of Pennsylvania in 1983, illustrates the point.

As a judge of the Court of Common Pleas of Philadelphia County, Joseph P. Braig had presided at the trial of a police officer accused of murdering a nineteen-year-old black man. Braig declared a mistrial on the ground of "intentional prosecutorial misconduct." His ruling was controversial and became the subject of discussion on a WKBS-TV public affairs program. An assistant district attorney said Braig was "no friend of the police brutality unit [of the prosecutor's office]. I don't care who we sent in to try that case, in my opinion, that case was going to get blown out." Braig took the position that the speaker accused him of being biased against the police and a party to a "fix." He sued both the assistant district attorney and the station for libel. A trial court granted a defense motion for summary judgment, holding that the remark quoted above was a statement of opinion. On appeal, the superior court held otherwise. Despite the speaker's qualifying "in my opinion," the statement, taken in context, emerged as a possible assertion of fact. The court said a jury should be permitted to decide whether the ordinary listener would conclude that Braig had conspired with police in a "fix."

Nevertheless, the First Amendment's protection for opinion has become a strong and frequently used defense in libel actions. If an allegedly defamatory assertion can be construed as opinion, courts are holding that it will not sustain a libel action. Whether courts have been using the "meat axe" approach deplored by Chief Justice Burger and Justice Rehnquist, or applying the contextual analysis advanced by Judge Starr, is open to debate. But there is no debate as to the current trend: Once courts have decided as a matter of law that allegedly defamatory material is an expression of opinion, it has absolute protection under the First Amendment. The common-law defense of fair comment has been supplanted by a defense that protects even unfair comment from libel actions.

---

115. National Rifle Association v. Dayton Newspapers, Inc., 555 F.Supp. 1299 (S.D.Ohio 1983).
116. Anton v. St. Louis Suburban Newspapers, Inc., 598 S.W.2d 493 (Mo.1980).
117. Haas v. Painter, 662 P.2d 768 (Or.App. 1983).
118. 456 A.2d 1366 (Pa. 1983).

Qualified Privilege

With the common-law defense of truth supplemented by the threshold requirement that the plaintiff must prove falsehood, and with the defense of fair comment giving way to the absolute protection afforded opinion, what has happened to the defense of qualified privilege? A survey of recent cases shows that it is thriving. (To review the meaning of the term "qualified privilege" in the context of a libel action, see page 95.)

In general, the purpose of qualified privilege is to protect the news media when they act as the eyes and ears of the general public in covering the actions of government and the statements of government officials. Under common law, as noted earlier, that protection applied only as long as the report was fair and accurate. With the added protection afforded by the actual malice holding in *New York Times*, and the negligence option offered by *Gertz*, the protection has become much stronger. A sampling of recent cases will illustrate the point.

In 1983, *Time* magazine won dismissal of a libel suit brought against it by Schiavone Construction Co.[119] The article in question reported that the construction company had made improper payments to labor union officials to prevent strikes. This allegedly happened when Raymond J. Donovan, President Reagan's first secretary of labor, was an officer of the company. Whether or not such payments were made—and if so, Donovan's knowledge of them—became subjects of news reports and congressional hearings during the secretary's tenure in office. *Time*'s article was based on testimony offered at the hearings. A federal district court held that because the report was a reasonably accurate account of that testimony it was protected by a qualified privilege. A federal circuit court affirmed that holding.

In a broader application of the privilege, a federal district court in Colorado, interpreting that state's law, held that letters written to a state agency, to various county officials, and even to a newspaper in connection with a rezoning proceeding carried absolute protection. The court held that the letters were written in response to a request from the county board of commissioners for comment on, and public participation in, the rezoning. Since they were a part of the board's search for facts on which to base its decision, they became a function of government and thus privileged.[120]

Statements made by public officials, including law enforcement officers, are protected by absolute privilege when the officials are acting in an official capacity. A United States district court's decision in *Moorhead* v. *Mullin*[121] in 1982 indicates that some courts interpret the scope of official duties quite broadly. In this instance, the lieutenant governor of the Virgin Islands wrote a letter criticizing the performance of the director of the Division of Utilities and Sanitation. Some of the allegations in the letter were false. Parts of the letter, including the false allegations, were published by a newspaper. When the director sued the newspaper for libel, the district court ruled that the lieutenant governor's letter was written as part of his official duties and therefore was protected by absolute privilege. It ruled further that the libel suit against the newspaper should be

---

119. Schiavone Construction Co. v. Time, Inc., 569 F.Supp. 614 (D.N.J. 1983); affirmed, 735 F.2d 94 (3d Cir. 1984).
120. Walters v. Linhof, 559 F.Supp. 1231 (D.Colo. 1983).
121. 542 F.Supp. 1614 (D.V.I. 1982).

dismissed because the director could not prove it had published the lieutenant governor's false assertions with actual malice.

A federal district court in Pennsylvania held in *Williams* v. *WCAU-TV* that the station was protected by privilege when it televised the arrest of a suspected bank robber, even though the suspect was released when police concluded he had no connection with the robbery. The court held that the arrest was an official action protected by the state's law defining privilege.[122]

Courts also operate under absolute privilege. This protects witnesses, lawyers, and judges in their testimony or comment during any legal proceedings. The privilege also extends to grand jury proceedings.[123] A federal court in Illinois held that a letter written to a judge by a psychologist in connection with a child custody proceeding was absolutely privileged because it was relevant to the proceeding.[124]

The news media are protected in covering legal proceedings as long as the reports are fair and accurate. This does not necessarily mean that the account must include everything that happened. For instance, a federal court in Massachusetts held that a magazine was protected in reporting that the defendant in a criminal prosecution had threatened a witness in court. There was a difference of opinion over the nature of the threat, and the defendant's attorney asserted that no threat had been made. The magazine article omitted the lawyer's disclaimer. The court ruled that the account still was fair and accurate because inclusion of his disclaimer would not have erased the derogatory sting of the report that a threat had been made.[125] A federal court of appeals held that CBS News did not abuse the privilege by illustrating its account of a court proceeding with videotapes taken outside the courtroom. The court held that the combination of words and pictures did not go beyond the bounds of a fair and accurate report.[126]

Qualified privilege can be abused, as is illustrated by a decision of a federal appeals court in 1982 in *Bufalino* v. *Associated Press*. The Supreme Court refused to review the case. It began with an Associated Press reporter's story about contributors to Richard L. Thornburgh's successful campaign for governor in 1978. The story featured the assertion

Bufalino v. **Associated Press**, 692 F.2d 266 (2d Cir. 1982).

that four of the fourteen thousand contributors were believed to have ties with organized crime. The reporter noted that Thornburgh had risen to fame "by battling organized crime." The governor-elect reacted by announcing the next day that he was returning the contributions made by three of the four persons identified in the story. The fourth contributor, who did not get his money back, was Charles J. Bufalino, a lawyer who also served as the appointed solicitor for a small town in northeastern Pennsylvania. He had given $140 to Thornburgh's campaign.

When Bufalino sued AP for libel, the reporter said he had included the lawyer in the story on the strength of assertions made to him by unidentified officials of the Pennsylvania Crime Commission. They told him that Charles was related to a Russell Bufalino who had been subjected to a deportation action because of his alleged actions

---

122. 555 F.Supp. 198 (E.D.Pa. 1983).
123. Reeves v. American Broadcasting Companies, Inc., 719 F.2d 602 (3d Cir. 1983).
124. Bond v. Pecaut, 561 F.Supp. 1037 (D.Ill. 1983).
125. Ricci v. Venture Magazine, Inc., 574 F.Supp. 1563 (D.Mass. 1983).
126. Lal v. CBS, Inc., 726 F.2d 97 (3d Cir. 1984).

as a Mafia leader. The sources said Charles's father and uncle had testified at Russell's hearing. The sources also told the reporter that Charles had represented organized crime figures as an attorney. A federal district court dismissed Charles Bufalino's libel suit, ruling that he was a public figure and could not prove actual malice. The appeals court reversed, holding that Bufalino was a private individual who need prove only negligence. The court also held that the information the reporter received from unidentified officials was not privileged. Nor could it be made privileged by records AP discovered later showing that Charles Bufalino may have had financial and social ties with organized crime figures. The court ruled that the story was written without such documentary support and would have to be judged for libel purposes on what the AP reporter knew at that time. The court said the reporter could not use the defense of qualified privilege unless he was willing to identify his sources. Only if he did so could the court determine whether they were acting within the scope of their official duties.

In any discussion of privilege and the courts, the question arises: Does privilege protect the reporting of information found in a petition or pleading initiating a lawsuit? The answer depends upon each state's common law. In the majority of the states that have ruled on the question, courts have held that such petitions are not protected by privilege until a court has taken some legal notice of them. This can come about through a decision made on a motion, either by the defense or the plaintiff. In these majority states, reporters who act too soon in basing a story on defamatory material taken from a petition filed in court may not be able to rely on qualified privilege as a defense.

The word "may" is used because of speculation in recent decisions that the modern trend is toward the position, still held in only a minority of the states, that protection should begin with the filing of the complaint.[127] An Illinois appeals court listed four reasons why this should be done:

1. The public has an interest in knowing what goes on in court, especially since many of society's problems are being attacked through litigation. Courts have been asked, for instance, to resolve issues affecting minority job rights, university admissions policies, wages paid to women, water and air pollution, and the safety of automobiles.

2. The majority states have taken the position that by deferring privilege until some judicial action has been taken, they will discourage the filing of suits for the sole purpose of putting defamatory accusations in circulation. However, there is no guarantee that a suit pushed forward to litigation has any substance, or was brought in good faith.

3. Starting in 1927,[128] courts have recognized a growing public awareness of the reality of what happens in court. Most persons know that those who file suit base that filing on a one-sided version of the facts. Thus, most readers will apply more than a few grains of salt to allegations contained in a story of a suit's being filed.

4. In all states, the filing of most suits produces a public record. Petitions are

---

127. For a discussion of this topic, see Newell v. Field Enterprises, Inc., 415 N.E.2d 434 (Ill. 1980).
128. Campbell v. New York Evening Post, 157 N.E. 153 (N.Y. 1927).

filed in the office of the clerk of courts where they are open to inspection by anyone. Thus, all publication does is extend the range of knowledge of the filing. In some states, records of paternity proceedings, of charges of incest, and, in a few states, of some kinds of divorce proceedings are sealed by law; therefore, they are not public records. Most juvenile courts also operate under a cloak of secrecy that can be breached only by order of the court.

Generally, however, professional communicators who are covering the actions of government and the activities of public officials enjoy double protection against libel suits. If a story accurately reflects a privileged situation, it is protected by qualified privilege. If the situation turns out not to have been privileged, or if some detail proves not to be accurate, the *New York Times* rule comes into play. At that point, the reporter's performance comes under examination. A public official or public figure plaintiff must offer clear and convincing evidence of actual malice. Private individuals in the states that have adopted the option offered by *Gertz* must prove negligence. In a few federal circuits, and in some states, reporters of public controversies enjoy an additional privilege—neutral reportage.

Neutral Reportage

Since 1977, courts in a few jurisdictions have recognized a First Amendment privilege for news media confronted with highly charged and newsworthy public controversies. In these jurisdictions, courts have held that when accusations are being flung back and forth, it is unreasonable to expect the media to investigate all of them and make reasonably certain that they are true. Therefore, as long as the media offer a neutral report of the accusations, and the reactions of the participants in the controversy, the media are protected. The protection will prevail even when reporters and editors may have had doubt as to the truth of the accusations. Such protection, called the privilege of **neutral reportage,** has not won general approval. Courts in a few jurisdictions have rejected it. The Supreme Court has refused to resolve the differences, rejecting opportunities to hear cases on both sides of the issue.[129]

The privilege was recognized first in 1977 by the United States Court of Appeals, Second Circuit, in *Edwards* v. *National Audubon Society*. The case began when a reporter for the *New York Times* read an editorial in a publication of the Audubon Society. The editorial said that some scientists who were defending the continued use of DDT as an insecticide were "paid liars." The reporter considered the allegation newsworthy, but so broad that it could hit a lot of innocent targets. He asked the society to be more specific. A vice-president of the society gave him five names, but insisted, as did the editor of the publication, that he did not know that the named scientists were

Edwards v. *National Audubon Society,* 566 F.2d 113 (2d Cir. 1977).

in fact "paid liars." What he did know was that the five continued to cite the society's annual bird count as proof of their assertion that DDT was not harmful to bird life. In the society's view, the count was increasing year by year, not because there were more

---

129. In Edwards and McCall, both discussed below.

birds, but because more watchers were participating in the count. The vice-president said the five scientists he named had ignored the society's efforts to impress them with this point. This list included three professors at highly regarded state universities, a Nobel Prize winner who had developed high-yield varieties of food grains, and a lecturer for the National Agricultural Chemical Association. The *Times* reporter sought comment from the five and obtained it from three of them. The resulting news story used the expression "paid to lie," attributed to an Audubon Society spokesman, and the reaction of the scientists. The three university professors sued the society and the *Times* for libel. A jury awarded two of them $20,000 each and the third $21,000.

On appeal, the circuit court reversed, holding that the *Times* was protected by an absolute **constitutional privilege** based on a right of neutral reportage. It defined that right:

> At stake in this case is a fundamental principle. Succinctly stated, when a responsible, prominent organization like the National Audubon Society makes serious charges against a public figure, the First Amendment protects the accurate and disinterested reporting of those charges, regardless of the reporter's private views regarding their validity. . . . What is newsworthy about such accusations is that they were made. We do not believe that the press may be required under the First Amendment to suppress newsworthy statements merely because it has serious doubts regarding their truth. Nor must the press take up cudgels against dubious charges in order to publish them without fear of liability for defamation. . . . The public interest in being fully informed about controversies that often rage around sensitive issues demands that the press be afforded the freedom to report such charges without assuming responsibility for them.

Edwards and subsequent decisions of other courts yield four elements that are essential to establish the privilege of neutral reportage:

1.   A public controversy must exist, or it must be created by serious and newsworthy charges.

2.   The allegations at issue must be made by a responsible person or organization, probably rising to the level of a public official or public figure.

3.   The assertion at issue must be directed at a public official or a public figure.

4.   It must be reported accurately and neutrally.

Decisions in the limited number of cases thus far indicate that the first two points are extremely important. The controversy must exist independently of the news media. The assertions at issue must be initiated by someone of stature who is seen by the media as both responsible and newsworthy. The media's role must be confined to that of a disinterested observer resisting the temptation to take sides or to add fuel to the controversy.

In *McManus* v. *Doubleday & Co.*,[130] a federal district court in New York City held that neutral reportage did not apply to charges resulting from investigative reporting. The court held that the charges were solicited by the reporter and that "no controversy raged around the libelous statement before the reporter entered the scene." The court

---

130. 513 F.Supp. 1383 (S.D.N.Y. 1981).

emphasized that "journalist-induced charges" do not come under the protection of the *Edwards* privilege. Nor does a story "particularly lacking in balanced reporting."[131]

The privilege of neutral reportage has been recognized in California,[132] the District of Columbia,[133] Florida,[134] Indiana,[135] Ohio,[136] Vermont,[137] and Wyoming.[138] Intermediate appeals courts in Illinois[139] and New York[140] have taken differing views on the privilege, adopting it in one district and rejecting it in another. The United States Court of Appeals, Tenth Circuit, seemed to endorse the privilege in libel suits brought by public officials or public figures, but rejected it in a case in which a private individual was the plaintiff. The court held that "the publisher may not escape liability for defamation when it takes words out of context and uses them to convey a false representation of fact."[141]

The privilege of neutral reportage has been rejected in dicta by the United States Court of Appeals, Third Circuit,[142] and directly by courts in Kentucky and Michigan.[143] The Kentucky Supreme Court's decision in *McCall* v. *Courier-Journal and Louisville Times* best illustrates the reasoning underlying the rejection.

The case began in 1976 when Kristie Frazier told a *Louisville Times* reporter that a lawyer, John Tim McCall, had promised to clear her of a drug charge if she paid him $10,000. She said he had talked about a "fix" and had bragged of going fishing with a

McCall v. Courier-Journal and Louisville Times, 623 S.W.2d 882 (Ky. 1981).

judge. Sensing a story, the reporter gave Frazier a tape recorder, small enough to hide in her purse, and coached her on the questions she should ask McCall on his next visit to his office. In the subsequent interview, McCall told Frazier there would be no bribe, no fix. He simply would work a lot harder for $10,000 than he would for his normal fee of $1,500. If his extra effort failed and she did have to go to jail, the fee would be only $1,500.

Frazier's account of the first interview, the tape recording of the second interview, and information obtained from other sources were converted into a page-1 story. The lead said McCall was "in possible violation of his professional ethics." That and eight other paragraphs, which were to become the basis of McCall's suit for libel and invasion of privacy, included such words as "fix," "illegal," "improper offers," and the like. The headline, spread across the top of the page, asked, "Lawyer's 'guarantee' to keep woman free for $10,000 unethical?"

A county court dismissed McCall's petition and a state court of appeals affirmed. But

131. Cianci v. New Times Publishing Co., 639 F.2d 54 (2d Cir. 1980).
132. Barry v. Time, Inc., 584 F.Supp. 1110 (N.D.Calif. 1984).
133. Bell v. Associated Press, 584 F.Supp. 128 (D.D.C. 1984).
134. El Amin v. Miami Herald, 9 Med.L.Rptr. 1079 (Fla.App. 1983).
135. Woods v. Evansville Press, 11 Med.L.Rptr. 2201 (S.D.Ind. 1985).
136. J.V. Peters & Co. v. Knight Ridder Co., 10 Med.L.Rptr. 1576 (Ohio App. 1984).
137. Burns v. Times Argus, 430 A.2d 773 (Vt. 1981).
138. Whitaker v. Denver Post, 4 Med.L.Rptr. 1351 (D.Wyo. 1978).
139. Krauss v. Champaign News Gazette, 375 N.E.2d 1362 (Ill.App. 1978) (Fourth District); Tunney v. ABC, 109 Ill.App.3d 769 (Ill.App. 1982) (First District).
140. Orr v. Lynch, 45 N.Y.2d 903 (N.Y.1978) (Third Department); Hogan v. Herald Publishing Co., 58 N.Y.2d 630 (N.Y.1982) (Fourth Department).
141. Dixson v. Newsweek, 562 F.2d 626 (10th Cir. 1977).
142. Dickey v. CBS, Inc., 583 F.2d 1221 (3d Cir. 1978).
143. McCall, below, and Postill v. Booth Newspapers, 118 Mich.App. 608 (Mich.App. 1982).

the state supreme court took the case and reversed, holding that there were issues of fact that a jury should be permitted to decide. It noted that when the reporters listened to the tape recording made by Frazier they "found no indication of any 'fix.' " But they published the allegation anyway, basing it on Frazier's account of the initial interview, supported by the word of a friend who had accompanied her. The court minced no words in condemning the newspaper for using the story:

> These allegations were published, *in spite of the fact that the newspaper knew—and admitted it knew—that there was no evidence of any crime on the part of McCall.*
>
> What we have here is a situation where the newspaper says to the reader, "We don't find any evidence of a crime on the part of McCall, but we heard some contrary stories and we are going to report them anyway."

The court held that McCall was a private individual who would have to do no more than prove "simple negligence" to prevail. The court rejected the newspaper's argument that it was protected by the privilege of neutral reportage applied in *Edwards.* It said it would have to ignore the Supreme Court's holding in *Gertz* in order to grant such a privilege. In that decision, the Court held that the news media can be held liable for falsehoods published with the requisite degree of fault. In the Kentucky court's view, that holding leaves no room for the publication of baseless charges, no matter where they originate or who they are aimed at.

The Supreme Court of the United States refused to review *McCall,*[144] as it also had refused to review *Edwards.*[145] Thus, it is uncertain how far courts will go in permitting journalists to offer a neutral report of doubtful allegations made in the heat of debate. As of this writing, courts seem disposed to interpret *Edwards* narrowly, limiting the privilege of neutral reportage to public allegations that are newsworthy not only for their content, but because of the stature of the people who made them and at whom they were made. The position of the courts that have adopted *Edwards* seems to be that when public officials and public figures begin hurling wild charges back and forth, the public is entitled to know about it. But, as the Kentucky Supreme Court pointed out in *McCall,* the *New York Times* rule suggests caution even then. That court said, in effect, that when reporters have serious doubts about a source's allegations, they ought to check further before they spread them. To publish with serious doubts is actual malice.

Two decades after *New York Times,* it is clear that that decision shifted the balance in libel cases toward the news media. Public officials and public figures who feel they have been defamed by the media must offer clear and convincing evidence of actual malice if they are to prevail. In more than half the states private individuals who sue the media for libel must, as a minimum, prove that the defendant was negligent. In a few states, private individuals who are defamed during the reporting of a public issue must prove actual malice—knowledge of falsity or reckless disregard for the truth—which remains a formidable task. In 1984, the Supreme Court held in *Bose* that while juries may be asked to determine whether there was actual malice when the facts are in dispute, their finding is subject to review by appellate courts. This created what one justice called

---

144. 456 U.S. 975 (1982).
145. 434 U.S. 1002 (1977).

a superquestion of law. The decision probably has increased the likelihood that trial court libel decisions, which run heavily against the news media, will be reversed on appeal, as the majority already were. In the decade after *Gertz,* most courts converted its dictum "Under the First Amendment there is no such thing as a false idea" into absolute protection for opinion, no matter how harsh and uncomplimentary. The effect has been to limit grounds for libel actions to false and defamatory assertions of fact. A statement is libelous only if it can be proved to be both false and defamatory. Like opinion, truth cannot be grounds for a successful libel action. Private individuals who feel they have been defamed by the media must prove not only some departure from accepted standards of ordinary care—negligence—but harm of some kind. If they can, the jury's award of damages is supposed to be only enough to compensate the plaintiff for the harm that was done to him. In some instances, however, juries have placed high values on such intangibles as humiliation and embarrassment. Private individuals cannot be awarded punitive damages unless they, too, can prove actual malice. Finally, a few jurisdictions are permitting the media to publish with doubt if they are covering a public dispute between public officials or public figure. As long as the allegations that are being bandied back and forth are presented without taking sides, the media are protected in those jurisdictions by the privilege of neutral reportage.

And yet, as of this writing, there are paradoxes. Libel actions are being brought against the media in record numbers. Judgments in six figures have become commonplace, and a few have survived appeal. Moreover, the costs of taking a libel action to trial have soared, largely because of the necessity of proving some degree of fault on the part of the defendant. Plaintiffs, relying on the Supreme Court's decision in *Herbert* v. *Lando,* conduct a searching inquiry into every phase of the editorial process. Reporters and editors can be required to recreate every step of the process that led to the completed story and to justify their editorial decisions. This takes large amounts of time, not only for the journalists involved, but for the lawyers for both sides. Thus, it is expensive. If these pretrial fact-finding procedures do not clearly establish a lack of fault on the defendant's part, the latter has no option except to try to settle out of court or go to trial, which can be even more expensive.

Thus in 1985 the *New York Times* rule, as supplemented by *Gertz,* was under fire from both sides. Victims of allegedly defamatory material in the media argued that the rules make it too difficult, and expensive, for them to clear their names. Even when they have established that they were victims of false and defamatory statements, they may still lose because they can't prove actual malice, as happened to Ariel Sharon. Defendants argue that they are put to great expense to counter libel suits because the focus is not so much on the nature of the offending item, as on editorial processes. Publishers and broadcasters see this not only as an intrusion into an area protected by the First Amendment, but as a potential damper on editorial vigor. Reports in the trade press indicate that some editors are discouraging investigative reporting because of the desire to avoid controversial stories.

In the Professional World

The lunch table topic was libel. "We get a libel suit filed against us almost every week," said an editor of a major metropolitan daily newspaper in the southeastern states. She may have been exaggerating, but maybe not. In Philadelphia, early in 1985, fifteen public officials had filed nineteen separate libel actions against newspapers, magazines, and broadcasting stations. Eugene L. Roberts, Jr., executive editor of the *Philadelphia Inquirer*, whose newspaper was the target of several of those suits, pointed out in his William Allen White Lecture at the University of Kansas that those officials were immune from libel suits because they enjoyed absolute privilege.[146] He argued that journalists ought to have a similar privilege when they write or talk about such officials. Under the actual-malice provision of *New York Times*, he said, officials are relying on the heavy costs of defending libel actions to intimidate their critics into silence. Roberts quoted several publishers who told him this is what had happened to them. One said, "I can't jeopardize my family business on balance against my First Amendment responsibilities as a publisher."

At about the same time Roberts was speaking in Kansas, retired General William C. Westmoreland wrote about libel, but in a different vein, for the *New York Times*.[147] After 110 days of trial, the general had just settled a libel action against CBS News. He had asked for $120 million, he and his backers having spent $3 million on the case; CBS had spent in excess of $15 million. Westmoreland received only a brief public statement by CBS acknowledging that he had conducted himself faithfully as the commander of troops in Vietnam. The statement said the network "never intended to assert, and does not believe" that he "was unpatriotic or disloyal in performing his duties as he saw them." But CBS also said it continued to stand behind the accuracy of its broadcast. At the time, Westmoreland said that if CBS had been willing to make a similar statement immediately after that telecast, he would have been satisfied.

However, the article in the *Times* left little doubt that the general still believed that a CBS documentary, "The Uncounted Enemy: A Vietnam Deception," had hit him below the belt. He called it "biased, misleading—far from objective." While he defended the right of the media "to expose misdeeds, bad judgments, acts against the public interest," Westmoreland also said that there are times when overzealous reporters or producers get carried away and come up with "what one would consider irresponsible reporting." In his instance, the documentary had accused him of "cooking the books," of lying to the president and Congress about enemy troop strength in Vietnam so that they would continue to support an immoral and unwinnable war. The general's decision to settle came after two of his former high-ranking colleagues in Vietnam had testified that the estimates of enemy troop strength he reported to Washington were not always what his subordinates had reported to him.

That did not take away evidence, produced by CBS News itself, that the documentary was biased, and that its producer had violated network policies in preparing it. Estimates of enemy troop strength in wartime, especially when guerrillas are involved, as in Vietnam, are always suspect. Commanders can alter such figures as an exercise of judgment, and CBS had interviewed persons of

---

146. Eugene L. Roberts, Jr., "On Collision Course," *Quill*, April 1985, excerpted from William Allen White Lecture at Kansas University, 8 February 1985. Cover and pp. 14 + .
147. William C. Westmoreland, "A Court's No Forum," *New York Times*, 24 February 1985.

stature who upheld Westmoreland. Their views were not included in the documentary. One witness who had opposed Westmoreland was given an opportunity to revise his taped interview in order to make it more damning. All of this and more was disclosed when Westmoreland's lawyer won pretrial discovery of CBS's staff investigation of complaints about the documentary.

Westmoreland's experience, and that of other public persons who have felt compelled to bring libel suits, makes a point. Even without the protection of the absolute privilege urged by Roberts, there are times when the media do offer falsehoods as fact. Sometimes this happens as the result of honest mistake. Sources do lie, or draw wrong conclusions from circumstantial evidence. But there are also occasions when the best professionals go with a story before they have pursued every lead to its end. This can happen even when journalists are trying hard to be fair and accurate. It is more likely to happen, however, when the pursuit of the story begins with the premise that its participants are up to no good. It also is more likely to happen when the goal is a story with "impact," defined as a story that will attract attention or win a prestigious journalism prize. When such stories defame individuals, high or low, what are the victims to do?

Westmoreland's first response was to call a news conference. It went largely unnoticed. His next step was a lawsuit. That ended inconclusively, with both sides bloodied. In retrospect, the general recalled that "many responsible editors and reporters" once supported the National News Council, which offered a powerless forum in which persons who believed themselves victims of unfair reporting could air their complaint and get a decision. But the council died because it could not win cooperation from some of the most powerful media institutions. That left General Westmoreland with the hope, shared with "many of my friends and supporters," that "in the future producers, writers and editors will demonstrate a greater sense of responsibility in dealing with issues of historical importance."

He has a point. Libel cannot be seen strictly as a legal problem. If the legal principles developed in the aftermath of *New York Times* and *Gertz* are applied strictly by the courts, public officials and public figures are not likely to win many lawsuits against the media. They will do so only in those instances in which communicators are caught in a knowing lie or in a grievous departure from accepted standards of journalism. Private individuals can prevail only if they can prove a careless violation of professional standards. By either of these tests, persons who have been the victims of demonstrably false assertions of fact can be left without compensation. But they can make it expensive for the media to win.

This suggests, then, that libel has become as much a question of ethics as of law. Is the public interest served by dissemination of false assertions? Do invective and name-calling, no matter how attention-getting, advance public debate on important issues? Does a biased story do any more than feed the public view that the media use the First Amendment as a shield for an arrogant abuse of power? Such questions are being confronted by editors, not only because of the number of libel actions, but in response to polls showing that media credibility with the public is low. This is especially true of newspapers. So serious was the concern with credibility in the mid-1980s that both the American Society of Newspaper Editors and the Associated Press Managing Editors Association commissioned major studies aimed at finding and correcting the causes of the problem. Both studies showed major differences between the public's assessment of the care journalists take to make certain that stories are correct and journalists' evaluation of their own performance. One conclusion that emerged from the APME study, and another conducted at about the same time for the *Los Angeles Times* by its media reporter, David Shaw, was that reporters and editors must not only set higher standards of professional performance—and stick to them—but must tell people how they do their jobs.[148] Noting that the news media are perceived as powerful institutions, Shaw argued that they should perform with the same degree of openness they demand from the institutions they cover. In his view, journalists ought to tell their audience how they developed controversial stories and why those stories took the form they did. Of course, this is precisely what plaintiffs' lawyers ask for when they file a libel action.

A study by three University of Iowa professors of libel plaintiffs, and of all libel and privacy cases decided between 1974 and 1984, suggests that such openness might help if it was coupled with a greater willingness to admit the occasional serious mistake.[149] The study showed that most libel plaintiffs believed they were the victims of a harmful falsehood, and that they went to court only after they had sought a correction and been rebuffed, sometimes rudely. In a summary of their findings, the authors said, "In a significant proportion of the cases, the *way* people were treated when they contacted the media seems to account for, or be a factor in, their anger and decision to sue." The authors attributed such treatment to a defensive attitude that seems inherent in the news business. Journalists spend so much of their time under pressure—from deadlines, from those attempting to get self-serving trivia into the news, and from others trying to prevent dissemination of real news—that they take pride in a tough independence. They especially like to show their independence to pressure from the sources most likely to bring libel suits—public officials, and persons, frequently in business, who have become powerful in the community. Journalists also share the human tendency to resist admitting mistakes. With journalists this tendency is compounded by the fact that an admission of mistake must be shared with the public. James D. Squires, editor of the *Chicago Tribune*, told the authors of the Iowa study:

> The people who sue us either are jerks looking into a deep pocket and never getting anywhere, so they're not that big of a problem—they're a nuisance—or people who are forced to sue us because we ignore them and kick them and refuse to deal with them.

Not surprisingly, the study recommended that media managers might reduce their vulnerability to libel actions if they took time to train reporters and editors in human relations. All of this suggests that in the real world, libel is being

---

148. "APME Credibility Research: What the Research Means," presentation by panel comprised of Roberto Goizueta, chairman of the board. Coca-Cola Co.; Norman Isaacs, former chairman, National News Council; and David Shaw, media reporter, *Los Angeles Times*, at the Associated Press Managing Editors Association's annual meeting in San Francisco, 29 October 1985.
149. Gilbert Cranberg, "Fanning the Fire: The Media's Role in Libel Litigation," *Iowa Law Review*, October 1985, pp. 221–25.

recognized as a problem that is as much a matter of ethics—of how people should be treated—as it is a matter of law.

---

1. With what is the law of defamation concerned? Distinguish between libel and slander; between libel *per se* and libel *per quod*.

2. At common law, what elements needed to be present in order to establish grounds for a lawsuit in defamation?

3. For purposes of a libel action, "defamation" has a precise legal meaning. What is it? What cannot be defamatory?

4. Outline the Supreme Court's decision in *New York Times* v. *Sullivan*. What effect did it have on the common law of defamation?

5. What are the meanings of the terms "public official," "public figure," and "public issue" as they relate to the law of defamation?

6   Outline the Supreme Court's decision in *Gertz* v. *Robert Welch, Inc.* What has been its principal effect on the law of defamation?

7. If you were a public official or public figure, what elements would you have to establish in order to bring a successful suit for libel? As a private individual, what would you have to establish?

8. With reference to the law of libel, distinguish between opinion and invective.

9. With reference to the criteria established by the Supreme Court, distinguish between public figures and private individuals. What is a public controversy?

10. What is "actual malice"? What legal standard must be met in proving it? Illustrate with a reference to a case in which actual malice was found.

11. How have courts defined "negligence" with respect to libel suits? What standard of care, if any, has been established in your state?

12. With respect to libel suits, what is the meaning of "absolute privilege"? Of "qualified privilege"? In what kinds of situations might they be used?

13. What is meant by the privilege of "neutral reportage"? What cautions must be observed with respect to it?

14. Define "harm" with respect to a libel suit. What is the significance of the term?

15. What is a retraction? What is its significance?

INVASION OF PRIVACY

When television cameras zoom in on people who have just learned that their friends or relatives were victims of an airplane crash, or when newspapers report, without apparent reason, that the man who deflected a shot aimed at the president is a homosexual, many people ask why. Are not such examples of journalistic enterprise an invasion of privacy?

It is not easy to answer that question when it is raised by critics of media performance. Twentieth-century law indeed recognizes that people have a right to be left alone. Persons who suffer humiliation or embarrassment because of the acts of others have a legal right of redress in most states. Problems arise, however, because the law varies widely from state to state and because the law recognizes that at some point an individual's asserted right to privacy limits the media's First Amendment right to inform the public. The problem is further compounded by a wide difference between the perception of the general public and that of media professionals as to what is an **invasion of privacy.** Polls show, for instance, that substantial majorities of the public think it is an invasion of privacy to publish photographs of accident victims, to report that a person committed suicide, or to give the addresses of burglary victims.[1] Obviously, the news media do all these things. It is equally obvious that none of them violate the law. Other studies show, however, that one factor in the media's low credibility with the public comes from the perception that journalists are invaders of privacy.[2]

This perception has resulted in lawsuits directed at the media, although by no means as frequently as libel actions. Nor have plaintiffs had the same degree of success. Major privacy judgments against media professionals are rare. However, the number of actions, and their nature, make privacy law a major area of concern not only for newspapers and television, but for photographers, advertisers, and public relations professionals as well.

Unlike the law of defamation, which has roots at least seven hundred years old, the law of privacy is of fairly recent origin. It was not recognized as a branch of tort law until early in this century, and has been recognized in some states only in the last decade. It is a product of both common law and statutes. Also unlike the law of defamation, it has not been federalized, nor has it been brought into the realm of First Amendment law, except in one of its aspects. Therefore, the law of privacy, to a greater extent than the law of defamation, varies from state to state. However, a few reasonably clear principles have been established by court decisions, and these will be the subject of this chapter.

The common law of privacy is concerned primarily with exploitation of the individual by the news media, by advertisers, and by public relations practitioners. Lawsuits can be brought by persons who believe that others have poked too deeply into their private lives, exposing facts that have caused them needless embarrassment. If such exposure is held not to be newsworthy, the plaintiff can win a judgment for damages. If facts are gathered by journalists who use intrusive methods—who go onto private property in pursuit of a story, or use hidden cameras or microphones—there may be a cause of action. In such instances, plaintiffs can recover damages even though the **intrusion** resulted in a bona-fide news story. Libel plaintiffs can recover damages only if they can

---

1. Sam Cremin, "Public Tells When News Media Invade Privacy," *Editor & Publisher*, 19 May 1979, p. 13.
2. *Journalists and Readers: Bridging the Credibility Gap*, commissioned by the Associated Press Managing Editors Association and conducted by MORI Research, Inc., Minneapolis, October 1985.

prove they have been victims of false and defamatory assertions of fact. Privacy plaintiffs can recover if an overly favorable story portrays them in a **false light** that would be embarrassing to a person of ordinary sensibilities. Finally, privacy law recognizes that people have a property right in their names and portraits. Thus, advertisers who rely on endorsements or on likenesses of real people to sell their products open themselves to privacy actions. In recent times, this branch of the tort has been expanded to protect performers or other famous persons from being exploited without their consent.

Government, too, has become involved in protecting privacy. States have enacted laws permitting persons who have been arrested and even convicted of crime, but who have gone straight, to expunge or seal the records dealing with their offenses. This has made it difficult in some instances for journalists to investigate allegations or wrongdoing, or the performance of prosecutors and judges.

Because of the nature of privacy law, none of the cases have the stature of *New York Times* v. *Sullivan* or *Gertz* v. *Robert Welch, Inc.* Rather, this chapter will present a number of significant cases, each of which illustrates one or more of the general principles mentioned above.

Major Cases

Bahr v. *Statesman Journal Co.* 624 P.2d 664 (Oreg.App. 1981).

Cantrell v. *Forest City Publishing Co.*, 419 U.S. 245, 95 S.Ct. 465, 42 L.Ed.2d 419 (1974).

Carson v. *Here's Johnny Portable Toilets*, 698 F.2d 831 (6th Cir. 1983).

Cher v. *Forum International, Ltd.*, 692 F.2d 634 (9th Cir. 1982).

Cox Broadcasting Co. v. *Cohn*, 420 U.S. 469, 95 S.Ct. 1029, 43 L.Ed.2d 328 (1975).

Diaz v. *Oakland Tribune, Inc.*, 188 Cal.Rptr. 762 (Calif.App. 1983).

Dietemann v. *Time Inc.*, 284 F.Supp. 925 (C.D.Calif. 1968), 449 F.2d 245 (9th Cir. 1971).

Galella v. *Onassis*, 487 F.2d 986 (2d Cir. 1973).

Jenkins v. *Dell Publishing Co.*, 251 F.2d 447 (3d Cir. 1958).

Kimbrough v. *Coca-Cola/USA*, 521 S.W.2d 719 (Tex.App. 1975).

National Bank of Commerce v. *Shaklee Corp.*, 503 F.Supp. 533 (W.D.Tex. 1980).

New Bedford Standard-Times Publishing Co. v. *Clerk of Third Dist. Court*, 387 N.E.2d 110 (Mass. 1979).

Newspapers, Inc., v. *Breier*, 279 N.W.2d 179 (Wis. 1979).

Oklahoma Publishing Co. v. *District Court in and for Oklahoma County*, 430 U.S. 308, 97 S.Ct. 1045, 51 L.Ed.2d 355 (1977).

Pearson v. *Dodd*, 410 F.2d 701 (D.C.Cir. 1969).

Shields v. *Gross*, 7 Med.L.Rptr. 2349 (Sup.Ct. N.Y.Co. 1981), modified, 451 N.Y.S. 419 (N.Y.App. 1982), affirmed as modified, 448 N.E.2d 108 (N.Y. 1983), 503 F.Supp. 533 (S.D.N.Y. 1983).

Sidis v. *F-R Publishing Corp.*, 113 F.2d 806 (2d Cir. 1940).

Smith v. *Daily Mail Publishing Co.*, 443 U.S. 97, 99 S.Ct. 2667, 61 L.Ed.2d 399 (1979).

Time Inc. v. *Hill*, 385 U.S. 374, 87 S.Ct. 534, 17 L.Ed.2d 456 (1967).

Virgil v. *Time Inc.*, 527 F.2d 1122 (9th Cir. 1975).

Zacchini v. *Scripps-Howard Broadcasting*, 433 U.S. 562, 97 S.Ct. 2849, 53 L.Ed.2d 965 (1977).

The Law of Privacy

Unlike libel law, which traces its lineage through at least six centuries of common law, the law of privacy is one of the few fields of law that can date its birth to a law journal article. The courts have drawn many of its principles from an article written by two Boston lawyers, Samuel D. Warren and Louis D. Brandeis, published in the *Harvard Law Review* in 1890.[3] Twenty-six years later, Brandeis was appointed to the Supreme Court of the United States, where his concern with privacy was reflected in some of his opinions.

When the article was written, Warren and Brandeis were young lawyers with entrée to Boston's top social circles. In their opinion, journalists were devoting too much attention to what happened in those circles. They wrote in protest:

> Instantaneous photographs and newspaper enterprise have invaded the sacred precincts of private and domestic life; and numerous mechanical devices threaten to make good the prediction that "what is whispered in the closet shall be proclaimed from the house-tops." . . .
>
> Of the desirability—indeed the necessity—of some . . . protection there can be, it is believed, no doubt. The press is overstepping in every direction the obvious bounds of propriety and decency. Gossip is no longer the resource of the idle and vicious, but has become a trade, which is pursued with industry as well as effrontery. To satisfy a prurient taste the details of sexual relations are spread broadcast in the columns of the daily papers. To occupy the indolent, column upon column is filled with idle gossip, which can only be procured by intrusion upon the domestic circle. The intensity and complexity of life, attendant upon advancing civilization, have rendered necessary some retreat from the world, and man, under the refining of influence of culture, has become more sensitive to publicity, so that solitude and privacy have become more essential to the individual; but modern enterprise and invention have, through invasions of his privacy, subjected him to mental pain and distress, far greater than could be inflicted by mere bodily injury.

---

3. Samuel D. Warren and Louis D. Brandeis, "The Right to Privacy," 4 *Harvard Law Review* 193, 15 December 1890.

The article suggested that the same principles that give property owners the right to protect their houses and lands from trespassers should give all persons the right to protect themselves from intrusion into their private affairs. The authors argued for a right to be left alone, for a right to control the extent to which others can pry into an individual's private life.

Within a decade, courts began to recognize such a right. Some of the early cases were decided on the theory of trespass, as the authors had suggested. Others were decided on the theory that an individual's identity is a form of property that the individual can control.

Some courts rejected the Warren and Brandeis reasoning, most notably the New York Court of Appeals in *Roberson* v. *Rochester Folding Box Co.*[4] The action had been brought by a young woman whose portrait was used without her permission to advertise flour. She won an order from a trial court preventing further use of her likeness, but the appeals court reversed, holding it could find no precedents to support a right of privacy. The legislature reacted in 1903 by enacting a law designed to prevent such exploitation.[5]

Today, eleven other states have statutes defining conditions under which individuals can bring suit for invasion of privacy. They are California, Florida, Massachusetts, Nebraska, Oklahoma, Rhode Island, Tennessee, Utah, Virginia, Washington, and Wisconsin. The statutes in Florida, Oklahoma, and Tennessee pertain only to protection of individuals from commerical exploitation.

In most, but not all, of the states not listed here, courts have established a common-law right of privacy. Indeed, in some of the listed states, courts have also recognized a supplemental common-law right of privacy.[6] Common law is court-made law. It is a product of court decisions, based on custom and a sense of what's right, in specific cases. Statute law is enacted by legislative bodies. An important difference is that courts interpreting statute law are bound by the language approved by the legislature. If that is not clear, they must try to determine the legislative intent. Common law is more flexible, leaving courts free to adapt to changing conditions. In large part, the law of privacy has developed largely as common law—through court decisions recognizing that people have an inherent right to be left alone.

The Four Elements of Invasion of Privacy

The phrase "invasion of privacy" seems simple, but under legal analysis in the courts it has proved to be highly complex. So much so that William L. Prosser, who for twenty years or so was a leading authority on torts law, finally concluded that invasion of privacy is not one tort but a bundle of four. His conclusions still are embodied in *Restatement of Torts*:[7]

---

4. 64 N.E. 442 (N.Y. 1903).
5. New York Civil Rights Law §§50–51.
6. Victor A. Kovner, "Recent Developments in Intrusion, Private Facts, False Light and Commercialization Claims," *Communications Law 1985* (New York: Practising Law Institute, 1985), pp. 563–92.
7. 3rd ed., 1964, vol. 3, §652a, p. 832.

The law of privacy comprises four distinct kinds of invasion of four different interests of the plaintiff which are tied together by the common name, but otherwise have almost nothing in common except that each represents an interference with the right of the plaintiff "to be let alone."

The four kinds of invasion comprising the law of privacy include:

(1) intrusion upon the plaintiff's physical and mental solitude or seclusion,

(2) public disclosure of private facts,

(3) publicity which places the plaintiff in a false light in the public eye,

(4) appropriation, for the defendant's benefit or advantage, of the plaintiff's name or likeness."

The summaries below point up the differences between the four elements that combine under the term "invasion of privacy."

Intrusion into Mental or Physical Solitude

Intrusion into a person's mental or physical solitude is closely related to the trespass mentioned by Warren and Brandeis. It involves entry without permission into another's private space. In 1983, an Oklahoma court upheld trespass convictions against reporters and photographers who followed antinuclear demonstrators onto a utility company's property.[8] Journalists who use subterfuge to gain entrance to a private home are vulnerable to suit as intruders. A photographer who harasses a newsworthy subject may also be an intruder. So may an eavesdropper or wiretapper. Publication is not an essential element in an action for intrusion. Courts have held that the harm lies in the act of intrusion itself. Some courts have rejected the argument that a First Amendment right to gather news ought to justify an intrusion, while others have held that the reporter's First Amendment interest must be balanced against the victim's right of privacy.

By 1985, thirty states and the District of Columbia had recognized intrusion as a cause of action in cases involving the news media, either by common law or by statute. They are Arkansas, California, Colorado, Connecticut, Florida, Georgia, Illinois, Indiana, Iowa, Kansas, Kentucky, Louisiana, Maine, Maryland, Massachusetts, Mississippi, Missouri, Nebraska, New Jersey, New Mexico, New York, Nevada, Oklahoma, Oregon, Pennsylvania, Rhode Island, Utah, Virginia, Washington, and Wisconsin.[9]

Disclosure of Private Fact

A disclosure of private fact occurs when some medium of communication disseminates personal information that the individual involved did not want made public. The information must be of a nature that would be offensive to a person of ordinary sensibilities. California courts held, for example, that a newspaper column commenting on a college student-body leader's sex-change operation was a disclosure of embarrassing private fact.[10] Disclosure is the only media-related tort for which truth is not an absolute

---

8. Stahl v. Oklahoma, 665 P.2d 839 (Okla.Ct.Crim.App. 1983).
9. Kovner, "Recent Developments," pp. 563–92.
10. Diaz v. Oakland Tribune, Inc., 188 Cal.Rptr. 762 (Calif.App. 1983).

defense. However, if the facts at issue are held to be newsworthy, or are taken from the public record of a court or other governmental agency, publication is not an invasion of privacy. The principal problem with this branch of the tort lies in defining what is newsworthy. Some courts leave this determination to a jury. Generally, courts have taken a broad view of newsworthiness, as we will see later in this chapter. However, a federal judge, ruling in a case involving publication of a nude photo, said, "I am not persuaded that a woman taking a bath is newsworthy."[11]

By 1985, disclosure of private fact had been recognized as an actionable tort, either through cases involving the media or by statute, in thirty-eight states and the District of Columbia. The states are Alabama, Arizona, Arkansas, California, Colorado, Connecticut, Delaware, Florida, Georgia, Idaho, Indiana, Iowa, Kansas, Kentucky, Louisiana, Maine, Maryland, Massachusetts, Michigan, Mississippi, Missouri, New Hampshire, New Jersey, New Mexico, New York, Nevada, Ohio, Oklahoma, Oregon, Pennsylvania, Rhode Island, South Carolina, Tennessee, Texas, Vermont, Washington, Wisconsin, and Wyoming.[12] However, in all but a few of the reported cases, courts held that publication was justified, either because the facts in question were newsworthy or because they had been found in a public record.

False Light

By definition, a person can be put in a false light only through publicity. He or she must be the subject of a publication, film, or broadcast that distorts his or her personality. Thus, this branch of the tort is related to defamation, and at some point merges into it. Short of that point, a false-light action can be based on neutral or even flattering statements. A baseball pitcher, a member of the sport's Hall of Fame, was able to stop publication of a book that falsely portrayed him as a war hero.[13] The essential element is that individuals must be portrayed as something other than they are to the point of embarrassment. To portray a Unitarian as a fundamentalist member of the Moral Majority, or vice versa, would defame neither, but probably would embarrass both. Such portrayal, then, could result in an action for false-light invasion of privacy.

In two cases brought by private individuals, the Supreme Court held that false-light plaintiffs must prove actual malice—knowledge of falsity or reckless disregard for the truth—if they were to prevail. Both preceded *Gertz*, and the Supreme Court has had no occasion since to rule on whether private individuals may prevail on a lesser showing of fault. However, in recent cases, courts in some states have held that private false-light plaintiffs need prove only negligence. The point is that courts treat false-light actions much like actions in libel, which means that the First Amendment stands as a strong barrier against a successful suit.

By 1985, false-light invasion of privacy had been recognized as an actionable tort, either through cases involving the media or by statute, in thirty-five states and the District of Columbia. The states are Alabama, Arizona, Arkansas, California, Connecticut, Florida, Georgia, Idaho, Illinois, Indiana, Iowa, Kansas, Kentucky, Louisiana, Maine, Maryland, Massachusetts, Michigan, Nebraska, New Jersey, New Mexico, New York,

11. McCabe v. Village Voice, 550 F.Supp. 525 (E.D.Pa. 1982).
12. Kovner, "Recent Developments," pp. 563-92.
13. Spahn v. Julian Messner, 18 N.Y.2d 324 (N.Y. 1966); 21 N.Y.2d 124 (N.Y. 1967).

Nevada, Ohio, Oklahoma, Oregon, Pennsylvania, Rhode Island, South Carolina, South Dakota, Texas, Virginia, Washington, West Virginia, and Wyoming.[14]

Appropriation and the Right of Publicity

Appropriation involves the unauthorized use of one person's name or likeness to benefit another. Commonly, such use occurs in an advertisement or in other promotional material designed to help the user make a profit. Thus, it is of particular importance to advertising and public relations professionals. Courts act on the theory that a person whose identity has been used without consent to sell a product is entitled to a share of the user's profit. Advertisers can avoid a lawsuit for appropriation by getting written consent from any person whose name or likeness will appear in an advertisement or other promotional material. In effect, such consent is a **contract,** which can be drawn broadly to cover any use, or narrowly to cover a specific use. Usually, the contract includes a schedule of fees to be paid to the person whose name or likeness is used.

In recent years, courts have been broadening the scope of appropriation to cover what is called the right of publicity. In defining this right, courts have recognized that entertainers, athletes, actors, and others whose names become household words acquire an identity that is of value and can be protected against unauthorized exploitation by others. In a few instances, courts have held that such protection can prevail even against a use by the news media, thus raising serious First Amendment questions.

As of 1985, the right to protect one's name or likeness against misappropriation by others had been recognized in thirty-eight states and the District of Columbia. The states are Alabama, Alaska, Arizona, California, Connecticut, Florida, Georgia, Hawaii, Idaho, Illinois, Indiana, Iowa, Kansas, Kentucky, Louisiana, Maine, Maryland, Massachusetts, Michigan, Missouri, Montana, Nebraska, New Jersey, New Mexico, New York, Nevada, North Carolina, Ohio, Oklahoma, Oregon, Pennsylvania, South Dakota, Tennessee, Texas, Utah, Virginia, West Virginia, and Wisconsin.[15]

Invasions of privacy may thus occur in four quite different ways, but intrusion stands alone in that publication is not necessary. There can be no action for disclosure of private fact, false light, or appropriation unless there has been some sharing of information with the public.

The four branches also differ in the role truth plays as a defense. Truth is not a factor one way or the other in an intrusion case; the focus is on the alleged intruder's methods. Truth works against defendants in disclosure cases. The plaintiff has no cause of action unless the information at issue is true. Obviously, then, truth alone is not a defense. The defendant can prevail only if the facts were taken from a public record or are held to be newsworthy. However, truth is an absolute defense in a false-light action. Just as persons cannot be libeled by publication of the truth about them, neither can they be put in a false light by the truth. With appropriation, or violation of the right of publicity, as with intrusion, truth is not a factor, unless there is some question as to the identity of a likeness used in an advertisement. Once it has been established that an individual's name or likeness has been used for another's commercial gain, the only defense is proof that there was valid consent for that use.

---

14. Kovner, "Recent Developments," pp. 563-92.
15. Ibid.

Intrusion

From the earliest recorded days of Anglo-Saxon jurisprudence, courts have shown great respect for private property. This respect is recognized in two places in the Bill of Rights. The Third Amendment forbids the quartering of troops in private homes. The Fourth protects individuals and their property "against unreasonable searches and seizures." The sanctity of property has long been recognized in the law of trespass. Property owners can take action against those who enter their premises without consent. Intrusion, as grounds for a civil action in invasion of privacy, is an extension of the law of trespass.

Professional communicators who keep in mind the origins of this branch of privacy law use caution whenever it seems necessary to enter private property to obtain information or make a photograph. In most instances, there are no problems. Most people are willing to consider a request for an interview, whether for print or for broadcast. If the request is granted, it is usually accompanied by an invitation to enter the source's home, office, or place of business. The vast majority of requests for information raise no privacy questions. But when the possessor of vital information, or a person suspected of violating the law, is unwilling to be interviewed or photographed, there can be problems.

Intrusion by Deception

The classic intrusion case, *Dietemann* v. *Time, Inc.*, involved a most reluctant source, a plumber who was believed to be practicing medicine without a license. He worked in

Dietemann v. Time Inc.,
284 F. Supp. 425
(C.D.Calif. 1968), 449 F.2d
245 (9th Cir. 1971).

his home and was careful to admit only persons he knew or who were referred to him by someone he knew. When an editor in the Los Angeles bureau of *Life* magazine heard about the plumber, he assigned a female reporter and a male photographer to pose as husband and wife seeking treatment from him. The couple consulted the district attorney, who decided to use them to get information that could be used in a criminal prosecution. The reporter and photographer agreed to cooperate.

The reporter packed a radio transmitter in her handbag and the man wore a tie-clip camera. They gained admission to the plumber's home by posing as friends of previous clients. After an examination, the plumber told the reporter she had cancer as a result of eating rancid butter eleven years, nine months, and seven days earlier. He prescribed a cure of minerals, herbs, and other harmless substances. Every word was transmitted to a tape recorder in a police car parked nearby, while the photographer was getting pictures of the diagnostic process. The plumber was arrested and charged with practicing medicine without a license. He pleaded no contest.

Life's article appeared after the arrest but before the plea. The plumber sued for invasion of privacy, and a federal district court in Los Angeles awarded him $1,000 in damages. On appeal, the Court of Appeals, Ninth Circuit, affirmed.

Both courts recognized there was a public interest in stopping Dietemann's crude practice of medicine, but they held that that did not justify the intrusion. The court of appeals condemned the *Life* team's reporting methods in strong terms:

Although the issue has not been squarely decided in California, we have little difficulty in concluding that clandestine photography of the plaintiff in his den and the recordation and transmission of his conversation without his consent resulting in his emotional distress warrants recovery for invasion of privacy. . . .

Plaintiff's den was a sphere from which he could reasonably expect to exclude eavesdropping newsmen. He invited two of defendant's employees to the den. One who invites another to his home or office takes a risk that the visitor may not be what he seems, and that visitor may repeat all he hears and observes when he leaves. But he does not and should not be required to take the risk that what is heard and seen will be transmitted by photograph or recording, or in our modern world, in full living color and hi-fi to the public at large or to any segment of it that the visitor may select.

Life's lawyers argued that the First Amendment protected the gathering of news as well as its dissemination. They argued that cameras and recording devices have become "indispensable tools" in investigative reporting. The court swept this argument aside:

The First Amendment has never been construed to accord newsmen immunity from torts or crimes committed during the course of newsgathering. The First Amendment is not a license to trespass, to steal, or to intrude by electronic means into the precincts of another's home or office. It does not become such a license simply because the person subjected to the intrusion is reasonably suspected of committing a crime.

The court thus condemned several methods that might be used by reporters who believe anything goes in pursuit of a good story. Foremost was the use of deception to gain entrance to Dietemann's house. There, if anywhere, he had the greatest expectation of privacy. While it was true that he also used his house as a medical office of sorts, it likewise was true that he normally accepted patients only if he knew them or knew someone who would vouch for them. Two other tools of the investigative reporter, the hidden microphone connected by radio to a tape recorder and the hidden camera, also were condemned by the court. We will see that there are times when reporters legally may use both. But in this instance, they were faulted because they were used in conjunction with an improper entry into private property.

The Camera and Intrusion

Photographers safely may use a camera to record anything they can see from a public place, provided they don't make nuisances of themselves. If people want to take off their clothes, or make fools of themselves in other ways, in places that can be seen from a public street or other public property, they are fair game. It needs to be emphasized that the subjects of such photographs must have done whatever it was they did of their own volition. But when photographers go onto private property to take their photographs, or harass their subjects, they may be open to an action in intrusion.

CBS News lost an action for criminal trespass because a camera crew entered an expensive French restaurant, Le Mistral, in New York City with camera running. Some of the videotape later used on WCBS-TV showed the restaurant's staff trying to eject the crew. Here, as in *Dietemann*, there was a reason for the intrusion. The restaurant was one of several cited by the New York City Health Service Administration for alleged health code violations. CBS was doing a news story on those violations.

The owners of Le Mistral did not like the way their restaurant was portrayed. They sued CBS for libel, false-light invasion of privacy, and trespass. A judge dismissed the first two counts, but in *Le Mistral* v. *Columbia Broadcasting System*,[16] decided in 1978, denied a motion to dismiss the trespass claim. Noting that the crew had entered the restaurant with no intention of eating and without permission to take photographs, he commented, "Patronizing a restaurant does not carry with it an obligation to appear on television." An appeals court sustained a $1,500 judgment against CBS.

While restaurants, like other businesses that cater to the public, normally are open to all, the New York courts held that those who patronize them retain some expectation of privacy. But when private property can be seen from public property, or a place normally open to the public, the camera may safely record what happens there. The Louisiana Supreme Court held in 1979, for instance, that the *Crowley Post-Signal* did not intrude when it published a photograph of one of the city's older homes along with a caption referring to it as "a bit weather worn and unkempt."[17] The photo had been taken from the street. In 1981, the Washington Supreme Court came to a similar conclusion in a privacy action against KING Broadcasting.[18] The action was brought by a pharmacist who was charged with fraud. When the pharmacist refused to be interviewed, a KING-TV camera operator stood in an alley alongside the store and photographed him through a window. Because the alley was open to the public, the court held there was no intrusion. The pharmacist could have been seen by anyone passing by.

Courts in Florida and Indiana have held that there are times when photographers safely may go onto private property in pursuit of a story. In both instances, the premises were under control of city officials during an emergency. The Florida case, *Florida Publishing Co.* v. *Fletcher*,[19] decided by the state's supreme court in 1976, involved a newspaper photographer who covered a fatal fire. He had gone with firefighters into a house where a young girl had died from smoke inhalation. A fire marshal asked the photographer to record the scene for the department's investigatory file. One of the photos was published in the photographer's paper, the *Florida Times-Union*. The girl's mother, who was not at home at the time of the fire, sued the newspaper for intrusion. In holding that she had no cause of action, the supreme court noted that photographers and reporters customarily accompanied police and firefighters to newsworthy events. The court held that this implied the latter's consent when an entry to private property occurred. In this instance, the fire marshal, not the dead girl's mother, was in control of the house during the fire. Thus, there was no illegal intrusion.

The same reasoning was used by a trial court in Indianapolis in 1976 when it held that a WISH-TV crew had not intruded during police investigation of a murder and attempted suicide.[20] The officer in charge had permitted the crew to enter the house and record the scene. In directing a verdict for the station, the judge noted that the event was a matter of public interest. Further, the police, not the owner, were in control of the premises at the time.

The narrow limits of these decisions are pointed up by an Oklahoma appellate court's

16. 402 N.Y.S.2d 815 (1st Dept. 1978).
17. Jaubert v. Crowley Post-Signal, Inc., 375 So.2d 1386 (La. 1979).
18. Mark v. KING Broadcasting, 635 P.2d 1081 (Wash. 1981).
19. 340 So.2d 914 (Fla. 1976).
20. Hoosier State Press Association, *Bulletin*, No. 26, 28 June 1976.

decision in the *Stahl* case mentioned earlier.[21] In that instance, photographers and reporters were arrested for following antinuclear demonstrators onto a utility company's property. The utility company had anticipated the demonstration and had set aside an area on its property for the news media. However, because the company was unhappy with coverage of a similar demonstration a year earlier, that area was out of sight of where guards and police confronted the demonstrators. The court rejected the argument that the utility's actions, coupled with the public interest in the event, justified the actions of the photographers and reporters who, along with the demonstrators, went over a fence to get into the property. Here, neither the company nor the police invited the intrusion.

In isolated instances, a photographer's methods, even in a public place, can reach nuisance level and thus become an intrusion. The classic example is found in *Galella* v. *Onassis*. The protagonists were Jacqueline Onassis, who first came to public attention as the wife and then the widow of President John F. Kennedy, and Ron Galella, a free-lance photographer who built a career on pictures of her and her family.

Galella v. *Onassis,* 353 F.Supp. 196 (S.D.N.Y. 1972); 487 F.2d 986 (2d Cir. 1973); 8 Med.L. Rptr. 1321 (S.D.N.Y. 1982).

The case report devotes several pages to a description of Galella's methods. Mrs. Onassis and her children, a son and daughter from her marriage to President Kennedy, could do little that Galella did not record on film and sell to various publications. He bumped into them in order to get interesting close-ups. He used telephoto lenses to record their actions when they sought refuge on private property. He would appear in the middle of the night to photograph Mrs. Onassis emerging from friends' apartments or to catch her with male friends.

Galella argued that the First Amendment gave him a right to take photographs of an admitted public figure like Mrs. Onassis. A federal district court in New York City conceded that she was indeed a public figure, but held:

> The First Amendment does not license Galella to trespass inside private buildings, such as the children's schools, lobbies of friends' apartment buildings and restaurants. Nor does that Amendment command that Galella be permitted to romance maids, bribe employees, and maintain surveillance in order to monitor defendant's leaving, entering, and living inside her home. . . . There is no general constitutional right to assault, harass, or unceasingly shadow or distress public figures.

The court ordered Galella to stay a specific distance away from Mrs. Onassis and her children, reduced on appeal to twenty-five feet from her and thirty feet from her children. In 1982, the district court found Galella in contempt for violating the terms of the order, giving him a choice between jail and an end to his photographic harassment. He chose the latter, promising never to take another picture of Mrs. Onassis "as long as I live."[22]

Tape Recording and Wiretapping

A reporter is within bounds, of course, in taking notes on a telephone conversation with a news source. Reporters in all media also commonly use tape devices to record

---

21. See note 8 above.
22. *Facts on File*, 18 June 1982, p. 447.

Photographer Ron Galella became the subject of an unusual court order in 1973 that restricted his right to take pictures of Jacqueline Onassis, widow of John F. Kennedy, and her children. Mrs. Onassis argued successfully that Galella's tactics invaded her privacy. He is shown here on the courthouse steps in New York City. (AP/Wide World Photos)

in-person interviews with news sources. But when a reporter uses a recording device without the source's consent, to record either a telephone conversation or an in-person interview, legal questions can be raised.

In the few cases arising out of the surreptitious recording of in-person interviews, the key question seems to be whether the subject had any expectation of privacy. In 1979, the United States Court of Appeals for the Eighth Circuit upheld dismissal of an intrusion action against a broadcasting station whose reporter had secretly recorded an interview with a prisoner in a city jail.[23] The court concluded that the prisoner, by pounding on bars and shouting loudly enough to be heard in the street, was seeking public attention.

23. Holman v. Central Arkansas Broadcasting, 610 F.2d 542 (8th Cir. 1979).

But in 1982, a federal district court in Illinois refused to dismiss an action against a TV crew that filmed an interview with a prisoner in his cell without his consent, even though the videotape was not used on the air.[24]

Wiretapping—the interception of a telephone conversation to which the reporter is not a party—is forbidden by federal law.[25] Violators can be fined up to $10,000 and sent to prison for as long as five years. The Federal Wiretap Statute does permit a party to a telephone call to tape-record without notice to the other party, but there is an exception that has been the subject of one court case. The exception makes it illegal to record "any wire or oral communication" without consent of the other party "for the purpose of committing any criminal or tortious act in violation of the United States Constitution or laws of the United States or of any State or for the purpose of committing any other injurious act."

In *Boddie v. ABC*, the United States Court of Appeals for the Sixth Circuit held in 1984 that this exception might have been violated by an episode of "20/20."[26] Producers of the ABC television news program were investigating allegations that an Ohio judge gave lenient sentences to female offenders in return for sex. One of the alleged participants agreed to be interviewed by an ABC reporter provided she was not videotaped. She alleged that ABC recorded the interview, using a hidden camera and microphone. She sued ABC for intrusion and false-light invasion of privacy. A jury returned a verdict for ABC. During litigation, the trial court held there had been no violation of the Federal Wiretap Statute. On appeal, the circuit court reversed, holding that because the plaintiff had established a valid cause of action against ABC for invasion of privacy, there was a triable issue of fact as to the news team's purpose. If that purpose was to commit a criminal, tortious, or illegal act, the law was violated. However, if the purpose was to preserve the woman's statements against future claims of distortion, there would be no cause of action. The record does not show what happened on remand. However, if the *Boddie* decision is followed in other jurisdictions, the purpose for which a surreptitious recording is made becomes an important factor. If it is done to harm a person who had not given permission, either direct or implied, to have the interview recorded, it could give rise not only to an action in intrusion, but a criminal action. However, the court also pointed out that recording to ensure the accuracy of the subsequent report is a lawful purpose.

The undisclosed use of tape recorders is further clouded by the fact that eleven states have laws prohibiting the secret recording of telephone conversations. They are California, Florida, Georgia, Illinois, Maryland, Massachusetts, Montana, New Hampshire, Oregon, Pennsylvania, and Washington.[27] Obviously, such laws are difficult to enforce because the violation can be disclosed only by the person who did the recording.

The cases make clear only that at some point, the use of surreptitious recording devices, audio or video, becomes an actionable intrusion. In the professional world, as we will see at the end of the chapter, the decision to resort to such methods is more a question of ethics than of law.

---

24. Smith v. Fairman, 98 F.R.D. 445 (C.D.Ill. 1982).
25. 18 U.S.C. §§2510–2520.
26. 731 F.2d 333 (6th Cir. 1984).
27. Kovner, "Recent Developments," p. 476.

Copied or Stolen Documents

Letters, reports, memoranda, and other written materials prepared by an individual are that person's private property. Like any property, they can be protected from theft. Looked at from the journalist's point of view, the information contained in documents may be something other than private property—it may be news. Can that news be made public without committing an intrusion? The answer is yes—provided that the reporter did not intrude in order to obtain it. Two cases involving the legendary investigative reporter and Washington columnist Drew Pearson make the point.

The first, *Liberty Lobby* v. *Pearson*,[28] decided by the United States Court of Appeals for the District of Columbia Circuit in 1968, involved information contained in documents stolen from a private lobbying organization and given to Jack Anderson, then Pearson's assistant. When the organization asked a federal court to prevent further publication of information taken from its files, the court refused to do so. On appeal, Warren Burger, then a circuit judge, held that Liberty Lobby was not entitled to relief unless it could prove that it owned the documents in Pearson's possession and could also show that either Pearson or Anderson had taken them from the files. Burger also held that there was a public interest in publication which, in a close case, would require a ruling in Pearson's favor.

The second case, *Pearson v. Dodd*, involved information taken from the files of a United States senator. Thomas Dodd of Connecticut was suspected of dipping into campaign funds to pay for his living expenses. Dis-

Pearson v. Dodd, 410 F.2d 701 (D.C.Cir. 1969).

gruntled members of his office staff copied documents supporting these suspicions and gave them to Pearson and Anderson, who published information taken from them. Dodd sued the columnists for intrusion and for conversion, the crime of using stolen property. A federal district court held that there had been a conversion, but an appeals court reversed, dismissing both counts of the lawsuit. It wrote:

> If we were to hold [Pearson and Anderson] liable for invasion of privacy on these facts, we would establish the proposition that one who received information from an intruder, knowing it has been obtained by improper intrusion, is guilty of a tort. In an untried and developing area of tort law, we are not prepared to go so far. A person approached by an eavesdropper would perhaps play the nobler part should he spurn the offer and shut his ears. However, it seems to us that at this point it would place too great a strain on human weakness to hold one liable in damages who merely succumbs to temptation and listens.

There was no conversion, the court held, because the documents themselves had never left Dodd's office. Thus, there had been no theft of property. The senator had not been deprived of the use of the documents, even though he had been embarrassed when the information they contained left his office through the magic of a handy copying machine.

To sum up, professional communicators run a risk of legal action when they enter a zone where another person has a legitimate expectation of privacy. The entry can be

---

28. 390 F.2d 489 (D.C.Cir. 1968).

physical and involve deception, as in *Dietemann,* or it can be an overt trespass, as in *Le Mistral.* However, we have seen that courts in some states have held that journalists who accompany police or firefighters onto private property are not intruders if they act with the consent of the officials. Normally, the camera can safely record whatever can be seen from a public place, but if a Ron Galella so persistently harasses a subject as to become a nuisance, a court may hold him to be an intruder.

The unannounced use of recording devices—concealed tape recorders, hidden video cameras, or recorders attached to a telephone—seems as much an ethical question as a legal one. The few cases seem to say that if the surreptitious recording enters a zone where the subject had an expectation of privacy, even though that zone might be a prison cell, it is an intrusion. The *Boddie* case also seems to say that surreptitious recording may even be a crime if its purpose is to harm the person whose words were recorded. But the same court said there can be no cause of action if the purpose was to ensure the accuracy of a report based on the encounter.

Information taken from copied, or even stolen, documents is fair game for journalists, provided the journalists themselves were not intruders. As the court of appeals said in *Pearson,* a reporter offered stolen information might "play the nobler part" by spurning the offer. But that court did not expect reporters to be noble. Nor did the Supreme Court in the Pentagon Papers case. Even though Justice Burger chastised the editors of the *New York Times* for not offering to return the obviously stolen secret documents to their owner, the Court said that any action for theft would have to be taken against someone other than the newspaper. The decisions thus recognize that there is a point at which the public's interest in the news must prevail. However, the cases also note an exception, pointed up most sharply in *Stahl:* Journalists who break the law in pursuit of a story can be expected to be treated like any other lawbreakers.

Disclosure of Embarrassing Private Fact

Courts have held that the news media can be required to pay damages to persons embarrassed by the publication of private facts. If such publication would "outrage the community's notions of decency," as measured by a jury, it can be an invasion of privacy. But courts have also held that the media cannot be found liable if the allegedly private facts, however outrageous, are newsworthy or are taken from a current public record. For journalists, the problem lies in the further holding by some courts that juries should decide when allegedly private facts become newsworthy. Thus, this branch of the tort is marked by considerable uncertainty. However, the news media have won more private-fact cases than they have lost. In the process, some guideposts have emerged to help journalists assess the hazards.

Constitutional Limits: Cox Broadcasting Co. v. Cohn

In the only private-fact case to reach the Supreme Court, the Court held that publication of facts found in the open records of a court cannot invade privacy. That holding has been broadened by subsequent decisions to cover matters found in the public records of any governmental agency. Further, the Supreme Court has indicated, in a decision not directly dealing with a privacy case, that the news media may safely use any "truthful information about a matter of public significance," provided it was obtained lawfully and does not violate "a state interest of the highest order."[29]

The Supreme Court, therefore, has given journalists some First Amendment protection in dealing with private-fact cases. The landmark decision is *Cox Broadcasting Co.* v. *Cohn*, decided in 1975. The case grew out of the rape and murder of a seventeen-year-old girl in Atlanta. In compliance with a state law making it a crime to publish or broadcast the name of a rape victim, the news media did not identify her. Eight months later, the six men accused of the crime appeared in court. As part of a plea bargain, five of them pleaded guilty to attempted rape. The sixth pleaded not guilty. A reporter for WSB-TV, the Cox station in Atlanta, was present. He asked the court clerk to show him the indictments so that he could get the names and the details of the charge correctly. Each indictment carried the victim's name, which the reporter also copied into his notes. On the news that evening, WSB-TV disclosed her name to the public for the first time.

Cox Broadcasting Co. v. *Cohn*, 420 U.S. 469, 95 S.Ct. 1029, 43 L.Ed.2d 328 (1975).

Normally, an action for disclosure of private fact can be brought only by the victim. But a provision in the Georgia statute forbidding publication of the name of a rape victim made it possible for close relatives to start a civil action in a deceased victim's behalf. Her father sued Cox Broadcasting for invasion of privacy, alleging disclosure of private fact. A trial court brushed aside First Amendment arguments and awarded summary judgment to the plaintiff, Cohn. The only question for the jury, the court ruled, was the amount of the judgment. Cox appealed, and the state supreme court upheld the verdict, ruling that the statute declared as state policy that a rape victim's name is not a matter of public concern. The statute, the state supreme court said, placed a limited, but legitimate, limitation on freedom of the press. Cox Broadcasting appealed to the United States Supreme Court, which took the case.

Justice Byron R. White, writing for himself and five other justices, focused the Court's decision on the question raised by the facts of the case: Could the news media be held liable for publishing facts found in the public records of a court? The majority held that a state neither can prevent such publication nor can it define such publication as an invasion of privacy. The Court gave two reasons for its holding:

1. The news media perform a valuable public service by covering news of government, including the courts. This is something few people have the time or the inclination to do for themselves. Therefore, the media, as surrogates for the general public, should not have needless limits placed on their coverage. In this instance, news of the crime of rape was of legitimate concern to the public.

2. Of particular importance is the right of the news media to report matters

---

29. Smith v. Daily Mail, 443 U.S. 97, 99 S.Ct. 2667, 61 L.Ed.2d 399 (1979).

on the public record. Courts have recognized "a privilege in the press to report the events of judicial proceedings." The majority concluded that there can be no liability for the accurate reporting of matters taken from public records, especially those of the courts.

Repeatedly, the Court emphasized that its holding was a narrow one, limited solely to the facts of this case. The Court held that the young woman's name was both on the public record and an element of a legitimate news event—a particularly brutal gang rape. Further, the majority made a point of noting that it was in no way limiting the authority of states to seal court records containing embarrassing facts. It noted that records of juvenile courts generally are considered private, subject to release only by a judge's order. Some states seal records in divorce and custody cases.

However, two subsequent decisions of the Supreme Court have raised questions as to whether even officially sealed records can protect the identity of victims of crimes, including rape. In 1979, in *Smith* v. *Daily Mail*,[30] the Court struck down a West Virginia law making it a crime for newspapers to publish the names of juvenile offenders. In that instance, the name of a junior high school student who shot another student to death in the school parking lot was obtained not from a public record but from police, a prosecutor, and other students at the scene. The Court noted that the name was obtained lawfully and that the juvenile was involved in "a matter of public significance." The Court held that the state's interest in seeking rehabilitation of juvenile offenders by shielding them from public knowledge was not sufficient to override the First Amendment interest in publication of offenders' names.

In 1982, in *Globe Newspapers* v. *Superior Court*,[31] the Court struck down a Massachusetts law excluding the news media from trials of sex crimes when minors were the victims. The Court held that the blanket exclusion swept too broadly. It indicated, however, that victims of sex crimes, particularly minors, might have a cause of action for disclosure under some circumstances. The Court also noted that in this instance, the names were "already in the public record." Left unsaid was whether protection of the victims of sex crimes from the trauma of public embarrassment is considered a state interest of sufficient importance to override a First Amendment interest in publication.

The ambiguity of the decision in *Globe Newspapers* indicates that how far the media can go in using the names of victims of sex crimes is more a matter of ethics than of law. That, at least, was the conclusion of a Florida appellate court in *Doe* v. *Sarasota-Bradenton Television*,[32] decided in 1983. The plaintiff, a rape victim, had been told that if she testified against her attacker, her name and photograph would not be published. However, when the case came to trial, the judge made no attempt to exclude or limit the media, and he permitted television coverage under rules of court in effect in Florida. The appellate court noted that, under the rules, the judge could have forbidden or limited photographers, and that the prosecutor could have asked him to do so. Because the judge did permit the televising of the victim's testimony, the appellate court held, she had no cause of action against the station for disclosure of private fact. However,

---

30. Ibid.
31. 457 U.S. 596, 102 S.Ct. 2613, 73 L.Ed.2d 248 (1982).
32. 9 Med.L.Rptr. 2074 (Fla.Ct.App.2d Dist. 1983).

the court strongly criticized the station's news director for being insensitive to the victim's plight.

While the Supreme Court in *Cox* carefully limited its holding to facts found in the public record of a court, the highest state courts in Kansas and Iowa have relied on its reasoning to hold that facts found in any public record cannot be the basis for an action in disclosure. The Kansas case, *Rawlins* v. *Hutchinson Publishing Co.*,[33] grew out of a newspaper's "Looking Backward" column. Such columns, found in many newspapers, are made up of brief summaries of stories appearing on the same date five, ten, twenty-five, or even fifty years earlier. In this instance, an item noted that ten years ago, Rawlins had been suspended from the police force while officials looked into a complaint that he had annoyed a woman. A few days later, the column noted that the city manager had fired the officer. In suing the newspaper for disclosure, Rawlins said he had lived an exemplary life since that episode, and that the publications recounting it had caused him and his family great embarrassment. A trial court held that he had no cause of action, and the state supreme court affirmed, holding that "under *Cox*, names, like facts, are in the public domain when available in public records. . . . Once facts become public the right of privacy ceases."

The Iowa case also involved a lapse in time, in this instance five years, but, unlike *Rawlins*, there had been no previous disclosure. In 1976, reporters for the *Des Moines Sunday Register* investigated allegations that residents of the Jasper County Home had died as a result of mistreatment. During their investigation, the reporters learned that a number of young women had been sterilized without their consent while they were wards of the home. The subsequent article identified one of them as Robbin Howard. Howard sued for disclosure, saying that she had lived a quiet life after she left the home among people who were not aware of her past. A state district court dismissed her suit, and the state supreme court affirmed in 1979 in *Howard* v. *Des Moines Register & Tribune*.[34] It noted that the sterilization was the subject of two public records. The governor had ordered a confidential investigation of the Jasper Home, which had produced information about Howard and others. When the investigators' report was filed in the governor's office, it became a public record by virtue of the state's Open Records Statute. The second record was in the files of the Jasper County auditor, who had paid the medical bills for the operation.

While the cases discussed above seem to indicate that journalists may use names and facts found in public records without fear of legal action, some exceptions must be noted. California courts, particularly, have held that under narrowly defined circumstances once-public facts can become private, even when they are a matter of record. The leading cases in point, *Melvin* v. *Reid*[35] and *Briscoe* v. *Readers Digest Association*,[36] involved persons who had been involved in crime, but who had been rehabilitated. In *Melvin* a former prostitute, who had been acquitted of murder and then found a place in respectable society, found herself the subject of a movie many years later. A state appellate court held that the use of her name was actionable, even though the events portrayed were matters of public record. As a young adult, Briscoe had helped hijack a

---

33. Rawlins v. Hutchinson Publishing Co., 543 P.2d 988 (Kans. 1975).
34. 283 N.W.2d 289 (Iowa 1979).
35. 112 Cal.App. 285 (1931).
36. 483 P.2d 34 (1971).

truck he was driving. California courts held that a magazine account of the event eleven years later was actionable because of the effect it might have on his efforts to lead a normal life. The court noted that the account of Briscoe's crime was used to illustrate a feature on truck hijackings and that there was no newsworthy purpose in using his name. Courts in other states have taken note of *Melvin* and *Briscoe* in deciding disclosure cases involving a time lapse, but have been reluctant to follow them.

The Measure of an Embarrassing Private Fact

Cox and its progeny deal with only one dimension of the tort of disclosure of embarrassing private fact. The cases discussed above tell us only that matters found on the public record can't be used as grounds for a disclosure action. Simply put, the decisions say that public facts aren't private. What, then, is an embarrassing private fact that will support a privacy suit if it is made public?

The Iowa Supreme Court said in *Howard* that a publication is actionable if (1) it concerns "the private, as distinguished from the public, life of the individual" and (2) it "is not of legitimate concern to the public." The second element was quoted from *Restatement (Second) of Torts,*[37] which also says that the facts in question must "be highly offensive to a reasonable person." What would offend a reasonable person usually is for a jury to decide.

Once they have determined that private fact is at issue, courts usually look to *Sidis v. F-R Publishing Corp.* for guidance as to whether it is actionable. At issue was a profile in the *New Yorker* magazine of William James Sidis, whose mathematical genius was such that he had attracted widespread attention as a child. He was graduated from Harvard at sixteen. He soon tired of life in the spotlight, however, and retreated from the academic world, became a recluse, and earned a bare existence as a clerk. More than twenty years later, a *New Yorker* writer caught up with Sidis. The resulting article was sympathetic in tone, but ruthless in detailing Sidis's rise and fall. He found it deeply offensive and sued the magazine for invasion of privacy. The courts were sympathetic, too, but not enough so to find in Sidis's favor. The appeals court noted that he was not an ordinary person, but a genius who, at one time, had attracted widespread public attention. That had made him a public figure. As such, he had lost most of his claim to a right of privacy. True, he had retreated into obscurity, but that, too, the court said, was "a matter of public concern." The article in the *New Yorker* "sketched the life of an unusual personality, and it possessed considerable popular news interest." The court added:

Sidis v. F-R Publishing Corp., 113 F.2d 806 (2d Cir. 1940).

> We express no comment on whether or not the newsworthiness of the matter printed will always constitute a complete defense. Revelations may be so intimate and so unwarranted in the view of the victim's position as to outrage the community's notion of decency. But when focused upon public characters, truthful comments upon dress, speech, habits, and

---

37. §652D.

the ordinary aspects of personality will usually not transgress this line. Regrettably or not, the misfortunes and frailties of neighbors and "public figures" are subjects of considerable interest and discussion to the rest of the population. And when such are the mores of the community, it would be unwise for a court to bar their expression in the newspapers, books and magazines of the day.

The publication of private facts is actionable, then, only if the disclosure would "outrage the community's notion of decency." The measure is not what would offend a sensitive person, like Sidis, but that composite known as the community, or the average person. A California jury found such outrage in a column that appeared in the *Oakland Tribune* in 1978. Columnist Sidney Jones thought there was news in his discovery that the female student-body president of the College of Alameda had had a sex-change operation. He wrote that the students would be surprised to learn that the president, Toni Ann Diaz, "is no lady, but in fact is a man whose real name is Antonio." The item added that students enrolled in a physical education class with her "may wish to make other showering arrangements." Diaz sued the newspaper and the columnist for invasion of privacy, alleging that the item disclosed private fact and was highly offensive. An Alameda county jury agreed, awarding her a $750,000 judgment against the *Tribune* and $25,000 against the columnist.

Diaz v. Oakland Tribune, Inc., 188 Cal. Rptr. 762 (Cal. Ct. App. 1st Dist. Div. 3 1983).

In 1983, a California appeals court reversed, not because it disagreed with the result, but because it concluded that the judge had not properly instructed the jury on the burden of proof. The court noted that the gist of the column was true. Toni had been Antonio until undergoing surgery in 1975. Then she had gone to great lengths to change all the usual forms of identification to show her as a woman. Only her closest relatives knew what had happened. The columnist had acted on a tip from confidential sources. The information was confirmed by Oakland police, who had arrested Antonio Diaz some years before. The columnist did not talk to Toni Diaz.

The *Tribune*, seeking support from *Cox Broadcasting*, argued that because the arrest of Antonio had led to a trial at which he was acquitted, its item was based at least in part on the public record of a court. The sex change was confirmed not only by police, but by later records in the name of Toni Diaz. The California court held that all such records were beside the point. The fact at issue was the sex-change operation, and that was not on the public record of a court.

The court also held that the publication of a private fact is an invasion of privacy if the fact in question "would be offensive and objectionable to [a] reasonable person" and if it were "not of legitimate public concern." The latter was the court's way of saying that even an offensive fact would be protected if it were newsworthy. The trial judge had told the jury that the newspaper had the burden of proving that Diaz's sex change was newsworthy. That, the appeals court ruled, was error. The judge should have required Diaz to prove that her operation was not newsworthy. It said that burden was mandated by the same First Amendment interest found in the *New York Times* rule. Those who would restrict the flow of news must carry the burden of proving a need to do so.

In sending the case back for retrial, the court said that the jury, given proper instructions as to the burden of proof, would have to balance the competing interests and decide whether the item was newsworthy. That decision, the court said, "depends upon contemporary community mores and standards of decency," which is the kind of factual judgment best left to a jury. However, the appeals court volunteered the opinion that the item was not newsworthy. It also said that the jury was correct in its finding that the columnist had acted with malice when he added the sentence about showering arrangements. He knew, or should have known, that Diaz was not enrolled in a physical education class. The sentence could have had no other purpose than to make fun of her. That, the court said, was enough to support the jury's award of punitive damages.

The record does not show what happened on remand. Nor do the case records show many instances in which plaintiffs have been able to bring successful disclosure actions against news media. In the few instances resulting in awards of damages, disclosure was coupled with other factors.

In 1964, the Georgia Supreme Court upheld a $4,166 judgment against the *Cullman Daily Times Democrat* based on a photograph taken at a county fair. It showed Mrs. Flora Bell Graham as she emerged from the fun house with her two young sons. An air jet had blown her skirt to her shoulders, and she was frantically trying to hold it down. The newspaper's editors thought the photo caught the spirit of the fair and used it on page 1. Mrs. Graham said she was mortified and sued the newspaper for disclosure of private fact. The newspaper argued that the photo was taken in a public place and was newsworthy. The supreme court held, in *Daily Times Democrat* v. *Graham*,[38] that it could find nothing newsworthy in a photo of Mrs. Graham's underpants. Further, it noted that they were exposed against her will. The court concluded that the jury properly concluded that such exposure outraged the public's sense of decency.

In 1982, a New Mexico court awarded a prison guard $200,000 for a story that appeared in the *Dallas Times Herald* describing his experiences as a hostage during a riot.[39] Prisoners had beaten, stabbed, and sexually assaulted him. The reporter had obtained much of the information by entering the guard's hospital room and eavesdropping on his conversation with a friend. The guard said he was very upset by publication of details of the assault and by a part of the story saying that he and his wife were living in near poverty. In this instance, the disclosure of embarrassing private fact was coupled with an intrusion.

The cases discussed thus far tell us that an individual has no cause of action for disclosure if the facts in question were taken from a public record, particularly the public record of a court. If a plaintiff's case is to survive summary dismissal, the embarrassing facts must have come from nonpublic sources, and they must be of such a nature as to outrage the community's sense of decency. But, as the courts noted in *Sidis* and *Diaz*, even outrageous facts are protected if they involve "a matter of public concern," if they possess "considerable popular news interest," if they are "of legitimate public concern," or if the subject of the article is a public figure. The record offers abundant proof that these elements offer the media powerful defenses against disclosure actions.

Newsworthiness and the Public Interest

From the beginning, courts have recognized a conflict between an individual's interest in privacy and the public's interest in being informed. When the Georgia Supreme

---

38. 162 So.2d 474 (Ga. 1964).
39. "Dallas Times Herald Loses $200,000 Suit," *Editor & Publisher*, 16 October 1982, p. 57; Schmitt v. Dallas Times Herald, No. 5781–582 (New Mexico Dist.Ct., Santa Fe. Co.).

Court recognized a common-law right of privacy more than eighty years ago, it grappled with that conflict. The court said, in *Pavesich* v. *New England Life Insurance Co.*,[40] that it believed the right of privacy to be one of the natural rights recognized by "the law of nature." But it also said that one of the stumbling blocks to its enforcement is that "it would inevitably tend to curtail the liberty of speech and of the press," which also is a natural right. The court added, "It will therefore be seen that the right of privacy must in some particulars yield to the right of speech and of the press." This has proved to be the case. In federal and state courts, newsworthiness—information deemed to serve a public interest—has become the strongest defense against an action for disclosure of embarrassing private fact.

Courts have tended to define newsworthiness broadly. In a decision that is still cited as a precedent, the United States Court of Appeals for the Third Circuit offered one of the broadest definitions of newsworthiness in 1958 in *Jenkins* v. *Dell Publishing Co.* The plaintiff was a widow who was noteworthy only because her husband had been beaten to death on the street by a pack of young hoodlums, leaving her with six young

Jenkins v. *Dell Publishing Co.*, 251 F.2d 447 (3d Cir. 1958).

children. Immediately after the incident, Mrs. Jenkins agreed to pose with her children for a Pittsburgh newpaper photographer. The picture appeared the next day along with a story about the murder of her husband. Three months later, the widow was shocked to find the same photograph in *Front Page Detective* magazine along with a brief, factual account of the murder. She sued the publisher for invasion of privacy, alleging, among other things, that the facts of her tragic loss were offered as entertainment for the magazine's readers, causing her embarrassment. A federal district court dismissed the action, and the appeals court affirmed, holding that "information and entertainment are not mutually exclusive categories." The court then sought to define news:

> A large part of the matter that appears in newspapers and news magazines today is not published or read for the value or importance of the information it conveys. Some readers are attracted by shocking news. Others are titillated by sex in the news. Still others are entertained by news which has an incongruous or ironic aspect. Most news is in various ways amusing, and for that reason of special interest to many people. Few newspapers or news magaines would long survive if they did not publish a substantial amount of news on the basis of entertainment value of one kind or another. This may be a disturbing commentary upon our civilization, but it is nonetheless a realistic picture of society which courts shaping new juristic concepts should take into account.

In 1975, the United States Court of Appeals for the Ninth Circuit also dealt with the line between news and entertainment. In a case,

Virgil v. *Time Inc.*, 527 F.2d 1122 (9th Cir. 1975).

Virgil v. *Time Inc.*, brought by a noted body-surfer, that court was less generous with the news media than the *Jenkins* court, but its decision, too, has become a frequently cited precedent.

Mike Virgil was said to be the most reckless member of a group who surfed at the Wedge, reputed to be the world's most dangerous spot for body-surfing. *Sports Illustrated*

---

40. 50 S.E. 68 (Ga. 1905).

assigned a writer to do a story on the sport. With Virgil as its focus, Virgil and his wife and others spoke freely with the writer. The completed article was rich in unusual facts about an unusual character. The article left no doubt that Virgil was as reckless on land as he was in the water. It said he had dived down a flight of stairs at a ski resort to "impress these chicks all around." He burned the back of his hand to win a bet that he could burn a hole with a cigarette in a dollar bill resting there. He ate spiders and insects. He injured himself deliberately on construction jobs so he could draw workers' compensation while he continued his surfing.

When one of the magazine's researchers telephoned Virgil to check on such details, he had second thoughts and asked that they not be published. Reasoning that whatever an adult says to a reporter is fair game, *Sports Illustrated* published the story. Virgil sued for invasion of privacy. A federal district court dismissed, but the appeals court reversed and remanded, holding that it thought a jury should decide whether details of Virgil's life out of the water were newsworthy. The court also held that one who speaks freely with a reporter does not necessarily consent to publication. If the subject of a story is given a chance to review it, as in this instance, and changes his or her mind about some of the revelations, the court said, "[T]he consequent publicity is without consent." Nevertheless, the court said Virgil could not recover damages if a jury decided that the public had a legitimate interest in the facts, that they had previously become public knowledge, or that they would not be offensive to a reasonable person of ordinary sensibilities.

Despite the circuit court's decision, Virgil never got a chance to present his case to a jury. On remand, the United States District Court for the Southern District of California granted summary judgment to *Sports Illustrated*.[41] Applying the circuit court's prescribed test of newsworthiness, the district judge concluded that no reasonable juror could find the story highly offensive. He conceded that the facts would embarrass Virgil, but he said they were neither morbid nor sensational. Nor were they published "for their own sake." The writer had a purpose, which was to give his readers an insight into Virgil's daring style of body-surfing. Thus the story fulfilled a legitimate public interest.

The *Diaz* court also offered jurors guidelines for determining when private facts become newsworthy, borrowing from the earlier decision in *Briscoe*.[42] It said the jury should "consider (1) the social value of the facts published, (2) the depth of the article's intrusion into ostensibly private affairs, and (3) the extent to which the party voluntarily acceded to a position of public notoriety. . . ."

Strict application of such guidelines has made it difficult for plaintiffs to win suits for disclosure of embarrassing private fact. Even when they have been able to convince a jury that the disclosure was not newsworthy, appeals courts have shown a disposition to hold otherwise. One case, *Cape Publications, Inc.*, v. *Bridges*,[43] decided by a district appellate court in Florida in 1983, illustrates the point. A woman was held hostage by her estranged husband. She managed to escape and ran into the street clutching a hand towel that just managed to conceal the fact that she was nude. A photographer for *Cocoa Today* took her picture as she fled, and the newspaper used it. She convinced a jury that the photo was not newsworthy and that the newspaper exceeded the limits of decency

---

41. Virgil v. Sports Illustrated and Time Inc., 424 F.Supp. 1286 (S.D. Calif. 1976).
42. Briscoe v. Reader's Digest Association, 483 P.2d 34, at 43 (Calif. 1971).
43. 423 So.2d 426 (Fla.App.Ct. 5th Dist. 1982).

in causing her extreme embarrassment. The jury awarded her $10,000. The appellate court reversed, holding:

> Just because the story and photograph may be embarrassing or distressful to the plaintiff does not mean the newspaper cannot publish what is otherwise newsworthy. At some point, the public interest in obtaining information becomes dominant over the individual's right of privacy.

This examination of newsworthiness and the public interest ends where it began: When an individual's asserted right of privacy collides with the public's right to be informed about matters of public interest, the latter almost always prevails. Courts have recognized that the public has a legitimate interest not only in the fate of nations but in human frailties, foibles, and misfortunes. The defenses against a disclosure action are not absolute, but they are nearly so. The successful plaintiff must prove that the facts in question were not found in the public record, that he did not make them public himself, that they would outrage the community's sense of decency, and that their revelation serves no legitimate public interest in the news. These are formidable barriers, but they reserve for the media what is perhaps the most important question of all: How far should the media go in publishing private fact that would embarrass any self-respecting person? In a free society, such questions can be answered only by those who are in the business of public communication. The ethical dimension of these questions will be discussed at the end of the chapter.

False Light

False light begins with offensive flattery at one end of the spectrum and merges into libel at the other. It is, in a practical sense, the realm of the communicator who melds fiction with fact. The harm comes in portraying individuals as something other than they are to a point that would be offensive to a person of ordinary sensibilities. The point to remember is that such portrayal need not be defamatory. If it is, courts have held that it should be the subject of a libel action, not a lawsuit for invasion of privacy.

Many of the legal principles that are applied to libel actions also apply to false-light litigation. A person cannot be put in a false light by the truth, so an action for false-light invasion of privacy, like an action for libel, must be grounded in a false assertion of fact. In libel actions, the false assertion of fact must be defamatory. In a false-light action, there is no defamation. There is nothing defamatory about being poor or soured on life, but to portray a person as one or both could result in a lawsuit for false-light invasion of privacy. The Supreme Court has held in two cases that plaintiffs in false-light actions must prove actual malice on the part of media defendants. Because the first of the decisions preceded *Gertz,* and the second clearly involved actual malice, the Court left open the degree of fault that must be proved by a private individual. Lower courts, in some instances, have required all false-light plaintiffs, public or private, to prove actual malice. In the most recent cases, however, courts in some jurisdictions have been distinguishing between public official/public figure plaintiffs and private individuals. The latter have been permitted to prevail on some lesser showing of fault, usually negligence.

Distortion of an individual's personality lies at the heart of a false-light action. A professional communicator who is careful with facts and slow to jump to broad characterizations has little to fear from this branch of the tort. Communicators run a risk only if they are tempted too casually to follow Tom Wolfe and Gay Talese into the kind of writing that purports to portray thought processes and recreate conversations that may not have occurred. To pass muster, such writing must be the product of exhaustive fact gathering, as it is with the writers named above. There must have been sufficient research to ensure that fictionalized passages are true to the character of the persons portrayed.

The first false-light case to reach the Supreme Court, *Time Inc.* v. *Hill*, grew out of a drama review in the old weekly version of *Life* magazine. The play, *The Desperate Hours*, portrayed the experiences of a couple and their two children, who were held hostage in their home by several escaped convicts. The play was based on a book by Joseph Hayes, who said he had taken his inspiration from several such real-life incidents. One of these involved Mr. and Mrs. James Hill and their five children, who had been held hostage in their home in suburban Philadelphia in 1952. The three escaped convicts who invaded their home treated the family courteously during a nineteen-hour standoff with the police. When the convicts left the house, two of them were shot and killed by police. The Hills were so shocked that they moved to Connecticut and resisted all efforts to publicize the experience.

Time Inc. v. *Hill,* **385 U.S. 374, 87 S.Ct. 534, 17 L.Ed.2d 456 (1967).**

When *The Desperate Hours* was playing in Philadelphia on its way to Broadway, an editor for *Life* had what seemed like a bright idea. Why not take the cast to what had been the Hill home and photograph them enacting several of the more dramatic scenes from the play? This would show the magazine's readers that the play was not altogether fiction. The play's producer and the new owner of the house were willing. Three of the resulting photographs accompanied a review of the play in a January 1955 issue of *Life*. One showed a son being roughed up by one of the convicts. Another showed the daughter biting a convict's hand to make him drop a gun. A third showed the father throwing the gun through a door. None of these things had happened to the Hills, and the copy written by the reviewer did not say that they had. But the editor who prepared the copy for publication changed both the review and the photo captions to make a direct association with the Hill family. He did so, he testified later, to "jazz up" the material. The changes gave readers the impression that the photographs portrayed the Hill family's experiences with the hostages. Hill sued for false-light invasion of privacy, setting in motion a legal yo-yo that remained in motion during more than a decade of litigation.

In the first round of the legal action, the Hills won a $75,000 judgment. An appellate court held that that was excessive. On retrial, they won a judgment for $30,000, which was affirmed on appeal. Time Inc. asked the Supreme Court to consider the case, arguing that its First Amendment rights were involved. The Supreme Court agreed that they were. Holding that the New York courts had not shown a proper regard for freedom of the press, the Court sent the case back for retrial. It said the Hills could win only if they could prove actual malice. At that point, they gave up.

At the time, the effect of the *Hill* decision was open to question. The Court was divided six-to-three, and only three members of the majority endorsed the actual malice standard. Two others would have held that the First Amendment rules out any false light actions. The sixth member of the majority would have permitted the Hills to prevail by proving negligence.

Seven years after *Hill*, in 1974, the Supreme Court reviewed a second false-light case, *Cantrell* v. *Forest City Publishing Co.*, and reiterated its actual malice holding, this time with the weight of a majority behind the decision. Mrs. Melvin Aaron Cantrell had been left a widow ten days before Christmas in 1967 when her husband was one of the forty-four victims of the collapse of the Silver Bridge, crossing the Ohio River at

*Cantrell v. Forest City
Publishing Co.*, 419 U.S.
245, 95 S.Ct. 465, 42
L.Ed.2d 419 (1974).

Point Pleasant, West Virginia. Several months later, a reporter for the *Cleveland Plain Dealer* decided to do a follow-up story on some of the survivors. He included Mrs. Cantrell because she had been the focus of one of the prize-winning stories he had written at the time of the disaster. She was not at home, but the reporter did interview several of her minor children. The resulting story, portraying the mother as embittered by broken promises and living in abject poverty, was written as though the reporter had talked with Mrs. Cantrell. One passage described her as wearing "the same mask of nonexpression she wore at the funeral." *Plain Dealer* editors featured the story in the newspaper's Sunday magazine.

Mrs. Cantrell sued for invasion of privacy, alleging that she had been placed in a false light. A federal district court jury awarded her a $60,000 judgment. The circuit court of appeals reversed, but the Supreme Court restored the original verdict. Eight justices held that a properly instructed jury had come to the correct conclusion in finding actual malice. There was enough evidence within the story to prove that the reporter's word portrait of Mrs. Cantrell was false. The story indicated that he had seen her and perhaps had talked with her. He had done neither.

Cantrell was decided about six months after *Gertz*. The majority took note of the latter decision but saw no need to decide whether the reasoning in *Gertz* with respect to private individuals should be applied to Mrs. Cantrell. Clearly, she was a private individual, but it was also clear that the *Plain Dealer*'s reporter had been caught in a knowing falsehood. Initially, lower courts confronted with false-light cases adopted the *Hill* rationale and required all plaintiffs to prove actual malice. Courts have so held in Arkansas,[44] California,[45] Connecticut,[46] Kentucky,[47] and Oregon.[48] More recently, courts in six jurisdictions have looked to *Gertz* for guidance and have held that only public official/public figure false-light plaintiffs need prove actual malice. They are the United States Courts of Appeals for the Fifth Circuit, applying Texas law,[49] and for the Sixth Circuit, applying Michigan law;[50] United States District Courts in the District of

---

44. Dodrill v. Arkansas Democrat, 590 S.W.2d 840 (Ark. 1979).
45. Fellows v. National Enquirer, 211 Cal.Rptr. 809 (2d Dist. 1985); review granted, 701 P.2d 1171 (1985).
46. Goodrich v. Waterbury Republican-American, 8 Med.L.Rptr. 2329 (Conn. 1982).
47. McCall v. Courier-Journal, 623 S.W.2d 882 (Ky. 1981).
48. Dean v. Guard Publishing Co., 699 P.2d 1158 (Ore.App. 1985).
49. Wood v. Hustler Magazine, 736 F.2d 1084 (5th Cir. 1984).
50. Bichler v. Union Bank, 715 F.2d 1059; vacated, 718 F.2d 802 (6th Cir. 1984).

Columbia,[51] the Northern District of Illinois,[52] and Kansas,[53] and the West Virginia Supreme Court.[54]

In 1984, the Supreme Court of North Carolina held that the First Amendment stands as an absolute barrier against false-light actions. In doing so, it took note of changes that have occurred in the practice of journalism since Warren and Brandeis wrote in 1890. The court said:

> Most modern journalists employed in print, television or radio journalism now receive training in ethics and journalism entirely unheard of during the era of "yellow journalism." As a general rule journalists simply are more responsible and professional today than history tells us they were in that era.[55]

The reported false-light actions in other jurisdictions fall into three categories:

1. False material is added to an otherwise accurate news or feature story resulting in a distorted portrayal of the subject of the story.

2. Material, commonly a photograph or videotape, is used in a context that results in a highly offensive portrayal of the subject.

3. Real people, either as themselves or thinly disguised, are used in fictional works.

The classic case illustrating the first of these categories is *Spahn* v. *Julian Messner*,[56] decided by New York's highest court in 1966. Warren Spahn was one of the best baseball pitchers of the late 1950s. A winner of baseball's top pitching award, he has long since entered baseball's Hall of Fame. At the height of his career, he became the subject of a biography to be published by Messner. The writer was not content to describe Spahn's career as it was, but said Spahn was a World War II hero, which he wasn't, and generally made him out to be larger than life. The pitcher brought suit for false-light invasion of privacy and eventually was able to win an injunction preventing distribution of the book.

The use of a photograph in a context that would make it highly offensive is illustrated by *Wood* v. *Hustler Magazine, Inc.*,[57] decided by the United States Court of Appeals for the Fifth Circuit in 1984. Lajuan Wood and her husband Billy took nude photographs of each other during an outing in a remote section of a Texas state park. They kept the prints in a dresser drawer in their bedroom. A neighbor thought it would be a great joke to send a photo of Lajuan to *Hustler* magazine for its "Beaver Hunt" section. He stole the print long enough to make a copy. The neighbor's wife, pretending to be Lajuan, sent the copy to *Hustler*, along with a letter saying that her secret fantasy was "to be screwed by two bikers." The editors of *Hustler* have a policy of calling persons who submit photos to it to make certain that the sender is who he or she claims to be and

---

51. Dresbach v. Doubleday, Inc., 518 F.Supp. 1285 (D.D.C. 1981).
52. Cantrell v. ABC, 529 F.Supp. 764 (N.D.Ill. 1981).
53. Rinsley v. Brandt, 446 F.Supp. 850 (D.C.Kans. 1977).
54. Crump v. Beckley Newspapers, 320 S.E.2d 70 (W.Va. 1983).
55. Renwick v. News and Observer, 312 S.E.2d 405 (N.Car. 1984).
56. 221 N.E.2d 543 (N.Y. 1966).
57. 736 F.2d 1084 (5th Cir. 1984).

does indeed want the photo published. In this instance, the policy was not followed strictly. The call to the neighbor's wife, pretending to be Lajuan, was perfunctory and resulted in a decision to publish.

The Woods learned what had happened when friends began to tease them. Both sued *Hustler* for invasion of privacy. Lajuan said she was so mortified by the experience that she had to have six weeks of psychological counseling. A jury awarded her $150,000 in damages and her husband, $25,000. The court of appeals threw out the award to the husband, holding that he could not collect damages for an invasion of his wife's privacy. But the court said there was no doubt that Lajuan had been put in a false light. It held further that as a private individual she had only to prove that the editors of *Hustler* were negligent in checking the identity of the person who submitted the photograph. That was evident, the court said, from the fact that they had not followed their own procedures.

The court apparently operated on the theory that given the mores of today, there is nothing particularly shocking about being photographed in the nude or even having that photograph used in a magazine. But when the photo was used in connection with the letter, the combination was offensive to any person of ordinary sensibilities.

Because Clarence W. Arrington was unable to prove that a use of his photograph was offensive, he lost a privacy action against the *New York Times*. An issue of the *Times Magazine* featured an article entitled "The Black Middle Class: Making It." The cover was a photo of a well-dressed black man striding along a city street carrying a brief case. Superimposed across the photograph was a promotional box for the featured article. Arrington was not identified in the photo credit lines, nor was he mentioned in the article. In suing the *Times* for invasion of privacy, Arrington argued that his photo was being used for commercial purposes, in violation of a New York statute, and that he had been put in a false light. He said he was associated with the article, parts of which portrayed him as other than he is. In 1982, the state's court of appeals upheld dismissal of both causes of action.[58] It noted that the photo was used as part of the news content of the magazine and thus was not for a commercial purpose. In dismissing the false-light claim, it held that there was no such cause of action in New York, and even if there were, the photo was not offensive, even if it could be connected with the article.

Several recent decisions indicate that there are false-light hazards in the "ambush" interviews sometimes conducted by investigative reporters for television news organizations. In 1982, in *Machleder* v. *Diaz*,[59] a federal district judge held that there was a cause of action in a street interview with a man who was asked about the dumping of chemicals on a nearby property. The judge held that the resulting portrayal of the man as evasive, ill-tempered, and responsible for the illegal dumping was highly offensive. The case went to trial and in 1985 resulted in a jury verdict awarding $1.25 million to the plaintiff, which was appealed.[60]

Fictionalization has been a problem largely for television "docudramas," which are mixtures of fact and fiction, with moving pictures, and with novels. The cases indicate that if the subject is a public figure, and the work deals with matters of public concern, courts will protect all but the grossest distortions. Because truth is elusive, and varies with the beholder, the First Amendment gives strong protection to works dealing with public figures and historical events.

---

58. Arrington v. New York Times, 56 N.Y.2d 284 (N.Y. 1983).
59. 538 F.Supp. 1364 (S.D.N.Y. 1982).
60. Kovner, "Recent Developments," p. 529.

Problems have arisen with the portrayal of peripheral figures, with those persons who surround public figures and play the supporting roles. For instance, an attorney who had represented a prominent figure in organized crime was held to have a false-light claim against the publisher of a novel in which his name was used.[61]

False light, like disclosure, is generating an increasing number of cases, but, also like disclosure, few are being won by plaintiffs. In false-light cases, there are two reasons for this: The distortion of the victim's personality must be highly offensive to a person of ordinary sensibilities, and it must have been done knowingly or negligently, depending on the jurisdiction and the circumstances. As a result of the Supreme Court's decisions in *Hill* and *Cantrell,* a public official or public figure cannot prevail in a false-light action without providing actual malice. Several states require private individuals to do so, too. False-light actions present courts with particularly troubling First Amendment problems because in most instances the plaintiffs have suffered no harm other than embarrassment. The false assertion that Warren Spahn was a war hero would take nothing away from the admiration in which he was held as a baseball pitcher.

Taken as a whole, the reported cases convey a straightforward message. Professional communicators who use words or pictures to portray individuals, and who take care to make certain that their work shows the individuals as they are, have little to fear. Indeed, if the subject of the work is a public figure, or an event of public importance, the law will tolerate material distortion before it will uphold a false-light privacy claim. The critical question is why a professional communicator would want to present a false picture of any individual.

Appropriation and the Right of Publicity

Appropriation, which for years was confined to the taking of a person's name or likeness for advertising purposes, is assuming a different form and taking on new life under what courts are calling "the **right of publicity**." That right means that individuals, particularly celebrities, have the right to control how others use their names. In effect, the courts are recognizing that a widely known name or likeness is a form of property and has a value that the possessor alone should be permitted to exploit. How far this right of publicity goes is still uncertain. Thus far, courts have found a violation of the right in advertisements, in the televising of a carnival act, in the promotion of feature stories, in film, in a variety show exploiting the memory of Elvis Presley, and even in the name of a company making portable toilets.

The principal and strongest defense against an action for appropriation or violation of the right of publicity is consent, preferably in writing. From the user's point of view, the best consent is written broadly enough to cover any conceivable use of a subject's identity in perpetuity. Short of that, any use of identity for commercial gain should be accompanied by the subject's specific consent. Consent can be implied in some instances, but usually only in connection with a news event, or only if commercial gain is incidental to the use.

Because this branch of invasion of privacy almost always hinges on the user's

---

61. Polakoff v. Harcourt Brace, 413 N.Y.S.2d 537 (1st Dept. 1979).

commercial gain, it is of concern mainly to advertisers, public relations practitioners, and photographers. In only a few instances has news or feature content been at issue in an appropriation or right of publicity action.

Appropriation

In its traditional form appropriation was fairly simple. An unsuspecting person who found his or her name or photograph in a commercial advertisement had a cause of action for damages. Courts usually fixed the award by determining what a model would have received for the same usage. In some instances, an attempt was made to calculate the commercial value of the subject's endorsement. On occasion, appropriation would become intertwined with false light, as when a young woman who posed for an advertisement for sheets found that the photograph had been altered in another usage to make it look as though she were reading a pornographic novel. In such instances, the award for damages might be higher than if appropriation alone were involved.

The experience of John Kimbrough, a former football player at Texas A&M University, illustrates the typical appropriation case. In it, a Texas appellate court held that a jury should decide whether his consent had been exceeded and, if so, how much he should receive in damages. Kimbrough was notified that he had been selected as his school's best former football player. As a result, *Texas Football* magazine and Coca-Cola had commissioned an artist to paint his portrait. He would get the original. One print would go to Texas A&M for permanent display and another would be placed in the Texas Football Hall of Fame. The letter also said in part:

Kimbrough v. Coca-Cola/ USA, 521 S.W.2d 719 (Tex. 1975).

> There is also contemplated use of these paintings [athletes from other Southwest Conference schools were also being honored] in a series of institutional advertisements in behalf of college football in Dave Campbell's *Texas Football* magazine.
> While no endorsement of any product is implied in the institutional nature of the proposed usage, we would not, of course, approach a project of this type without your complete approval.

Kimbrough replied that he was honored at being chosen and would sit for his portrait. Sometime later his daughter called to tell him she had found a reproduction of his portrait in the program for the Southern Methodist–Wake Forest football game—as part of an advertisement for Coca-Cola. Kimbrough reacted by suing everyone connected with the promotion for invasion of privacy. A state district court in Dallas dismissed the action, but an appeals court reversed.

Coca-Cola based its case on two grounds: As a public figure, Kimbrough had lost any claim to a right of privacy, and, in any event, he had given his consent. The court said that while it is true that public figures do surrender much of their privacy, they still are entitled to protection against appropriation for commercial purposes. The court also concluded that the ambiguous wording of the original letter raised a jury question as to whether Kimbrough's consent had been exceeded. Here there was a real possibility that his consent was for noncommercial uses only.

National Bank of Commerce v. *Shaklee Corp.*, 503 F.Supp. 719 (W.D.Tex. 1980).

A case decided by a United States District Court in San Antonio in 1980 illustrates how complicated an appropriation action can be. The court's decision is of particular value because it illustrates two aspects of appropriation law:

1. The difficulty of determining how far a subject's consent goes.

2. The application of this branch of the law to both advertising and public relations.

For many years, Heloise Bowles wrote a widely syndicated column of sometimes zany household tips, "Hints from Heloise," which since her death has been carried on by her daughter. At the height of its popularity, it was used by 580 to 600 newspapers in the United States and abroad, it had an estimated readership of 30 million, and it generated 4,000 to 5,000 letters a month. Heloise's popularity was aided by two policies from which she never deviated: She never mentioned any product by brand name, and she never published a household tip until she had tried it and found that it worked.

Under a complicated agreement with her syndicate, King Features, she also wrote books, largely collections of her columns, which were published in hardcover by Prentice-Hall and in paperback by Pocket Books. Still another company was involved in bulk and premium sales of some of the books for promotional purposes. Under her contract with King Features, Heloise had to approve any commercial use of her work.

However, without her knowledge, an agent for the bulk sales organization made a deal with Shaklee Corporation, which distributes home care products through a network of independent distributors who deal directly with consumers. Shaklee agreed to buy 100,000 copies of *All Around the House*, one of Heloise's most popular books, for thirty-eight cents each. After it had placed advertising messages on the front and back covers and at the end of each chapter, it offered to resell the books for fifty cents each to its more than 200,000 distributors to use as "door-openers." The front cover proclaimed in large type, "Welcome a new Shaklee Woman," and in even larger type, "Heloise." Two articles in the company's magazine for its distributors hailed Heloise as "an excellent addition to your sales group."

Heloise herself first learned of this promotion when she went to California on a speaking trip. Members of the audience confronted her with questions about when she began to endorse Shaklee products. She testified later that she was "humiliated," and "shocked to death." She also became angry and asked King Features what was going on. It, too, had not been advised. Heloise later testified that when she saw Shaklee's version of her book and the articles promoting it, she "nearly had a heart attack and called Kellis, my lawyer." She was so agitated, she said, that she "took nitro." (Heloise had been under treatment for a heart condition in which nitroglycerine tablets are used.)

Heloise sued Shaklee for invasion of privacy on appropriation grounds, for unfair competition, and for violation of her copyright. During the discovery process, she died, but the suit was pushed forward by the National Bank of Commerce as executor of her estate. Shaklee argued that a dead person has no privacy, but the district court pointed to a section of Texas law that permits an action in torts to survive the death of the person who began it.

Shaklee also argued that because Heloise was a public figure she would have to prove actual malice if she were to prevail. The court rejected that argument. Nothing false was involved. At issue was simply a blatant use by Shaklee of Heloise's name and good will to promote its products. Thus it was a clear case of invasion of privacy by appropriation.

But, Shaklee argued, there was consent for its use. It had made what it thought was a bona-fide business deal with a bona-fide agent of Heloise, her syndicate, and her publisher. It was doing all of them a favor by buying her book at what it assumed was a profit for them and was using the book to help make a profit for itself. The court held that if that were all that had happened, there would be no case. But when the book was altered to make it look as though Heloise were pushing Shaklee's products, and when the house organ hailed her as a new member of the firm's sales team, the terms of the agreement were exceeded. Therefore, Shaklee was guilty of invasion of privacy by appropriation.

In filing her suit, Heloise had asked for $2 million in actual damages for invasion of privacy, $5 million in special damages as the value of her endorsement, $350,000 for mental and physical pain and suffering, and $5 million in exemplary or punitive damages. Her estate was awarded a total of $135,000 in damages plus the award of profits from the copyright violation.

Consent

Professional advertisers, photographers, and public relations practitioners usually know enough about their business to obtain consent from their subjects. For that reason, as the cases examined above suggest, most appropriation actions are based on attempts to revoke or limit consent or on allegations that the consent was exceeded. Some plaintiffs have learned that consent given too readily and too broadly can not only embarrass the giver but deny him legal relief, as the following episode illustrates.

In 1975, when Brooke Shields, the actress and model, was ten years old, she posed for a series of nude photographs taken by Gary Gross for Playboy Press. She was portrayed in and out of a bathtub for a book, *Sugar and Spice*, designed "to depict the woman in the little girl to highlight the sensuality of prepubescent youth." Brooke was photographed with the cooperation of her mother, Mrs. Teri Shields, who signed a standard "model release" and in return received $450.

Shields v. *Gross*, 7 Med.L. Rptr. 2349 (Sup.Ct. N.Y.Co. 1981).

Neither the photos of Brooke nor the book in which they appeared was in any way pornographic. Larger-than-life reproductions of two of the bathtub photos were displayed for weeks in the windows of a Fifth Avenue salon.

Five years later, after Brooke had begun to appear in movies in which she played sensual roles, the nude photos resurfaced. Some appeared in a magazine published in France. Others were used in various American magazines. When "publications of dubious respectability" began proclaiming that they offered photographs of "Brooke Shields Naked," Mrs. Shields tried to buy the negatives from Gross. When that failed, she went to court, asking that the photographer be prevented from selling or using the nude photographs of her daughter. The court granted her a temporary injunction, heard her lawyer's arguments, then turned her down flat, except to put into legal form Gross's agreement not to sell the photos to pornographic magazines or those designed to appeal predominantly to a prurient interest.

Judge Edward J. Greenfield of the New York Supreme Court—a trial court—told Mrs. Shields in blunt language that she could not have it both ways. She could not exploit her daughter's "extraordinary genes," her "exceptional beauty and engaging personality," and then complain when others sought to cash in on the same qualities. He reminded Mrs. Shields that the release she had signed so eagerly, without even reading it, in 1975 had given Gross an absolute right to use and publish the products of the photo session in any way he liked. She also had waived her right "to inspect or approve" the finished photographs and had agreed to give up any right to recover damages for their use, even if that use "should subject me to ridicule, scandal, reproach, scorn or indignity." In short, she would have to be satisfied with the $450 she had taken in 1975, while Gross was free to sell the photos for whatever the market would offer.

Mrs. Shields proved to be a persistent adversary. She appealed first to the supreme court's appellate division, which found in her favor and gave her part of what she sought, and then to the state's highest court, which rebuffed her by restoring the trial court's order.[62] This litigation took two years to move through the courts, during which time a series of temporary injunctions prevented Gross from further sales of the photographs. When Mrs. Shields lost her last round in the state courts, she went immediately to the United States District Court in New York City. The judge dismissed her suit summarily, accusing her lawyer of abusing the legal system to deny Gross profits that were rightfully his under terms of the consent.[63]

Two contradictory points emerge: Photographers and advertisers who use live models should ask them for the broadest possible terms of consent. Persons who are asked to lend their names and likenesses to others who will try to profit from that use should try to limit the terms of the consent to the specific use. It is a general rule of law, as the New York Court of Appeals reminded Mrs. Shields, that "a defendant's immunity from a claim for invasion of privacy is no broader than the consent executed to him." In short, no one can be compelled to give up more of his privacy than he is willing to give, at least for purposes of advertising or trade.

The Right of Publicity: An Expanding Tort

Until 1977, courts generally held that there could be no appropriation if a person's name or photograph was used primarily for news or feature purposes. Courts were even willing to tolerate some use of a newsworthy person's identity to promote sales of a newspaper or magazine. Courts took the view that publications must make a profit if they are to remain in operation. Editors choose news, feature, photo, and other content with the expectation that it will help the publication prosper. But it does not follow that persons who are featured in such content have been victims of appropriation. For instance, a New York court held that Joe Namath, then a highly successful football quarterback, could not recover from *Sports Illustrated* when his photo was used to promote the magazine.[64] The photo had originally appeared on the cover of one issue

---

62. Shields v. Gross, 451 N.Y.S.2d 419 (N.Y.App. 1982); 448 N.E.2d 108 (N.Y. 1983).
63. Shields v. Gross, 503 F.Supp. 533 (S.D.N.Y. 1983).
64. Namath v. Sports Illustrated, 1 Med.L.Rptr. 1843 (N.Y. 1st Dept. 1975).

of the magazine. That cover was one of several included in the promotional brochure. The court held that Namath's likeness was being used only to show prospective readers the kind of editorial content they could expect to enjoy if they became subscribers.

The nature of appropriation law was changed abruptly in 1977 by the United States Supreme Court's decision in *Zacchini* v. *Scripps-Howard Broadcasting.* The plaintiff,

***Zacchini* v. *Scripps-Howard Broadcasting,* 433 U.S. 562, 97 S.Ct. 2849, 53 L.Ed.2d 965 (1977).**

Hugo Zacchini, made his living by being shot out of a huge cannon into a net 200 yards away. When he appeared at the Geauga County Fair in Chardon, Ohio, a crew from WEWS-TV in Cleveland recorded his dramatic flight. Zacchini protested that the station was stealing his act, but that night it was broadcast as part of the news from the fair. Zacchini sued, asking for $25,000 as the value of the performance.

Three Ohio courts came to as many different conclusions as to the merits of his suit, with the state supreme court holding that because the act had news value, the station had a right to show it. Zacchini took his case to the Supreme Court, which reversed, holding that the station had appropriated the act, violating the performer's "right of exclusive control over the publicity given to his performance."

The Court conceded that the station's newscast was protected in its entirety by the First Amendment. It conceded also that there was news value in the fact that Zacchini had performed at the fair. However, Justice White, writing for six members of the Court, held that the First Amendment could not be stretched to justify appropriation of the entire act. He compared the newscast with the usual form of appropriation:

> [T]he broadcast of petitioner's entire performance, unlike the unauthorized use of another's name for purposes of trade or the incidental use of a name or picture by the press, goes to the heart of petitioner's ability to earn a living as an entertainer. Thus in this case, Ohio has recognized what may be the strongest case for a "right of publicity"—involving not the appropriation of an entertainer's reputation to enhance the attractiveness of a commercial product, but the appropriation of the very activity by which the entertainer acquired the reputation in the first place.

The Court's minority argued in vain that the small segment of the newscast devoted to the Human Cannonball's flight contributed little, if anything, to the station's revenue and should be treated as an incidental use. Justice Lewis F. Powell, Jr., predicted that the decision would have unforeseen consequences at the point where news and entertainment meet. His prediction has proved correct, as the next two incidents show.

The television "docudramas" that became popular in the 1970s brought legal problems with them. As noted in the section on false light, when these fictionalized treatments of history dealt with public figures and public events, the persons who are portrayed had little chance of recovery. Courts held that unless the fictionalized portrait was deliberately highly offensive, it was protected by the First Amendment.

The Supreme Court's decision in the *Zacchini* case seems to have given celebrities a new legal weapon against producers of docudramas. When Elizabeth Taylor learned in 1982 that ABC Television was preparing a movie based on her life, her lawyers set to work to keep it off the air. Using the rationale on which *Zacchini* was based they argued that her life story was a form of commercial property she alone has the right to exploit. She argued that she might some day decide to write or film her autobiography with the expectation of profiting from the work. In her eyes, she told a *New York Times* reporter, ABC, by beating her to the punch, was "taking away from my income."[65] Floyd Abrams, a noted First Amendment lawyer, told the same reporter that if the courts were to adopt Miss Taylor's argument, they would take away some of the freedom of the press. He argued that there is news in the lives of celebrities that serves the public interest, even when some aspects of those lives are fictionalized. To hold otherwise, he said, would not only prevent the telecasting of unauthorized docudramas, but would raise questions about books and articles dealing with the careers of living persons. Nevertheless, confronted with the prospect of going to court to defend its right to show its version of Miss Taylor's colorful life, ABC put the project on hold. It was still there at the end of 1985.

Cher v. Forum International, Ltd., 692 F.2d 634 (9th Cir. 1982). A case decided by the United States Court of Appeals for the Ninth Circuit in 1982 gave some support to Abrams's concern. In *Cher* v. *Forum International, Ltd.*, the court held that *Forum* magazine could be held liable for the unauthorized use of a taped interview bought from a free-lance writer.

The writer originally had been hired by *Us* magazine to interview Cher for a cover story. Cher consented, but retained the right to approve any other uses of the material. The interview did not go as Cher expected, and she asked *Us* not to base an article on it. Subsequently, the writer sold copies of the tape to *Forum* and to the publisher of the *Star*, a tabloid sold at supermarket checkout counters. Both magazines prepared articles and promoted them heavily. *Forum* used Cher's photo on the cover, along with promotional copy that said, "There are certain things that Cher won't tell *People* and would never tell *Us*." The magazine invited readers to "join Cher and *Forum*'s hundreds of thousands of other adventurous readers today." The *Star*'s cover promotional copy was more direct. It simply said, seeming to quote Cher, "My Life, My Husbands, and My Many, Many Men."

Cher reacted by suing both magazines for violating her right of publicity. A trial court held in her favor and awarded her $600,000.[66] The appellate court cleared the *Star*, but upheld a judgment against *Forum* for $269,117. Although both articles were written in the first person, as though by Cher herself, the court said the *Star*'s deceit was not great enough to overcome the news value of the story. However, the court said *Forum* had not only misrepresented the exclusive nature of the interview—Cher had intended it originally for *Us*—but indicated in its promotional material that she endorsed the magazine. This, the court held, amounted to exploitative appropriation of the publicity value of Cher's identity.

Courts dealing with right of publicity cases have shown some doubt as to the definition of the identity a celebrity may protect. This is illustrated by a disagreement within a three-judge panel of the United States Court of Appeals for the Sixth Circuit in 1983.

Carson v. Here's Johnny Portable Toilets, 698 F.2d 831 (6th Cir. 1983). The suit was brought by John W. Carson, introduced for more than twenty years with a drawn-out "Here's Johnny!" to viewers of NBC's "Tonight" show. The owner of a Michigan firm that manufactured and distributed portable toilets admitted he had that in-

---

65. Tamar Lewin, "Whose Life Is It, Anyway? It's Hard to Tell," *New York Times*, 21 November 1982.
66. 7 Med.L.Rptr. 2593 (C.D.Calif. 1982).

troduction in mind when he named his company "Here's Johnny Portable Toilets." Lest there be any doubt, he added to his advertising the phrase, "The World's Foremost Commodian," considering it "a good play on a phrase."

Carson alleged that the firm name infringed the "Here's Johnny" trademark identifying a line of clothing made by a firm in which he held a minority interest. He also said he was embarrassed because he found it odious to be associated with the manufacturer's product. The court rejected both grounds as a basis for suit, but held that the firm clearly was exploiting Carson's identity to its advantage, thus violating his right of publicity. He alone had the right to exploit his name for commercial advantage.

The firm had argued that it was not using Carson's name. It noted that toilets have been known as "johns" for many years. "Here's Johnny," it asserted, is a phrase commonly used, and therefore not subject to protection. The court conceded that the phrase was not strongly enough identified with Carson's line of clothing to become protected as a trademark. But it said each of his appearances since 1957 had been preceded by a distinctive "Here's Johnny," thus indelibly making those words a symbol of his identity. Therefore, the firm's use of "Here's Johnny" in its name violated Carson's right of publicity, and he was entitled to prevent such use or get paid for it.

Judge Cornelia G. Kennedy argued in dissent that the majority went much too far in defining the identity Carson is entitled to protect. She argued that the sentence in question is a part of the public domain, and thus can be used by anyone. She warned that the court's decision could open the way for an almost limitless expansion of a celebrity's identity, leading to many more claims under a right of publicity.

Her warning may have been prophetic. A survey of recent reported cases shows that the right of publicity has become a frequently litigated branch of invasion of privacy. Its potential for expansion has been enhanced by statutes and by court decisions holding that the right survives the death of the individual. States with such laws are California, Florida, Nebraska, Oklahoma, Tennessee, Utah, and Virginia. The California law is the most generous, permitting the legal heirs of a celebrity to protect and profit from his or her right of publicity for fifty years after the celebrity's death.

Courts are divided over whether the right of publicity survives death in the absence of a statute. Illustrative of those holding that it does is a decision of the United States Court of Appeals for the Eleventh Circuit in 1983. It held, in *Martin Luther King, Jr., Center for Social Change, Inc.*, v. *American Heritage Products, Inc.*,[67] that the right of publicity in the identity of the civil rights leader survived his assassination and, like any other form of property, could be protected by his heirs.

How far the courts will go in expanding on the Supreme Court's decision in *Zacchini* is not clear at this writing. What is clear is that the decision has given celebrities an additional weapon with which to make certain that they control the right to profit from the exploitation of their status. It also is clear that advertisers, photographers, and public relations practitioners no longer are the only likely media targets of actions in appropriation. Movie and television scriptwriters, film and television producers, broadcasting news editors, magazine publishers, and others need to be aware that celebrities have acquired a property right in their identities and that courts will protect it against exploitation by others.

---

67. 694 F.2d 674 (11th Cir. 1983).

Privacy and Government Records ══════════

At one level, the Supreme Court's 1975 decision in *Cox*, followed by *Smith* and *Globe Newspapers*, expanded the media's right to use names and facts. Anything found on the public record can be used without invading someone's right of privacy. But, at another level, the decisions may have restricted information in the public domain. The Court suggested in *Cox* that Georgia might have prevented publication of the name of the rape victim by sealing the records in which it was found. Indeed, at the time that decision was written, federal and state legislative bodies were enacting statutes designed to restrict access to government files containing certain personal information. These statutes took two forms.

One form, exemplified by the federal Privacy Act of 1974, is designed to prevent disclosure by government agencies of personal data about employees and others on whom files are kept. Because such laws restrict media access to information, their effect will be examined in chapter 8, which deals with that topic.

The second form of statutory protection deals with the kinds of information journalists have always considered public—police and court records of adult offenders. In most states, statutes provide that under certain circumstances public records of arrests, and even of convictions, can be either sealed or expunged. These laws vary in their scope, but generally cover arrests that do not result in convictions or guilty pleas, long-past convictions of persons who have gone straight, and records of juvenile offenses. The purposes of these laws, which have been adopted by forty-eight states, the District of Columbia, and Puerto Rico, are to encourage rehabilitation of wrongdoers and to protect the privacy of persons who have been arrested but never convicted. In a sense, they are a legislative adoption of the reasoning used by the California courts in *Melvin* and *Briscoe*, discussed earlier. At some point, a person who was caught in a law violation, but who went straight thereafter, should no longer have to fear having that infraction called to public attention.

Journalists see such laws as restrictions on freedom of the press. Persons have been known to revert to crime after many years of normal life. Should journalists be denied the opportunity to inform the public that one of the candidates for director of a day-care center was once arrrested on suspicion of child molesting? Or that a candidate for county auditor had once been convicted of embezzlement? Journalists also argue that they cannot properly assess the performance of police, prosecutors, and judges unless they can get access to all arrest and disposition records. For instance, it would be difficult to check reports that a prosecutor took it easy on men accused of beating their wives or women friends if the records of arrests not resulting in prosecution were sealed.

Expunging or Sealing of Criminal Records

The Illinois statute represents one of the common forms an expungement law takes.[68] The pertinent part states:

---

68. Ill.Rev.Stat. 1975, ch. 38, par. 206–5.

All photographs, fingerprints, or other records of identification so taken shall, upon the acquittal of a person charged with the crime, or, upon his being released without being convicted, be returned to him. Whenever a person, not having previously been convicted of any criminal offense or municipal ordinance violation, charged with a violation of a municipal ordinance or a felony misdemeanor, is acquitted or released without being convicted, the Chief Judge of the circuit wherein the charge was brought, or any judge of that circuit designated by the Chief Judge, may upon verified petition of the defendant order the record of arrest expunged from the official records of the arresting authority.

The Massachusetts law goes further and establishes elaborate safeguards designed to keep anyone but police and courts from having access to criminal dossiers on individuals. The only case testing the law also made clear that it is a limitation on investigative reporting. Under the law, reporters and the public have access only to the day-to-day records of arrests and of public judicial proceedings. Any compilation of records in alphabetical order or any alphabetized index to police or court files is available only to law enforcement officers.

The *New Bedford Standard-Times* saw the law as an obstacle when it undertook an investigation of individuals believed to be in violation of building, sanitary, or housing laws and regulations. Its reporters were unable to check the records readily to see whether any given individual had been arrested or even convicted at some time in the past. To do so, reporters would have to go through docket books day by day, looking for individual names. The newspapers asked, therefore, to look at an alphabetical case file compiled by the clerk of the Third District Court of Bristol County to make the court's work easier. Cards in that file contained a reasonably complete arrest and disposition record for each offender. When the clerk refused the request, the *Standard-Times* filed suit, arguing that the section of the law barring public inspection of alphabetical files was unconstitutional. The newspaper was rebuffed both by a district court and the supreme judicial court.

New Bedford Standard-Times Publishing Co. v. *Clerk of Third Dist. Court,* 387 N.E.2d 110 (Mass. 1979).

The latter viewed the dispute in narrow terms. The only question, it said, was how far the state should go in making it easy for the newspaper to obtain information from public records. The court conceded that the newspaper had difficulty in assembling arrest records, particularly of offenses that had occurred in the distant past. This was as it should be, it concluded, for there is less news value in long-past convictions. In any event, the legislature had decided that the public interest in rehabilitation of offenders requires protection of their privacy. The court held that the right of privacy "weighs more heavily" than the purpose of the newspaper's investigation.

Newspapers, Inc., v. *Breier,* 279 N.W.2d 179 (Wis. 1979).

However, the Supreme Court of Wisconsin held in 1979 that an interest in the privacy of criminal suspects cannot be carried too far. In *Newspapers, Inc.,* v. *Breier,* it ruled that the Milwaukee police chief could not deny reporters access to his department's daily arrest log or "blotter."

Chief Harold A. Breier took the position that an arrest does not mean that the suspect is guilty. Indeed, the prosecutor may decide there is not enough evidence to take the suspect to court, or, if there is, a court may acquit him or her. Therefore, publication of the details of an arrest, including the name of the suspect, may only result in needless embarrassment of an innocent person. Therefore, the chief adopted a policy of releasing the names of arrested persons only on demand, but even then, police would not release the nature of the charge.

Joseph W. Shoquist, managing editor of the *Milwaukee Journal*, took the chief to court, arguing that arrest records are public records. The trial court would have permitted a forty-eight-hour delay in release of arrest records, but the state's highest court said even that was too much. The power to arrest, it said, "is an awesome weapon for the protection of the people, but it also is a power that may be abused." One way of preventing abuse is to make the people aware of it when it happens. Under the chief's policy, even as modified by the trial court, this could not be done. The supreme court said it would be "a travesty of our judicial and law enforcement system" to report that persons had been arrested, but fail to give the reasons for it.

As of this writing, no reported privacy case has hinged on facts contained in an expunged record, but a libel case decided by an Oregon appellate court in 1981 did. The decision, in *Bahr* v. *Statesman Journal Co.*, was an interesting victory for the newspaper involved. The Oregon expungement law **Bahr** v. **Statesman Journal** specifies that a person whose record has been removed **Co.**, 624 P.2d 664 (Ore. from the public files can say, if asked, "I have no **App. 1981).** criminal record." Les Bahr, a candidate for county commissioner, used that response when a reporter for the newspaper in Salem asked him if he had been convicted of embezzlement several years previously. As a matter of fact, Bahr had been convicted and had served four months in jail. When he had gone three years without committing another offense, he had had his record expunged.

When the reporter, relying on the newspaper's files, reported Bahr's conviction for embezzlement, the candidate sued for libel. The trial court granted the newspaper's request for dismissal, and the appellate court affirmed. A part of Judge Betty Robert's decision for the defendant offers an interesting commentary on Oregon's expungement law:

> The statute does not . . . impose any duty on members of the public who are aware of the conviction to pretend that it does not exist. In other words, the statute authorizes certain persons to misrepresent their own past. It does not make that misrepresentation true. . . .
>
> While plaintiff was entitled to deny his conviction . . . defendant, in this civil defamation case, was entitled to rely upon the fact that a conviction did occur as a defense. . . . Because plaintiff admitted in his complaint that he had been convicted, two things follow from the allegations of the complaint and the provisions of [the law]. First, that defendant's statement that plaintiff had been convicted was true, and secondly, that it was true that plaintiff had lied in denying his conviction, despite the fact the lie was authorized by statute.

Pertinent comment will be left to Joseph Heller should he care to write a sequel to *Catch-22*.

Juvenile Offenders

All states have laws restricting the release of information that would identify juvenile offenders. In their usual form, the statutes forbid release of such information by the juvenile system unless it is authorized by a judge. The rationale is that young offenders should be given every opportunity to be rehabilitated and should not be haunted for the rest of their lives by the mistakes of their youth. In a few states, courts and legislatures have attempted to protect juveniles further by imposing penalties on the news media for disclosing their names. In two decisions, the Supreme Court has held that such attempts impose an impermissible prior restraint if the juvenile was identified in open court or if the state's only interest is rehabilitation of the offender.

One of the cases, *Smith* v. *Daily Mail Publishing Co.*, was discussed earlier in the chapter. In it, the Court struck down a West Virginia law making it a crime for newspapers to disclose the names of juvenile offenders. The asserted state interest was in rehabilitation. The second case, *Oklahoma Publishing Co.* v. *District Court in and for Oklahoma County*, decided in 1977, struck down a judge's order forbidding publication of the name and photograph of an eleven-year-old boy who was accused of murder. When the boy was taken into custody, the judge permitted reporters to attend the hearing, at which the offender's name was used. When the boy was taken out of the courthouse, newspaper and television photographers recorded the scene. News reports of the arrest in all media identified the suspect.

Oklahoma Publishing Co. v. District Court in and for Oklahoma County, 430 U.S. 308, 97 S.Ct. 1045, 51 L.Ed.2d 355 (1977).

When the boy was arraigned at a closed hearing four days later, the judge issued an order forbidding the news media to use the name or photograph of any minor child involved in a pending proceeding. Clearly, the order was designed to prevent any further use of the name or photograph of the murder suspect. The news media appealed the judge's edict, arguing that the boy's identity already was common knowledge, owing largely to the court's own actions. Pointing to *Cox* v. *Cohn*, they argued that a name made public during the official proceedings of a court could not later be made private. The Oklahoma Supreme Court rejected that argument, but on further appeal, the United States Supreme Court reversed, issuing only a brief *per curiam* decision. It noted that the news media had obtained their information legally, with the state's implicit approval. Therefore, the judge's subsequent order was a clear violation of the First Amendment's guarantee of freedom of the press.

The Supreme Court's decision in *Cox*, discussed earlier, has cut two ways. Beyond question, it has immunized the media from successful actions for disclosure of facts found in the public records of courts or disclosed in open court. Other court decisions have extended the *Cox* rationale to protect media reliance on facts found in other kinds of public records, if they are obtained legitimately. But in *Cox* a majority of the Court also suggested that courts and legislatures could protect the privacy of rape victims and others by sealing records or closing proceedings in which they are identified. At the time of *Cox*, juvenile records already were sealed in all states. All but two states have also enacted laws providing for expunging or sealing long-past arrest records or even records of convictions. They have done so to encourage rehabilitation and to protect privacy. Courts have upheld such laws, but also have held that they cannot be carried so far as to permit withholding of information about current arrests.

In the *Newspapers* case, the Wisconsin court held that the abuses that could occur if arrests were kept secret outweighed the privacy interest inherent in the fact that charges against many persons arrested by police are dismissed by the prosecutor. An Oregon court held that a person once convicted of a crime could not sustain a libel action against a newspaper which reported that fact after the record had been expunged. What once was true still was true despite a state law permitting the plaintiff to say it wasn't. Finally, the Supreme Court itself has held, in *Oklahoma Publishing* and in *Smith*, that the media can neither be restrained from nor punished for publishing the identity of an offender whose record is sealed, provided the information is obtained legally.

In the Professional World

When professional journalists get together—whether at formal meetings or informally over drinks—few topics arouse more discussion than invasion of privacy. These discussions are usually inconclusive because opinions and practices with respect to the line between private fact and news vary widely. An elaborate subterfuge used by one newspaper to catch city employees in the act of taking bribes was condemned as unethical by others.[69] A story seen as a journalistic scoop by some editors was shunned as an intolerable revelation of private fact by others.[70] Sometimes the conflict between good journalism and bad ethics occurs in the same individual. One editor said he would nominate for a Pulitzer Prize a photograph he considered a grossly insensitive intrusion into a family's grief.[71]

Codes of ethics adopted by organizations of journalists contain sections on privacy. The code embraced by the Society of Professional Journalists–Sigma Delta Chi says, "The news media must guard against invading a person's right to privacy." That is followed by a less strongly worded sentence that says, "The media should not pander to morbid curiosity about details of vice and crime." The Associated Press Managing Editors code also advises respect for the individual's right of privacy. The code of the Radio-Television News Directors Association is somewhat broader. It says that "broadcast journalists shall at all times display humane respect for the dignity, privacy and the well-being of persons with whom the news deals." Such language obviously leaves the individual professional wide latitude in dealing with questions of privacy.

As we have seen, the law also gives journalists a wide field in which to work. Courts have shown little sympathy for reporters who trespass or break the law to get a story. In *Dietemann*, two federal courts condemned a reporter's and a photographer's use of deception. However, the decision is clouded by the fact that the deception was used to gain entry to the private sanctuary offered by Dietemann's home. Courts have not condemned other kinds of deception used to obtain news stories. Journalists who are usually quick to condemn the deceptions of others have on occasion used subterfuge themselves.

---

69. H. Eugene Goodwin, *Groping for Ethics in Journalism* (Ames: Iowa State University Press, 1983), pp. 135–36, 138–40.
70. The *San Francisco Chronicle's* revelation that Oliver W. Sipple was a member of that city's homosexual community is but one example. Sipple made news in 1976 by deflecting a shot aimed at President Ford.
71. Bob Greene, "News Business and Right of Privacy Can Be at Odds," *1985-86 Journalism Ethics Report*, National Ethics Committee, Society of Professional Journalists, Sigma Delta Chi, p. 15.

In one instance, editors of the *Dayton Journal Herald* asked a reporter new to the city to try to get a job as an orderly at a state mental hospital. The purpose was to investigate reports of patient mistreatment. The reporter got the job and emerged from cover thirty days later with material for a series of sensational stories resulting in changes in the hospital's administration. The series also won two journalism prizes.[72] In another instance in the late 1970s, editors of the *Chicago Sun-Times* asked two reporters to buy and operate a tavern, The Mirage, to investigate tips that city building inspectors were shaking down owners of small businesses. The reporters-turned-barkeepers soon learned that the tips were true. They could not stay open without paying off wiring and plumbing inspectors. Hidden microphones and cameras recorded the transactions. The operation produced stories that ran for four weeks.

Were these stories the fruits of unusual enterprise? Or were the unwary officials led into a trap and baited into making demands they might not otherwise have made? If dishonesty was indeed rampant in city officialdom, could it have been exposed only by tactics that were not quite on the level themselves? Those questions were raised at the time by David Halvorsen, then managing editor of the *San Francisco Examiner*, who asked two editors of stature to respond to them.[73] Clayton Kirkpatrick, whose *Chicago Tribune* was scooped by the series, defended his competitor's methods. He said he was convinced there was no entrapment. There are times, he said, when direct, convincing evidence of wrongdoing can be obtained only through the reporter's involvement. He saw The Mirage operation as different only in degree from instances in which reporters posing as ordinary consumers obtain evidence on dishonest television and automobile repair services. Eugene Patterson of the *St. Petersburg Times* disagreed. Like Kirkpatrick, he recognized that there are occasions when reporters need not proclaim who they are. A newspaper's restaurant critic can best serve by seeming to be an ordinary diner. Applying what he called "a scale of distinctions," Patterson said his newspaper would not ask reporters to go undercover to investigate conditions in nursing homes. He said he believed that with hard work, open reporting methods could get the same information. He said, "We've inflicted pretty high ethical standards on public and private institutions with our editorials in recent years and I worry a lot about our hypocrisy quotient if we demand government in the sunshine and practice journalism unnecessarily in the shade." However, he reserved the right to use deception if that proved to be the only way to obtain a story of "vital public interest."

Where dissemination of private facts are at issue, journalists differ widely. The *Diaz* case represents one extreme. Some editors take the position that people who seek the public's approval, either by entering politics or by becoming celebrities, have little or no right of privacy. Others act on the belief that even persons of prominence are entitled to raise a family, drink, or even philander in private as long as what they do does not affect their duty to the public. In this area, there

---

72. Jack Vincent of the *Dayton Journal Herald* during the author's association with that newspaper in the 1950s.
73. *Bulletin of the American Society of Newspaper Editors*, September 1979, p. 12.

has been a marked changed in journalistic ethics in the last twenty-five years. When John F. Kennedy was president, every Washington correspondent who was halfway alert heard stories of his womanizing, but no one reported it. Reporters also knew that Wilbur Mills, then chairman of the House Ways and Means Committee and one of the most powerful men in Washington, had a drinking problem. That did not get into the news until police arrested him for cavorting drunkenly in public with a stripper. Two incidents in 1985 illustrate how the times have changed. The *Wall Street Journal* broke the story that John Fedders, the top enforcement officer of the Securities and Exchange Commission, was a confessed, chronic wife-beater. The story came out through a divorce action, not because of any problems Fedders was having with his job. In that same year, when actor Rock Hudson's desperate attempt to obtain treatment for AIDS led to the disclosure that he was a homosexual, CBS and NBC led their evening news telecasts with the story. Also in 1985, the American Society of Newspaper Editors got the results of a year-long study of newspaper credibility. It found that 78 percent of a rather large sampling of the general public believe that reporters "don't worry much about hurting people."

When private individuals are drawn into the news, the definition of a right of privacy becomes even more difficult. This is illustrated by the experience of John Harte, a photographer for the *Bakersfield Californian*, and his managing editor,

Reporters and photographers surrounded Mrs. Leon Klinghoffer when she disembarked from the cruise ship *Achille Lauro* in Port Said, Egypt, after it had been hijacked by Arab terrorists in 1985. Her husband, who was confined to a wheelchair as a result of a stroke, was shot and thrown overboard. Although the journalists' intrusive disregard for Mrs. Klinghoffer's grief is not a violation of privacy law, polls show that many persons consider such actions a breach of ethics. (B. Bisson/Sygma)

Bob Bentley.[74] Harte was present when the body of a five-year-old drowning victim was dragged from a lake. He photographed the victim's father, mother, and older brother at the moment the body bag was opened to reveal the boy's face. The father is crouched over the body, his fists pressed tightly against his eyes. The older brother stands screaming in his mother's arms. Her face is distorted by a sob. The *Californian* used the photograph. It was offered to Associated Press, which distributed it nationally. In the next two days, the newspaper received more than 500 calls from people protesting what they saw as an invasion of the family's privacy. A bomb threat forced evacuation of the newspaper building. Bentley wrote a column, apologizing to the paper's readers. If he had it to do over, he said, he would not have run the photograph. He told Bob Greene, columnist for the *Chicago Tribune*:

> To me, this case is the strongest validation I've ever seen that newspapers are out of touch with their readers. We did something we thought was right, and the overwhelming majority of our readers thought it was wrong. They told us that by printing the picture, we had violated that child's memory. . . . By running that picture we alienated the hell out of our readers, and if we don't respond to that, we're stupid.

Photographer Harte disagreed. "I'm proud of the shot," he said, adding that it stood as a powerful reminder to others to be careful in the water.

Bentley did not fault the photographer for taking the picture or for being proud of it. He agreed that it was a powerful and dramatic shot, so good that he told Greene he intended to nominate it for a Pulitzer Prize. If he did, it was not among the winners announced in April 1986. However, the winning photographs, taken by Carol Guzy and Michel DuCille of the *Miami Herald*, also portrayed death and grief—that of the victims of mudslides that followed the eruption of Nevado del Ruiz volcano in Colombia.

The dilemmas represented by Bentley's ambivalence are all too common in the professional world. Questions of privacy present more hard decisions than any others. Policies can be adopted and guidelines drafted, but they cannot cover all eventualities. For instance, most news organizations have a policy forbidding publication of the name of a rape victim. But of what use is such a policy if the victim is widely publicized on television? That happened in 1984 when Cable News Network televised most of the trial of six men accused of raping a young woman on a pool table in a bar in New Bedford, Massachusetts. The camera focused on the victim throughout her testimony, and her name was used repeatedly. The following year, a rape victim became something of a celebrity when she said she had lied about being raped several years previously and now wanted her alleged attacker released from prison. A few newspapers publish names of rape victims in the belief that by doing so they may prevent some women from making false charges for vindictive purposes.[75]

Obviously, any generalizations made about journalism professionals and their attitude toward privacy are likely to be fallacious. And yet one observation may be

---

74. See note 71 above.
75. Goodwin, *Groping for Ethics*, pp. 224–27.

more valid than not. In recent years, journalists are talking more about ethical considerations than once was the case. In the mid-1980s, both the American Society of Newspaper Editors and the Associated Press Managing Editors Association commissioned credibility studies that were concerned in large part with the ethics of privacy. The Society of Professional Journalists issues annual reports surveying what it sees as the ethical lapses of the media. Several textbooks on journalism ethics, designed for college courses, have been published. All of this activity seems to suggest an increased awareness of ethical considerations. Perhaps it indicates that some journalists are becoming less concerned with how much the law will let them get away with and more concerned with what a sense of compassion tells them they should do. Within the author's experience as a reporter and editor, journalists turned aside requests to keep embarrassing facts out of the paper or off the air with, "I don't make the news, I only report it." During the discussion of APME's credibility study at the association's annual meeting in San Francisco in October 1985, one editor said he now asks, on occasion. "How would I feel if this story were about me, or someone close to me?" That question will not resolve all privacy dilemmas—some embarrassing facts must be reported in the public interest— but it represents another, and welcome, approach.

FOR REVIEW

1. What is meant by "the right of privacy"? Why is the concept of particular interest to journalists?

2. List and define the four branches of invasion of privacy identified by William L. Prosser. Distinguish each from the others in terms of the elements of the offense.

3. How far can a reporter go in gathering news that takes place on private property? In obtaining information from reluctant news sources?

4. Define the limits of a photographer's right to take and use pictures for news purposes. Would the limits be any different if the photographs were to be used for feature purposes?

5. How have the courts defined an "embarrassing private fact"? How far can the news media go in reporting intimate details of a news subject's life?

6. What meaning does *Cox* v. *Cohn* have for journalists?

7. Does the term "public figure" have the same meaning in connection with invasion of privacy as it has in connection with libel?

8. Distinguish between false light and libel. What is the meaning of the *Hill* and *Cantrell* decisions?

9. List and justify a set of rules for use by an advertising agency planning to use identifiable persons in an advertising campaign.

10. What meaning does "the right of publicity" have in law? What hazards does it raise for television news directors? For writers of magazine articles?

11. Expand on the meaning of newsworthiness, illustrating with examples from cases.

12. Expand on the meaning of consent, illustrating with examples from cases.

13. What is an expungement law? A sealed record? How do they relate to the work of the journalist?

14. In all states, records of juvenile offenders are kept secret unless released by a judge. Does this mean that the news media can be kept from disseminating names of juveniles who have committed crimes? Why or why not?

CHAPTER *6*

A FAIR AND PUBLIC TRIAL

"Jazz Age journalism" was born in the 1920s when most American cities had two or more highly competitive newspapers striving for a share of the audience. Sensationalism was considered the key to winning readers, and the era was made to order for it. Prohibition, which spanned the twenties, and the Depression, which ended them, spawned gangland wars and such figures as Al Capone, John Dillinger, Pretty Boy Floyd, and Bonnie and Clyde. Their crimes, and the crimes of others, were the subjects of breathlessly written stories bannered under screaming headlines on page 1. When a suspect was arrested, particularly on a charge of murder, reporters outdid each other to gather evidence that would prove him guilty. In this trial by newspaper they were aided by police officers and prosecutors, eager to win a conviction and get their names in the papers. Defense attorneys, not to be outdone, sought to build backfires by giving reporters any shred of evidence that would help their clients. Most judges looked the other way. Only an occasional civil libertarian argued that the system violated the suspect's right to a fair trial. Once in a while it was discovered that an innocent person had been punished because prejudicial publicity pushed a jury to an improper conviction.

This system began to change about 1960, partly because of changes in journalism. Few cities were left with competitive newspapers, while television, although highly competitive, did not cover crime in detail. College-trained reporters and editors, a minority in most newsrooms prior to World War II, became the rule.

The audience had changed, too. Readers were better educated and more sophisticated in their concept of news. In any event, if they were interested in crime, they could see more of it in prime time television than in the real world—and the film version was a lot more exciting.

But a more important factor in the decline of trial by newspaper was the Warren Court. The term is a tribute to Earl Warren, who was appointed chief justice by President Eisenhower in 1953 and who served until 1969. Under his leadership, the Supreme Court of the United States did more to enlarge and protect the rights of criminal suspects than in any other time in its history. Two of its decisions, *Irvin* v. *Dowd*[1] in 1961 and *Sheppard* v. *Maxwell*[2] in 1966, served notice on judges everywhere that they should not permit prejudicial publicity in the news media to interfere with a suspect's right to a fair trial. The Court found that mandate in the Sixth Amendment:

> In all criminal prosecutions, the accused shall enjoy the right to a speedy and public trial, by an impartial jury of the State and district wherein the crime shall have been committed, which district shall have been previously ascertained by law, and to be informed of the nature and cause of the accusation; to be confronted with the witnesses against him; to have compulsory process for obtaining witnesses in his favor, and to have the assistance of counsel for his defense.

In this chapter, the focus will be on just four words of this amendment: "impartial jury" and "public trial." We will see that, starting with *Irvin*, the Court sought first to define what trial by an impartial jury is. In the process, it established criteria for determining whether a trial has been fair. With the *Sheppard* decision five years later, attention was focused on measures judges are expected to take to ensure that a defendant gets a fair trial. In response to *Sheppard*, judges experimented with restraints, popularly called "gag orders," designed to cut off prejudicial information at the source. These took two forms: One was directed at participants in the trial—attorneys for both sides, witnesses,

---

1. 366 U.S. 717, 81 S.Ct. 1639, 6 L.Ed.2d. 751 (1961).
2. 384 U.S. 333, 86 S.Ct. 1507, 16 L.Ed.2d 600 (1966).

and court employees; the other was directed at reporters covering court proceedings at which prejudicial information was disclosed. Appellate courts have upheld restraint of participants, but only when the threat to a fair trial is clear. The Supreme Court has held that journalists can be subjected to restraint only under conditions that make such a step highly unlikely. However, in so holding, the Court suggested that judges might solve their problem by closing some court proceedings so that highly prejudicial information could be kept from reaching the public. This brought into question the meaning of the Sixth Amendment's guarantee of a public trial. In resolving that issue, the Supreme Court held that the First Amendment implies a right of journalists and the public to attend court proceedings. That right can be overcome only by evidence that the suspect cannot get a fair trial unless some specific part of the legal process is closed.

Reduced to a brief outline, the Court's twenty-five-year struggle to ensure that trials are both fair and open to the public is stripped of the strong feelings it has aroused. At the height of the struggle, lawyers and judges stood behind the Sixth Amendment, arguing that circulation- and ratings-hungry newspapers and broadcasters were trampling on the rights of criminal suspects. Opposing them, reporters and editors stood behind the First Amendment, arguing that courts and the bar were trampling on the people's right to be informed. Relations between the two sides were so strained at one point that it was news when a press-bar committee was formed in the state of Washington to attempt to reach some middle ground. Skirmishes still are being fought, but there is a middle ground now, and a better understanding on both sides of the accommodations that must be made if defendants are to be assured a fair and public trial, and the people are to be informed. This chapter therefore is a study of what happens when two rights, each directly guaranteed by the Bill of Rights, come into conflict.

Major Cases

Estes v. Texas, 381 U.S. 532, 85 S.Ct.. 1628, 14 L.Ed.2d 543 (1965).

Federated Publications, Inc. v. Swedberg, 633 P.2d 74 (Wash. 1981).

Gannett, Inc. v. DePasquale, 443 U.S. 368, 99 S.Ct. 2898, 61 L.Ed.2d 608 (1979).

Globe Newspaper Co. v. Superior Court, County of Norfolk, 457 U.S. 596, 102 S.Ct. 2613, 73 L.Ed.2d 248 (1982).

In re Russell, 726 F.2d 1007 (4th Cir. 1984).

Irvin v. Dowd, 366 U.S. 717, 81 S.Ct. 1639, 6 L.Ed.2d 751 (1961).

Murphy v. Florida, 421 U.S. 794, 95 S.Ct. 2031, 44 L.Ed.2d 589 (1975).

Nebraska Press Association v. Stuart, 427 U.S. 539, 96 S.Ct. 2791, 49 L.Ed.2d 683 (1976).

Press-Enterprise Co. v. Superior Court of California, Riverside County, 464 U.S. 501, 104 S.Ct. 819, 78 L.Ed.2d 629 (1984).

Richmond Newspapers, Inc. v. *Virginia,* 448 U.S. 555, 100 S.Ct. 2814, 65 L.Ed.2d 1973 (1980).

Rideau v. *Louisiana,* 373 U.S. 723, 83 S.Ct. 1417, 9 L.Ed.2d 229 (1963).

Sacramento Bee v. *United States District Court,* 565 F.2d 477 (9th Cir. 1981).

Sheppard v. *Maxwell,* 384 U.S. 333, 86 S.Ct. 1507, 16 L.Ed.2d 600 (1966).

United States v. *Dickinson,* 465 F.2d 496 (5th Cir. 1972).

United States v. *Tijerina,* 412 F.2d 661 (10th Cir. 1969).

THREATS TO A FAIR TRIAL

The Legal Process

The trial of a person accused of committing a crime is a ritual, with roots embedded deep in Anglo-Saxon history. However informal the process may sometimes seem, it is surrounded by safeguards designed to prevent the defendant's being railroaded into prison on flimsy evidence or in response to public clamor.

An individual is brought into the criminal justice system in most cases by an *arrest,* which is defined as "the taking of a person into custody for the purpose of charging him with a crime."[3] It is at this point that the nature of the crime and the identity of the suspect become known to the news media because arrests are matters of public record.

This public record is created by a process known as *booking,* that is, the formal entry into the police records system of the date, the time, the nature of the charge, the name of the person arrested, and the name of the arresting officer.

The arrested person is now under custody, and the next step usually is *detention* in jail or a holding cell. If the charge is minor, the suspect may be released on posting **bail,** or, if he has strong roots in the community, on his own recognizance—that is, on his promise that he will show up for such further proceedings as may be scheduled. If the crime is a serious one, the setting of bail may be the subject of a **hearing** conducted by a judge. If the charge is murder, the suspect may be denied bail as a matter of law.

The next step is the drafting of the *formal accusation,* or *charge.* If the suspect was arrested on a **warrant,** that step was taken in advance. The formal accusation, which takes varying forms, depending on its origin, is a statement in legal language precisely defining the crime with which the suspect is accused. In federal cases involving serious crimes, the formal accusations must come from a *grand jury,* because the Fifth Amendment so requires. A grand jury is a group of persons whose names have been chosen at random and brought together for the purpose of deciding whether a crime has been committed and, if so, identifying the likely suspect. At the state level, the formal accusation can come from a grand jury or from the prosecutor, acting either on his own

---

3. A. C. Germann, Frank D. Day, Robert R. J. Gallati, *Introduction to Law Enforcement and Criminal Justice* (Springfield, Ill.: Thomas, 1976), p. 192.

or on the basis of complaints from the victim, the police, or others. A formal accusation of crime resulting from a grand jury's investigation is called a bill of *indictment*, sometimes referred to as a "true bill." If the suspect is not already in custody, the indictment may be sealed until he can be arrested.

What happens next varies from state to state and also varies with the manner in which the formal accusation was brought. A prompt *preliminary hearing* is generally required, although this can be waived by the defendant, and usually is if a grand jury has returned an indictment. If the hearing is not waived, the suspect is brought before a judge and the prosecution is required to (1) show that a crime has been committed; and (2) offer sufficient evidence to convince the judge there is a reasonable basis for connecting the accused with the crime. Such hearings are informal. The prosecution is permitted to present evidence that may not be admissible at trial. Because such information may be highly prejudicial to the defendant, the preliminary hearing has become one of the points of contention between the courts and the news media.

If the preliminary hearing results in a finding of "probable cause," the next step is *arraignment*. Again the suspect is brought before a judge. The charge is read and explained, and the suspect is asked how he pleads. If the defendant pleads guilty, all that remains is sentencing. If he pleads not guilty, the next step is the trial.

However, trial is the exception. In most instances, while the steps above are taking place, the prosecutor and the defense attorney will have been engaged in *plea bargaining*. A defendant charged with armed robbery, a serious crime, may balk at pleading guilty to that charge, but may agree, through his attorney, to do so to a lesser charge of simple assault. Or a defendant charged with driving under the influence, and facing a possible loss of his driver's license, may agree to plead guilty to reckless driving. Most cases are disposed of in this way because neither prosecutors' staffs nor the courts themselves could otherwise cope with the large numbers of persons charged with crime.

If the decision is made to go to trial, the defendant may choose to be tried by a judge, or a panel of judges in a serious case, or by a jury. If there is to be a jury, the first day or days of the trial will be concerned with selection of its members. Prospective jurors are chosen by lot from lists of registered voters, taxpayers, or telephone owners, and are supposed to represent a cross section of the community. The judge has the duty of questioning each candidate closely to weed out those who may be prejudiced for or against the defendant. This questioning is called *voir dire*—a French phrase meaning literally, "to say truly." Practically, in the voir dire prospective jurors are questioned closely by the judge, in the presence of the defendant and counsel for both sides. The purpose is to discover any prejudices or personal information that might influence a juror's decision.

Once the jury has been chosen, the trial itself is as rigidly structured as a Bach fugue. Here is a summary of its elements:

THE OPENING STATEMENTS   First the prosecutor and then the defense attorney tells the court his version of the facts and the likely testimony. What is said is argument, not evidence, and the judge will caution the jury to avoid drawing conclusions from it.

THE STATE'S CASE   The prosecutor calls witnesses whose testimony is designed to prove the defendant guilty beyond reasonable doubt. Each witness is subject to **cross-examination** by defense counsel, who will do all he can to raise doubt about the credibility of each.

If the cross-examination produces new information, the prosecutor may follow with redirect examination, which may open the witness to recross-examination.

This process, niggling and repetitive as it may seem, is the heart of the trial. The burden of proof is on the prosecutor, and it is a strong one. He cannot win a guilty verdict unless his evidence can convince each member of the jury beyond a reasonable doubt. In contrast, the defense attorney's job is much simpler. All he must do is raise doubt in the mind of one strong-willed juror. If he can do so, the worst he can get is a hung jury—that is, a jury that cannot agree. A few states permit majority verdicts if the offense is minor, but in most the jury's verdict must be unanimous. If the jury cannot agree, then the state must decide whether to go to the time and expense of another trial, or dismiss the charge.

THE DEFENSE CASE   If the defense attorney thinks the prosecution's case is weak, he will move to dismiss. If the judge agrees, the defendant is freed. If not, the defense presents its case. Its witnesses may merely attack the credibility of the state's case, or they may offer an affirmative defense, such as alibi or self-defense. The defendant is not required to testify. Indeed, if he is a repeat offender, it is unlikely he will be called. If he doesn't testify, the rules of the court forbid any mention of his criminal record. The court operates on the theory that a prior arrest record, or even a term in prison for a similar offense, has nothing to do with proving guilt in the current case. However, if the defendant does choose to testify, the prior record may be introduced by the prosecution to impeach his testimony—that is, to raise doubt in the minds of the jurors as to how far he can be trusted to tell the truth.

REBUTTAL   Witnesses may be offered to respond to allegations made by the defense, or to answer questions raised by it. If the process discloses new evidence, the defense has an opportunity for surrebuttal.

SUMMATION OR CLOSING ARGUMENT   After all the evidence is in, first the defense counsel and then the prosecutor offers his summary of the case. Again, the jury is cautioned that what is said is not evidence. Each attorney summarizes the testimony in a manner calculated to lead the jury to the desired conclusion.

INSTRUCTING THE JURY   The judge is responsible for seeing that the trial is conducted in accord with pertinent law and constitutional safeguards. It is the jury's duty to decide what the evidence means. However, that decision cannot be made without some awareness of the law. The judge may tell the jury, for instance, that it cannot find the defendant guilty if it concludes he was legally insane at the moment the crime was committed. He probably will instruct the jury further on the legal criteria involved in determining insanity. The jury is the ultimate finder of fact. It alone can decide which witnesses to believe, which versions of two or more conflicting stories to accept. The judge also "charges" the jury by seeking to impress it with the duty to bring in a verdict based solely on the evidence seen and heard in court.

DELIBERATION   The jury retires to a jury room where it remains until it reaches a verdict. The jurors select one of their number to act as foreman, who seeks to lead them to a verdict. If the judge's instructions on the law permit, the jury may find the defendant guilty of a lesser offense.

MOTIONS   If the defendant is found guilty, motions are in order. Usually at this point, the defense will allege that the judge erred in rulings on points of law raised during the trial. This provides grounds for a possible appeal.

JUDGMENT   The judge issues the decision of the court, making formal the verdict of the jury. Imposition of the penalty usually is deferred pending an investigation designed to guide the judge to a choice of several alternative sentences ranging from release on probation to a long term in prison.

The process is designed to make the state prove its case through valid evidence that goes to the point of the offense with which the defendant is charged. Evidence that does not bear directly on the offense, or that has been obtained in violation of the defendant's rights, is not supposed to be submitted to the jury. For instance, a confession is not admissible as evidence if the defendant had not been advised of his Fifth Amendment right to remain silent and the right to consult a lawyer. Sometimes a hearing on the admissibility of evidence may be the most important element in the criminal process. If a confession is the strongest evidence the prosecution has, a ruling excluding it from the trial may mean that the defendant goes free.

Fair-trial issues are raised when the news media report the existence of evidence that cannot, under the rules, be used at the trial. Jurors are screened at the start of the trial to find out whether they have knowledge of such evidence. Once chosen, they are admonished not to read or listen to news accounts of the trial. But on occasion courts have found that news reports of inadmissible evidence were so pervasive that the jurors could not have been impartial. In such instance, the defendant either must be submitted to a new trial, or go free.

Defining an Impartial Jury

The concern with prejudicial publicity and its presumed effect on the right to a fair trial is not new. Aaron Burr, a former vice-president of the United States, raised the question in 1807 when he was tried for treason because of his alleged part in a conspiracy to set up an independent nation somewhere between the Ohio and Mississippi rivers. He asked that the indictment be dismissed, arguing that inflammatory articles in the *Alexandria* (Va.) *Expositor* and other newspapers had turned the minds of potential jurors against him. The great Chief Justice John Marshall, sitting as a trial judge, rebuffed that argument, setting standards used to this day in selecting juries. He wrote in *United States* v. *Burr:*[4]

> The great value of trial by jury certainly consists in its fairness and impartiality. Those who most prize the institution prize it because it furnishes a tribunal which may be expected to be uninfluenced by an undue bias of the mind. I have always conceived [that] . . . an impartial jury . . . must be composed of men who will fairly hear the testimony which

---

4. 25 Fed.Cas. 49 (No. 14,692g) (1807).

may be offered to them, bring in their verdict according to that testimony, and according to the laws arising on it.

Marshall noted the obvious: Persons who have made up their minds in advance about the defendant's guilt or innocence cannot be impartial. This does not mean, he added, that potential jurors must be completely ignorant of the defendant or of the crime. Even in the society of 1807, that would be too much to expect. Therefore, jurors can be considered impartial if they hold "light impressions [as to guilt or innocence] which may fairly be supposed to yield to the testimony . . . which may leave the mind open to a fair consideration of that testimony. . . . "

An impartial juror, then, is one whose mind is not made up in advance, but who is willing to listen to the evidence and evaluate it fairly. In Burr's case, jurors chosen by Marshall's criteria listened to the evidence for six months and found the defendant not guilty.

The passage of nearly two centuries has not materially changed Chief Justice Marshall's definition of an impartial jury. It is made up of men and women whose minds are open to the testimony offered in court and who will base their decision solely on that evidence. In the America of the early 1800s, sources of information that might prejudice members of a jury were confined largely to the weekly newspapers and to word of mouth. Today, we are surrounded by communications media that use graphic devices, market research, and the latest discoveries of the communications theorists in an attempt to get us to pay attention to them. Not surprisingly, this has raised new questions about the influences that can prevent people from being impartial jurors.

Some of these questions have focused on what makes a potential juror biased. In a University of Chicago study, judges noted that suspects were denied a fair trial because jurors had read or heard about confessions that were made in violation of constitutional safeguards. Other jurors were prejudiced by reading or hearing about the results of lie detector tests, which are not admissible as evidence, the defendant's prior criminal record, or evidence seized in violation of the suspect's right of privacy.[5] By an overwhelming majority, these judges said they believed it "inappropriate" for the news media to publish such information in advance of a trial. However, they also said, as Marshall had many years earlier, they they did not believe jurors needed to be altogether ignorant of the facts of a case in order to be impartial.

Studies of jury performance are inconclusive. One researcher concluded that "the jury is a pretty stubborn, healthy institution not likely to be overwhelmed either by a remark of counsel or a remark of the press."[6] A federal appeals court judge in Chicago once told an audience of newspaper editors that he had learned during his days as a trial judge that most potential jurors hadn't paid much attention to stories of crime. He said very few had made up their minds as to guilt or innocence because of what they read.[7]

5. Fred S. Siebert, "Trial Judges' Opinions of Prejudicial Publicity," in Chilton R. Bush, ed., *Free Press and Fair Trial* (Athens: University of Georgia Press, 1970), pp. 2–19. The poll was conducted by the National Opinion Research Center at the University of Chicago.

6. Walter Wilcox, "The Press, the Jury and the Behavioral Sciences," in *Free Press and Fair Trial*, pp. 67–102, quoting Harry K. Kalven, Jr., coauthor with Hans Zeisel of *The American Jury* (Boston: Little, Brown, 1966).

7. "Notable and Quotable," *Wall Street Journal*, 5 May 1976, quoting Judge William J. Bauer of the United States Court of Appeals, Seventh Circuit, in a speech to the American Society of Newspaper Editors.

But the fact remains that in a significant number of cases since 1960 federal and state courts have found that pervasive media publicity given to inadmissible evidence and prior criminal records has caused jurors to come to the trial with their minds not only closed, but with their opinion as to guilt or innocence already formed. Thus, they have not been impartial jurors, as required by the Sixth Amendment. As a result of such findings, some criminal defendants have been set free, and others have had to go through new trials with some juries confirming the original verdict, and others coming to opposite conclusions.

Factors Causing an Unfair Trial

A little-noted decision of the Warren Court in 1959 marked the beginning of a new attitude toward trial by newspaper. In *Marshall* v. *United States*,[8] the Supreme Court reversed the conviction of a drug dealer. It held that the jurors had been improperly influenced by reading that Marshall had two prior convictions, one of them for practicing medicine without a license. The case was of limited interest because the conviction had been in a federal court, so that the decision applied only to the federal court system, which was not heavily involved with criminal cases at the time.

Two years later, in 1961, the Court won a great deal of attention with its reversal of a murder conviction that came up to it from the state courts in Indiana. In its decision, the Court announced, as a principle of federal constitutional law applicable to all courts, that decisions reached by jurors who have been influenced by prejudicial publicity violate the Sixth Amendment guarantee of trial by an impartial jury. The defendant in this instance was Leslie Irvin, who was accused of killing six persons in and near Evansville, Indiana, in 1954 and 1955. Some of the newspaper stories compared his actions to those of a mad dog. Copy editors picked up on the theme, writing headlines about "Mad Dog Irvin." So pervasive was the publicity in Evansville itself that the trial was moved to Princeton in adjoining Gibson County, where a jury found Irvin guilty and imposed the death penalty.

Irvin v. *Dowd,* 366 U.S. 717, 81 S.Ct. 1639, 6 L.Ed.2d 751 (1961).

The Supreme Court agreed to review the conviction, holding in *Irvin* v. *Dowd* that he had been the victim of a prejudiced jury. In this instance, the Court was able to point to tangible evidence proving bias on the part of nine of the twelve jurors. Prejudicial publicity had been so pervasive, even in Gibson County, that although more than four hundred potential jurors were examined, and the defense used up all its challenges, most of those who were accepted believed Irvin guilty. Under such conditions, the Supreme Court held, a fair trial was impossible. On remand, Irvin again was tried, this time in Central Indiana, where he was again found guilty, this time sentenced to a life term in prison.

In its *Irvin* decision, the Supreme Court held that a conviction in a highly publicized case should be reversed on appeal on a showing of evidence that one or more of the

---

8. 360 U.S. 310, 79 S.Ct. 1171, 3 L.Ed.2d 1250 (1959).

jurors had been prejudiced against the defendant. The decision put the burden of proof on the defense to demonstrate a direct connection between harmful news stories and the jury's decision.

Within two years, in its decision in *Rideau v. Louisiana*, the Supreme Court modified that standard. It did so in a case originating in Lake Charles, Louisiana, where Wilbert

Rideau v. Louisiana, 373 U.S. 723, 83 S.Ct. 1417, 9 L.Ed.2d 229 (1963).

Rideau robbed a bank, took three of its employees as hostages in his getaway, and killed one of them before he was captured. The morning after his arrest, Rideau was visited in his jail cell by the sheriff, followed by a camera crew from KPLC-TV of Lake Charles. With the sheriff asking the questions, Rideau talked about his exploits, readily admitting that he had killed the hostage. The television station broadcast its tape of his confession three times in two days.

As Rideau's trial date approached, his lawyer asked for a change of venue to a court beyond the reach of KPLC-TV's signal. The request was denied. Prospective jurors were asked if they had seen any of the telecasts. Three said they had, but they were permitted to serve anyway. Two other members of the jury were honorary deputy sheriffs. The jury found Rideau guilty. On appeal, the Supreme Court of the United States agreed to review the verdict. It held that Rideau was entitled to a new trial in a location where the televised confession had not been seen.

Justice Potter Stewart, writing for the Court, said that for the tens of thousands of persons who saw the telecasts, Rideau's trial had taken place in his jail cell, and his own words had proved his guilt. The Court held that where there was such pervasive exposure to such prejudicial publicity, a trial could not be fair. In effect, the Court held that the telecasts had created an atmosphere of prejudice, making the selection of an impartial jury impossible. Under this standard, it was not necessary for the defense to prove that any member of the jury had been influenced by the publicity, as the *Irvin* test required. The defense need only show that there was enough prejudicial publicity to lead appellate judges to the conclusion that jurors probably were influenced by it.

Irvin and *Rideau* dealt with publicity that occurred before the trial. In 1965, the Court took a case in which a change of venue had been granted to get away from the effects of pretrial publicity. But because parts of the trial had been televised, the Supreme Court held in *Estes v. Texas*, in a close decision, that the defendant had not received a fair trial, and that the mere presence of the television cameras in the courtroom, even

Estes v. Texas, 381 U.S. 532, 85 S.Ct. 1628, 14 L.Ed.2d 543 (1965).

though they were largely shielded from view by a false wall, created a presumption of unfairness. Although there was no evidence that the jurors had been influenced in any way, five members of the Court concluded that people are affected in unpredictable ways when they know they are on camera. The decision was so lacking in firm guidelines for lower court judges trying to assess its meaning that Richard Cardwell, counsel for the Hoosier State Press Association, characterized it as encouraging "gut jurisprudence."[9] By that he meant that fair trial decisions were based on neither evidence of prejudice nor the application of clearly established criteria, but on nothing more tangible than the judge's feelings.

---

9. *Bulletin* No. 36, HSPA, 7 September 1970.

At the time, the *Estes* decision was important for two reasons. As already indicated, it seemed to leave appeals judges free to use their own judgment as to whether a trial was fair or not. If they found that media coverage created a "probability of prejudice," they were to conclude that the trial was "inherently lacking in due process." The *Estes* decision also seemed to suggest that judges should keep cameras, particularly television cameras, out of the courtroom. The Court's message was clouded by the fact that only four justices signed the leading opinion, written by Justice Tom C. Clark. Those four condemned televised trials:

> [T]he chief function of our judicial machinery is to ascertain the truth. The use of television, however, cannot be said to contribute materially to this objective. Rather its use amounts to the injection of an irrelevant factor into court proceedings. In addition, experience teaches that there are numerous situations in which it might cause actual unfairness—some so subtle as to defy detection by the accused or control by the judge.

Clark speculated that jurors would be distracted by the cameras and their "telltale red lights," and by the awareness that others were seeing and hearing the trial. He predicted that some witnesses might become demoralized, while others might become "cocky and given to overstatement" if they knew they were on television. Judges and lawyers might become actors, seeking public approval. But, in Clark's opinion, the defendant would be the biggest loser. Televising his trial would subject him to a "form of mental—if not physical—harassment" violating his "personal sensibilities, his dignity, and his ability to concentrate on the proceedings before him—sometimes the difference between life and death. . . . " Clark concluded:

> A defendant on trial for his life is entitled to his day in court, not in a stadium, or a city or a nationwide arena. The heightened public clamor resulting from radio or television coverage will inevitably result in prejudice. Trial by television is, therefore, foreign to our system.

The day was saved for photojournalism by Justice John Marshall Harlan. He conceded that Estes had not had a fair trial. But he was not prepared to conclude that the presence of cameras in the courtroom would always violate the defendant's right to due process. Television, he noted, was a fairly recent development at the time of the Estes trial in 1962. It was reasonable to expect improvement in cameras and in recording processes. The Supreme Court, he argued, ought not to issue a decision that would prevent the states from experimenting with television coverage of trials. Harlan's words proved to be prophetic. Fifteen years later, a majority of the Court took guidance from him in holding that there is nothing inherently prejudicial in televising a trial.[10] The current state of the law with respect to cameras in the courtroom will be discussed in chapter 8.

In deciding *Marshall, Irvin, Rideau,* and *Estes,* the Court had, in effect, locked the garage after the automobile had been stolen. It had expanded the meaning of an unfair trial dramatically in six years, but had paid little attention to steps that might be taken to neutralize media influence on jurors. While it was deciding these cases, a murder conviction was smoldering in the Ohio and federal courts on its way to the Supreme

---

10. Chandler v. Florida, 449 U.S. 532, 101 S.Ct. 802, 66 L.Ed.2d 740 (1980).

Court. There it would become the vehicle not only for further definition of the meaning of an unfair trial, but for the Court's prescription of remedies. The Court would not fashion any new legal devices, but it would reiterate in strong terms the responsibility imposed on all judges to confine criminal trials to evidence produced in the courtroom and to enforce the safeguards contained in the Sixth Amendment. The case it chose for this purpose had been conducted in a carnival atmosphere in which some elements of the media literally had demanded the suspect's death.

Dr. Sam Sheppard, a young osteopathic surgeon, had been found guilty in 1954 of murdering his wife. Because Sheppard's family was socially prominent and was able to shield him for awhile from police investigation, the case attracted widespread attention in the news media. From the beginning, the doctor asserted his innocence. He said his wife had been beaten to death by a bushy-haired stranger whom he had surprised in the act and who had fled from the house onto a beach along nearby Lake Erie. Because no one else had seen such a stranger, and because it was known that Sheppard and his wife were having marital problems, he quickly became the center of suspicion. When police did not act on that suspicion, Cleveland's three newspapers demanded that

Sheppard v. *Maxwell,* 384 U.S. 333, 86 S.Ct. 1507, 16 L.Ed.2d 600 (1966).

When Dr. Sam Sheppard was tried for murder in a Cleveland courtroom in 1954, photographers waited outside the doors, creating what the Supreme Court later described as "a carnival atmosphere." The Court held that to ensure a fair trial judges could banish photographers from the courthouse and closely limit the number and activities of reporters. (AP/Wide World Photos)

they do so. One headline proclaimed, "Somebody Is Getting Away with Murder." Another demanded, "Why Isn't Sam Sheppard in Jail?" His arrest followed within hours.

During the weeks leading up to his trial, Cleveland's newspapers and radio and television stations laid down a barrage of stories designed to prove Sheppard's guilt. It was alleged that he had had affairs with a number of women, and that his wife lived in fear of him, but had refused to give him a divorce. One story reported as fact that Sheppard had delayed reporting his wife's murder while he washed away a trail of blood leading from the bedroom and disposed of the murder weapon. When jurors were chosen for the trial, the newspapers published their names and addresses. All said they received letters and telephone calls from persons trying to influence them. So many reporters wanted to cover the trial that the judge, Herbert Blythin, ordered an extra press table set up inside the bar of the court. It was so close to the defense table that Sheppard had to confer with his lawyers in a whisper to avoid being overheard. Newspaper and radio reporters took over adjacent courthouse offices. Television cameras kept a vigil on the sidewalk outside the courthouse where interviews were conducted with witnesses. The judge would not permit cameras in the courtroom while court was in session, but he made an arrangement with photographers that made the ban a mockery. At each recess, they would burst through the doors, cameras ready, and take their pictures before the witness could leave his chair.

Through more than six weeks of trial, the jurors were permitted to go home each evening. Judge Blythin told them not to read, view, or listen to any reports about the case, but made only the most perfunctory attempts to find out whether his order was being obeyed. If the jurors did disobey him, they read and heard about an altogether different trial from the one conducted in the courtroom. News media, local and national, consistently reported "evidence" from "witnesses" who were not even called to testify. Newscasters of prominence argued on radio that the evidence proved Sheppard guilty long before the trial had ended.

Shortly before Christmas 1954, the jury found Sam Sheppard guilty of the murder of his wife. He was sentenced to life in the Ohio State Penitentiary at Columbus. Sheppard appealed to the Ohio Supreme Court and then to the U.S. Supreme Court, arguing that he had not received a fair trial. With the decision in *Irvin* still seven years in the future, both courts rejected his plea. Therefore, the doctor spent the next ten years in prison, where he gained favorable attention by volunteering as a subject for medical experimentation. In 1964, Sheppard's family hired F. Lee Bailey, then one of the nation's leading criminal defense attorneys, to make another attempt to clear Sheppard. He was able to persuade a recently appointed federal judge that the surgeon's trial had been unfair when measured against the standards set long afterward in *Irvin*, *Rideau*, and *Estes*. An appeals court disagreed, but on further appeal the Supreme Court took the case and, in *Sheppard* v. *Maxwell*, reversed. In holding that Sheppard had been the victim of a biased jury, the Court reiterated a basic principle of jurisprudence: A judge's first responsibility is to make certain that a trial is conducted fairly, solely on the basis of admissible evidence.

Justice Clark, writing for seven members of the Court, started with praise for "a responsible press." Over the years, he said, the media have guarded "against the miscarriage of justice by subjecting police, prosecutors, and judicial processes to extensive scrutiny and criticism." Clark endorsed that coverage, noting that the press had been "the handmaiden of effective judicial administration."

He turned next to Judge Blythin's conduct of the trial. Here, he was more critical, holding that the judge had not done as much as he should to protect the jurors from media influences. Indeed, he had permitted the media to turn them into celebrities of a sort by publicizing their names, addresses, and photographs. As a result, the jurors had been exposed "to expressions of opinion from both cranks and friends."

Additionally, by giving reporters and photographers almost free rein in and around the courtroom, the judge had deprived Sheppard of the "judicial serenity and calm to which [he] was entitled." Clark wrote:

> The fact is that bedlam reigned at the courthouse during the trial and newsmen took over practically the entire courtroom, hounding most of the participants in the trial, especially Sheppard. . . . [T]he judge lost his ability to supervise the environment. The movement of the reporters in and out of the courtroom caused frequent confusion and disruption of the trial.

Thus, the Court, which had found television cameras a distracting influence in *Estes*, found reporters and photographers, whatever their medium, to be a problem when they were permitted to take over the courtroom and its environs. Because reporters entered and left the courtroom as they pleased, because photographers congregated in the corridors ready to pounce when the courtroom doors were opened, because witnesses and other participants were fair game for on-the-spot interviews, the "judicial serenity" that should have surrounded the trial was lost. Further, by giving publicity to members of the jury, the media had ensured that they would be subjected to pressure from anyone who felt moved to pick up a telephone and call them. All this was in addition to a massive barrage of prejudicial tips, rumors, and speculation pointing to Sheppard's guilt. The Court concluded that a trial conducted under such circumstances could not possibly have been fair. Sam Sheppard's life sentence was set aside. He was entitled to a new trial.

So serious was the problem of prejudicial publicity seen to be that the Court had moved in five years from a holding that convictions in criminal cases should be set aside if the defendant could show that the jury was prejudiced by media publicity to a much looser position. It had held in *Rideau* that convictions might be reversed if the jury was chosen from a locality permeated by prejudicial publicity. With *Estes* and *Sheppard*, courts seemed to be told to decide on a case-by-case basis whether publicity before and during a trial, coupled with distracting conduct on the part of the media, raised a presumption that jurors were prejudiced. If so, there must be a new trial or the suspect must be set free. All four decisions, and the earlier *Marshall* decision as well, accepted as a given that publicity given to such things as prior criminal records—Irvin had a long one, for example—and inadmissible evidence has an unacceptable influence on jurors. At the time, judges reading the Supreme Court's decisions were acting on the assumption that juror exposure to news stories of any kind dealing with the case at hand made a fair trial unlikely. Given the pervasive penetration of the media in modern society, questions were being raised about the trial system itself. Could not a clever criminal escape punishment by committing a crime on television, as when Jack Ruby shot down Lee Harvey Oswald, the suspected assassin of President John F. Kennedy at Dallas? Nearly a decade was to pass before the Supreme Court sought to answer this question.

Nonprejudicial Publicity

Need jurors be completely uninformed about the case they are asked to decide? That question has confronted judges since Chief Justice Marshall dealt with it in the *Burr* case. In that instance, he said they need not be completely uninformed, but they do need to have their minds open to the testimony they will hear in the courtroom. He recognized that some defendants, like former Vice-President Burr, might be so widely known that only the least intelligent, or least involved, members of society would have no knowledge of them. Could such persons be entrusted with resolving difficult cases? Would they be likely to understand the issues, or give them serious attention?

To resolve such questions, the Supreme Court agreed in 1975 to review a Florida court's conviction of Jack Murphy, one of the most flamboyant criminals of the era. Murphy first gained media attention in 1964 for his role in stealing the Star of India sapphire from an elaborately protected case in a New York City museum. That episode became the subject of a movie. Later, he went to *Murphy* v. *Florida*, 421 U.S. 794, 95 S. Ct. 2031, 44 L.Ed.2d 589 (1975). Miami Beach, where he became known as "Murph the Surf." He was handsome and had a way with women. He used those attributes to gain entry to the homes of the wealthy, from which he took jewels and cash. One such episode resulted in murder, for which Murphy was convicted. All these escapades were given heavy news coverage. When Murphy resumed his criminal career after a prison term, police captured him and three accomplices as they fled from a robbery in a Miami Beach home.

At the trial, Murphy's lawyer argued that news coverage of his client's activities made a fair trial impossible. He supported that position by offering the court a voluminous file of newspaper clippings and transcripts of news broadcasts. The judge conducted a careful voir dire and seated a jury he believed to be impartial. Murphy's lawyer took little part in the trial, resting his case on the belief that any conviction would be reversed on appeal because of publicity given to his client. The jury did indeed convict Murphy. A state appellate court confirmed. Murphy's lawyer turned to the federal courts for relief, arguing that his client was a victim of the news media. When he was rebuffed there, he went to the United States Supreme Court which, in *Murphy* v. *Florida*, affirmed the conviction with only one dissent.

Justice Thurgood Marshall wrote for the Court. He said that the earlier decisions in *Irvin*, *Rideau*, *Estes*, and *Sheppard* do not stand for the proposition that juror exposure to factual information about a defendant and his crime is prejudicial on its face. Reasoning as Chief Justice John Marshall had in *Burr*, he wrote that jurors need not come into the courtroom "wholly ignorant of the *facts*, for this would establish an impossible standard." Thurgood Marshall added that voir dire must be used diligently to find out whether exposure to factual information has led a potential juror to a fixed conclusion about the defendant's guilt or innocence. Further, the judge selecting the jury must look beyond the courtroom into the community. Only if the "general atmosphere . . . is sufficiently inflammatory" should the judge disregard a prospective juror's assertions of impartiality.

The Court found no evidence of such an atmosphere in Miami. Nor could it find anything in the clippings submitted by Murphy's lawyer likely to arouse strong emotions against his client. The news stories merely recited the facts of a criminal career.

This decision sent a clear message to trial and appeals courts: A mere showing of factual news stories will not alone support the conclusion that an impartial jury cannot be had. Reinforcing what Clark had said in *Irvin*, the Court emphasized that jurors need not be completely ignorant of a case in order to be fair. Beyond that, the court was reiterating its faith in the ability of careful, conscientious judges to use voir dire to screen out those potential jurors who would resist the impressions conveyed by the evidence.

That voir dire does work is illustrated by the trial of former attorney general John Mitchell and of former White House aides John Ehrlichman and H. R. Haldeman on charges of obstructing justice in connection with the Watergate burglaries. They were found guilty in a District of Columbia trial court in 1975. The trial had been preceded not only by the *Washington Post's* Pulitzer Prize–winning stories, but by widely televised congressional hearings, and blanket coverage by all news media. The defendants pointed to that publicity in asking an appellate court to reverse. In *United States* v. *Haldeman*,[11] it refused to do so:

> We find in the publicity here no reason for concluding that the population of Washington, D.C., was so aroused against the appelllants and so unlikely to be able objectively to judge their guilt or innocence on the basis of evidence presented at trial that their due process rights were violated.

The court based its conclusion in large part on the careful voir dire conducted by Judge John J. Sirica, who spent many days questioning each prospective juror at length, observed by attorneys from both sides.

In 1984, the Supreme Court reinforced its decision in *Murphy*, upholding the conviction of a high school teacher who had twice been found guilty of the stabbing death of a female student. Both the crime and the trials received heavy news coverage. Arguing that the publicity kept him from getting a fair trial, the teacher appealed to the Supreme Court for relief. In *Patton* v. *Yount*,[12] the Court quoted from both *Irvin* and *Murphy*. It noted that there was no clamor in the community demanding the teacher's conviction at the time of the second trial, nor did the media try to create one. Further, as in *Murphy*, the publicity that preceded that trial was "purely factual . . . generally discussing not the crime or prior prosecution, but the prolonged process of jury selection."

In *Patton* as in *Murphy*, the court said it is not the amount of publicity about a crime, but the nature of that publicity, that determines whether the atmosphere has been so infected with prejudice as to make a fair trial impossible. If the news stories are factual in nature, if there is no attempt on the part of the news media to convict the defendant before he goes on trial, a fair trial in the courtroom is possible, even though prospective jurors have read or heard the stories. The law does not expect jurors to be ignorant of the facts. It requires that their minds be open to the evidence, and that they base their decision on it.

---

11. 559 F.2d 31 (D.C.Cir. 1976).
12. 467 U.S. 1025, 104 S.Ct. 2885, 81 L.Ed.2d 847 (1984).

ENSURING A FAIR TRIAL ══════════════════

The Supreme Court's decision in *Sheppard* in 1966 went beyond its previous fair-trial decisions in that the Court prescribed steps trial judges might take to counteract prejudicial media publicity. In doing so, it recognized that reversal, and a new trial years after the crime had been committed, did not always lead to justice.

The prescriptions in *Sheppard* began with such basic remedies as a more vigorous voir dire, which always had been part of the jury selection procedure, and change of venue, the moving of the trial to another locality not reached by news stories about the crime and the defendant. These remedies have aroused little controversy, but some of the others have. For instance, some judges reading *Sheppard* have imposed "gag orders." These are orders of the court directing witnesses, lawyers, defendants, and others involved in a trial not to talk to outsiders about the case. Such orders, which are classic prior restraints of the kind discussed in Chapter 3, have also been imposed on journalists who have become aware of prejudicial information through court proceedings. Judges have sought, too, to cut off prejudicial publicity at its source by closing legal proceedings at which prejudicial information might be disclosed or discussed. The latter measures have led to serious conflict between the legal establishment, as it has sought to protect the Sixth Amendment rights of defendants, and journalists, as they have sought to protect First Amendment freedoms. At least half a dozen times in the twenty years after *Sheppard* the Supreme Court has felt compelled to try to resolve various aspects of that conflict.

The Supreme Court Prescribes Remedies ══════════════════════

In the Court's *Sheppard* decision, it had concluded that Judge Blythin had lost control of the proceedings. Because he had given reporters and photographers a free rein in and out of the courtroom, he had sacrificed the "judicial serenity and calm" that are essential to a fair trial. Thus, Sam Sheppard was entitled to a new trial at which his right to trial by an impartial jury must be protected.

At that point in the decision, Justice Clark turned to a discussion of remedies that Judge Blythin should have used to ensure a fair trial orginally. Clark wrote that the judge had compounded the problems arising from the conduct of reporters and photographers by making no effort to cut off the flood of prejudicial news stories at their source. At the start of the trial, he had announced "that neither he nor anyone else could restrict prejudicial news accounts." He repeated the view many times thereafter. But, said Clark, Blythin looked at the wrong target when he saw the news media as the sources of that problem. What he should have done, and could have done, was to take steps to prevent prejudicial information from reaching the news media. Clark made some specific suggestions:

> The carnival atmosphere at trial could easily have been avoided since the courtroom and courthouse premises are subject to the control of the court. . . . Bearing in mind the massive pretrial publicity, the judge should have adopted stricter rules governing the use of the courtroom by newsmen, as Sheppard's counsel requested. The number of reporters

in the courtroom itself could have been limited at the first sign that their presence would disrupt the trial. They certainly should not have been placed inside the bar. Furthermore, the judge should have more closely regulated the conduct of newsmen in the courtroom. . . .

Secondly, the court should have insulated the witnesses. All of the newspapers and radio stations apparently interviewed prospective witnesses at will, and in many instances disclosed their testimony. . . .

Thirdly, the court should have made some effort to control the release of leads, information, and gossip to the press by police officers, witnesses, and the counsel for both sides. Much of the information thus disclosed was inaccurate, leading to groundless rumors and confusion. . . .

Defense counsel immediately brought to the court's attention the tremendous amount of publicity in the Cleveland press that "misrepresented entirely the testimony" in the case. Under such circumstances, the judge should have at least warned the newspapers to check the accuracy of their accounts. . . . The prosecution repeatedly made evidence available to the news media which was never offered in trial. Much of the "evidence" disseminated in this fashion was clearly inadmissible. The exclusion of such evidence in court is rendered meaningless when the news media make it available to the public. . . .

More specifically, the trial court might well have proscribed extrajudicial statements by any lawyer, party, witness, or court official which divulged prejudicial matters, such as the refusal of Sheppard to submit to interrogation or take any lie detector tests; any statement made by Sheppard to officials; the identity of prospective witnesses or their probable testimony; any belief in guilt or innocence; or like statements concerning the merits of the case. . . . [T]he court could also have requested the appropriate city and county officials to promulgate a regulation with respect to dissemination of information about the case by their employees. In addition, reporters who wrote or broadcast prejudicial stories could have been warned as to the impropriety of publishing material not introduced in the proceedings. . . . In this manner, Sheppard's right to a trial free from outside interference would have been given added protection without corresponding curtailment of the news media. Had the judge, the other officers of the court, and the police placed the interest of justice first, the news media would have soon learned to be content with the task of reporting the case as it unfolded in the courtroom—not pieced together from extrajudicial statements.

. . . Given the pervasiveness of modern communications and the difficulty of effacing prejudicial publicity from the minds of jurors, the trial courts must take strong measures to ensure that the balance is never weighed against the accused. And appellate courts have the duty to make an independent evaluation of the circumstances. Of course, there is nothing that proscribes the press from reporting events that transpire in the courtroom.

Clark ended by mentioning other steps judges might take in cases like this one, "where there is a reasonable likelihood that prejudicial news prior to trial will prevent a fair trial." The start of the trial can be postponed until the publicity dies down, or the judge can order a change of venue, that is, transfer of the trial to a court not reached by the publicity. If prejudicial publicity continues during the trial, the judge can **sequester the jury** or declare a **mistrial** and start over. But Clark emphasized that the cure lies with trial judges, who must "protect their processes from prejudicial outside interferences."

Sam Sheppard was freed from prison and retried late in 1966. Witnesses had died. Memories had faded. A jury acquitted him. Sheppard tried to resume his practice of osteopathy, but was the subject of several malpractice suits. He quit his practice and turned to other things. Immediately after his release from prison, he had married a

German immigrant with whom he had corresponded. That ended in divorce. Not long before he died of liver disease in 1970, he became a professional wrestler in the stable of a promoter working out of Columbus, Ohio. He married the promoter's nineteen-year-old daughter, who became his widow. A book and a television movie later portrayed him as the innocent victim of a vendetta inspired by the *Cleveland Press*.[13] Others remained convinced the first jury was right.

Courts have found nine remedies implicit or explicit in Justice Clark's decision. Six of these either were noncontroversial because they had always been part of the trial process, or have been upheld so firmly by appellate courts that they have become taken for granted. The other three remain controversial. Here is a summary of the nine remedies:

1. Continuance to allow the effect of an initial burst of publicity to subside. However, the Supreme Court has ruled that undue delay violates the speedy trial clause of the Sixth Amendment.[14] Rules of court now require dismissal of cases that do not reach trial within a specified time after arraignment, unless the delay is attributable to the defense. Six months is a common limit.

2. Change of venue, now quite common.

3. Rigorous use of voir dire to screen out prospective jurors who have made up their minds as a result of pretrial publicity.

4. Restrictions on the number of reporters who are permitted to cover trials that attract massive attention in the media, and on the comings and goings of reporters in the courtroom while court is in session.

5. Banishment of photographers from the courtroom and its environs. However, there have been significant changes in attitude on the part of judges in more than half the states, and of the Supreme Court itself, with respect to the photographing of trial proceedings.

6. Sequestration of the jury. Most judges consider this a tool of last resort. Jurors resent being kept virtual prisoners for the duration of a trial, especially if it is a long one.

The remedies that have generated continuing controversy are:

7. Gag orders directed at participants in the trial, including attorneys. These restrictive orders have raised First Amendment questions. However, most appeals courts have upheld the right of trial judges to order participants in the proceedings to refrain from talking to reporters and others, provided that a sufficient need is demonstrated. Some courts require evidence of a clear and present danger to the right of the accused to a fair trial.

---

13. Jack H. Pollack, *Dr. Sam: An American Tragedy* (Chicago: H. Regnery Co., 1972). The television movie, *Guilty or Innocent: The Sam Sheppard Murder Case*, was presented by NBC on 17 November 1975.

14. Barker v. Wingo, 407 U.S. 514, 92 S.Ct. 2182, 33 L.Ed.2d 101 (1972).

Additionally, attorneys who talk to reporters and disclose prejudicial information are subject to discipline by the bar and the courts. The Code of Ethics of the American Bar Association defines the kinds of information likely to be prejudicial and establishes guidelines for the release of information by lawyers involved in criminal cases. Generally, it says that lawyers should confine their public disclosures to factual information of the kind likely to be admitted as evidence without much question at trial. Lawyers are not supposed to talk about such things as confessions, tests, the possibility of a guilty plea, and witnesses and their likely testimony because these are matters to be resolved during the trial process.[15] Occasionally, a lawyer will be punished for violating the guidelines. For instance, F. Lee Bailey, who conducted Sam Sheppard's successful appeal, was suspended from the practice of law in New Jersey for one year for violating state judicial canons against pretrial publicity.[16]

8. Gag orders directed at reporters. This led to a decision of the Supreme Court that makes it difficult, if not impossible, for judges to justify such orders.

9. Closing to the press and public of certain parts of the trial process—**preliminary hearings,** bail hearings, and hearings on the admissibility of evidence. After four Supreme Court decisions in this area, the controversy continues, but the decisions make clear that court proceedings presumptively are open. They are to be closed only as a last resort to ensure a fair trial.

By applying the above remedies conscientiously, trial court judges have reduced considerably the number of reversals based on prejudicial publicity. As we will now see, they also have generated some notable media-bar confrontations.

Restraining Participants in a Trial ══════════════════

In *Sheppard,* Justice Clark suggested that Judge Blythin should have tried to cut off some of the flood of prejudicial publicity at its source by "proscrib[ing] extrajudicial statements by any lawyer, party, witness or court official. . . ." He acted on the theory that the media don't create news; they only report what sources are willing to disclose. If there are no prejudicial disclosures, there will be no prejudicial stories.

This sometimes is easier said than done. A judge can enforce a gag order only against persons within the jurisdiction of the court. This includes employees of the court; witnesses appearing under **subpoena,** which is an order of the court; parties to the action, or attorneys representing them. Further, the judge must make a finding, based on evidence, that there is "a clear and present danger, or a reasonable likelihood, of a serious and imminent danger to the administration of justice."[17] Such findings must be

---

15. American Bar Association Legal Advisory Committee on Fair Trial and Free Press, *The Rights of Fair Trial and Free Press* (1969).
16. "Jersey Suspends F. Lee Bailey from Practice," *New York Times*, 9 February 1971.
17. 16 Corpus Juris Secundum, 1981 Supplement, p. 264.

made on a case-by-case basis. For instance, the United States Court of Appeals, Seventh Circuit, rejected an attempt to impose gag orders in all trials through a standing order of the court.[18]

In two cases with strong political overtones, federal appeals courts have held that gag orders do not unduly violate the First Amendment rights of participants. The first, *United States* v. *Tijerina,* involved five members of a Spanish-Mexican civil rights group. All were charged with assault on federal forest rangers and damage of government-owned trucks. The five had led an attempt to occupy federal parklands that they contended had been taken illegally from the original native owners. Because feelings were running high, the federal district court judge assigned to the case issued an order forbidding the defendants and other participants in the trial from making any public statement about it.

United States v. Tijerina, 412 F.2d 661 (10th Cir. 1969).

When the civil rights group conducted a meeting some days later, two of the defendants spoke, urging members to demonstrate against their arrest, which they viewed as political. Police gave the trial judge a tape of the speeches. He found the speakers in contempt for violating his order.

The speakers, Tijerina and Noll, appealed, arguing that they had a right under the First Amendment to plead their case where they wished. They also argued that because the order had been issued to protect their right to a fair trial, they could disregard it if they chose. The United States Court of Appeals, Tenth Circuit, held that they were wrong on both counts. Their proper course was to appeal the gag order, not defy it. In any event, the public also has an interest in insisting on a fair trial. In this instance, that right could be thwarted unless the gag order was obeyed by all to whom it applied, including both the prosecution and the defense. The court observed that the Sixth Amendment requires that the trial be in a courtroom, not in a convention hall, and that the outcome be determined by a jury, not by a mob.

In 1984, in *In re Russell,* the United States Court of Appeals, Fourth Circuit, upheld a gag order imposed on seventeen potential witnesses in the trial of several members of the Ku Klux Klan and the Nazi party. The defendants were involved in a shooting in Greensboro, North Carolina, in 1979 that resulted in the deaths of five persons, most of them members of the far-left Revolutionary Communist Party. The victims were protesting Klan activities. Some of the witnesses had been participants in the protest, and others were related to the victims. Many of the witnesses also were plaintiffs in civil actions related to the shootings. In an attempt to keep highly charged emotional and racial currents from reaching the jury trying the criminal case, the judge imposed a gag order on the witnesses. Not only did he forbid them to talk to reporters, but he forbade them to talk to others with the intent to relay their words to the media.

In re Russell, 726 F.2d 1007 (4th Cir. 1984).

In justifying the order, the judge noted that the trial was the "subject of intense local and national publicity." Documents presented to the court showed that the witnesses had strong feelings which led them to make highly prejudicial statements. Some of these

---

18. In re Oliver, 452 F.2d 111 (7th Cir. 1971).

already had been in the news. Because the publicity was widespread, and was likely to be repeated wherever the trial might be held, the judge rejected change of venue as a means of ensuring a fair trial. He concluded that the gag order was his only alternative. Arguing that their First Amendment rights were being violated, the witnesses appealed.

The court of appeals upheld the trial court's order, finding that it was drafted narrowly to prohibit only those activities and statements likely to prevent a fair trial. The court concluded:

> The tremendous publicity attending this trial, the potentially inflammatory and highly prejudicial statements that could reasonably be expected from petitioners (and had indeed been openly forecast by their counsel in proceedings before the trial judge), and the relative ineffectiveness of the considered alternatives, dictated the "strong measure" of suppressing speech of potential witnesses to ensure a fair trial.

Such decisions leave no question about the right of trial judges to impose prior restraints on participants in a criminal trial if the demonstrated need is great enough. There must be a showing that the prejudicial statements are likely to be made by the participants, that the order will prevent prejudicial publicity resulting from such statements, that no other means will ensure a fair trial, and that the order will restrict only that speech likely to create a prejudicial atmosphere.

Restraining the News Media

Some trial judges who read *Sheppard* and tried to follow the Supreme Court's mandates concluded that the Supreme Court might condone prior restraint if that were necessary to ensure a fair trial. Headlines culled from *Editor & Publisher*, the newspaper trade magazine, during the mid-1970s indicate media reaction. They include such terms as "gag order," "curb on newsmen," "censorship law," and "more curbs on press." Two decisions from that era remain worthy of note. One prescribes the proper course of action for journalists who may be confronted with an order not to publish prejudicial information. The other makes such an order highly unlikely, although not impossible.

In the first case, *United States* v. *Dickinson*, a federal district court judge in Baton Rouge, Louisiana, was confronted with a highly charged situation. A young man active in the civil rights movement during the early 1970s was accused of conspiring to kill the mayor of the city. The judge had to conduct a preliminary hearing to determine if there was enough evidence to hold the suspect for trial. He

United States v. *Dickinson,* **465 F.2d 496 (5th Cir. 1972).**

knew that police would offer evidence at that hearing that might not be admissible at the trial, but would point strongly at the young man's guilt. He also knew that reporters would be present, ready to spread that evidence through the city. Thinking ahead to the problem of selecting an impartial jury if the young man were tried, the judge concluded that his only recourse was to cut off harmful publicity at its source. He ordered the reporters present not to publish anything about the hearing except his decision, which was to hold the young man for trial.

Reporters for the two Baton Rouge newspapers consulted their editors, who told them to write stories covering the hearing in full. The editors reasoned that the public was more likely to be inflamed by a lack of fact than by a straightforward account of the evidence presented at the hearing. Without the facts, rumor would take over. When the stories were published, the judge held the reporters in contempt for violating his order and fined each $300. They appealed to the United States Court of Appeals for the Fifth Circuit.

Chief Judge John R. Brown held that "even the merest breeze blowing across the First Amendment" was enough to lead to the conclusion that the gag order was improper. It was a prior restraint, based not on a heavy showing of necessity, but on a series of improbable assumptions—that the suspect would go to trial; that the prejudicial publicity, if any, would be pervasive; and that voir dire would not work. Further, the court held, the public had a right to know as much as the media could learn about a situation as highly charged as that which prevailed in Baton Rouge.

With that said, the court also held that journalists, like everyone else, must obey a judge's order or appeal to a higher court for relief. The First Amendment gives them no special right to disobey a judge, even when they are convinced he is wrong.

On remand, the trial judge stuck to his guns, reimposing the $300 fines. He conceded that his order may have been improper, but reiterated that he would not tolerate defiance. On further appeal, the apppelate court upheld the fines. The Supreme Court refused to review.[19]

Despite that part of the *Dickinson* decision condemning prior restraint, trial judges persisted in trying to tell reporters what to omit from their stories. The most notable of these attempts took place in a small county seat in western Nebraska in 1975. Erwin Charles Simants had killed six members of the Henry Kellie family and then had confessed to anyone who would listen. One of the victims was a ten-year-old girl, who also had been raped. All this took place in Sutherland, a town with a population of 840 in Lincoln County, which has a population of 36,000, of whom 24,000 live in North Platte, the county seat. The crime was highly publicized by the media in the county and elsewhere.

Nebraska Press Association v. Stuart, 427 U.S. 539, 96 S.Ct. 2791, 49 L.Ed. 2d 683 (1976).

When Simants was scheduled to appear in court in North Platte for a preliminary hearing, his attorney and the county attorney joined in asking the judge to issue an order restricting what could be reported about the case. They said that details highly prejudicial to Simants would be presented at the hearing. They considered these details so inflammatory that it probably would be impossible to select an impartial jury when Simants came to trial. The county court judge agreed and issued a restrictive order.

The news media, represented by the Nebraska Press Association, appealed for relief to a district court in Lincoln, the state capital. Judge Hugh Stuart of that court proposed an alternative. He noted that the press association and most of the media in the state had adopted a voluntary set of guidelines, patterned on the *Sheppard* decision and the American Bar Association guidelines, for the coverage of news of crime and the courts. Media subscribing to these guidelines promised not to publish information that might prejudice a defendant's right to a fair trial. Stuart said he would make the guidelines mandatory by adopting them as rules of the court. Finding a clear and present danger

---

19. 476 F.2d 373 (5th Cir. 1973); cert. den., 414 U.S. 979 (1973).

to Simants's right to a fair trial, the judge issued an order, to be in effect until a jury was chosen, prohibiting media within the court's jurisdiction from mentioning the defendant's several confessions. The judge also forbade publication of medical information indicating that some of the victims had been sexually assaulted. Finally, he also ordered the media not to report that they were operating under a gag order.

Appeals were filed in all directions, with the U.S. Supreme Court eventually agreeing to consider the case. Its decision in *Nebraska Press Association* v. *Stuart* erected three high hurdles between courts and a prior restraint of the news media in the interest of ensuring a fair trial. Chief Justice Warren E. Burger wrote for a Court that was unanimous in condemning Judge Stuart's order, but was divided as to whether all such orders violate the First Amendment.

The chief justice began by noting that the drafters of the Bill of Rights guaranteed both freedom of the press and the right to trial by an impartial jury. When the two rights conflict, how can each be preserved without harming the other? Burger suggested that voluntary press-bar guidelines like those in effect in Nebraska and several other states offered one answer. However, such guidelines may fail when the need for them is greatest. The chief justice noted that "even the most ideal guidelines are subjected to powerful strains when a case such as Simants' arises." Some editors will observe them. Others will not.

Confronted with that fact, Judge Stuart sought to protect Simants's Sixth Amendment right to a fair trial by restraining the media's First Amendment rights. The Court held that he went too far. At the same time, Chief Justice Burger rebuffed those who would resolve the fair-trial issue by holding that First Amendment rights should never be restricted. He wrote:

> The authors of the Bill of Rights did not undertake to assign priorities as between First Amendment and Sixth Amendment rights, ranking one as superior to the other. . . . [I]f the authors of these guarantees . . . were unwilling or unable to resolve the issue by assigning to one priority over the other, it is not for us to rewrite the Constitution by undertaking what they declined. It is unnecessary, after nearly two centuries, to establish a priority applicable to all circumstances.

The Court proceeded to hold that gag orders could be imposed on the media only as a last resort to ensure a fair trial. Such orders can be imposed, a majority of the Court held, only if three conditions are met. A judge proposing a restraint on the media must offer convincing evidence of these three criteria:

1. There is, or is likely to be, widespread prejudicial publicity.

2. None of the usual methods of ensuring a fair trial—voir dire, change of venue, continuance, and the like—will work.

3. The prior restraint will stop the flow of prejudicial publicity.

The chief justice said that Judge Stuart had satisfied only the first of these criteria. There was ample evidence of widespread prejudicial publicity, and the promise of more. But Judge Stuart could only speculate on the effect of that publicity. There was no evidence to prove that rigorous voir dire or a change of venue could not result in selection of an impartial jury. Nor was there any evidence that a gag order imposed on the media would cut off news of the confessions or of the sordid nature of the crime. Word of mouth, Burger noted, would spread such information quickly through a town of only 840 persons. The news also had been poured into the county by outside broadcasting stations and newspapers. Therefore, Judge Stuart's order was an improper restraint, violating the First Amendment.

In 1983, a United States District Court judge in California attempted to comply with the *Nebraska Press Association* guidelines in imposing a gag order on CBS News. John DeLorean, a former General Motors executive who organized a British company to build a sports car carrying his name, was about to go on trial for conspiracy to sell cocaine. Federal agents had videotaped him apparently in the act of making the deal. Government prosecutors alleged that he resorted to the cocaine deal to raise money to save his failing automobile business.

A few days before the trial was to begin, KNXT, the CBS affiliate in Los Angeles, broadcast excerpts from the government's videotape. One segment showed DeLorean

This segment of a videotape broadcast on the CBS network shows John DeLorean at the moment of his arrest by FBI agents on charges of conspiring to sell cocaine. A federal judge attempted to block the showing of the tape on the grounds that it would prevent the former automobile manufacturer from getting a fair trial. He was overruled on appeal. A jury later found DeLorean not guilty. (UPI/Bettmann Newsphotos)

examining a shipment of cocaine in a hotel room. Another showed FBI agents arresting him. The station said it would show other segments later. Judge Robert M. Takasugi postponed the start of the trial and issued an order forbidding CBS News from broadcasting any part of the tape. He said he feared that the portion already shown would make it difficult for him to find an impartial jury.

On appeal, the United States Court of Appeals, Ninth Circuit, overruled Judge Takasugi. It held that his gag order was an unconstitutional prior restraint. The court said the judge had failed to prove that further publicity would so distort the views of potential jurors that an impartial panel could not be seated.[20] Events proved that the judge was able to pick a jury, which heard the evidence during many weeks of trial and found DeLorean not guilty. The jury concluded that federal agents had initiated the cocaine transaction and therefore were guilty of **entrapment**.[21]

The CBS case illustrates the difficulty any court is likely to have in fulfilling the criteria established in *Nebraska Press Association*. It is easy to illustrate the likelihood of prejudicial publicity. But how does a judge prove in advance that such ordinary measures as change of venue and voir dire will not result in finding a dozen persons who can decide the case on its merits? And with satellites, cable, and even the mails bringing in news reports and commentary prepared by individuals who need not come within hundreds of miles of the judge who issues a gag order against the media, how can prejudicial information be cut off by court order? A judge cannot reach out beyond the limits of his jurisdiction, usually limited to a county or district, and punish those who disseminate information he has proscribed. It is for these reasons that the media are unlikely to be restrained to ensure a fair trial any longer than it takes to carry an appeal to the next higher court.

Closing Court Proceedings

Gannett v. *DePasquale*

It was precisely because of the unlikelihood of prior restraint of the media that some courts began using a new technique—the closing of court proceedings at which prejudicial information was likely to be disclosed. Traditionally, trials and other court proceedings were open to the public. The Sixth Amendment guarantees suspects not only the right to trial by an impartial jury but "to a speedy and public trial." In *Sheppard*, Justice Clark had noted, almost as an aside, "Of course, there is nothing that proscribes the press from reporting events that transpire in the courtroom." Nor was there any reason in 1966 to doubt that court proceedings would be conducted in public in all but the most unusual circumstances, usually involving divorce and custody cases or embarrassing testimony in sex crime trials.

By 1976, when *Nebraska Press Association* was decided, some judges, in their attempt to ensure a fair trial, had begun to experiment with closing **pretrial proceedings**. The most common closures were of preliminary, sometimes called probable cause, hearings

---

20. Columbia Broadcasting Systems, Inc. v. U.S. District Court, Central District of California, 729 F.2d 1174 (9th Cir. 1984).
21. "DeLorean: Not Guilty," *Newsweek*, 27 August 1984, pp. 22–23.

where police and prosecutors can offer evidence that would not be admissible at a formal trial. The gag order in *Nebraska Press Association* was issued at such a hearing. In his decision in that case, Chief Justice Burger took note of the experiments with closing in a way that seemed to approve them. He wrote:

> The county court could not know that closure of the preliminary hearing was an alternative open to it until the Nebraska Supreme Court so construed state law; but once a public hearing had been held, what transpired there could not be subject to prior restraint.

Burger was referring to a decision of the Nebraska court holding that the judge who conducted the preliminary hearing, and who imposed the original gag order, might have solved his problem by conducting the hearing in private. Some judges read the first branch of the sentence quoted above and found in it the Supreme Court's endorsement of such closings. One who did was Daniel DePasquale, judge of the Seneca County Supreme Court, a trial court, in upstate New York. He was confronted with the duty of conducting a highly unusual murder case—one without a corpse. The case began when Wayne Clapp, a former police officer, disappeared from his home near Rochester. He had gone fishing in Lake Seneca, forty miles away, with two male companions. When Clapp failed to return, police began a search. His boat, riddled with bullets, was found in Lake Seneca, and his pickup truck was found outside a motel in Jackson, Michigan. Officers arrested Kyle Greathouse and his wife, both sixteen, and David Ray Jones, twenty-one, who were in the motel. The suspects surrendered Clapp's credit cards and a .357 Magnum revolver. They also made statements to police describing how and why they had killed Clapp. Police returned the trio to Seneca County, New York, where the two men were charged with murder.

As the trial date approached, their attorneys filed two motions with the county court. One asked that the statements be suppressed on the ground that they had not been given voluntarily. The other asked for suppression of the credit cards and the revolver. When these motions came up for a hearing, the attorneys made a third motion. Pointing to seven news stories that had appeared in the two Rochester newspapers, they argued that "the unabated buildup of adverse publicity has jeopardized the ability of the defendants to receive a fair trial." They asked that spectators, including reporters, be excluded from the suppression hearing. The district attorney made no objection, and Judge DePasquale granted the request. Only one reporter, Carol Ritter, a stringer for the Rochester newspapers, was present. She left the courtroom at the judge's request, and the hearing proceeded behind closed doors. Judge DePasquale held that critical evidence had been obtained in violation of the defendants' rights and ordered it withheld from trial. This led to an agreement under which Greathouse and Jones pleaded guilty to lesser offenses.[22] They were sentenced to short terms in prison.

Meanwhile, Ritter had consulted her editors in Rochester. They advised her to protest Judge DePasquale's order. She wrote a letter to the judge, asserting her "right to cover this hearing," and asking to see a transcript of the proceedings. The judge reserved a decision on her request. An attorney for the Gannett Company, owner of the Rochester newspapers, filed a formal motion, repeating Ritter's request.

---

22. Gannett, Inc. v. DePasquale, 43 N.Y.2d 373, 396 (N.Y. 1977).

At the hearing on the motion, Judge DePasquale said he, too, believed the press had a constitutional right of access to court proceedings. He said it was unfortunate that Ritter had not objected at the time the closure motion was made. However, he said her right under the First Amendment was not absolute and would have to be balanced against the right of the defendants to a fair trial. In this instance, he said he would hold that the right to a fair trial outweighed the reporter's right to cover the suppression hearing. He refused to release the transcript.

Gannett's unsuccessful course through the New York state court system led eventually to the U.S. Supreme Court, resulting in a decision that divided the justices as have few others, and that created a furor in the media and legal profession. The Court held, five-to-four, in 1979 in *Gannett* v. *DePasquale*, that the judge had acted properly. The Court's majority decided the case on Sixth Amendment grounds, holding that the

Gannett v. DePasquale, 443 U.S. 368, 99 S.Ct. 2898, 61 L.Ed.2d 608 (1979).

guarantee of a public trial was designed to protect the rights of the defendant. Justice Stewart, who wrote the leading opinion signed by only one other justice, held that because the right is for the defendant's benefit, it may be waived at his request if the trial judge approves. If such a request is made, Justice Stewart wrote, the Sixth Amendment gives the media and the public no right to object. They may or may not have such a right under the First Amendment. If so, it is not absolute, and Judge DePasquale fulfilled any duty he may have had under it by listening to Gannett's request for access to the transcript of the testimony given at the suppression hearing. His denial of access was held to be proper.

At the time, the decision seemed to deliver a devastating blow to those who believe that justice is more likely to be done in the open than behind closed doors. The decision was made all the more devastating by the grounds on which it was decided. At issue when the case reached the Supreme Court was the question as to whether a judge can close a hearing on the suppression of evidence. Strictly speaking, such hearings are not a part of the trial. However, the language of the Sixth Amendment speaks only of a trial. Justice Stewart began by writing about suppression and other nontrial hearings, but quickly picked up the language of the Amendment. Thus, when he finished he had written an opinion which seemed to say that trials could be conducted behind closed doors if the defendant wanted it that way and the judge agreed to it. Many judges read it that way. In the year after the decision was handed down, defendants in forty-nine cases asked to have all or parts of their trial closed and about half the requests were granted.[23]

Because of decisions that will be discussed in the next section, the scope of *Gannett* has been narrowed considerably. However, the decision still is worth some attention. Its original sweep obviously troubled the Court itself, as is evidenced by both the five-four split and the fact that the nine justices wrote five different opinions. Chief Justice Burger agreed with the verdict but emphasized in a separate concurrence that the proceeding at issue was "not a *trial*," but "a *pre*trial hearing." He clearly sought to limit *Gannett's* reach. Justice Lewis F. Powell, Jr., agreed with Stewart's Sixth Amendment reasoning, but argued that First Amendment considerations give reporters an interest in being

---

23. *News Media and the Law*, August/September, November/December, 1979, pp. 7–9, 10–23.

present, not only at trials, but at suppression hearings. That right is not absolute, Powell concluded, and he suggested guidelines judges might use in deciding when the public could be barred. Justice William H. Rehnquist, the most conservative member of the Court on First Amendment issues, wrote separately to reject Powell's position. As he saw it, the Sixth Amendment was the only ground on which the case could be decided. He said there is nothing in the First Amendment that gives "the public a right of access to meetings of government agencies."

Justice Harry A. Blackmun wrote for the four dissenters, calling the decision "an unfortunate one." In his view, the majority had written a rigid rule that would offer defense lawyers the temptation to seek closed hearings for their clients. He predicted that judges would take the easy course and agree to such requests. Arguing that the majority had underestimated the value of open court proceedings, and the public's interest in them, Blackmun would have held that the Sixth Amendment mandates a hearing before any proceeding is closed. At such hearings, "full and fair consideration" should be "given to the public's interest . . . in open trials."

As further evidence of the Court's doubts about *Gannett*, four justices took the unusual step in the weeks following the decision of offering public comment on it. The chief justice and Justices Blackmun, Powell, and John Paul Stevens, who had joined in Stewart's opinion, all pointed out that *Gannett* involved only a suppression hearing, not a trial.[24]

An immediate result of the decision was to reopen the battle between courts and the media over the fair-trial issue. The question this time was whether the public and the media had a right to object to a motion to close a hearing or the trial itself. The four dissenters and Powell had said they should have such a right. The leading opinion was equivocal, but clearly said there was no such right under the Sixth Amendment.

Nevertheless, in October 1979 the legal department of the American Newspaper Publishers Association suggested that any reporter confronted with a closure motion make the following statement in court:

> "Your honor, my name is ——————. I am a reporter for the ——————, and I would like the court to note my objection to the motion to close this courtroom to the press and the public. I believe that I have the right to be present in this court and to observe the administration of justice by your honor and counsel for both sides. Supreme Court Justice Powell, writing in *Gannett* v. *DePasquale*, stressed the importance of affording those present in the courtroom an opportunity to be heard on a question of this nature."[25]

Subsequently, many newspapers, broadcasting stations, and news agencies had that statement printed on "Gannett cards" to be carried by their court reporters.

The decision also provoked a bit of doggerel written by Ashton Phelps, president and publisher of the *New Orleans Times-Picayune* and *States-Item*, and a lawyer, during a meeting of the ANPA's Press/Bar Relations Committee:

---

24. I. William Hill, "Justice Stevens Discounts Fears of Secret Trials," *Editor & Publisher*, 15 September 1979, p. 9.
25. "Courts: Pretrial or trial?" *Presstime*, October 1979, pp. 17–21.

Ode to the Gannett *Decision*

The Burger Court surpassed itself
And reached the height of follies.
The court they should have closed was theirs
Instead of DePasquale's.[26]

Opening Court Proceedings

Richmond Newspapers v. *Virginia*

Even as Phelps's "ode" was being published, the Supreme Court seized the opportunity to clarify what it had done in *Gannett*. Since early 1976, a troublesome murder case had been bouncing up and down through the Virginia courts. It began with the stabbing death of a motel manager in Hanover, a hamlet twenty miles north of Richmond. A Hanover County grand jury indicted John Paul Stevenson on a charge of murder, on the basis of the principal piece of evidence connecting Stevenson with the crime, a bloodstained shirt. It belonged to Stevenson, but he contended police had seized it in violation of his rights. The shirt was introduced as evidence at the trial, and a jury found Stevenson guilty of second-degree murder. On appeal, the Virginia Supreme Court ruled that the shirt should not have been used as evidence and ordered a new trial. Two subsequent trials resulted in mistrials. When Stevenson's fourth trial began, his lawyer asked that it be closed to the public. He argued that a member of the victim's family seemed to be coaching the witnesses. The prosecutor made no objections to the closing. The judge noted that the courtroom was not well designed. The jurors could see the spectators and, the judge reasoned, might be influenced by them. When he ordered the courtroom cleared, two reporters for the Richmond newspapers were among those evicted.

At the time, the *Gannett* case had not been decided by the Supreme Court. The Virginia judge acted on his reading of a state law authorizing judges in criminal trials to "exclude from the trial any persons whose presence would impair the conduct of a fair trial, provided that the right of the accused to a public trial shall not be violated."[27]

There is nothing unusual in the statute. As the Supreme Court reminded judges in *Sheppard*, courts have always had a duty to keep prejudicial influences out of the courtroom. However, even a cursory survey of the cases in this area leads to the conclusion that the right to exclude individuals from the courtroom has been used infrequently and limited narrowly. Attempts by judges to stretch the rule into a blanket exclusion order usually were rebuffed.[28]

In the Virginia case, counsel for the Richmond newspapers asked the trial judge later that day for a hearing on the closure order. He agreed to hear the lawyer's argument, listened to him in private, and ruled that the trial would proceed behind closed doors. The trial ended the next day when the judge granted a defense motion to strike the

---

26. Ibid., p. 17.
27. Virginia Code §19.2-266.
28. E. W. Scripps Co. v. Fulton. 125 N.E.2d 896 (Ohio 1955), and Oliver v. Postel, 282 N.E.2d 306 (N.Y.App. 1972).

prosecution's case from the record. The judge then found Stevenson not guilty. His written order gave no reason for his decision.

When the state supreme court rejected an appeal of the closure order, the Richmond newspapers took their case to the U.S. Supreme Court. The petition reached the Court within weeks after *Gannett* had been decided. It seized the opportunity to limit that decision and held, with only one dissent, that the Virginia judge had acted improperly. Justice Powell, who had practiced law in Richmond, took no part in the case.

Richmond Newspapers v. *Virginia*, 448 U.S. 555, 100 S.Ct. 2814, 65 L.Ed.2d 1973 (1980).

The Court's seven-to-one decision in *Richmond Newspapers* v. *Virginia* was not nearly as unanimous as the vote suggests. While the majority found common ground in holding that the closure was unwarranted, the justices wrote six different opinions to explain why they did so. Some clearly would have preferred to have grounded the decision in the Sixth Amendment guarantee of a public trial. But the leading opinion, written by Chief Justice Burger and signed by Justices Stevens and White, was grounded in the First Amendment. The justices reasoned that because of the historical origins of trials, and a long tradition of openness, trials have become public assemblies where the business of government is conducted. Therefore, the freedom of assembly clause of the First Amendment gives journalists and the public a right to attend trials. It is not an absolute right, but it does give people a right to argue against a motion to close a trial or any part of it, with the presumption in favor of openness.

This represented an important advancement in First Amendment theory. Previously, as Justice Rehnquist had pointed out in *Gannett*, the Court had steadfastly rejected the argument that the right to disseminate news implies a right to gather it. In a few of its previous decisions the Court had spoken in general terms about First Amendment protection for newsgatherers, but it had not upheld any specific right. One aspect of this protection will be the subject of the next chapter.

Chief Justice Burger began his judgment for the Court in *Richmond Newspapers* by putting as much distance as he could between this case and *Gannett*. Using italic type to lend emphasis to his writing, he noted repeatedly that "*pre*trial" proceedings were at issue in *Gannett* while *Richmond* dealt with a "*trial*."

Burger reviewed the history of trials, quoting from both British and Colonial American documents to make the point that by tradition trials have been open to the public. There are compelling reasons why this should be so, Burger wrote. When spectators are present, they can see for themselves whether the defendant is treated fairly. Witnesses will be less likely to lie. Decisions reached in open court are more likely to command public support than those reached in secret. Public trials also serve as an outlet for community concerns when an especially shocking crime has been committed. The trial will provide an outlet for their anger. If the people see that justice is being done, they are less likely to take the law into their own hands. Burger concluded by observing that "the appearance of justice can best be provided by allowing people to observe it."

The chief justice then made a significant shift in his reasoning. He wrote that "[i]n earlier times, both in England and America, attendance at court was a common mode of 'passing the time.'" Thus, a courtroom was, in a sense, a place of public assembly. People went to court for the drama it offered as well as to observe one branch of their government in action. In more recent times, however, people have come to rely on "the press, cinema, and electronic media" for "the real life drama once available only in the courtroom," Burger wrote. They also rely on the media to cover trials for them. This, Burger said, "validates the media claim of functioning as surrogates for the public." Judges have recognized that role by giving reporters "special seating and priority of entry so that they may report what people in attendance have seen and heard."

Noting that a "core purpose" of the First and Fourteenth Amendments is to assure "freedom of communication on matters relating to the functioning of government," Burger moved to a position he had not previously taken. He concluded that this freedom must imply a right to gather news on the functioning of government. Specifically, he said that because trials are a function of government, and because they have traditionally been open, they are public assemblies that the public has a right to attend. It is not an absolute right, and the chief justice described it as follows:

> What this means in the context of trials is that the First Amendment guarantees of speech and press, standing alone, prohibit government from summarily closing courtroom doors which had long been open to the public at the time that amendment was adopted. . . .
>
> It is not crucial whether we describe this right to attend criminal trials to hear, see, and communicate observations concerning them as a "right of access," or a "right to gather information," for we have recognized that "without some protection for seeking out news, freedom of the press could be eviscerated." . . . The explicit, guaranteed rights to speak and to publish concerning what takes place at a trial would lose much meaning if access to observe the trial could, as it was here, be foreclosed arbitrarily.
>
> Subject to the traditional time, place, and manner restrictions, . . . streets, sidewalks, and parks are places traditionally open, where First Amendment rights may be exercised . . . ; a trial courtroom also is a public place where the people generally—and representatives of the media—have a right to be present, and where their presence historically has been thought to enhance the integrity and quality of what takes place. . . .
>
> We hold that the right to attend criminal trials is implicit in the guarantees of the First Amendment; without the freedom to attend such trials, which people have exercised for centuries, important aspects of freedom of speech and "of the press could be eviscerated."

Burger concluded by holding that the Virginia judge had not given enough attention to the remedies recommended in *Sheppard* before he decided to close the courtroom in order to ensure a fair trial. He added:

> Absent an overriding interest articulated in findings, the trial of a criminal case must be open to the public. Accordingly, the judgment under review is reversed.

While Justice White signed Burger's opinion, he could not resist chiding the chief justice for voting with the majority in *Gannett*. If Burger had endorsed the minority view in that case, the Court would have construed the Sixth Amendment "to forbid excluding the public from criminal proceedings except in narrowly defined circumstances." Thus it could have avoided the First Amendment issue.

Justice Stevens, who also had put his name on Burger's opinion, wrote separately to expand on White's reservations about the creation of a new First Amendment right of access. Noting that the Court previously had rejected suggestions that the Amendment implies such a right, he added:

> Today, . . . for the first time, the Court unequivocally holds that an arbitrary interference with access to important information is an abridgment of the freedoms of speech and of the press protected by the First Amendment.

Even such strong advocates of First Amendment freedoms as Justices Marshall and Brennan seemed worried by the sweep of Burger's position. Writing for both of them, Brennan agreed that there is a First Amendment right of access to trials, and to some other kinds of news as well, but he would have had the Court set limits to that right. He suggested, for instance, that lower-court judges should not read *Richmond Newspapers* as granting a right of access to secret information vital to the nation's security. He would have confined the right of access to information about what Brennan called the "structures" of government. In his view, people have a right to find out how well the institutions of government—of which the courts are one—are functioning.

Even Justice Stewart, who was seeing much of his year-old opinion in *Gannett* reduced to dicta, concurred in the Court's judgment. He said that his earlier decision had left open the question as to whether other parts of the Constitution might guarantee a right of access. That right had now been found in the First Amendment, and he was willing to go along with that. However, Stewart said that right should not be construed as absolute. Judges should be able to "impose reasonable limitations upon the unrestricted occupation of a courtroom by representatives of the press and members of the public."

Justice Blackmun, who had led the dissenters in *Gannett*, made no effort to hide his exasperation with both Stewart and the chief justice. With his position—that the Sixth Amendment gives the public some right of access to court proceedings—rejected, he concurred in the Court's verdict. He wrote that he was happy to see the Court paying some attention to legal history, and added:

> It is gratifying . . . to see the Court wash away at least some of the graffiti that marred the prevailing opinion in [*Gannett*]. No less than twelve times in the primary opinion in that case, the Court (albeit in what seems now to have become clear dicta) observed that the Sixth Amendment closure ruling applies to the *trial* itself. The author of the first concurring opinion [Burger] was fully aware of this and would have restricted the Court's observations and rulings to the suppression hearing. Nonetheless, he *joined* the Court's opinion with its multiple references to the trial itself; the opinion was not a mere concurrence in the Court's judgment. And Mr. Justice Rehnquist, in his separate concurring opinion, quite understandably observed, as a consequence, that the Court was holding "without qualification," that "members of the public have no constitutional right under the Sixth and Fourteenth Amendments to attend criminal trials." The resulting confusion among commentators and journalists was not surprising.

Justice Blackmun said he still believed that the right of access to a trial, or to a suppression hearing, lies "where the Constitution explicitly placed it—in the Sixth Amendment." But because he could not persuade a majority of the Court to his position, he wrote that he was driven "to conclude, as a secondary position, that the First Amendment must provide some measure of protection for public access to the trial."

Justice Rehnquist alone remained unconvinced. He believed his colleagues mistaken and he said so bluntly:

In the Gilbert and Sullivan operetta *Iolanthe*, the Lord Chancellor recites:

"The law is the true embodiment
of everything that's excellent,
It has no kind of fault or flaw,
And I, my lords, embody the law."

It is difficult not to derive more than a little of this flavor from the various opinions supporting the judgment in this case. . . .
. . . I do not believe that either the First or Sixth Amendments, as made applicable to the States by the Fourteenth, require that a State's reasons for denying public access to a trial, where both the prosecuting attorney and the defendant have consented to an order of closure approved by the judge, are subject to any additional constitutional review at our hands.

However, Rehnquist stood alone. As Stevens emphasized in his concurring opinion, the Court, for the first time, had found in the First Amendment a right of the press and public to attend trials. It is not an absolute right, but the various opinions make clear that it is a right that can be abridged only by a strong showing of evidence that the defendant's right to a fair trial can be protected only by closing the courtroom. Further, representatives of the public and the news media have a right to argue against closing. Because the plurality grounded that right in the First Amendment, the decision implies that there may be other functions of government that historically have been so open that the same reasoning could be applied to them. For that reason Stevens called *Richmond Newspapers* "a watershed case." For that reason Brennan suggested the new right of access be limited to probing the structures of government. And for that reason Blackmun found the decision "troublesome." It is not possible, until courts have had an opportunity to act in properly presented cases, to know how far a First Amendment right of access to government information might reach. The issues of access presented in *Gannett* and *Richmond Newspapers* split the Court as have only two other First Amendment questions: the definition of obscenity and the prior restraint imposed in the Pentagon Papers case. The justices wrote twelve different opinions in the two access cases. However, through all the disagreements and reservations expressed in those opinions, one point comes clear: Eight of the nine justices concluded in varying degree that some right of access to news sources is implicit in the First Amendment and can be applied to the states through the due process clause of the Fourteenth. Rehnquist was the only holdout.

Globe Newspaper, Press-Enterprise, and *Waller*

Reacting to the confusion created in the minds of lower-court judges by its decisions in *Gannett* and *Richmond Newspapers*, the Supreme Court has on three occasions since felt compelled to decide cases involving access to court proceedings. In each instance, it has expanded the scope of its holding in *Richmond Newspapers*.

In the first of the cases, *Globe Newspaper Co.* v. *Superior Court, County of Norfolk*,[29] decided in 1982, the Court held that a Massachusetts law closing courtrooms during the testimony of certain sex-crime victims violated the First Amendment.

In the second, *Press-Enterprise Co.* v. *Superior Court of California, Riverside County*,[30] decided in 1984, the Court held that because the voir dire traditionally is part of the trial, it, too must be conducted in the open unless convincing evidence shows it must be closed to ensure a fair trial.

In the third, *Waller* v. *Georgia*,[31] also decided in 1984, the Court held that a pretrial suppression hearing can be closed over the defendant's objections only if there are compelling reasons to do so. More importantly, the Court held that the people's First Amendment right of access to such proceedings rests on the same factors as the defendant's Sixth Amendment right to a public trial.

The effect of these decisions has been to reinforce the conclusion that all court proceedings are presumed to be open; that closing, even of nontrial hearings, is the exception; and that each must be justified by evidence showing that a fair trial is unlikely unless the proceeding is closed. A survey of cases decided in 1984 and 1985 showed decisions running about two-to-one in favor of open proceedings. In all instances, appellate courts held that closure motions should be disposed of on a case-by-case basis with clearly articulated reasons and evidence supporting a decision to close. Because these decisions were based on *Globe Newspaper* and *Press-Enterprise*, in addition to *Richmond Newspapers* and *Gannett*, the former need to be examined.

Globe Newspaper Co. v. *Superior Court, County of Norfolk,* **457 U.S. 596, 102, S.Ct. 2613, 73 L.Ed.2d 248 (1982).** At issue in *Globe Newspaper* was a Massachusetts law that required judges presiding at the trials of certain sex crimes to exclude the public and the media during the testimony of victims under the age of eighteen. The Court held six-to-three that any such arbitrary closing of a courtroom during a trial violates the First Amendment right of access defined in *Richmond Newspapers.*

The law had been invoked during the trial of a man accused of raping three girls, all of whom were under eighteen. When it came time for the victims to testify, the judge closed the courtroom, despite objections by a reporter for the *Boston Globe*. In response to that challenge, the state sought to justify the law on two grounds: It protected "minor victims of sex crimes from further trauma and embarrassment," and it encouraged those victims "to come forward and testify in a truthful and credible manner."

The Supreme Court's majority conceded that both interests were important, but held that they can be served by measures less restrictive than a mandatory law. The court said that while the right of access to criminal trials is not absolute,

> the circumstances under which the press and public can be barred from a criminal trial are limited; the State's justification in denying access must be a weighty one. Where, as in the present case, the State attempts to deny the right of access in order to inhibit the disclosure of sensitive information, it must be shown that the denial is necessitated by a compelling governmental interest, and is narrowly tailored to serve that interest.

---

29. 457 U.S. 596, 102 S.Ct. 2613, 73 L.Ed.2d 248 (1982).
30. 464 U.S. 501, 104 S.Ct. 819, 78 L.Ed.2d 629 (1984).
31. 467 U.S. 39, 104 S.Ct. 2210, 81 L.Ed.2d 31 (1984).

In this instance, the law swept too broadly. The Court said that Massachusetts could protect minor witnesses through judicial action on a case-by-case basis. In that way, the judge could weigh the interest in privacy and a fair trial against the public's interest in the testimony and reach a suitable decision. Thus, the Court did not rule out the possibility that the courtroom could be closed during the testimony of the young victims, but it could be done only after a hearing at which the media could plead their case. Then the judge would have to conclude, on the basis of clear evidence, that the victims would not testify fully unless reporters and the public were barred.

The *Press-Enterprise* case had its origins in the selection of a jury for the trial of a suspect accused of rape and murder. The crime was the subject of intense media coverage, and the judge took special pains to make certain that the voir dire was as searching as possible. The first three days were conducted in open court. Then the prosecutor asked that the process be closed, arguing that otherwise, the prospective jurors might not respond to questions with sufficient candor to disclose their biases. The judge agreed, and the questioning continued in private for six weeks before a jury was seated.

Press-Enterprise Co. v. Superior Court of California, Riverside County, 464 U.S. 501, 104 S.Ct. 819, 78 L.Ed.2d. 629 (1984).

When the *Press-Enterprise* sought a copy of the transcript of the voir dire, the defendant's attorney objected, arguing that some of it would violate the jurors' right of privacy. The prosecutor joined in the objection, arguing that prospective jurors had answered questions under an "implied promise of confidentiality." The judge upheld the objections, noting that much of the transcript was "dull and boring," and that a few persons had disclosed matters that might prove embarrassing if made public. The *Press-Enterprise* appealed, but was rebuffed by two state appellate courts.

The Supreme Court overruled the California courts, with Chief Justice Burger writing for the majority. Reviewing much of the same historical ground he had covered in *Richmond Newspapers*, he concluded that jury selection, like the trial itself, traditionally has been conducted in public. In his view, open proceedings are more likely to ensure fairness than they are to promote prejudice. The chief justice wrote:

> No right ranks higher than the right of the accused to a fair trial. But the primacy of the accused's right is difficult to separate from the right of everyone in the community to attend the *voir dire* which promotes fairness.

However, the Court stopped short of holding that jury selection never should be conducted in private. It established the following guidelines:

> Closed proceedings, although not absolutely precluded, must be rare and only for cause shown that outweighs the value of openness. . . . The presumption of openness may be overcome only by an overriding interest based on findings that closure is essential to preserve higher values and is narrowly tailored to serve that interest. The interest is to be articulated along with findings specific enough that a reviewing court can determine whether the closure order was properly entered.

The passage above has been cited frequently by lower courts seeking guidance in access cases. The Supreme Court itself reiterated the *Press Enterprise* test a few months later in 1984 in its decision in *Waller* v. *Georgia,* adding one element. It said a court contemplating closure of a proceeding would have to demonstrate that alternative remedies had been considered. The Court emphasized that whether the proceeding in question is a trial, or a hearing related to a trial, the presumption is that it will be open.

That presumption was reinforced in June 1986 when the Court decided a second Press-Enterprise case, this one involving a judge's closing of a preliminary hearing to ensure a fair trial. In a seven-to-two decision, the Court held that the qualified First Amendment right of access to criminal proceedings applies to preliminary hearings as conducted in California. The Court said such hearings cannot be closed unless the judge makes specific findings demonstrating a "substantial probability" that the right to a fair trial will be prejudiced by publicity and that reasonable alternatives cannot protect that right (*Press-Enterprise Co.* v. *Superior Court of California for Riverside County,* No. 84-1560, 30 June 1986).

The circumstances under which closed proceedings still may be tolerated are illustrated by two earlier cases in which closure to ensure a fair trial was upheld. In both instances, the Supreme Court refused to accept the cases for review.

Sacramento Bee v. *United States District Court* grew out of a long and newsworthy trial of seven persons accused of dealing in heroin. The trial judge knew from the start that the trial would last for weeks and that prejudicial information might be disclosed during that time. He considered ordering the jurors sequestered, but changed his mind when he learned it would take two weeks to make the arrangements. Four weeks into the trial, counsel for one of the defendants moved to suppress some of the evidence. The judge cleared the courtroom while he heard arguments from attorneys for both sides. Four days later, a second request for suppression of evidence was made. The judge sent the jurors to the jury room and ordered reporters to leave the courtroom, but he permitted other spectators to remain and hear the arguments. The *Sacramento Bee* challenged the order. The judge said he was certain he would rule that the evidence in question was not admissible, and he didn't want to run a risk that the jurors would read about it in the newspapers. The judge offered to discuss his problem with the *Bee's* lawyer. He asked the lawyer repeatedly what the latter would do to make certain that the long and expensive trial would not end in mistrial through juror exposure to prejudicial information about inadmissible evidence. If he was hoping that the lawyer would volunteer to ask the *Bee's* editor to suppress news of such evidence, he was disappointed. The attorney said if he had the judge's problem, he would sequester the jury. Because the judge considered that impractical, he said he would continue to exclude reporters during suppression hearings.

Sacramento Bee v. United States District Court, 565 F.2d 477 (E.D.Calif. 1981).

The *Bee* asked the United States Court of Appeals, Ninth Circuit, to overrule the judge. It refused to do so, holding that the judge had acted properly in assessing the likelihood that prejudicial information would reach the jurors through the newspapers. It commended the judge for seeking the *Bee's* cooperation, and lectured the newspaper for refusing it. The court wrote:

> We are puzzled . . . that representatives of the press failed to suggest a logical and workable alternative to solve the court's dilemma. An easy solution would have been to

acknowledge that immediate publication was unnecessary and that the *Bee* would await later developments in the trial until the material withheld from the jury might be printed without prejudice to any defendant and without inconveniencing the jury.

In *Federated Publications, Inc.* v. *Swedberg*, the news media were asked to promise in writing that they would abide by their own fair trial guidelines. Judges, lawyers, and media representatives in Washington were pioneers in seeking an accommodation that would ensure fair trials without infringing First Amendment freedoms. A committee representing the three groups drafted voluntary guidelines defining what each could do to keep prejudicial publicity to a minimum. News media subscribing to the guidelines pledged not to publish or broadcast prejudicial information while a trial was pending. The agreement was considered a model of what conciliation could accomplish and was adopted in several other states.

Federated Publications, Inc. v. Swedberg, 633 P.2d 74 (Wash. 1981).

In Washington, the guidelines were put to the test when a woman was arrested and tried on a charge of attempted murder. The case drew considerable attention because she was alleged to be a friend of the "Hillside Strangler," who had committed several murders in Seattle. The woman's lawyer moved to suppress some of the evidence and moved further that the hearing be closed. He said the evidence in question was of such a nature that any disclosure of it would prejudice jurors against his client. Judge Byron L. Swedberg conceded that it probably would, but he was reluctant to close the hearing. He offered a deal to the reporters who were present. If they would agree in writing to abide by the Bench-Bar-Press Guidelines, he would let them stay. If they didn't, they would have to leave. He was making the offer, he said, because he knew from experience that people are more likely to keep a promise if they make it in writing. To show his good faith, he said he would not use his contempt powers to punish any reporter who signed the agreement and then violated it. Several journalists, including the reporter for the *Bellingham World*, owned by Federated Publications, refused to sign. When Judge Swedberg excluded them from the suppression hearing, Federated challenged his action as a prior restraint. The Supreme Court of Washington held that it was not. It noted that Washington's Constitution guarantees the public access to trial and pretrial hearings. It also imposes on judges a duty to see that defendants get a fair trial. The court said Judge Swedberg acted reasonably when he balanced the two requirements and concluded that the woman's right to a fair trial forced him to act as he had.

The cases in this section illustrate the process judges must follow in considering motions to close any legal proceeding. They start with the assumption that it should be open. Their first step is to assess the likelihood that prejudicial information will be disclosed during the proceeding and that it will be disseminated to the public. They must offer proponents and opponents of closing an opportunity to present their arguments. They must consider alternatives that would ensure a fair trial even if the prejudicial information were disseminated. If they conclude that closure alone will do the job, they must state the reasons for that conclusion and the evidence that supports it. Finally, the closure order must go no further than is necessary to keep the prejudicial information from the jurors or potential jurors until the trial has ended.

In The Professional World

A criminal trial is not a sporting event, nor is it a television drama. In fact, most trials tend to be more boring than dramatic. They drone to a conclusion, unattended by anyone except a few friends and relatives of the defendant and the victim, and courthouse hangers-on. Only the occasional celebrated case, involving a prominent defendant or victim, or a particularly monstrous crime, attracts full-time attention from the news media. Yet, whether the case is boring or celebrated, it has one common element: The defendant is gambling his freedom, and perhaps even his life, on the outcome. Criminal trials, then, are serious business.

Media professionals treat them as such. With most newspapers, Jazz-Age coverage of the police beat and the courts can be found only in the microfilmed copies of front pages from another era. Police and court beats still are covered on a daily basis, but with an eye for stories that illustrate trends, that will alert the public to problems with a particular kind of crime, or that will serve as a check on the performance of police, prosecutor, and judges. Much of the information is simply reduced to a listing for the record of offenses reported, arrests made, and of court action.

It is that occasional celebrated case that raises tensions between the legal system and the media. Judges who must try such cases are very much aware of the duty imposed by *Sheppard*. They must do all they can to protect the defendant's rights or risk having the verdict overturned on appeal. No judge likes being overruled by a higher court. And prosecutors must be cautious in talking with reporters lest they disclose information that might be seen later as grounds for reversal. If there has been any publicity at all, defense attorneys are under an obligation at the start to seek a change of venue. If that fails, they are likely to appeal a conviction on grounds that the publicity prevented the defendant from getting a fair trial. A defense lawyer who does not raise such questions runs the risk of being accused of offering inadequate counsel. These pressures on the lawyers and the judge may well result in pressures on the news media also, as the cases in this chapter illustrate.

The cases also illustrate that the media are free to publish or broadcast any scrap of information they can learn about the crime, the suspect, the victim, and the possible witnesses. It is unlikely that any judge seeking to order the media not to use information in their possession can meet the test prescribed in *Nebraska Press Association*. Editors supervising coverage of a celebrated case act in the knowledge that the only restraints are those they impose on themselves.

All of the major professional organizations representing journalists, print or electronic, have adopted codes of ethics. All recognize that prejudicial publicity can interfere with the right to a fair trial and suggest that it be minimized. However, all of these codes are written in general terms, and journalists have resisted attempts to enforce them.

As cases like *Murphy* and *Patton* suggest, much crime and court coverage is not sensational and prejudicial. It is not unusual for the media to withhold such information as a defendant's prior criminal record, either until the trial ends or the record has been introduced in court. Many editors understand that coverage that results in a change of venue or a reversal of a conviction only adds to the costs of supporting the courts, costs the taxpayers must bear.

And yet there are limits to the self-restraint of even the most conscientious editors. In a competitive market, if one outlet uses leaked information, no matter how prejudicial, others will scramble to get it, too. KNXT's use in Los Angeles of a videotape supposedly showing John DeLorean caught up in a cocaine deal was followed by news stories describing the taped scene in detail.

Nor is competition the only factor that may lead editors to ignore a code of ethics. When someone runs amok, kills several persons, and then talks about it, as in *Nebraska Press Association*, it is illogical to believe that no one will publish or broadcast those facts. As the Supreme Court pointed out, if the facts aren't used by the media, word of mouth not only will circulate them, but enlarge on them. The potential for harmful rumor also was a factor in the editors' decision to publish in *Dickinson* (page 235). If the police think seriously enough that someone is plotting to kill the mayor so that they make an arrest to prevent it, the public ought to know. In that instance, the editors thought the facts might defuse racial tensions that already were running high. Clearly, there are times when the news media should make every effort to get the facts of a crime and share them with the public.

If the criminal justice system is working as it should, there is not much point in trying cases in the newspapers or on the air. It is doubtful that "scoops" on the police and court beats sell many newspapers or win many ratings points. The public interest is served if the news is reported as it breaks. If the system is not working properly, different considerations come into play. If the police are corrupt, the prosecutor lazy, judges incompetent, the public needs to know. One way to expose such problems is for the news media to dig out the facts pointing to the guilt of suspects who go free or to the innocence of an occasional suspect who is convicted wrongfully. In such situations, editors can hope that, given the facts, the voters will set things right at the next election.

In any event, as the cases in this chapter suggest, whether they are covering the occasional highly newsworthy crime or the routine, professional journalists are aware that someone, at some point, may try to hide things from them. When that happens, professionals usually are quick to assert a right of access, even though they may decide not to use the information. As the earlier cases in this textbook tell us, the First Amendment long has meant that each of us, journalist or not, has a right to decide what information we will share with others. The cases in this chapter also tell us that the First Amendment gives us the right to insist on access to news of the courts.

FOR REVIEW

1. Distinguish between a hearing and a trial. As far as a right of access is concerned, is that difference significant?

2. Plea bargaining sometimes becomes an issue in states where judges and prosecutors are elected. Why might that be?

3. Define "voir dire." What is its purpose?

4. Define "impartial juror." Why is the term important?

5. What kinds of information are considered likely to induce prejudice in jurors?

6. Outline and define the procedures a judge is expected to take to ensure a defendant's right to a fair trial. (*Sheppard* v. *Maxwell*)

7. What did the Supreme Court's decision in *Murphy* v. *Florida* contribute to the definition of a fair trial?

8. What is meant by the term "gag order"? Is such an order ever proper?

9. Assess the likelihood that a gag order might be imposed on journalists covering a trial. What should be done if such an order is issued? Why?

10. What is meant by a First Amendment right of access to the courts? How did the Supreme Court rationalize such a right? Why did some justices have reservations about it?

11. If you had been a Supreme Court justice, how would you have voted in *Globe Newspaper* and *Press-Enterprise*? Why?

CHAPTER 7

THE JOURNALIST'S PRIVILEGE: CONFIDENTIALITY

It is a legal principle of long standing that "the public . . . has a right to every man's evidence." This means that courts are entitled to summon as witnesses any persons who may have direct knowledge of a crime or the subject matter of a civil action. The Sixth Admendment, which gives suspects a right to a public trial by an impartial jury, also gives them the right "to have compulsory process for obtaining witnesses" in their behalf. This is a reference to the subpoena power—the power of a court to issue an official order summoning witnesses to appear and testify. One who refuses to obey such an order is in contempt and may be punished by the judge. The subpoena power is based on the theory that a court is more likely to reach a proper verdict if it hears evidence from all who have knowledge of the case in point than it is if some are excused.

Therefore, the courts have been reluctant to grant exceptions to the principle that all should testify. Certain exceptions, called "privileges," have been granted in recognition of special circumstances. The strongest of these is found in the Fifth Amendment, which says, in part: "No person . . . shall be compelled in any criminal case to be a witness against himself. . . ." It was put there as a guard against the use of torture to force confessions and it means what it says: No matter how guilty a suspect may be, any confession must be completely voluntary and made in full knowledge of the consequences. If the suspect does not want to plead guilty, he has the right to remain silent and make the prosecutor prove the charge against him.

Other privileges have been recognized by decisions of the courts to respect confidential relationships. Some states have written them into rules of court or into statute law. The most common is the husband-wife privilege. Few courts will require one spouse to testify against the other. Other common-law privileges involve lawyer-client, physician-patient, and clergy-penitent relationships. The courts recognize that a lawyer cannot adequately protect a client who tells him less than the truth. A physician may make a wrong diagnosis if the patient withholds information. A priest cannot grant full absolution to a pentitent who does not confess fully. In all instances, the receivers of the information are bound by codes of ethics not to disclose it to others without permission. Generally, courts have converted these codes into privileges, but they are not absolute. Physicians, for instance, are required to report suspicious wounds to the police and contagious diseases to the Board of Health.

For years, journalists sought with little success to have courts recognize their confidential relationship with some of their news sources and protect it as privileged. They argued that they served a public purpose when they investigated wrongdoing, particularly on the part of public officials, and called public attention to it. They argued further that some of their information came from sources who would disclose it only on condition that the reporter not identify them. Such sources feared they might lose their jobs or suffer physical harm if their identity became known to anyone other than the reporter. Through the years, the promise to protect a source has become a part of the journalistic code. Journalists asked to identify confidential sources argued that were they to do so, few would trust them again, and their effectiveness would be ended. Until recent times, few courts recognized a privilege for journalists, so some reporters and editors have gone to jail or paid fines rather than break their word to a source.

As far back as 1896, the Maryland Legislature gave enough credence to the journalists' arguments to enact a law defining reporters and giving them a right in some instances to protect their sources. This was the first state **shield law.** Twenty-five other states now have such laws. They range from near-absolute to limited in their protection.

Journalists served with subpoenas to appear as witnesses also argued for recognition of either a common-law privilege or one grounded in the First Amendment. Until 1972, they did so with little success. In that year, in *Branzburg* v. *Hayes*,[1] the Supreme Court told three reporters that they were like everyone else and would have to honor subpoenas ordering them to appear before grand juries seeking information about possible crime. In doing so, the Court appeared to reject the reporters' argument that the First Amendment should give some protection to their promises to their confidential sources. However, the justices were so divided in their reasoning that most courts now read the decision as creating a limited First Amendment privilege for journalists. Some state courts, reluctant to invoke the First Amendment, are holding that journalists have a common-law right to protect confidential sources and information. So strong have these privileges become in a relatively short time that, in the year ending in mid-1985, journalists won thirty-eight cases while losing only eight.[2]

Statutory and court-granted privileges have raised four questions:

1. Who is entitled to invoke the privilege? This involves the definition of a reporter and questions as to who is entitled to be considered as one.

2. What is protected? The privilege commonly enables journalists to refuse to identify confidential sources. It may also permit them to protect confidential information.

3. How far does the privilege extend? In the usual context, it can be used to challenge a subpoena, whether to appear before a grand jury or as a witness in a trial. However, courts also have used search warrants and have directed subpoenas at third parties to get information from journalists.

4. To what kinds of situations can the privilege be applied? Most commonly, journalists are asked to testify because they seem to have direct knowlege of a crime or the subject matter of a civil action. But in some instances, as in libel cases, the journalist may be a party to the action.

We will find that the extent of the privilege varies widely and is determined on a case-by-case basis. In a few jurisdictions, it is considered to be absolute. In four states, as of this writing, it has been rejected flatly. Even in states that recognize the privilege, journalists may be subjected to punishment if a court rules that it does not apply to their situation. For instance, in July 1984 Richard Hargraves, an editorial writer for the *Belleville* (Ill.) *News-Democrat*, spent three days in jail because he refused to identify his sources.[3] He had written an editorial accusing the chairman of a county board of supervisors of lying and refusing to keep campaign promises. Hargraves's sources became an issue when the chairman sued for libel. When the writer refused to name them, a judge sentenced him to jail until he was willing to do so. The ordeal ended when the

---

1. 408 U.S. 665, 92 S.Ct. 2646, 33 L.Ed.2d 626 (1972).
2. James C. Goodale and Joseph P. Moodhe, "Reporter's Privilege Cases," *Communications Law 1985* (New York: Practicing Law Institute), vol. 2, p. 11.
3. Mark Fitzgerald, "Editorial Writer Freed," *Editor & Publisher*, 14 July 1984, p. 10.

chairman's lawyer identified them by other means. In 1985, an Illinois circuit court found that Hargraves and his employer, Capital Cities Communications, had libeled the board chairman. It awarded him $450,000 in compensatory damages and $600,000 in punitive damages.[4]

Despite wide variations in the application of the privilege, three questions have come into general use in the courts when a request is made to quash a subpoena:

1. Does the journalist have information bearing directly on the case?

2. Can it be obtained from other sources?

3. Is it crucial to the determination of the case?

Major Cases

Baker v. *F & F Investment*, 470 F.2d 778 (2d Cir. 1972).

Branzburg v. *Hayes*, 408 U.S. 665, 92 S.Ct. 2646, 33 L.Ed.2d 626 (1972).

Bruno & Stillman v. *Globe Newspaper Co.*, 633 F.2d 583 (1st Cir. 1980).

Carey v. *Hume*, 492 F.2d 631 (D.C.Cir. 1974).

Commonwealth v. *Corsetti*, 387 Mass. 1 (Mass. 1982).

Grand Forks Herald v. *District Court*, 322 N.W.2d 850 (N.D. 1982).

Greenberg v. *CBS Inc.*, 419 N.Y.S.2d 988 (N.Y.App. 1979).

In re Vrazo, 423 A.2d 695 (N.J.Super. 1980).

Miller v. *Transamerican Press, Inc.*, 621 F.2d 721 (5th Cir. 1980).

Reporters Committee for Freedom of the Press v. *American Telephone & Telegraph Co.*, 593 F.2d 1030 (D.C. Cir. 1979).

Silkwood v. *Kerr-McGee Corp.*, 563 F.2d 433 (10th Cir. 1977).

United States v. *Cuthbertson*, 630 F.2d 139 (3d Cir. 1980), 651 F.2d 189 (3d Cir. 1981).

Zurcher v. *Stanford Daily*, 436 U.S. 547, 98 S.Ct. 1970, 56 L.Ed.2d 525 (1978).

THE ORIGINS OF THE PRIVILEGE

Reporters and Grand Juries

The Supreme Court's decision in 1972 in *Branzburg* v. *Hayes* was widely viewed by journalists as a slap in the face. Three reporters had asked the Court to give them a

---

4. Costello v. Capital Cities Communications, 11 Med.L.Rptr. 1738 (Ill.Cir.Ct. 1985).

qualified First Admendment privilege to protect them from grand jury subpoenas, and the Court had turned them down. The leading opinion told them that, like any other persons who were properly summoned, they would have to appear and testify. But that leading opinion was signed by only four justices. The fifth member of the majority in the five-to-four decision invited journalists who felt harassed by the legal process to challenge subpoenas by filing a **motion to quash,** that is, to request a hearing on the propriety of the subpoena. Three of the four justices in the minority would have granted the reporters a qualified privilege, while the fourth would have made it absolute.

Branzburg v. Hayes, 408 U.S. 665, 92 S.Ct. 2646, 33 L.Ed.2d 626 (1972).

Very quickly, as journalists acted on the invitation to challenge subpoenas, lower courts began reading *Branzburg* as establishing a qualified First Amendment privilege very much like the one the Court had told the three reporters they could not have. Thus, in an ironic way, *Branzburg v. Hayes* has become one of the more important decisions expanding the rights of journalists. Although they can't count on it in every instance, it has given journalists additional credibility when they promise sources that their names will not be revealed to authorities.

The three reporters who were brought together in *Branzburg* came from widely separated parts of the country and had only a few things in common—they were

When the Supreme Court handed down its decision in *Branzburg* v. *Hayes* in 1972, the three reporters involved were widely regarded as losers. They are, from the left, Paul Pappas of television station WTEV in New Bedford, Massachusetts; Earl Caldwell, West Coast bureau chief of the *New York Times,* and Paul Branzburg, a reporter for the *Louisville Courier-Journal.* The Court held that they had no right to refuse to identify confidential sources or to withhold information from a grand jury. With the passage of time, however, the principles established in that case have led to the creation of a widely recognized journalist's privilege. (AP/Wide World Photos)

investigative reporters; they were interested in people who lived at the fringes of society; they had won the trust of their sources. As a result, they were able to produce stories offering insights into lifestyles that were viewed with distrust by much of the public.

Paul Branzburg was a reporter for the *Louisville Courier-Journal*. He won entry to the subculture of drug abusers in Louisville and Frankfort, the Kentucky capital, and wrote a series of revealing stories for his newspapers in which he sought to describe why the children of middle-class Kentuckians were using narcotics. Earl Caldwell was one of the first black reporters employed by the *New York Times*. Assigned to the newspaper's West Coast bureau, he won the confidence of Black Panthers in the San Francisco area. At a time when that organization was widely believed to be plotting guerrilla warfare against white society, Caldwell was able to explore the forces that moved some blacks to take up arms. He found that the Panthers had some real grievances and sought some positive goals. Paul Pappas was a reporter-photographer for a television station in New Bedford, Massachusetts. In a city torn by racial strife, he, too, won the confidence of a Black Panther group. Members, fearing that police would attack their headquarters and kill them, let Pappas spend a night with them on condition that he would report nothing unless the attack took place. When it didn't, he kept his word.

All three reporters were served with subpoenas by grand juries investigating criminal activity. Branzburg was asked to tell county grand juries in Louisville and Frankfort what he knew about the traffic in illegal drugs. Kentucky had a shield law that protected reporters who refused to identify confidential sources of information. When Branzburg tried to use it, two separate state courts held that he could not. His stories, and the photographs illustrating them, made clear that Branzburg had been present when drug laws were violated. That made him an eyewitness to crime. He was the source of much of the information in his stories, and there was nothing confidential about his identity. Therefore, the courts ruled that he would have to appear before the grand juries and name the persons who had committed crimes in his presence. Caldwell was subpoenaed to appear before a federal grand jury in San Francisco looking into charges that the Black Panthers were plotting to kill President Nixon. He argued that if he were to appear before the jury, he would forever lose the trust of his sources, even though he said nothing. That would cut off important information about the black community, having a "chilling effect" on First Amendment freedoms. Both a federal district court and the Ninth Circuit Court of Appeals were willing to permit Caldwell to refuse to identify his sources, but they were not willing to grant him an absolute right to refuse to meet with the grand jury. Pappas worked in a state that had no shield law. When he was asked to appear before a county grand jury and tell about his night in the Panther headquarters, he asked the courts to excuse him. Massachusetts's highest court held that he would have to honor the summons or be held in contempt.

The Supreme Court took all three cases and treated them as one. Five-to-four it held that the reporters must honor the summonses and tell the grand juries what they knew. But aside from that, the Court's message was not at all clear. The justices wrote four opinions in which they differed sharply over how far the First Amendment should go in protecting newsgathering. Because the justices were split so many ways, and so evenly, in their reasoning, lower courts have been able to read *Branzburg* as both rejecting and supporting the journalist's privilege, with the majority favoring the latter view. To see how that has happened, we need to study the opinions of the justices.

Justice Byron R. White wrote the opinion of the Court, in which he was joined by three others. He began by making an important concession, one that has been quoted frequently in court decisions, most notably in *Richmond Newspapers*, with results examined in the previous chapter. Noting that the reporters had argued that the First Amendment ought to protect them in gathering the news as well as in disseminating it, White wrote that he did not question the Amendment's value to society. He added:

> "Nor is it suggested that news gathering does not qualify for First Amendment protection; without some protection for seeking out the news, freedom of the press could be eviscerated.

He followed that concession by defining the issue in this case in narrow terms, and by holding that no important First Amendment interests were at stake. He wrote:

> The sole issue before us is the obligation of reporters to respond to grand jury subpoenas as other citizens do and to answer questions relevant to an investigation into the commission of a crime. Citizens generally are not constitutionally immune from grand jury subpoenas; and neither the First Amendment nor any other constitutional provision protects the average citizen from disclosing to a grand jury information that he has received in confidence. The claim is, however, that reporters are exempt from these obligations because if forced to respond to subpoenas and identify their sources or disclose other confidences, their informants will refuse or be reluctant to furnish newsworthy information in the future. This asserted burden on news gathering is said to make compelled testimony from newsmen constitutionally suspect and to require a privileged position for them.
>
> It is clear that the First Amendment does not invalidate every incidental burdening of the press that may result from the enforcement of civil or criminal statutes of general applicability.

White noted that state courts consistently had held that journalists have no right, other than that granted by shield laws, to protect confidential sources and information. He wrote:

> These courts . . . have concluded that the First Amendment interest asserted by the newsman was outweighed by the general obligation of a citizen to appear before a grand jury or at trial, pursuant to a subpoena, and give what information he possesses.

Grand juries, White noted, play an important role in the criminal justice system. Jurors listen to allegations of wrongdoing and decide whether an individual should be charged with a crime. To help them in getting at the truth, grand juries have broad powers to subpoena witnesses. This authority, White wrote, is essential, but it is not unlimited. If it is abused, it may be restricted by a judge. However, the justice added that the "longstanding principle that 'the public . . . has a right to every man's evidence,' . . . is particularly applicable to grand jury proceedings."

At this point, White took notice of the testimonial privileges noted at the start of this chapter—the Fifth Amendment privilege against self-incrimination, and the common-law privileges cloaking marital, physician-patient, lawyer-client, and clergy-penitent relationships. Such testimonial privileges are so deeply rooted, he noted, as to be almost beyond challenge. Then he wrote:

> We are asked to create another [privilege] by interpreting the First Amendment to grant newsmen a testimonial privilege that other citizens do not enjoy. This we decline to do.

In rejecting the reporters' argument, White and the three justices who joined him balanced the public's interest in law enforcement against the journalists' interest in access to sources of news. Because they were not convinced that confidential sources play an important role in newsgathering, the justices came down on the side of law enforcement. They took the position that it is better to do something about crime than to write about it. In their view, anyone, including reporters, with direct knowledge of a crime has a duty to share that knowledge with law enforcement officers. As White put it,

> [W]e cannot accept the argument that the public interest in possible future news about crime from undisclosed, unverified sources must take precedence over the public interest in pursuing and prosecuting those crimes reported to the press by informants and in thus deterring the commission of such crimes in the future.

White further justified the plurality's position by arguing that a testimonial privilege grounded in the First Amendment could be abused. Journalists could use it to "protect a private system of informers . . . , a system that would be unaccountable to the public, would pose a threat to the citizen's justifiable expectations of privacy," and would also protect those tempted for pay or otherwise to "betray their trust to their employer or associates." Under the First Amendment, media informants would enjoy a higher degree of protection than do police informants. The latter have no constitutional protection, White noted. If a police informant's testimony is sought by a grand jury, or is needed in court, police either must identify him or drop the prosecution. In a footnote, White suggested that if reporters were granted a First Amendment shield for their sources, groups of criminals might establish newspapers and hire themselves as reporters so as to cloak their illegal activities.

Nor were White and his colleagues willing to grant journalists a qualified privilege based on common law rather than the First Amendment. To do that, they said, would "embark the judiciary on a long and difficult journey to . . . an uncertain destination." Courts would have to determine who would be entitled to claim the privilege. That would put the courts in the position of deciding who is a bona-fide journalist. Such decisions would be made difficult by the fact that the Supreme Court has held that freedom of the press is a "fundamental personal right not confined to newspapers and periodicals." Lecturers, political pollsters, novelists, academic researchers, and dramatists also gather information and offer it to the public.

However, the plurality said it had no objection to legislators attempting to define journalists and grant them a testimonial privilege by statute. Thus, the four justices gave their approval to the shield laws then in effect in seventeen states.

Only at the end did White and his associates temper their strong rejection of a journalist's privilege. They wrote:

> Finally, as we have earlier indicated, news gathering is not without its First Amendment protection, and grand jury investigations, if instituted or conducted other than in good faith, would pose wholly different issues for resolution under the First Amendment. Official harassment of the press undertaken not for purposes of law enforcement but to disrupt a reporter's relationship with his news sources would have no justification. Grand juries are subject to judicial control and subpoenas to motions to quash. We do not expect courts will forget that grand juries must operate within the limits of the First Amendment as well as the Fifth.

Justice Lewis F. Powell, Jr., voted with White and his colleagues to hold that the three journalists had no right to refuse to answer a grand jury's questions. But he wrote separately to enlarge on the point made in the paragraph above. That he did so has proved to be of utmost importance to journalists who receive subpoenas, not only to testify before grand juries, but in other legal proceedings, both criminal and civil. The majority of the courts considering challenges to such subpoenas have found in Powell's concurrence support for a qualified journalist's privilege. Because this is the case, Powell's reasoning merits careful attention.

The justice noted that a majority of the Court had indeed refused to give journalists an absolute privilege that would protect their refusal to testify in any legal proceeding. However, not even the plurality had said that journalists must testify under all circumstances. It had conceded that the right to gather news has some degree of First Amendment protection. Public officials and courts must respect that right, Powell wrote. If they should not, the justice invited journalists to seek redress in court:

> As indicated in the concluding portion of the opinion, the Court states that no harassment of newsmen will be tolerated. If a newsman believes that the grand jury investigation is not being conducted in good faith he is not without remedy. Indeed, if the newsman is called upon to give information bearing only a remote and tenuous relationship to the subject of the investigation, or if he has some other reason to believe that his testimony implicates confidential source relationships without a legitimate need of law enforcement, he will have access to the court on a motion to quash and an appropriate protective order may be entered. The asserted claim to privilege should be judged on its facts by the striking of a proper balance between freedom of the press and the obligation of all citizens to give relevant testimony with respect to criminal conduct. The balance of these vital constitutional and societal interests on a case-by-case basis accords with the tried and traditional way of adjudicating such questions.
>
> In short, the courts will be available to newsmen under circumstances where legitimate First Amendment interests require protection.

Powell thus sought to define how far the First Amendment might go in protecting the right to gather news. He suggested that grand juries ought not to subpoena journalists unless there is reason to believe the latter have some substantial knowledge about the subject of the investigation. Further, Powell suggested that grand juries should respect the confidentiality of reporters' sources unless "a legitimate need of law enforcement" requires disclosure. These suggestions were stated with more precision by Justice Potter Stewart, writing in dissent. He was joined by Justices William J. Brennan, Jr., and Thurgood Marshall. The language was blunt:

> "The Court's crabbed view of the First Amendment reflects a disturbing insensitivity to the critical role of an independent press in our society. The question whether a reporter has a constitutional right to a confidential relationship with his source is of first impression here, but the principles that should guide our decision are as basic as any to be found in the Constitution. While Mr. Justice Powell's enigmatic concurring opinion gives some hope of a more flexible view in the future, the Court in these cases holds that a newsman has no First Amendment right to protect his sources when called before a grand jury. The Court thus invites state and federal authorities to undermine the historic independence of the press by attempting to annex the journalistic profession as an investigative arm of

government. Not only will this decision impair performance of the press' constitutionally protected functions, but it will, I am convinced, in the long run, harm rather than help the administration of justice.

White, in writing for the plurality, had responded to the arguments advanced by Branzburg, Caldwell, and Pappas by focusing on the role of the grand jury. Stewart and his colleagues focused on the role of the news media. They seized on the majority's recognition that newsgathering has some First Amendment protection and enlarged on that theme:

> A corollary of the right to publish must be the right to gather news. . . .
> . . . News must not be unnecessarily cut off at its source, for without freedom to acquire information the right to publish would be impermissibly compromised. Accordingly, a right to gather news, of some dimensions, must exist. . . .
> The right to gather news implies, in turn, a right to a confidential relationship between a reporter and his source. This proposition follows as a matter of simple logic once three factual predicates are recognized: (1) newsmen require informants to gather news; (2) confidentiality—the promise or understanding that names or certain aspects of communications will be kept off the record—is essential to the creation and maintenance of a newsgathering relationship with informants; and (3) an unbridled subpoena power—the absence of a constitutional right protecting, in *any* way, a confidential relationship from compulsory process—will either deter sources from divulging information or deter reporters from gathering and publishing information.
> It is obvious that informants are necessary to the newsgathering process as we know it today. If it is to perform its constitutional mission, the press must do far more than merely print public statements or prepared handouts. Familiarity with the people and circumstances involved in the myriad background activities that result in the final product called "news" is vital to complete and responsible journalism, unless the press is to be a captive mouthpiece of "newsmakers."
> It is equally obvious that the promise of confidentiality may be a necessary prerequisite to a productive relationship between a newsman and his informants. An officeholder may fear his superior; a member of the bureaucracy, his associates; a dissident, the scorn of majority opinion. All may have information valuable to the public discourse, yet each may be willing to relate that information only in confidence to a reporter whom he trusts, either because of excessive caution or because of a reasonable fear of reprisals or censure for unorthodox views. The First Amendment concern must not be with the motives of any particular news source, but rather with the conditions in which informants of all shades of the spectrum may make information available through the press to the public. . . .
> . . . Commentators and individual reporters have repeatedly noted the importance of confidentiality. And surveys among reporters and editors indicate that the promise of nondisclosure is necessary for many types of news gathering.
> Finally, and most important, when governmental officials possess an unchecked power to compel newsmen to disclose information received in confidence, sources will clearly be deterred from publishing it, because uncertainty about exercise of the power will lead to "self-censorship." . . . The uncertainty arises, of course, because the judiciary has traditionally imposed virtually no limitations on the grand jury's broad investigatory powers.

Stewart sought to avoid the uncertainty, and the resulting self-censorship, by proposing a three-point test that must be met before a journalist could be required to testify. He wrote:

Accordingly, when a reporter is asked to appear before a grand jury and reveal confidences, I would hold that the government must (1) show that there is probable cause to believe that the newsman has information that is clearly relevant to a specific probable violation of law; (2) demonstrate that the information sought cannot be obtained by alternative means less destructive of First Amendment rights; and (3) demonstrate a compelling and overriding interest in the information.

This is not to say that a grand jury could not issue a subpoena until such a showing is made, and it is not to say that a newsman would be in any way privileged to ignore any subpoena that was issued. Obviously, before the government's burden to make such a showing were triggered, the reporter would have to move to quash the subpoena, asserting the basis on which he considered the particular relationship a confidential one.

Stewart presented the reasoning behind his three-part test. He said the test of relevance would protect those sources who have neither committed a crime nor have direct knowledge of a crime. Anything such sources might have to say would be **hearsay** at best and not admissible in court if an indictment were returned. And if relevant helpful information could be obtained without subpoenaing a reporter, why do so? He added:

No doubt the courts would be required to make some delicate judgments in working out this accommodation. But that, after all, is the function of courts of law. Better such judgments, however difficult, than the simplistic and stultifying absolutism adopted by the Court in denying any force to the First Amendment in these cases.

Justice William O. Douglas wrote separately in dissent to advance an absolute view of the First Amendment. He would have held that journalists have a constitutional right to refuse to take part in any legal proceeding. If they chose to testify, they could do so on their own terms. No other member of the Court was willing to go that far.

Judges applying *Branzburg* have found the elements of a First Amendment journalist's privilege in three places:

1. White and the three justices who voted with him recognized that news-gathering has some First Amendment protection. While he was unwilling to convert that protection into a privilege in this case, he warned that "[o]fficial harassment of the press . . . would have no justification." Where a legitimate interest in coping with crime ends and harassment begins is, of course, a matter of judgment.

2. Powell, whose vote made the decision possible, emphasized White's warning against harassment. He made the further points that journalists ought not to be asked for "information bearing only a remote and tenuous relationship to the investigation," and ought not to be asked to identify confidential sources without good reason.

3. Where White and Powell were vague, Stewart was specific. The former can be read as recognizing that a privilege exists. Stewart had no doubts. The three-part test he suggested for determining when the privilege can be invoked has been adopted almost verbatim by many courts. In most jurisdictions, persons seeking a journalist's testimony must prove that the

journalist has firsthand information about the matter at issue, that the information can't be obtained from other sources, and that it is essential to a proper resolution of the case.

The Privilege in the Federal Courts ==========

In reaction to the Supreme Court's decision in *Branzburg*, Congress considered adoption of a federal shield law. But when journalists themselves were unable to agree on how far such a law should go, or even on the need for any law at all, the proposal was dropped.[5] At about the same time, the U.S. Department of Justice adopted guidelines designed to limit the use of journalists as witnesses in federal grand juries and in trials in federal courts.[6]

The guidelines start with the premise that federal law enforcement officers will make no attempt to subpoena journalists until they have made "all reasonable attempts . . . to obtain information from nonmedia sources." If such attempts fail, the next step is negotiation with the media. If that fails, a subpoena cannot be issued without "the express authorization of the Attorney General."

That authorization is not to be given in criminal cases unless information from nonmedia sources indicates that a crime has been committed and that a reporter has information directly bearing on a suspect's guilt or innocence. Even then, the government is not supposed to issue a subpoena to the reporter unless it has been unable to get that information from nonmedia sources. Questioning of reporters who are subpoenaed is to be limited to verification of published information and to establishing its accuracy. The directive advises government attorneys to avoid the appearance of harassing journalists and to limit their requests to specific kinds of information. The same restrictions apply to civil cases with the added provision that journalists are not to be drawn into such lawsuits unless the issue is "of substantial proportions."

Clearly, the attorney general's guidelines are based on the Stewart-Powell opinions in *Branzburg*. How diligent Justice Department attorneys have been in observing them has been the subject of debate in a committee of Congress,[7] and of a few court cases.

However, whatever their effect, the guidelines have been overshadowed in the last decade by court decisions protecting journalists who have been given subpoenas. Early decisions by the U.S. Courts of Appeals in three circuits established precedents that have been followed in many cases, not only in federal courts, but in state courts as well. These influential cases are *Baker* v. *F & F Investment*,[8] decided by the Second Circuit in 1972; *Carey* v. *Hume*,[9] decided by the District of Columbia Circuit in 1974; and *Silkwood* v. *Kerr-McGee Corp.*,[10] decided by the Tenth Circuit in 1977. The cases illustrate how courts, in line with Powell's suggestion in *Branzburg*, have balanced the

---

5. Martin Arnold, "Watergate Stalls Press Shield Law Effort," *Louisville Courier-Journal*, 4 July 1973.
6. 28 C.F.R. Part 50.
7. *Newsmen's Privilege*: Hearings, Subcommittee on Courts, Civil Liberties, and the Administration of Justice, Committee on the Judiciary, House of Representatives, 94th Congress, 1st sess., on H.R. 215, 23 and 24 April 1975, pp. 6–36 and 94–102.
8. 470 F.2d 778 (2d Cir. 1972).
9. 492 F.2d 631 (D.C.Cir. 1974).
10. 563 F.2d 433 (10th Cir 1977).

journalists' interests in freedom of the press against the courts' interest in justice. In *Baker* and *Silkwood*, the balance favored the journalist. In *Carey*, the court recognized the existence of a privilege, but held that the balance of interests required the journalist to identify his confidential source.

In *Baker*, the plaintiff in a civil action sought information from a magazine writer who was not involved in the litigation. Alfred Balk, an editor of the *Columbia Journalism Review*, had written an article on blockbusting for the *Saturday Evening Post*. Relying in part on information obtained from confidential sources, Balk described tactics used by some real estate firms to provoke panic selling of homes by white owners when a black family moved into the neighborhood. The real estate firms involved would buy from the white owners at low prices and then sell to black families at much higher

Baker v. F & F Investment, 470 F.2d 778 (2d Cir. 1972).

prices. Baker, representing himself and other black buyers, sued F & F, seeking damages as alleged victims of racial discrimination. Seeking support for his case, Baker asked a federal district court in New York City to compel Balk to identify the sources interviewed for his article. The court refused to do so, holding that Baker had not shown that he could not obtain the same information from other sources. That holding was affirmed on appeal. The circuit court further buttressed its verdict by holding that Balk's information did not go to the "heart of the claim" advanced by Baker. The circuit court distinguished *Baker* from *Branzburg* by noting that the former was a civil action. In *Branzburg*, the government had been seeking the reporters' information about criminal activity. The circuit court held that in a civil action, a journalist's interest in freedom of the press carries more weight than in a criminal proceeding.

Carey, too, was a civil action, but differed from *Baker* in that the journalist was directly involved as a libel defendant. Carey, a lawyer for the United Mine Workers union, was the subject of a Jack Anderson column alleging that he had taken a box of union records from the union's office and then reported it stolen. The column was based on information given to one of Anderson's reporters by a confidential source. During the preliminary stages of the resulting libel action, Carey said he could not prove actual

Carey v. Hume, 492 F.2d 631 (D.C.Cir. 1974).

malice unless he knew the identity of Anderson's sources. A federal district court agreed and ordered Anderson and the reporter to name their sources. On appeal, the District of Columbia Circuit Court affirmed. Applying the balancing test endorsed by Justice Powell, and recognizing the existence of a qualified privilege, the court held that the journalists' interest would have to yield. In this instance, the information sought by Carey went to the heart of his case. He could prove actual malice only if he could show that Anderson "had no reliable sources, that he misrepresented the reports of his sources, or that reliance upon these particular sources was reckless." That issue could be resolved only if the court knew who the sources were.

Silkwood v. Kerr-McGee Corp., 563 F.2d 433 (10th Cir. 1977).

Silkwood, like the two previous cases, was a civil action. In this instance, as in *Baker*, the journalist was not a party to the action. The case is of special interest because the court expanded the definition of a journalist to include producers of television documentaries.

Karen Silkwood had been employed by Kerr-McGee at a plant processing plutonium. Her body became contaminated by plutonium radiation, which she alleged was a result of her employer's negligence. While she was driving in her car to meet a *New York Times* reporter to talk about conditions in the plant, her car left the road under mysterious circumstances, and she was killed. The administrator of her estate sued Kerr-McGee for damages, alleging that the company had violated Miss Silkwood's civil rights by conspiring to prevent her from organizing a labor union and from filing official complaints over safety conditions, and by contaminating her with radiation. Arthur Hirsch, a producer of television documentaries, was one of several journalists who investigated Miss Silkwood's complaints and the circumstances of her death. He had relied on confidential sources in preparing his report. In preparing to defend itself against the lawsuit, Kerr-McGee sought to question Hirsch about his sources and about confidential information that had not been used in the documentary. When Hirsch moved to quash the subpoena, a federal district court ruled that he was not a journalist and therefore was not covered by a privilege that would permit him to refuse to answer questions. Hirsch appealed to the Tenth Circuit, which ruled that the Supreme Court in *Branzburg* had not limited the privilege to newspaper reporters. It said that Court "has in fact held that the press comprehends different kinds of publications which communicate to the public information and opinion."

In sending the case back to the district court for resolution, the circuit court said that court should apply Justice Stewart's three-part test in determining whether to compel Hirsch to testify. It said the district court should consider the nature of the information being sought, its relevance and significance to the case, and its availability from alternative sources. The district court had no opportunity to rule because Kerr-McGee withdrew its subpoena.

These cases have served as models for other courts confronted with a request to recognize the journalist's privilege. As of this writing, U.S. Courts of Appeals in five other circuits have endorsed the privilege, and none has rejected it in recent decisions.

Thus, despite the lack of a federal shield law, journalists who are developing stories on matters within the jurisdiction of the federal courts have a considerable degree of protection for their confidential sources. If the government is a party to the action, they can rely in the first instance on the attorney general's guidelines. These say, in effect, that subpoenas are to be served on journalists only as a last resort, and then only with the attorney general's approval. If the attorney general does approve, a motion to quash can be filed with the appropriate district court. If a journalist is summoned in connection with a civil action to which the government is not a party, his or her appeal is also to the district court. Motions to quash can be filed with the knowledge that no circuit has refused to recognize a journalist's privilege, while eight of the twelve have done so. In response to a motion to quash, a federal court is likely to require the party seeking a journalist's testimony to apply Stewart's three-part test:

1. Does the journalist have information of substance that is relevant to the case?

2. Does the information go to the heart of the question at issue?

3. Can the information be obtained from other sources?

If the answer to either of the first two questions is no, or to the third question is yes, the journalist is not likely to be required to testify. The recent decisions indicate that federal courts are willing to grant strong protection to journalists who are served with subpoenas. Results in state courts have been mixed, but there, too, the trend has been running in favor of the journalist's privilege.

State Shield Laws

At the time of the *Branzburg* decision in 1972, seventeen states had enacted shield laws granting a testimonial privilege to journalists. In reaction to that decision, nine other states enacted such laws, making a total of twenty-six in effect in 1986. This is not the end of it, however. State courts have been looking not only to the First Amendment, but to their own state constitutions and to common law to find support for journalists seeking to protect their sources and information. Courts in fifteen of the states without shield laws have held that there is a qualified privilege for journalists served with a subpoena. In only four states, Colorado, Georgia, Hawaii, and Massachusetts, have state courts held that journalists have no privilege.[11] Courts in five states, Maine, South Carolina, South Dakota, Utah, and Wyoming, have had no reported cases dealing with a reporter's privilege.

States with shield laws are Alabama, Alaska, Arizona, Arkansas, California, Delaware, Illinois, Indiana, Kentucky, Louisiana, Maryland, Michigan, Minnesota, Montana, Nebraska, Nevada, New Jersey, New Mexico, New York, North Dakota, Ohio, Oklahoma, Oregon, Pennsylvania, Rhode Island, and Tennessee. Their terms vary widely. All define the kind of journalist who qualifies for the privilege. Some permit journalists to protect only confidential sources of information. Some are operative only if the information is published or broadcast. Others protect not only sources, but information, whether or not it is published or broadcast. A few are inoperative if the journalist is the target of a libel suit. Other laws make exceptions if a fair trial is at stake, or if the court finds a public interest in the journalist's testimony. About half the laws are written in absolute terms, but courts have not always found them so. New Jersey's law, as interpreted by its Supreme Court, may be the strongest.[12] The court held that the law gives journalists an absolute right to refuse to name their sources, or to discuss editorial processes, in a libel action. Indiana's law, which is limited to the identity of confidential sources, has also been held to be absolute, even when the journalist is a defendant in a libel action.[13]

States in which courts have looked to *Branzburg* or other sources to find a journalist's privilege are Alaska, California, Connecticut, Delaware, Florida, Idaho, Illinois, Iowa, Kansas, Michigan, Mississippi, Missouri, New Hampshire, New Jersey, New York, North Carolina, Ohio, Oklahoma, Texas, Vermont, Virginia, Washington, West Virginia, and Wisconsin. A comparison between this list and the shield-law listing above shows that journalists in nine states may find protection from more than one source.

---

11. State court cases are listed in *Communication Law 1985*, James C. Goodale, chairman (New York: Practicing Law Institute, 1985), vol 2, pp. 310–355.
12. State v. Boiardo, 414 A.2d 14 (N.J. 1980), 416 A.2d 793 (N.J. 1980); In re Vrazo, 423 A.2d 695 (N.J.Super 1980), and Maressa v. New Jersey Monthly, 445 A.2d 376 (N.J. 1982).
13. Jamerson v. American Newspapers, Inc., 469 N.E.2d 1243 (Ind.Ct.App. 1984).

These states are Alaska, California, Delaware, Illinois, Michigan, New Jersey, New York, Ohio, and Oklahoma.

Like shield-law protection, court-granted privileges also vary widely in their application. Most are qualified, with some being quite limited. Florida seems to have gone further than any of the non–shield-law states in protecting journalists from subpoenas. Decisions in thirty-six reported cases between 1974 and 1983 forged an absolute privilege for journalists in civil litigation and in cases involving disclosure of sealed grand jury materials. Courts have based the privilege on the First Amendment and on the free press section of the Florida Constitution.[14]

The dimensions of the protection granted by state shield laws and by the decisions of state courts will be examined in subsequent sections of this chapter. However, because this can be done only in a general way in a textbook, journalists are advised to acquaint themselves with decisions of the courts in the states where they are employed.

QUALIFYING FOR THE PRIVILEGE

The Definition of a Journalist

Shield laws generally define journalists in broad terms so as to include anyone who is able to get an article in print with a recognized publisher, or on the air over a radio or television station. In the past, a few of the laws have extended protection only to persons who are employed by a publisher or broadcaster or who are paid on a free-lance basis. Such laws raise questions as to whether they cover student newspapers, publications produced by community organizations, and other media with nonpaid staffs. The modern tendency is to broaden the laws to cover anyone whose primary purpose is to gather information for dissemination to the public. For instance, the New York law[15] was amended in 1981 to include free-lancers, still and movie photographers, authors of books, employers of journalists, and persons connected with noncommercial media.

Where the law leaves doubt as to whether the person who receives a subpoena qualifies as a journalist, courts look at the circumstances. If such persons were acting as journalists, and were seeking information for dissemination to the public, then courts have tended to hold that they can invoke the privilege. If not, they may not be protected, as the following two cases illustrate.

The first case grew out of the discovery process during General William Westmoreland's libel action against CBS News.[16] The general contended that he was defamed by a segment of "60 Minutes," which portrayed him as part of a conspiracy to understate enemy troop strength in Vietnam. When complaints were made about the segment, CBS conducted an internal study, which concluded that some of its news policies had been violated in preparing the report. During pretrial discovery, Westmoreland's lawyers

---

14. Morgan v. State, 337 So.2d 951 (Fla. 1976).
15. N.Y. Civ. Rights Law §79-h (McKinney 1981).
16. Westmoreland v. CBS, 9 Med.L.Rptr. 2316 (S.D.N.Y. 1983); 97 F.R.D. 703 (S.D.N.Y. 1983), and 10 Med.L.Rptr. 1214 (S.D.N.Y. 1984).

asked for a copy of the study, along with notes and materials used in preparing it. When CBS resisted, the district court ordered the information released, holding that the writer of the study was not engaged in newsgathering. Later, the order was modified to exempt sources who had spoken to the writer under promises of confidentiality.

In the second case, an Indiana appellate court denied a claim of privilege under that state's shield law to a part-time reporter. It held that she was performing as an activist, not a journalist, when she obtained a copy of a confidential Environmental Protection Agency report. As further evidence of her nonjournalistic role, the court cited the fact that she had not used the report in the newspaper to which she contributed articles but had given it to a television reporter. The television station's use of the report led to a libel suit. The court said the woman would have to answer the plaintiff's questions about who had given her the EPA document.[17]

Cases like these are rare, indicating that courts generally have little difficulty in deciding who is a bona-fide journalist entitled to invoke a privilege against disclosure of sources. At this point, there has been no evidence to support Justice White's suggestion in *Branzburg* that, if a privilege were recognized, bands of criminals would establish a newspaper to protect their members from testifying against one another.

The Protection of Sources and Information

Two questions lie at the heart of every privilege case:

1. What kind of information is being sought by the issuer of the subpoena?

2. What kinds of information does the shield law, or the court-defined privilege, permit the journalist to withhold?

The decisions that have dealt with the answers to these questions are not always precise, but they sort out into six categories, three dealing with sources and three with information. With reference to sources, the categories are as follows:

1. Some shield laws and some court decisions protect all of a journalist's sources, regardless of circumstances. This is the broadest possible protection of sources. With such protection, a journalist cannot be asked to identify any of the persons consulted during the preparation of a story.

2. Other courts require that there be some evidence to show that the reporter promised not to identify a source. In some instances, the relationship between reporter and source is seen almost as a contract. If both sides did not clearly understand that the source's name was not to be disclosed, the court will not respect the reporter's attempt to keep the identity of the source confidential.

3. A few courts have narrowed source protection almost to the vanishing

---

17. Northside Sanitary Landfill, Inc. v. Bradley, 462 N.E.2d 1321 (Ind. App. 1984).

point by holding that it applies only to sources whose information was not included in the final story.

With respect to information, the decisions also vary widely in the scope of the protection they give the journalist:

1. Some courts have held that reporters cannot be asked to testify about any information not in the story that was published or broadcast. This means that if they are summoned, they cannot be asked to do any more than verify that the story is theirs and that it reflects the information they obtained.

2. Others have held that reporters can't be asked to testify as to unpublished information they obtained from others, but they can be asked to tell what they saw and heard, but did not include in the story. This limitation would come into play if the reporter had been a witness to a crime or had been present during an action that led to a civil suit.

3. Still other courts have limited the privilege to unpublished information obtained from sources who were promised confidentiality.

The strength of any shield law, or court-established privilege, from the journalist's point of view, can be measured by reference to these six categories. Thus, a privilege that protects all sources and all information not published or broadcast would be the strongest. Most of the decisions involve mixtures of the six, as the cases that follow illustrate.

The nature of promises made to the reporter's sources became the key question in *Bruno & Stillman v. Globe Newspaper Co.*, decided by the U.S. Court of Appeals, First Circuit, in 1980. Bruno & Stillman, a shipbuilding company, sued the *Boston Globe* for libel over articles commenting unfavorably on commercial fishing vessels it had produced. During **discovery,** the company asked the

Bruno & Stillman v. Globe Newspaper Co., 633 F.2d 583 (1st Cir. 1980).

reporter to give it the notes and materials he used in preparing his stories. Discovery is a pretrial process in which lawyers obtain information from participants and potential witnesses in an effort to narrow the issues to be resolved at trial. The newspaper surrendered about 1,500 pages of the reporter's handwritten notes, but it refused to disclose the identity of three confidential sources and the unpublished information they gave the paper. A federal district court ordered disclosure of the withheld information.

On appeal, the circuit court remanded with instructions that the district court apply a balancing test before deciding whether to repeat the disclosure order. It said the court should first satisfy itself that the libel action was not frivolous. Then it should determine whether there was a jury issue as to the falsity of the allegedly defamatory statements in the articles. Finally, it should determine whether the requested information was more than remotely relevant to proving Bruno's case. But that did not end the matter.

If the court concluded, after applying the three-part test, that the information might be essential to the case, it should examine the circumstances under which the reporter obtained it. If the reporter could prove that the information had been obtained under a promise of confidentiality, that promise would be given consideration. Otherwise, disclosure would be ordered. The court made some pertinent points about the nature of newsgathering:

> Not all information as to sources is equally deserving of confidentiality. An unsolicited letter may be received with no mention of an interest in anonymity; such a letter may casually mention the wish for confidential treatment; it may specifically condition use on the according of such treatment; or it may defer communication of any substance until a commitment to confidentiality is received. Oral communications could also range from the cavalierly volunteered to the carefully bargained-for undertaking. . . . In the present case a number of facts need to be sorted out and others need to be developed. For example, although one source sent an unsolicited letter, there was a subsequent promise to protect not only all notes of conversation with the source but the intitial letter. Whether and to what extent such a *nunc pro tunc* undertaking merits protection by the court is a matter for its discriminating judgment. The existing record is silent as to the reasonable expectation of confidentiality on the part of the other two sources.

The term *nunc pro tunc* refers to an attempt to modify an existing arrangement, and to proceed on the assumption that the modifications had been in effect from the beginning. In this instance, information about Bruno & Stillman had been offered to the reporter without any request for confidentiality. At a later date, the source and the reporter did enter into a confidential relationship. The question the court raised was whether that relationship could be made retroactive to include the material offered originally.

United States v. Cuthbertson, 630 F.2d 139 (3d Cir. 1980); 651 F.2d 189 (3d Cir. 1981).

In two decisions, in 1980 and 1981, the United States Court of Appeals, Third Circuit, dealt with an attempt by CBS News to withhold unused information. At issue in *United States* v. *Cuthbertson* were "outtakes"—that is, videotape taken but not used—in an episode of "60 Minutes."

The episode examined complaints about Cuthbertson's franchising of Wild Bill's Family Restaurants. Later, a federal grand jury indicted Cuthbertson on charges of conspiracy and fraud. A month before the trial was scheduled, Cuthbertson's lawyers issued a subpoena to CBS asking for all of the outtakes used in preparing the program. They believed that the unused tape included interviews with persons who might appear as witnesses for the government and might be useful in challenging their testimony. When CBS asked the trial court judge to quash the subpoena, he ruled that CBS would have to let him review any outtakes dealing with government witnesses. If he concluded information on any of them might be useful to the defendant, he would turn those parts of the outtakes over to his lawyers. At that point, the lawyers asked the judge to review additional tapes dealing with about a hundred other persons. When the judge agreed to do so and asked CBS to produce the outtakes, it refused. He found the network in contempt and fined it one dollar a day until it complied with his order.

On appeal, the Third Circuit Court recognized a qualified privilege in the news media to protect confidential sources of information. But it said that was not the end of it, adding:

The compelled production of a reporter's resource materials can constitute a significant intrusion into the newsgathering and editorial processes. . . . Like the compelled disclosure of confidential sources, it may substantially undercut the public policy favoring the free flow of information to the public that is the foundation of the privilege. . . . Therefore, we hold that the privilege extends to unpublished materials in the possession of CBS.

The court told the district court judge that he could not compel CBS to surrender its outtakes until, in each instance, he had balanced the need for the material against the inhibiting effect his order would have on First Amendment freedoms. He also was told to consider whether the information sought by Cuthbertson could be obtained from other sources. The court held further that CBS could be required to give up for the judge's inspection only those tapes on which government witnesses were interviewed.

On remand, CBS submitted pertinent outtakes to the judge. He concluded that, while some of the tapes would help determine whether witnesses had told CBS one thing and said something else in court, all of them would help the defense with its case. When he ordered them to be given to the defense, CBS again appealed to the circuit court. It reversed, holding there had been no showing that specific evidence would be admissible in court or that it could not be obtained by other means.

The decisions above are significant because they are being looked to by other courts for guidance. In *Bruno & Stillman*, the court was willing to protect a reporter's confidential sources in a libel action, but only if it was clear he had promised in advance not to disclose their names. In *Cuthbertson*, the court held that First Amendment interests also require that some degree of protection be given to information obtained by reporters but not used in their stories. In that instance, the ruling was in a criminal case and the question was whether the unused information would help the defense raise doubt about the testimony of government witnesses. The decision shows a willingness on the part of some courts to protect the editorial process—decisions that shape the final version of a story—as well as confidential sources.

Search Warrants and Third-Party Subpoenas

The *Branzburg* case began when three reporters received subpoenas directing them to appear before grand juries to answer questions about crimes of which they were believed to have knowledge. The other cases looked at thus far have also dealt with attempts to obtain information from journalists. They have been asked to identify their confidential sources, as in *Baker*, *Carey*, and *Bruno & Stillman*, or they have been asked to provide information, as in *Silkwood* and *Cuthbertson*. As these instances suggest, a subpoena directed to individuals who are supposed to have direct knowledge of a crime or the substance of a civil action is the most common method of obtaining testimony from reluctant witnesses.

Courts also have other methods of obtaining information, two of which have seen limited use against journalists. One of these is the **search warrant,** and the other is a subpoena directed at third parties who have information that might identify a journalist's sources. Search warrants are authorized by the Fourth Amendment, which was drafted to protect people's property and possessions from arbitrary seizure by police. The amendment says that searches of private property can be made only if authorized for good cause by a magistrate. Usually, warrants are issued only to seize evidence of a crime, such things as a stash of drugs, stolen property, or weapons believed to have been used in committing a crime. Third-party subpoenas sometimes are served on banks to obtain financial information about a suspected criminal, or on the telephone company to obtain records of a user's long-distance calls.

The Privacy Protection Act of 1980

Until the advent of photojournalism, search warrants seldom were a problem for the news media. Few journalists have been involved in crime, and most newsrooms are unlikely hiding places for criminal contraband. The era of political activism that reached a climax during the latter years of the Vietnam War brought police search teams into newsrooms in disturbing numbers. Usually, they were seeking unpublished photographs, still or video, that would help them identify persons who had caused personal injury or property damage during riots. The most notable of these searches saw police rummaging through desk drawers and wastebaskets in the office of the *Stanford* (Cal.) *Daily*, a student newspaper, in 1971. They were seeking photographs that would help them identify students and others who had occupied the Stanford University Hospital, and who had severely beaten several police officers. The searchers found nothing that would help them, but their actions led first to a significant Supreme Court decision and then to congressional enactment of the Privacy Protection Act of 1980. The latter has made it unlikely that police again will search a newsroom.

The Supreme Court decision, in *Zurcher* v. *Stanford Daily*, written in 1978, was seen at the time as a serious blow to First Amendment freedoms. The editors of the newspaper had reacted to the search by filing suit against those responsible, alleging violation of freedom of the press and abuse of the search warrant provision of the Fourth Amendment. They argued that because there was no evidence that anyone on the *Daily* had been involved in a crime, the police should have used a subpoena, not a search warrant, to obtain the unused photographs. Lower federal courts found in the students' favor, but the Supreme Court took the case and reversed.

Zurcher v. *Stanford Daily,*
436 U.S. 547, 98 S.Ct.
1970, 56 L.Ed.2d 525
(1978).

Justice White, writing for a majority of the Court, noted that search warrants had been used on other occasions to seize printed materials. His reference was to instances, mainly during the Cold War era after World War II, when police seized books and pamphlets alleged to be subversive. The court held that any First Amendment interest in protecting the newsroom from police intrusion had been taken into account by the magistrate who issued the search warrant.

White noted further that the Fourth Amendment requires only that the warrant describe specifically "the place to be searched." He found nothing in that language exempting newsrooms. If police believe helpful evidence can be found in a place, and if they further believe that a subpoena would result in destruction of that evidence, issuance of a search warrant is justified. The First Amendment, in the Court's view, cannot create sanctuaries beyond the reach of the police.

The decision encouraged police and prosecutors to conduct twenty-three other newsroom searches in ten states within the year after it was handed down.[18] It also helped persuade Congress to enact the Privacy Protection Act of 1980.[19] The law, which applies to federal, state, and local law enforcement agencies, strictly limits the circumstances under which a warrant can be issued to search for the "work products" and "documentary materials" of persons "engaged in First Amendment activities." Translated from legal jargon, the Act protects photographs, audio and video tapes, notes on interviews, drafts of articles, and notes used in preparation of articles.

The law does not raise absolute barriers against newsroom searches. A warrant can be issued to seize any materials if there is probable cause to believe a journalist is using them to commit a crime, or if seizure is necessary to prevent death or serious injury. Further, such things as photos, tapes, and notes on interviews can be seized if there is reason to believe they would be destroyed in response to a subpoena or if they have not been handed over in response to a court order and further delay would stand in the way of justice.

As of this writing, there have been no cases testing the limits of the Act.

Limitation on Privacy

In the 1970s and in 1980, a few journalists learned that Justice Department attorneys had been studying a listing of their long-distance calls. The listings, showing the telephone numbers of persons called by the journalists, had been obtained under subpoena to the telephone companies serving the reporters' homes and offices. The attorneys sought the records in an attempt to find out who gave the Pentagon Papers to the *New York Times*, how Jack Anderson obtained copies of a classified report on relations between the United States, India, and Pakistan, and on how the *Times* obtained an income tax audit and access to secret grand jury proceedings.

Reporters Committee for Freedom of the Press v. *American Telephone & Telegraph Co.*, 593 F.2d 1030 (D.C. Cir. 1979).
Believing that such subpoenas were both an invasion of privacy and a violation of First Amendment freedoms, a group of journalists challenged the practice in court. However, the United States Court of Appeals for the District of Columbia Circuit upheld the Justice Department's position. Its decision, in *Reporters Committee for Freedom of the Press* v. *American Telephone & Telegraph Co.*, rejected both grounds for the lawsuit.

The court said that the search warrant provision of the Fourth Amendment implies a right of privacy that will be protected as long as people stay on their own property. But when people venture off their property, or even use the telephone to call others, they give up some of their privacy. In this instance, the telephone company had made records of long-distance calls for billing purposes. Those records belonged to the company, not to the callers. Because the callers gave up their expectations of privacy when they placed the calls, they could not prevent the phone company from surrendering its records to the government under subpoena.

---

18. *News Media Update*, 19 October 1981.
19. 42 U.S.C. §§2000aa-2000aa-12.

The circuit court referred to White's opinion in *Branzburg* in rejecting the reporters' First Amendment argument. The government's purpose in seeking the long-distance billing records was to investigate a crime. In this instance, it seemed likely from their stories that journalists had sought information from persons who had committed crimes. As long as the investigation was conducted in good faith, the subpoena for the long-distance records did not violate the journalists' First Amendment interests.

However, in 1980, the Justice Department adopted guidelines that reduced the likelihood of further subpoenas for records of journalists' long-distance calls.[20] Except in unusual circumstances, department attorneys are expected to seek the journalist's consent to obtain the records. If that fails, a subpoena can be issued only with the attorney general's approval. The department can proceed in criminal cases if it has "reasonable grounds to believe, based on information obtained from nonmedia sources, that a crime has occurred, and that the information sought is essential to a successful investigation." Subpoenas also may be issued in a civil action if the case is of "substantial proportions" and there is reason to believe the information is "essential to [its] successful completion."

The case reports show no recent instances in which journalists have contested subpoenas for their long-distance telephone records.

THE SCOPE OF THE PRIVILEGE

Journalists in Criminal Proceedings

Journalists who break the law are treated like any other violators. It goes without saying that they are subject to arrest, and, if arrested, that they have no more, and no less, protection than anyone else. However, in most jurisdictions, journalists who have knowledge of crimes committed by others are treated differently from other kinds of witnesses. It is increasingly likely that they can avoid testifying, if they want to do so, whether they be summoned by a grand jury or as a witness for the defense or the prosecution. In federal proceedings, the right to avoid testifying is grounded in the First Amendment interpretation of *Branzburg*. In state courts, it may be grounded in the First Amendment, in the freedom of press clause of the state's constitution, in a shield law, or in common law. Because of the varying sources of the privilege, it varies widely and is granted or denied on a case-by-case basis. Therefore, the cases chosen for treatment in this section can be considered only as illustrative.

Grand Jury Subpoenas

A review of twenty or so recent cases in which reporters have contested subpoenas asking them to testify before grand juries shows that they are least likely to be excused if they have witnessed a crime. However, they can argue that the court must show an overriding need for their testimony, and, in a few instances, subpoenas have been quashed. Much depends upon whether a state shield law can be invoked, as the following case shows.

---

20. 28 C.F.R. §50.10.

Fawn Vrazo, a reporter for the *Philadelphia Bulletin*, had written a series of stories on corruption in government in southern New Jersey. A grand jury was asked to look into the allegations, and it summoned Vrazo to testify. Her stories had relied heavily on confidential sources, but it also appeared that the reporter had been present when illegal acts were committed. Vrazo moved to squash the summons, citing New Jersey's strong shield law. The prosecutor argued that the law did not protect reporters who were eyewitnesses to a crime. He argued further that Vrazo had waived any claim to privilege with respect to information by publishing some of it. In *In re Vrazo*, the state's Superior Court rejected both arguments. It held that the eyewitness exception applied only to crimes involving physical violence or property damage. Further, the law defines a journalist's privilege as protecting both sources and information. The court held it could not be waived so far as the grand jury was concerned by disclosing privileged information in the newspaper. Vrazo was not required to testify.

In re Vrazo, 423 A.2d 695 (N.J.Super. 1980).

In a New York case, *In re Grand Jury Investigation*,[21] a public official had violated a state law by giving a sealed report to a television reporter. The reporter might also have been subject to prosecution as a witness to an illegal act. A special grand jury, called to look into the release of the report, issued a subpoena to the reporter. A motion to quash ultimately was upheld by the Court of Appeals, New York's highest court. It held that the shield law was written to give journalists an absolute right to protect the identity of their confidential sources, even when the journalist might be involved in the crime. Since the reporter had obtained the sealed document under a promise not to identify the source, he could not be compelled to testify, the appeals court held, even though a guilty public official might go unpunished as a result.

Reporters who have not seen a crime committed, but who have talked to those who have, may have to testify if they are summoned by a grand jury. Here, too, much depends upon the existence of a shield law.

The experience of Paul Corsetti, a reporter for the *Boston Herald*, illustrates the worst that can happen when a journalist bases a story on a conversation with a criminal. Corsetti talked by telephone with a man suspected of murder. He wrote that the man had confessed to the crime. A grand jury summoned Corsetti to testify about the interview. Corsetti filed a motion to quash, arguing that the grand jury could get the same information from a police officer. A judge concluded that Corsetti's testimony would indeed duplicate the officer's, but ordered the reporter to testify anyway. Massachusetts had no shield law. On appeal, the state's highest court ruled that because the grand jury had completed its work, there was no reason to decide the case.[22] That did not end Corsetti's problems, as we will see shortly.

Reporters whose stories disclose a direct knowledge of a crime open themselves to the possibility of a grand jury subpoena. At that point, reporters have two options: They can agree to testify, or they can hire a lawyer and file a motion to quash. This could lead to bargaining, and an agreement that would limit the scope of the grand jury's questions. The alternative is a hearing in which a judge would decide how far a state shield law,

---

21. 460 N.Y.S.2d 227 (N.Y.Co.Ct. 1983); rev'd. Beach v. Shanley, 466 N.Y.S.2d 725 (3d Dept. 1983), rev'd motion granted, 476 N.Y.S.2d 765 (N.Y. 1984).
22. Corsetti v. Commonwealth, 411 N.E.2d 466 (Mass. 1980).

common law, or a First Amendment privilege would go in protecting reporters. The cases decided thus far indicate that most judges will order the reporters to testify. At that point, they have three options. If they are being asked only to identify sources of information, they can try to persuade the sources to identify themselves. Otherwise, the reporters either must testify or be held in contempt. The latter opens the way for appeal to a higher court. At that stage, the cases show that some reporters have escaped punishment either because the grand jury's investigation was dropped, or it obtained enough evidence from other sources to support an indictment.

As Prosecution Witnesses

Reporters whose stories disclose knowledge of a crime run a risk not only of being summoned by a grand jury, but of being called as a witness by the prosecution. In such instances, the fifteen or so recent reported cases show that reporters have a fifty-fifty chance of getting the subpoena quashed. Again, much depends upon the existence of a shield law and the degree of privilege recognized by the court involved.

Paul Corsetti's experience, which began with a summons to testify before a grand jury, was renewed when the murder suspect with whom he had talked was brought to trial. The prosecutor subpoenaed the reporter as a witness. Corsetti appeared in court as ordered, but testified only as to the fact that he had written the story that appeared in the *Boston Herald*. When he was pressed for details of his interview with the suspect, Corsetti said he had promised that he would not testify in court as to the substance of the conversation. The judge found Corsetti in contempt and sentenced him to ninety days in jail, the maximum permitted by law. On appeal, the Supreme Judicial Court indicated, in *Commonwealth* v. *Corsetti*, that it might be willing to recognize a common-law journalist's privilege, but had no need to do so in this instance. Corsetti had identified his source, and had disclosed much if not all of the information, when he wrote the article. Therefore, he had waived any claim to a privilege. Corsetti spent about a week in jail before the governor commuted his sentence to time served and ordered his release.

Commonwealth v. *Corsetti*, 387 Mass. 1 (Mass. 1982).

In a Maryland case, neither the state's shield law nor the court's recognition of a qualified privilege protected a television station served with a subpoena. A reporter for WBAL-TV had interviewed a suspected criminal. Part of it was used in the station's news programs. An assistant state's attorney who was preparing for the suspect's trial issued a subpoena to the station for its outtakes, the portions of the videotape not used on the air. The station resisted, arguing that the fact that the suspect had already been convicted in a federal court proved that whatever might be on the outtakes was not needed as evidence. When the attorney insisted, a trial court judge looked at the videotape in the privacy of his office and ruled that it was needed. When the station persisted in its refusal to surrender the videotape, the judge found it in contempt. On appeal, the Maryland Court of Appeals in 1984, in *WBAL-TV Division, The Hearst Corporation* v. *Maryland*,[23] upheld the trial court judge's order. The court said the videotape offered

---

23. 477 A.2d 776 (Md.App. 1984).

evidence "frozen in time" that could be duplicated in no other way. Thus, despite the court's recognition of a three-prong test similar to that advanced by Stewart in *Branzburg*, the court said the state's need for the tape was overriding.

While most of the reported decisions are in accord with *Corsetti* and *WBAL-TV*, reporters involved in two separate cases in Florida were the victors under that state's common-law privilege. In *Florida* v. *Taylor*,[24] decided in 1982, the reporter had talked to a suspect at the scene of the crime. When the prosecutor summoned the reporter as a witness, the reporter filed a motion to quash, which was upheld by a state circuit court. It held that the prosecutor had failed to show the reporter's evidence was relevant, that it could not be obtained from other sources not protected by the First Amendment, that the prosecutor had tried in vain to get the evidence from other sources, and that there would be a miscarriage of justice if the reporter was not compelled to testify. In the second case, *Tribune Co.* v. *Green*,[25] decided in 1983, a state appellate court applied a shortened version of the same test and held that the reporter, who also had interviewed a suspected criminal, should not be required to testify.

Journalists who are subpoenaed as prosecution witnesses in other states should not place too much reliance on the Florida decisions. That state does not have a shield law, but its courts have forged one of the strongest privileges for journalists in effect anywhere. Courts in Michigan, Pennsylvania, and Texas have joined Maryland and Massachusetts in holding that journalists must offer evidence for the prosecution if asked to do so. Courts in California and Idaho have joined Florida in excusing journalists who were given subpoenas by the prosecution. So did a United States District Court in Miami. Courts in New York have ruled both ways, depending on how essential the reporter's information is deemed to be.

As Defense Witnesses

When a reporter is believed to have evidence that will help prove a criminal defendant not guilty, two constitutional rights may come into conflict. A clause in the Sixth Amendment gives a criminal defendant a right "to have compulsory process for obtaining witnesses in his favor." That process is exercised through the subpoena power. A reporter summoned as a reluctant witness can argue that the Supreme Court, in *Branzburg*, recognized that newsgathering is protected to some extent by the First Amendment. With some notable exceptions, the reported cases show that reporters generally are successful in resisting defendants' subpoenas.

The decision of an Ohio appeals court in 1982 in *People* v. *Monica*[26] is illustrative of the majority position. A reporter for the *Cleveland Plain Dealer* had written that a murder was arranged by Mafia chieftains. When a suspect in the murder was brought to trial in California, he sought a subpoena to compel identification of the reporter's confidential sources and information. He argued that the information would show that he was not the Mafia figure who had arranged for the murder. An Ohio trial court judge refused to issue the subpoena and the appeals court affirmed. It held that the defendant

---

24. 9 Med.L.Rptr. 1551 (Fla.Cir.Ct. 1982).
25. 440 So.2d 484 (Fla.Dist.Ct.App. 1983).
26. Ohio Court of Appeals, 8th Dist., No. 39950 (1979).

had failed to prove that the reporter was a necessary and material witness. The court said that the reporter's First Amendment privilege could be overcome only if the defendant were able to show that: (1) the material sought from the reporter would help establish guilt or innocence; (2) alternative sources of helpful information had been exhausted; (3) an effort had been made to obtain the reporter's testimony as to nonconfidential information; and (4) a request had been made to a judge to examine confidential information in private to determine if it was relevant.

Without stating quite so elaborate a test, courts in Delaware, Florida, New Hampshire, New York, Vermont, Washington, and Wisconsin have upheld a reporter's right to refuse to serve as a defense witness in a criminal case. On the other hand, a Georgia appeals court, citing earlier state court decisions and *Branzburg*, held in 1982 that journalists have no right under the First Amendment to refuse to testify.[27] In a case involving a television news team, an Oregon court held in the same year that neither that state's shield law nor the First Amendment could be invoked to resist a criminal defendant's subpoena.[28] The crew had covered a decoy operation conducted by an undercover police officer and had witnessed an attempt to steal money from the officer. The defendant issued a subpoena to the station, asking for the names of the members of the news team. The station resisted, asserting an absolute privilege under Oregon's shield law and under the First Amendment. A circuit court judge ruled that a First Amendment privilege did not apply under the facts of the case. Nor, he ruled, would the seemingly absolute language of the shield law prevail, because it was overridden by the defendant's right to compulsory process under both the Sixth Amendment and a section of the Oregon Constitution.

Myron Farber, a reporter for the *New York Times*, spent forty days in jail in 1978 because he refused to let a New Jersey state court judge examine his notes on a murder investigation. Farber had written a series of stories about the deaths of several patients in a New Jersey hospital. As a result, a grand jury indicted a former physician at the hospital on a charge of murder. The physician's lawyer subpoenaed Farber as a witness, alleging that he had information that would help the defendant's case. Subpoenas also were issued for Farber's notes and for any memoranda in the newspaper's files bearing on the investigation. The judge was willing to examine the materials in private to see whether any of them would indeed help the physician. When Farber and the *Times* refused his offer, the judge found both in contempt, sending the reporter to jail and fining the newspaper $5,000 a day until each complied with his order.[29] Farber's jail term and the *Times's* fine ended when a jury found the physician not guilty. In 1982, Governor Brendan Byrne pardoned Farber and the newspaper. He also returned $101,000 of the fine.

As a result of Farber's ordeal, the New Jersey Legislature greatly strengthened the state's shield law, and state courts have construed it as near absolute in its effect, as noted earlier.

On the basis of the reported decisions, reporters are more likely to be able to invoke

---

27. Hurst v. Georgia, 8 Med.L.Rptr. 2374 (Ga.App. 1982).
28. Oregon v. Knorr, 8 Med.L.Rptr. 2067 (Cir.Ct. 1982).
29. In re Farber, 394 A.2d 330 (N.J. 1978).

Myron Farber, a *New York Times* reporter, spent 40 days in a New Jersey jail in 1978 because he refused to let a judge examine his notes. Farber's stories in the *Times* had led to the indictment on murder charges of a physician accused of giving fatal injections to hospital patients. A jury acquitted the physician. (UPI/Bettmann Newsphotos)

a privilege against testifying for criminal defendants than they are if they are summoned by the prosecution or by a grand jury. Taken together, the cases illustrate the wide range of possibilities faced by reporters who receive subpoenas in criminal cases and who do not wish to testify. *Vrazo* shows that New Jersey's courts are willing to uphold the absolute language of that state's shield law. *Taylor* and *Tribune Co.* are only two of a number of decisions in which Florida courts have forged an absolute privilege without help from a shield law. *Corsetti* illustrates the opposite extreme. As of this writing, Massachusetts does not have a shield law and its courts have shown no willingness to find a privilege either in the Constitution or in common law. *Monica* illustrates what happens in most instances, with most judges willing to seek an accommodation. Some start, as in *Cuthbertson* and *Farber*, by offering to review the reporter's evidence in their chambers to see whether any of it indeed is pertinent to resolution of the case. If it is, they may try to find out whether it is obtainable from other sources, or whether the case can be resolved without the reporter's evidence. Obviously, the decision as to whether the reporter should be required to honor the subpoena becomes a judgment call, but, as Justice Stewart pointed out in *Branzburg*, that's what courts are for.

Journalists in Civil Actions

Judging from the large number of cases in point, a journalist is far more likely to be summoned in connection with a civil action than a criminal proceeding. The decisions make clear that most courts not only recognize, but respect, a journalist's privilege in civil lawsuits. Litigants seeking a journalist's testimony are likely to have to prove that the journalist has information essential to their case and that it cannot be obtained from other sources. This is true even when the government is one of the parties to the civil action. The following cases exemplify the majority holdings.

When five states brought a civil antitrust action against seventeen oil companies, they acted on the theory that price movements were coordinated through a trade publication, *Platt's Oilgram Price Report*. Consequently, the states obtained a subpoena directing the newsletter and two of its reporters to provide the names of their confidential sources of price information. In response to a motion to quash, a U.S. District Court judge in New York ordered disclosure. One reporter gave the court four names. The other refused. The court held the newsletter's publisher, McGraw-Hill, in contempt and imposed a fine of $100 a day until its order was complied with. On appeal, the U.S. Court of Appeals, Second Circuit, reversed. Its decision in *In re Petroleum Products Antitrust Litigation*, decided in 1982, was emphatic.[30] The court said journalists could not be forced to identify confidential sources unless there was "a clear and specific showing that the information is highly material and relevant, necessary or critical to the maintenance of the claim, and not obtainable from other available sources." In this instance, the court said the states had offered no evidence that the newsletter was involved in any price fixing scheme. It was not enough to suggest that the reporters may have been unknowing conduits for information through which the oil companies fixed prices.

Playboy magazine was able to invoke California's shield law when it was caught in the middle of a dispute between the comedy team of Cheech and Chong and their former accountants. The comedians sued the accounting firm for damages, charging it with fraud. While the case was pending, a *Playboy* reporter interviewed the comedians. In the course of the interview, Richard ("Cheech") Marin allegedly made statements about the accountants. When the interview was published, two things happened. The accountants subpoenaed *Playboy*, asking for all notes and tape recordings taken in connection with the interview. They were seeking information that could be used to cast doubt on Marin's testimony at trial and to support their side of the case. Also in response to publication of the article, Marin said he had not made some of the statements attributed to him. *Playboy* moved to quash the subpoena. In 1984, a state appeals court ordered the subpoena dismissed except for one element: The magazine would have to give the accountants the address and telephone number of the reporter. Otherwise, the appeals court ruled that California's shield law protected any unpublished information known to the interviewer or any unpublished information in documentary form. The accounting firm did not have an interest strong enough to overcome the shield's protection.[31]

A few courts have balked at excusing journalists who are asked to testify in civil

---

30. 680 F.2d 5 (2d Cir. 1982).
31. Playboy Enterprises, Inc. v. Superior Court, 201 Cal.Rptr. 207 (Cal.App. 1984).

actions, but have held that they could assert a privilege on a question-by-question basis. This is illustrated by a federal district court's decision in 1984 in *Continental Cablevision, Inc.* v. *Storer Broadcasting Corp.*[32] The two firms were competitors for a cable television franchise in Florissant, Missouri, a suburb of St. Louis. When Continental's bid was rejected by the city council, the firm sued Storer for libel, based on a written statement given to members of the council. As a part of its pretrial discovery, Continental issued a subpoena to a *St. Louis Globe-Democrat* reporter who had written a story about Storer's statement. She moved to quash, arguing that she was protected by a federal common-law privilege. The court held that because the plaintiff and defendant were from different states, the common-law privilege was not applicable. Nor did the base states of the parties—Massachusetts and Missouri—have shield laws. The court then relied on First Amendment principles. It held that the reporter would have to respond to the subpoena and submit to questioning by Continental's lawyer. At that point, the balancing test proposed in *Branzburg* would come into play. With help from her lawyer, the reporter would decide which questions she would answer and which she would not, following detailed guidelines set by the court.

When a litigant in a civil action seeks a newspaper's unpublished photographs neither a shield law nor a journalist's privilege may be of much help if other courts follow the example of the North Dakota Supreme Court. In *Grand Forks Herald* v. *District Court*, decided in 1982, that state's highest court denied a motion to quash a subpoena for unpublished photographs. The newspaper's photographer had taken several pictures of an accident, which became the subject of an action for damages. Only one of the photos was published. One of the parties to the damage suit sought the others, thinking they might help his case. When the newspaper resisted, the supreme court ruled against it, noting that the litigant had tried without success to find other photographs of the accident. Further, it held there was nothing confidential involved. The photographer had taken the pictures in a public place. His editors might have selected any one, or all of them, for publication. Further, the photos offered evidence that could not be presented in any other way. Finally, surrender of the photos would be less intrusive into First Amendment rights than requiring the photographer to testify as to what he had seen at the site of the accident.

Grand Forks Herald v. *District Court*, 322 N.W.2d 850 (N.D. 1982).

Grand Forks Herald is an exceptional case. Most attempts to draw journalists into civil actions as witnesses have resulted in rulings that the evidence should be sought from other sources. In several instances, cases have been continued for as long as a year while alternative sources were sought.

Libel and Confidential Sources

When journalists' reliance on confidential sources subjects them to a libel suit, courts vary widely in their treatment of such sources. Some will not permit defendants to use information from such sources as part of their defense. A few have instructed juries to

---

32. 583 F.Supp. 427 (E.D.Mo. 1984).

decide cases on the assumption that the source did not exist. More recently, courts have begun to apply balancing tests similar to Justice Stewart's three-part test in *Branzburg*.

The first two of these three approaches can be traced to the Supreme Court's 1979 decision in *Herbert* v. *Lando*,[33] which is summarized in chapter 4. In that case, the Court held that journalists who are sued for libel do not have a privilege to protect their editorial processes. These are the decisions that go into the shaping of a story—to include some facts while omitting others, and to believe some sources more than others. In *Herbert*, the court held that libel plaintiffs can ask detailed questions about such decisions during discovery leading up to trial and during the trial itself. It did so, it said, to avoid making it impossible, or nearly so, for plaintiffs to prove the requisite degree of fault.

Some courts have read that decision to apply not only to the editorial process, but to the identity of confidential sources. This has led these courts to impose harsh restrictions on media defendants in libel actions growing out of stories in which confidential sources were used. One of these approaches, to deny the defendant the use of any information obtained from such sources, has been applied in shield-law states. The following case is illustrative.

A segment of "60 Minutes" entitled "Over the Speed Limit" included an interview with an unidentified woman who said a Dr. Greenberg had prescribed more than eighty pills a day to help her lose weight. When the physician sued for libel, CBS tried to verify the patient's allegation by offering affidavits from other unidentified sources. It acted in the belief that New York's shield law gave it absolute protection against being required to identify its sources. Both sides moved for summary judgment. The trial court rejected CBS's motion, and the appeals court affirmed. It conceded that because of the shield law, it could not make CBS identify any of the sources. But it held that when the case went to trial, CBS would have two options. It could continue to stand behind the shield law. In that instance, it could use none of the evidence it had obtained from confidential sources. Or it could waive the shield law, identify its sources, and use their evidence to refute Greenberg's assertion that CBS was grossly negligent.

Greenberg v. *CBS Inc.*, 419 N.Y.S.2d 988 (N.Y.App. 1979).

The second approach, to instruct the jury that it is to assume no source existed, has been taken by appellate courts in California and New Hampshire. It is equivalent to a holding that the reporter acted in actual malice. The California case, *Rancho La Costa, Inc.* v. *Penthouse*,[34] was decided in 1980. It was based on a story in *Penthouse* alleging that the owners of a luxury golfing resort had ties to organized crime. The owners sued for libel and asked the magazine to identify confidential sources on whom it had relied for part of its information. *Penthouse*, relying on California's strong shield law, refused to do so. The trial judge conceded he had no means of compelling the magazine to name its sources. But he said that when the case came to trial, he would instruct the jury to act on the assumption they did not exist. On appeal, the appellate court modified the form of the order without changing its effect. It said the judge should tell the jury that *Penthouse*'s only sources were those it was willing to identify in court.

The New Hampshire case, *Downing* v. *Monitor Publishing Co.*,[35] also was decided

---

33. 441 U.S. 153, 99 S.Ct. 1635, 60 L.Ed.2d 115 (1979).
34. Rancho La Costa, Inc. v. Penthouse, 165 Cal.Rptr. 347 (Cal.Super.Ct. 1980).
35. 415 A.2d 683 (N.H. 1980).

in 1980. Downing, a police chief, was the subject of a newspaper article in which an unidentified source said he had failed a lie detector test. When Downing sued for libel, he said he could not prove actual malice unless he knew who the source was. The newspaper insisted on keeping its source confidential. Although the state has no shield law, the New Hampshire Supreme Court said it would not compel disclosure until the chief had offered proof that the story was false. Holding that he already had done so, the court said that if the reporter chose to go to jail rather than identify the source, the trial judge should proceed on the assumption that none existed.

More commonly, courts have shown a willingness to look past *Herbert*, if the key issue is identity of a source, and apply a balancing test. One element of such tests was applied by the New Hampshire court in *Downing*. It would not act to compel disclosure of the source's identity until the plaintiff had established that he was the target of a defamatory falsehood. Other courts have held that the plaintiff must prove that his suit is not frivolous or brought for purposes of harassment. *Bruno & Stillman*, discussed earlier, illustrates how such threshold tests are applied.

The United States Court of Appeals, Fifth Circuit, carried balancing still further in 1980 in *Miller* v. *Transamerican Press, Inc.* A trade publication reported that Miller, a trustee of the Teamsters' pension fund, had mishandled the fund's assets. The article was based on information from a confidential source. Miller sued the magazine for libel and sought, during discovery, to learn the identity of the source. On three occasions, a federal district court ruled that Miller could not compel discovery from the writer or the magazine's editor until he could prove that the information was not available from other

Miller v. Transamerican Press, Inc., 621 F.2d 721 (5th Cir. 1980).

sources. One of Miller's fellow trustees gave him a sworn statement saying he knew nothing to indicate the fund's assets had been mishandled. Miller gave the court a sworn statement asserting that the article was false. At that point, the trial judge ruled that Miller could not prove actual malice unless he knew who the source was. Because that went to the heart of his case, the judge ordered Transamerican to name its source. On appeal, the Fifth Circuit court modified the order, limiting disclosure to Miller's lawyer. On rehearing, the circuit court said its order would not go into effect until Miller had proved that the article was false and defamatory, that he had made reasonable, but unsuccessful, efforts to identify the source on his own, and that his case could not proceed unless the source were identified.

Anyone seeking certainty will not find it in the law defining the journalist's privilege. There are several reasons for this. One is that it is a relatively new area of law. Until 1972, few courts except in the seventeen shield-law states had recognized that there might be sufficient value in news from unidentified sources to justify permitting reporters to protect such sources. A second comes out of the several grounds on which the privilege is based. In twenty-six states, it is defined by statute. In the federal courts, it is grounded in the First Amendment interpretation of *Branzburg*. State courts also find support for a privilege in state constitutions, common law, and even rules of court. A third reason for uncertainty comes out of the way the privilege is applied. If a court insists on a journalist's testimony, and the journalist chooses to resist, the outcome depends on a balancing of interests. Weighed on one side are the confidence and trust upon which reporters rely for "touchy" stories of the kind that point to wrongdoing. Weighed on the other is the judicial system itself. Journalists may believe they have proved wrongdoing. But only the courts can make an official finding of wrongdoing, and that may not be possible if some evidence is withheld because reporters will not identify their sources or share their information with the court. Finally, there is uncertainty because the scope of the privilege still is being defined. In some states, it covers only the identity of sources who have been promised confidentiality. In others, it covers any source the reporter refuses to identify for whatever reasons. Some states interpret the privilege to cover not only confidential sources, but any information the reporter obtained in confidence and chose not to use. A few go so far as to permit reporters to refuse to testify about crimes they have witnessed.

However, for all the uncertainties, several points have come clear. Foremost is the fact that a journalist's privilege does exist. In most jurisdictions where courts have had occasion to rule on the matter, they have recognized a public interest in permitting journalists to protect confidential sources. In a few states, that interest has been interpreted as supporting an absolute privilege. More commonly, journalists' interest in keeping confidences can be overcome if a court concludes they have information that is crucial to the case at bar and if that information cannot be obtained from other sources.

In the Professional World

Journalists who investigate wrongdoing by public officials or others enter a legal and ethical minefield. If they do their work well, they may win a Pulitzer Prize for meritorious public service. That's what the *Washington Post* did in 1973 for showing that a burglary at Democratic headquarters was linked to President Nixon's personal staff. Without the help of a still-unidentified source known as "Deep Throat," that connection might not have been traced. In 1981, that same newspaper had to return a Pulitzer Prize when its editors discovered that one of its reporters had made up a touching story about a young boy who was being injected with heroin by his mother and her boyfriend. That story, too, was based on reports from anonymous sources. When Washington police began looking for the boy to save him from almost certain death, the reporter still refused to identify him and her editors backed her up. Only when the story won the prize was the deception discovered.

They were not the first, nor the last, editors to be duped. Editors at the *New York Times*, the *New York Daily News*, and *The New Yorker* magazine have run as fact stories later discovered to be part fiction because quoted sources did not exist. No doubt other editors have been taken in, too. The temptation to make a good story better, to achieve superficial balance, or to cover for a missing fact is more than some writers can resist. Unfortunately, there is more than a little truth in the cynical newsroom advice, "Never let the facts stand in the way of a good story."

It is because of such temptations that both professional editors and the courts have looked askance at stories based on anonymous sources. When Carl Bernstein and Bob Woodward were developing their prize-winning Watergate stories for the *Washington Post*, no fact obtained from a confidential source was published unless it was corroborated by at least two other sources. Stylebooks for both wire services caution against using material from sources who do not wish to be identified. Many newspaper editors permit the use of anonymous sources only if their information serves an important public purpose and cannot be obtained on the record. Professionals are aware that not all sources who insist on anonymity are motivated by the highest principles of public service. Many are self-serving and are engaged in nothing more noble than an attempt to use the news media to get even for a real or imagined wrong.

The threshold question, then, for journalists is whether and to what extent they will rely on confidential sources. Some news organizations advise reporters to promise confidentiality only with an editor's approval. This approval is usually based on evidence that the story can't be obtained otherwise. Even then, information obtained from confidential sources is treated with care and may not be used unless it can be confirmed by on-the-record sources. As the cases discussed in this chapter indicate, courts are more likely to grant the journalist's privilege when they are convinced that the source and the reporter reached a clear agreement on confidentiality. However, the experience of Richard Hargraves also suggests that there should be room for reconsideration if the reporter is cited for contempt. It is one thing to break a good story. It is another to become a martyr for it.

If a journalist's investigation, with or without the help of confidential sources, does uncover evidence of wrongdoing, new ethical and legal problems arise. Once the story or stories have been published, does that end the journalist's responsibility to society? As this chapter makes clear, shield laws in some of the states and court decisions in others answer that question with a qualified yes. They do so, in most instances, in recognition of the fact that if a reporter, working without the subpoena power, can uncover wrongdoing, police, prosecutors, and grand juries, with all the resources at their command, ought to be able to do so, too. This is especially true if the journalist has done a thorough reporting job. Since the purpose of journalism is public exposure, all the facts that police need ought to be in the newspaper or magazine, or in the televised newscast. However, as the cases in this chapter again suggest, that is not always true. Drug pushers made sales and converted marijuana into hashish in Paul Branzburg's presence. They would not knowingly do so in a police officer's presence. When the reporter may be the only witness to a crime, does his or her duty to society end with the production of a no-names story? That question clearly troubled Justice White when he wrote his opinion in *Branzburg*. In his view, "The crimes of news sources are no less reprehensible and threatening to the public interest when witnessed by a reporter than when they are not." In fashioning testimonial privileges, courts think of the worst possible "what ifs": "What if a reporter was the only person who knew who shot the governor—and for whatever reason chose not to testify?"

The other side of the coin is illustrated by the *Farber* case. There, Myron Farber's stories for the *New York Times* resulted in revival of a long-dormant murder investigation and the arrest of Dr. Mario E. Jascalevich. The stories relied heavily on unidentified sources and may or may not have revealed all that the reporter knew about the case. Acting on the theory that the identity of some of the sources and unpublished information might help his client, Dr. Jascalevich's lawyer issued a subpoena for Farber, his notes, and such notes as the *Times* itself might have. Standing on First Amendment principle, Farber and the *Times* resisted to the point of being held in contempt. Farber spent forty days in jail and the *Times* was fined heavily to defend a principle. In the end, the jury found the doctor not guilty. But what if Farber had been hiding the only evidence that would have proved his innocence?

As this brief look at the ethical dilemmas suggests, professional journalists tend not to nod politely when a potential news source says, "Don't quote me, but . . ." or "This is off the record." They react by trying to find out why such a request is made and the subject matter that prompts it. Promises of confidentiality are not made lightly.

Sophisticated news sources and reporters have developed commonly understood terms that convey degrees of meaning with respect to confidentiality. "Off the record" means that the source does not want to see the information in print or hear it on the air. The reporter is expected to use it only for guidance to avoid misstating the thrust of the news. Information offered "for background only" is designed to help the reporter understand a complex situation and may be reflected, but not directly included, in the story. If the source offers information "not for attribution," he or she wants to see it in print or hear it on the air, but does not want to be connected with it. Public officials sometimes use this means "to float a trial balloon," that is, to disclose a policy option and see how the public reacts to it before making it official. If the policy is shot down, it is the reporter, not the official, who takes the flak.

Journalists are of two minds about confidential sources and information. The Jack Andersons, and other commentators on the political labyrinth that is the federal government, could not survive without them. Indeed, we would not know as much as we do about the inside doings of government at any level if it were not for good reporters' "informed sources." Part of the art of reporting is knowing who to go to for the straight story when the official, on-the-record version is laced with doubletalk.

There also are reporters who receive all off-the-record requests with skepticism or even distrust. They are afraid of being used, and they don't want to have their hands tied if they can get the same information on the record. This difference of opinion among journalists is part of the reason there is no federal shield law. Reporters and editors who testified before committees of Congress not only could not agree on how far the law should go, but on whether there should be one at all. Also a factor in Congress's failure to act was the fact that Woodward and Bernstein's Watergate stories were written without the protection of a shield law.

The opinions written by Justices White and Stewart in *Branzburg* reflect the differences among journalists. In White's view, confidential sources play a minor role in journalism. To him, it was incredible that a press that had flourished for more than 150 years without the ability to protect its sources suddenly had need for a First Amendment privilege. To Stewart, that was a "crabbed view" that might reduce the news media to serving as a transmission belt for the official views of official spokesmen. In his view, confidential sources are important simply because now and then one of them does help the news media expose incompetence, mistaken policies, or outright wrongdoing on the part of public officials. In Stewart's eyes, the possibility for abuse is a small price to pay for the public benefit that might flow from even a limited journalist's privilege.

FOR REVIEW

1. What is the journalist's privilege? Is it comparable with other testimonial privileges recognized by the courts?

2. What did the Supreme Court decide with respect to the three journalists who were involved in *Branzburg* v. *Hayes*? Identify the elements in that case that can be construed as creating the journalist's privilege.

3. List and discuss arguments for and against the journalist's privilege. What is your opinion? Why?

4. What is a shield law? If your state has one, what are its terms?

5. Has your state recognized a privilege for journalists other than that established by a shield law? If so, what are its terms?

6. Assess the likelihood that a newsroom will be searched by police.

THE RIGHT TO KNOW

As its Preamble declares, the Constitution established a government of the people. It is easy to postulate, then, that there must have been some intent on the part of the authors of that document to provide for access to information about government. After all, if the people are to make wise decisions about how they are to be governed, they must have access to information about the performance of government and government officials. This idea is embodied today in the phrase "the right to know."

However, if the founders intended that there be public access to government information, they did not write that intention into the Constitution. Nor did they act as if they believed government should be conducted in the open. The Constitutional Convention itself was conducted in secrecy. Once the finished product had been announced to the public and the new government established, the Senate met behind closed doors for the first five years of its existence.[1] Only two paragraphs in the Constitution mandate any degree of openness on the part of the federal government. Both are found in Article I, which established the Congress and defines its powers:

> Each House shall keep a journal of its proceedings, and from time to time publish the same, excepting such parts as may in their judgment require secrecy; and the yeas and nays of the members of either House on any question shall, at the desire of one-fifth of those present, be entered on the journal. [Section 5, paragraph 3]

> No money shall be drawn from the Treasury, but in consequence of appropriations made by law; and a regular statement and account of the receipts and expenditures of all public money shall be published from time to time. [Section 9, paragraph 7]

The first requirement is met by publication of the *Journal*, a summary listing of actions taken by both houses of Congress, and, in an expanded form, by the *Congressional Record*. The second requirement is met by publication of the annual budget, which includes actual receipts and expenditures by categories in the last previous fiscal year, an estimate for the current year, and planned spending for the next year. That is all the information the Constitution requires the government to give its people. Until 1966, citizens who approached government officials in quest of information had to be content with what they got. Vance Trimble, a reporter for the Scripps-Howard News Service, learned in 1959 that even the First Amendment was no help to him when he tried to find out whether members of the Senate were violating the law by putting relatives on their office payrolls.[2] He had won a prize for distinguished reporting with a series of articles naming House members who illegally funneled tax money to their relatives. But when he sought the same information from the clerk of the Senate, Felton Johnston turned him down flat. When Trimble went to the United States District Court for the District of Columbia for an order directing Johnston to let him examine the Senate payroll, Judge Alexander Holtzoff told him the court could not create a duty where neither the Constitution nor Congress had established one. The First Amendment, he said, would protect Trimble in publishing any news he might find, but it could not be used to pry news from reluctant officials. Nor would Article I, section 9, paragraph 7 help him. The Senate payroll, in total amount—without names—was in the budget, as that paragraph required.

1. Robert A. Diamond, ed., *Origins and Development of Congress*, (Washington, D.C.: Congressional Quarterly, 1976), pp. 178–80.
2. Trimble v. Johnston, 173 F.Supp. 651 (D.D.C. 1959).

Today, reporters who approach federal agencies for information find help from two sources that were unavailable in Trimble's day. Beginning in 1972, when it decided *Branzburg* v. *Hayes*,[3] the Supreme Court has been finding that the First Amendment does give some protection to the right to gather news as well as to disseminate it. As we saw in the previous chapter, the *Branzburg* opinions have been interpreted to permit journalists to protect their confidential sources and information in legal proceedings. In 1980, in *Richmond Newspapers* v. *Virginia*,[4] which was discussed in chapter 6, the Court held that the First Amendment also gives journalists and the public a right to insist that they be admitted to court proceedings. In this chapter, we will see an extension of the principle to give journalists a right of access to audio tapes made by police for use as evidence in a prosecution. It is a limited right and perhaps could not yet be stretched far enough to give a 1980s' Vance Trimble access to the Senate payroll.

Meanwhile, in 1966, Congress enacted the Freedom of Information Act, which establishes as policy that government records, with designated exceptions, should be open to the public. The law applies to all federal agencies except the Office of the President, the courts, and the Congress. Thus, while it too would not help a latter-day Trimble, it has helped journalists and others gain access to information that in earlier years might have been conveniently lost in government files.

This chapter begins with a survey of the decisions in which the courts have ruled on a claimed First Amendment right of access to news about the federal government. Such right as there is seems at this writing to be confined to court records. The Supreme Court, in something of a change from its ruling in *Estes* v. *Texas*,[5] discussed in chapter 6, held in 1981 that, while the Sixth Amendment does not ban photographers from courtrooms, neither does the First Amendment mandate that they be admitted. That left the states free to do what they please, and most have opened at least some courtrooms, under some conditions, to news photographers.

The middle part of the chapter covers statutory rights of access to news of the federal government. Extensive analysis is given to court decisions interpreting the Freedom of Information Act. We will see that the exemptions have given agencies rather wide discretion to withhold information sought by journalists and others, and that the courts have supported them more often than not. Congress also has enacted a "Government in the Sunshine" Act, which requires that administrative decision-making bodies meet and act in public.

The latter part of the chapter deals in a general way with state open records and open meetings laws. It attempts more specifically to answer particularized questions of access to police records, welfare rolls, and the proceedings of juvenile courts.

Major Cases

Chandler v. *Florida*, 449 U.S. 560, 101 S.Ct. 802, 66 L.Ed.2d 740 (1981).

Chrysler Corp. v. *Brown*, 441 U.S. 281, 99 S.Ct. 1705, 60 L.Ed.2d 208 (1979).

---

3. 408 U.S. 665, 92 S.Ct. 2646, 33 L.Ed.2d 626 (1972).
4. 448 U.S. 555, 100 S.Ct. 2814, 65 L.Ed.2d 973 (1980).
5. 381 U.S. 532, 85 S.Ct. 1628, 14 L.Ed.2d 543 (1965).

Consumer Product Safety Commission v. *GTE Sylvania, Inc.*, 447 U.S. 102, 100 S.Ct. 2051, 64 L.Ed.2d 766 (1980).

Department of the Air Force v. *Rose*, 425 U.S. 352, 96 S.Ct. 1592 48 L.Ed.2d 11 (1976).

Federal Bureau of Investigation v. *Abramson*, 456 U.S. 615, 102 S.Ct. 2054, 72 L.Ed.2d 376 (1982).

Forsham v. *Harris*, 445 U.S. 169, 100 S.Ct. 978, 63 L.Ed.2d 293 (1980).

Kissinger v. *Reporters Committee for Freedom of the Press*, 445 U.S. 136, 100 S.Ct. 960, 63 L.Ed.2d 267 (1980).

United States Department of State v. *Washington Post Co.*, 456 U.S. 595, 102 S.Ct. 1957, 72 L.Ed.2d 358 (1982).

The Right of Access to Government Information

In 1959, a federal judge surveyed the Supreme Court's First Amendment decisions and told Vance Trimble he could find in them nothing to require government officials to divulge information they wished to withhold. Twenty years later, Justice William H. Rehnquist, writing in *Gannett* v. *DePasquale*,[6] said that neither he nor the Court could find anything in the First Amendment that gives the public a right of access to news of government. One year later, a majority of the Court held in *Richmond Newspapers* that the First Amendment does give the public a right of access to the courts and to any news that is generated there. Justice John Paul Stevens hailed the decision as "a watershed case." He said, "[T]he Court unequivocally holds that an arbitrary interference with access to important information is an abridgment of the freedoms of speech and of the press protected by the First Amendment."

As of this writing, the dimensions of a constitutional right of access to the news are still undefined. If it has not been carried as far as Justice Stevens suggested it might go, neither is it nonexistent, as Justice Rehnquist averred. This is evidenced by the 1981 decision of a U.S. District Court in New York City in *United States* v. *Carpentier*.[7] The court held that the First Amendment grants a right of access to audio tapes made by police during an investigation of a crime. The tapes at issue had been made by the Federal Bureau of Investigation during the events that led to the "Abscam" cases. The investigation produced evidence that seven members of the House of Representatives, a United States senator, and several local government officials were willing to take bribes to do favors for foreign nationals who, in reality, were FBI agents. Voice recordings of one transaction were admitted in evidence during the trial, but they were not played in court. At the end of the trial, the defendants' attorney moved to seal the tapes for sixty

---

6. 443 U.S. 368, 99 S.Ct. 2898, 61 L.Ed.2d 608 (1979).
7. 7 Med.L.Rptr. 2332 (S.D.N.Y. 1981).

days. The *New York Times* and the *New York Daily News* objected. Looking at a line of Supreme Court cases ending with *Richmond Newspapers*, the court found "an emerging right of the public to know what happens in court." It ordered the tapes released.

Meanwhile, until they are overruled, five earlier Supreme Court cases stand as counters to *Richmond Newspapers*. Therefore, they need to be noted briefly.

The most recent of these, *Nixon v. Warner Communications, Inc.*,[8] decided in 1978, also dealt with audio tapes, in this instance, the famous Nixon tapes, secret recordings the president made of conversations in his office. Twenty-two hours of those recordings were played in open court during the trial of several of his top aides, who were found guilty of conspiring to cover up White House complicity in the Watergate burglary of Democratic National Headquarters. Transcripts of the tapes were distributed to the news media during the trial and were quoted widely. When the trial ended, the television networks asked to copy the tapes so that they could be broadcast. Warner Communications, which has holdings in cable television and in the entertainment field, joined in the request. Nixon, arguing that excerpts from the tapes would be exploited for commercial purposes, asked a federal district court to prevent their release. Lower courts disagreed, with the Supreme Court eventually upholding Judge John J. Sirica's refusal to permit copying. The Supreme Court held that Nixon's fears that the tapes might be exploited were justified. The Court reasoned that its decision did not restrict the public's right to know, since the information on the tapes had been released and still was available to anyone who wanted to obtain a transcript. Copies of the tapes were also in the National Archives and could be listened to there.

Four earlier Supreme Court decisions rejected the argument that the First Amendment gives journalists a right to visit prisons and interview prisoners. In *Pell v. Procunier*,[9] decided in 1974, and *Houchins v. KQED, Inc.*,[10] decided in 1978, the Court held that journalists have no more right to visit jails or prisons than does anyone else. The Court said there is no First Amendment right to places where prisoners are kept. In *Procunier v. Martinez*[11] and *Saxbe v. Washington Post Co.*,[12] both decided in 1974, the Court held there is no right to interview prisoners, even when they are willing to be interviewed. The Court said the principal duties of prison officials are to maintain order and encourage rehabilitation. Therefore, if prison officials conclude that an interview would detract from these duties, they can forbid it.

The effect of these decisions is to affirm the right of prison officials to control access to prisons and prisoners by outsiders, except for lawyers who have free access to their inmate clients. In *Houchins*, the Court's majority took pains to insist that the decision did not limit First Amendment freedoms. It said reporters could still learn about prison conditions by interviewing former prisoners and others. They could also receive letters from inmates or join public tours of prisons.

Thus, the right of access to government information implicit in the First Amendment seems limited to the courts at this writing. This right is supplemented, particularly at the state level, by a common-law right of access to court records. This is not an absolute

---

8. 435 U.S. 589, 98 S.Ct. 1306, 55 L.Ed.2d 570 (1978).
9. 417 U.S. 817, 94 S.Ct. 2800, 41 L.Ed.2d 495 (1974).
10. 438 U.S. 1, 98 S.Ct. 2588, 57 L.Ed.2d 553 (1978).
11. 416 U.S. 396, 94 S.Ct. 1800, 40 L.Ed.2d 224 (1974).
12. 417 U.S. 843, 94 S.Ct. 2811, 41 L.Ed.2d 514 (1974).

right and may be restricted if wiretap evidence is sought,[13] if trade secrets might be disclosed,[14] or if records have been sealed to protect privacy.[15]

The Photographer and the Courtroom

The Supreme Court's decision in *Estes*, discussed in chapter 6, condemned still and television photographers as contributors to an atmosphere of prejudice in the courtroom. The Court came within one vote of holding that their presence would always make a fair trial impossible by denying the defendant the due process guaranteed by the Fifth and Fourteenth Amendments. At that point, in 1965, the future of courtroom photography appeared bleak.

The *Estes* case occurred because at the time Texas, with Colorado, was one of two states that permitted photographers to use their cameras in courtrooms. The decision was, in part, a reaction to the obstrusive nature of the still and television cameras then in use. Photographic equipment was bulky, sometimes noisy, and required special lighting. However, technical advances even then were leading to smaller cameras and to film and videotape that could be used in available light. Justice John Marshall Harlan took note of these advances in writing his concurring opinion in *Estes*. Although he agreed with four other justices in holding that the use of cameras in the courtroom had kept Estes from getting a fair trial, he was not willing to join them in holding that that would always be the case. He argued that further advances in technology might permit unobtrusive photography in the courtroom. Therefore, he wrote, he was unwilling to close the door on future experimentation with courtroom photography.

In time, Florida was one of several states that took up Harlan's invitation to experiment further with photojournalism in courtrooms. The Florida Supreme Court decided, in response to a request from the Post-Newsweek television stations in Jacksonville and Miami, to permit televising of court proceedings on an experimental basis.[16] Reaction was favorable, and the rule was made permanent.[17]

The guidelines regulating photography in Florida are quite strict.[18] Only one camera and one operator are permitted inside the courtroom. Once placed, the camera cannot be moved during the trial. Nor can the operator change lenses, film, or videotape while court is in session. Sound may be recorded only through the court's own audio pickup system. Operators are forbidden to record conferences between the lawyers, between parties and counsel, and with the judge. The judge can, without being subject to appeal, forbid televising or recording of the testimony of certain witnesses. The jury cannot be filmed under any circumstances. In short, television is limited to covering only what members of the jury can see and hear, and sometimes not all of that. Judges are admonished that their first obligation is to ensure the defendant a fair trial. Judges who conclude that television would prevent that can keep cameras out of the courtroom.

---

13. In re Application of Kansas City Star, 7 Med.L.Rptr. 2353 (8th Cir. 1981).
14. "Court Refuses to Unseal All of Records of Shaklee Case Despite Dow Jones Plea," *Wall Street Journal*, 21 January 1982.
15. The sealing of court records is discussed in Chapter 5, pp. 000–00.
16. Petition of the Post-Newsweek Stations, Florida, Inc., 327 So.2d 1 (Fla.App. 1976); 347 So.2d 402 (Fla. 1976).
17. 370 So.2d 764 (Fla. 1979).
18. Post-Newsweek Stations, 370 So.2d 764, at 778-779, 783-784.

During the experimental period a judge of a Dade County court permitted limited televising of a trial that had attracted a great deal of attention. Two Miami Beach police officers were charged with burglary after an amateur radio operator had heard them talking over their walkie-talkie while they committed the crime. When they were brought

Chandler v. *Florida,* 449 U.S. 560, 101 S.Ct. 802, 66 L.Ed.2d 740 (1981).

to trial, a television camera recorded part of the testimony of the radio operator. It also recorded the closing arguments of counsel for both sides. Only two minutes and fifty-five seconds of videotape was used on the air, and the editor selected only those parts depicting the prosecution's side. When the police officers, Noel Chandler and Robert Granger, were found guilty, they used the presence of the television camera as the basis for an appeal. They got nowhere in the Florida courts, but on further appeal, the Supreme Court took their case. In *Chandler* v. *Florida*, it affirmed the convictions.

The attorney for Chandler and Granger argued that the Supreme Court had held in *Estes* that no televised trial could be fair. Chief Justice Warren Burger, writing for a majority of the Court, rejected that argument. He noted that only four justices had taken that position. The fifth member of the majority in *Estes*, Justice Harlan, confined his reasoning to the facts of that case. While Harlan agreed that the presence of cameras had kept Estes from getting a fair trial, he made a point of noting that smaller, less obtrusive cameras might not interfere with a fair trial in the future. Focusing on Harlan's concurring opinion in *Estes*, Chief Justice Burger said the burden was on Chandler's and Granger's attorney to prove that their trial had not been fair.

The chief justice's conclusions in *Chandler* can be summarized as follows: The Supreme Court has no supervisory authority over state courts. Therefore, they are free to permit photography in the courtroom if they wish. The only limiting provisions at the federal level are that clause in the Sixth Amendment to the Constitution guaranteeing trial by an impartial jury and the clause in the Fourteenth Amendment forbidding deprival of life, liberty, or property without due process of law. As long as the presence of cameras cannot be shown to violate either of those provisions, federal courts have no basis for interfering.

There is no firm evidence, Burger continued, to prove that the mere presence of cameras in the courtroom has an effect on the participants. It follows that federal courts cannot ban state experiments with photographic coverage of trials on the mere suspicion that prejudice will somehow occur. Therefore, the Supreme Court had no basis for concluding that the trial of Chandler and Granger had been inherently unfair.

Nor, the Supreme Court concluded, could the defendants offer facts to prove that they had been the victims of a prejudiced jury. Jurors were asked during voir dire whether the presence of cameras would keep them from deciding the case solely on the basis of the evidence. The fact that a jury was seated demonstrated that the judge and lawyers for both sides believed that the jurors could do so.

The Supreme Court's decision in *Chandler* clearly rejected the many assumptions about the effects of television that are found in the leading opinion in *Estes*. The effect of *Chandler* has been to encourage state courts to adopt rules permitting still photographers and television crews to cover their proceedings; and by 1985, courts in forty states had done so.[19] Some have limited photo coverage to appellate courts, which ordinarily do

---

19. National Center for State Courts, Summary of Cameras in the Courtroom, 1 March 1985.

not hear witnesses and take testimony. In all instances, rules of court give the judge broad authority to regulate use of cameras so as not to cause a disturbance or otherwise interfere with the fairness of the proceeding.

Federal rules of criminal procedure continue to forbid photography in federal courts. In 1982, Alcee Hastings, a federal district court judge who was accused of accepting a bribe, challenged the rules by asking that his trial be covered by television. In 1983, the Court of Appeals, Eleventh Circuit, held that only a minimal First Amendment interest would be served by such coverage and rejected his request.[20] Hastings was tried without the presence of cameras and was acquitted.

Thus, while the First Amendment ensures that the public and reporters have a right of access to courtrooms and news of the courts, it does not go so far as to mandate a right to photograph court proceedings. On the other hand, neither the fair-trial clause of the Sixth Amendment nor the due process clause of the Fifth and Fourteenth Amendments stand as barriers against their use. Thus, it can be said that the Constitution is neutral toward photography in the courtroom as long as the judge takes proper steps to ensure a fair trial.

The Freedom of Information Act

Governments at all levels both acquire and create vast amounts of information. Much of it is routine and of little interest to anyone. Only the police care, for instance, who has been issued which license plate number, and then only if they are trying to trace a hit-and-run driver or a stolen car. Some records are highly personal. The federal government has tax files showing the reported income of everyone who files a return. Many business firms and journalists might find such information interesting, and even helpful, but it is kept secret by law. Other kinds of information are classified as secret by executive order because disclosure might harm national security. The Defense Department, no doubt, has contingency plans covering such things as another outbreak of war in the Middle East or any one of a dozen other trouble spots. It would be interesting to know what those plans are, but exposure would ensure our defeat if one of them had to be used.

Government files also hold vast amounts of information that might serve a public interest if released. Government agencies collect information on the safety of products ranging from face creams to prescription drugs to automobiles. The Department of Agriculture assesses periodically the expected annual production of farm crops and the number of animals being readied for market. Other agencies collect voluminous data measuring every aspect of the economy. The kinds of information above are released routinely. As any Washington correspondent will attest, federal agencies release a torrent of information every day, far more than any one news medium can keep up with.

Without question, the government of the United States is one of the most open in the world. And yet aside from the kinds of information for which the need for secrecy is apparent, there have been times when the public has been denied access to data in which it has had a legitimate interest. Usually, such information is withheld because it would point to inefficiency, stupidity, or outright wrongdoing on the part of government

---

20. United States v. Hastings, 695 F.2d 1278 (11th Cir. 1983).

officials. Until 1966, reporters seeking such information had no legal means of getting access to it. Their alternative was to cultivate sources in Congress or in the agencies themselves who might be willing to "leak" the desired data. Even then, the reporters would never know whether they got the full story, or only that part serving the source's purposes. That was changed, at least in part, when Congress passed the Freedom of Information Act,[21] which declared as a policy of government that the public should have access to information in the files of government agencies.

How helpful the law was to journalists in its early years is open to debate. No doubt, its mere presence did some good. However, government officials could also use it to justify their refusal to release some documents. This happened because the Act listed nine categories of information that were exempted from disclosure, including investigatory records of such agencies as the Federal Bureau of Investigation and the Central Intelligence Agency and documents classified as confidential or secret to protect national security.

Even members of Congress found it difficult or impossible to penetrate the wall of secrecy erected by the latter exemption. In the early 1970s, the government announced that it was going to conduct a nuclear weapons test beneath one of the Aleutian Islands off the coast of Alaska. Representative Patsy Mink of Hawaii and other members of Congress feared that escaping radiation might pollute the waters of the Pacific. But when they asked the Defense Department for a copy of the environmental impact statement prepared for the test, they were told it was part of a sheaf of documents classified top secret. When they filed suit under the Freedom of Information Act, the Supreme Court eventually held, in *Environmental Protection Agency* v. *Mink*,[22] in 1973 that the Act had to be interpreted as Congress had written it. The courts had no power to review an agency's refusal to release classified material.

The decision came at a time when Democrats controlled both houses of Congress. Richard Nixon was president, and Republicans controlled the administrative agencies, but the Watergate disclosures had already cast a pall over the White House. A Senate committee chaired by Senator Frank Church of Utah had uncovered CIA intelligence gathering within the United States, in violation of law. Vice-President Spiro Agnew resigned in 1973 and pleaded no contest to income tax evasion. President Nixon resigned the next year when release of tapes he had made secretly showed he was lying when he had said he had no knowledge of his staff's involvement in the Watergate burglaries. All these events fueled a drive in Congress to strengthen the Freedom of Information Act. Amendments seeking to force more openness were passed over President Gerald Ford's veto and took effect in 1975.[23]

The Act requires that federal agencies make available for inspection and copying the decisions of administrative tribunals, policy statements, and staff manuals of instructions affecting the public. Agencies may delete information that would clearly invade an individual's privacy, but must explain such deletions in writing. To make the search for information easier, each agency is required to publish an index to its files and update it every three months.

---

21. 5 U.S.C. §552.

22. 410 U.S. 73, 93 S.Ct. 827, 35 L.Ed.2d 119 (1973).

23. Edward Karam, "The FoI Act Gets Teeth," Freedom of Information Center Report No. 337, School of Journalism, University of Missouri at Columbia, May 1975. The House voted to override President Ford's veto, 371-31; the Senate, 65-27.

Requests for information do not have to be justified and must be disposed of within ten working days. If the agency decides not to release information, the seeker is entitled to appeal to an agency review officer, and the appeal must be granted or denied within twenty working days. Thus, the maximum delay, if the law is observed, is limited to thirty working days, or six weeks. However, because some agencies have been swamped with large numbers of requests, or with requests for huge volumes of documents, the law permits a ten-day extension. The seeker must be notified of the delay in writing, and must be given a reason.

If the time limits are not met, or if the seeker meets a final refusal, the next step is appeal to a federal district court. Such appeals must be given expedited treatment. If the plaintiff wins, the government must pay all costs, including attorneys' fees. However, in some recent cases, judges have refused to award legal fees to plaintiffs who have obtained information that will aid them in their businesses. Business firms have become major users of the Freedom of Information Act.

Agencies are permitted to charge fees for providing copies of records, but the law says these must be reasonable and limited to recovery of direct costs. If a request is deemed in the public interest, the agency can reduce its fees or even waive them altogether.

The act defines the covered agencies:

> [T]he term "agency" . . . includes any executive department, military department, Government corporation, Government controlled corporation, or other establishment in the executive branch of the Government (including the Executive Office of the President), or any independent regulatory agency.

The language above includes all but three parts of the government. The Freedom of Information Act cannot be used to obtain documentary information in the possession of

— the president and his immediate advisers

— Congress, its committees, and the few agencies under its direct control, principally the Library of Congress and the General Accounting Office

— the federal judicial system

The revised version of the Act continues the nine exemptions written into the original. However, exemptions 1 and 7 were modified in 1975 so as to provide some degree of access to classified documents and investigatory records. The exemptions are as follows:

1. Materials properly classified under executive order "to be kept secret in the interest of national defense or foreign policy."

2. "Internal personnel rules and practices of an agency."

3. Materials exempted from disclosure by a specific statute worded in such a way as to leave no doubt of the intent of Congress.

4. "Trade secrets and commercial or financial information obtained" with the assurance that it will be kept confidential.

5. "Inter-agency or intra-agency memorandums or letters" that would not ordinarily be available to outsiders except in connection with a lawsuit.

6. "Personnel and medical files and similar files the disclosure of which would constitute a clearly unwarranted invasion of privacy."

7. "Investigatory records compiled for law enforcement purposes." However, the law requires disclosure of records that will not interfere with an ongoing investigation, identify confidential sources or methods of gathering information, invade privacy, interfere with a fair trial, or endanger lives.

8. Materials bearing on the operating conditions, regulation, or supervision of financial institutions.

9. "Geological and geophysical information and data, including maps, concerning wells."

It needs to be emphasized that the Freedom of Information Act does *not* apply to state and local governments. These are covered by their own laws, which vary from state to state and city to city. However, the federal law does cover local branches of federal agencies, several of which are to be found in any city of any size.

One other limit on access to information at the federal level needs to be noted. The Privacy Act of 1974[24] applies directly to the Freedom of Information Act. It seeks to limit access to personal files collected by government. Such files are defined as those that link an individual's name with "his education, financial transactions, medical history, and criminal or employment history . . ."

The Act is a product of concern over the possibilities for abuse inherent in computerized record-keeping systems. It establishes procedures under which each of us can examine any files kept on us by the federal government and correct errors found there. It also establishes civil and criminal procedures that can be used to prevent or punish invasions of privacy resulting from misuse of personal records kept by the government. The law forbids agencies of government to keep records bearing on how an individual uses First Amendment rights, unless such information is pertinent to a bona-fide law enforcement activity. It also forbids sale of names and addresses to compilers of mailing lists.

There is no question that the revised version of the Freedom of Information Act has greatly increased public access to the files of government agencies. So many requests are made, in fact, that some agencies have been unable to keep up with them. In mid-1983, the FBI and five other units of the Department of Justice came under criticism for failing to meet the Act's deadlines. The General Accounting Office reported that the FBI was taking an average of 139 calendar days to process requests for information, and other units of the Justice Department were taking four to fifteen months to process complex requests.[25]

Differences of opinion over the scope of the Act have led to hundreds of lawsuits, more than a dozen of which have reached the Supreme Court. The Court has held that the exemptions in the Act should be construed as written, in line with traditional rules

---

24. 5 U.S.C. §552a.
25. "Report Raps Justice on FoI Requests Delays," *Editor & Publisher*, 11 June 1983, p. 30.

of statutory interpretation. As a consequence, lower court decisions during the twenty months between July 1981 and February 1983 were running three-to-one against the seekers of access to information.[26]

Nevertheless, there were complaints—principally from the Defense and State Departments, the FBI, the CIA, and from business firms seeking to protect trade secrets—that too much information was being released. President Reagan reacted in 1982 by issuing Executive Order 12356, which made it easier for agencies to classify documents to protect national security.[27] The new criteria were intended to make it more difficult to prove that documents were classified improperly, thus strengthening Exemption 1. His administration also asked Congress to amend the Act to cut down the release of information from the investigatory files of the FBI and the CIA and of information that might give a business firm's trade secrets to its competitors. In its final form, however, the measure did no more than exempt the CIA's operational files from disclosure.[28]

Thus the Freedom of Information Act remains as a legal means through which journalists and others can obtain access to records in the files of government agencies. In practice, business firms and agencies serving special interests have been major users of the Act. Law violators also have used the Act in large numbers in an attempt to discover how much information the FBI and the Drug Enforcement Administration have on their activities.[29] However, journalists also have been using the Act to obtain access to information previously denied them.

Interpreting the Freedom of Information Act

Court decisions interpreting the Freedom of Information Act have fallen into three categories:

1. Defining an **"agency record."** This is important, because the Act uses that term in referring to the kinds of information subject to its provisions.

2. Defining the ability of third parties, usually firms that have supplied information to the government, to prevent disclosure of government information.

3. Defining the nine exemptions. By far the largest number of cases is in this category. In line with the judicial rules of statutory interpretation, the Supreme Court has taken the lead in insisting that the language of the exemptions must be interpreted literally and in accord with the intent of Congress. Consequently, in most instances the courts have upheld an

---

26. Author's compilation from case summaries reported in *West's Federal Case News.*
27. Denise Kalette, "SDX Lobbying against Reagan's FOIA Order," *Editor & Publisher,* 4 September 1982, p. 9.
28. "Senate Clears FOIA Exemption Bill," *Congressional Quarterly,* 6 October 1984, p. 2459.
29. U.S. Congress, House Subcommittee on Government Operations, *Freedom of Information Act Oversight,* 97th Cong., 1st sess., 15 July 1981, p. 165. Assistant Attorney General Jonathan C. Rose testified that 40 percent of the requests for information received by the Drug Enforcement Administration were believed to come from prisoners and another 20 percent from law violators not yet in custody.

agency's refusal to release information coming within the scope of the exemptions.

Defining an "Agency Record"

The Supreme Court has held in two instances that the Freedom of Information Act can be used only to obtain records in the physical possession of an agency. This is true even though the agency may have disposed of the records in violation of a statute. Nor can the Act be used to compel an agency to obtain records from a contractor doing research for it. Thus, the threshold question in any request for information is, "Is it in a document officially considered to be an 'agency record'?" Usually, that question can be answered by consulting the agency's index to its files.

In the first of the two Supreme Court cases, journalists sought access to notes of telephone conversations made while Henry Kissinger was serving, first, as foreign policy adviser to President Nixon, and later as secretary of state. The Supreme Court held in 1980 that neither set of notes need be released. The Court ruled that the notes made while Kissinger was an adviser to the president were not subject to the FOI Act because

Kissinger v. Reporters Committee for Freedom of the Press, 445 U.S. 136, 100 S.Ct. 960, 63 L.Ed.2d 267 (1980).

the president and his immediate advisers are exempt from its terms. Ordinarily, notes made of the secretary of state's conversations would be subject to disclosure because the Department of State is an "agency" within the scope of the Act. However, in this instance, the notes had been transferred to the Library of Congress under terms that gave Kissinger strict control over their release. Kissinger, who left office before the legal action began, had acted in good faith in consigning his official papers to the Library, but a recently enacted law had made his action illegal. The Reporters Committee pointed to this fact in asking a federal district court to compel the State Department to regain custody over the former secretary's papers. The district court issued such an order and was upheld by a circuit court of appeals.

The Supreme Court held that both courts were wrong. There is nothing in the Freedom of Information Act, the Supreme Court ruled, that requires an agency to sue a third party to recover records no longer in its possession, even though the transfer to that third party may have been illegal. The Act, the Court held, applies only to records in the physical possession of an agency. The Act's terms cannot be used to compel an agency to release records it does not have. Nor, the Court held, does the law give persons outside of government a right to sue to compel an agency to return documents it might be holding illegally. Only the attorney general can initiate such action. In this instance, he did not choose to do so. Nor could the reporters obtain Kissinger's notes from the Library of Congress without his permission because as an agency of Congress it is not covered by the FOI Act. One effect of the decision was to prevent other authors from using information that Kissinger chose to disclose in his memoirs, the first volume of which was published while this case was making its way through the courts.[30]

---

30. Henry Kissinger, *White House Years* (Boston: Little, Brown, 1979). The second volume, *Years of Upheaval*, was published in 1982.

The second case, *Forsham* v. *Harris*, also was decided in 1980. It involved an attempt to gain access to raw data collected by a private organization hired by the government to study thousands of diabetes patients. The focus of

Forsham v. Harris, 445 U.S. 169, 100 S.Ct. 978, 63 L.Ed.2d 293 (1980).

the study was on the side effects of drugs used to control the disease. Under its contract, the research organization was required to summarize its findings and report periodically to the Department of Health, Education and Welfare. Although the department had the right to obtain the raw data gathered during the study, it did not do so.

When the summaries indicated that the oral medicines commonly used as alternatives to injected insulin might cause heart disease, the study became a subject of controversy. The committee on the Care of the Diabetic and other groups resorted to the FOI Act to compel the Department of Health, Education and Welfare to obtain and release the raw data so that other researchers could analyze it and come to their own conclusions. When HEW refused to do so, the groups went to court. The department's decision was upheld.

The Supreme Court ruled that a private organization, even one working under a $15 million contract with the government, is not an "agency" as defined by the FOI Act. Nor can that Act be used to compel a federal agency to obtain data from a private contractor if it does not choose to do so.

At least nine times thereafter, lower courts looked to *Kissinger* and *Forsham* for guidance in determining whether information sought through the FOI Act was contained in "agency records." The decisions show that the term is being construed to mean that not only must the actual physical record—a document, report, or letter—be in the possession of the agency, but one court has held that the subject matter must be pertinent to the agency's work.[31] In six of the nine cases, courts ruled that the materials sought were not agency records.

Defining the Ability of Third Parties to Prevent Release of Information

In an action brought by Chrysler Corporation, the Supreme Court held in 1979 that the nine exemptions contained in the Act can be enforced only by the government. In order to obtain a weapons contract, Chrysler had to file data with the Defense Department showing that it did not discriminate against women and minorities. When a labor union sought release of the data under the FOI Act, Chrysler filed suit, arguing that disclosure was forbidden by Exemption 4, which protects trade secrets and commercial and financial information. It said that the employment figures could be used unfairly by the unions

Chrysler Corp. v. Brown, 441 U.S. 281, 99 S.Ct. 1705, 60 L.Ed.2d 208 (1979).

representing its employees or by its competitors. Chrysler won a partial victory in the lower courts, but the Supreme Court reversed, holding that it was seeking a remedy in the wrong forum and with the wrong means. The purpose of the FOI Act, the Court said, was to encourage release of information. And

---

31. Illinois Institute for Continuing Education v. U.S. Department of Labor, 545 F.Supp. 1229 (N.D.Ill. 1982).

while it did exempt certain kinds of information from disclosure, language in the Act was permissive, not mandatory. Thus, if an agency in its discretion decided to release information arguably subject to one of the exemptions, it could do so. If, as in this instance, a corporation or an individual believed it would be harmed by such release, it should first seek relief through the agency's administrative procedures. Only if that failed could the victim resort to the courts. However, the Supreme Court said that such action would have to be based on some law other than the FOI Act.

The decision conveys two messages to government officials and to users of the FOI Act. In the narrower sense, the decision said that third parties cannot invoke the Act to prevent release of information they have given to a covered government agency. In the broader sense, the Court also told government officials that the exemptions are not mandatory. If officials decide to release information within the scope of one of the exemptions, they can do so, provided some other restrictive law does not apply. There is no way of finding out whether many officials have read the *Chrysler* decision and have been moved by it to release information subject to one of the exemptions. However, there are quite a large number of cases in which courts have looked at the FOI Act and upheld an official's decision to invoke one or more of the exemptions. Some decisions have gone the other way, too.

Defining the Nine Exemptions

The nine exemptions were crafted with two objectives: (1) to permit the government to protect secrets it must keep if it is to carry out its functions; (2) to protect the privacy of government employees and of persons or business firms who provide information to the government. The first objective covers such things as secrets bearing on national security, current investigations by law enforcement officers, the working papers of government lawyers, and memoranda proposing government policies. The second covers such things as personnel records, medical records, trade secrets, financial data used in compiling economic statistics, tax returns, and other kinds of information obtained in confidence. What follows is a sampling of the decisions interpreting seven of the nine exemptions. There are no media-related cases involving the last two, which pertain to the regulation of financial institutions and to geological data concerning wells.

CLASSIFIED INFORMATION   In a world bristling with political, economic, and religious animosities, it is obvious that government must try to keep some secrets. The Defense and State Departments particularly generate information every day that other governments would dearly love to have. The ultimate responsibility for keeping such information limited to those who must have it rests with the president. By executive order, each president in modern times has established guidelines to be followed in deciding what kinds of information need to be safeguarded by being classified as "Confidential," or "Secret." In general, access to such information is limited to those who must have it so that they can carry out their duties. It is a crime for a person authorized to have access to restricted materials to disclose them to an unauthorized person.

Until the Freedom of Information Act was revised in 1975, restricted information was treated like the holiest of holies, protected by the most fearsome taboos. Judges could not even examine restricted documents to determine whether they had been

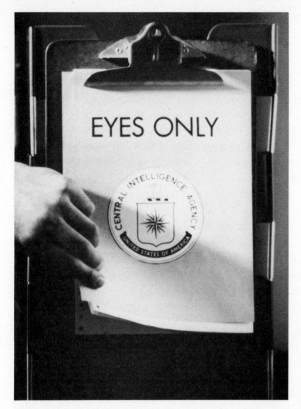

"Eyes Only" is only one of the classifications used by government agencies to protect secrets considered vital to national security. Such materials are usually exempt from disclosure to reporters and others by limitations contained in the Freedom of Information Act. (Stanley Tretick/Sygma)

classified properly, or to sort out of a packet of classified documents those that contained no secrets whatsoever.[32]

Since 1975, the FOI Act has permitted courts to examine documents withheld under Exemption 1 to determine whether they were classified properly. However, an examination of the cases shows that this has not resulted in widespread release of sensitive information dealing with foreign policy and defense. In some instances, courts have upheld a refusal to release information that on the face of it seemed to have more to do with history than current events.[33] In determining whether documents have been classified properly, courts give great weight to affidavits offered by government officials asserting a need for secrecy. However, judges can, and have, examined documents in the privacy of their chambers to resolve doubts. That process was used in *Alfred A. Knopf, Inc.* v. *Colby*,[34] which was discussed in chapter 2. The message implicit in that decision is that declassification of secret documents is a job for experts, not for judges who may not be widely informed in foreign policy or the intricacies of national defense.

More recently, the Supreme Court upheld the view that great weight must be given

32. Environmental Protection Agency v. Mink. See note 22 above.
33. Miller v. Casey, 730 F.2d 773 (D.C.Cir. 1984), in which the U.S. Court of Appeals, District of Columbia Circuit, upheld the CIA's refusal to disclose information on alleged attempts to infiltrate potential guerrillas into Albania between 1945 and 1953.
34. 509 F.2d 1362 (4th Cir. 1975).

to the claims of officials who assert a need for secrecy. In *Weinberger* v. *Catholic Action of Hawaii/Peace Education Project*,[35] the Court upheld in 1981 the navy's refusal to prepare an environmental impact statement for a weapons storage area in Hawaii. The only claimed environmental impact was that which would come from an accidental detonation if the navy decided to store nuclear weapons in the facility. By law, the location of nuclear weapons storage depots is classified. The mere filing of an impact statement, which would be open to inspection under the Freedom of Information Act, would confirm supposition about the depot's purpose. Thus, Justice Rehnquist wrote, the Court would have to take the navy's word for its claim that it had complied with environmental protection law "to the fullest extent possible." Any more than that was "beyond judicial scrutiny" for security reasons.

Reporters and others seeking access to classified documents do not face an impossible task, but most of the assumptions work against them. This is illustrated by a sampling of Exemption 1 cases reaching federal courts from 1982 through mid-1984. The decisions were ten-to-three against disclosure, with partial disclosure in another case. In the most notable instance, the U.S. District Court for the District of Columbia upheld the refusal of the State Department to release records bearing on an alleged plot by exiled French Secret Army terrorists to assassinate President Kennedy.[36]

INTERNAL PERSONNEL INFORMATION   Every agency of government has a body of rules to guide its employees as they carry out the duties imposed on them by law. Some may be so picayune as to limit what may be stacked on desks. Others may detail procedures to be followed in auditing income tax returns. Each agency also maintains files on its employees, which include such things as educational background, work history, and pertinent medical data. The question is, how far does Exemption 2 go in shielding the internal operations of an agency from public view?

The Supreme Court dealt with that question in 1976 when it decided *Department of the Air Force* v. *Rose*, an access suit brought by the student editors of the *New York University Law Review*. In preparing an article on disciplinary procedures at the service academies, the editors asked for summaries of honor and ethics hearings. These are

Department of the Air Force v. Rose, 425 U.S. 352, 96 S.Ct. 1592, 48 L.Ed.2d 11 (1976).

informal proceedings, conducted by the students themselves, to look into allegations that cadets have lied, cheated, or otherwise broken the strict code of conduct governing them. The air force refused to hand over summary reports of these proceedings at the Air Force Academy even with the names of the offending cadets deleted. It argued that the offenders still might be identifiable, with consequences that would haunt them the rest of their lives. Disclosure, the air force contended, would violate Exemptions 2 and 6. The latter permits agencies to withhold records that would pose "a clearly unwarranted invasion of personal privacy."

Lower courts disagreed on withholding, but the Supreme Court ruled that the summaries should be released without the names. Justice William J. Brennan, Jr., wrote that neither exemption should be read as an absolute barrier against disclosure. Each

---

35. 454 U.S. 139, 102 S.Ct. 197, 70 L.Ed.2d 298 (1981).
36. Shaw v. U.S. Department of State, 559 F.Supp. 1053 (D.D.C. 1983).

requires a balancing of the public's interest in the requested information against the agency's or the individual's interest in withholding it.

In the present instance, the Court held, the public had an interest in cheating and dishonesty in the service academies. Some cadets had been discharged. Others were being disciplined. The summaries in question were posted routinely on bulletin boards within the living areas of all three service academies. Clearly, rumor abounded. Therefore, release of the facts, carefully edited to protect individual cadets, was in the public interest.

With this decision as their guide, lower courts have ordered release of such things as manuals used to guide internal revenue service agents in approving or disallowing certain deductions. In most recent Exemption 2 decisions, courts have required those seeking access to agency rules to prove that an important public interest will be served by disclosure.

INFORMATION EXEMPTED BY LAW   In about a hundred instances, Congress has written provisions into federal law prohibiting disclosure of certain kinds of information. In many such instances, the intent is to protect an individual's privacy. Thus, there is considerable overlap between Exemption 3 and Exemption 6, which permits agencies to withhold information to protect privacy. Recent court decisions interpreting both exemptions show a reluctance by both federal agencies and the courts to release data that would permit others to intrude into an individual's private life.

However, the one Exemption 3 case that has reached the Supreme Court did not involve privacy. At issue was an attempt by Consumers Union, publisher of *Consumer Reports* magazine, to obtain government data on possibly dangerous television sets. The magazine's editors learned that the Consumer Product Safety Commission was investi-

Consumer Product Safety Commission v. *GTE Sylvania, Inc.,* 447 U.S. 102, 100 S.Ct. 2051, 64 L.Ed.2d 766 (1980).

gating reports that some people had been injured when the picture tube of their television set had exploded. When *Consumer Reports* asked the agency for its data, the commission was willing to release it, but some television manufacturers objected. Led by GTE Sylvania, Inc., they went to court, arguing that the law under which the Consumer Product Safety Commission operated forbade disclosure. The United States District Court in Delaware agreed and issued an order forbidding the commission from releasing the data sought by *Consumer Reports*. The magazine countered by filing suit to compel release of the data in compliance with the Freedom of Information Act. Both actions reached the Supreme Court.

In *Consumer Product Safety Commission* v. *GTE Sylvania, Inc.,* the Court upheld the Delaware court's order forbidding release of the information. It noted that the law establishing the commission put restrictions on the release of information reflecting unfavorably on a product. Under the law, such information cannot be released until the manufacturer has been notified and given an opportunity to defend its product. The commission's news release describing the problem is required to include the manufacturer's response. Nor can the commission issue any release until it is satisfied that its report is accurate "and that disclosure is 'fair in the circumstances and reasonably related' " to the purpose of the law, which is to protect consumers from hazards. The Supreme Court held that the commission had not complied with the law when it expressed its willingness to give *Consumer Reports* unfavorable information about television sets.

The commission reminded the Court that it had held in the *Chrysler* case that agencies of government are permitted to release information covered by the exemptions if they choose to do so. In some instances, that could be done, Justice Rehnquist replied, but not here. The law establishing the commission specifically limited the circumstances under which it could release information. That law must be obeyed. Therefore, the injunction issued by the district court was proper.

In recent years, most Exemption 3 cases decided by the courts have involved Section 6102 of the Internal Revenue Code, which forbids release of tax return information to a third party. Courts will permit release of such information only if the data are presented in a way that will not identify individual taxpayers.

TRADE SECRETS AND OTHER CONFIDENTIAL DATA   The Supreme Court has not ruled directly on this exemption. In the *Chrysler* case, it conceded that release of trade secrets may have been involved, but advised the company to seek a remedy through the administrative processes of the Defense Department. In 1983, the Circuit Court of Appeals for the District of Columbia held that a consumer advocacy group was not entitled to Food and Drug Administration records on intraocular lenses because the records contained trade secrets.[37] The lenses are implanted in patients' eyes to correct vision after cataract operations. Earlier, a federal district court upheld the refusal of the Federal Aviation Administration to give aircraft certification records to the Air Line Pilots Association.[38] The court held that disclosure would result in considerable competitive harm to the McDonnell-Douglas Corporation.

MEMORANDA   Stripped of its legal terminology, Exemption 5 applies primarily to working papers used in preparing a legal case, or to memoranda exchanged by government officials in laying the groundwork for decisions on policy. If release of such information would give persons in litigation with the government, or persons subject to a proposed governmental policy, an unfair advantage, withholding is justified. In recent years, Exemption 5 has been the subject of more than twenty-five federal court decisions, almost all of which have upheld an agency's refusal to release memoranda. Three cases have reached the Supreme Court. In all three, that Court supported an agency's refusal to release information.

The first of these decisions, *Federal Open Market Committee* v. *Merrill*,[39] decided in 1979, permits the Federal Reserve Board to delay for one month the public disclosure of its decisions on buying or selling government securities. Such decisions, made monthly, have an effect on interest rates, the availability of credit, and the value of the dollar in foreign exchange. The Supreme Court agreed with the Federal Reserve Board's contention that prompt release of its buying and selling plans would thwart their purpose, which is to keep the economy on an even keel.

The second Supreme Court decision, in 1983, in *Federal Trade Commission* v. *Grolier, Inc.*,[40] protects the working papers of government lawyers. The commission had sued Grolier, alleging that its sales representatives were using deceptive methods to sell encyclopedias. The lawsuit was dismissed before it reached trial. Grolier then filed a

---

37. Public Citizen Health Research Group v. Food and Drug Administration, 704 F.2d 1280 (D.C.Cir. 1983).
38. Air Line Pilots Association v. Federal Aviation Administration, 552 F.Supp. 811 (D.D.C. 1982).
39. 443 U.S. 340, 99 S.Ct. 2800, 61 L.Ed.2d 587 (1979).
40. 462 U.S. 19, 103 S.Ct. 2209, 76 L.Ed.2d 387 (1983).

request under the Freedom of Information Act for memoranda prepared by FTC lawyers in preparation for trial. The firm's admitted purpose was to find out how much the agency had learned about sales methods through its surveillance of Grolier's sales representatives. Two lower courts ordered disclosure of the data on grounds that the litigation had ended, thus ending any need to protect strategy planned for the trial. The Supreme Court overruled them, holding that the wording of Exemption 5 says nothing about the status of litigation. It protects the working papers of government lawyers at all times.

The third decision, in 1984, in *United States* v. *Weber Aircraft Corp.*,[41] upheld the air force's refusal to disclose statements obtained during investigation of an aircraft accident. The pilot, who suffered serious injuries, sued Weber, manufacturer of the plane's ejection seat, for damages. To support his case, he sought access to the data collected by air force investigators. The air force readily released factual information gathered under oath during its attempt to find the cause of the crash, but it refused to surrender supplementary data gathered in an attempt to prevent similar accidents in the future. Much of that data was gathered under assurances that the identity of the sources would not be made public. The Supreme Court held that confidential statements gathered in an attempt to formulate safety regulations clearly are intra-agency memoranda of the kind Congress sought to protect when it approved Exemption 5. Therefore, they did not have to be released.

Lower courts have shown a similar reluctance to order release of memoranda that contain no more than the suggestions and supporting data that are the raw materials of government policy. In one sense, this can be seen as beneficial. If government policy makers are going to reach sound conclusions, they must have input from as many sources as possible. Some of those sources must be willing to play the devil's advocate. Others should be encouraged to offer proposals that may sound farfetched, or off-the-wall, especially if taken out of context. In another sense, Exemption 5 does, of course, restrict the public's right to know. Journalists can find much of interest in policy position papers and sometimes serve a public interest by disclosing information found in them. However, the court decisions make clear that to obtain such information reporters must rely on leaks from their sources rather than on the Freedom of Information Act.

DISCLOSURES THAT INVADE PERSONAL PRIVACY   The concern for individual privacy written into Exemption 6 is not absolute. It erects a barrier only against "a clearly unwarranted invasion of personal privacy," thus requiring agencies and the courts to balance an individual's interest in privacy against the public interest served by release of data. Increasingly in recent years, courts have upheld a refusal to release information on privacy grounds.

The leading case interpreting Exemption 6 is *United States Department of State* v. *Washington Post Co.*, decided by the Supreme Court in 1982. It began when a reporter

United States Department of State v. Washington Post Co., 456 U.S. 595, 102 S.Ct. 1957, 72 L.Ed.2d 358 (1982).

for the *Post* received a tip that two officials prominent in Iran's revolutionary government held valid United States passports. The *Post* asked the State Department for information in its files that would prove or disprove the tip. The department refused, citing Exemption 6. While passport data did not qualify as "personnel

---

41. 465 U.S. 792, 104 S.Ct. 1488, 79 L.Ed.2d 814 (1984).

or medical files," the department's lawyers argued that it qualified as "similar files the disclosure of which would constitute a clearly unwarranted invasion of personal privacy." When lower federal courts rejected that argument, the State Department took its case to the Supreme Court.

Writing for the Court, Justice Rehnquist noted that Exemption 6, unlike the other eight, is written in general rather than specific terms. This means, he reasoned, that Congress intended that agencies and courts give special consideration to protecting data bearing on personal privacy. The general purpose of Congress, Rehnquist wrote, "was to provide for the confidentiality of personal matters."

In this instance, the Court gave great weight to the State Department's claim that disclosure of any information about the two Iranians might very well sign their death warrants. Not long after the *Post* made its original request, the Khomeini government's rabid anti-Americanism had led to capture of the United States Embassy in Teheran and the taking of its employees as hostages. The Supreme Court directed the district court to conduct another hearing on the *Post*'s request, at which it should consider the danger to the Iranians' lives. Such danger, the Court said, was an important element in determining whether "similar files" contained private information that ought to be withheld from the public.

A search of the case reports in 1986 disclosed no further action on the *Post*'s request. It did show that lower courts have been citing *Department of State* in expanding the scope for the definition of "similar files" entitled to privacy. United States courts of appeals in two instances have upheld refusals to disclose information that would identify investigators and thus open them to possible harassment.[42] In another instance, a federal appeals court upheld the refusal of the Veterans Administration to disclose details of VA-guaranteed loans on homes in Cleveland Heights, Ohio.[43] A community organization sought the information so that it might check allegations that loans were being steered to whites and blacks in such a way as to resegregate the city. The court ruled that the borrowers' interest in privacy outweighed the organization's interest in promoting racial integration. Decisions in two circuits have upheld an agency's refusal to disclose the mailing addresses of individuals. In one instance, a labor union asked for the addresses of Social Security employees so that it might solicit them as members.[44] In the other, a resort owner was refused the names and addresses of persons who had obtained government permits to boat on a stretch of scenic river on which his resort was situated.[45]

However, the U.S. Court of Appeals for the District of Columbia ordered release to a reporter of the names and amounts of prescription drugs supplied to the Office of the Attending Physician of the Congress.[46] The reporter was investigating allegations that members of Congress were obtaining undue amounts of prescription medicines commonly used by drug abusers. Because the Office of the Attending Physician obtained its supply from the National Naval Medical Center, records of the center were subject to the FOI Act. The center refused the reporter's request, arguing that specific drug orders might

---

42. Kiraly v. Federal Bureau of Investigation, 728 F.2d 273 (6th Cir. 1984), and New England Apple Council v. Donovan, 725 F.2d 139 (1st Cir. 1984).
43. Heights Community Congress v. Veterans Administration, 732 F.2d 526 (6th Cir. 1984).
44. American Federation of Government Employees, AFL-CIO, Local 1923, v. U.S. Department of Health and Human Services, 712 F.2d 931 (4th Cir. 1983).
45. Minnis v. U.S. Department of Agriculture, 737 F.2d 784 (9th Cir. 1984).
46. Arieff v. U.S. Department of the Navy, 712 F.2d 1462 (D.C.Cir. 1983).

be traceable to individual members of Congress. The appellate court ruled that that possibility was too remote to overcome the public interest in knowing what quantities of various medicines were being dispensed to members of Congress.

INVESTIGATORY RECORDS   Because the battleground over the meaning of this exemption lies in the exceptions to it, a reading of its full text is essential. Exemption 7 applies to information

> in the nature of investigatory records compiled for law enforcement purposes, but only to the extent that the production of such records would (a) interfere with enforcement proceedings, (b) deprive a person of a right to a fair trial or an impartial adjudication, (c) constitute an unwarranted invasion of personal privacy, (d) disclose the identity of a confidential source and, in the case of a record compiled by a criminal law enforcement authority in the course of a criminal investigation, or by an agency conducting a lawful national security intelligence investigation, confidential information furnished only by the confidential source, (e) disclose investigative techniques and procedures, or (f) endanger the life or physical safety of law enforcement personnel.

Until 1975, Exemption 7 was much briefer and less complicated, ending at the comma after the word "purposes." Consequently, about 60 percent of the FOI Act requests made to the Federal Bureau of Investigation were rejected.[47] Addition by Congress of the lettered exceptions has made investigatory records far more accessible to the news media and others. The exceptions have also resulted in considerable litigation, with two cases reaching the Supreme Court.

The first of the cases, *National Labor Relations Board* v. *Robbins Tire and Rubber Co.*,[48] was decided in 1978. In it, the NLRB charged Robbins with unfair labor practices and scheduled a hearing. The company filed a request under the Freedom of Information Act to obtain records of NLRB staff interviews with Robbins employees who were to be witnesses at the hearing. The board refused to release the records, arguing that to do so would interfere with its investigation. The Supreme Court agreed, reasoning that disclosure might lead to coercion of the witnesses by the company.

The second case, *Federal Bureau of Investigation* v. *Abramson*, was decided in 1982. It was begun by a journalist, Howard Abramson, who was investigating allegations that President Nixon had used federal agencies for political purposes. Specifically, he had heard that the president had asked the FBI to collect information on people whose only crime was that Nixon considered them his political enemies. As part of his investigation, Abramson asked the FBI to give him all data in its files concerned with such individuals. The FBI rejected the request. It said that release of such information would be an unwarranted invasion of privacy and thus was covered both by Exemption 6 and Exemption 7(c). When

Federal Bureau of Investigation v. **Abramson,** 456 U.S. 615, 102 S.Ct. 2054, 72 L.Ed.2d 376 (1982).

---

47. U.S. Congress, Joint Committee Print, *Freedom of Information Act and Amendments of 1974* (P.L. 93-502); *Source Book: Legislative History, Texts, and Other Documents*, 94th Cong., 1st sess., March 1975, pp. 104–05, and 192.

48. 437 U.S. 214, 98 S.Ct. 2311, 57 L.Ed.2d 159 (1978).

Abramson appealed to a United States district court for help, the FBI gave him eighty-four pages of information, from which some names and facts had been deleted.

However, Abramson did not get what he wanted most, sixty-three pages of data on eleven political figures, which were contained in a memorandum sent personally by J. Edgar Hoover to John D. Ehrlichman, one of the president's closest aides. When the journalist again went to court, the district court upheld the FBI, but the court of appeals sided with Abramson. It held that because the White House is not involved in law enforcement duties the memorandum in question could not have been compiled for law enforcement purposes. Therefore, it was not covered by Exemption 7.

Five justices of the Supreme Court disagreed. They held, in a decision written by Justice Byron R. White, that the circuit court had lost sight of the origins of the data at issue and thus had been led into error. It was true, White conceded, that the document sent to the White House was not an investigatory record, nor had it been compiled for law enforcement purposes. But the information it contained had been collected by the FBI, a law enforcement agency, presumably for investigatory purposes. Congress had written the exemptions to protect information, not pieces of paper containing information. And, since all of the information on the papers sent to Ehrlichman had been compiled for law enforcement purposes, it was covered by Exemption 7. Further, no one had argued that the data would not invade privacy. Therefore, the FBI properly had invoked Exemption 7(c) in denying Abramson's request.

The decision stands as further evidence of the tendency of the courts to be protective of investigatory information and to show concern for alleged invasions of personal privacy. Here, the Court chose to focus not on what the data had to say about White House intrusion into civil rights, but on what it had to say about potentially embarrassing events in the private lives of the subjects of that data.

A sampling of the cases in the lower courts shows that journalists have scored some partial victories in their attempts to gain access to investigatory files, and have suffered defeats, too. National Public Radio was denied access to the FBI's files on the death of Karen Silkwood,[49] who was killed in an automobile accident en route to an interview with a union official and a *New York Times* reporter. Her friends alleged her car was forced off the road by someone who wanted to keep her from talking about plutonium contamination at the plant in which she had been working. The *Providence Journal* was denied access to FBI wiretap information on an alleged patriarch of organized crime.[50] The *St. Louis Post-Dispatch* and its Washington bureau chief, Richard B. Dudman, won and lost when they sought access to nearly a hundred documents in the files of the FBI. Most of them concerned Dudman, who had come under investigation because he was on President Nixon's "enemies list," and because he had traveled in Vietnam and China. In the end, a federal district judge went through some of the documents and decided that parts of them could be released without invading the privacy of third parties or disclosing investigatory methods or confidential sources.[51]

Undoubtedly, the 1975 amendments to the Freedom of Information Act have forced a great deal more openness in federal agencies. The number of cases filed in the federal

---

49. National Public Radio v. Bell, 431 F.Supp. 509 (D.D.C. 1977).
50. Providence Journal Co. v. Federal Bureau of Investigation, 460 F.Supp. 778 (D.R.I. 1978), reversed, 602 F.2d 1010 (1st Cir. 1979).
51. St. Louis Post-Dispatch v. Federal Bureau of Investigation, 447 F.Supp. 31 (D.D.C. 1977).

district courts indicates that some of the openness has been grudging. There is no question that the amendments have been of help to reporters, although business firms account for the largest number of litigated requests. But any reader of a major newspaper, or of wire service material, has seen the clause, "information disclosed by a Freedom of Information Act request."

"Government in the Sunshine"

In 1976, Congress enacted what it called the "Government in the Sunshine" Act.[52] It was a straightforward attempt to open most of the decision making of federal administrative agencies to the public. Generally, it has served that purpose, and courts have had to deal with few cases alleging that its terms have not been met.[53] Therefore, it is enough simply to note its major provisions.

The law applies to

> any agency . . . headed by a collegial body composed of two or more individual members, a majority of whom are appointed to such position by the President with the advice and consent of the Senate, and any subdivision thereof authorized to act on behalf of the agency.

The list of such agencies is long. It includes some obvious ones, like the Federal Communications Commission and the Federal Trade Commission, along with some obscure ones, like the Harry S. Truman Scholarship Foundation and the Overseas Private Investment Corporation.

In effect, a meeting takes place any time a quorum gets together to discuss or act on any item that is properly the business of the agency. No such meetings are to be held without prior notice to the public.

There are exceptions, of course. These roughly parallel the exemptions contained in the Freedom of Information Act. The Sunshine Act also outlines highly detailed procedures that must be followed if a meeting is to be closed. A decision to close must be accompanied by a written explanation. the agency must keep detailed minutes of closed meetings and make an edited version available as soon as possible. All agencies subject to the law have been required to draft regulations applying to their meetings and publish these in the *Federal Register*.

Federal courts have been asked in only a handful of instances to interpret the Sunshine Act. In one instance, the courts held that the Act did not prevent the Atomic Safety and Licensing Board from meeting in secret to prepare a report on the nuclear steam supply system to be used in a proposed power plant.[54] In another case involving nuclear licensing, the Tenth Circuit Court of Appeals held that the Sunshine Act did not protect demonstrators who chained themselves to the door of a meeting room to prevent a secret meeting.[55] The Court of Appeals for the District of Columbia held that the Chrysler

---

52. 5 U.S.C. §552b.
53. 5 U.S.C.A., 1981 supplement, pp. 125–26.
54. Hunt v. Nuclear Regulatory Commission, 468 F.Supp. 817 (N.D.Okla. 1979); affirmed, 611 F.2d 332 (10th Cir. 1979); cert. den., 445 U.S. 906 (1980).
55. United States v. Rankin, 616 F.2d 1168 (10th Cir. 1980).

Loan Guarantee Board was not an agency subject to the law. While it was true that each of its members was an official appointed by the president and confirmed by the Senate, it also was true that the appointments were to other positions within the federal government.[56]

There remain times, of course, when even the most dedicated government officials, acting in full awareness of the law's commitment to openness, feel compelled to sound the waters before embarking on a potentially stormy sea of public controversy. There is no way of checking on telephone calls that are made from one board member to others in advance of a public meeting. Nor does the law forbid members of an administrative tribunal from talking with one another if they meet at a cocktail party or at lunch. On occasion, reporters have argued that because they saw a majority of a board's members having lunch together they were holding an unlawful meeting, but such complaints seldom get far. The fact remains that, taken together, the Sunshine Act and the Freedom of Information Act stand as remarkable commitments to public access to the activities and files of government.

Access to State and Local Decision Making

Every state has access statutes of varying strength and complexity. In addition, there is a large body of common law which, for more than a century, has mandated some degree of access. Thus, reporters covering local and state governments, like those covering the federal government, have legal tools that can be used to force access to meetings and to information. The differences are in the details of the state and local laws, not in the principles applying to their interpretation. Because the specifics of each state's laws are beyond the scope of a general text, the rest of this chapter will focus on principles.

At the state and local level, as at the federal, the need for access to some records is so obvious that no one questions it. People cannot know what the law is unless they have ready access to statutes enacted by legislatures, ordinances passed by city councils, and regulations adopted by administrative agencies. People also need access to court decisions interpreting the law. If government is to be kept honest, records of money spent and received should be open to inspection. So should detailed election results. No prudent person would buy property without a rigorous title search. If taxes are owed on the land, or if it is subject to an unpaid mortgage, the would-be purchaser needs to know. All the kinds of information listed above, customarily and as a matter of legal right have long been freely available. Indeed, in some states, laws require that local governments buy newspaper advertising space once a month to list their receipts and expenditures.

Other kinds of records—such as birth and death certificates, complaints filed with police, accident reports, welfare rolls—may or may not be freely available for public inspection. It depends on whether a law defines them as public records, or whether courts, applying common law, have defined them as such. Because the common-law definition of a public record has been incorporated into the statutes of some states, it is

---

56. Symons v. Chrysler Loan Guarantee Board, 7 Med.L.Rptr. 2363 (D.C.Cir. 1981).

worth a look. *Corpus Juris Secundum*, a legal encyclopedia, states that definition as follows:

> A public record is one required by law to be kept, or necessary to be kept in the discharge of a duty imposed by law, or directed by law to serve as a memorial and evidence of something written, said or done, or a written memorial made by a public officer authorized to perform that function, or a writing filed in a public office.[57]

The problem with the common-law definition was that it required a study of each record sought by a journalist or others to determine whether it qualified as a public record. Sometimes such a determination required weeks of litigation. The public records statutes now in effect in each state attempt to define and classify state and local records, listing those that are freely available, those that may be made available at an official's discretion, and those that are not to be made public because they might invade an individual's privacy, interfere with an investigation, or lead to other kinds of harm.

At common law, there was also a right of access to most meetings of governmental bodies. State legislatures traditionally have opened their sessions to the public, although some committees may meet in secret occasionally. City and county legislative bodies usually have met in public, as have school boards. However, at the local level, governing bodies have made a practice of going into "executive session" to discuss, and even come to conclusions on, sensitive matters. The term is a euphemism for secret meeting. Such sessions usually involve sensitive issues that the members don't want to discuss in public.

The open-meetings laws now in effect in every state have been enacted in an attempt to end the practice of conducting public business behind closed doors. Such laws require legislative and administrative bodies to meet in public, with closed meetings permitted only for limited purposes. Most such laws define a public agency in broad enough terms to include any agency spending public funds. To enforce openness, they provide that any final action taken during an executive session is null and void. They also provide for use of the injunction to mandate openness.

An open-meeting law is of limited use if agencies can call special meetings with little or no notice. Therefore, most such laws require adequate advance notice of such meetings, usually forty-eight hours. News organizations that want to receive notice of special meetings provide agencies with addressed postcards that can be used for this purpose. Open-meetings laws also require posting a notice of special meetings, including the topic to be considered.

Open-meetings laws narrowly restrict executive sessions. The Indiana law, for instance, requires forty-eight-hour notice of such meetings and a statement, in general terms, of the topic to be discussed. Subject matter considered proper for closed meetings is limited to such things as the strategy to be followed in collective bargaining, or in a pending legal action. The law also permits executive sessions to discuss possible purchase of land or buildings, or to interview industrial or commercial prospects who may be thinking of locating in a community. Most such laws permit confidential discussion of personnel matters, including complaints against individual employees. But any action taken on matters discussed in executive session must take place at a subsequent open meeting.

The number of cases still reaching the courts is proof of the fact that statutes mandating

---

57. 76 C.J.S., Records, §1, p. 112.

access to public records and the meetings of public bodies are no open-sesame. But they do give journalists legal keys that can, and should, be used to open the activities of government officials to public inspection, even when the officials might wish otherwise.

Specific Problems in Journalistic Access

When records are clearly public and customarily open to inspection by anyone, journalists have no problems. But when records are not clearly defined as public, or when a journalist makes an unusual request for information, questions can arise. The most common of these are dealt with in the following part of the chapter.

Do Journalist Have a Special Right of Access to Records and Meetings?

Legally, no. Public records laws define a right of access for all persons, including journalists. However, by earning the trust of their sources, reporters may be able to obtain access to records that the law defines as available only at the discretion of an official, or even to records defined as nonpublic.

Nor do reporters have any special legal right of access to meetings of government agencies. However, as a courtesy, and in the interest of ensuring a greater degree of accuracy, governing bodies usually provide special seating for reporters where they can see and hear all that goes on. Governing bodies also commonly give reporters copies of proposed legislation and other documents scheduled for consideration. Reporters who are going to do more than cover the surface of events also seek to gain the confidence of individual members of government agencies. Only by doing so can they learn about the wider, and sometimes hidden, interests that mold government policy at all levels.

Do Journalists Have a Right to Inspect Police Records?

It depends on the kind of record sought, state law, and the terms of the state constitution. The police agencies' policies also are a factor. In all states, arrest records of adults are required to be kept by law. Therefore, they are public records and anyone can inspect the log, or "book," in which arrests are listed. While the fact that the police have made an arrest is noteworthy, it is not the end of the matter. All arrests are subject to review by prosecutors or district attorneys who may dismiss the preliminary charge if they conclude there is not enough evidence to prove guilt beyond a reasonable doubt.

Police also receive and investigate many complaints that may or may not result in an arrest. Officers file written reports of such activities. Reporters may or may not be given access to these reports, depending on a variety of factors. How much journalists can do to force disclosure of information when police use their discretion and withhold it depends on state law. Unless there is a law requiring disclosure of specific police records, or defining complaints recorded by police as public records, there is little journalists legally can do to gain access.[58] If a law does grant a right to inspect complaints filed with police, its terms may give them some latitude for discretion. In Florida, for instance, a court has held that police records are open except where secrecy is required as a matter of public policy.[59]

Texas courts have found a limited constitutional right of access to police records.[60] The Texas legislature drafted a law designed to open police and other records to public inspection. However, like the federal Freedom of Information Act, it contained a list of exemptions. The Houston police relied on the exemptions to justify withholding records that previously had been open to reporters. When the *Houston Chronicle* challenged the police action, an appeals court took a positive view of the First Amendment and held that it required police to make certain information public, despite the wording of the law. This includes the location of the crime, identification and description of the person making the complaint, the time of occurrence, the property involved, details of the offense, and the names of the investigating officers. However, the court held that the news media's right to inspect such records must be balanced against the police interest in law enforcement. And it further held that police could withhold a part of the complaint record containing a listing of evidence. statements made by the suspect, and the investigating officer's conclusions.

A California court has rejected a claim that the First Amendment ensures a right to inspect complaint or investigatory records of police agencies.[61] At issue was a statute exempting such records from the state's Freedom of Information Act in the interest of protecting privacy. The court said it would not disturb the legislature's conclusion that the right of privacy outweighed the public's right to know.

As noted earlier, an arrest record is a public record. And if the arrest leads to conviction, that too, is a matter of public record. But when police compile an individual's criminal history, the compilation may not be a public record. The answer must be sought in individual state law and policy. Since 1978, the Federal Bureau of Investigation has sought to discourage release of criminal histories by threatening to deny offending local police agencies access to its information system.[62] The effect has been to confine legal histories to records of convictions. And, if a state has a law under which the record of a years-old conviction can be expunged, that list may not be complete. The intent is to protect privacy and encourage rehabilitation. However, some states have recognized a countervailing interest in denying certain kinds of employment to persistent lawbreakers and have mandated a right to inspect criminal histories.[63]

Do Journalists Have a Right of Access to Juvenile Court Proceedings?

Generally, no, although many states give judges of such courts wide discretion over access to their proceedings. The juvenile justice system is a product of the idealism that

---

58. See, for example, Gallagher v. Marion County Victim Advocate Program, Inc., 401 N.E.2d 1362 (Ind.App. 1980). In 1983, the state legislature enacted a Public Records Law which, among other things, opened some police records to inspection (Indiana Code 5-14-3, effective 1 January 1984).
59. Lee v. Beach Publishing Co., 173 So.2d 440 (Fla. 1937).
60. Houston Chronicle Publishing Co. v. City of Houston, 531 S.W.2d 177 (Civ.App.14th Dist. 1975).
61. Black Panther Party v. Kehoe, 117 Cal.Rptr. 106 (Cal.App.3d Dist. 1974).
62. " 'Rap Sheet' Availability?" *Bulletin*, Hoosier State Press Association, No. 13–16, 29 March–19 April 1982.
63. Indiana Public Law 23, Acts of 1981.

suffused this country in the early part of the century. It is based on the theory that youngsters go wrong not because they are evil, but because they have not been shown the right way to go. Therefore, the purpose of the system is seen as educational rather than punitive. Offenders are put on probation. If that doesn't work, they are sent to "reform schools." They are held in "detention facilities" rather than in jails. Traditionally, the system has been cloaked in secrecy on the theory that publicity for juvenile offenders would stigmatize them and make it more difficult for them to go straight.

The theory on which the juvenile justice system is based has been tested sorely in the latter part of the twentieth century. In 1980, for instance, twenty-two out of every hundred arrests were of a boy or girl under eighteen years old.[64] For crimes of violence against people or property, the proportion was twenty-five out of one hundred. To give these figures their full meaning, it needs to be noted that the census of that same year found that only nine of each one hundred persons was in the fifteen-to-nineteen-year-old age group.[65] Given, then, the fact that young people account for more than their share of crime, pressures have been generated to force some aspects of the juvenile justice system into the open.

Thus, in the case of particularly vicious crimes, a juvenile court judge may order offenders tried as adults in the regular court system. When that happens, there is no question about a right of access to the records and disposition of that particular offense. Legislatures also have given judges of juvenile courts authority to open some of their own proceedings and records to inspection. In some states, juvenile courts are releasing edited versions of their proceedings, designed to show the nature of the offense and the disposition by the court, but to protect the identity of the offender. In part, such arrangements are a response to accusations that nothing happens to punish persistent offenders.

State laws designed to protect juveniles from publicity usually apply only to the courts, leaving police free to release names if they wish. In other states, the statutory cloak extends even to police records. However, the Supreme Court has held that neither a judge's order nor a state law can prevent publication of a juvenile offender's name, if it has been acquired legally.[66]

Do Journalists Have a Right of Access to the Scene of a Crime?

It depends. The police investigation takes first priority. Whether the crime took place on public or private property, the police have a duty to protect the scene while evidence is being gathered. Thus, they can prevent access in the interest of preserving evidence. If a crime or accident takes place on public property, there is nothing to prevent reporters and photographers from coming as close as the police will permit. And, while it is not uncommon for police to attempt to forbid photography of particularly gruesome scenes, or of situations that may make them look bad, they have no legal right to do so. An

---

64. Uniform Crime Report, Federal Bureau of Investigation.
65. *1980 Census of Population and Housing*, U.S. Bureau of the Census.
66. Oklahoma Publishing Co. v. District Court of Oklahoma County, 430 U.S. 308, 97 S.Ct. 1045, 51 L.Ed.2d 355 (1977); Smith v. Daily Mail Publishing Co., 443 U.S. 97, 99 S.Ct. 2667, 61 L.Ed.2d 399 (1979).

While police are investigating a crime, reporters and photographers have no right of access to the scene beyond what officers are willing to give them. Courts have held that police have a right to control premises in which a crime has been committed to protect the gathering of evidence. This photo suggests what might happen if the courts were to rule otherwise. (Owen Franken/Stock, Boston)

officer who grabs the camera of a photographer who is not interfering with an investigation, or who shoves him or her, has committed an assault. The news media can take prompt legal action in all such cases.

If the crime or accident takes place on private property, there is no right of access except that granted by whoever is in control of the property. Courts in Florida and Indiana have held that if police or firefighters are in control of the property, and are willing to admit reporters and photographers, they may do so.[67]

All police forces of any size have policies regulating actions by officers at the scene of a crime. Usually these state that the news media shall be given information and permitted

---

67. Fletcher v. Florida Publishing Co., 319 So.2d 100 (Fla.App.1st Dist. 1975); quashed as Florida Publishing Co. v. Fletcher, 340 So.2d 914 (Fla. 1977); cert. den., 97 S.Ct. 2634 (1977); *Bulletin,* Hoosier State Press Association, No. 26, 28 June 1976.

to take photographs as long as there is no interference with the investigation.[68] However, reporters and photographers who refuse to obey a valid order by police in charge of the scene of a crime or accident risk arrest.

Can Journalists Find Out Who Is Receiving Welfare Payments?

In modern times, whether the economy is good or bad, large numbers of people have been able to exist only because government supports them in some way. In the 1984 fiscal year, for instance, two dollars of each five spent by the federal government went for what the Treasury Department lists as "income security."[69] This represents payments to individuals and the cost of administering the various programs, including Social Security. In that same year, one person in ten received food stamps.[70] When government money is available, there are bound to be some who will lie and cheat to get it. Periodically, then, editors will ask reporters to look into allegations of welfare fraud. This can't be done very well unless the reporters can find out who is getting how much.

Although the bulk of the financing for welfare programs comes from the federal government, local governments share the costs and are responsible for administering most of the programs. Thus, access is governed both by federal and state laws. Since the early 1950s, a federal law[71] has permitted states to open certain designated welfare rolls to public inspection. However, it does not apply to all programs, most conspicuously, Medicaid, the government's medical care program for the poor.[72] Medicare is not a welfare program but a part of the Social Security system's insurance program. Therefore, its records of individual payments, like Social Security payment records, are not open to public inspection.

Do Journalists Have a Right to Find Out What Grand Juries Are Doing?

A grand jury is made up of persons chosen by lot whose duty is to hear evidence indicating that a crime has been committed. If the jurors find reasonable cause to believe that a named individual has violated a specific law, they put their names to an indictment, or "charge." If the individual is not already in custody, the indictment serves as a warrant for that person's arrest.

Since at least 1681, grand juries have met in secrecy. All states and the federal government prescribe this secrecy either by statute, by rule of court, or by common law.[73] There are several reasons for this. Grand juries operate informally, and, at the state level, have broad authority to look into what they will. They are not bound by the

---

68. The Indiana State Police policy statement issued in November 1975 is typical.
69. Treasury Department, Financial Management Service, *The World Almanac*, 1986, p. 101.
70. "Federal Food Program Costs," *The World Almanac*, 1986, p. 164.
71. 42 U.S.C. §1306(a).
72. "No Wonder," *Bulletin*, Hoosier State Press Association, No. 45–46, 2–9 November 1981.
73. Yale Kamisar, Wayne R. LaFave, and Jerold H. Israel, *Modern Criminal Procedure*, 4th ed. (St. Paul, Minn.: West Publishing Co., 1974), pp. 884–93.

strict rules of evidence prevailing in the courts. Proceedings are informal. Witnesses are free to report unfounded gossip or voice their suspicions. Grand juries hear witnesses whose lives would be in peril, or who would be ostracized by their neighbors, if word of their testimony leaked out. Secrecy also protects the jurors from those who might try to influence them, and it protects those who have been investigated and cleared. Finally, if a grand jury does decide to indict a person who is not in custody, secrecy may be essential to keep him or her from fleeing.

Secrecy is enforced through an oath given to members of the grand jury and to those stenographers and officers of the court who work with it. The record of the jury's deliberations, including the testimony it hears, is sealed. Thus, a juror who talks to a reporter about the proceedings, or an official who leaks all or part of a transcript, faces punishment for contempt. Some reporters have been punished for contempt, not for publishing information leaked from a grand jury, but for refusing to identify the source of the leak.[74]

However, most states do not require witnesses who appear before a grand jury to take an oath of secrecy. Courts recognized long ago that it is next to impossible to prevent persons who talk to a grand jury from talking to others if they are of a mind to do so. When a judge in Akron, Ohio, ordered grand jury witnesses not to talk to reporters, an appeals court reminded him that the rules of court of that state forbid imposing an oath of secrecy on witnesses.[75] Therefore, there is nothing to prevent reporters from waiting out side a grand jury room and trying to talk to witnesses as they emerge. Nor is there anything to prevent reporters, once they have identified the topic of an investigation, from going after the news in their own ways. There is one further caution. If the grand jury does not return an indictment, reporters who have written stories about the target of an investigation cannot rely on privilege as a defense if they are sued for libel. The record of the testimony will remain sealed and therefore unavailable for use as evidence to support the accuracy of the story.

In the Professional World

While there is no question that the Freedom of Information Act has opened many previously closed federal agency files to public inspection, it is by no means a magic key. Doug Lee, writing in the 1985–86 *Freedom of Information* report on the Society of Professional Journalists, Sigma Delta Chi, said reporters who use the Act must persist in their quest for information.[76] He said first-time users of the Act can expect to encounter delay, and then may obtain only a heavily edited document. Despite the seemingly rigid timetable written into the Act, release of requested data may be delayed for as long as six months, depending on the agency's backlog. Reporters also told Lee that the agencies' interpretation of the exemptions seems arbitrary and inconsistent.

---

74. For the experiences of reporters who defy court orders, see Chapter 7.
75. Beacon Journal v. Unger, 8 Med.L.Rptr. 1338 (Ohio App. 1982).
76. Doug Lee, "The Many Benefits of the FOIA," *Freedom of Information*, 1985–86 Report of the Society of Professional Journalists, Sigma Delta Chi; SPJ, SDX, Chicago, 1986, p. 9.

Reporters who seek information from a federal agency are advised to telephone the agency's FOIA officer to get an estimate of the likely delay. The next step is to consult the agency's index to identify the documents in which the needed information is likely to be found. This search may also uncover documents containing other helpful information. When the documentary sources have been identified, the next step is the filing of a formal request, which should be in writing. It should state that the request is being made under the terms of the Freedom of Information Act, it should list the documents requested, and it should suggest some limit to the search and copying fees the requester is prepared to pay.[77] The law mandates that such fees be "reasonable," but in instances where large numbers of documents are sought they can run into thousands of dollars.

At the state and local level, access procedure usually is less formal. In part this is because the volume of requests is not as great. Reporters also are more likely to have frequent contact with the officials controlling release of the documents. Ready access also is related to the fact that many state press associations, individual publishers and broadcasters, and the Society of Professional Journalists have shown a willingness to go to court to enforce the terms of state open-records and meeting laws. For instance, in 1985 the Society awarded grants to establish or maintain freedom-of-information hotline services in Wisconsin, Wyoming, Utah, Colorado, Montana, Nevada, and New Mexico.[78]

Because reliance on legal procedures can be slow, experienced reporters also continue to cultivate sources. Any controversy has losers as well as winners. The losers in an intra-agency battle over policy may be willing to carry an appeal to the public through a trusted reporter. Inefficiencies, and even corruption, in public agencies have been brought to light because a conscientious employee was willing to give information to journalists under a promise of confidentiality. In such instances, access laws can be used to obtain supporting or supplementary data.

Reporters assigned to cover police news are particularly dependent on their sources. As mentioned earlier, laws in most states provide only for limited access to complaints filed with police and may give no right of access to investigatory records. In larger police agencies, the degree of access may be defined by a formal policy. In smaller departments, the relation between police and reporters may be quite informal. But whatever the surface relationships and the policy, there are inescapable tensions between police on one side and the news media and the public on the other.

More than a century ago, Gilbert and Sullivan noted in their comic opera *The Pirates of Penzance* that "a policeman's lot is not a happy one." The opera makes light of that fact. Today, it is a factor that reporters assigned to the police beat take into account. Several recent studies indicate that the police feel that courts make their jobs difficult and the general public does not appreciate what they do.[79] One study of police news indicates that police and journalists have almost completely

---

77. A suggested request letter is included in the report in note 76 above and in "How to Use the Federal FOI Act," a publication of the FOI Service Center, 800 18th St., N.W., Washington, D.C. 20006. In 1986, the cost of the latter publication was $3.
78. Peter Prichard, "Progress on Several Fronts in 1985," *Freedom of Information* Report, p. 2.
79. See, for instance, Robert M. Fogelson, *Big-City Police* (Cambridge: Harvard University Press, 1977), pp. 219–42.

opposing views as to what is news.[80] The police officers surveyed believed there was news in the things they did to help people. Not surprisingly, they did not see much news value in their mistakes. Perhaps also not surprisingly, journalists saw more news in police mistakes than in their good deeds.

Because the law in most states permits police to withhold some information, reporters seek to develop the trust of sources within the agency. Professionals do this by building a reputation for fairness and impartiality. They recognize that there is news in some of what the police do to help people, but they also insist on full disclosure when police mistakes must be covered. Professionals seek to avoid either becoming press agents for police agencies or chronic second-guessers. Because the actions of police officers affect more people more frequently than any other agency of government, police coverage is important. Much of it is no more than a routine listing of arrests and reports of crime and accidents. But most editors today also expect police reporters to be monitors of police performance, on the alert for trends in crime and enforcement as well as for laxity or wrongdoing.

At a point, the questions of access go beyond law and enter the realm of ethics. At this point it should be clear that professional journalists can obtain access to virtually any information government has in its files, either by forcing its release by law or gaining access by ingenuity. As we saw in the discussion of the Progressive case in chapter 3, newspapers and magazines have published what was purported to be the top-secret key to building a hydrogen bomb. The Supreme Court has held that even when the law mandates secrecy, as in the punishment of juvenile offenders, the news media can publish protected information if they can obtain it legally. Does this mean that anything goes?

With all editors, the answer is no. But no safe generalization can be made beyond that point. Perhaps there is the greatest agreement on not publishing names of juvenile offenders. Exceptions are made only for murder or a crime of such a public nature that there is no point in not using the offender's name. Some editors rationalize, "Any kids who are old enough to kill are old enough to get their names in the paper."

Arrest records for adults are public, and many newspapers by policy print all arrests. Today, even some small weekly newspapers also routinely advise their readers that an arrest is not a conviction.[81] Other newspapers also attempt to follow up and report the disposition of all arrests. Thus, if an arrest is dismissed, or leads to acquittal, the public is told about that, too.

Access laws at the federal, state, and local levels have made more information available to the public than ever before. Editors of necessity are highly selective, choosing those items that will be of most interest to the greatest number of their readers or viewers, along with those that will shed the most light on government policy and the abilities of public officials.

---

80. Virginia Dodge Fielder, "Priorities for the Coverage of Law Enforcement News: Perceptions of Citizens, Police, and Media Gatekeepers" (Ph.D. diss., Indiana University, 1976).

81. The *Brown County Democrat*, Nashville, Indiana, uses this paragraph at the head of its listing of persons arrested: "All persons listed here are presumed innocent of these preliminary charges until proven guilty in court."

FOR REVIEW ▨▨▨▨▨▨▨▨▨▨▨▨▨▨▨▨▨▨▨▨▨▨▨▨▨▨▨▨▨▨▨▨▨▨

1. What is meant by "a First Amendment right of access"? How far does it seem to go?

2. With respect to photography in the courtroom, distinguish between the Supreme Court's decisions in *Estes* (1965) and in *Chandler* (1981). Do photographers have a right to take pictures in any courtroom at any time? Why or why not?

3. What is the Freedom of Information Act? In general, what is its purpose?

4. What is an "agency record"? Why is the term important?

5. What is the meaning of the term "classified information"? Is there any right of access to such information?

6. What is the significance of the Supreme Court's decision in the case in which the *Washington Post* sought access to the State Department's passport records?

7. Discuss the likelihood of a journalist's being able to obtain records from the files of the Federal Bureau of Investigation.

8. What is the purpose of the "Government in the Sunshine" Act?

9. What is a "public record"? What is the significance of the term to journalists?

10. What is an "executive session" of a public agency?

11. What rights do journalists and others have to examine arrest records? To examine complaints filed with police? Explain the difference.

12. Is there a right of access to juvenile court proceedings? Should there be? Why or why not?

13. If you needed to use the Freedom of Information Act, how would you go about it?

PART 3

LEGAL REGULATION OF THE MEDIA

CHAPTER 9

OBSCENITY

Supreme Court Attempts to Define Obscenity

Raw Sex or Redeeming Social Importance?

Community Standards of Obscenity

Obscenity Law since *Miller* and *Paris*

Refining the Definition of Obscenity / Defining Child Pornography / Defining and Limiting the Use of Zoning Laws / Limiting the Use of Prior Restraint

---

The urge to censor portrayals of human sexuality has run deep in American society since colonial times. Courts have upheld such censorship as a necessary step to protect public morality in the belief that obscene publications lie outside the realm of ideas protected by the First Amendment. That belief was reinforced by the Supreme Court's 1931 decision in *Near v. Minnesota*[1] in which Chief Justice Charles Evans Hughes wrote that "the primary requirements of decency" may permit prior restraint to prevent circulation of obscene materials (see Chapter 2, p. 33).

The problem with the suppression of obscenity has been in defining what it is. Through most of America's history, until after World War II, any description of sexual activity, no matter how delicately phrased, was likely to draw a censor's frown. James Joyce's *Ulysses*, now studied as a classic, was banned as obscene until a federal judge held in 1933 that it was literature, not pornography.[2] *Lady Chatterley's Lover*, the novels of Henry Miller, and Edmund Wilson's *Memoirs of Hecate County* were among the works that drew official disapproval. Even Norman Mailer had to be wary of the censor when he wrote *The Naked and the Dead*, a realistic account of small-unit combat in World War II. To avoid having his work labeled as obscene, he invented the word "fug" to substitute for one of the two most common epithets of the war. The four-letter version

---

1. 283 U.S. 697, 51 S.Ct. 625, 75 L.Ed. 1357 (1931).
2. United States v. One Book Entitled "Ulysses," 5 F.Supp. 182 (D.N.Y. 1933).

did not win the Supreme Court's approval until 1971.[3] By that time, the Court had lowered the barriers against literary and pictorial portrayals of sexual activity, but it had not abolished them.

Over the years, persistent attempts to suppress obscenity have pitted religious groups against civil libertarians, citizens' groups fearing human degradation against citizens' groups fearing suppression of healthy sexual expression, and prosecutors against a multi-billion-dollar industry that makes and sells explicit sexual movies, videotapes, printed materials, and devices. This says nothing of the even larger flood of materials, including advertising, that exploits sex appeal short of the limits set by obscenity law. Recently, feminists have entered the fray, arguing that much explicit sexual material encourages rape by portraying women as inviting and enjoying the most degrading kinds of sexual assault. Cases requiring courts to interpret obscenity laws have divided judges as have few other issues.

The controversy over the enforcement of obscenity laws centers on the fact that prosecutors seeking a conviction need not prove that anyone has suffered physical harm. The crime is one of the few that is committed in the mind. The Supreme Court has held that material is obscene if it "appeal[s] to a prurient interest in sex" by portraying "sexual conduct in a patently offensive way."[4] Traced to its Latin roots, "prurient" means literally "to itch," therefore, figuratively, "to yearn for, to be lascivious." As the courts use it, the word means that material is considered obscene if a jury concludes that it arouses an obsessive or morbid interest in sex. Since virtually all humans feel, and even welcome, an interest in sex at some point, the critical determination is when an interest becomes obsessive.

Those who oppose the traffic in obscenity argue that it degrades society by corrupting the morals of persons who are exposed to it, particularly young people. Critics of stature have argued that the ready availability of magazines, moving pictures, and videotapes devoted to infinite varieties of sexual gratification encourages sexual permissiveness and weakens the bonds that hold society together.[5] Scientific evidence to support such conclusions is harder to come by. In 1970, the President's Commission on Obscenity and Pornography concluded that there was no relationship between exposure to erotic

---

3. Cohen v. California, 403 U.S. 15, 91 S.Ct. 1780, 29 L.Ed.2d 284 (1971), held that the four-letter word avoided by Mailer was protected speech when it was printed on the back of a man's jacket to show his opposition to the Vietnam War. Hess v. Indiana, 414 U.S. 105, 94 S.Ct. 326, 38 L.Ed.2d 303 (1973), held that the same word was not actionable when it was directed at a deputy sheriff during an antiwar demonstration.
4. Miller v. California, 413 U.S. 15, 93 S.Ct. 2607, 37 L.Ed.2d 419 (1973).
5. Edwin McDowell, "The Critics Descend on Pornotopia," Wall Street Journal, 15 May 1973.

materials and antisocial behavior.[6] More recently, Edward Donnerstein and Daniel Linz, psychology professors at the University of Wisconsin, reported that there is evidence to support the conclusion that "exposure to even a few minutes of sexually violent pornography, such as scenes of rape and other forms of sexual violence against women, can lead to antisocial attitudes and behavior."[7]

However, courts generally have chosen to sidestep the question of harm in dealing with allegedly obscene materials. They have focused on the idea content—or lack of it—of sexually explicit matter. In 1957, in *Roth* v. *United States*,[8] the Supreme Court of the United States held that obscenity can be suppressed because it is devoid of idea content and therefore "not within the area of constitutionally protected speech or press." Materials are obscene, the Court said, if their dominant purpose is to arouse a prurient interest in sex. However, the Court added that "sex and obscenity are not synonymous." Materials dealing with sexuality in a responsible way are protected because they do deal in ideas. In 1973, the Court clarified its position, holding in *Miller* v. *California* that portrayals of sexual activity are not obscene if they have "serious literary, artistic, political, or scientific value." What constitutes such value is for a jury to determine, applying the standards of the community from which its members were selected.

This chapter will trace the development of obscenity law, focusing on the *Roth* and *Miller* decisions. Although the Supreme Court has decided numerous obscenity cases in the past thirty years, these are the landmarks. In them, the Court established, as precisely as words can do, the line at which sexually explicit materials leave the realm of ideas and can be suppressed because they are obscene. We will find that the line is not a sharp one, nor can it be fixed with certainty. This is because the Supreme Court held in *Miller* that juries must apply their notion of community standards in determining whether sexually explicit materials are obscene. Thus, it is possible that magazines, movies, and the like condemned as obscene in one community may be freely available in another a few miles away.

Major Cases

Hamling v. *United States*, 418 U.S. 87, 94 S.Ct. 2887, 41 L.Ed.2d 590 (1974).

Jenkins v. *Georgia*, 418 U.S. 153, 94 S.Ct. 2750, 41 L.Ed.2d 642 (1974).

Memoirs v. *Massachusetts*, 383 U.S. 413, 86 S.Ct. 1975, 16 L.Ed.2d 1 (1966).

Miller v. *California*, 413 U.S. 15, 93 S.Ct. 2607, 37 L.Ed.2d 419 (1973).

New York v. *Ferber*, 458 U.S. 747, 102 S.Ct. 3348, 73 L.Ed.2d 1113 (1982).

Paris Adult Theatre I v. *Slaton*, 413 U.S. 49, 93 S.Ct. 2626, 37 L.Ed.2d 446 (1973).

6. 1970 *Report of the Presidential Commission on Obscenity and Pornography* (New York: Bantam Books, 1970).
7. Edward Donnerstein and Daniel Linz, "Sexual Violence in the Media: A Warning," *Psychology Today*, January 1984, p. 14+.
8. 354 U.S. 476, 77 S.Ct. 1304, 1 L.Ed.2d 1498 (1957).

Roth v. *United States*, 354 U.S. 476, 77 S.Ct. 1304, 1 L.Ed.2d 1498 (1957).

Stanley v. *Georgia*, 394 U.S. 557, 89 S.Ct. 1243, L.Ed.2d 542 (1969).

Supreme Court Attempts to Define Obscenity

Congress enacted its first obscenity law in 1873 at the urging of Anthony Comstock, who came out of Union Army service in the Civil War as a one-star general to devote the rest of his life to the suppression of vice. The law, which bears his name, is still in effect. It prohibits, subject to a fine of up to $5,000 and up to five years in prison, the mailing of "every obscene, lewd, lascivious, indecent, filthy or vile article, matter, thing, device or substance."[9]

An examination of the language of the law illustrates the difficulty in defining the crime of obscenity. Murder can be defined as the act of taking the life of another person. Obscenity is defined with other words, each of which involves a value judgment as to what might be offensive or arouse sexual excitement, neither of which need result in an overt act.

The vagueness of the language of the Comstock Law did not keep it from being enforced. For decades, trial courts translated its generalities by applying a standard borrowed from England. In 1868, in *Regina* (the Queen) v. *Hicklin*,[10] Lord Chief Justice Cockburn ruled that a work is obscene if "the tendency of the matter . . . is to deprave and corrupt those whose minds are open to such immoral influences and into whose hands a publication of this sort might fall."

In the United States, the test was made even stronger by rulings that it could be applied to isolated passages, even if they were taken out of context. A few lurid passages in any book, no matter how serious its overall purpose, could condemn the work as obscene. Obscenity laws in every state supplemented the Comstock Law. Their combined effect was to drive the traffic in sexually explicit materials under the counter. Few tried to argue that a First Amendment issue might be at stake.

The first break in the high barriers against sexually explicit materials came in 1957 when, for the first time, the Supreme Court accepted two obscenity convictions for review. One of the cases, *Butler* v. *Michigan*,[11] involved a bookseller who had been fined $100 for violating that state's obscenity law. The judge had held that the book in question contained "obscene, immoral, lewd, lascivious language, or descriptions tending to incite minors to violent or depraved or immoral acts, manifestly tending to the corruption of the morals of youth." The Supreme Court found two things wrong with the judge's decision: (1) the book had been sold to an adult police officer, not a minor, and (2) the Michigan law, by defining obscenity in terms of material that would corrupt minors, would reduce the people of the state "to reading only what is fit for children." The Court added, "Surely this is to burn the house to roast the pig."

Later that year, the Court decided two cases as one and, for the first time, applied

---

9. 18 U.S.C.A. §1461.
10. 6 L.R. 3 Q.B. 360 (1868).
11. 352 U.S. 380, 77 S.Ct. 524, 1 L.Ed.2d 158 (1957).

First Amendment theory to materials considered obscene. One case came out of New York City where Samuel Roth had been found guilty in U.S. District Court of violating the federal law forbidding the sending of obscenity through the mails. The other case came out of Beverly Hills, California, where David S. Alberts was found guilty in a state court of "lewdly keeping for sale obscene and indecent books," in violation of state law. Roth's name appeared first in the Supreme Court's decision and thus he has achieved a sort of immortality by lending his name to the test still being used to determine obscenity.

Roth v. *United States*, 354 U.S. 476, 77 S.Ct. 1304, 1 L.Ed.2d 1498 (1957).

Justice William J. Brennan, Jr., wrote for himself and four others in upholding the convictions of both men. He began by asking "whether obscenity is utterance within the area of protected speech and press":

> Although this is the first time the question has been squarely presented to this Court, either under the First Amendment or under the Fourteenth Amendment, expressions found in numerous opinions indicate that this Court has always assumed that obscenity is not protected by the freedom of speech and press.

Brennan reviewed the history of laws curbing speech and came to the usual conclusion: The First Amendment is not absolute. He also concluded that the purpose of the amendment is to protect "unfettered interchange of ideas" designed to bring about social and political change. He elaborated on that theme:

> All ideas having even the slightest redeeming social importance—unorthodox ideas, controversial ideas, even ideas hateful to the prevailing climate of opinion—have the full protection of the guarantees, unless excludable because they encroach upon the limited area of more important interests. But implicit in the history of the First Amendment is the rejection of obscenity as utterly without redeeming social importance. This rejection for that reason is mirrored in the universal judgment that obscenity should be restrained, reflected in the international agreement of over 50 nations, in the obscenity laws of all of the 48 states, and in the 20 obscenity laws enacted by the Congress from 1842 to 1956. . . . We hold that obscenity is not within the area of constitutionally protected speech or press.
>
> It is strenuously urged that these obscenity statutes offend the constitutional guarantees because they punish incitation to impure sexual *thoughts*, not shown to be related to any overt antisocial conduct which is or may be incited in the persons stimulated to such *thoughts*.

The Court said the answer to that argument lies in the finding that a work is obscene. Once that finding has been made, the consequences that might flow from the work are irrelevant. The point is that once material has been found obscene, it carries no First Amendment protection whatsoever. The Court then turned to defining the obscene:

> However, sex and obscenity are not synonymous. Obscene material is material which deals with sex in a manner appealing to prurient interest. The protrayal of sex, *e.g.*, in art, literature and scientific works, is not itself sufficient reason to deny material the constitutional protection of freedom of speech and press. Sex, a great and mysterious motive force in

human life, has indisputably been a subject of absorbing interest to mankind throught the ages; it is one of the vital problems of human interest and concern.

With that passage, Brennan made clear his belief that sex in itself is not obscene. In some of its aspects, sex is a matter of public concern that requires public discussion. Such discussion is within the realm of ideas protected by the First Amendment. Courts, then, must be on guard lest the prosecution of obscenity intrude into the realm of protected speech. If the material in question "does not treat sex in a manner appealing to prurient interest," it must be safeguarded. Brennan noted that some American courts had adopted the *Hicklin* rule under which a work was judged by the effect an isolated excerpt might have on particularly sensitive persons. He wrote:

> [L]ater decisions have rejected it and substituted this test: whether to the average person, applying contemporary community standards, the dominant theme of the material taken as a whole appeals to prurient interest.

Brennan footnoted that sentence to a series of recent decisions in federal and state courts. It is not found in so many words in any of them. His formulation has come to be known as the *Roth* test, and, despite many subsequent decisions, it remains the key to a finding that a work is obscene. Although the test did not exist until Brennan wrote it in *Roth*, the Court held that it had been applied properly by the juries that convicted Roth and Alberts.

Brennan's decision for the Court established a precedent that lower courts were required to follow. However, the concurring and dissenting opinions in *Roth* are worth attention because they embody the deep differences that would divide the Court on obscenity cases for the next two decades.

Chief Justice Earl Warren voted to uphold the convictions of Roth and Alberts, but he was troubled by the majority's reasons for doing so. He would not have gotten the courts involved in condemning books and photographs as obscene. He wrote that crimes are committed by persons, not by words or pictures. He argued that the critical test in obscenity cases should be the conduct of the seller of the materials. In this instance, Warren concluded, Roth and Alberts "were plainly engaged in the commercial exploitation of the morbid and shameful craving for materials with prurient effect." Therefore, the chief justice viewed *Roth* as a pandering case that did not involve a First Amendment question.

Justice John Marshall Harlan had no doubt about Alberts's conviction under California law, but would have reversed Roth's conviction under federal law. In his view, a national standard for determining obscenity is dangerous. It is one thing if a state court bans a book—readers will be able to buy it in other states—but it is an altogether different matter if a book is banned as obscene by a national standard. Then it could not be obtained legally anywhere in the United States. Nor was Harlan comfortable with the majority's willingness to let a jury decide what might appeal to a prurient enterest. What would happen if a jury were to find *Ulysses* or the *Decameron* obscene? Such decisions, Harlan wrote, would raise for him "the gravest constitutional problems, for no such verdict could convince me, without more, that these books are 'utterly without redeeming social importance.'" In obscenity cases, he argued, judges should reserve the right to review the facts that led a jury to find a work obscene.

Only Justices William O. Douglas and Hugo L. Black would have reversed both convictions. In a vehement dissent, Douglas raised questions that persist in obscenity cases to this day. He wrote:

> The tests by which these convictions were obtained require only the arousing of sexual thoughts. Yet the arousing of sexual thoughts and desires happens every day in normal life in dozens of ways. Nearly 30 years ago a questionnaire sent to college and normal school women graduates asked what things were most stimulating sexually. Of 409 replies, 9 said "music"; 18 said "pictures"; 29 said "dancing"; 40 said "drama"; 95 said "books"; and 218 said "man." Alpert, Judicial Censorship of Obscene Literature, 52 Harv. L. Rev. 40, 73.
>
> The test of obscenity the Court endorses today gives the censor free range over a vast domain. To allow the State to step in and punish mere speech or publication that the judge or the jury thinks has an *undesirable* impact on thoughts but that is not shown to be part of unlawful action is drastically to curtail the First Amendment.

Douglas examined some of the psychological and sociological literature on delinquency and concluded none of it showed any link to the reading of obscene literature. One conclusion of the studies, he said, is that delinquents don't do much reading of anything. Then he turned on the community standard test, finding it

> too loose, too capricious, too destructive of freedom of expression to be squared with the First Amendment. Under that test, juries can censor, suppress, and punish what they don't like, provided the matter relates to "sexual impurity" or has a tendency "to excite lustful thoughts." This is community censorship in one of its worst forms. It creates a regime where in the battle between the literati and the Philistines, the Philistines are certain to win. If experience in this field teaches anything, it is that "censorship of obscenity has almost always been both irrational and indiscriminate." . . . The test adopted here accentuates that trend.

Despite Douglas's protests, the decision in *Roth* settled one question: Materials found to be obscene do not have First Amendment protection. Because Roth and Alberts properly had been found guilty of selling such materials, they had to take their punishment. The decision also established a test for obscenity: "[W]hether to the average person [a jury], applying contemporary community standards, the dominant theme of the material taken as a whole appeals to prurient interest." Further, the material must be, in Brennan's words, "utterly without redeeming social importance." The Court held that materials that fail the *Roth* test are outside the realm of ideas and therefore outside the realm of the First Amendment. The test does not require any proof that the materials in question harmed anyone. Indeed, Brennan noted that obscenity laws "punish incitation to impure sexual thoughts." He was willing to accept punishment of thought, he said, because the effect of the materials is beside the point. If a work is obscene, that is enough. It can be condemned out of hand, and those who traffic in it can be punished.

Raw Sex or Redeeming Social Importance?

Experience was to prove that the Supreme Court's decision in *Roth* raised more questions than it answered. Producers of sexually oriented materials studied the decision

Hugh Hefner's *Playboy* was one of the first magazines to take advantage of Supreme Court decisions holding that nudity and portrayals of sexual activity are not necessarily obscene. By its thirtieth anniversary in 1982, it had begun to lose circulation. Hefner sought to change with the times by producing video cassettes featuring the same kinds of materials that had made the magazine popular. (AP/Wide World Photos)

and found a challenge. How far could they go in linking portrayals of sex with ideas before they crossed the line into a raw appeal to prurient interest?

The decision came at a time when attitudes toward sex, and portrayals of sexuality, were becoming more relaxed. Hugh Hefner was one of the first to capitalize on that change. He founded *Playboy* magazine in 1953, four years before the Court decided *Roth*. The magazine has never been the subject of a successful obscenity action, but the nature of its content in its early years gives some clues as to the effect *Roth* had in legitimizing sexual portrayals previously considered improper. Starting with its first issue, the magazine featured photographs of bare-breasted young women. A nude Marilyn Monroe, photographed from the side and rear, was the subject of the first centerfold. Other women followed her, month after month. However, it was not until November 1959, two years after *Roth*, that a man appeared in the same photograph with a partially nude woman. And it was not until 1968, long after others had tested the legal waters to find out how much sex might be deemed of social importance, that a *Playboy* photograph showed a woman's pubic hair. Meanwhile, other publishers and filmmakers were offering far more explicit material with little or none of the serious content that helped make *Playboy* one of the most successful magazines of the era. Their offerings led to more than a dozen Supreme Court obscenity decisions in the fifteen years after *Roth*. These decisions raised more questions than they resolved because in only a few instances could as many as five justices agree on any point of law. Therefore, only a few of the cases remain worthy of note.

Memoirs v. Massachusetts,
383 U.S. 413, 86 S. Ct.
1975, 16 L.Ed.2d 1 (1966).

One of these, *Memoirs v. Massachusetts,* decided in 1966, was important at the time because it greatly expanded the scope of permissible sexual portrayals. It also needs to be examined in order to understand *Miller,* which repudiated *Memoirs* in 1973.

At issue in *Memoirs* was that durable classic of erotic literature, John Cleland's *Memoirs of a Woman of Pleasure,* commonly known as *Fanny Hill.* Although it contains no four-letter words, it abounds in descriptions of many kinds of sexual activity. The heroine, who was cast adrift in eighteenth-century England, quickly discovered that her fair face and full figure had value that could earn her a livelihood. When an edition of the book was produced and distributed in 1963 by a reputable publisher, Massachusetts courts condemned it as obscene, just as they had more than a century earlier.[12] Several professors of literature at distinguished New England universities argued in vain during the trial that the book had "redeeming social value," and thus could not be obscene under the *Roth* test. In their eyes, it was "a minor work of art," having "literary merit" and "historical value" and containing "deliberate, calculated comedy." One of the professors said it was "social history of interest to anyone who is interested in fiction as a way of understanding society in the past." Further, as another of the witnesses put it, the work was redeemed by its moral: Sex in marriage is more desirable and enjoyable than sex in a brothel. The jury chose to believe the prosecution's only expert witness, the headmaster of a private school in New England. He had read the book and found no redeeming social value in Fanny's fictional account of her life. To him, the book was "obscene, impure, hard-core pornography, and patently offensive." Massachusetts appeals courts agreed, upholding the jury's verdict.

The Supreme Court took the case and reversed, but no more than three of the justices could agree on any one reason for doing so. The leading opinion, written by Justice Brennan, sought to define the role of "redeeming social value" in the test used to define obscenity. Writing for himself and two others, Brennan said it was not enough for a jury, "applying contemporary community standards," to find that "to the average person . . . the dominant theme of the material taken as a whole appeals to prurient interest." The prosecution also must prove to the jury's satisfaction that the work in question was "utterly without redeeming social value." Further, the social-value finding should be made independently. If a jury found such value in a work, then it would make no difference if the work also were found to have "prurient appeal" or "patent offensiveness." In Brennan's view, the First Amendment protection given to "socially redeeming" ideas was sufficient to override the accompanying portrayals of sexual activity. He was willing to make only one concession: If the seller advertised the materials as sexually provocative, courts should take him at his word and consider them obscene.

The Court's decision in *Memoirs* seemed to signal a virtual end to successful prosecutions for obscenity, provided care were taken in offering sexually explicit materials to the public. That conclusion was reinforced a year later, in 1967, by the Supreme Court's *per curiam* decision in *Redrup* v. *New York.*[13] At issue were the kinds of magazines then appearing on newsstands in response to the decisions in *Roth* and *Memoirs.* The titles

---

12. Commonwealth v. Peter Holmes, 17 Mass. 336 (Mass. 1821).
13. 386 U.S.767, 87 S.Ct. 1414, 18 L.Ed.2d 515 (1967).

are suggestive of the contents: *Lust Pool*, *High Heels*, *Spree*, *Gent*, and *Bachelor*, among others. The Supreme Court held that Redrup and others found guilty of obscenity for selling such materials should go free. The convictions must be reversed, the Court said, because the lower courts had failed to consider three factors:

1. In none of the cases was there any evidence that the works were available to juveniles, or that there was a law defining what might be kept from them.

2. Nor was there any evidence that the materials were thrust upon unsuspecting adults.

3. Nor was there any evidence of pandering.

The Court seemed to have adopted the conduct test first suggested by Chief Justice Warren in *Roth*. It seemed to be saying that if sellers took care to exclude minors from their stores, if they avoided displays that could be seen from a public place, and if they refrained from portraying their wares as intended to turn anyone on, they could sell what they pleased. In short, the Court seemed to be giving its approval to so-called adult bookstores and theaters.

Two years later, in 1969, the Supreme Court struck down another bastion of obscenity law. Many states had statutes making mere possession of obscene materials a crime. One of these was Georgia, where Robert E. Stanley was found guilty of possessing three reels of pornographic film. His arrest had come about in an unusual way. Police suspected Stanley of conducting a betting operation from his home. They obtained a search warrant authorizing them to enter his premises to look for evidence of gambling. The search found no such evidence, but in a desk drawer in Stanley's bedroom, an officer found three reels of eight-millimeter film. Using Stanley's projector and screen, police spent about fifty minutes looking at the film. That was enough to convince them it was obscene. Unable to make a gambling arrest, police arrested Stanley for possessing an obscene film. A county court found him guilty. The Supreme Court agreed to review the conviction and, in *Stanley* v. *Georgia*, reversed, holding the Georgia law unconstitutional.

Stanley v. *Georgia*, 394 U.S. 557, 89 S.Ct. 1243, 22 L.Ed.2d 542 (1969).

This was one of the few instances in that era when a majority of the Court could agree on the rationale for an obscenity decision. Writing for the Court, Justice Thurgood Marshall held "that the mere private possession of obscene matter cannot constitutionally be made a crime." Applying First Amendment principles to the facts of Stanley's arrest, Marshall found absolute protection for the "right to receive information and ideas." That protection is such that it forbids "state inquiry into the contents of a person's library." Marshall wrote:

If the First Amendment means anything, it means that a State has no business telling a man, sitting alone in his own house, what books he may read or what films he may watch. Our whole constitutional heritage rebels at the thought of giving government the power to control men's minds.

When some observers, including lower-court judges, looked at *Stanley* in conjunction with *Redrup*, *Memoirs*, and *Roth*, they concluded that obscenity laws were dying, if not dead.[14] The Supreme Court had held that individuals were entitled to read and view what they pleased in the privacy of their homes. If there were some who wished to peruse what others believed obscene, did they not have a right to obtain such fare? Did that not imply a right to make and sell sexually oriented materials? If *Redrup* meant what it said, the answer to the latter question appeared to be yes, provided that the materials are not sold to minors or exposed to unsuspecting adults, and provided the seller does not pander them.

But even as *Stanley* was being celebrated, the tide began to turn. The Supreme Court would continue to respect the privacy of the home and its occupants' choices in reading or viewing matter, but it would change its mind about what could be seen or sold in public, even in limited public places like those defined in *Redrup*. It did so, in part, as a result of appointments made to the Court by President Nixon. Warren E. Burger replaced Warren as chief justice in 1969. Harry L. Blackmun replaced Abe Fortas in 1970. Lewis F. Powell, Jr., and William H. Rehnquist replaced Black and Harlan in 1971. As a group, the new justices were more conservative on social issues than those they replaced.

Also, other forces were at work. The new wave of sexual candor in film and print generated controversy, not only in the courts but in public discussion. As the 1970s began, sexually explicit materials were widely available. An article in the *Wall Street Journal* reported the situation and the reaction to it: [15]

> A half block from the Justice Department, a variety of photomagazines sell briskly at an "adult bookstore." "Nude Mood," "Cycle Orgy," and "Male Lovers" are some of the milder titles.
>
> Down the street from the White House, a bar offers "two of the most amazing sex films ever shown." On Capitol Hill, a theater packs them in with "Censorship in Denmark: A New Approach." Despite the title, the film's content suggests there is very little censorship in Denmark—or the U.S. either.

The article described "a rising public clamor for action" to stem the tide of sexually explicit materials. Members of Congress were quoted as saying they were receiving more outraged letters on obscenity than on any other subject. More than two hundred bills that would place stricter curbs on obscenity had been introduced in Congress. The president was calling for a "citizens' crusade against the obscene."

In 1967, President Johnson had appointed an eighteen-member commission to study the traffic in obscenity and make recommendations. Its report, released in September 1970, only fueled the fire. Twelve members recommended that government give up its attempt to censor what adults might see or read. They said they had been unable to find any link between explicit sexual materials and sexual arousal, to say nothing of a link to antisocial behavior. Meanwhile, the ambiguous approach mandated by the courts was

---

14. See, for instance, Charles Rembar, *The End of Obscenity* (New York: Bantam Books, 1968). Rembar was counsel for G. P. Putnam's Sons in *Memoirs*.
15. Ronald G. Shafer, "What Is Obscenity? Lack of a Definition Stymies a Crackdown against Smut Dealers," *Wall Street Journal*, 19 August 1970.

simply adding to the profits of the exploiters, who charged premium prices to cover costs of defending themselves against prosecution. The laws were also being used to censor serious works, the majority said. Three of the dissenters filed a minority report in which they quoted police officers in an attempt to prove a link between possession of obscene materials and delinquency. If the majority had its way, they said, America would become "pagan, animalistic, and base."[16]

But the wind was blowing against the commission's majority. Earlier that year, a *Wall Street Journal* reporter had written about the new chief justice and the Supreme Court's likely approach to obscenity.[17] The reporter predicted that Burger would use the obscenity issue to "reverse a major decision of the Warren Court," and thus signal the beginning of a more conservative approach to First Amendment law.

The prediction proved to be accurate. Three years later, Chief Justice Burger found an obscenity case behind which he could muster a majority of the Court. The decision, which he wrote, would make it easier for prosecutors to obtain obscenity convictions.

Community Standards of Obscenity

In the late 1960s, the young manager of a restaurant in Newport Beach, California, was opening the day's mail while his mother stood near. He opened an envelope and found it stuffed with advertising brochures that were not like the usual "junk" mail. These brochures described a film, *Marital Intercourse*, and four books, *Intercourse*, *Man-Woman*, *Sex Orgies Illustrated*, and *An Illustrated History of Pornography*. The brochures were illustrated with photographs leaving no doubt that the materials offered for sale portrayed sexual activity.

The manager and his mother gave the brochures to the police, who arrested Marvin Miller, the sender, on a charge of mailing unsolicited sexually explicit material, a violation of state law. A trial court found him guilty, and a state appeals court affirmed. A further appeal was taken to the U.S. Supreme Court. Chief Justice Burger had found the case on which he could muster a majority. For the first time since *Roth*, sixteen years earlier, five justices would agree on a definition of obscenity.

Like the decision in *Roth*, the new decision was to be laced with irony. The Court had upheld Roth's conviction. But its decision was *Miller* v. *California*, 413 to clear the way for others to do legally what Roth U.S. 15, 93 S.Ct. 2607, 37 was punished for doing illegally. Now the Court L.Ed.2d 419 (1973). would find that Miller's conviction was improper because the California courts had used the wrong standard to determine obscenity. But in doing so, the majority would write a decision that would make it even easier to obtain future convictions.

The chief justice himself wrote the decision in *Miller* v. *California*. He was joined by the three other Nixon appointees—Blackmun, Powell, and Rehnquist—and by Byron R. White, who had been appointed in 1962 by President Kennedy. The majority began

16. *1970 Report*, note 6 above.
17. Louis M. Kohlmeier, "High Court to Review Post Office's Power to Ban Obscene Materials from the Mails," *Wall Street Journal*, 3 March 1970.

by focusing on the origins of the case. "Aggressive sales action" had been used to thrust "sexually explicit materials" on an unwilling recipient. Burger wrote:

> This Court has recognized that the States have a legitimate interest in prohibiting dissemination or exhibition of obscene material when the mode of dissemination carries with it a significant danger of offending the sensibilities of unwilling recipients or of exposure to juveniles.

This was a reference to the Court's decision in *Redrup*. Burger turned next to a review of the decisions in *Roth* and *Memoirs*, noting that the latter had imposed a nearly impossible burden of proof on prosecutors in obscenity cases. They were required to prove a negative, that is, "that the material was '*utterly* without redeeming social value.' " He noted that the *Memoirs* decision, like all other obscenity decisions since *Roth*, had been the product of a divided court. At no time had a majority of the Court endorsed the "redeeming social value" test. Nevertheless, it had been widely used by lower courts, including, Burger said, the California court that had convicted Miller. Then came his clincher: "But now the *Memoirs* test has been abandoned as unworkable by its author, and no member of the Court today supports the *Memoirs* formulation."

That was the truth, but a somewhat misleading one. Brennan was the author of the plurality opinion in *Memoirs*. He had also written the *Roth* test. In *Miller*, he wrote a strong dissent in which he indeed abandoned the *Memoirs* formulation. But that did not mean that he wanted to make it easier for prosecutors to obtain obscenity convictions. On the contrary, he had moved close to the absolute position of Black and Douglas. In part, this was out of revulsion against the Court's role as a "Supreme Board of Censors," which required it to look at sleazy books, photographs, and films to decide whether they would appeal to prurient interest. Brennan, joined by Marshall and Potter Stewart, urged the Court to adopt the decision in *Redrup* as its sole guide, thus making the test of obscenity the conduct of the vendors rather than the content of their wares.

The majority chose another course. It rejected the *Memoirs* test, and then wrote its own three-part test to be applied by lower courts in future obscenity prosecutions. One of its purposes was to hand back to the states the major responsibility for controlling the traffic in pornography. States could do this without infringing on First Amendment freedoms, Burger wrote, if they acted under statutes specifically defining obscenity. Such statutes would have to be "carefully limited" and confined to "works which depict or describe sexual conduct." Further,

> A state offense must also be limited to works which, taken as a whole, appeal to the prurient interest in sex, which portray sexual conduct in a patently offensive way, and which, taken as a whole, do not have serious literary, artistic, political, or scientific value.

Within a paragraph, a majority of the Court had rewritten the law of obscenity. Lest that point be missed, Burger set down three guidelines for juries to apply:

> (a) whether "the average person, applying contemporary community standards," would find that the work, taken as a whole, appeals to the prurient interest,
> (b) whether the work depicts or describes, in a patently offensive way, sexual conduct specifically defined by the applicable state law, and

(c) whether the work, taken as a whole, lacks serious literary, artistic, political, or scientific value.

The newly proclaimed three-point test retained Brennan's formulation in *Roth*, but rejected his plurality opinion in *Memoirs*. Henceforth, purveyors of sexually explicit materials could avoid an obscenity conviction only if they could prove that the items in question had some serious value to society.

The Burger majority offered advice to state legislatures in drafting statutes that would comply with the new test and to courts interpreting them. It listed "a few plain examples" of the kinds of works that would be obscene under "the standard announced in this opinion":

(a) Patently offensive representations or descriptions of ultimate sexual acts, normal or perverted, actual or simulated.

(b) Patently offensive representations or descriptions of masturbation, excretory functions, and lewd exhibition of the genitals.

The majority expanded on these examples:

Sex and nudity may not be exploited without limit by films or pictures exhibited or sold in places of public accommodation any more than live sex and nudity can be exhibited or sold without limit in such public places. At a minimum, prurient, patently offensive depiction or description of sexual conduct must have serious literary, artistic, political, or scientific value to merit First Amendment protection. . . . For example, medical books for the education of physicians and related personnel necessarily use graphic illustrations and descriptions of human anatomy. In resolving the inevitably sensitive questions of fact and law, we must continue to rely on the jury system, accompanied by the safeguards that judges, rules of evidence, presumption of innocence, and other protective features provide, as we do with rape, murder, and a host of other offenses against society and its individual members.

The majority proceeded to give the jury a central role in obscenity cases:

Under a National Constitution, fundamental First Amendment limitations on the power of the States do not vary from community to community, but this does not mean that there are, or should or can be, fixed, uniform national standards of precisely what appeals to the "prurient interest" or is "patently offensive." These are essentially questions of fact, and our Nation is simply too big and too diverse for this Court to reasonably expect such standards could be articulated for all 50 States in a single formulation, even assuming the prerequisite consensus exists. When triers of fact [a jury] are asked to decide whether "the average person, applying contemporary community standards" would consider certain materials "prurient," it would be unrealistic to require that the answer be based on some abstract formulation. The adversary system, with lay jurors as the usual ultimate fact-finders in critical prosecutions, has historically permitted triers of fact to draw on the standards of their community, guided always by limiting instructions on the law. To require a State to structure obscenity proceedings around evidence of a *national* "community standard" would be an exercise in futility. . . .

It is neither realistic nor constitutionally sound to read the First Amendment as requiring that the people of Maine or Mississippi accept public depiction of conduct found tolerable in Las Vegas, or New York City. . . . People in different States vary in their tastes and attitudes, and this diversity is not to be strangled by the absolutism of imposed uniformity.

Thus, the Court sought to define "community" as the place from which a jury was drawn to hear an obscenity case. It also sought to define the "community standard" as the jurors' collective estimate of the level of sexual candor tolerated by them, their friends, and their neighbors.

Justice Douglas, writing in dissent, protested that the majority was giving juries of lay citizens a task that even Supreme Court justices had shown remarkably little talent for doing; that is, determining what is obscene. In his view, the new test "would make it possible to ban any paper or any journal or magazine in some benighted place." He added:

> The idea that the First Amendment permits punishment for ideas that are "offensive" to the particular judge or jury sitting in judgment is astounding. No greater leveler of speech or literature has ever been designed . . .
>
> We deal with highly emotional, not rational, questions.

Douglas's protest had no effect. The Court returned the case against Miller to the California courts for retrial under the new standard.

Paris Adult Theatre I v. Slaton, 413 U.S. 49, 93 S.Ct. 2626, 37 L.Ed.2d 446 (1973).

On the same day, the Court decided *Paris Adult Theatre I* v. *Slaton*, an obscenity case aimed at an adult theater operator in Georgia. Again Chief Justice Burger was able to muster a majority, this time to repudiate the Court's *per curiam* decision in *Redrup*.

Lewis R. Slaton, district attorney of Fulton County, Georgia, had brought a civil action to prevent the showing in an adult theater of two films, *Magic Mirror* and *It All Comes Out in the End*, which a judge had declared obscene. However, the judge had held that he could not prevent the theater from showing them because it operated within *Redrup* guidelines, that is, it excluded minors and unsuspecting adults, and it did not pander. The Georgia Supreme Court overruled him, and the U.S. Supreme Court affirmed that decision.

The chief justice moved directly to the attack on *Redrup*:

> We categorically disapprove the theory, apparently adopted by the trial judge, that obscene, pornographic films acquire constitutional immunity from state regulation simply because they are exhibited for consenting adults only. . . . Although we have often pointedly recognized the high importance of the state interest in regulating the exposure of obscene materials to juveniles and unconsenting adults, . . . this Court has never declared these to be the only legitimate state interests permitting regulation of obscene material. The States have a long-recognized legitimate interest in regulating the use of obscene material in local commerce and in all places of public accommodation, as long as these regulations do not run afoul of specific constitutional prohibitions. . . .
>
> In particular, we hold that there are legitimate state interests at stake in stemming the tide of commercialized obscenity. . . . These include the interest of the public in the quality of life and the total community environment, the tone of commerce in the great city centers, and possibly, the public safety itself. . . .

If we accept . . . the well nigh universal belief that good books, plays, and art lift the spirit, improve the mind, enrich the human personality, and develop character, can we then say that a state legislature may not act on the corollary assumption that commerce in obscene books, or public exhibitions focused on obscene conduct, have a tendency to exert a corrupting and debasing impact leading to antisocial behavior?

Lawyers for the theater had pointed to the Court's decision in *Stanley*, arguing that it established a right of privacy protecting the viewing of obscene materials. Burger replied that the decision in *Stanley* clearly confines that right to the home:

The idea of a "privacy" right and a place of public accommodation are, in this context, mutually exclusive. Conduct or depictions of conduct that the state police power can prohibit on a public street do not become automatically protected by the Constitution merely because the conduct is moved to a bar or a "live" theatre stage, any more than a "live" performance of a man and woman locked in sexual embrace at high noon in Times Square is protected by the Constitution because they simultaneously engage in a valid political dialogue.

At that point, *Redrup* and the broader implications some had seen in *Stanley* had been torn to ribbons. States and localities might permit so-called adult bookstores and films if they wanted to, but if states chose to ban obscenity, the makers and the sellers of it could not look to the United States Supreme Court for help. If the materials in question portrayed explicit sexual or excretory activity, and did so in a manner that a jury found patently offensive, they could be condemned as obscene, unless they were redeemed by serious literary, artistic, political, or scientific value. Nor could obscene materials find sanctuary behind doors marked "adults only." If state officials chose to do so, they could prosecute purveyors of obscenity if a state law defined the crime in terms of specific sexual conduct.

Obscenity Law since *Miller* and *Paris*

In the aftermath of the *Miller* and *Paris* decisions, newspaper and magazine writers sought comment from publishers, film producers, authors, artists, law enforcement officers, and others. They found what one reporter described as "confusion and chaos."[18] *Playboy*, *Oui*, and *Penthouse* were seized by police in Macon, Georgia. *Playboy* became an under-the-counter item in Fort Wayne, Indiana. A city board of film censors in Dallas, one of the few remaining such agencies in the country, declared *Paper Moon* "not suitable for children" despite its rating as a PG film. The board found it objectionable because the script required ten-year-old Tatum O'Neal to swear and smoke cigarettes. Russ Meyer, whose films featuring well-endowed naked young women drew large audiences in the 1960s, shelved plans for *Foxy*. He said the Supreme Court's decisions made the $400,000 investment too risky.

Robert A. Wright of the *New York Times* found considerable uneasiness among the

---

18. Earl C. Gottschalk, Jr., "Pornography Ruling Causing Confusion and Chaos, Many Traditional Publishers and Filmmakers Say," *Wall Street Journal*, 16 July 1973.

major writers of fiction.[19] Kurt Vonnegut, Jr., Hoosier-born author of best-selling satire on middle-class mores, feared that some of his works might be condemned by some jury, somewhere. Such a decision, he said, would "hurt personally." Irving Wallace, Joyce Carol Oates, Ross Macdonald, Dan Wakefield, Jacqueline Susann, John Updike, and Truman Capote also were interviewed. None had any intention of changing his or her writing style, but all saw the Court's decisions as a step backward. Miss Oates predicted *Miller* would lead to repression of the arts. Macdonald pointed to an ambiguity in Burger's reasoning in *Paris:*

> Burger's strange suggestions that nothing can be described or expounded in a work of art which couldn't be performed in Times Square at high noon—well, this doesn't apply to any other aspect of what goes on in a work of art. The fact, for example, that murder is a crime when it takes place in real life has nothing to do with whether it is proper to describe it in fiction.

In the immediate aftermath of the *Miller* and *Paris* decisions, two currents worked at cross purposes. Police and prosecutors moved against obscenity with renewed vigor. But some judges, reading *Miller*, were finding state statutes unconstitutional because they did not define obscenity in terms of explicit sexual conduct. For instance, a federal district court in Alabama ruled that the state's obscenity law was unconstitutional in a case involving *Last Tango in Paris*, which starred Marlon Brando.[20] In another case, the Minnesota Supreme Court struck down that state's law, which included, word-for-word, the formulation in *Roth*.[21] Pointing to *Miller*, the court said the law was flawed because it did not describe sexual conduct in specific terms.

It also quickly became apparent that with its decisions in *Miller* and *Paris* the Court had not succeeded in ridding itself of obscenity cases. In the years since, it has decided at least one, and as many as four, in several of its terms. It also has refused to review many others. The Court has felt a need to deal with problems in several areas, which are summarized and categorized below.

Refining the Definition of Obscenity

Brennan had predicted that local juries would condemn as obscene works that were seen elsewhere as art. Even as he wrote that passage in *Miller*, a case bearing out his prediciton was on its way to the Court. In 1971, a jury in Albany, Georgia, had found the movie *Carnal Knowledge* obscene. The exhibitor was fined $750 and placed on probation for a year. The film, starring Jack Nicholson, was a serious look at the sexual fantasies and later hangups of college friends who go their separate ways into early middle age. Most reviewers found it an honest look at the process and problems of maturing. Some thought well enough of it to place it on their lists of the ten best films of 1971.

Jenkins v. *Georgia*, 418 U.S. 153, 94 S.Ct. 2750, 41 L.Ed.2d 642 (1974).

---

19. Robert A. Wright, "Broad Spectrum of Writers Attacks Obscenity Ruling," *New York Times*, 21 August 1973.
20. United Artists Corp. v. Wright, 368 F.Supp. 1034 (M.D.Ala. 1974).
21. State v. Welke, 216 N.W.2d 641 (Minn. 1974).

After the Georgia Supreme Court had upheld the Albany jury, the *Miller* decision came down. In light of that verdict, the Supreme Court of the United States agreed to review.

In its decision in *Jenkins* v. *Georgia*, the Court reiterated two points it had made in *Miller*:

1. The Georgia Supreme Court was correct in holding that a jury need not be told to apply a state-wide standard. Local standards of sexual candor are to be used in determining whether a film is obscene.

2. However, local juries do not have "unbridled discretion" in deciding what is obscene. Material can be obscene only if it depicts or portrays "patently offensive 'hard core' sexual conduct."

Therefore, *Carnal Knowledge* was not obscene. Justice Rehnquist explained why:

   While the subject matter of the picture is, in a broader sense, sex, and there are scenes in which sexual conduct including "ultimate sexual acts" is to be understood to be taking place, the camera does not focus on the bodies of the actors at such times. There is no exhibition whatsoever of the actors' genitals, lewd or otherwise, during these scenes. There are occasional scenes of nudity, but nudity alone is not enough to make material legally obscene under the *Miller* standards.

On the same day, in *Hamling* v. *United States*, the Court upheld prison terms imposed on two men who had used the mails to distribute 55,000 brochures advertising *The Illustrated Presidential Report of the Commission on Obscenity and Pornography*.

Hamling v. **United States,**
418 U.S. 87, 94 S.Ct. 2887,
41 L.Ed.2d 590 (1974).

The sample illustrations used in the brochure showed a wide variety of heterosexual and homosexual activity, and of humans engaged in sexual activity with animals. The convictions had taken place in a federal district court and had been upheld by the court of appeals before *Miller* was decided. The Court held that in such instances convicted defendants were entitled to any help *Miller* might give them, but concluded that in this instance it gave them none.

Three points emerged from the decision:

1. Although federal laws define obscenity in general terms, they were made specific by the Supreme Court's decision in *Miller*. Under well-established principles of constitutional law, statutes mean what the courts say they mean. Thus, the federal law must be interpreted and applied in the light of the "few plain examples" provided by Chief Justice Burger in *Miller*.

2. Juries deciding obscenity cases brought under federal law are not required to apply a national standard. They are to draw on their knowledge of the standard of sexual candor prevailing in the communities from which jurors are selected.

3. Nor are jurors required to pay any attention to expert witnesses who testify as to what they believe the standard is. The jurors are considered the experts.

The effect of *Hamling* has been to strengthen the role of the locally drawn jury in determining what is obscene. The jury's discretion is limited only by the proviso, reinforced by *Jenkins*, that the material at issue must portray, in words or pictures, specific sexual activity lacking "serious literary, artistic, political or scientific value."

In 1977, in *Ward* v. *Illinois*,[22] the Court broadened the definition of obscenity to include portrayals of sadomasochistic practices. Wesley Ward thought he had found a loophole in the law because his materials did not fit the "few plain examples" listed by the chief justice. Nor, he argued, did Illinois law describe prohibited sexual acts in explicit terms. Neither argument prevailed. The Court held that the Illinois Supreme Court had construed the state obscenity law properly in *Roth-Miller* terms. And the "few plain examples" were just that. The list was not intended to be exhaustive.

Also in 1977, in *Splawn* v. *California*,[23] the Court upheld a California judge who had told a jury it could consider the seller's methods in coming to the conclusion that two reels of film were obscene. This revived and affirmed the pandering test first proposed by Chief Justice Warren in *Roth* and endorsed by the Court nine years later in *Ginzburg* v. *United States*.[24] The decisions mean that a seller who tells customers his materials will arouse their prurient interest is likely to be taken at his word if an obscenity prosecution results.

Defining Child Pornography

Some adults see children as exciting sexual objects who can be exploited because of their immaturity. Such adults are willing to pay well for photographs of children engaged in sexual action. In 1977, the traffic in such materials led to passage by Congress of a law providing for prosecution of persons who make or sell such photographs.[25] Under its terms, violators can be sentenced to as long as ten years in prison for a first offense. All fifty states have similar laws.

Most such laws describe the crime of child pornography in terms of specific sexual acts. Even an isolated portrayal of a proscribed act is subject to prosecution if it involves a minor. For that reason, the laws do not precisely fit the *Roth-Miller* mold, which requires that a work charged with being obscene must be looked at as a whole.

In 1982 in *New York* v. *Ferber*, the Supreme Court upheld that state's child pornography law. The Court said that in protecting children from sexual exploitation, states can go beyond the limits imposed by *Miller*. It held flatly that there is no First Amendment protection for portrayals of specifically described sex acts performed by boys or girls under sixteen years of age. Justice White said the Court could find no value whatsoever in encouraging children to engage in sex. On the contrary, it would uphold the legislature in its conclusion that "the use of children as subjects of pornographic materials is harmful to the physiological, emotional, and mental health of the child. That judgment, we think, easily passes muster under the First Amendment."

New York v. *Ferber*, 458 U.S. 747, 102 S.Ct. 3348, 73 L.Ed.2d 1113 (1982).

---

22. 431 U.S. 767, 97 S.Ct. 2085, 52 L.Ed.2d 738 (1977).
23. 431 U.S. 595, 97 S.Ct. 1987, 52 L.Ed.2d 606 (1977).
24. 383 U.S. 463, 86 S.Ct. 942, 16 L.Ed.2d 31 (1966).
25. Protection of Children Against Sexual Exploitation Act of 1977, 18 U.S.C. §§2251–2253.

The decision is of further interest in that all nine justices agreed that Ferber should be punished. However, four of them wrote opinions in which they differed with White on some elements of his reasoning. Justices Stevens and Brennan, for instance, did not join that part of the decision holding that all depictions of minors engaged in sexual activity are without First Amendment protection. They would have held open the possibility that sometime, somehow, a work portraying sexual activity by teenagers might be a work of art.

Defining and Limiting the Use of Zoning Laws

Zoning laws can be used to confine adult theaters and bookstores to specified parts of a city, but they cannot be used as a subterfuge to ban all such establishments. The Supreme Court's decisions in this area point up the variety of approaches to obscenity law made possible by *Miller*. In some states, or even in parts of states, anything goes. Either there is no law making obscenity a crime, or, if there is a law, local prosecutors do not bother to enforce it. Some states, formally or informally, condone establishments that operate within the *Redrup* guidelines. In still other states and localities, obscenity laws are enforced and juries return convictions. In states that continue to apply *Redrup*, some local authorities have turned to zoning laws to control the location of adult establishments.

In 1976, in *Young* v. *American Mini Theatres*,[26] the Supreme Court upheld a Detroit ordinance that confined adult bookstores and theaters to commercial areas of the city. Its terms were held to be a reasonable restriction of time, place, and manner on First Amendment activities. But in 1981, in *Schad* v. *Borough of Mount Ephraim*,[27] the Court said a New Jersey community went too far when its zoning law forbade live entertainment. The law's target was an adult bookstore in which a woman danced in the nude behind a glass screen. The Court said the law also could be used to restrict other forms of expression. In 1986, in *City of Renton* v. *Playtime Theatres, Inc.*,[28] the Supreme Court expanded on its holding in *Young*. It upheld a zoning ordinance that prohibited adult theaters from locating within a thousand feet of any dwelling, church, park, or school. Thus, zoning laws may be used to concentrate sexually oriented businesses in a particular part of a city and to prevent them from expanding into designated neighborhoods.

Limiting the Use of Prior Restraint

Repeatedly, the Supreme Court has said that materials found to be obscene are outside the realm of the First Amendment. This means, among other things, that such materials are subject to prior restraint. For instance, a film found to be obscene can be subjected to the ultimate in restraint. It can be destroyed. However, the Supreme Court has also held in at least three instances that no restraint can be imposed until a trial has resulted

---

26. 427 U.S. 50, 96 S.Ct. 2440, 49 L.Ed.2d 310 (1976).
27. 452 U.S. 61, 101 S.Ct. 2176, 68 L.Ed.2d 671 (1981).
28. __U.S.__, 106 S.Ct. 925, 89 L.Ed.2d 29 (1986).

in a finding of obscenity. However, if a theater's showing of sexually explicit films attracts undesirables to a neighborhood to the point of becoming a public nuisance, it can be closed by court order.

In 1975, in two instances, the Court struck down attempts to restrain allegedly obscene exhibitions. One involved a ruling by Chattanooga city officials preventing a performance of the rock musical *Hair* in a municipal auditorium.[29] Although the musical contained one scene in which the cast stripped on stage, it had not been held to be obscene. In the other case, the Court struck down an ordinance of the city of Jacksonville, Florida, forbidding outdoor theaters to show movies containing nudity. The Court pointed out that nudity in itself is not obscene.[30] In 1980, the Court held unconstitutional a Texas law permitting authorities to close theaters in which an obscene film had been shown. The Court said that the fact that one such film had been shown could not justify preventing the showing of other films that might or might not be obscene.[31]

However, in its next term the Court upheld a California court's decision to close an adult theater for one year on the ground that it had become a public nuisance.[32] The decision was not based on a judgment of the kinds of films the theater offered, but on the type of patrons it attracted and their effect on the neighborhood. The Court said authorities can act under a state's police powers to abate a nuisance.

The decisions in this section point in several directions. *Jenkins* and *Hamling* further defined the role of the jury in deciding what is obscene. Jurors are the experts on the community's standards of sexual candor. They fix the point at which depictions of sexual activity become patently offensive. In doing so, they think in terms of the community with which they are familiar, without being required to think either of a national standard or of a statewide standard. But *Jenkins* stands as a reminder that juries cannot go too far in limiting what their neighbors may read or see. If a book, magazine, or movie does not portray explicit sexual activity, it cannot be obscene.

If children under sixteen years of age are used to portray sexual activity, those who traffic in the portrayals can be punished without any need for a jury to find the materials obscene. In *Ferber*, the Court held that the state interest in protecting minors from psychologically harmful exploitation is strong enough to overcome any First Amendment values that might be found in child pornography. Apparently, such laws are limited to photographs of child models. Two justices said it was not the Court's intent to condemn Shakespeare's *Romeo and Juliet*, in which both the title characters were under sixteen.

The Court's decisions on zoning regulations and prior restraint merely applied principles dealt with earlier in this book. Communities can regulate the time, place, and manner in which establishments can offer sexually explicit wares to the public, but they cannot forbid their distribution without first finding, through an adversary process in the courts, that they are obscene.

Thus, after thirty years of litigation, frequently reaching the nation's highest court, obscenity law can best be described as a hodgepodge. The *Roth-Miller* test reads almost like a mathematical formula when it is encountered in the pages of the Supreme Court reporters:

---

29. Southeastern Promotions, Ltd. v. Conrad, 420 U.S. 546, 95 S.Ct. 1239, 43 L.Ed.2d 448 (1975).
30. Erznoznik v. City of Jacksonville, 422 U.S. 205, 95 S.Ct. 2268, 45 L.Ed.2d 125 (1975).
31. Vance v. Universal Amusement Co., 445 U.S. 308, 100 S.Ct. 1156, 63 L.Ed.2d 413 (1980).
32. Cooper v. Mitchell Brothers' Santa Ana Theater, 454 U.S. 90, 102 S.Ct. 172, 70 L.Ed.2d 262 (1981).

During the 1970s, *Deep Throat* became one of the classic porn movies. That it could be shown publicly at all was one of the products of a series of Supreme Court decisions greatly relaxing obscenity law. The Court's *Miller* decision in 1973 gave local communities greater leeway to prosecute obscenity. Among the victims of this decision was Harry Reems, one of the "stars" of *Deep Throat*, who was found guilty of obscenity by a federal jury in Memphis. (Michael Weisbrot and Family/Stock, Boston)

> A state offense . . . must be limited to works which, taken as a whole, appeal to the prurient interest in sex, which portray sexual activity in a patently offensive way, and which, taken as a whole, do not have serious literary, artistic, political, or scientific value.

The reality of defining each of the elements of the formula in the hurly-burly of the courtroom has proved to be something less than precise. Obviously, many prosecutors don't bother to try. It is equally obvious that some do. Larry Flynt, publisher of *Hustler* magazine, has been prosecuted in several states and found guilty of obscenity in at least two, Georgia[33] and Ohio.[34] Despite such actions, the magazine continues to be published and is widely available, along with more explicit materials. Harry Reems, one of the "stars" of *Deep Throat*, which has become one of the classics of porn movies, was found guilty by a federal jury in Memphis of conspiring to transport obscene material—the movie—across state lines.[35] More recently, the same movie was shown several times on the Indiana University campus as a fund-raiser for a student residence hall. But when a residence hall showed another porn classic, *Insatiable*, in 1985, police moved in at the

33. Flynt v. State, 264 S.E. 2d 669 (Ga. App. 1980).
34. Stephen Grover, "Pornography and Community Standards," *Wall Street Journal*, 2 February 1977.
35. Ibid.

second showing and confiscated the film. The student who arranged the showing was subsequently charged with a violation of the Indiana obscenity law.[36]

The widely varying attitudes toward enforcement of obscenity laws reflect not only varying community standards, but society's ambiguity toward the public treatment of human sexuality. One extreme is illustrated by the widespread opposition to sex education in the public schools. The other is illustrated by a series of interviews on ABC's "Good Morning America" with teenagers who said sexual activity was common among their peers.[37]

Currently, this battle against sexual materials has taken a new tack. Feminist groups, backed by evidence obtained in the psychological studies of Edward Donnerstein and others, have attacked pornography as contributing to violence against women. City councils in Minneapolis and Indianapolis were impressed enough by the arguments to enact ordinances in 1984 treating obscenity as a violation of women's civil rights.[38] The mayor of Minneapolis vetoed that city's ordinance, acting on his belief that it was unconstitutional. Two federal courts held that the Indianapolis law was unconstitutional because it did not define obscenity in *Roth-Miller* terms.[39] As written, the law defined pornography as the "graphic sexually explicit subordination of women," which it then said was a form of discrimination against women. The courts said government does have an interest in preventing sexual discrimination, but that interest is not great enough to overcome the First Amendment interest in freedom of speech and press.

In the Professional World

The Supreme Court said in *Paris* that legislators are free to act on the assumption that obscenity detracts from "the quality of life, . . . the tone of commerce in the great city centers, and, possibly, the public safety itself." But in its own definition of obscenity, the Court has limited that term to sexually explicit materials and has avoided any consideration of the question of harm. Under *Roth-Miller*, those who deal in sexually explicit materials can be punished, not because it can be proved that the dealers have caused any harm, but because, in the opinion of a jury, their wares are devoid of serious ideas.

But also in *Paris*, Chief Justice Burger, writing for a majority of the Court, referred to "the well nigh universal belief that good books, plays, and art lift the spirit, improve the mind, enrich the human personality, and develop character. . . ." Communications theorists disagree over the extent to which that belief can be proved, but all agree that visual messages do have some effect on some people some of the time. Our educational system is grounded in the belief that words and pictures can impart knowledge, and can modify beliefs and behavior. World-wide religious institutions have been built on the power of the word. Business firms

---

36. Author's knowledge of the events.
37. Week of 10–14 February 1986. Some of the segments focused on parental objections to sex education in the schools; others, on what teenagers themselves knew and thought about sexual activity.
38. "Minneapolis Mayor Vetoes Porn Bill," *Facts on File*, 20 January 1984, p. 35F2; "Indianapolis Porn Law Challenged," *Facts on File*, 6 July 1984, p. 488D3.
39. American Booksellers Association v. Hudnut, 598 F.Supp. 1316 (S.D.Ind. 1984); affirmed, 771 F2d. 323 (7th Cir. 1985). In 1986, the Supreme Court affirmed, six-to-three, without writing an opinion.

spend billions of dollars every year on messages designed to win friends and persuade customers to buy their products or services. Governments spend other billions on information services and public relations. In this country, most mass media could not exist without the support they receive from advertisers seeking to influence an audience. Still more billions are spent on various forms of entertainment, which may have more influence on behavior than any other medium.

The belief, supported by considerable evidence, that communications has an effect on society raises interesting questions for professional communicators of all kinds. Despite the fears of the authors interviewed by the *New York Times* at the time of the *Miller* decision,[40] few professionals will ever come close to being prosecuted for obscenity. One has only to read some of the best-selling fiction or watch an R-rated movie to know that. So, for most communicators, the possibility of a prosecution for obscenity is not an issue.

However, anyone who is moderately aware of events knows that the portrayal of sex in the mass media is an issue. And so, to a perhaps lesser extent, is the portrayal of violence. The short-lived ordinances in Minneapolis and Indianapolis, and the experiments of Edward Donnerstein indicate that still other issues are raised when sex and violence are linked. Professional communicators ranging from reporters through advertising and public relations practitioners to recording artists deal with one or both in a variety of situations, sometimes without much thought for the consequences, at other times after calculating them closely. A short section of this kind cannot deal with all of the questions raised by portrayals of sex and violence in the mass media. It can only point to some of the problems.

The spectrum begins with the treatment of words considered profane or vulgar. The Supreme Court has held that even the "strongest" of such words is protected by the First Amendment.[41] However, the *Associated Press Stylebook* advises journalists not to use them "unless they are part of direct quotations and there is a compelling reason for them."[42] Many editors have learned that it may not be advisable even then. When the *Louisville Courier-Journal* ran an unexpurgated version of a report on the causes of the riot in Chicago during the Democratic National Convention in 1968, Norman Isaacs, executive editor, said he wrote hundreds of letters of apology to protesting readers.[43] They were offended by the report's frequent use of variations on the vulgarism for sexual intercourse, which the demonstrators used to provoke the police. More recently, the wives of several highly placed federal officials formed a nationwide organization—Parents Music Resource Center—to protest the use of explicit sexual language and hatefulness on rock recordings. They succeeded in getting some recording companies to agree to a labeling system, something like the rating system for movies, to advise buyers as to the nature of the content.[44]

Questions of another kind are raised by portrayals of sex designed to sell products or attract viewers to a form of entertainment. It is a truism of both the advertising

---

40. See note 19 above.
41. See note 3 above.
42. Christopher W. French, Eileen Alt Powell, and Howard Angione, eds., *The Associated Press Stylebook* (New York: The Associated Press, 1984), p. 143.
43. Interview with Norman Isaacs at the time.
44. Michael Cieply, "Records May Soon Carry Warning that Lyrics Are Morally Hazardous," *Wall Street Journal*, 31 July 1985.

and entertainment worlds that sex sells. This is despite the fact that some church groups have organized campaigns against what they consider television's overexposure of women's breasts and buttocks. When the owner of a weekly newspaper in rural southern Indiana announced that he was going to build a cable television system, he said he was the target of two questions: "You are going to show R-rated movies, aren't you?" and, "You aren't going to show R-rated movies, are you?"[45] He decided he wouldn't.

One of the many valid questions about sex in the media is, "To what extent does it contribute to reinforcing of stereotypes about sexual roles?" What of the brewers' television ads that show trim, virile young men trooping off the job into a bar where they have a great time while ordering beer by the pitcher? The only women in sight either are looking at the men adoringly or are waitresses, who not only serve the men but are the objects of their playful pranks. Other ads hold out the promise of loving attention from seductive women to the man who uses the right shaving cream or who drives the right car.

It is obvious that in the professional world there are no clear limits as to how far media managers will go in the exploitation of sex. Few newspapers carry cigarette advertising. But many carry advertising for X-rated movies. Most confine such advertising to a listing of the movie titles. Only a few permit illustrations. If these portray the actors and actresses in the nude, most advertising departments will use an air brush to clothe them. There is no way of knowing whether such delicacy is dictated by ethical considerations or by an unwillingness to offend some portion of the newspaper's subscribers.

Whatever their standards with respect to the treatment of sex, very few of the mainstream mass media will show the act that creates life. Any allusions to it are treated delicately, even by the columnists who specialize in sexual, medical, and personal advice. In part, this is because depictions of sexual activity are at the threshold of a finding of obscenity. In part, it is also because, until recent times, sex was not considered a topic for polite conversation. Further, as Chief Justice Burger pointed out in *Paris*, it is a crime to engage in sexual intercourse "at high noon in Times Square"—or in any other public place. The same reasoning that makes public intercourse a crime, Burger wrote, justifies making public portrayal of it a crime if that portrayal serves no serious purpose.

Author Ross Macdonald, in the *Times* article referred to above, noted the inconsistency in the chief justice's reasoning. Murder is also a crime, whether committed in Times Square at high noon or in private. Further, murder occurs more frequently in the United States, by most measures, than in almost any other nation. In 1984, nearly 19,000 Americans had their lives taken by another person.[46] As a cause of death, murder ranked twelfth in frequency, just behind suicide and ahead of deaths resulting from pregnancy, kidney disease, congenital defects, and blood disease.[47] As a problem of our society, violent death would seem to be somewhat comparable to the problems associated with sexual activity.

And yet there is no outcry against the portrayal of violent death—whether on

---

45. Conversation with the author.
46. Federal Bureau of Investigation, U.S. Crime Reports, *World Almanac*, 1986, p. 791.
47. National Center for Health Statistics, Leading Causes of Death by Sex and Race, *World Almanac*, 1986, p. 782.

television, in the movies, in the news, or in books—comparable to the outcry over the portrayal of sexual activity. Murder has been a staple of drama and fiction from earliest times. Homer's *Odyssey*, written three thousand years ago, describes in gory detail the manner in which Odysseus killed his wife's suitors when he returned home in disguise after the siege of Troy. And any well-done version of Shakespeare's *Macbeth* literally drips blood.

However, it is only in recent times that filmmakers and television scriptwriters have produced works in which violence as violence plays the leading role. Special-effects technicians have become experts in showing what happens when a chain saw cuts through flesh and bone, an ax cleaves a skull, or a bullet smashes through a brain. Films like *Texas Chainsaw Massacre, Maniac,* and *The Slumber Party Massacre* have become cult movies for younger people. Television producers, responding to pressure from some groups, have cleaned up their scripts somewhat from the days when viewers could see twenty or so persons killed in one evening's prime time,[48] but dramas featuring various kinds of skullduggery continue to dot the upper levels of the Nielsen ratings. Statistics measuring the effects of violence in the media probably are no more reliable than statistics measuring the effects of sexually explicit materials. And yet there are research studies showing that people who watch a lot of television tend to believe crime is more prevalent than it is,[49] and that exposure to filmed violence, especially when it is linked with sex, tends to desensitize the members of the audience toward sex crimes.[50] This is not to suggest, in a textbook devoted in large part to First Amendment freedoms, that obscenity laws should be broadened to include portrayals of violence. It is to suggest that professionals in a position to control what the media offer to the public may need to think beyond a consideration of what sells as entertainment or what will sell a product. Sex and death are inescapable realities. Treated with respect, sex can unite two persons like no other force. Treated with respect, death can be a sublime escape, or a tragedy reminding the survivors that life is too precious to waste. Trivialized, both sex and the taking of life can become meaningless acts.

FOR REVIEW

1. Outline the arguments for and against restrictions on obscenity.

2. What is the nature of the crime of obscenity?

3. How did the Supreme Court define obscenity in *Roth* v. *United States?*

4. List and explain the changes in obscenity law resulting from the Court's decision in *Miller* v. *California.*

5. Outline and explain the role of the jury in obscenity cases. Is it true that a jury has unbridled discretion in determining what is obscene? Why or why not?

6. What is the "community" in an obscenity case? How are its standards of sexual candor determined?

---

48. Author's count during one evening as a relative's captive audience in the 1960s.
49. George Gerbner et al., "The 'Mainstreaming' of America: Violence Profile No. 11," *Journal of Communication*, vol. 30, 1980, No. 3, pp. 10–29.
50. "Sexual Violence in the Media," note 7 above.

CHAPTER 10

THE ELECTRONIC MEDIA

Broadcasting—AM and FM radio, and television—is the only medium of communication licensed by the federal government. Radio stations are licensed for periods of seven years; television stations, for five. Renewal is not automatic. Broadcasters must be prepared to prove, if challenged, that they have operated their stations in the public interest.

Licensing has been in effect for more than fifty years. It was imposed at the request of broadcasters themselves and grew out of the nature of the medium. Broadcasting stations operate on wavelengths, or frequencies, in an electromagnetic spectrum. If two stations within range of each other try to operate on the same frequency, the result is interference, which may prevent both from being heard. In 1927 Congress established the Federal Radio Commission and gave it authority to license broadcasting stations to operate on a specified frequency. Congress acted on the theory that the airwaves—the electromagnetic spectrum—belong to the people, and therefore should be regulated in the public interest. The frequencies in that spectrum were seen as a scarce resource to be doled out by federal officials to those who offer the best service to the public.

Over the years, the focus of the government's concern shifted from prevention of electronic interference to assuring variety in programing. During the 1930s, when Adolf Hitler used radio to help him rise to power in Germany, broadcasting was recognized as a powerful means of reaching people and persuading them to a point of view. As a result, government's power to assign frequencies was broadened to cover the way those frequencies could be used. Rules were adopted that were designed to prevent one political candidate, or one point of view on public issues, from dominating the airwaves. Although these rules raised serious First Amendment questions, they were upheld by the courts, acting on the theory that it is more important for a diversity of opinion to reach the audience than it is for license holders to exercise unrestricted freedom of speech. Thus it became well established that owners of broadcasting stations did not enjoy the same editorial freedom enjoyed by owners of newspapers and magazines. Regulation of the content of broadcasting was justified in the belief that it was in the public interest to do so.

For decades, broadcasting prospered under this regulatory system. While the number of daily newspapers remained stable at about 1,750, broadcasting stations showed spectacular increases in numbers. By the mid-1980s, there were more than 9,500 stations, about equally divided between AM and FM bands. Television, which did not become commercially feasible until the 1950s, reached 98 percent of the people through about 630 UHF stations and 80 VHF.[1] VHF stations operate over the air on channels 2 through 13; UHF, on channels 14 through 83. The audience for many of the television stations has been extended by means of cable television systems, which by 1985 reached about 40 percent of the viewers. In more than 18,000 communities, sophisticated antennas were used to pluck distant signals from orbiting satellites and give cable subscribers their choice of a dozen or more stations. Cable systems also offered their subscribers channels devoted exclusively to news, movies, sports events, and rock music groups. Some cable users could tune in daily to the activities of Congress. Newspaper

---

1. The number of broadcasting stations licensed by the Federal Communications Commission is listed regularly in *Broadcasting* magazine.

publishers and others experimented with interactive systems capable of delivering news and information to subscribers on a demand basis.

The rapid proliferation of electronic media, coupled with a change in the political climate as the 1980s began, raised challenges to the federal regulatory system. Were broadcasting frequencies still a scarce commodity? Only about three dozen cities were left with competing newspapers. But the owner of even the cheapest radio could tune in to several stations. Most television viewers had access to three or more stations; those on cable could get several times that many. With so many competing broadcasters, was it still necessary to use the power of government to ensure variety in content?

In response to such questions, President Jimmy Carter suggested toward the end of his term that the Federal Communications Commission, successor to the original Federal Radio Commission, consider deregulating broadcasting. Studies begun in 1980 were carried forward during the administration of President Reagan. In 1981, the FCC lifted many restrictions from commercial radio.[2] It followed in 1984 with a similar lifting of restrictions on commercial television.[3] Both steps were challenged by groups who believed that the quality of public debate on the air would decline and that easier license renewal procedures would make it more difficult for minority groups to acquire licenses to broadcast. Critics of deregulation also decried the disappearance of wholesome children's programing and what they perceived as an increase in the amount of sexually oriented programing, especially on cable.

Broadcasting regulation is in a state of flux as this is being written. In response to what appeared to be an invitation from the Supreme Court, broadcasters are challenging the long-established rationale supporting regulation. They are arguing that because broadcast frequencies no longer are a scarce commodity, programing can be regulated more fairly and more efficiently in the public interest by market forces than by a government agency.

Because of the uncertainties, this chapter focuses on those aspects of broadcasting regulation that were in effect in 1986 and on the principles on which they were based. We will begin by looking at the history of broadcasting in order to get an understanding of why it is the only medium of communication licensed by government. We will find that the courts consistently have held that federal regulators have broad powers to ensure that persons who obtain a license to broadcast must use it in the public interest. We will also see that Congress and the courts have been particularly aware of broadcasting's power as a political medium. By law, political candidates must have an **equal opportunity** to reach the public by radio or television. In practice, this has meant that a station that sells time to one candidate for a public office must stand ready to sell equivalent time to his or her opponents. Under certain limited circumstances, it sometimes means that a station must give time to candidates. Congress requires stations to sell reasonable amounts of time to candidates for federal offices.

The equal opportunities requirement does not apply to bona-fide news coverage of political campaigns. However, a section of broadcast law called the **fairness doctrine** does, as of this writing. It requires broadcasters to identify controversial public issues and present various points of view on them. The doctrine is applied to all aspects of a station's

---

2. Report and Order (BC Dkt. No. 79-219), 84 F.C.C.2d 968; recon., 87 F.C.C.2d 797 (1981).
3. Report and Order (BC Dkt. No. 81-496), F.C.C. 84-294, 22 August 1984.

programing and requires that the treatment of issues be balanced over time. Thus, in a real sense, it has restricted the First Amendment freedoms of station owners. While enforcement of the doctrine seldom has led to a station's losing its license, its very presence has served to get viewpoints on the air that otherwise might have been ignored. Critics of the doctrine argue that it either has led to a false balance, in which extremist views get more attention than they are worth, or has led broadcasters to ignore issues so as to avoid bringing the doctrine into play. In 1985, the Federal Communications Commission joined the fray, recommending that the doctrine be repealed because it "chills and coerces speech."[4]

While the fairness doctrine has required stations to present different points of view, the Supreme Court has held that it does not give any particular person or group a right of access to the airwaves, except for victims of personal attacks. Thus, the Court has upheld the right of stations to refuse to sell time for cause advertisements.

Broadcasters also are more restricted than owners of print media in their right to present sexual materials or language some people consider offensive. Publishers and film makers cannot be punished unless their wares are found to be obscene by *Miller-Roth* standards. (See Chapter 9.) The Supreme Court has held that broadcasters are subject to censure by the FCC if their offerings are in bad taste, especially at times when children might be listening or watching.

The closing sections of the chapter will deal with the movement toward deregulation of broadcasting and with the rapid rise in cable and satellite systems. Cable particularly raises new kinds of First Amendment questions because in the future it may be a monopolistic means of delivering not only entertainment but information of all kinds.

Major Cases

CBS, Inc. v. *Federal Communications Commission*, 453 U.S. 367, 101 S.Ct. 2813, 69 L.Ed.2d 706 (1981).

Columbia Broadcasting System v. *Democratic National Committee*, 412 U.S. 94, 93 S.Ct. 2080, 36 L.Ed.2d 772 (1973).

Democratic National Committee v. *Federal Communications Commission*, 717 F.2d 1471 (D.C.Cir. 1983).

Federal Communications Commission v. *Pacifica Foundation*, 438 U.S. 726, 98 S.Ct. 3026, 57 L.Ed.2d 1073 (1978).

National Broadcasting Co. v. *United States*, 319 U.S. 190, 63 S.Ct. 997, 87 L.Ed.2d 1344 (1943).

Office of Communication, United Church of Christ v. *Federal Communications Commission*, 359 F.2d 994 (D.C.Cir. 1966).

Paulsen v. *Federal Communications Commission*, 491 F.2d 887 (9th Cir. 1974).

---

4. In the Matter of Inquiry into Section 73.1910 of the Commission's Rules and Regulations Concerning the General Fairness Doctrine Obligations of Broadcast Licensees (Gen. Dkt. No. 84-282), F.C.C. 85-459, 7 August 1985.

LICENSING IN THE PUBLIC INTEREST

The Regulation of Broadcasting

There is no doubt about the government's authority to regulate broadcasting in the public interest. The legal challenges to that authority were met and overcome more than forty years ago.

The first questions were raised in the 1920s, when the government, in cooperation with Canada and Mexico, adopted an orderly process for assigning frequencies, prescribing limits on transmitter power, and setting hours of operation. Ninety-six of the 107 channels on the AM band were reserved for stations in the United States. Forty of these were set aside for clear-channel operation; that is, for the exclusive use of one powerful station. The rationale was that the clear-channel stations could reach out, especially at night, and provide news and entertainment for listeners in even the most remote parts of the country. The remaining fifty-six channels were assigned to low-power local stations on a zoned basis. The result was supposed to be a system of broadcasting that would serve the entire nation with a minimum of electronic interference.

Stations that were forced to change frequencies or reduce power if they were to retain their licenses challenged the government's authority. This led to court decisions holding that broadcasters were engaged in interstate commerce and therefore were within the reach of federal regulation.[5] Owners threatened with loss of their licenses because they refused to comply with the new regulations argued that the government was taking their property without due process of law, thus violating the Fifth and Fourteenth Amendments to the Constitution. Courts held that a broadcasting license was not a form of property belonging to the station owner. It was only a token of the station owner's right to use a frequency belonging to the people. That right was valid only as long as the station owner served the "public interest, convenience, and necessity." However, a broadcaster faced with nonrenewal or revocation of his license was entitled to a hearing before the Federal Radio Commission. If the commission then acted within its powers in deciding not to renew or to revoke, the due process requirement was met.[6]

Can a refusal to renew a broadcasting license violate the station owner's First Amendment right to freedom of speech? That question was raised in *Trinity Methodist Church, South v. Federal Radio Commission*,[7] decided by the U.S. Court of Appeals for the District of Columbia Circuit in 1932. Radio station KGEF in Los Angeles was owned by the church, whose pastor, Rev. R. P. Shuler, used it as an extension of his pulpit. He was an opinionated, outspoken preacher who mixed politics with religion and became one of few persons held in contempt of court for statements made over the air.[8] His targets included gamblers, bootleggers, labor unions, judges, the bar association, Jews, and Roman Catholics. As he saw it, all were involved in ungodly immorality, and he said so in strong terms, using the station to spread his views. When KGEF's license

---

5. United States v. American Bond & Mortgage Co., 31 F.2d 448 (N.D.Ill. 1929).
6. Technical Radio Laboratory v. Federal Radio Commission, 36 F.2d 111 (D.C.Cir. 1929).
7. 62 F.2d 850 (D.C.Cir. 1932).
8. Ex parte Shuler, 292 P. 481 (Calif. 1930).

came up for renewal in 1930, some listeners objected. After hearing more than ninety witnesses, the FRC refused to renew. The church appealed, arguing that the commission's action was a prior restraint of the kind the Supreme Court recently had condemned in *Near* v. *Minnesota* (see page 33).[9]

The Court of Appeals rejected that argument, holding that the commission was acting within its powers when it refused to renew the license. The court said that a license to broadcast did not give the holder an unlimited right to spread hatred "from one corner of the country to the other." If licensees could do so, "then this great science, instead of a boon, will become a scourge, and the nation a theater for the display of individual passions and the collision of personal interests." The court said the commission's action was "neither censorship nor previous restraint," nor was it "a whittling away of the rights guaranteed by the First Amendment." It was simply an exercise of the FRC's authority to make certain that the airwaves were used in a way that served the public interest. It was in the public's interest to deny use of one of those frequencies to spread Dr. Shuler's strong opinions.

These early lower-court decisions, handed down when broadcasting was in its infancy, proved influential in shaping judicial attitudes. They established that broadcasters must obtain a license from the federal government before they can go on the air. To obtain a license, they must promise to serve the public interest. To retain it, broadcasters must prove that they have done so. No matter how much broadcasters may invest in buildings and equipment in order to go on the air, they do not own the license that permits them to do so. The license is merely a permit to use a frequency that belongs to the people as a whole, a permit that may not be used at the whim of the holder. If it should be used in a one-sided way to spread a message that violates the public's concept of decency and fair play, the right to use a frequency can be taken away. This has not happened often. But the possibility has been there since 1932 and has had an effect on broadcasting for more than fifty years.

Thus, almost from the beginning, the courts have applied a different set of rules to broadcasters than to other media. A newspaper publisher's right to express a point of view is limited only by the willingness of the people to keep on buying the publication. As we have seen, the courts have given publishers and film makers wide latitude to say what they please, particularly about public issues. Broadcasters have not enjoyed that same degree of freedom because they must go to government for a license that gives them a right to use an assigned frequency on which to transmit their messages to the public.

Broadcasting and the Supreme Court

Radio came to maturity in World War II. Germany's conquest of Poland, France, Denmark, and Norway under direction from Adolf Hitler was brought to Americans step by step through shortwave transmissions that were rebroadcast over networks of domestic stations. The voice of Hitler himself came directly from his carefully orchestrated Nazi party rallies. Correspondents such as William L. Shirer, H. V. Kaltenborn, and Edward

---

9. 283 U.S. 697, 51 S.Ct. 625, 75 L.Ed. 1357 (1931).

Radio, carrying news and entertainment over the airwaves, reached even remote farm families like this one, photographed in Hood River County, Oregon, in 1925. To ensure that scarce frequencies were used in the public interest, Congress established the Federal Radio Commission in 1927. (Culver Pictures)

R. Murrow broadcast dramatic accounts of these and other events. When London came under massive German air attacks in 1940, Americans sitting in their living rooms could hear by radio the crack of antiaircraft guns, the wail of air raid sirens, and the thud of bombs, while a reporter described the action.

Radio also served other purposes. During the Great Depression it became the only source of entertainment for many who no longer could afford to go to the movies. Networks of local radio stations were formed by the National Broadcasting Company and the Columbia Broadcasting System to carry entertainment and news across the country. So great was the demand for such programing that NBC broke its network into two, called the Blue and the Red networks. Radio also provided a nationwide audience for championship boxing matches, college football, and the World Series of baseball. A ruckus over the broadcasting of the latter event gave the Supreme Court its first opportunity to review the powers of the Federal Communications Commission, which had replaced the Federal Radio Commission in 1934. With the change in name came broadened responsibilities, not only for radio, but for interstate telephone and telegraph systems.

In 1938, the FCC became concerned enough about the growth of network broadcasting to conduct seventy-three days of hearings, spread over more than a year. While it was pondering the mass of evidence gathered by the hearings, a new network, Mutual, bid for and obtained the right to broadcast the World Series of 1939 between the New York Yankees and the Cincinnati Reds. Because Mutual stations were relatively few, baseball fans in some parts of the United States were unable to hear the games. Stations affiliated with CBS and NBC were willing to air the games in areas not served by Mutual affiliates, but were blocked by terms of their network contracts. The resulting furor was reflected in the chain broadcasting regulations drafted by the FCC to take effect in 1941.

The Federal Communications Commission conceded that it could not regulate the networks directly because they did not require a license to operate. However, it proceeded on the theory that it could regulate network practices by imposing restrictions on the affiliated stations. The new rules said that any station that was a party to a network contract containing certain prohibited conditions would not have its license renewed. NBC and CBS joined forces in asking a federal court to nullify the rules. The court dismissed their plea. In *National Broadcasting Co.*

National Broadcasting Co. v. United States, 319 U.S. 190, 63 S.Ct. 997, 87 L.Ed. 1344 (1943).

v. *United States*, the Supreme Court affirmed. It held that to protect the public interest, the FCC can impose reasonable regulations on broadcasters consistent with the powers given it by Congress.

The Court began its analysis by noting that NBC and CBS had gained an almost complete monopoly over programing, especially at night. Together, they controlled more than 85 percent of the night-time wattage, a measure of a station's ability to reach its audience. The Court also took note of the fact that this control had prevented persons in some parts of the country from hearing the 1939 World Series.

Justice Felix Frankfurter, writing for five members of the Court, proceeded to an examination of each of the eight abuses found by the FCC and that it sought to correct:

1. A station affiliated with NBC or CBS could not broadcast a program originated by any other network. The effect of this restriction was to make it difficult for other networks to be formed. It also had the effect of denying certain programing to persons in some parts of the country. The FCC proposed to correct this by refusing to renew the license of any station signing an exclusive affiliation agreement.

2. Both networks had agreed not to sell programs to any other station in an area covered by an affiliate. Thus, if a local station chose for some reason not to carry a network offering, no other station in the same area could pick it up. The FCC rules would permit other stations to carry such rejected programing.

3. Affiliation agreements were for five-year periods. The FCC wanted to limit them to two years, or one year less than the three-year license period then in effect.

4. All three networks required their affiliates to take a certain number of hours of network programing each day, thus limiting the time available for local programing. These required hours included prime time, when the station's potential audience was the largest. The FCC proposed cutting back this mandatory time.

5. Affiliates were restricted in the number of network offerings they could refuse. Thus local stations were captives of the networks, which, in turn,

let their advertisers dictate program content. The public, then, was being offered programing over which local license holders had little, if any, control. The FCC saw this as an abdication of the public interest role of broadcasting. The proposed regulations gave local stations the right to refuse any network program.

6. The networks also were becoming station owners. NBC owned ten; CBS, eight. These included some of the most powerful stations in the country, operating on the most desirable frequencies. The FCC said that if it could start over, it would not license any stations owned by a network. Since it could not do that it would simply limit a network to one station in any given market and reserve for later the decision as to the maximum number a network might own.

7. NBC operated two networks out of the same studios in Rockefeller Center in New York City. The FCC said this was one too many, but took no action on a recommendation that NBC be required to sell one of them. Later, the FCC adopted the recommendation, and one of NBC's two networks became the American Broadcasting Company.

8. NBC went as far as to control the local advertising rates its affiliates might charge for commercials inserted into network programs. The FCC would leave local stations free to charge what they would for advertising.

The networks argued that these proposals went beyond the powers Congress had given the Federal Communications Commission. If they were carried into effect, the government would violate the networks' First Amendment freedoms. The majority of the Court disagreed. In doing so, it adopted and amplified the public interest theme that had run through the lower-court decisions summarized in the first section of this chapter.

Reviewing the history of radio, Frankfurter said that the old FRC was brought into existence not merely to act as a sort of scientific traffic officer, policing frequencies and transmitter power, but to make certain that the new medium operated in the "public interest, convenience, and necessity." These words, he wrote, were not an empty litany, but a grant of power authorizing the commission to use its judgment in coping with the medium's complications. He continued:

> The "public interest" to be served under the Communications Act is thus the interest of the listening public in "the larger and more effective use of radio."
>
> The avowed aim of the Communications Act of 1934 was to secure the maximum benefits of radio to all of the people of the United States. To that end Congress endowed the Federal Communications Commission with comprehensive powers to promote and realize the vast potentialities of radio.

Thus the Court gave its endorsement to a principle that had emerged more than a decade earlier. Broadcasting is regulated so that it will serve the public in the broadest possible way. Those who are fortunate enough to obtain a license must use it first to serve their audiences and then to serve their own interests.

But surely, the networks argued, this mandate did not extend to them. They were not licensed. They merely provided needed programing to stations that were.

Frankfurter reminded the networks that their practices had denied some of that programing to people who had wanted it very badly. Thus, the FCC had intervened properly to make certain that the networks, too, served the public interest. To ensure that radio does serve the public, he wrote, Congress "gave the Commission not niggardly but expansive powers." This included authority to impose special rules on stations "engaged in chain broadcasting."

Frankfurter turned next to the argument that the regulations proposed by the FCC would abridge the networks' freedom of speech. He wrote: "If that be so, it would follow that every person whose application for a license to operate a station is denied by the Commission is thereby denied his constitutional right of free speech."

But that is not the case, the justice continued. Radio is not like newspapers or magazines. It operates in a medium that imposes physical limits on the number of stations that can use the available frequencies. It is not open to all who have the desire and the money to erect a transmitter. Some who would like to go on the air must be turned down. Congress gave the authority to make such choices to the Federal Communications Commission, acting for the people as a whole. Frankfurter said that if the FCC were to use the authority "to choose among applicants upon the basis of their political, economic or social views, or upon any other capricious basis," it would violate its trust.

But that was not the case in this instance, Frankfurter concluded. The FCC was using its licensing powers to strike down restrictive network rules that clearly had prevented member stations from serving the public interest. In doing so, he said, it had acted well within the authority given to it by Congress. The reasonable use of that authority did not violate the First Amendment.

The Court's decision was a solid victory for the Federal Communications Commission. Its proposed network regulations were put into effect and have carried over into the television era. But, in a broader sense, the *National Broadcasting Co.* decision has become a part of the foundation of the commission's power. The Court said that its grant of authority from Congress is to be construed broadly. The commission's authority is to be used to ensure that broadcasters serve the public, in the full meaning of that term. When broadcasters raise First Amendment questions, courts look first at the interests of the audience. Because not everyone who wants to do so can go on the air, those who are able to get a license must bow to the free-speech needs of those who cannot.

Serving the Public Interest

The *National Broadcasting Co.* decision firmly established that holders of broadcasting licenses must operate in the public interest. Strangely, more than twenty years would pass before courts would hold that the listening and viewing public has a voice in deciding what that means. Until the mid-1960s, the Federal Communications Commission rejected attempts by public interest groups to offer testimony at license renewal time on a station's programing. It changed its position only under prodding from the U.S. Court of Appeals for the District of Columbia Circuit in one of the rare instances in which a station lost its license for fairness doctrine violations.[10] The doctrine requires

---

10. Office of Communication, United Church of Christ v. Federal Communications Commission, 359 F.2d 994 (D.C.Cir. 1966).

stations to identify controversial issues and to carry a balanced version of the competing points of view.

This seems not to have happened on television station WLBT in Jackson, Mississippi, during the early years of the civil rights movement that began in the 1950s. Although nearly half its audience was made up of blacks, the station allegedly reflected a segregationist point of view. In response to complaints, the Office of Communication of the United Church of Christ joined civil rights organizations in monitoring the station's programing. From 1955 on, they noted a peculiar pattern of technical problems at the station. When black and white entertainers appeared on the same network television program, WLBT's viewers saw only a blank screen and the message "Sorry, cable trouble." The same trouble occurred when the station's network presented a documentary on racial integration. The station offered time to the White Citizens Council to argue the case for continued segregation in the schools. It refused black groups time to present the case for integration. When the station's license came up for renewal in the early 1960s, the Office of Communication asked the FCC to hear its evidence. The commission refused, noting that it granted a right to intervene only to station operators who could show either electronic interference or unfair economic competition from the license holder seeking renewal. However, the commission took note of fairness doctrine complaints that had been submitted to it in writing and renewed WLBT's license for only one year, instead of the normal three, making further renewal contingent on a showing of fairness in racial programing.

Office of Communication, United Church of Christ v. Federal Communications Commission, 359 F.2d 994 (D.C.Cir. 1966)

That was not good enough for the Office of Communication and its allies. They asked the court of appeals for an order permitting them to intervene in the renewal proceeding. Judge Warren E. Burger, then three years away from his elevation to chief justice of the United States, held that the FCC must permit them to do so.

Burger noted that the FCC had permitted intervention to protect a financial interest. He rationalized that television viewers, as well as owners of competing stations, had such an interest. He calculated that viewers had invested nearly $40 billion in receiving sets. That was twenty times the owners' investment in transmitters. Therefore, the viewers had a stake in making certain that those transmitters served their interests. If viewers could intervene at license renewal time, broadcasters would have an additional inducement to be "responsive to the needs of the audience."

Broadcasters argued that to the extent that viewers were given a voice in programing decisions, their own right to control content would be diminished. If that principle were carried to an extreme, broadcasters would be reduced to carrying whatever programs were demanded by some segment of the audience. Burger said his decision did not go that far. It simply stood as a reminder that when a "broadcaster seeks and is granted the free and exclusive use of a limited and valuable part of the public domain," he accepts a "franchise . . . burdened by enforceable public obligations." One of these obligations is to present balanced programing on controversial public issues, including points of view with which the owner disagrees. Burger added: "After nearly five decades of operation the broadcast industry does not seem to have grasped the simple fact that a broadcast license is a public trust subject to termination for breach of duty."

Burger said that by giving members of a station's audience a right to be heard at license renewal time, he was limiting the FCC's role in programing decisions. In the future, it could act as an impartial umpire when it received complaints about a station's service to the public. No longer need it be both prosecutor and judge.

The court emphatically disapproved the commission's decision to renew WLBT's license, even temporarily:

> We recognize that the Commission was confronted with a difficult problem and difficult choices, but it would perhaps not go too far to say it elected to post the Wolf to guard the Sheep in the hope that the Wolf would mend its ways because some protection was needed and none but the Wolf was handy. This is not a case, however, where the Wolf had either promised or demonstrated any capacity and willingness to change, for WLBT had stoutly denied . . . charges of programing misconduct and violations.

He sent the case back to the commission with orders that it listen to the complaining civil rights organizations. It did so, rejected the claims as not proved, and in 1968, renewed WLBT's license for three years. Again, there was an appeal to Judge Burger's court. This time, he rebuked the FCC, withdrew WLBT's license, and invited new applicants for the frequency.[11] The Wolf no longer was permitted to guard the Sheep.

The cases stood as a warning that a station could lose its license if it did not fairly serve the programing needs of its audience. They also stood for the right of members of that audience to pass judgment on programing and to make their views known to the commission as a part of license renewal proceedings. Seeing the prospect of endless hearings that would tie up license renewals indefinitely, the FCC tightened its rules to require public interveners to offer specific proof of fairness violations before they could ask for a hearing.

In a few other instances stations have lost their license, either for fairness doctrine complaints or for other reasons having to do with public service or undue concentration of media ownership. But, with more than 9,000 licenses in use, it is obvious that most are renewed routinely. If one listens at the right time, one can hear stations announcing that their license is about to expire and inviting comments on programing. Such announcements are made in response to the ruling in WLBT. But it is a rare exception to the rule if a complaint leads to a hearing. No station operator can be 100 percent certain of renewal. But the certainty is somewhere above 99 percent.

REGULATION OF BROADCAST CONTENT

The Equal Opportunities Law

Beginning with the Radio Act of 1927, the statutes have contained language designed to prevent radio, and now television, from being dominated by any political candidate

---

11. Office of Communication, United Church of Christ v. Federal Communications Commission, 425 F.2d 543 (D.C.Cir. 1969).

or party. Currently, §315 of the Broadcasting Act defines what is known as the equal opportunities requirement. Under its terms, a station that permits any candidate for public office to use its facilities to reach an audience must stand ready to permit equivalent use by the candidate's opponents. "Use" is defined in terms that exclude "bona fide" newscasts, documentaries, news events, and news interviews. As a practical matter, then, a political "use" is limited to paid messages in which the candidate is a participant, and to appearances in non-news programing, whether it be entertainment or a talk show not normally devoted to newsworthy issues. Under §315, no station is required to permit itself to be used by any candidate. If it does so, it can not censor the content of the candidate's message. And, of course, if it permits a use, paid or free, by one candidate, the equal opportunities provision comes into effect with respect to that candidate's opponents.

Other provisions of §315 require stations that elect to sell time to political candidates to do so at the lowest rate offered commercial advertisers. "Broadcasting stations" are defined to include cable television systems.

In 1972, Congress added a subsection to §312, not §315, that requires broadcasting stations to sell "reasonable amounts of time" to candidates for federal elective offices. Refusal to do so can result in loss of license. Thus broadcasting stations must make themselves available for use as a public forum by candidates for president, the House of Representatives, the Senate, and a few other elective federal offices, if they can pay for the time. Obviously, §§312 and 315 impose on broadcasters both duties and restrictions with respect to political campaigns that are not imposed on newspapers and magazines.

Broadcasters have chafed at these duties and restrictions. They have argued that they could do a more meaningful job of covering political campaigns if they did not have the FCC looking over their shoulders and applying a stopwatch to each use by a candidate. In 1981, at the urging of Mark S. Fowler, a chairman appointed by President Reagan, the commission asked Congress to repeal §315. The commission said repeal would put broadcasters in a position of "First Amendment parity" with the print media and make possible "greater opportunity for presentation of significant candidates' views to the public."[12] Congress refused to act on the proposal.

To qualify for access to air time under §315, a candidate must meet three criteria:[13]

1. He or she must be eligible for election to the office sought. In one instance, the FCC held that a thirty-one-year-old was not a legally qualified candidate for president because the Constitution says a president must be at least thirty-five.

2. He or she must be an announced candidate.

3. He or she must have taken the steps required by law to qualify for a place on the ballot. Candidates who seek write-in votes must show that they are conducting a campaign.

These criteria apply equally to primary and general elections. A primary is a preliminary election at which members of a political party select their candidates for office. If

---

12. F.C.C. Legislative Proposals, Track II, 17 September 1981, p. 22.
13. Material in this section and the next is drawn from *The Law of Political Broadcasting and Cablecasting*, Federal Communications Commission, 43 *Federal Register* 36342-36399, 16 August 1978.

nominations are made by convention or caucus, the candidate must make a serious showing of an effort to win the nomination.

In legal terms, a political spot announcement is a "use" if the candidate or the candidate's voice is identifiable in it. On the other hand, a political commercial of any length is not a "use" if the candidate's likeness or voice is not a part of it. The key to a use that will trigger §315 is the candidate's identity. If the candidate can be recognized by the viewer or listener, and the appearance is not covered by one of the four exemptions listed in the Act, it is a "use." If the candidate or his backers did not pay for such a use, then his or her opponents are entitled to a similar free use if they ask for it. It makes no difference if the original candidate's use had nothing to do with politics.

"Equal opportunities" goes beyond a counting of minutes. It starts there—if one candidate for governor buys thirty minutes of air time, the station must be willing to sell thirty minutes to his opponent—but also takes into account the potential audience. Thus, thirty minutes at 1 A.M. is not equal in opportunities to thirty minutes at 8 P.M. Usage must be scheduled so that each candidate can reach approximately the same number of persons. If a station offers help to one candidate in preparing for a use—in staging, graphics or whatever—it must offer the same help to his or her opponents. However, none of these provisions is self-triggering. A candidate who is seeking to balance an opponent's use, free or paid, must apply to the station within seven days of that use.

The equal opportunities provision balances paid time against paid time, free time against free time. There is no crossover between the two. If one candidate is able to buy a great deal of time, and the other can afford little or none, the station is under no obligation to balance the scales by giving the latter free time. If it were to do so, it would be obligated to give the first candidate free time if he or she asked for it, as almost certainly would happen.

The FCC has been quite liberal in defining bona-fide news programs subject to the four exemptions. Any station's regular news programs are exempt from equal opportunities requirements. Even in an instance in which one candidate for office was interviewed on a newscast five days in a row, the FCC ruled that §315 could not be invoked.[14] It has held that NBC's "Today,"[15] and CBS's "60 Minutes"[16] are bona-fide news programs.

To qualify as a "bona fide news interview," the interview must take place during a regularly scheduled, continuing series of programs devoted to newsworthy topics. Thus, such long-established programs as "Meet the Press," "Face the Nation," and "Issues and Answers" are exempt from the equal opportunities requirement.[17] A call-in show has been held to be exempt if it is regularly scheduled and is under the control of the station's news department.[18] But talk shows not primarily devoted to newsworthy topics do not qualify for exemption from §315. The commission looked at one such program and found that its content had ranged from "monsters in films to sexual fantasies to psychic healing and TV soap operas." Therefore, it held, a candidate's appearance on

---

14. Letter to Citizens for Reagan (WCKT-TV), 58 F.C.C.2d 925 (1976).
15. Lar Daly, 40 F.C.C. 314 (1960).
16. Letter to CBS, 58 F.C.C.2d 601 (1976).
17. Letters to Andrew J. Easter, 40 F.C.C. 307 (1960); Lar Daly, 40 F.C.C. 310 (1960); Hon. Frank Kowalski, 40 F.C.C. 355 (1962), and telegram to Yates for U.S. Senator Committee, 40 F.C.C. 368 (1962).
18. Socialist Labor Party, 7 F.C.C.2d 857 (1967).

the program had not resulted in a "bona fide news interview,"[19] and therefore was a "use."

There has been little dispute over the meaning of a "bona fide news documentary." If such programs are under the control of a station's or network's news department and are devoted to a newsworthy topic, they qualify for exemption.

However, there has been considerable dispute over the meaning of "on-the-spot coverage of bona fide news events." Some complaints have grown out of broadcasts by presidents to announce or comment on news events when they were candidates for reelection. In such instances, the commission generally has upheld the broadcaster's "reasonable, good-faith judgment" that the occasion was newsworthy. Debates among candidates for the same office are considered bona-fide news events, even when they are arranged by a broadcaster, and may be covered without triggering the equal opportunities requirement.[20] Press conferences held by candidates for public office also are considered news events.

Obviously, the FCC's interpretation of the bona fide-news exemptions written into §315 has given broadcasters considerable leeway to cover political campaigns as they see fit. Usually, this means that news coverage focuses on the candidates of the two mainstream political parties, Democrat and Republican. Thus, only the most diligent student of presidential campaigns is likely to know that at least four candidates other than Ronald Reagan and Walter Mondale aspired to the presidency in 1984, even though one of them, carrying the banner of the Libertarian Party, was on the ballot in thirty-eight states.

Few cases involving the equal opportunities provision have reached the courts. One of the more interesting of these raised this question: Should an actor who appears regularly on television be required to give up his job if he becomes a candidate for public office? Pat Paulsen, a comedian, argued that no one else must give up his or her occupation when he becomes a candidate. As he saw it, §315 discriminates against TV and radio performers. Paulsen's problem began in 1972 when he entered the New Hampshire primary as a candidate for the Republican nomination for president. His purpose was to poke fun at the news media's heavy focus on a mid-winter primary usually involving fewer than 200,000 voters. Shortly before his flirtation with politics, he had signed a contract with Walt Disney Productions to appear in a TV series, "The Mouse Factory." One episode would be telecast during the primary campaign. When the producer learned of Paulsen's candidacy, he asked the FCC whether that would raise equal opportunities problems. The FCC ruled that it would. When Disney canceled Paulsen's contract, the actor appealed first to the FCC and then to the U.S. Court of Appeals for the Ninth Circuit. In *Paulsen* v. *Federal Communications Commission*, the court upheld the producer and the FCC.

Paulsen v. *Federal Communications Commission*, 491 F.2d 887 (9th Cir. 1974).

The Court said the purpose of §315 was to require broadcasters to treat all candidates alike. Paulsen argued that he should be treated differently because his appearance in

---

19. Socialist Workers Party, 65 F.C.C.2d 234 (1976).
20. *The Law of Political Broadcasting and Cablecasting: A Political Primer—1984 Edition*, 100 F.C.C.2d 1476.

"The Mouse Factory" would be nonpolitical, he would have no control over the script, and, because he already was well known, the program would have no effect on his candidacy. The court said that if it were to accept his arguments, it would plunge the FCC into passing judgment on program content to distinguish between political and nonpolitical appearances. Further, it also would open a loophole that ingenious candidates could exploit by creating entertainment programs for no other purpose than to help them win election.

Nor did Paulsen get anywhere with his argument that §315 discriminates against TV and radio actors, thus denying them the equal protection of law guaranteed by the Fourteenth Amendment. The court held that the interest of Congress in "preventing unfair and unequal use of the broadcast media" for political purposes was important enough to outweigh such discrimination as might result.

The equal opportunities provision thus withstood an attempt to have it declared unconstitutional. In 1980 and 1984, prudent television station managers took care not to schedule Ronald Reagan movies for the duration of the presidential campaigns. One who did not take such care found himself required to give thirty-three minutes of air time—"enough to make me sick"—to one of Reagan's opponents in the Michigan Republican presidential primary.[21] That's how long actor Ronald Reagan had been on screen in the 1957 movie "Hell Cats of the Navy," which the manager had chosen to air. Thus, even an actor who was destined to become president of the United States does not enjoy special treatment under the equal opportunities provision of §315.

Political Candidates and Censorship

Section 315 flatly forbids broadcasters to censor a political candidate's use of their stations. Until 1984, the commission and the courts interpreted that provision to mean exactly what it says, no matter how crude or libelous the candidate's remarks. In that year, an unusual candidate, Larry Flynt, publisher of *Hustler* magazine, who proposed an unusual campaign message, led to an FCC staff conclusion that broadcasters could not be required to use obscene political advertisements.[22] The staff analysis pointed to another section of the Communications Act that makes it a crime to air obscenities. Short of that, broadcasters can exercise no control over the content of a political use, as is illustrated by an FCC ruling and a Supreme Court decision.

In 1972, one of the candidates in the Democratic primary for governor of Georgia was J. B. Stoner, an ardent segregationist. He made a series of spot announcements for radio and television in which he made blatant and vulgar attacks on blacks, vowing to "put them in their place" if he were elected. He used the epithet "nigger" repeatedly. The Atlanta unit of the National Association for the Advancement of Colored People, arguing that airing of the commercials was likely to incite racial violence, appealed to the FCC to ban them. The commission ruled that the stations could not keep them off the air unless they could show a "clear and present danger of imminent violence,"[23]

---

21. "Equal Time at Work," *Wall Street Journal*, 25 February 1980.
22. "Stations Needn't Show Political Ads with Obscenities," *Wall Street Journal*, 26 January 1984.
23. Atlanta N.A.A.C.P., 36 F.C.C.2d 635 (1972).

which they could not do. The commercials were broadcast on Georgia stations throughout the campaign. Most stations preceded and followed them with an advisory explaining that by law, and under orders from the FCC, they could not censor political broadcasts. Some stations also told listeners to direct complaints to the Stoner campaign headquarters or to the FCC rather than to the station.

During the 1980 presidential campaign, Barry Commoner, candidate of the Citizens Party, caused a brief stir by authorizing use of a radio spot announcement containing what the *New York Times* called "a barnyard expletive."[24] An announcer twice used the word to describe the political rhetoric of President Carter and his leading opponents, Ronald Reagan and John Anderson. The commercial was broadcast on the CBS and NBC radio networks, producing an immediate reaction. The networks and the Federal Communications Commission reported receiving thousands of letters and telephone calls from persons objecting to the use of the expletive. With the Stoner precedent firmly behind it, the FCC didn't bother to make a formal ruling. A press officer announced that §315 forbids broadcasters "from exercising any censorship on the use of air time by bona fide candidates." Bill Zimmerman, campaign director for Commoner, noted an irony in the attention the commercial received. He said the media had paid more attention to it than to the candidate's repeated attempts to deal seriously with the major problems facing the country. Commoner received about 234,000 votes in the District of Columbia and the thirty-two states where his name appeared on the ballot.

The Supreme Court held in 1959 that a station cannot be sued for a libel spoken during a political use. Ruling in *Farmers Educational and Cooperative Union of America v. WDAY*,[25] the Court said lawsuits must be directed at the candidate. The case grew out of an equal opportunity demanded by a minor candidate for United States senator from North Dakota after WDAY had given time to the two major-party candidates. The speaker devoted part of his time to an attack on the Farmers Union, accusing it of trying to establish "a Communist Farmers Union Soviet right here in North Dakota." The Union, which was a farmers' cooperative marketing organization and a strong political force in the state, sued both the candidate and the station for libel. When state courts dismissed the suit against the station, the Supreme Court agreed to take the case. It upheld the state courts, five-to-four. The majority noted that in writing §315 Congress had given broadcasting stations no option. If they gave or sold time to one candidate for political office, they had to be willing to give or sell time on request to his or her opponents. The law also said they could not censor a candidate's remarks.

The "Reasonable Time" Requirement

Section 312(a)(7) of the Communications Act requires broadcasters to sell reasonable amounts of time to candidates for federal offices. Congress adopted the provision because broadcasters in some large cities, where there are a number of congressional districts, had refused to sell time to candidates for the House. In 1981, the Supreme Court upheld the law and an FCC interpretation of it.

---

24. Bernard Weinraub, "One Word Is Worth a Thousand Speeches to Obscure Presidency Hopeful," *New York Times,* 16 October 1980.
25. 360 U.S. 525, 79 S.Ct. 1302, 3 L.Ed.2d 1407 (1959).

In October 1979, the Carter-Mondale Presidential Committee asked all three networks to sell it thirty minutes of air time during the first week of December. The purpose was

***CBS, Inc.* v. *Federal Communications Commission,* 453 U.S. 367, 101 S.Ct. 2813, 69 L.Ed.2d 706 (1981).**

to announce the start of President Carter's reelection campaign. For various reasons, including the assertion that it was too early to start the 1980 political campaign, the networks refused to sell the requested time. The committee complained to the FCC, which ruled that the networks had violated §312(a)(7) by denying reasonable access to the airwaves. The networks took their case to the court of appeals, which affirmed the FCC's ruling. On further appeal, the Supreme Court did likewise.

Chief Justice Burger, writing for six members of the Court, held that the networks did not have the right to determine when a political campaign ought to begin. That is a decision to be made by politicians. However, the majority held that stations could refuse time to candidates for federal offices if they acted on some rational basis. It offered guidance as follows:

> In responding to access requests . . . broadcasters may also give weight to such factors as the amount of time previously sold to the candidate, the disruptive impact on regular programing, and the likelihood of requests for time by rival candidates under the equal opportunities provision. . . . These considerations may not be invoked as pretexts for denying access; to justify a negative response, broadcasters must cite a realistic danger of substantial program disruption—perhaps caused by insufficient notice to allow adjustments in the schedule—or of an excessive number of equal time requests. Further, in order to facilitate review by the Commission, broadcasters must explain their reasons for refusing time or making a more limited counteroffer. If broadcasters take the appropriate factors into account and act reasonably and in good faith, their decisions will be entitled to deference even if the Commission's analysis would have differed in the first instance. But if broadcasters adopt "across-the-board policies" and do not attempt to respond to the individualized situation of a particular candidate, the Commission is not compelled to sustain their denial of access.

The Court brushed aside CBS's argument that the reasonable access provision violated its First Amendment rights. The section was written, Burger said, to enhance the ability of candidates for federal office to present their views to the voting public. Thus it served the more important First Amendment interests of the people in receiving "information necessary for the effective operation of the democratic process."

The Fairness Doctrine

From the earliest days of federal regulation of broadcasting, critics of the medium, members of Congress, and others have been both awed and troubled by its potential as a mass medium of communication. In a way that carries more impact than words on paper, it can convey a message from Maine to California, Florida to Washington state, instantly, and with whatever emotional content the sender desires. Television has enhanced the impact, because the spoken word can be supported by pictures and graphic devices that carry the ring of truth. Television has shown the ability to pull the nation together, as it did with its 24-hours-a-day coverage of the assassination of President Kennedy and its aftermath. Or it can contribute to forces that have seemed to tear the nation apart, as with its coverage of the Vietnam War and the violent reaction to it on the nation's college campuses. Every president in modern times has resorted, first, to radio, as with Franklin D. Roosevelt, and then to television to go over the heads of the print media to reach the people.

The *Trinity Methodist Church* case (see p. 358) was an early manifestation of concern over the power of broadcasting to inflame public passions. That same concern was evidenced in 1941, during intense debate over whether the United States should enter World War II, in the FCC's ruling in *Mayflower Broadcasting Corp.*[26] The commission ruled that broadcast license holders could not use their stations to air their own views on public issues. But after the war ended, the FCC changed its mind. In its 1949 Report on Editorializing by Broadcast Licensees,[27] it held that broadcasters could argue a point of view, provided that air time also was made available to persons holding other points of view. This led to a series of commission rulings that formulated what has come to be known as "the fairness doctrine." In 1959, Congress gave the doctrine official sanction by amending §315(a) of the Communications Act to include this sentence:

> Nothing in the foregoing [the equal opportunities provision] shall be construed as relieving broadcasters, in connection with the presentation of newscasts, news interviews, news documentaries, and on-the-spot coverage of news events, from the obligation imposed upon them under this Act to operate in the public interest and to afford reasonable opportunity for the discussion of conflicting views of issues of public importance.

The doctrine is based on the same principles that underlie all governmental regulation of broadcasting. Broadcasters reach the public by sending signals through a medium that belongs to the people. The government, acting for the people, must decide who can use these scarce frequencies and on what terms. One of the terms is that the holder of a frequency must operate in the public interest. A most important public interest is " 'uninhibited, robust, wide-open' debate on public issues."[28] If such issues are to be resolved logically, broadcasters must open their microphones to all shades of opinion so that viewers and listeners can make up their minds on the basis of a balanced presentation of the facts and arguments. Thus the fairness doctrine is based on an affirmative theory of the First Amendment, which recognizes a responsibility on the part of government to encourage freedom of expression. In applying this theory to broadcasters, the courts have drawn a sharp distinction between broadcasting and all other media. As the Supreme Court demonstrated in *Miami Herald Publishing Co.* v. *Tornillo*, newspapers and other print media cannot be required by government to carry items rejected by their editors.[29] In that case, a majority of the Court said that the "treatment of public issues and public officials—whether fair or unfair"—is solely a matter of editorial judgment. News directors of broadcasting stations also have wide latitude for editorial judgments, but there is a federally imposed requirement that public issues and officials be treated fairly.

---

26. 8 F.C.C. 333 (1941).
27. 13 F.C.C. 1246 (1949).
28. *New York Times* v. *Sullivan*, 376 U.S. 254, quoted in the Introduction to the *Fairness Report*, 48 F.C.C.2d 1 (1974). The *Report* is the result of a three-year study of the fairness doctrine begun in 1971.
29. 418 U.S. 241, 94 S.Ct. 2831, 41 L.Ed.2d 730 (1974). See p. 431 of this book.

In the simplest terms, the elements of the fairness doctrine are as follows:

1. Broadcasters have a duty to identify controversial issues of public interest and to present programing dealing with them.

2. This can be done on the station's regular newscasts, supplemented by documentaries, panel discussions, special interviews, or call-in programs featuring persons advocating a particular point of view.

3. On any given issue, such programing must give proponents of all shades of opinion a good-faith opportunity to be heard. This need not be done all at once, but balance must be achieved within a reasonable time.

4. Broadcasters are to exercise reasonable news judgment in seeking out advocates of various points of view and in determining when balance and fairness have been achieved.

5. Broadcasters may sell time to advocates of a particular point of view on a controversial public issue, but if they do, they must achieve balance either by selling time to others with differing views or by offering other points of view in their own programing.

6. Broadcasters also are permitted to editorialize, advocating a particular solution to a public issue. But if they do, they must make an offer of free time to proponents of other points of view so as to balance the presentation.

7. The system is policed through complaints made to the FCC. However, the reality is that only a very few of these are considered serious enough to survive summary rejection by the commission's staff.

8. Compliance with the fairness doctrine is one of the factors taken into account when a station's license is being renewed. Theoretically, a station can lose its license for serious breaches of fairness. This has happened in a few instances.

9. Persons who become victims of a personal attack during the broadcast discussion of a controversial public issue must be notified and given an opportunity to respond. Thus, there is a strictly limited right of personal access to the airwaves under the fairness doctrine.

The fairness doctrine should not be confused with the equal opportunities provision discussed earlier. The two are related, and even intertwined, but there are also marked differences between them. The equal opportunities provision of §315 is concerned solely with candidates for public office, that is, with *human beings*. It applies only to specified uses of the air time by those candidates—either paid commercial time or appearances outside of bona-fide news programs.

The fairness doctrine is concerned with *ideas* and *issues*. Station owners are charged with identifying controversial public issues and offering discussion of them from differing points of view. The doctrine is not concerned with who does the discussing. It can be station personnel or outsiders chosen for the insights they can present. The choice of speakers is left to management's news judgment. The fairness doctrine applies to all of a station's public affairs programing. It requires that all such programing dealing with controversial issues of public importance come to a reasonable balance over time. Such balance is not measured with a stopwatch. It is a product of station management's news judgment, subject to review by the Federal Communications Commission on the basis of complaints from the audience. Such review is limited by court decisions to two questions:[30]

1. Were station management's judgments on achieving balance reasonable?

2. Were they made in good faith?

Decisions on fairness doctrine questions are highly subjective, both at the station and at the commission levels. When passions run high—on such issues as racial, religious, or sexual discrimination—what strikes one side as eminently fair may strike another as grossly unfair. It is not surprising, then, that the FCC has shown great reluctance to intervene in all but the most serious complaints. During three recent sample years, for instance, the commission sustained only thirteen of 15,189 fairness doctrine complaints.[31] The only penalty imposed was a letter from the commission to the broadcaster, noting the infraction. Such statistics can be misleading as to the effect of the doctrine. Evidence indicates that it influences some broadcasters simply because it is there. There is no telling how many talk-show appearances, or how many public service announcements, are designed to head off a fairness doctrine complaint.

The Fairness Doctrine in the Supreme Court

As interpreted by the Federal Communications Commission, the fairness doctrine guards against personal attacks during the discussion of a controversial issue of public importance. It does so by requiring that the victim of such an attack be notified, be given a tape or script of the offending remarks, and be offered an opportunity to reply. The FCC's attempt to enforce this rule led to a Supreme Court decision that upheld not only the right to reply, but the fairness doctrine itself. The decision, *Red Lion Broadcasting Co. v. Federal Communications Commission*,[32] has become a cornerstone of broadcast law, although it did little more than pull together the various currents flowing through court decisions examined earlier in this chapter.

In 1964, Fred J. Cook, a journalist who wrote books and magazine articles, learned that he was the target of a fifteen-minute radio broadcast carried by more than three hundred stations. The speaker was the Rev. Billy James Hargis, a radio and television evangelist, creator of the "Christian Crusade" series. In the Rev. Mr. Hargis's eyes, Cook was twice a sinner: He had written a campaign tract in 1964 that was highly critical of Barry Goldwater, the Republican candidate for president, and he had written an article attacking J. Edgar Hoover, for years director of the Federal Bureau of

---

30. Democratic National Committee v. Federal Communications Commission, 717 F.2d. 1471 (1983).
31. David Burnham, "F.C.C. to Examine Fairness Doctrine," *New York Times*, 12 April 1984.
32. 395 U.S. 367, 89 S.Ct. 1794, 23 L.Ed.2d 371 (1969).

Investigation. Hargis denounced Cook as a communist sympathizer, in the process distorting the circumstances that had led, years earlier, to Cook's departure from a New York City newspaper. The author considered filing a libel suit, then decided it would cost less to seek redress under the personal attack rule of the fairness doctrine. He prepared a letter asking for response time and mailed it to every station that had carried the Hargis broadcast. Some offered time without question, but WGCB, in the small town of Red Lion, Pennsylvania, was among those that sent Cook a rate card. WGCB took the position that because Hargis had paid for his time, Cook should pay for the response time. Cook appealed to the Federal Communications Commission for an order requiring WGCB to give him reply time without charge.

While this was going on, the FCC was in the process of redrafting the personal attack rule to make it more precise. It also sought to qualify the rule to forestall its use by political candidates as a means of getting free time on the air. It did so by stating that if a political candidate was the subject of a personal attack, the reply would have to be given by someone else. The commission limited the rule to attacks "upon the honesty, character, integrity or like personal qualities of an identified person or group."

The proposed rule was opposed strongly by broadcasters. Their fears were heightened when the FCC ordered WGCB to give Cook time for a reply to Hargis. The station appealed to the U.S. Court of Appeals for the District of Columbia. The Radio-Television News Directors Association, anticipating an unfavorable verdict by that court, began litigation in Chicago with a view to having both the personal attack rule and the fairness doctrine held in violation of the First Amendment. The Court of Appeals for the Seventh Circuit, based in Chicago, had a reputation for conservatism and the RTNDA believed that it would view the doctrine as a form of governmental intrusion into broadcasters' freedoms. The court did as expected, striking down the personal attack rule and the fairness doctrine. At about the same time, however, the District of Columbia circuit court also did as expected and upheld both, ordering WGCB to give Cook time on the air. The Supreme Court agreed to take both cases. It combined them under the *Red Lion* title, reversed the seventh circuit decision and upheld the ruling of the District of Columbia court.

Red Lion Broadcasting Co. v. Federal Communications Commission, 395 U.S. 367, 89 S.Ct. 1794, 23 L.Ed.2d 371 (1969).

Justice Byron R. White, writing for a unanimous Court except for one justice who abstained, reviewed the scarcity rationale for broadcast regulation. The First Amendment, he noted, gives no one the right to obtain a license. Nor does it give one who succeeds in getting a license greater First Amendment rights than those who do not. Then White reached the heart of the decision:

> Because of the scarcity of radio frequencies, the Government is permitted to put restrictions on licensees in favor of others whose views should be expressed on this unique medium. But the people as a whole retain their interest in free speech by radio and their collective right to have the medium function consistently with the ends and purposes of the First Amendment. It is the right of the viewers and listeners, not the right of the broadcasters, which is paramount. . . . It is the purpose of the First Amendment to preserve an uninhibited marketplace of ideas in which truth will ultimately prevail, rather than to countenance monopolization of the market, whether it be by the Government itself or a private

licensee. . . . It is the right of the public to receive suitable access to social, political, esthetic, moral and other ideas and experiences which is crucial here. That right may not constitutionally be abridged either by Congress or the F.C.C.

With the *Red Lion* decision, the Court upheld the fairness doctrine and the personal attack rule. On a narrower base, it upheld Fred Cook's right to use without charge a few minutes of WGCB's air time to defend his integrity as a journalist.

Right of Access to the Airwaves

In *Red Lion*, the Supreme Court said that because the airwaves belong to the public, those who have a license to use them must offer the public a wide variety of views on controversial public issues. Thus, the fairness doctrine can be seen as guaranteeing the public access to all shades of opinion. On the other side of the coin, the doctrine can be seen as guaranteeing those who hold varying opinions a right to have them expressed on the air. Flowing from these guarantees is a logical question: Does the fairness doctrine give any particular proponent of a point of view a right of access to radio or television? In the early 1970s, two political groups argued that it does. The United States Court of Appeals for the District of Columbia Circuit agreed with them, but the Supreme Court reversed.

The groups involved were Business Executives' Move for Vietnam Peace and the Democratic National Committee. Each had sought to buy time to carry its message to the people. Each had been rebuffed. Nor were they able to persuade the Federal Communications Commission that the fairness doctrine required the broadcasters to sell time to them. A divided appellate court ordered the FCC to devise a right of access to radio and television stations, but the Supreme Court held that such an attempt would put the commission too deeply into control over content.

Columbia Broadcasting System v. *Democratic National Committee*, 412 U.S. 94, 93 S.Ct. 2080, 36 L.Ed.2d 772 (1973).

The case, *Columbia Broadcasting System* v. *Democratic National Committee*, gave the Court an opportunity to explore in detail the line that separates the FCC as a regulator of broadcasting from a role that would make it a regulator of content. Lower courts continue to look to the decision for guidance in deciding broadcasting cases.

Chief Justice Burger, writing for a majority of the Court, reviewed *Red Lion*, making the point that broadcasters have only limited First Amendment rights, which are secondary to those of the audience. But the legislative record, he wrote, makes it clear that broadcasters are not stripped of all right to make content judgments. At various times, in considering changes in the Communications Act, Congress has rejected the following attempts:

1. To make broadcasters "common carriers," like a telephone company or a bus line. Common carriers are required to offer service to anyone able to pay the required fee.

2. To mandate a right of reply for political candidates or public officials who are dissatisfied with a station's news treatment of them.

From the beginning, Burger concluded, government regulators have walked a tight wire with respect to broadcasting, teetering between control of content by government and absolute freedom for broadcasters. And, while broadcasters have not been given absolute freedom,

> Congress appears to have concluded . . . that of these two choices—private or official censorship—Government censorship would be the most pervasive, the most self-serving, the most difficult to restrain and hence the one to be most avoided.

Burger also found in the legislative history an intent on the part of Congress to "preserve the values of private journalism under a regulatory scheme which would insure fulfillment of certain public obligations." This is done mainly through the equal opportunities and fairness provisions of §315. Government power is to be brought into play, the chief justice continued, "(o)nly when the interests of the public are found to outweigh the private journalistic interests of the broadcasters." Even then, the government's power is not to be exerted directly but in license renewal proceedings, "in which the listening public can be heard."

The chief justice next turned to the central question of this case: Does the public interest require "broadcasters to sell commercial time to persons wishing to discuss controversial issues"? Burger said that his former colleagues on the District of Columbia appeals court were wrong in holding that it did. If their view was to prevail, the right of access would be "heavily weighted in favor . . . of those with access to wealth." This would raise "the substantial danger . . . that the time allotted for editorial advertising could be monopolized by those of one political persuasion."

Nor could that imbalance be righted by application of the fairness doctrine to editorial advertising. Because the weight of the Constitution would be behind those seeking to buy time, it would be they, not the broadcasters, who would set the agenda for discussion of controversial public issues. Burger expanded on the theme:

> The result would be a further erosion of the journalistic discretion of broadcasters in the coverage of public issues, and a transfer of control over the treatment of public issues from the licensees who are accountable for broadcast performance to private individuals who are not. The public interest would no longer be "paramount" but, rather, subordinate to private whim. . . . Under such a regime the congressional objective of balanced coverage of public issues would be seriously threatened.
>
> Nor can we accept the Court of Appeals' view that every potential speaker is "the best judge" of what the listening public ought to hear or indeed the best judge of the merits of his or her views. All journalistic tradition and experience is to the contrary. For better or worse, editing is what editors are for; and editing is selection and choice of material. That editors—newspaper or broadcast—can and do abuse this power is beyond doubt, but that is no reason to deny the discretion Congress provided. Calculated risks of abuse are taken in order to preserve higher values. The presence of these risks is nothing new; the authors of the Bill of Rights accepted the reality that these risks were evils for which there was no acceptable remedy other than a spirit of moderation and a sense of responsibility—and civility—on the part of those who exercise the guaranteed freedoms of expression.

The passage above is a strong endorsement both of the right of broadcasters to exercise news judgment without interference by the FCC, and of the role of editors in general.

However, Burger did not stop there. As he has done on other occasions,[33] he proceeded to blunt the seemingly absolute tone of his opinion. There might come a time, he wrote, when Congress and the commission could draft some limited right of access.

Justice Potter Stewart concurred in the result but he would have gone beyond the chief justice in upholding the rights of broadcasters. He focused on the question raised by Jerome Barron[34] and others: Does the rise of media giants require government to play an affirmative role in helping speakers who are outside the mainstream reach an audience? Stewart wrote:

> The First Amendment prohibits the Government from imposing controls on the press. Private broadcasters are surely part of the press. Yet here the Court of Appeals held, and the dissenters today agree, that the First Amendment *requires* the Government to impose controls on private broadcasters—in order to preserve First Amendment "values." The appellate court accomplished this strange convolution by the simple device of holding that private broadcasters *are* government. This is a step along a path that could eventually lead to the proposition that private *newspapers* "are" government. Freedom of the press would then be gone. In its place we would have such governmental controls upon the press as a majority of this Court at any particular moment might consider First Amendment "values" to require. It is a frightening specter.

The Democratic National Committee and the anti-Vietnam War group had argued that the right of access could be limited to responsible individuals or groups. Stewart wrote that if that point of view were endorsed by the courts, someone in government would have to decide who is responsible and who is not, He asked: "Since when has the First Amendment given Government the right to silence all speakers it does not consider 'responsible'?"

Three members of the majority wrote separately to attack the fairness doctrine itself. Justice Harry A. Blackmun, joined by Justice Lewis F. Powell, Jr., said the First Amendment does not permit the FCC to substitute its view of fairness for that of the broadcaster. Justice Hugo L. Black put it more bluntly:

> The fairness doctrine has no place in our First Amendment regime. It puts the head of the camel inside the tent and enables administration after administration to toy with television or radio in order to serve its sordid or its benevolent ends.
> . . .[T]he regime of federal supervision under the fairness doctrine is contrary to our constitutional mandate and makes the broadcast licensee an easy victim of political pressures and reduces him to a timid and submissive segment of the press.

Justice William J. Brennan, Jr., joined by Justice Thurgood Marshall, dissented. They agreed with the court of appeals in its view that the First Amendment requires broadcasters to accept cause advertising. They took the position that the holder of a

---

33. See, for example, Nebraska Press Association v. Stuart, 427 U.S. 539, 96 S.Ct. 279, 49 L.Ed.2d 683 (1976), and Richmond Newspapers v. Virginia, 448 U.S. 555, 100 S.Ct. 2814, 65 L.Ed.2d 973 (1980).
34. Professor of law at George Washington University. See "Access to the Press—A New First Amendment Right," 80 *Harv. L. Rev.* 1641 (1967), and *Freedom of the Press for Whom?* (Bloomington, Ind.: Indiana University Press, 1973). Also see the discussion of Barron's views in Chapter 11 of this book, p. 428.

broadcasting license receives a form of subsidy from the government and therefore becomes an agent of government. That would make a broadcaster's decision denying paid access to the airwaves a form of prior restraint forbidden by the First and Fourteenth Amendments.

But it was the majority view that carried the day. It should be noted that the Court did not say that broadcasting stations cannot accept cause or editorial advertising. They are free to do so if they wish. However, if a paid advertisement deals with a controversial subject of public importance, its message must be balanced over time by presentation, in the station's public affairs programing, or in other paid advertisements, of opposing points of view. The decision gave the Supreme Court's endorsement to the position that broadcasters should be given great latitude in making decisions on both news and advertising content. As long as these judgments are made in good faith and are reasonable, the Federal Communications Commission must respect them. In *Columbia Broadcasting System*, a majority of the Court said as clearly as it could that both fairness and diversity are more likely to flow from the decisions of thousands of individual station operaters than from the decisions of a government agency.

Resolving Fairness Doctrine Complaints

Justice White's words in *Red Lion* have a noble ring: "It is the right of the viewers and listeners, not the right of the broadcasters, which is paramount." Coupled with Burger's opinion in *United Church of Christ*, they conjure a vision of concerned viewers and listeners insisting that broadcasters inform them fairly on the complexities of political and economic issues. However, writing as chief justice in the *CBS* case, Burger recognized that there is another side to the fairness coin. If broadcasting is to be free of government control, news judgments should be made by editors, because "editing is what editors are for." But he also noted that "editors . . . can and do abuse this power." When a station's viewers or listeners believe that its editors have abused their power, how is the question resolved? What is the role of the Federal Communications Commission in deciding what is fair? The commission's procedures in considering fairness complaints focus on two questions:

1. Did the alleged unfairness occur during the discussion of a controversial public issue?

2. If so, were the station's decisions as to choice of content made in good faith and were they reasonable?

Defining a Controversial Public Issue

Most of the fairness complaints made to the commission involve the allegation that a station presented one side of a controversial public issue and refused to provide time for other views. If there appears to be substance to the allegation, the commission's inquiry begins with an attempt to define the issue. If it is not controversial and has no public importance, no fairness doctrine question has been raised. Both the commission and the courts have observed that this frequently is the most difficult question to resolve.[35] In its 1974 *Fairness Report*, the FCC declined to set criteria for identifying issues, but it did make what it called "general observations" on the problem.[36] The *Report* says that an issue is not necessarily important simply because it has been in the news, although that is a factor to be considered. The broadcaster must look beyond newsworthiness to find whether the issue has been receiving attention from government officials and community leaders. Even more important is the impact "the issue is likely to have on the community at large." The *Report* concedes that this is a subjective evaluation. The same "observations" are to be used in determining whether an issue is controversial, but the *Report* suggests that this finding can be made with some degree of objectivity. If the issue "is the subject of vigorous debate" pitting "substantial elements of the community in opposition to one another," it is controversial.

In one instance, in 1976, the FCC found that a radio station not only had failed to identify a controversial issue of public importance, but was ignoring it to an extent that violated the fairness doctrine. In *Patsy Mink*,[37] the commission, for the first time, ordered a station to carry issue-oriented programing. At the time, Patsy Mink was a representative to Congress from Hawaii. She had introduced a bill designed to put strict federal controls on strip mining. To gain support for her bill, she prepared an audio tape summarizing her position and sent copies to radio stations, among them WHAR in Clarksburg, West Virginia. Although that city was in a strip mining area, the station did not broadcast the tape. When Representative Mink objected, the station manager said WHAR was relying on its Associated Press news wire to present a balanced report on the strip mining issue. Mink complained to the FCC, alleging that the station had aired arguments opposing her bill while refusing to present her arguments for it. She also noted that when WHAR's license had been renewed, the station had identified strip mining as one of the controversial public issues it intended to cover. After a hearing, the FCC concluded that WHAR had acted unreasonably in failing to cover "an issue which clearly may determine the quality of life in Clarksburg for decades to come." It gave the station twenty days to inform the commission of plans for programing on strip mining.

In this instance, the station itself had helped define the controversial public issue by identifying strip mining as one of the concerns of its audience. Not all such decisions are as clear-cut. As the FCC noted in its 1974 *Fairness Report*, the determination is subjective, and involves a case-by-case examination of issues to determine whether the public is affected by them and divided over their proper resolution.

Determining Reasonableness and Good Faith

If the commission's staff decides that a complaint has substance and was directed at coverage of a controversial public issue, it moves to an examination of how the alleged

---

35. National Broadcasting Co. v. Federal Communications Commission, 516 F.2d 1101, at 1117 (D.C.Cir. 1974).
36. 48 F.C.C. 1, paragraphs 29–35.
37. 59 F.C.C.2d 984 (1976).

offender reached its decisions on content. The purpose of the examination is to determine whether such decisions were reasonable and were made in good faith. This focus on method rather than content is designed to limit the FCC's role in shaping a station's programing.

Democratic National Committee v. *Federal Communications Commission,* 717 F.2d 1471 (D.C.Cir. 1983).

The commission's approach to fairness doctrine complaints has been defined by court decisions. The principles derived from these were summarized in 1983 by the United States Court of Appeals for the District of Columbia Circuit in its *per curiam* decision in *Democratic National Committee* v. *Federal Communications Commission.*

The case began when the Democratic party organization concluded that neither CBS nor NBC news was giving fair treatment to critics of President Reagan's economic policy. During the fall of 1981 both networks carried a series of 30-second spot advertisements supporting tax and spending cuts advocated by the president and then being considered by Congress. The party's researchers analyzed the two networks' news coverage of the issue and concluded that when the advertisements were taken into account, Republican views had outweighed Democratic views, by four-to-one on NBC and by more than three-to-one on CBS.

Acting in accord with procedures established by the FCC, the Democratic National Committee complained first directly to the networks. Each network responded by saying that it believed it had complied with the fairness doctrine, because it had aired the views of Democratic opponents to the Reagan program. Disagreeing, the committee filed a formal complaint with the FCC.

The Democratic Committee offered evidence to support its complaint. In addition to the analysis summarized above, it offered affidavits from four of its officials and from four persons outside the party. All said they had been regular watchers of NBC and CBS news for at least a six-month period. They said they had noticed some news reports opposing the Reagan program, but that in their opinion the proponents had dominated the coverage. In addition, the committee listed persons who had appeared on "Face the Nation" and "Meet the Press," arguing that on those programs, too, the balance was in the president's favor.

The FCC dismissed the complaint. It held that the Democratic party had not proved that the networks' coverage of the issue was unreasonable. Even if the differences in covering the two sides were as great as the committee contended, the "imbalance could hardly be considered a 'glaring' disparity." The FCC also said it found it "difficult to envision a case in which a major political party would raise an issue of public importance ignored by the electronic press." Still dissatisfied, the Democrats took their case to the court of appeals.

Quoting largely from previous decisions, the court noted that it had approved the FCC's decision to raise a "formidable procedural barrier" to fairness doctrine complaints. The purpose is to "preclude the chilling effect" that would result from asking stations to respond to "insubstantial complaints." The fairness doctrine requires only that broadcasters provide a "reasonable opportunity" for all points of view to be heard. The court noted, "What constitutes a 'reasonable opportunity' is largely left to the discretion of broadcasters." The main purpose of the fairness doctrine "is that *the American public must not be left uninformed.*" That purpose might be frustrated if there were "an egregious imbalance in presentation of competing viewpoints" so that one side was virtually ignored. Or it could happen if one point of view was presented regularly in prime time and opposing points of view when no one was watching. The court added:

> The Commission and the courts have emphasized, however, that the balance required in the context of the fairness doctrine is measured, not in terms of equal time or identity of treatment, but rather in terms of good faith and reasonableness, with ample deference given to a broadcaster's conception of what reasonableness entails.

To do otherwise would involve an agency of government too deeply in deciding how public issues are presented and discussed on the air.

In applying the above standards to the facts of a case, the court said it "must give considerable weight to the Commission's expert judgment." In this instance, it agreed that the Democratic National Committee had not made the required showing of unfairness. The court noted that the FCC had based its decision on the conclusion that the Democratic party had presented no evidence to show that the audience who had seen its views was not comparable to that who had seen the Republican view. The court said that that conclusion was reasonable.

The court specifically rejected the Democratic National Committee's argument that the time devoted to the opposing points of view was grossly unbalanced. The court said that implicit in that argument was an attempt to convert the fairness doctrine into the equal opportunities law. Quoting an earlier decision, it said, "[T]he fairness doctrine 'nowhere requires equality but only reasonableness.' " It also rejected the Democrats' argument that the message in political advertisements has such a high impact that it cannot be balanced by the message content in regular news and public affairs programs. The court said that broadcasters have wide discretion in selecting offsetting programing and are expected to use it.

This decision illustrates why a fairness doctrine complainant has only about one chance in a thousand of winning.[38] Both the FCC and the courts generally are reluctant to impose their news judgments on broadcasters lest the power of government be used to distort debate on public policy. Thus the test employed in determining whether a broadcaster is fair is focused on how the decision was reached rather than on its nature. If news judgments are reasonable and made in good faith, they are fair. Only "an egregious imbalance in presentation of competing viewpoints" will draw a reprimand from the FCC.

And yet the effect of the fairness doctrine ought not to be dismissed. In 1985, during FCC hearings on the fairness doctrine, several witnesses testified as to its usefulness.[39] The organization People for the American Way was able to persuade a Los Angeles television station to give it time to respond to political statements made by religious broadcasters. In Oregon, the Public Interest Research Group was able to get air time to counter public utility company advertising. Liberals and conservatives were united in arguing that without the fairness doctrine broadcasters would give less time to viewpoints from the far left and the far right of the political spectrum.

---

38. Steven J. Simmons, *The Fairness Doctrine and the Media* (Berkeley: University of California Press, 1978), pp. 210–11.
39. Jeanne Sadler, "Right and Left Find Common Ground: Backing Fairness Rule for Broadcasters," *Wall Street Journal*, 8 February 1985.

The commission reacted to the hearings by recommending unanimously that the doctrine be repealed by Congress or struck down by the Supreme Court.[40] Its report said that the large number of over-the-air stations, coupled with the rapid growth of cable systems, has undercut the scarcity theory used by the Supreme Court in 1969 in *Red Lion*. At the end of 1985, a group of broadcast organizations including CBS, Inc., asked the U.S. Court of Appeals for the District of Columbia Circuit to declare the fairness doctrine in violation of the First Amendment.[41] They were encouraged not only by the FCC, but by a reading of the footnotes in the Supreme Court's 1984 decision in *Federal Communications Commission* v. *League of Women Voters of California*.[42] In that case, the Court struck down a law forbidding public broadcasting stations to editorialize. Justice Brennan, writing for five members of the Court, held that the law was an impermissible restriction on political speech. In two footnotes expanding on his views he also criticized the fairness doctrine and the Court's decision in *Red Lion*. Brennan noted that in upholding the fairness doctrine the Court had acted on the theory that frequencies are scarce and that the doctrine enhances debate on public issues. Evidence suggests that neither theory is valid today. Cable and satellite technology have greatly increased the number of available channels. Further, critics of stature argue that the fairness doctrine inhibits, rather than enhances, debate. Brennan added, however, that the Court was not prepared "to reconsider our longstanding approach without some signal from Congress or the FCC that technological developments have advanced so far that some revision of the system of broadcast regulation may be required." The FCC has given such a signal. As of this writing, Congress has not.

Therefore, until the Court has an opportunity to consider the challenge begun in the lower courts, the doctrine remains in effect. It continues to require broadcasters to identify controversial public issues and present varying points of view on them. Although the doctrine obviously is out of favor with the Federal Communications Commission, its 1985 report said it will continue to enforce it. This means that station operators must continue to make a good faith effort to offer a reasonably balanced presentation of public issues.

Indecent Programing

One afternoon in October 1973, a disc jockey on the Pacifica Foundation's FM radio station in New York City played all twelve minutes of a George Carlin monologue entitled "Filthy Words." It was recorded before a nightclub audience that howled in appreciation as Carlin repeated in many contexts "the curse words and swear words . . . you couldn't say on the public, ah, airwaves, um, the ones you definitely wouldn't say." He proceeded to say them, and the station put them on the airwaves. One listener was not amused. His complaint to the Federal Communications Commission led to a Supreme Court decision, *Federal Communications Commission* v. *Pacifica Foundation*, that again made

Federal Communications Commission v. *Pacifica Foundation*, 438 U.S. 726, 98 S.Ct. 3026, 57 L.Ed.2d 1073 (1978).

40. Reginald Stuart, "Fairness Doctrine Assailed by F.C.C.," *New York Times*, 8 August 1985.
41. Reginald Stuart, "Challenge to the Fairness Doctrine Is Planned," *New York Times*, 23 October 1985.
42. ___U.S.___, 104 S.Ct. 3106, 82 L.Ed.2d 278 (1984).

the point: Broadcasters do not enjoy the same degree of First Amendment freedom as do editors and publishers of print media.

The FCC reprimanded Pacifica, holding that the Carlin monologue violated 18 U.S.C. §1464, which forbids the use on the air of any "obscene, indecent, or profane language." Pacifica argued that because the monologue was not obscene according to the *Miller-Roth* standard,[43] the station should not be punished. A badly divided Court upheld the commission, five-to-four.

Writing for himself and two other members of the majority, Justice John Paul Stevens said that the three elements of §1464 must be looked at separately, not as a unit. Thus, a station could be punished if it broadcast matter that was indecent or profane, without being obscene. The three justices also held that §1464 must be considered independently of the language in §326 of the Communications Act that forbids the FCC to censor broadcasting stations. When the two sections are looked at together, Stevens wrote, they mean that the FCC can't prevent a station from broadcasting "obscene, indecent, or profane language," but it can take such material into consideration at license renewal time in deciding whether a station has operated in the public interest.

The Court conceded that the Carlin monologue was not obscene, despite repeated use of the vulgar terms for excretion and sexual intercourse. However, it agreed with the commission's finding that the recording was "indecent."

The plurality defined "indecent" as "nonconformance with accepted standards of morality," and held that the monologue failed that test. It made much of the fact that the recording was put on the air at a time of day when children were likely to be in the audience.

Pacifica argued that the definition of "indecent" was so broad that it might well cover language protected by the First Amendment. The broadcaster argued further that because the recording admittedly was not obscene under the *Miller* test, the Constitution forbade "any abridgment of the right to broadcast it on the radio."

The Court rejected both arguments. Even granting that there were some First Amendment values in Carlin's words, Stevens wrote, "surely [they] lie at the periphery of First Amendment concern." Such value as there might be was not enough to overcome the fact that "of all forms of communication it is broadcasting that has received the most limited First Amendment protection."

Stevens advanced two major reasons for his conclusion, both grounded in privacy considerations. He wrote:

First, the broadcast media have established a uniquely pervasive presence in the lives of all Americans. Patently offensive, indecent material presented over the airwaves confronts the citizen, not only in public, but also in the privacy of the home, where the individual's right to be let alone plainly outweighs the First Amendment rights of an intruder. Because the broadcast audience is constantly tuning in and out, prior warnings cannot completely protect the listener or viewer from unexpected program content. To say that one may avoid further offense by turning off the radio when he hears indecent language is like saying that the remedy for an assault is to run away after the first blow. One may hang up on an

43. Miller v. California, 413 U.S. 15, 93 S.Ct. 2607, 37 L.Ed.2d 419 (1973).

indecent phone call, but that option does not give the caller a constitutional immunity or avoid a harm that has already taken place.

Second, broadcasting is uniquely accessible to children, even those too young to read. . . . Other forms of offensive expression may be withheld from the young without restricting the expression at its source. Bookstores and motion picture theaters, for example, may be prohibited from making indecent materials available to children. We held in *Ginsberg* v. *New York*, that the government's interest in the "well being of its youth" and in supporting "parents' claim to authority in their own household" justified the regulation of otherwise protected expression. The ease with which children may obtain access to broadcast material, coupled with the concerns recognized in *Ginsberg*, amply justify special treatment of indecent broadcasting.

The plurality ended by emphasizing the narrowness of its decision. It said it had no intention of making it impossible for a station to broadcast unexpurgated versions of Shakespeare's more earthy comedies. Nor was it saying that a taxi company could be punished if a frustrated driver uttered a curse into an open microphone. It was simply reminding broadcasters that their medium entered homes where children and unsuspecting adults might be listening. Therefore, discretion is in order. To many, the Carlin monologue would be a nuisance, which Justice George Sutherland had once described as "a right thing in the wrong place—like a pig in the parlor instead of the barnyard." To which Stevens added: "We simply hold that when the Commission finds that a pig has entered the parlor, the exercise of its regulatory power does not depend upon proof that the pig is obscene."

In *Pacifica*, the Court spoke to broadcasters at two levels. At one level, it was merely telling them that they run a risk at license renewal time if they persist in airing sexually oriented material when children are likely to be in the audience. While the Supreme Court was deciding this case, the Court of Appeals for the District of Columbia reinforced that warning with its decision in *Illinois Citizens Committee for Broadcasting* v. *Federal Communications Commission*.[44] The Committee had objected to an FCC order fining Sonderling Broadcasting Corporation $2,000 for airing material the commission considered obscene. The host for an afternoon call-in show had encouraged his female listeners to talk about their experiences with oral sex. The appeals court held that the Committee had a right to be heard, but also that the FCC was correct in holding that the program violated 18 U.S.C. §1464. The decisions marked the end of a brief experiment with "blue" radio.

At another level, the Court's decision in *Pacifica* has assumed new importance in the 1980s because it lends support to those who believe government should continue to regulate broadcasting in the interest of public decency. The effort to rescind the fairness doctrine, noted above, is part of a broad movement to free broadcasters from government regulation. Some of the opponents of this effort point to MTV on cable and to R-rated movies on pay television and argue that the rule on which the *Pacifica* decision was based should be retained along with the FCC's authority to deny license renewal in the public interest.

---

44. 515 F.2d 397 (D.C.Cir. 1974).

DEREGULATION OF BROADCASTING

The Relaxation of Standards for License Renewal

As of this writing, the movement toward deregulation of broadcasting has proceeded unevenly. Acting on its own authority, the Federal Communications Commission has given commercial radio and television stations freedom to decide how much of their time will be devoted to news and public affairs programing. It also has removed limits on the amount of time that can be devoted to commercial advertising. License renewal has been simplified. The FCC has increased the number of stations that any one individual or corporation may own. However, it has continued to insist that stations employing five or more persons must have an equal employment opportunities program and show progress in the hiring and promoting of racial minorities and women. With the help of Congress, the FCC has clarified the extent of its control over cable systems.

The courts have contributed to the movement toward deregulation. As noted earlier, the Supreme Court struck down a law that prevented public broadcasting stations from editorializing. In 1985, the U.S. Court of Appeals for the District of Columbia Circuit overturned an FCC rule requiring cable systems to carry all local television stations.[45] The court said the rule violated the First Amendment rights of the owners of the systems. As of this writing, the fairness doctrine is under attack in the courts.

Changes in response to deregulation have been gradual in most instances. Cable viewers may find access to only one public television station or one affiliate of a given network. Discerning listeners to radio may notice that some stations play packaged audio tapes all day long with only minimal breaks for sketchy news bulletins and weather. Popular stations may have squeezed in another commercial or two during those times of the day that attract the largest viewing or listening audience. Sunday morning listeners may notice fewer reports from the statehouse, or interviews with the mayor and other local officials.

With commercial radio, such changes as have occurred are in response to a *Report and Order on Deregulation of Radio*[46] issued by the FCC in 1981. Commercial television was the subject of a somewhat narrower *Report and Order*[47] released on August 21, 1984. The next day, the FCC issued an order removing all programing requirements from public television stations except for the restriction forbidding them to accept payment for airing specific programs or announcements.[48] The more significant provisions of these orders are summarized as follows:

1. Previously, radio stations were required to devote specified percentages of their time to news and public affairs programing. Under deregulation, they are required only to devote a reasonable amount of time to public issues. Stations in large markets, where there are many other broadcasters, can

---

45. Quincy Cable TV, Inc., v. Federal Communications Commission, 768 F.2d 1434 (D.C.Cir. 1985).
46. 50 R.R.2d 93 (1981).
47. MM Dkt. No. 893-670, F.C.C. 84-293.
48. Report and Order (BC Dkt. No. 81-496) F.C.C. 84-294.

meet this obligation by focusing on issues of concern to their particular listeners. Thus, a station catering to a black or to a Hispanic audience can concentrate its public affairs programing on black or Hispanic issues.

2. Previously both radio and television stations were required to comply with elaborate polling procedures designed to identify controversial issues of public importance. They also were required to offer a plan for airing programing on these issues. Now, radio broadcasters seeking license renewal need only show that they have somehow identified issues facing their community. Also, they must place in their "**public file**" a listing of five or ten issues that have been the subject of programing. This can be supported with examples. The commission requires only that the methods used to identify issues be reasonable. Television stations must compile on a quarterly basis a list of five or more issues that the station featured during the quarter and report how it dealt with them.

3. Under the old rules, radio stations were limited to eighteen minutes of commercials in any hour; television stations to sixteen. Those limits have been removed.

4. Broadcasters were required to keep, and place in their "public file," detailed logs showing, minute by minute, what was put on the air. The purpose was to provide a ready means of checking the public service offerings of each station. When that provision was abolished for commercial radio in 1981, many interest groups objected, arguing that stations would devote less time to public service. Even the National Association of Broadcasters was made uneasy by the change, but for other reasons. Station owners were left wondering how much public affairs programing they would have to offer in order to be "reasonable," and how they could prove they were reasonable if challenged.

Because the old rules had specified minimum percentages for various categories of public service programing, many broadcasters had felt comfortable with the logging requirements. They knew that if they were challenged they could add up the minutes devoted to news, discussion, religion, and public service, divide the total by the number of minutes the station was on the air, and get a figure that was at or over the minimum requirement for such programing. Such mathematical precision tended to foreclose questions as to the quality of the programing. Under the new rules, licensees no longer have a quick and easy way to counter a Petition to Deny, the one thing they fear most. Such petitions may be filed at renewal time by persons or groups seeking to take over a licensee's frequency. They are grounded in an allegation that the current holder has failed to serve the public interest.

If a petition offers evidence of substantial failure to offer public service programing, the FCC may require the station to defend its record in a hearing. During the hearing, the competing applicant may attempt to persuade the commission it would do a better job of serving the public if it were granted the license. Only rarely has a new applicant succeeded in taking a license from an established operator. However, the expense of going through a hearing can eat deeply into an owner's profit. Two close observers of the FCC's performance have noted, "Designating a license renewal for hearing is considered by both key staff people and most commissioners almost as drastic as taking a license away."[49]

Thus there is nothing automatic about license renewal, although it is nearly so. Under deregulation, the renewal process has been simplified considerably, but, under pressure from minority and women's groups, and of critics of commercial broadcasting, the way has been left open for challenge.

Persons or organizations seeking a broadcasting license must convince the Federal Communications Commission that they are best qualified to use the available frequency in the public interest. Several factors go into the commission's decision:

1. Diversity in the marketplace of ideas. The commission's policy encourages competitive points of view. An applicant who owns no other media properties in the same area will be favored over one who does. In the most favored position is an applicant who owns no other stations. Since 1975, daily newspapers have been barred from acquiring broadcasting stations within their own circulation area.[50]

2. Owner participation in the station's operation. The commission's policy assumes that owners who live in the same community and who take part in the station's operation are more likely to focus on local issues than are absentee owners.

3. Ownership by minorities and women. Ownership groups including blacks, Hispanics, other minorities, or women are given preference over those that do not.

4. Programing. A prospective licensee must have a plan to offer programing that will serve the needs of the station's audience.

5. Efficiency of operation. This is a technical factor involving the quality of the station's signal.

6. The character of the owners. The keys here are honesty and candor. Because the FCC's enforcement procedures rely to a great extent on reports prepared by station management, and endorsed by the owner or owners, any proven record of sharp dealings probably will disqualify an applicant. In a few instances, such a record also has resulted in refusal to renew or in renewal for less than the full license term.

7. Financial stability. Prospective broadcasters not only must prove they have funding to obtain a studio and erect a transmitter, but must be able to fund the first year's operation.

Radio licenses are granted for seven-year periods; television, for five. Under deregulation, station owners may obtain renewal simply by sending a postcard in the proper form to the FCC.[51] However, 5 percent of the television and noncommercial radio

49. B. Cole and M. Oettinger, *Reluctant Regulators* (Reading, Mass.: Addison-Wesley, 1978), p. 213.
50. "Multiple Ownership of Standard, FM and Television Broadcast Stations," 50 F.C.C.2d 1046 (1975).
51. Memorandum Opinion and Order, 46 Fed. Reg. 26236 (1981).

Renee Ferguson was graduated from Indiana University, Bloomington, with a degree in journalism in 1971. She began her career as an on-the-air reporter with WTHR in Indianapolis and has since been employed by WBBM-TV in Chicago and as a correspondent by CBS News in Atlanta and New York City. (Courtesy of CBS)

licenses are selected at random for more intensive scrutiny. Stations in this sample must submit program audit forms designed to show how they operated in the public interest. They also are subject to on-site inspection of their public file.

Licensees also must be prepared to show that they are in compliance with the commission's policies on employment of women and minorities. Each year, stations employing five or more persons must file detailed reports listing employees by employment category, race, and sex. The FCC's goal is employment equity, that is, a staff that mirrors the community in terms of race and sex mix.[52] As part of the move toward deregulation, the commission has ruled that stations serving an area in which minorities make up less than 5 percent of the labor force need not file equal opportunities reports.[53]

For more than thirty years, FCC rules forbade any one entity from owning more than seven stations in each of three categories—television, AM radio, and FM radio. The purpose of the rule was to discourage chain ownership of broadcasting stations, particularly by the networks. This has prevented the rise of broadcasting empires akin to Gannett, Knight-Ridder, Thomson, Scripps-Howard, and other chain newspaper owners. In 1984, the FCC proposed to raise ownership limits to twelve stations in each category. This drew opposition from television and movie producers, which resulted in a vote of disapproval by the Senate Appropriations Committee.[54] After Congress adjourned, the FCC modified its rule with respect to television stations. Any company can own twelve

52. "Nondiscrimination in the Employment Policies and Practices of Broadcast Licensees," 60 F.C.C.2d 226 (1976).
53. "Amendment of Broadcast Equal Employment Opportunity Rules and F.C.C. Form 395," 49 R.R.2d 1295 (1981).
54. Jeanne Sadler, "Senate Panel Votes to Bar Application of New Rule on TV-Station Ownership," *Wall Street Journal*, 3 August 1984.

stations as long as the combined audience does not exceed 25 percent of the nation's TV audience.[55] A company that has UHF stations among its holdings is permitted to count only half their potential audience against its 25 percent limit. To encourage minority participation in ownership, companies whose holdings include stations more than half owned by minorities can exceed the twelve-station limit.

During the 1970s, the Federal Communications Commission, the U.S. Court of Appeals for the District of Columbia Circuit, and broadcasters were at odds over the role of programing in license renewal and in the transfer of a license from one owner to another. The conflict began in 1972 when Zenith Radio sold an FM station in Chicago. Zenith had operated the station with a classical music format. The new owner announced that it would adopt a contemporary sound format. Listeners appealed to the FCC to disapprove the transfer, arguing that they would be left without access to classical music on radio. The FCC ruled that they weren't even entitled to a hearing. The listeners took their case to the court of appeals, which held that if a proposed format change causes "public grumbling of significant proportions," the FCC must conduct a hearing.[56] Two years later, a new challenge to a station's change in format gave the FCC an opportunity to adopt a policy toward the problem.[57] It took the position that programing changes beyond the news and service elements required in the public interest are best left to the forces of the market. Again, the court of appeals disagreed. However, the Supreme Court held that the FCC's policy reflected the intent of the Communications Act: The commission's role in programing should be minimal.[58] That decision has left stations free to decide for themselves the kinds of programing they will offer.

This led some critics to complain that deregulation had encouraged neglect of worthwhile programing, especially for children.[59] One of the casualties was Bob Keeshan, whose *Captain Kangaroo* CBS had cut back from thirty minutes five mornings a week to shorter weekend spots. All three networks had canceled educational children's programing that had been developed under pressure from the more activist-minded FCC of the early 1970s. Interviewed by a reporter for the *Wall Street Journal*, Mark Fowler, the Reagan-appointed chairman of the FCC, conceded that deregulation might not be best for children. But he said he did not think it the role of the commission to order the networks to do a better job. The policy adopted at his urging, he said, marked the end of "regulation by raised eyebrow." His reference was to a period when the FCC used its powers subtly—and sometimes overtly—to influence the nature of programing, in its opinion for the better.

In less than a decade, the extent to which the Federal Communications Commission regulates broadcasting has changed dramatically. "Regulation by raised eyebrow" and more overt measures designed to encourage "better" programing, whether entertainment or discussion of public affairs, have been replaced by the belief that market forces should shape the content of broadcasting. A majority of the FCC, as it was constituted in 1986,

---

55. "FCC Revises Limit on TV Stations One Firm Can Own," *Wall Street Journal*, 20 December 1984.
56. Citizens Committee to Save WEFM v. Federal Communications Commission, 506 F.2d 246 (D.C. Cir. 1974).
57. "Changes in the Entertainment Formats of Broadcast Stations," 41 Fed. Reg. 32950 (1976).
58. Federal Communications Commission v. WNCN Listeners Guild, 450 U.S. 582, 101 S.Ct. 1266, 67 L.Ed.2d 521 (1981).
59. Jane Mayer, "Networks Are Accused of Neglecting Children in Era of Deregulation," *Wall Street Journal*, 17 March 1983.

made no secret of its belief that broadcasters should be permitted to offer what the audience wants. With radio particularly, the policy induced a scramble among station owners to carve out some segment of the audience to which they could lay claim and thus sell to advertisers. Stations offered highly specialized programing, with FM outlets focusing on music—rock of varying degrees of hardness, country-western, easy listening, golden oldies, contemporary, or whatever. Classical music became a rarity, except in the big cities and on public radio stations. On AM, which could not match FM in sound quality, some stations became outlets for radio evangelists, others used former disc jockeys to prime the audience to call in and talk about the problem of the day, while a few offered nothing but news.

Television station owners, particularly of VHF outlets affiliated with one of the major networks, did not have to scramble quite so hard. The networks continued the programing formats that had proven an ability to attract large audiences. Local stations had learned that news was their largest "profit center." Many offered two hours of local news each day, along with two hours of network-originated news, weather, and talk to start the day, and another half-hour of network news in the evening.

But television station owners also were living with the knowledge that they were reaching a smaller portion of the potential audience then they had been a decade earlier.[60] This was because of the rapid growth of cable systems offering viewers specialized programing in music, sports, movies, and even news, including gavel-to-gavel coverage of the daily sessions of Congress. The common use of video recorders gave many viewers the options of taping programs off the air to view at leisure and of renting or buying movies. Others used dish antennas to pluck programing from the air, while a few were connected to two-way information systems capable of bringing them everything from stock market quotations to the full content of a major encyclopedia. In short, the FCC's hands-off approach to radio and television was encouraging a revolution in how the public receives both entertainment and information, and also raising new First Amendment questions.

New Technologies and the First Amendment

Within the memory of persons now living, broadcasting has moved from an interesting curiosity to a pervasive influence in society. When radio began in the 1920s, America was a collection of isolated communities. People had to leave home and travel to find out what life was like in some other part of the country. Major events that were destined to make history were something we read about in the newspapers. Until radio came along, Americans could not hear what their president had to say unless they were in the president's presence. Today, we can sit in our homes and not only hear, but see, the president, along with any other of the world's leaders who may be making news in front of a television camera. However, advancements in the same technology that has brought the world into our homes are also making it possible for us to shut out the world. Individuals with access to highly specialized channels of entertainment and information

60. "Cable TV Is Found a Respectable Rival of Networks' Fare," *Wall Street Journal*, 13 January 1982.

may become tuned in to one to the exclusion of all others. This prospect has been made possible by cable, satellite dishes, VCRs, computer links to data bases, and even Sony's Walkman and its imitators. Clearly, the proliferation of communications delivery systems raises First Amendment considerations of a different kind than those that guided the Supreme Court in 1943 when it decided the *NBC* case, or in 1969 when it decided *Red Lion*. Communications channels no longer are a scarce commodity.

In 1985, about 45 percent of the 85 million homes with television sets were on cable.[61] The better systems were capable of bringing a hundred or more channels into the home, far more than there was programing to fill. This put cable system owners in a position where they could offer to serve as a carrier for others seeking to reach people with a service that could be sold at a profit.

Newspaper publishers had to be considered as one of the potential customers. Newsprint costs rose past the $500-a-ton mark, making the cost of the paper in a Sunday *New York Times* more than the price of the newspaper. Publishers also were having difficulty finding and keeping dependable carriers to deliver their newspapers to doorsteps. A decade earlier, some publishers had begun raising questions about the wisdom of cutting down acres of trees to deliver tons of newsprint to readers who quickly turned it into waste paper. Some publishers experimented with cable delivery systems, offering viewers frequently updated summaries of the news. Dow Jones, Knight-Ridder, the *Los Angeles Times*, Associated Press, and others experimented with two-way systems. Subscribers could use a terminal attached to a video screen or electronic printer to consult an index and order delivery only of those items of interest to them. Others experimented with electronic delivery of classified advertising. Some of the experiments proved unprofitable and were abandoned.

But even the experiments raised significant questions. If a newspaper converts to electronic delivery, does it become subject to the equal opportunities provisions of §315 and to the fairness doctrine? Could material considered indecent, even though it was not obscene, be barred from such systems? Would cross-ownership rules prevent newspaper publishers from acquiring an electronic medium that might offer the most efficient means of delivering information to their subscribers?

At this writing, the law with respect to cable television can best be described as unsettled. Even though a cable system does not use the people's airwaves, the Federal Communications Commission, with the backing of Congress and the courts, has assumed some jurisdiction. It has done so because most of the news and entertainment offered by cable systems comes from stations that do use the air. This is somewhat the same rationale the FCC used in the 1940s to bring the networks under its jurisdiction. However, because a cable system must run wires along and over the streets of the community it serves, it must also obtain a franchise from local units of government before it can operate. Local governments, therefore, can and do impose conditions such as certain technical standards that franchise holders must meet. In all instances, the holder must pay a fee to the city or county served. Bidding for the right to serve a community can become intensely competitive.

The winner of a franchise must file a registration statement with the FCC. Since

---

61. Thomas Whiteside, "Onward and Upward With the Arts: Cable—1," *The New Yorker*, 20 May 1985, p. 45.

1965, cable operators have had to agree that they would comply with the commission's signal carriage rules. These require in part that systems carry all local stations with "significant" numbers of viewers in the area. The rules also permit local stations to ask the cable operator to block out distant signals that duplicate local offerings.[62] As noted earlier, in July 1985 the U.S. Court of Appeals for the District of Columbia Circuit held that the must-carry rule violated the First Amendment rights of cable operators.[63] Some reacted by dropping local stations with low ratings in order to add programing that might attract more viewers. This resulted in complaints from CBS, NBC, the cities of Boston and New York, and more than forty groups claiming to speak for disappointed TV viewers.[64] Representatives of the cable industry met with broadcasters in February 1986 to seek a compromise, but were unable to do so.[65] Meanwhile, the Supreme Court was considering a request that it review the appellate court's decision.

Cable operators who initiate their own programing are required to comply with the equal opportunities law, the fairness doctrine, and the indecency restrictions upheld by the Supreme Court in *Pacifica*.[66] They must also meet the same hiring standards for minorities and women that the FCC has set for broadcasting stations.

To end some of the uncertainty surrounding cable operations, Congress in 1984 adopted a law establishing a greater degree of federal control.[67] Under its provisions, local governments will lose control over cable subscriber fees in 1987. The law also established standard procedures for renewal of cable franchises. Operators complained that they were at the mercy of local governing bodies who sometimes made decisions arbitrarily or for political reasons. The first draft of the bill would have forbidden newspapers from owning cable systems in their circulation areas. That restriction was removed before the bill became law.

Almost universally, local governments have awarded cable operators exclusive franchises for their service areas. Larger cities may be served by more than one cable system, but usually each is exclusive in its assigned area. The effect is to grant franchise holders a monopoly. In March 1985, the U.S. Court of Appeals for the Ninth Circuit held that Los Angeles could not grant an exclusive franchise in an area where existing pole systems could support more than one cable.[68] The court held that the city's refusal to permit competitive service violated the First Amendment. In June 1986, the Supreme Court affirmed the decision.[69]

As this brief survey suggests, the law as it applies to cable television systems is in a state of flux. This is equally true of other aspects of the new communications technology. In an attempt to draft guidelines for resolution of the problems, more than sixty persons met in Leesburg, Virginia, in 1982 for a seminar called "First Amendment Values in a Changing Information System." The participants included educators, lawyers, journalists, broadcasters, cable system operators, government administrators, scientists, and members

---

62. 47 C.F.R., §§76.92–76.99 (1981).
63. Quincy Cable TV, note 45 above.
64. Peter W. Barnes and Laura Landro, "Cable Firms, TV Stations to Meet Today in Bid for Compromise on Access Rules," *Wall Street Journal*, 7 February 1986.
65. "Cable Firms, TV Stations Fail to Set Must-Carry Pact," *Wall Street Journal*, 10 February 1986.
66. 47 C.F.R. §§76.205 through 76.221; 76.311 (1981).
67. "Congress Limits Local Control of Cable TV," *New York Times*, 12 October 1984.
68. Preferred Communications, Inc., v. City of Los Angeles, 754 F.2d 1396 (9th Cir. 1985).
69. *City of Los Angeles* v. *Preferred Communications, Inc.*, 106 S.Ct. 2034 (1986).

of special interest groups. Their assignment was to peer beyond the present into the world of tomorrow, to visualize the future of information delivery systems, and to think about the rules that ought to regulate them. They assumed that in the not too distant future cable may be the principal means of bringing news and entertainment to the homes of most Americans. Beyond that, they differed sharply, reaching agreement on only a few general principles. Among them were the following:[70]

1. "The First Amendment bars, and ought to bar, 'content regulation' in any form, for print or broadcasting or any combination of the two."

2. Regulatory law must be reexamined in the light of new technologies.

3. "The fairness doctrine and equal time rules are relics of the past, and their elimination would not be mourned."

4. Print publishers who move into electronic transmission of text materials should retain the same degree of First Amendment freedom they now enjoy.

Later in 1982, Arthur Ochs Sulzberger, chairman of the New York Times Company, joined William S. Paley, chairman of CBS, in calling for repeal of §315 and the fairness doctrine. Both spoke in the same week at meetings in New York City.[71] Paley had long been a critic of the regulations, but Sulzberger's speech signaled the growing awareness that, in his words, "the line between print and electronic journalism is thin at best and getting thinner." He argued that the great number of radio, television, and cable outlets has made the fairness doctrine obsolete, adding, "It is time for print publishers to join with their electronic brethren to close this First Amendment gap."

At their spring meeting the following year, the directors of the American Newspaper Publishers Association approved a resolution flatly condemning "the so-called fairness doctrine and equal time requirements."[72] They pledged their support for efforts to repeal laws "which permit government content regulation," particularly as they affect coverage of political issues and public affairs.

At this writing, the debate over further deregulation of broadcasting is continuing. So is the jockeying for advantage among those seeking to become the primary means of delivering news, advertising, entertainment, information, banking services, and catalog merchandising directly into the home or office. To journalists, the argument for total deregulation of content is strong. Government has no business exercising any control over the debate on public issues, even when its purpose is to encourage debate and keep it within the bounds of fairness. Given the multiplicity of electronic voices, the scarcity rationale for government regulation no longer makes any sense.

There are strong arguments on the other side, too. The most basic starts with a premise that has not changed since the first station went on the air. Broadcasting operates in a medium that should no more be made private property than should the high seas.

---

70. First Amendment Congress, "Special Report," The Newspaper Center, Washington, D.C. (1982).
71. "Sulzberger, Paley Call for End of the Equal Time Rule," *Editor & Publisher*, 27 November 1982, p. 10.
72. "ANPA Supports Repeal of Fairness Doctrine," *Editor & Publisher*, 30 April 1983, p. 20.

The airwaves either belong to the people, who can insist that they be used for the benefit of all, or they belong to no one. When, in the early days of broadcasting, society acted on the latter premise, the result was chaos.

Further, broadcasting is intrusive. Persons who buy a newspaper, magazine, or book have a pretty good idea what they are bringing into their homes. But those who tune across a radio band, or switch from channel to channel on television, do not know with certainty what will suddenly appear in the home. Conventional television fare has come under fire from some groups who see on the screen sex, violence, and scorn for religious values. Some cable channels go beyond the conventional, offering the strong language, simulated sex, nudity, and crude violence of R-rated movies. In 1981, the Utah Legislature, prodded by politically active Mormons, enacted a law banning delivery of "any pornographic or indecent material" by wire or cable. A federal court quickly struck it down as too vague. But the fight moved into local communities, some of which drafted more carefully worded ordinances.[73] In 1983, a grand jury in Cincinnati indicted the Warner Amex cable system serving part of that city on a charge of pandering obscenity because the system had offered its subscribers programing provided by Playboy Enterprises.[74] The charge, a misdemeanor, was dismissed in exchange for Warner's promise not to offer X-rated programing, which it had not offered. The Playboy channel had been dropped before the indictment was issued.[75]

Deregulation is opposed by such groups as the Media Access Coalition and the Office of Communication of the United Church of Christ for other reasons. They find too little sense of social responsibility in most newspapers and magazines, and are convinced broadcasters would go the same route if they could. Minority groups, in particular, feel they would be less well served by a deregulated system. Andy Schwartzmann, executive director of the Media Access Coalition, said, "Experience shows that unless broadcasters have their feet held to the fire, they will not prove significantly more responsible to local needs than other communicators—and often less."[76]

A current characteristic of cable raises another question. As noted earlier, cable systems usually are monopolistic. Even with the Supreme Court's decision in the Los Angeles case, that is not likely to change significantly. The costs of stringing cable and of extending service to individual dwellings are so great that operators are not likely to enter a market without an exclusive franchise. Because of the costs, small operators, who once dominated the cable industry, are selling out to larger organizations.

Cable is monopolistic in another way, too. Once a family plugs their set into a cable system, they are not likely to use the set to bring in television stations through the air. That still leaves radio and the print media as competitors for the family's entertainment and information time. But what might happen at some time in the future if the cable system's hundred or so channels also are used to carry high-fidelity, stereophonic music in several varieties, classified advertising, and an around-the-clock print news service? Could not the cable—perhaps by then completely unregulated—become the only medium in town? To some, that is an attractive possibility. Through a connection with

---

73. Norman Thorpe, "Utahans Fight Over Decency in Cable TV," *Wall Street Journal*, 23 September 1982.
74. "Warner Amex Cable Unit in Cincinnati Indicted for Obscenity," *Wall Street Journal*, 15 June 1983.
75. Information provided by Warner Cable's attorney, 21 March 1986.
76. Tony Schwartz, "F.C.C. Battleground: Deregulation of TV," *New York Times*, 22 October 1980.

the bank and a mail-order store, viewers might even save time spent on paying bills and shopping. But the prospect of an all-purpose cable system, guided by no other force than the pursuit of a market, also is a specter haunting conventional broadcasters, newspaper publishers, and anyone who thinks about the meaning of community and a of a free society.

In the Professional World

Rapid technological change has done far more than alter the nature of the electronic media. It also has changed the way news is presented on television. Electronic newsgathering techniques have made it possible for minicameras to go almost anywhere and, with the help of microwave links sometimes bounced off satellites, put news on the air as it is happening. The live remote has become a staple of television news in the last decade.

When the space shuttle Challenger exploded seconds after liftoff in 1986, television viewers shared the shock and surprise of the event. They also shared the intrusion into the privacy of the next of kin of the astronauts as the cameras shifted focus to record their stunned reaction to the tragedy. In the hours that followed, viewers who stayed tuned also shared the tedium as the networks strove to fill time between interviews with officials speculating on what went wrong, or with persons who wanted to talk about the victims. The live coverage of that event and others reinforced the observation once made by Elmer Lower, a retired president of ABC News and a veteran of service with all three networks. He said, "We are the only journalistic medium that does its reporting and editing right in front of the audience."[77]

Television's ability to present the news raw, before it can be tested and refined to an approximation of truth by the checking and rechecking of skilled reporters and editors, raises special ethical considerations that apply to no other medium. So, too, does the ring of truth television conveys by giving viewers the sense of being present as news is made. When a newspaper or magazine presents one version of a news event and television another, it is difficult to argue with the viewer who says, "I saw it with my own eyes." And yet television professionals live with the knowledge that their medium has an infinite capacity to distort the news. Tom Pettit, an award-winning television newsman and executive vice-president of NBC News, wrote, "Today, technology permits producers to speed up or slow down actual events, actual voices. This is alteration of reality akin to forging a check."[78]

To forestall such forgery, the news divisions of all three networks and of many local television stations have adopted codes of ethics that are more detailed than that of their professional organization, the Radio-Television News Directors Association. That code starts with the assertion that the primary purpose of broadcast

---

77. Richard D. Yoakam and Charles T. Cremer, *ENG: Television News and the New Technology* (New York: Random House, 1985), p. 248.
78. Ibid., p. xi.

journalists is "to inform the public of events of importance and appropriate interest in a manner that is accurate and comprehensive." That purpose, the code says, overrides all others. The code also says that stories should be given sufficient background to make them meaningful and should not be sensationalized. Further, it says broadcast journalists "shall at all times display humane respect for the dignity, privacy and the well-being of persons with whom the news deals."

It is at this point that the code seems to part company with the realities generated by the intense competition among television news organizations. The television reporter who thrusts a microphone at the grieving survivors of disaster victims to catch their response to "How do you feel?" has become a cliché. That approach to news, and the ambush interview used on ABC's "20/20" and other news shows, have contributed to the public's perception that reporters are callous invaders of privacy. There is enough truth in that perception to make some journalists sensitive about it, but it may in part be a factor of what is not seen on the air. The more detailed codes of ethics adopted by CBS and NBC news advise against interviewing survivors on the air unless their permission is obtained in advance. And even with permission, the codes say that such interviews should be used only if they produce information essential to a proper telling of the story.

Fred Friendly, a former president of CBS News who became a professor at Columbia University, once told WBBM-TV that the ambush interview "is the dirtiest trick department of broadcast journalism."[79] In such interviews, a subject suspected of having something to hide is confronted suddenly in front of a live camera and is asked a question akin to "Why don't you stop beating your wife?" Even persons with nothing to hide are likely to look as though they have. Producers of television news shows are divided in their opinions as to the propriety of such interviews.[80] All concede they can be abused. Most prefer not to use an ambush interview with people who are not generally in the news. But all feel there are times when it should be used with public officials and others who are accountable to the public for their performance.

Television journalists live with the knowledge that their reporting methods are more obtrusive than those of their colleagues in the print media. Print reporters carry nothing more noticeable than a tape recorder, and these are usually so small they can be slipped into a pocket or purse. Television reporters are part of a team. At the very least, a camera operator will be in evidence, and somewhere nearby there will be a technician to see that the words and pictures get back to the studio. Although cameras have become small enough to carry in one hand, they are difficult to hide. Even in the fifth decade of the television era, a camera tends to draw a crowd. As John Premack, a prizewinning photojournalist with WCVB-TV in Boston, said, "We must recognize that a television camera tends to create its own reality. Part of our job as photojournalists is to understand that our mere presence can inflame, incite, initiate, and otherwise alter events we wish to cover."[81] Everyone in the news business is very much aware that some events,

79. Interviewed on "Watching the Watchdog" documentary, WBBM-TV, Chicago, 20 April 1981.
80. H. Eugene Goodwin, *Groping for Ethics in Journalism* (Ames: Iowa State University Press, 1983), pp. 181–82, 301.
81. Yoakam and Cremer, *ENG*, p. 261.

including press conferences, are staged solely in the expectation that cameras will be there. When all television news was recorded in advance and edited before it appeared on the air, such events could be cut to a size commensurate with their importance, or even ignored. Today, when television news producers emphasize "live from the scene" reports, there is little opportunity to screen out the exhibitionists. Their possible presence requires a higher degree of awareness on the part of the reporter on the scene, the camera operator, the electronic coordinator, the anchor, and the news director to detect the point at which the news event is taken over by someone with an ax to grind or a personal score to settle.

No other medium can bring news into the home with the impact of television. No words, no still picture, could duplicate television's portrayal of the awful moment when Challenger disappeared behind a glistening white cloud of smoke. But television news has its shortcomings, too. It tends to magnify stories high in emotional content and visual impact. The taking of hostages by anyone, anywhere, for whatever purpose, seems more important on television than it does reduced to a few paragraphs in a newspaper—especially if the hostages are interviewed in front of cameras. Stories of far greater importance may pass almost unnoticed because they are complex or do not lend themselves to pictorial treatment. It is difficult to simplify and glamorize a revision of the tax code or a proposal to reduce the federal deficit. If the latter must be explained in forty-five seconds, it is apt to come out in terms of what it might do to a mother of two small children who fears that reduction of her rent subsidy will drive her into the streets.

Despite its shortcomings, polls indicate that some people get all their news from television. For most of us, television and radio are the first to bring us breaking news. All of us rely on it for such impression as we have of the world's newsmakers. Television professionals are aware that theirs is a serious and important business demanding more thought and care than time sometimes permits.

FOR REVIEW

1. What is the rationale for the regulation of broadcasting?

2. Compare and contrast the First Amendment rights of broadcasters and of print publishers.

3. What did the Supreme Court say in *National Broadcasting Co.* v. *United States* with respect to the powers of the Federal Communications Commission?

4. List the principal provisions of the equal opportunities sections of the Communications Act. To whom do they apply? Under what circumstances? How much discretion does a station owner have in deciding whether to grant time to a candidate for public office? Can a station owner exercise control over the content of political usages? Why or why not?

5. Describe the fairness doctrine. On what rationale is it based?

6. Describe the role of the FCC in investigating complaints of violations of the

fairness doctrine. How far can it go in imposing its view of fairness on a broadcaster?

7. What two points with respect to the fairness doctrine were established by the court of appeals decision in the first *United Church of Christ* case?

8. Describe the personal attack rule. What was the rationale and principal effect of the Supreme Court's decision in *Red Lion?*

9. What did the Supreme Court say in the *CBS* case about an individual or corporate right of access to the airwaves?

10. What did the Supreme Court tell broadcasters in the *Pacifica* case?

11. How far has the FCC gone toward the deregulation of the broadcasting media? What is the rationale of the movement? What arguments have been offered in opposition to it?

12. Outline some of the issues raised by the growth of cable television systems.

CHAPTER 11

ADVERTISING

Advertising, after word of mouth, is the most pervasive means of communication. It makes up a substantial part of the content of newspapers and magazines. Without advertising, radio and television would not exist in their present form. Makers of commercial products, providers of services, and advocates of causes spend in excess of $60 billion a year to catch the public's attention. A major part of this amount supports the news media.

Despite this intimate relationship, until recent times advertising had little or no legal protection except that afforded by the **law of contracts and commercial transactions.** As far as the First Amendment was concerned, advertising was in exile, along with obscenity, fighting words, sedition, and other kinds of speech condemned by courts as lacking in valid idea content. Thus advertising, unlike news and opinion, could be subjected to prior restraint and other legal punishments with little hindrance.

This is not to say that advertising suffered from many restrictions. Any history student who has scanned the advertisements in turn-of-the-century newspapers has noted that any claim, no matter how preposterous, could be, and was, made for products like patent medicines. Until well into this century, the rule in advertising was "anything goes," reflecting the age-old rule of commercial transactions—*caveat emptor* ("Let the buyer beware"). The law assumed that buyers and sellers, advertisers and their audiences, were of equal intelligence. Anyone who was stuck with a bad bargain or taken in by a flowery ad was out of luck. It was assumed that victims of sharp practices would learn from their experience and not be taken in the next time. Not until 1906 did Congress take a first small step toward control of deceptive advertising. In that year it passed the Pure Food and Drug Act, which gave a federal agency authority to regulate claims made on package labels. This was followed in 1914 by the Federal Trade Commission Act. One of the duties of the commission was to regulate advertising claims. The Federal Trade Commission has become one of several weapons used against deceptive advertisers.

This chapter deals with four major themes of advertising law:

1. The Supreme Court's recognition in the 1970s that advertising is **commercial speech** entitled to limited First Amendment protection. That protection extends to advertisements for legal products and services as long as the ad is not deceptive. Government can regulate protected advertising only if it can demonstrate an overriding public interest in doing so.

2. The role of the Federal Trade Commission in regulating advertising to prevent deception. This role peaked in the 1970s in response to consumer activism and declined in the 1980s as a part of the government's move toward deregulation of business. Other federal and state agencies play a minor role in the regulation of advertising. Further, some firms have responded to a competitor's allegedly misleading advertising by seeking legal relief in the courts.

3. The media's right to refuse advertising, whether it be for a commercial product or to persuade others to adopt a point of view on a public issue. Courts generally have rejected the argument advanced by Jerome Barron and others that people should have a right under the First Amendment to

compel the media to carry their messages. However, courts have held that media under direct control of government officials can be required to accept advertising advocating a point of view on public issues. This applies mainly to public high school and college newspapers. The Supreme Court has held that municipalities may forbid outdoor advertising for aesthetic or safety reasons, but not for reasons of content.

4. The right of corporations to spend corporate funds on advertising intended to influence opinion on a public issue. The Supreme Court has held that corporations may advertise a point of view even when the issue will not have a direct effect on their business.

Major Cases

Bates v. *State Bar of Arizona*, 433 U.S. 350, 97 S.Ct. 2691, 53 L.Ed.2d 810 (1977).

Bigelow v. *Virginia*, 421 U.S. 809, 95 S.Ct. 2222, 44 L.Ed.2d 600 (1975).

Bolger v. *Youngs Drug Products Corp.*, 463 U.S. 60, 103 S.Ct. 2875, 77 L.Ed.2d 469 (1983).

Central Hudson Gas & Electric Corp. v. *Public Service Commission*, 447 U.S. 557, 100 S.Ct. 2343, 65 L.Ed.2d 341 (1980).

Chicago Joint Board, Amalgamated Clothing Workers of America, AFL-CIO v. *Chicago Tribune Co.*, 307 F.Supp. 422 (N.D.Ill. 1969).

First National Bank of Boston v. *Bellotti*, 435 U.S. 765, 98 S.Ct. 1407, 55 L.Ed.2d 707 (1978).

Lee v. *Board of Regents of State Colleges*, 306 F.Supp. 1097 (W.D.Wis. 1969).

Miami Herald Publishing Co. v. *Tornillo*, 418 U.S. 241, 94 S.Ct. 2831, 41 L.Ed.2d 730 (1974).

Pittsburgh Press Co. v. *Pittsburgh Commission on Human Relations*, 413 U.S. 376, 93 S.Ct. 2553, 37 L.Ed.2d 669 (1973).

Shuck v. *The Carroll Daily Herald*, 247 N.W. 813 (1933).

Valentine v. *Chrestensen*, 316 U.S. 52, 62 S.Ct. 920, 86 L.Ed. 1262 (1942).

Village of Hoffman Estates v. *Flipside, Hoffman Estates*, 455 U.S. 489, 102 S.Ct. 1186, 71 L.Ed.2d 362 (1982).

Virginia State Board of Pharmacy v. *Virginia Citizens Consumer Council*, 425 U.S. 748, 96 S.Ct. 1817, 48 L.Ed.2d 346 (1976).

Warner-Lambert Co. v. *FTC*, 562 F.2d 749 (D.C.Cir. 1977).

THE DOCTRINE OF COMMERCIAL SPEECH

Advertising and the First Amendment

Not long before the United States entered World War II in 1941, F. J. Chrestensen bought a surplus navy submarine and towed it from one East Coast port to another, charging admission to visitors. In 1940, he arrived in New York City, where he was refused the right to tie up at a city-owned pier. Finding dockage elsewhere, he began distributing handbills in Times Square, soliciting business. A police officer stopped him, explaining that by law he could solicit for a cause in the streets, but he could not solicit business. Chrestensen had a bright idea. He was still mad at the city for refusing him space at its pier. So he had his handbills reprinted. On one side, the message protested the city's action. On the other, it invited visitors to tour his submarine, now tied up at a state-owned pier. The ploy didn't work. Police arrested Chrestensen and charged him with violating a section of the Sanitary Code forbidding distribution of commercial handbills on the streets.

***Valentine* v. *Chrestensen*, 316 U.S. 52, 62 S.Ct. 920, 86 L.Ed. 1262 (1942).**   On appeal, the Supreme Court of the United States affirmed. Justice Owen J. Roberts, writing for a unanimous Court in *Valentine* v. *Chrestensen*, noted that the Court had long held that the streets are proper forums for the communication of ideas, subject only to restrictions of time, place, and manner. Then he added:

> We are equally clear that the Constitution imposes no such restraint on government as respects purely commercial advertising. Whether, and to what extent, one may promote or pursue a gainful occupation in the streets, to what extent such activity shall be adjudged a derogation of the public right of the user, are matters for legislative judgment.

With those few words the Court reinforced the assumption that "purely commercial advertising" lay outside the realm of speech protected by the First Amendment.

For more than twenty years that assumption went unchallenged. Lawyers for L. B. Sullivan, police commissioner of Montgomery, Alabama, cited *Valentine* in their brief to the Supreme Court to support Sullivan's libel suit against the *New York Times*. The statement accusing him of aiding in the mistreatment of the Rev. Martin Luther King, Jr., and the black students at Alabama State College had appeared in a paid advertisement. Therefore, the lawyers argued, it was not protected by the First Amendment. But, as noted in Chapter 4, the Court held that this ad was different. It was not selling a product. It was arguing a cause of vital interest to the nation's welfare. Publishers should be encouraged to print such ads to further the debate on desegregation. Therefore, the Court held that cause or editorial advertising—advertising designed to sell an idea rather than a product—does have the full protection of the First Amendment.[1] But the Court

---

1. New York Times v. Sullivan, 376 U.S. 254, 84 S.Ct. 710, 11 L.Ed.2d 686 (1964).

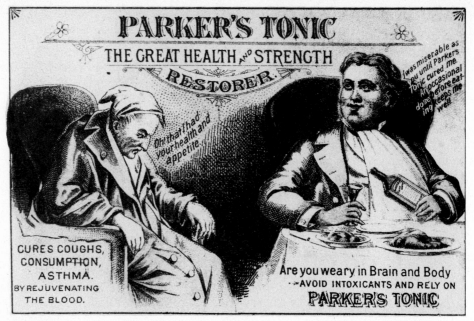

Wild claims made by patent medicine advertisers at the turn of the century contributed to adoption of the Pure Food and Drug Act in 1906. Eight years later the Federal Trade Commission was created and was given authority to regulate deceptive advertising. (The Bettmann Archive)

was silent on "purely commercial speech." It appeared, then, that the Court had divided paid communication into two classes, depending upon the purpose of the ad. If the purpose was to sell an idea, the ad was protected by the First Amendment. If the purpose was to sell a product, or a service, it was not.

This neat classification persisted for nearly a decade before another aspect of the civil rights movement raised questions about it. In the *Pittsburgh Press Co.* v. early 1970s, Pittsburgh, like many other cities, estab-*Pittsburgh Commission on* lished a Commission on Human Relations. One of *Human Relations,* 413 U.S. its purposes was to attack discrimination in whatever 376, 93 S.Ct. 2553, 37 form it might take, but particularly in the sensitive L.Ed.2d 669 (1973). areas of housing and hiring. The ordinance establishing the commission made it illegal, for instance, to discriminate in hiring on sexual grounds, or to abet such discrimination.

The commission charged that the two daily newspapers in Pittsburgh, jointly published by the Pittsburgh Press Co., were violating the law in their classified advertising sections. Ads seeking or offering employment were printed under three headings: "Male Interest," "Female Interest," and "Male-Female." This, the commission concluded, was furthering stereotyped job classifications, thus abetting discriminatory hiring. Not at all, the newspapers responded. They were merely performing a service for their readers. Some jobs clearly were the kind that appealed more to women than to men, and vice versa. By recognizing this, the newspapers' advertising department was simply making it easier for both employers and job seekers to find what they were looking for. The department's decisions, the newspapers argued, were editorial judgments protected by the First Amendment.

Neither the commission nor a county court bought that argument, and the newspapers were ordered to comply with the law, which all but forbade any sexual references in employment advertising. The newspapers carried their case to the Supreme Court, and in *Pittsburgh Press Co.* v. *Pittsburgh Commission on Human Relations*, the Court upheld the commission, five-to-four.

Because the Pittsburgh Press Co. had raised the First Amendment question, the Court had to deal with it. Looking at both *Valentine* and *New York Times*, the majority concluded that the ads in question were commercial in nature. Therefore, they were not entitled to First Amendment protection. But Justice Lewis F. Powell, Jr., writing for the majority, could not quite reject the suggestion that editorial decisions were involved in classifying the ads:

> Under some circumstances, at least, a newspaper's editorial judgments in connection with an advertisement take on the character of the advertisement and, in those cases, the scope of the newspaper's First Amendment protection may be affected by the content of the advertisement.

In this case, he continued, he was not convinced that there was enough judgment involved to lift "the newspapers' actions from the category of commercial speech." In any event, such judgments as were involved "probably do help employers who are of a mind to discriminate in hiring." Then he wrote the kind of sentence that lawyers love to explore for further meaning:

> Any First Amendment interest which might be served by advertising an ordinary commmercial proposal and which might arguably outweigh the governmental interest supporting the regulation is altogether absent when the commercial activity itself is illegal and the restriction on advertising is incidental to a valid limitation on economic activity.

Stripped to its essentials, the statement seemed to say that some kinds of "purely commercial advertising" might enjoy some First Amendment protection under some circumstances. But in this case, the statement clearly said, there was no such protection because the ads promoted an illegal purpose, that is, discrimination in employment.

Within two years, the Court was offered an opportunity to clarify Powell's reference to advertising and the First Amendment. That case, too, had civil rights origins, and had been moving through the courts for four years. It began when the *Virginia Weekly*, an "underground newspaper" at the University of Virginia, carried an advertisement for an abortion clinic operating legally in New York City. At the time, abortions not only were illegal in Virginia, but it was likewise a crime to advertise to perform an abortion. Jeffrey Bigelow, the *Weekly*'s managing editor, was arrested, found guilty of advertising an abortion service, and fined. When Virginia persisted in prosecuting Bigelow, even after the Supreme Court had legalized abortions, the Court agreed to review his conviction. It held, in *Bigelow* v. *Virginia*, that the state law forbidding abortion advertising was unconstitutional.

Bigelow v. Virginia, 421 U.S. 809, 95 S.Ct. 2222, 44 L.Ed.2d 600 (1975).

Justice Harry A. Blackmun wrote for seven members of the Court. He tackled head-on "[T]he central assumption . . . that commercial speech does not enjoy First Amendment protection." When he had finished writing, that assumption was all but demolished. The Virginia courts, he said, had read too much into *Valentine*, on which they had relied in convicting Bigelow. That decision never had done any more than uphold New York City's restriction on commercial handbills. It did not mean "that all statutes regulating commercial advertising are immune from constitutional challenge." Stating it the other way, Blackmun wrote, "Our cases . . . clearly establish that speech is not stripped of First Amendment protection merely because it appears [in an advertisement]."

In Bigelow's case, the Court held, the abortion ad did more than propose a simple commercial transaction—that is, "If you come to New York City you can get a legal abortion at our clinic." It informed women in Virginia that there were places outside that state where abortions were being performed legally. Virginia could not close its borders to those of its residents who might want to have a legal abortion elsewhere. Nor could it arrest them when they got back, even though abortions were illegal in Virginia when the ad appeared. Therefore, because the ad conveyed an idea as well as a commercial proposition, and because it offered a service that was within the law, it was not without First Amendment protection.

This negative approach stopped short of saying that any ad for any legal product or service is protected by the First Amendment. The justices were looking for information content, for a message that conveyed a noncommercial idea. Within less than a year, Virginia was to offer the Court another commercial speech case, this one involving advertising that offered a commercial transaction in its starkest terms: "We will sell you a specific product for a stated price."

Virginia, like other states, has a body of law regulating licensed professions. Such laws generally define "unprofessional conduct," and provide for disciplining practitioners who violate the code. In Virginia, pharmacists are among the licensed professionals. In the early 1970s, the law said that advertising the price of a prescription drug was unprofessional conduct. Thus a patient who required a prescription drug was, in effect, a blind buyer forced to pay whatever price was charged at the time of purchase. If all drug stores charged the same price for the same drug, this would make no difference. However, surveys conducted by various consumer groups, and by the American Medical Association, showed price variations in commonly prescribed drugs of up to 1,200 percent. One study showed, for instance, that the price of a commonly prescribed antibiotic ranged from $1.20 to $9 for the same number of capsules. Persons with prescriptions could shop around for a good price only if they had the time, and the will, to use the telephone or go from store to store.

Virginia State Board of Pharmacy v. Virginia Citizens Consumer Council, 425 U.S. 748, 96 S.Ct. 1817, 48 L.Ed.2d 346 (1976).

In the early 1970s, several drug firms began to challenge laws defining price advertising as unprofessional conduct. They did so discreetly, merely posting the prices of commonly prescribed drugs. In Virginia they were joined by a consumer group, the Virginia Citizens Consumer Council. It filed suit in a federal district court asking that the price law be declared unconstitutional. The court did so. An appeal went to the U.S. Supreme

Court, which affirmed, eight-to-one, in *Virginia State Board of Pharmacy* v. *Virginia Citizens Consumer Council.*

Again Justice Blackmun wrote for the Court. Again he fished for information content to justify the conclusion that price advertising is worthy of First Amendment protection. Again he found it. He posed the key question:

> Here, in contrast [to the earlier cases], the question whether there is a First Amendment exception for "commercial speech" is squarely before us. Our pharmacist does not wish to editorialize on any subject, cultural, philosophical, or political. He does not wish to report any particularly newsworthy fact, or to make generalized observations even about commercial matters. The "idea" he wishes to communicate is simply this: "I will sell you the X prescription drug at the Y price." Our question, then, is whether this communication is wholly outside the protection of the First Amendment.

Justice Blackmun rationalized that in inflationary times, when prescription drug purchasers, many of them elderly pensioners, were being squeezed financially, price information became significant. Indeed, he wrote, the consumer's interest in prices "may be as keen, if not keener by far, than his interest in the day's most urgent political debate." Be that as it may, when he had finished writing, the doctrine of commercial speech seemed to include advertising for any legal purpose. Chief Justice Warren E. Burger was not prepared to go that far. He concurred in the judgment, but wrote separately to note that he was not ready to let the First Amendment permit advertising by lawyers and physicians. And Justice Potter Stewart, also concurring in the result, wondered whether Blackmun had not written so broadly as to cancel laws regulating deceptive advertising. These reservations soon would be answered.

Defining the Amendment's Scope

For decades, lawyers and judges can move serenely along, unaware that a given area of law may offer legal or constitutional problems. Then some court will be persuaded to accept and decide a case where no precedents exist. That will lead to others, and soon there will be a flood of similar cases surging through the courts. And so it has been with commercial-speech cases. Few years have passed since 1976 in which the Supreme Court has not had to decide one or more such cases. With few exceptions, these have done little more than fill in the gaps left by the two Virginia cases.

In 1977, the Court decided *Linmark Associates,* v. *Township of Willingboro*[2] and *Bates* v. *State Bar of Arizona.*[3] In the former, a New Jersey township had forbidden posting of "For Sale" or "Sold" signs in residential neighborhoods. It had done so to halt the flight of white home-owners from racially integrated neighborhoods. The Court ruled the law unconstitutional. Home-owners traditionally have used yard signs to tell others that their houses are for sale. There are other ways of doing so, but all are more expensive and may not be as effective. If home-owners can be prevented from using the most direct way to tell others their house is for sale, Justice Thurgood Marshall wrote,

2. 431 U.S. 85, 97 S.Ct. 1614, 52 L.Ed.2d 155 (1977).
3. 433 U.S. 350, 97 S.Ct. 2691, 53 L.Ed.2d 810 (1977).

"then every locality in the country can suppress any facts that reflect poorly on the locality, so long as a plausible claim can be made that disclosure would cause the recipients of the information to act 'irrationally.' " The decision did, however, introduce a new factor into the commercial-speech equation. Marshall said that the township might be able to regulate the signs if it could demonstrate a compelling need to do so. This idea would become a major idea in some of the later decisions.

In the *Bates* case, the Court dealt with Chief Justice Burger's reservations in *State Board of Pharmacy*. John R. Bates and Van O'Steen were fledgling lawyers in Phoenix. They placed an ad in the *Arizona Republic* that got right to the point. "DO YOU NEED A LAWYER?" it asked in big, bold type. In smaller type it proclaimed, "Legal Services at very reasonable fees." Under an illustration representing the scales of justice, the ad proceeded to list basic prices for half a dozen services, including divorce and bankruptcy. The lawyers' ad flew squarely in the face of the Canons of the American Bar Association, which in Arizona were also a rule of court embedded in the state's statutes.

Bates v. State Bar of Arizona, 433 U.S. 350, 97 S.Ct. 2691, 53 L.Ed.2d 810 (1977).

The president of the state bar himself charged the lawyers with soliciting clients in violation of the code of ethics. A hearing committee recommended they be suspended from the practice of law for not less than six months. On appeal, the state supreme court reduced the penalty to censure. On further appeal, the Supreme Court said even that was too much. The ban on advertising by lawyers violated the First Amendment.

Because Justice Blackmun, who again wrote for the Court, was touching his fellow lawyers in a tender spot—their means of obtaining clients—he wrote a great deal about the nature of the practice of law. What it boils down to is the conclusion that lawyers may have made themselves too remote and mysterious. Persons with a great deal of money have learned to consult them in time of trouble. The Supreme Court has held that poor folk who are accused of a crime must have a lawyer at public expense. Congress has established legal aid societies that help the poor with civil problems. But the great middle classes hold back from seeking legal advice, perhaps because they fear it may be too expensive. Therefore, Blackmun reasoned, ads like that run by Bates and O'Steen could help such persons defend their legal rights when they need to do so. Again, the Court resorted to the rationale that whatever its commercial aspects, the ad conveyed valuable information: "You, too, can afford a lawyer."

Blackmun also dealt with Stewart's reservation in *Virginia Pharmacy*, that the doctrine of commercial speech might condone misleading advertising. He wrote:

> Advertising that is false, deceptive, or misleading of course is subject to restraint. . . . Since the advertiser knows his product and has a commercial interest in its dissemination, we have little worry that regulation to assure truthfulness will discourage protected speech. . . . And any concern that strict requirements for truthfulness will undesirably inhibit spontaneity seems inapplicable because commercial speech generally is calculated. Indeed, the public and private benefits from commercial speech derive from confidence in its accuracy and reliability. Thus, the leeway for untruthful or misleading expression that has been allowed in other contexts has little force in the commercial arena.

In other words, Blackmun was serving notice that there was no room in the doctrine of commercial speech for the *New York Times* rule. The First Amendment protection given to commercial advertising did not contain the "breathing space" for falsehood enjoyed by speech commenting on the activities of public officials and public figures. This left open the possibility, suggested in *Linmark* and *Bates*, that government could regulate advertising if there were some "compelling need" to do so, or if it were misleading. Thus, while commercial speech had been admitted to the First Amendment community, its status seemed to be that of a second-class citizen. Three years after the Supreme Court decided *Bates*, it took another commercial-speech case and sought to define with greater precision what that status is.

Regulating Commercial Speech

Middle Eastern Arab countries, exasperated by United States policy toward Israel, cut off oil exports to this country in 1973. The resulting temporary shortages of petroleum products caused more irritation than hardship, but they did serve to focus attention on oil as a dwindling resource. New York's Public Service Commission reacted by forbidding all advertising by electric companies promoting the use of electricity. Its rationale was straightforward. Most of the electrical generating plants in the state burned fuel oil. If the companies sold less electricity, they would need less oil. Therefore, they should not be advertising to obtain more customers, or to urge their present customers to buy appliances that would use more electricity. The Arab embargo was lifted in March 1974, but the New York advertising ban remained in effect.

The Central Hudson Gas & Electric Corp., acting for itself and other New York state electric companies, asked a state court to end the ban. Looking at the Supreme Court's commercial speech cases, the utilities argued that it violated their First Amendment right to advertise. The state court disagreed, holding that there was a continuing need for oil conservation, which was great enough to justify the restriction. When state appeals courts affirmed, Central Hudson carried its case to the Supreme Court. In *Central Hudson Gas & Electric Corp.* v. *Public Service Commission*, it reversed, with only one dissenting vote.

Central Hudson Gas & Electric Corp. v. *Public Service Commission*, 447 U.S. 557, 100 S.Ct. 2343, 65 L.Ed.2d 341 (1980).

Justice Powell, writing for the Court, reviewed the commercial speech cases and found in them protection even for advertising that "communicates only an incomplete version of the relevant facts." The First Amendment, he said, "presumes that some accurate information is better than no information at all." Therefore, the state cannot prohibit all commercial speech, even though the Constitution gives it less protection than it does most other kinds of speech. The degree of protection for commercial speech, Powell wrote, "turns on the nature both of the expression and of the governmental interests served by the regulation." The Court has brought the First Amendment into play to protect "the informational function of advertising." Thus, if a commercial message does "not accurately inform the public about lawful activity," it may even be suppressed, as in the *Pittsburgh Press* case.

But if the commercial message does not mislead, and it concerns lawful activity, the government's power to regulate it is limited. Here, Powell outlined the points that must be taken into consideration in determining whether such regulation is proper:

The State must assert a substantial interest to be achieved by restrictions on commercial speech. Moreover, the regulatory technique must be in proportion to that interest. The limitation on expression must be designed carefully to achieve the State's goal. Compliance with the requirement may be measured by two criteria. First, the restriction must directly advance the state interest involved; the regulation may not be sustained if it provides only ineffective or remote support for the government's purpose. Second, if the governmental interest could be served as well by a more limited restriction on commercial speech, the excessive restrictions cannot survive.

Powell wrote that the state cannot impose regulations that only indirectly advance its interests. Nor can it regulate commercial speech that poses no danger to a state interest. He concluded:

> In commercial speech cases, then, a four-part analysis has developed. At the outset, we must determine whether the expression is protected by the First Amendment. For commercial speech to come within that provision, it at least must concern lawful activity and not be misleading. Next, we ask whether the asserted governmental interest is substantial. If both inquiries yield positive answers, we must determine whether the regulation directly advances the governmental interest asserted, and whether it is not more extensive than is necessary to serve that interest."

Powell applied this four-step analysis to the New York commission's regulation and concluded that it violated the utility company's First Amendment rights. Clearly, Central Hudson's proposed advertising was not inaccurate, nor did it promote unlawful activity. But the utilities commission argued that Central Hudson, like all electric companies, was a monopoly. If people in its territory wanted electricity, they had to get it from Central Hudson. The New York courts had looked at that fact and concluded there was little point to advertising by electric companies. Therefore, such advertising was of little First Amendment value and must yield to a larger state interest in conservation.

Powell said the lower courts had looked at the issue too narrowly. For some purposes, fuel oil and natural gas are in direct competition with electricity. And even in uses where there is no competition, advertising serves some purpose. The electric company may wish to offer new services, or inform its customers of new terms of doing business. Further, it might also wish to advertise new lines of appliances that use less energy than those now in use. Powell concluded that there are substantial reasons why electric companies should be permitted to advertise.

The state of New York had argued that it was serving two important interests by banning advertising: It was encouraging conservation of a scarce resource, and it was keeping rates lower than they otherwise would be. If the companies' advertising led to increased use of electricity, they would have to build new plants to meet peak demands. These building costs would be reflected in higher rates.

Powell conceded that both interests were substantial. But he dismissed the latter with a few sentences:

> The link between the advertising prohibition and [Central Hudson's] rate structure is, at most, tenuous. The impact of promotional advertising on the equity of [the company's] rates is highly speculative. . . . Such conditional and remote eventualities simply cannot justify silencing [its] promotional advertising.

He took the conservation argument more seriously, noting a direct link between promotional advertising and increased use of electricity. But it is well established, Powell said, that a restriction on speech cannot go beyond what is needed to protect a vital state interest. New York's ban was not limited to promotional advertising. It applied to all advertising by electric utilitites. This swept too broadly, and thus was in violation of the First Amendment. The utilities commission had made no showing that it could not encourage conservation by some more limited restriction. Therefore, its broad ban on advertising must fall.

The Court has used Powell's four-point analysis in deciding more recent commercial-speech cases. In 1981 it struck down an ordinance of the city of San Diego banning commercial billboards.[4] The Court said the city council could rationally conclude that billboards created a traffic hazard and detracted from the city's beauty. Therefore, it might ban all billboards on those grounds. But when the ordinance divided billboards into two classes—commercial and noncommercial—and permitted those showing non-commercial messages, it infringed on free speech. The city could not choose topics it considered fit for public display on billboards.

In 1984, in *Members of City Council* v. *Taxpayers for Vincent*,[5] the Supreme Court upheld a Los Angeles city ordinance forbidding erection of advertising signs on public property. The action was brought by Roland Vincent, a candidate for city council, whose campaign signs were removed from utility poles by city employees. The Court held that the city had a right to protect aesthetic values by prohibiting advertising signs on public property as long as it applied to all signs. The Court said the ordinance would fall, as it applied to political campaign signs, only if Vincent could demonstrate that he had no other effective means of calling attention to his candidacy. The Court concluded he could not do that.

Twice since *Bates*, the Supreme Court has seen fit to further define its holding that lawyers have a right to advertise. In 1982, in *Matter of R ____ M. J ____*,[6] the Court struck down a Missouri Supreme Court rule narrowly restricting the content of advertisements placed by attorneys. A lawyer was facing disbarment because his listing of practice areas did not use precisely the words prescribed by the rules. The Court held that as long as there was nothing misleading in the wording of a lawyer's ad, it could be couched as the advertiser saw fit. In 1985, in *Zauderer* v. *Office of Disciplinary Council*,[7] the Court struck down a section of the Ohio Professional Code prohibiting the use of illustrations in ads placed by attorneys. Philip Q. Zauderer, a lawyer practicing in Columbus, had used a drawing of a Dalkon shield, a birth control device, in an advertisement seeking clients who had suffered harm from its use. The Court said illustrations serve "important communicative functions" and thus "are entitled to the First Amendment protections afforded verbal commercial speech." However, the Court held that Zauderer could be disciplined because he had omitted information about plea bargaining and the charging of expenses that made his ads misleading.

If advertising messages and the editorial content of books and magazines are linked

---

4. Metromedia v. City of San Diego, 453 U.S. 490, 101 S.Ct. 2882, 69 L.Ed.2d 800 (1981).
5. 466 U.S. 789, 104 S.Ct. 2118, 80 L.Ed.2d 772 (1984).
6. 455 U.S. 191, 102 S.Ct. 929, 71 L.Ed.2d 64, (1982).
7. ___U.S.___, 105 S.Ct. 2265, 85 L.Ed.2d 652 (1985).

with commercial activity in a manner that seems to promote use of harmful drugs, the state may intervene. In 1982, the Supreme Court held that its commercial-speech doctrine would not protect a "head shop" from complying with a licensing ordinance enacted by the village of Hoffman Estates, Illinois. The village required shops selling materials "designed or marketed for use with illegal cannabis or drugs" to pay $150 a year for a license. Owners also were required to take the names of persons buying such materials and to make the list available to police. By the terms of the ordinance, a shop qualified for a license if it displayed such things as cigarette papers, roach clips, water pipes, and the like in conjunction with literature, signs, graphic designs, or other materials encouraging the use of illegal drugs.

Village of Hoffman Estates v. Flipside, Hoffman Estates, 455 U.S. 489, 102 S.Ct. 1186, 71 L.Ed.2d 362 (1982).

A shop called Flipside was cited for not obtaining a license. It stocked not only an array of items commonly associated with drug usage but such publications as A *Child's Garden of Grass, Marijuana Grower's Guide,* and *High Times.* The shop's owner asked a federal district court to declare the licensing law unconstitutional on First Amendment grounds. That court dismissed the action, but the United States Court of Appeals for the Seventh Circuit reversed, holding that the ordinance swept too broadly into protected First Amendment speech. The Supreme Court took the case and restored the district court's verdict, thus upholding the ordinance.

Justice Marshall, writing for the Court, said the ordinance imposed neither a prior

In 1982 the Supreme Court held that local communities may license "head shops" and restrict their advertising messages. The Court said that when advertising promotes illegal activity it may be regulated or banned entirely. (Frank Siteman/ Stock, Boston)

restraint nor an unacceptable restriction on commercial speech. It did nothing more than look to the nature of advertising messages and editorial content as guides to the purposes for which certain items were being sold. The purpose of the ordinance was to discourage illegal drug use. If speech was at issue, it was speech promoting an illegal purpose, "which a government may regulate or ban entirely."

Bolger v. *Youngs Drug Products Corp.*, 463 U.S. 60, 103 S.Ct. 2875, 77 L.Ed.2d 469 (1983).

In 1983, the Supreme Court struck down a federal law prohibiting the mailing of unsolicited advertisements for contraceptives. The decision, in *Bolger* v. *Youngs Drug Products Corp.*, offers a classic example of the application of Powell's four-step *Central Hudson* test.

Youngs Drug Products is a manufacturer of condoms. It used three kinds of circulars to promote sales of its products through the mails. When the Postal Service warned Youngs that its mailings violated the law, the manufacturer asked a federal district court to hold that the law violated its First Amendment rights. When the district court did so, the Postal Service appealed directly to the Supreme Court. It affirmed unanimously, with one justice taking no part in the case.

Justice Marshall, writing for the Court, held that the advertising circulars were not deceptive. They advertised a legal product. Therefore, the message they bore was a form of protected commercial speech. That speech had value because it promoted a product that could prevent venereal disease or an unwanted pregnancy.

The Postal Service argued that its ban on advertising served two important state interests: It shielded recipients from materials that some would find offensive, and it helped parents control the manner in which their children were to be informed about birth control. Marshall dismissed the first interest as insubstantial. People who opened an envelope and found the contents offensive could avert their eyes. Marshall held that the second interest had merit. But the law reached too far in trying to serve that interest. Parents who did not want their children exposed to the condom advertisements could ask the Postal Service to cut them off at the source.[8] This was the preferred remedy, Marshall held. The law prohibiting all mailing of birth control advertisements was defective because it purged "all mailboxes of unsolicited material that is entirely suitable for adults. . . . The level of discourse reaching a mailbox simply cannot be limited to that which would be suitable for a sandbox."

It is well established, then, that advertising for any legal product or service is protected by the First Amendment as long as the contents are not deceptive. Government may regulate such advertising, but only if it finds a "compelling need" to do so. The proposed regulation must serve a substantial governmental interest. Further, the regulation must directly advance that interest and it must not sweep more broadly than necessary. In developing the doctrine of commercial speech, the Supreme Court has rejected the suggestion that advertisers be given the leeway that *Near* and *New York Times* give to political speech. In *New York Times* particularly, the Court held that speech directed at government officials or influential public figures cannot be punished even if it is false,

---

8. Under 39 U.S.C. §3008, people who do not want to receive sexually oriented mailings may notify the Postal Service, which, in turn, is required to notify the offending advertisers. They must honor such requests or face penalties.

unless the victim can prove knowledge of falsehood or reckless disregard for the truth. This is the rule even when the offending speech appears in an advertisement. But when an ad promotes a commercial product or service, there is no margin of forgiveness for error. Justice Blackmun addressed that question directly in *Bates*, concluding that "the leeway for untruthful or misleading expression that has been allowed in other contexts has little force in the commercial arena." The implications of this dual standard will be examined next.

THE REGULATION OF ADVERTISING

The Rise of the Federal Trade Commission

When the Federal Trade Commission was established in 1914, its mission was to protect business firms from each other. It did so in part by seeking to stop deceptive advertising, which was held to give the offending firm an unfair advantage over its more honest competitors. This focus on unfair competition was reinforced by the Supreme Court in 1931 when it held in *Federal Trade Commission* v. *Raladam*[9] that the law creating the commission did not give it the authority to act to protect consumers. Not until 1938 was the law changed to permit the FTC to act to protect consumers from deceptive advertising.

Even with that change, the Federal Trade Commission (FTC) was destined to labor in obscurity for more than thirty years. It was limited on one side by anemic budgets and on the other by news media that usually ignored its work. Its occasional findings that certain advertisements were deceptive and would have to be withdrawn or changed went largely unreported except in a few consumer-oriented magazines of limited circulation.

That began to change in the 1960s when the same ferment that produced the civil rights and anti-Vietnam War movements also produced a consumer movement. In the beginning, it was largely the work of one man, Ralph Nader, who made himself highly visible by taking on such giants as General Motors. Nader's book *Unsafe at Any Speed*[10] documented charges of engineering and design problems that led GM to stop production of its rear-engined Corvair. The consumer movement gathered strength from several other sources. Inflation, which became an uncomfortable factor of American life in the late 1960s, made everyone more conscious of value. It also was a time when authority generally was being questioned. Young people particularly were asking why those who were in charge of business firms and other institutions couldn't do things right. The media, particularly television, contributed to the questioning mood. For years, most people took it for granted that there was a certain amount of puffery in print ads. But even children could see that there sometimes was a considerable difference between the

---

9. 283 U.S. 643, 51 S.Ct. 587, 75 L.Ed. 1324 (1931).
10. Ralph Nader, *Unsafe at Any Speed* (New York: Grossman, 1972).

way a product performed in a television commercial and the way it performed in actual use. In 1969, the American Bar Association appointed a committee headed by Miles Kirkpatrick to study the FTC's role in policing advertising. The result was a scathing expose' of the agency's ineffectiveness accompanied by recommendations for reform.[11] President Richard M. Nixon followed up by appointing Kirkpatrick to the commission. Congress responded by increasing the FTC's budget.

Thus began in the early 1970s a decade of what one observer called "trench warfare" between the FTC and the advertising business.[12] By 1982, the FTC was under attack on four fronts—from business, the Congress, President Ronald Reagan, and even from its own chairman. James Miller, appointed by Reagan, asked a Senate committee to limit the agency's power to challenge ads as deceptive. He said it operated under such broad authority that "virtually any ad can be found to be deceptive."[13]

A look at the FTC's rulings during the previous decade might lead one to that conclusion. A sampling of the files shows the following:

— Kroger Co.'s "price patrol" advertising, featuring the results of comparison shopping, was held deceptive in 1981 because it was not based on a broad enough sampling.[14]

— Sterling Drug Co. ads for Bayer, Bayer Children's Aspirin, Cope, Vanquish, and Midol were found to promise more than they could deliver in the way of headache and tension relief.[15]

— Standard Brands agreed to stop advertising that "every 15 seconds, a doctor recommends Fleischmann's" margarine. It could not produce valid survey results supporting the claim.[16]

— Control Data Corp. ads for its computer-programing courses were found to be misleading. The ads had said a college education was not an advantage in getting a job in the computer field.[17]

— Mobil Corporation agreed to warn users of its Mobil 1 oil, touted as reducing oil consumption up to 25 percent, that it might actually increase oil usage in some kinds of cars.[18]

These instances could be multiplied many times. Other targets of FTC deceptive

11. *Facts on File*, vol. 29, no. 1507, 11–17 September 1969, p. 597; vol. 30, no. 2556, 20–26 August 1970, p. 608.
12. Bruce Fohr, "War: FTC v. Advertisers," Freedom of Information Center Report No. 535, School of Journalism, University of Missouri at Columbia, June 1976.
13. "New Chief of FTC Urges Congress to Limit Commission's Authority to Challenge Ads," *Wall Street Journal*, 19 March 1982.
14. "FTC Says Kroger's Ads Were Deceptive; Company Comparing Food Prices to Competitors'," *Wall Street Journal*, 1 October 1981.
15. "Sterling Drug, Inc., Gets Big Headache from an FTC Judge," *Wall Street Journal*, 11 February 1981.
16. Margaret Gerrard Warner, "Standard Brands Settles FTC Charges over Margarine Ads," *Wall Street Journal*, 7 January 1981.
17. "Control Data Settles with FTC on Claims for Computer Courses," *Wall Street Journal*, 9 October 1980.
18. "Mobil Agrees to Warn Consumers on Results of Synthetic Motor Oil," *Wall Street Journal*, 19 September 1980.

advertising rulings during the decade included AMF bicycles and tricycles, Litton microwave ovens, Sears appliances, Bristol-Myers pain relievers, Sanka, Fresh Horizons, Wonder and Profile breads, Geritol tonic, Warner-Lambert's Listerine, STP oil treatment, and the most common acne remedies. As the list suggests, the FTC managed to step on some very important toes in the business world.

It would be misleading, however, to suggest that the FTC was working wonders in that era. Its budget had been increased, but it was still minute in comparison with expenditures on advertising. It was receiving a great deal of attention in newspapers, many of which routinely covered FTC actions. But in many of the instances above, the advertising campaigns held to be deceptive had been discontinued months or even years before the finding was issued. Under its administrative procedures, the commission was always operating after the fact. That is, it could do nothing, of course, until an allegedly deceptive advertising campaign had come to its attention. Then its investigation, and the hearings designed to meet the need for **due process**, would take still more time. Meanwhile, the advertisements in question would continue in use either until the campaign ran to its scheduled end or was terminated just ahead of an adverse commission ruling. The Kroger price patrol campaign, for instance, ended two years before the FTC held it deceptive. One of the concerns of the revitalized commission was to find procedures that would either forestall deception or permit it to be attacked and ended at an early stage.

Any action by the Federal Trade Commission begins by determining whether the advertisement has a capacity to deceive. If the commission's staff concludes that it does, that sets in motion a chain of procedures designed to end the problem.

Deceptive Advertising

Over the years, the Federal Trade Commission has used varying standards to determine whether an advertisement has the capacity to deceive consumers. At one point, ads were considered deceptive if they could mislead "the ignorant and unthinking and credulous, who, in making purchases, do not stop to analyze but too often are governed by appearances and general impressions."[19] However, the standard used in more recent years was written into a policy statement adopted by the commission in 1983:

> The Commission will find an act or practice deceptive if there is a misrepresentation, omission or other practice, that misleads the consumer acting reasonably in the circumstances, to the consumer's detriment.[20]

This standard is known as the "reasonable person" test. Such persons are assumed to know enough about the ways of advertisers to tolerate a bit of puffery as long as the claims are not demonstrably false.[21]

The law under which the FTC operates is so written as to give the staff considerable leeway in determining what might be deceptive. When the staff decides to act on a

---

19. United States v. 95 Barrels of Vinegar, 265 U.S. 438, 44 S.Ct. 529, 68 L.Ed. 1094 (1924).
20. CCH Trade Regulation Reports (Current) ¶50,455, p. 56,079.
21. Kircher, 63 F.T.C. 1282 (1963).

complaint, it looks not merely at the words of the ad, but at the overall impression it might convey. The basic test is the capacity, or tendency, to deceive. There need be no proof that the ad has deceived anyone. The FTC staff is not required to survey consumers, either for evidence of deception or to determine how the ordinary person perceives the ad. Thus, the staff has the initial authority to decide that an ad is deceptive. The law assumes that staff members are experts in the field, and their findings are to be given great weight. [22]

An advertisement can be literally true and still be considered misleading. Truth can be used, for instance, to create a misleading impression, to promise more than the product will deliver. If the ad conveys a misleading innuendo, it is in trouble. If a statement can be read two ways, one perfectly proper but the other misleading, the ad is to be judged by the latter interpretation. Finally, it makes no difference what the advertiser intended. Intent is not a factor in determining whether deception is present. The test is of the ad, and the meaning found in it by the staff of the FTC.

The catalog of deceptive advertising listed in such legal reference works as *American Jurisprudence* and *Corpus Juris Secundum* is long and interesting. [23] Courts have held that widely advertised "free gifts" had costly hidden strings attached; that a product advertised at a ridiculously low price is bait designed to lure customers into the store so that salespersons can try to switch them to a higher priced model, and that encyclopedia salespersons should not pose as pollsters. The decisions show that some "diet breads" have fewer calories per slice, not because of their ingredients, but because the slices are thinner than with regular bread. Courts also have held that despite advertising claims, no golf club in itself will convert a duffer into a crack golfer; that "shockproof, waterproof" watches should not be worn in a shower (to say nothing of a snorkeling expedition), and that some "Havana" cigars were made in Pennsylvania after Fidel Castro came to power in Cuba. There is much, much more.

This is not to say that all advertising is deceptive. The great bulk of it is not. Advertising and public relations agencies subscribe to codes of ethics and usually follow them. Newspapers, magazines, broadcasting stations, and television networks have codes of acceptance designed to turn away fraudulent or misleading advertising. The problems occur at the fringes where sharp operators are to be found in any business, and in a genuine difference of opinion over the meaning of "deception" and as to whether a given ad has a capacity to deceive. The Federal Trade Commission takes a literal view of those terms. If a product is advertised as capable of removing "even the most stubborn sink stains with a single application," then it must do so, or the ad is subject to being ruled deceptive. But the FTC has been unwilling to find deception in ads that portray a mouthwash's ability to combat bad breath as the key to romance, even though most users will not be kissed by the next attractive man or woman they meet. Even in its most active period, the commission rejected suggestions that psychological manipulation of people's anxieties and desires might be a form of deceptive advertising. And, in light of the First Amendment decisions discussed earlier in this book, it is clear that the FTC has no authority over political advertising, no matter how distorted or deceptive it may be.

---

22. This paragraph and the next are based on 55 Am. Jur. 2d 740, pp. 51–53.
23. 55 Am. Jur. 2d 750–76, pp. 56–75; 87 C.J.S. 92–120, pp. 325–405.

Even within the rather narrow range in which it operates, the Federal Trade Commission's authority to rule ads deceptive is limited by several safeguards. Staff findings are subject to review by administrative law judges, who in turn are subject to review by the commission itself. Beyond that, an advertiser displeased by the commission's verdict can go to the United States Courts of Appeals for further review.

Coping with Deceptive Advertising

The Federal Trade Commission is made up of five members, appointed by the president, subject to confirmation by the Senate, for seven-year terms. No more than three can be members of the same political party. The president designates one of the members to serve as chairman. Although the term of each member spans almost two presidential terms, each president in recent times has been able to appoint enough members to have an influence on the commission's approach to its duties. By the fifth year of the Reagan administration, that approach was to let the competitive forces of the marketplace carry the burden of coping with deceptive advertising.[24]

The commission has concerns in two major areas. Its Bureau of Competition is concerned with antitrust law violations and with restraint of trade. The Bureau of Consumer Protection is concerned with deceptive advertising and unfair trade practices. Therefore, the commission is able to devote only a little more than half its budget, which was about $66 million in 1984, to helping the consumer. The FTC's spending for all purposes in any year is about .1 percent of the amount spent on advertising. According to figures prepared for *Advertising Age* and published in the *World Almanac*, this amount was about $60 billion a year in the mid-1980s. According to the same sources, each one of the top fifty advertisers was spending more on its attempts to sell its products than the FTC had available for all its duties. Although the agency has offices in eleven cities from Boston to Honolulu, staff and budget limitations require it to act largely on a basis of complaints.

If the staff decides a complaint is worth investigation, it notifies the advertiser. At that point, the commission may be willing to settle for a *letter of compliance*, which is simply a written promise that the advertiser will change its ads to remove the alleged deception. This does not involve an admission of deception on the part of the advertiser.

If the advertiser decides to contest the action, it is entitled to a hearing before an administrative law judge. The procedure is informal. The judge's conclusions are drafted as a *consent agreement*, outlining what the advertiser must do, if anything, to comply with the law. If the advertiser is willing to accept its terms, that ends the matter. Again, acceptance does not involve a confession of wrongdoing. It can mean no more than unwillingness to go to the expense of further litigation. Or it can mean that the campaign in question has ended.

There are compelling reasons why both the advertiser and the FTC try to avoid going beyond the consent agreement level. For an advertiser, further attempts at vindication not only become expensive but can result in protracted unfavorable publicity. For the government, the prospect of a court action can raise its level of proof from capacity to

---

24. John Koten, "More Firms File Challenges to Rivals' Comparative Ads," *Wall Street Journal*, 12 January 1984.

deceive to a showing that the advertisement at issue actually has deceived consumers. Circuit courts have varied on this point.[25] However, whatever the reasons, about three-quarters of the actions begun by the FTC do not go beyond the consent agreement level.

Advertisers who do elect to proceed begin to risk penalties. The next step up the enforcement ladder leads to the possibility that the commission will issue a *cease and desist order*. This is precisely what the name implies. The advertiser who gets such an order has only two courses open: immediate compliance or an appeal to the U.S. Court of Appeals. Failure either to comply or appeal can lead to an injunction and fines.

Working within this simple framework, the FTC has relied on an early decision of the Supreme Court[26] to devise a wide variety of remedies designed to cope with deceptive advertising. Congress further strengthened its hand in 1975, at the height of the consumer movement, with passage of the Magnuson-Moss Warranty-Federal Trade Commission Improvement Act.[27] Some of its remedies are examined below.

Broadened Cease and Desist Orders

The traditional order merely forbade repetition of a specific deception by a single advertiser for a single product. As a result of the Supreme Court's decision in *FTC v. Colgate Palmolive Co.*[28] in 1965, the commission has been able to issue cease and desist orders covering a specific deceptive practice but applying to all advertisers who might be tempted to use it. Such orders have had their greatest effect on television commercials. If a product is demonstrated, it must be shown as is and under conditions of normal usage. If there is a time lapse between the application of that new, improved detergent and the disappearance of the "ring around the collar," the announcer must say so, or a graphic must indicate it.

Affirmative Disclosure

Sometimes a truth is not the whole truth. For years, the J. B. Williams Co. advertised Geritol as the great rejuvenator of the aging. For that tired feeling, brought on by "iron-poor blood," there was no better remedy than regular doses of iron-rich Geritol. There were truths in the commercials. People do tend to tire more easily as they grow older. And persons who suffer anemia, an iron deficiency, will tire more easily than others. However, most tiredness has nothing to do with iron deficiency. For such persons, the only "pickup" they might find in Geritol would be in its alcohol content. The FTC found the Geritol ads deceptive and ordered J. B. Williams to state in future advertising that iron-poor blood is only rarely the cause of tiredness.[29] This affirmative disclosure was required to supply the element of truth that the advertiser had left out of the original message.

---

25. National Commission on Egg Nutrition v. Federal Trade Commission, 517 F.2d 485 (7th Cir. 1975); Federal Trade Commission v. Simeon Management Corp., 391 F.Supp. 697 (D.Calif. 1975); affirmed, 532 F.2d 708 (9th Cir. 1976).
26. Jacob Siegel Co. v. FTC, 327 U.S. 374, 66 S.Ct. 758, 90 L.Ed. 888 (1946).
27. 15 U.S.C. §§2301–12, 2345–58.
28. 380 U.S. 374, 85 S.Ct. 1035, 12 L.Ed.2d 904 (1965).
29. J.B. Williams Co. v. FTC, 381 F.2d 884 (6th Cir. 1967).

This principle has been applied in other contexts. Many stores will sell a person an appliance on a deferred-payment schedule. However, most merchants don't carry their own accounts. They sell their installment contracts to banks or finance companies. Thus a purchaser of a faulty product may try to force the seller to make repairs by withholding payments, only to find this has no effect except for a nasty letter from the holder of the note. There was a time when stores did not have to tell customers what they did with their notes. The FTC now requires affirmative disclosure of the sale of installment contracts to financial institutions. [30]

Affirmative Acts

Sometimes the fault lies not in the advertising, but in the advertisers' willingness to do what they promised to do. In such instances, the FTC has ordered specific performances to carry out the terms of an ad. This remedy has been applied most commonly to promotional games and contests, including the multitude of major prize offers that are sent to millions of persons through the mails. The FTC concluded that such promotions were being abused. For instance, winning numbers might be distributed only in cities where the promoter was hard pressed by competitors. Or the list of winners might be posted in an inconvenient place, so that most prizes would not be claimed.

In the late 1960s, the FTC looked into a promotion conducted by the McDonald's hamburger chain. Advertisements said the chain would give away 15,610 prizes worth $500,000. The FTC learned that only 227 prizes worth about $13,000 were claimed by McDonald's customers. [31] However, a divided commission rejected the staff's conclusion that advertising for the sweepstakes was deceptive. The majority concluded that if one accepted the literal meaning of the ads, McDonald's had not promised to give away all of the prizes.

However, the investigation of that and similar sweepstakes led to adoption of a Trade Regulation Rule for Games of Chance in the Food Retailing and Gasoline Industries. [32] This requires that customers be notified of the exact number of prizes to be given away in each category and the approximate odds against winning. If the sweepstakes continues more than thirty days, participants must be told how many prizes remain. Winning tickets must be distributed solely by chance, and the list of winners must be made available.

In addition, as a result of a case involving the *Reader's Digest* sweepstakes, the FTC held that if advertising promises that all prizes will be awarded, drawings must be continued until they are. [33]

Corrective Advertising

In the early 1970s, a group of law students at George Washington University in Washington, D.C., came up with a brilliantly original remedy for deceptive advertising:

---

30. See, for example, Seekonk Freezer Meats, Inc., 82 F.T.C. 1019 (1973).
31. McDonald's Corp. 78 F.T.C. 606 (1971).
32. 16 C.F.R. §419, 17 October 1969.
33. Reader's Digest Association, 79 F.T.C. 696 (1971); modified, 83 F.T.C. 1356 (1974).

Why not require advertisers to confess and correct their deceptions? They were outraged at television commercials for a new line of Campbell's Soups—Chunky Soups, so thick with meat and vegetables that the solid ingredients stuck up through the liquid in the bowl. What the camera didn't show was the layer of marbles on which the meat and vegetables rested. The FTC staff accused Campbell's of misleading advertising.

Into the fray charged the law students, calling themselves Students Opposing Unfair Practices, or SOUP. Why, they argued at the hearing, should Campbell's, or anyone else, be permitted to profit from the impression left by a misleading ad campaign? Why not require an errant advertiser to erase the impression by confessing his sin in subsequent commercials? This would be a form of penance that would indeed carry a sting likely to make other would-be sinners mend their ways. The commission, by a three-to-two vote, rejected the need for corrective advertising in this instance, but a majority agreed that it was an idea worth looking into.[34] Chairman Caspar W. Weinberger wrote:[35]

> We have no doubt as to the Commission's power to require such affirmative disclosure when such disclosures are reasonably related to the deception found and are required in order to dissipate the effects of that deception. . . . All that is required is that there be a "reasonable relation to the unlawful acts found to exist."

Very shortly, the FTC began to carry the idea into effect. Several companies were even willing to accept consent orders requiring them to run corrective advertising. One of the notable pioneers was ITT Continental Baking Co., bakers of Profile bread, widely touted in advertising as an aid in weight reducing. A series of television commercials featured slender young women, who were being admired by handsome young men while an announcer extolled the virtues of Profile bread. Eat two slices, of it, plain or toasted, before lunch and dinner, the announcer said, and you, too, can lose weight. The FTC staff held that the ads conveyed the misleading impression that Profile bread had fewer calories than other kinds of bread and had some special value in taking off weight. In reality, bread is bread, and all brands of a given kind of bread contain essentially the same number of calories an ounce. If Profile had any value in a weight-reducing program it was because it was sliced thinner than other breads and therefore had about four and a half fewer calories a slice.

ITT Continental agreed to a consent order requiring it to include a corrective statement in all of its advertising for the next year. It was required to spend not less than 25 percent of its advertising costs on messages proclaiming that "Profile is not effective for weight reduction, contrary to possible interpretations of prior advertising."[36] The effect was sobering. Sales of Profile bread dropped 20 to 25 percent. Some store owners relegated it to the least favorable shelf positions.[37] Such an effect was noted by other prospective targets for corrective advertising. Foremost among these was the Warner-Lambert Co.,

---

34. Gerald J. Thain, "Corrective Advertising: Theory and Cases," N.Y. Law Forum, 19:1–34, Summer 1973.
35. Campbell Soup Co., 77 F.T.C. 664, at 668 (1970).
36. ITT Continental Baking Co., Inc., 79 F.T.C. 248 (1971).
37. John Holusha, "Baking Firm Beats False Ad Charge," *Louisville Courier-Journal*, 28 December 1972. The headline referred to a subsequent FTC staff finding that ITT Continental had misrepresented the nutritional qualities of Wonder Bread and Hostess Snack Cakes. This time, ITT fought it out and an administrative law judge found in its favor.

makers of Listerine antiseptic mouthwash, which fought the FTC all the way to the Supreme Court. The case was a straightforward test of the authority of the FTC in light of the doctrine of commercial speech.

Listerine had been on the market since 1879 with a formula that remained unchanged for a hundred years. Starting in 1921, it had been advertised as beneficial in preventing colds and sore throats, and in alleviating their symptoms. It became one of the most widely sold mouthwashes. Several times, the FTC had studied Listerine's advertising claims and had taken no action.[38] But in 1972 it began another study that led to a formal complaint. Warner-Lambert asked for a hearing, which lasted four months and produced four thousand pages of testimony. The administrative law judge upheld the complaint as did the full commission in 1975.

Warner-Lambert Co. v. *FTC*, 562 F.2d 749 (D.C. Cir. 1977).

The commission found that Listerine did indeed kill millions of bacteria in the mouth and throat, but it left many millions more. However, this had no effect on colds, because colds are caused by viruses, which are immune to the ingredients in Listerine. The commission therefore ordered Warner-Lambert to cease and desist from all advertising that claimed or implied that its mouthwash would cure colds or sore throats, or help its users avoid either. Further, it ordered the company to include in future advertising a corrective sentence: "Contrary to prior advertising, Listerine will not help prevent colds or sore throats or lessen their severity." It was to do so until it had spent on such advertising a sum equal to its average annual expenditures on Listerine advertising during the preceding ten years. This was about $10 million.

Warner-Lambert appealed to the Court of Appeals for the District of Columbia Circuit, arguing in part that the First Amendment protected its claims for Listerine and that the penalty was excessive. The result was a nearly complete victory for the FTC. In *Warner-Lambert* v. *FTC*, a divided court held that the commission had not exceeded its powers in ordering corrective advertising. Nor could it find any relief for Warner-Lambert in the First Amendment. In the commercial-speech cases decided up to that time, the Supreme Court had said several times that false or misleading advertising does not merit First Amendment protection. Warner-Lambert tried to take its case to the Supreme Court, but was denied **certiorari**.[39]

Long before the decision was handed down, Warner-Lambert had shifted the thrust of its advertising campaign for Listerine. It was being touted as the perfect remedy for bad breath, because it kills the bacteria that produce unpleasant odors in the mouth. The corrective sentence was incorporated as part of this new approach.

Relying on the *Warner-Lambert* decision, the FTC ordered other firms to use corrective advertising in 1980 before the advent of the Reagan administration led to a general relaxation of its campaign against allegedly deceptive advertising. Among them were two marketers of products designed to treat acne. Both were ordered to stop advertising their products until they had agreed to run specific corrective advertising. Hayoun Cosmetique of New York City had been advertising a kit offering four of its

---

38. Listerine's advertising was reviewed by the FTC in 1932, 1940, 1951, 1958, and 1962. Warner-Lambert Co. v. FTC, 562 F.2d 749, at 763, n. 70 (D.C.Cir. 1977).
39. 435 U.S. 950, 98 S.Ct. 1575, 55 L.Ed.2d 800 (1978).

products as a cure for acne. It was ordered to stop suggesting that the products would eliminate the blemishes associated with the teenage affliction. Nor could it advertise in any way unless for the next six months its advertising clearly proclaimed, "No product can cure acne."[40] AHC Pharmacal of Miami, marketer of AHC Gel and Dr. Fulton's Acne Control Regimen, was the target of an even more specific order. The FTC said it could not advertise further until it had run ads in Sunday newspaper supplements in six cities proclaiming in 48-point type, "No product can cure acne." The prescribed type is two-thirds of an inch high.[41]

Substantiation of Advertising Claims

Advertisers who make performance claims for products must be prepared to back them up. Advertising of gasoline mileage claims for automobiles offers one example. Because mileage can vary greatly with the way a car is driven, automobile manufacturers lean heavily on the ratings the federal government requires for all new cars. But because these figures are products of laboratory tests, the FTC requires that their use in advertising be qualified by the notice that actual mileage will depend on the individual driver, road conditions, and weather.

Advertisers who claim that their product tastes better than others must be able to support that claim with data collected from a representative sampling of consumers. Because such sampling is costly, and is certain to show that some portion of the sample did not like the product, television has seen the rise of the blind taste test. The viewer sees the blinding sleeve come off the can of beer or cup of cola, and the look of surprise as the drinker recognizes that he or she has just been a traitor to a favorite brand. No mention need be made of how many samplers made the wrong choice.

Since 1971, the FTC has insisted that any claims for product performance be backed by valid survey results. It has taken a dim view of surveys conducted exclusively among dealers for a product, or by the manufacturer of a product. The Kroger-conducted price survey, mentioned earlier, is one example.

Until 1984, the FTC periodically asked all major companies in certain industries to send the agency their data supporting advertising claims. These were studied by agency staff members looking for discrepancies. After five thousand hours of study over several years produced not a single case, FTC Chairman James Miller proposed that the substantiation program be dropped. After hearing from protesters, the agency agreed to continue to require advertisers to collect data to support their claims, but it no longer requires that the data be submitted routinely. The agency will seek supporting data only as part of a specific investigation.[42]

Trade Rules

All the above remedies share a common problem. None can be imposed until a complaint has been made and an investigation conducted by the FTC staff. If the

---

40. Hayoun Cosmetique, Inc., 95 F.T.C. 794 (1980).
41. AHC Pharmacal, Inc., 95 F.T.C. 528 (1980).
42. "Running the Government Right," *Wall Street Journal*, 27 March 1984; "FTC Reaffirms Policy Requiring Advertisers to Prove Their Claims," *Wall Street Journal*, 30 July 1984.

advertiser resists, there is further delay until a hearing can be scheduled and conducted by an administrative law officer. Further resistance can lead to a hearing before the full commission and thence into the federal courts. In the Listerine case, the procedure took six years. Thus, all remedies, except for corrective advertising, amount to little more than locking the garage door after the car has not only been stolen, but has been stripped and the remains sent to the crusher. Many television advertising campaigns, for instance, run for no more than thirteen weeks.

The FTC began in the early 1970s to establish trade regulation rules (**trade rules**) with the idea that they could be used to bring quick action against errant advertisers. Doubts about the commission's authority to do this were resolved by Section 18 of the FTC Improvement Act of 1975. However, the history of trade rules has been an uneven one. The procedure works as follows:

The FTC staff tries to identify misleading practices on an industrywide basis. Then it proposes a set of rules designed to cope with such practices. These are published in the *Federal Register* and distributed within the affected industry with a request for comment. A hearing is scheduled. When all sides have been heard, the proposed trade rules are put in final form. These, too, are published and distributed. From that point on, the FTC acts on the theory that all of those involved know what the rules are and should be expected to obey them. Thus, an infraction is considered willful. If one occurs, the FTC can move at once with a cease and desist order backed by the ability to impose an injunction or fines that can run up to $10,000 a day.

In some areas, trade rules have met with little objection. In others, they have been fought. The oil industry, for instance, fought a trade rule requiring the posting of octane ratings on gasoline pumps. It lost.[43] The clothing industry, on the other hand, accepted a rule that requires placement of a cleaning instruction label in garments.[44]

But when the FTC tried to establish trade rules for the advertising of over-the-counter drugs, it ran into a storm of protest that led it, six years later, to retreat from the field.[45] At one point, the agency proposed that drug advertisers be required to use approved medical terms. Thus, a cough remedy would have to be described as an "antitussive." A mint tablet designed to quell digestive gases would have to be described as an "antiflatulent." Ads no longer could offer "relief for that burning sensation due to hyperacidity," nor could they present a remedy for "that bloated feeling due to excess gas."[46] After years of argument, the FTC abandoned the proposed regulation, in part because of its patent absurdity and in part because the drug industry and its advertising agencies resisted vigorously.

An attempt to write rules regulating nutritional claims for food came to the same end after another six-year effort.[47] However, the agency was able to write rules for claims that a food is "natural." That term can be used only for foods that contain no artificial

---

43. National Petroleum Refiners Association v. FTC, 482 F.2d 672 (D.C.Cir. 1973); cert. den., 415 U.S. 951, 94 S.Ct. 1475, 39 L.Ed.2d 567 (1974).
44. Care Labeling of Textile Wearing Apparel, 16 C.F.R. §423, 3 July 1972.
45. FTC Kills Proposal on Ads for Drugs Sold over Counter," *Wall Street Journal*, 12 February 1981.
46. Burt Schorr, "How the FTC Plans to Cure Synonymity (Or Is It Synonymy?)," *Wall Street Journal*, 13 February 1978.
47. "FTC to End Six-Year Bid to Write a Rule on Nutrition Claims in Food Industry," *Wall Street Journal*, 3 April 1980.

ingredients and have been subjected to no processing other than what could be done in a home kitchen.[48]

Attempts to impose trade rules can step on sensitive toes. When the FTC proposed rules for funeral directors, used-car dealers, and television advertising aimed at children, the affected industries took their objections not only to the agency, but to Congress. This resulted in legislation giving Congress the power to veto any trade rule adopted by the FTC.[49]

However, in June 1983, in a case involving another agency, the Supreme Court held that Congress exceeded its authority when it wrote legislation giving it the right to nullify executive decisions like those embodied in the FTC's trade regulations.[50] Chief Justice Burger, joined by five other justices, said such legislative vetoes violate the separation of powers mandated by the Constitution. Thus, Congress no longer has the authority to override FTC trade regulations.

During President Reagan's first term, Congress approved annual reductions in the Federal Trade Commission's budget. That, coupled with the antiregulatory philosophy of the Reagan appointees, led to a noticeable slowing of work on trade rules and in the number of deceptive advertising orders issued by the FTC. For the time being, the consumer activism that had made the agency more than a paper tiger had run its course. However, the trade commission, and the law under which it operates, survive. So do the remedies devised to check deceptive advertising. The activist era clearly established that the FTC can order advertisers to substantiate claims made for their products. They can be required to provide missing facts needed to overcome deception by omission. If a deception is blatant and of long standing, the commission can order the offending company to correct its misleading statements in subsequent advertising. Deceptive practices can be made the subject of trade rules, which can be enforced without second-guessing from Congress.

Other Means of Coping with Deceptive Advertising

While the Federal Trade Commission has been the most visible and most active agency dealing with deceptive advertising, it is not alone in the field. Other federal agencies have some control over certain kinds of advertising. Every state except Alabama has given either an administrative agency or its attorney general authority to act to prevent or punish deception. In several instances in recent years, manufacturers have gone to court to seek an injunction or damages in actions directed at a competitor's advertising.

Federal agencies involved in financing housing and enforcing civil rights have adopted guidelines for real estate advertising placed in newspapers.[51] The purpose is to prevent

---

48. "U.S. Issues Rules for Advertising 'Natural' Foods," *New York Times*, 13 October 1980.
49. Pub. L. 96–252, 94 Stat. 393, 28 May 1980; 15 U.S.C.A. §57a-1.
50. Immigration and Naturalization Service v. Chadha, 462 U.S. 919, 103 S.Ct. 2764, 77 L.Ed.2d 317 (1983).
51. *Publication Guidelines for Compliance with Title VIII of the Civil Rights Act of 1968*, 37 Fed.Reg. 6700 (1 April 1972); 45 Fed.Reg. 57102 (22 September 1980).

discrimination based on race, religion, color, sex, or national origin of the buyer or renter. The Securities and Exchange Commission imposes narrow limits for advertisements of securities. Also at the federal level, agencies regulate food and drug labeling, the labeling of alcoholic beverages, and the warning labels that must be placed on potentially dangerous tools, machinery, and appliances.

State laws regulating advertising take various forms. Most common are the so-called *Printers' Ink* statutes that provide penalties for deceptive advertising. They are named for a trade publication that took the lead in urging publishers to stand behind their advertising. Most of the laws are aimed at business firms or agencies that prepare and place advertising, but courts have held that they can be used against media that knowingly accept false or deceptive advertising.

Recently, some business firms have gone to court to attack what they believe to be deceptive advertising by their competitors. In 1984, the weekly marketing column of the *Wall Street Journal* ascribed such actions to the popularity of comparative ads which then accounted for 35 percent of all television commercials. In addition to legal action, business firms also were complaining to the networks, to the Better Business Bureau, and to the Federal Trade Commission. As one example, the column noted that Mars, Inc., had withdrawn its claim that the Three Musketeers candy bar offered "more of what you buy chocolate for." A competing firm had complained to the Better Business Bureau that its "perception test" showed that most people thought this meant the bar contained more chocolate than competing bars. That was not true.[52]

ACCESS TO THE MEDIA

The Right to Refuse Advertising

The news media, with few exceptions, are supported by advertising. Therefore, in the normal course of events, it can be assumed that the purpose of the advertising department of a newspaper, magazine, or broadcasting station is to sell as much advertising as possible. Yet there are times when management feels compelled to refuse an ad. Most broadcasting stations, for instance, won't accept advertising for hard liquor. Some newspapers won't print cigarette advertising. Others won't advertise X-rated movies. Some have rules against advertising that is used to attack another business or an individual. Some won't accept advertising on topics considered too controversial.

As long as advertising was considered to be without First Amendment protection, there was little question about the right to refuse advertising. Publishers could point to article I, section 10, paragraph 1 of the Constitution which states in part: "No State shall . . . pass any bill of attainder, ex post facto law, or law impairing the obligation of contracts."

Advertising is sold under contract. If a state can't impair a contract already made, it certainly can't force an unwilling party to enter into one. That ended the matter as long as most towns of any size had competing newspapers. With the advent of one-newspaper towns in mid-century, efforts were begun to change the rule. The argument was advanced

---

52. John Koten, "More Firms File Challenges to Rivals' Comparative Ads," *Wall Street Journal*, 12 January 1984.

that the news media are like **common carriers**—a bus line, the telephone company, or a ferry. If a newspaper was the only carrier of advertising in town, then it ought to be required to accept an ad from anyone who could pay the established price. One low-level Ohio court accepted that reasoning in 1919 in *Uhlman* v. *Sherman*,[53] but no other court has done so.

The classic case in this area is *Shuck* v. *The Carroll Daily Herald*, decided by the Supreme Court of Iowa in 1933. In that instance, the newspaper's agent went so far as

Shuck v. The Carroll Daily Herald, 247 N.W. 813 (1933).

to accept money for an ad brought in by the owner of a dry cleaning store. The publisher decided not to publish it, and returned the money. The dry cleaner, Shuck, sued to force the publisher to run the ad. The trial court refused, and the state supreme court affirmed unanimously. Rejecting the common-carrier argument advanced by Shuck and supported by reference to the *Uhlman* case, the court held:

> The newspaper business is an ordinary business. It is a business essentially private in its nature—as private as that of the baker, grocer, or milkman, all of whom perform a service on which, to a greater or lesser extent, the communities depend, but which bears no such relation to the public as to warrant its inclusion in the category of businesses charged with a public use. If a newspaper were required to accept an advertisement, it could be compelled to publish a news item. If some good lady gave a tea, and submitted to the newspaper a proper account of the tea, and the editor of the newspaper, believing that it had no news value, refused to publish it, she, it seems to us, would have as much right to compel the newspaper to publish the account as would a person engaged in business to compel a newspaper to publish an advertisement. . . .
>
> Thus, as a newspaper is a strictly private enterprise, the publishers thereof have a right to publish whatever advertisement they desire and to refuse to publish whatever advertisements they do not desire to publish.

The many decisions since have added nothing to the principle. They have established that publishers can classify advertisements as they see fit,[54] or can change an ad to meet their standards of acceptability.[55] However, to avoid conflict over whether a contract is in force, the wording of advertising contracts should reserve to the publisher or advertising director the final right of approval and should state the kinds of advertising that are unacceptable. Any prospective advertiser should be given a copy of the terms at the first inquiry.

What can happen if the terms of the contract are not clearly understood is illustrated by an Indiana Court of Appeals decision in *Herald-Telephone* v. *Fatouras*.[56] A candidate for a local school board paid for an ad that was to be run on the day before the election. She submitted the copy late, and the newspaper bent its normal deadlines to accept it. When the publisher's representative reviewed the copy, he rejected it on the ground that it made serious charges against persons who would have no opportunity to respond before voting began. The candidate persuaded a county judge to hold court on Sunday evening

---

53. 31 Ohio Dec. 54 (1919).
54. Staff Research Associates v. Tribune Co., 346 F.2d 372 (7th Cir. 1965).
55. Camp-of-the-Pines v. New York Times, 53 N.Y.S.2d 475 (S.Ct., Albany Co. 1945).
56. 431 N.E.2d 171 (Ind.App. 1982).

to hear her argument that the publisher not only had refused to honor a contract, but had violated her First Amendment rights. Deciding that a contract had been reached when the candidate's money was accepted and the copy delivered to the newspaper, the judge ordered the ad run the following day. The newspaper did so. The court of appeals eventually held that if a newspaper imposes conditions on the acceptance of advertising copy, advertisers must be told about them in advance.

The right to refuse advertising also is subject to antitrust law. The landmark case in this area is *Lorain Journal Co.* v. *United States.*[57] It grew out of an attempt by the publisher of the *Lorain Journal* to freeze out a newly established radio station in an adjoining city. The publisher ordered the newspaper's advertising department to monitor the station and cancel the advertising contract of any Lorain merchant who bought time on the station. Because the newspaper's circulation reached 97 percent of the households in the area, and the station could demonstrate nowhere near such coverage, this was a potent threat. The Supreme Court held there was no doubt that the purpose of the policy was to preserve the newspaper's monopoly, and therefore it was a violation of the law.

However, barring a pattern of refusal that points to an intent to harm a competitor, any news medium may refuse commercial advertising for any reason or for no reason.

Who May Refuse Cause Advertising?

What happens if people have a serious grievance against society, or a great idea for saving the world, but can't get a reporter to listen? If the media are to be a true marketplace of ideas, shouldn't they be required to carry all points of view? During the civil rights and anti–Vietnam War disturbances of the 1960s, Jerome Barron, a professor of law at George Washington Law School, pondered those questions and concluded there should be a right of access to the media. He first argued his thesis in the *Harvard Law Review* in 1967[58] and expanded it into a book published six years later.[59] He also acted as counsel in several cases testing his theory. However, courts at every level, including the Supreme Court, have rejected his argument as it applies to privately owned media. Courts have held that public officials cannot order newspapers owned by public high schools or state universities to refuse cause-related advertising unless they can prove that the ad is likely to cause harm. In the cases in point, decisions were made by a school principal, a full-time publisher employed by a state university to run its newspaper, and a state board of regents. However, one federal circuit court upheld the right of a student editor to refuse cause-related advertising offered to a state university newspaper. In the former instances, courts held that the refusal was a form of state action, thus violating the First Amendment through the Fourteenth. In the latter instance, the court ruled that the editor was not an officer of the state and had not acted under pressure from one. Thus the decision was not the kind of state action restricting speech that the Supreme Court has condemned.

Briefly summarized, Barron's argument is as follows: The news media have become big businesses engaged in pursuit of an audience. This pursuit makes the managers of the media cautious. They don't want to make people angry, lest they lose part of their

---

57. 342 U.S. 143, 72 S.Ct. 181, 96 L.Ed. 162 (1951).
58. "Access to the Press—A New First Amendment Right," 80 Harv. Law Rev. 1641 (1967).
59. *Freedom of the Press for Whom?* (Bloomington, Ind.: Indiana University Press, 1973).

audience and their advertisers. The results of this caution are bland media that largely ignore the ills of society. As Barron saw it, the violence of the 1960s was in part a reaction to the media's indifference. Frustrated groups of individuals resorted to public demonstrations to call attention to their grievances.

Barron read *New York Times* v. *Sullivan* and found in its grant of First Amendment protection to cause advertising a mandate that such ads should be accepted by publishers. He also found support for his belief in the fairness doctrine, which requires broadcasters to present news and public affairs programing on controversial topics of public interest. Barron argued that if the First Amendment is to have any real meaning in the modern world, it must be changed from a passive defense for matter already published to an active weapon for forcing all shades of opinion into the media. Otherwise, the concept of the marketplace of ideas is a mockery. Barron wrote:

> At the very minimum, the creation of two remedies is essential—(1) a nondiscriminatory right to purchase editorial advertisements in daily newspapers, and (2) a right of reply for public figures and public officers defamed in newspapers. These remedies could be instituted by either legislative or judicial action. They represent the very least of what ought to be done to broaden public participation in the press.[60]

Despite the facts and logic Barron used to support his thesis, courts generally have held that he has failed to overcome two barriers, both grounded in the Constitution.

1. Most media are privately owned. This is true even of broadcasting, the one medium that is regulated by government. Thus, any attempt by government to tell an owner that an article or an ad must be accepted and used could be taking of property without due process of law, violating the Fifth Amendment.

2. Further, an attempt by the state to tell media owners that they must accept an article or an ad violates the freedom of the press protected by the First Amendment.

The cases below illustrate how these principles have been applied to the print media. Their application to broadcasting stations will be treated in the next chapter.

Privately Owned Newspapers

In the 1960s, the Amalgamated Clothing Workers union became concerned about an influx of foreign-made men's clothing. In reaction, the union's Chicago Joint Board began picketing stores selling imported garments. To call attention to its campaign, it tried to buy display advertising in the then four Chicago daily newspapers. All refused to accept the ads. The union went to a U.S. district court and asked it to order the newspapers to do so.

Chicago Joint Board, Amalgamated Clothing Workers of America, AFL-CIO v. Chicago Tribune Co., 307 F.Supp. 422 (N.D.Ill. 1969).

In *Chicago Joint Board, Amalgamated Clothing Workers of America, AFL-CIO v. Chicago Tribune Co.*, the court rejected the argument.

---

60. Ibid., pp. 6–7.

The union's lawyers pointed to cases in which the Supreme Court had held that there is a right to distribute religious tracts on the streets of a company-owned town,[61] and to picket in a privately owned shopping center.[62] They also pointed to laws that forbid restaurants and other places of public accommodation to refuse service on racial or religious grounds. They argued that newspapers enjoy special privileges granted by government, such as free working space in police headquarters, city hall, and the state capitol. They are the beneficiaries of legal advertising and are the only commodity that may be sold legally on the streets and sidewalks. All of this, the lawyers argued, makes newspapers "quasi-public entities" that come under the scope of the First Amendment by way of the Fourteenth. Their refusal to accept cause advertising is akin to state action abridging freedom of speech.

Judge Abraham L. Marovitz met each argument squarely. A newspaper is not like a company town, a shopping center, or a restaurant, none of which is given special protection by the Constitution. Newspapers are. Nor has the state annexed newspapers by giving them special privileges designed to help them gather and disseminate the news. The press, he wrote, "does not wear the cloak of a function of government."

> Quite simply, the business of newspapers is not inherently governmental. . . . [T]he reporting of the day's events and related commentary is not a governmental function. Indeed, the opposite is true. While the government and its officials make news, they do not publish it. . . . [T]here is no state press, no American equivalent to *Izvestia* or *Pravda*.
>
> Rather than regarded as an extension of the state exercising delegated powers of a governmental nature, the press has long and consistently been recognized as an independent check on governmental power.

Nor can *New York Times* v. *Sullivan* and the fairness doctrine be put together to support a right of access to newspapers, Marovitz said. The fairness doctrine requires broadcasters to identify controversial public issues and present varying opinions on them. Judge Marovitz noted that broadcasters operate under license from the federal government and therefore are subject to a different set of rules than are newspapers. In any event, broadcasters retain editorial control over who will present the varying points of view. As to the *New York Times* decision, the judge said it stands for no more than the fact that a publisher is protected against libel suits if he does accept cause advertising. "[T]he right of free speech was never intended to include the right to use the other fellow's presses."

The U.S. Court of Appeals for the Seventh Circuit affirmed.[63] Other courts have come to the same conclusion: A privately owned newspaper cannot be compelled to accept editorial advertising any more than it can be required to accept commercial advertising, unless it has contracted to do so.

The Right of Reply

Privately owned newspapers also cannot be required to publish unpaid editorial matter submitted by public officials or political candidates who feel they have been victims of

---

61. Marsh v. Alabama, 326 U.S. 501, 66 S.Ct. 276, 90 L.Ed. 265 (1946).
62. Amalgamated Food Employees Local 590 v. Logan Valley Plaza, Inc., 391 U.S. 308, 88 S.Ct. 1601, 20 L.Ed.2d 603 (1968).
63. 435 F.2d 470 (7th Cir. 1970); cert. den., 402 U.S. 973 (1971).

unfair attacks, either in a news story or an editorial. Pat Tornillo, a candidate for the Florida Legislature in 1972, was the subject of a harsh editorial in the *Miami Herald.*

Miami Herald Publishing Co. v. Tornillo, 418 U.S. 241, 94 S.Ct. 2831, 41 L.Ed.2d 730 (1974).

Noting that he had led a teachers' strike at a time when such strikes were illegal, the editorial called Tornillo a "czar" and a lawbreaker. Under a Florida law that granted a right of reply under such circumstances, Tornillo submitted a long statement to the editor of the *Herald* and asked that it be published. When the editor refused, Tornillo went to court. A county court turned him down, holding that the law was unconstitutional, but on appeal, the Florida Supreme Court reversed, six-to-one. In doing so, it adopted Barron's reasoning. The U. S. Supreme Court took the case and reversed without dissent. Barron represented Tornillo as counsel. Chief Justice Burger wrote for the Court.

He reviewed with some sympathy Barron's argument that the press has changed drastically since the First Amendment was written. The chief justice conceded that it has become a big business and has taken on some of the aspects of a monopoly. Then he added:

> However much validity may be found in these arguments, at each point the implementation of a remedy such as an enforceable right of access necessarily calls for some mechanism, either governmental or consensual. If it is governmental coercion, this at once brings about a confrontation with the express provisions of the First Amendment and the judicial gloss on that amendment developed over the years.

Burger held that any attempt by government to force newspapers to publish material their editors would reject violates the Constitution in four ways:

1. The Court has held in a number of decisions that an attempt to force publication of "that which 'reason' tells [editors] should not be published" violates the First Amendment. The chief justice added, "A responsible press is an undoubtedly desirable goal, but press responsibility is not mandated by the Constitution and like many other virtues it cannot be legislated."

2. Compelled publication is a kind of prior restraint. If editors are forced to put something in a newspaper, they will be forced to leave out something else. "Governmental restraint on publishing need not fall into familiar patterns to be subject to constitutional limitations."

3. The alternative to leaving something out is to increase the number of pages to accommodate the material mandated by government. This increases the publisher's costs for paper, ink, and composing time, thus imposing an economic penalty amounting to a taking of property in violation of the Fifth Amendment.

4. Finally, it is likely that the factors above would lead some editors to "conclude that the safe course is to avoid controversy and . . . political and electoral coverage would be blunted or reduced."

Burger concluded by enlarging on the first point, in the process upholding the rights of editors:

> A newspaper is more than a passive receptacle or conduit for news, comment, and advertising. The choice of material to go into a newspaper, and the decisions made as to limitations on the size of the paper, and content, and treatment of public issues and public officials—whether fair or unfair—constitutes the exercise of editorial control and judgment.

Any intrusion by government into that function, the chief justice wrote, "fails to clear the barriers of the First Amendment."

The Court's decision not only nullified the Florida right of reply law but served notice to legislators generally that they cannot interfere with editorial decisions by imposing some official version of fairness.

Government-Owned Media and the Right of Access

The First Amendment stands as a barrier against government interference with news and opinion media. As written, the amendment forbids Congress to make laws abridging freedom of speech and press. Since the 1920s, the Supreme Court has interpreted the language of the Fourteenth Amendment to forbid state action abridging freedom of speech and press. In neither application is the barrier absolute, as this text illustrates. The two cases immediately above illustrate another point that has been implicit thus far. The First Amendment does not stand as a barrier against individual editorial decisions to omit items from the news and editorial columns or from advertising space. On the contrary, it protects the owners and employees of privately owned media from government interference.

When media are owned by government, the application of First Amendment law changes. When decisions on content are made by a government official, state power is used to determine what shall and shall not enter the arena where truth and falsehood grapple. Thus, courts have held that such decisions are subject to challenge as prior restraints. One case illustrates the reasoning involved.

In 1967, three groups—a labor union, black students protesting racial discrimination, and opponents of the Vietnam War—tried to place editorial ads in the student newspaper at Wisconsin State University-Whitewater and were refused. The newspaper, *The Royal Purple*, was owned by the university and controlled by a publications board comprised of students and faculty. Ultimately, the board was answerable to the president of the university and the Board of Regents of State Colleges. The board, with the president's knowledge, had adopted a policy refusing all cause advertising. In this instance, representatives of the groups were told to summarize their views in letter form for publication as letters to the editor. They rejected that alternative and, after an unsuccessful appeal to the president, went to court.

Lee v. Board of Regents of State Colleges, 306 F.Supp. 1097 (W.D.Wis. 1969).

The U.S. District Court for the Western District of Wisconsin held that the policy violated the First Amendment. The court brushed aside arguments that the *Royal Purple* was not a newspaper but only a laboratory for the school's journalism students. It was, the court held, "an important forum for the dissemination of news and expression of opinion. As such a forum, it should be open to anyone who is willing to pay to have his views published therein—not just to commercial advertisers." Nor were letters to the editor an adequate substitute. Different type sizes and styles can be used to give advertisements greater impact than a letter.

The court's holding was not absolute. The newpaper could refuse an ad if it presented a clear and present danger of arousing harmful conduct. There was no such danger in this instance.

The key to the court's holding lay in the fact that the decision to reject the ad was made under color of state authority, by a board acting with the support of the university president who, in turn, was responsible to the board of regents. On appeal, the U.S. Court of Appeals for the Seventh Circuit supported the district court's reasoning.[64]

In other decisions, courts have held that student editors of newspapers published by state universities cannot be punished arbitrarily for disobeying an order of a faculty adviser not to publish an editorial,[65] nor can a state university president require a student editor to submit copy to him for approval, even though the newspaper is funded completely by the university.[66]

When student editors act on their own, without coercion from state employees, courts have upheld their right to make decisions on content. An editor can refuse to publish an article submitted by a would-be contributor.[67] Student editors also have been upheld when they refused to accept cause advertising. In *Mississippi Gay Alliance* v. *Goudelock*,[68] a federal circuit court took note of the fact that the decision to reject an ad offering counseling and legal aid to gay students at Mississippi State University was the editor's alone. The majority quoted from *Tornillo* to support its conclusion that government ought not to interfere with editorial decisions.

The Supreme Court refused to review *Mississippi Gay Alliance*, nor has it accepted any other case involving access to a state-owned publication. However, in *Lehman* v. *City of Shaker Heights*,[69] the Court held in 1974 that a municipal transit system can refuse political advertising. The five-justice majority noted that the Court has been "jealous to preserve access to public places for purposes of free speech," but held that the buses were not public forums. Therefore, the city did not violate First Amendment freedoms when it limited car card advertising to commercial messages. The principle underlying Shaker Heights's ban on political advertising was expanded ten years later when the Court held in *Taxpayers for Vincent*, summarized on page 411, that Los Angeles could forbid the posting of political signs on public property. In that case, the city did not permit signs of any kind on public property for aesthetic reasons.

It seems, then, that the right of access to state-owned media rests on a narrow base. If the medium is considered a public forum, and accepts advertising, persons seeking to

---

64. 441 F.2d 1257 (7th Cir. 1971).
65. Dickey v. Alabama State Board of Education, 273 F.Supp. 613 (M.D. Ala. 1967).
66. Antonelli v. Hammond, 308 F.Supp. 1329 (D.Mass. 1970).
67. Avins v. Rutgers, State University of New Jersey, 385 F.2d 151 (3d Cir. 1967); cert. den., 88 S.Ct. 855 (1968).
68. 536 F.2d 1073 (5th Cir. 1976); reh. den., 541 F.2d 281; cert. den., 97 S.Ct. 1678 (1977).
69. 418 U.S. 298, 94 S.Ct. 2714, 41 L.Ed.2d 770 (1974).

argue a cause cannot be denied access by action of a state official. However, in the case of student newspapers, student editors can make decisions as to content, whether it be an article or a cause ad. But if the medium is not a public forum, it cannot be opened up to political advertising as long as the ban on such ads is absolute.

Corporate Cause Advertising

Because political speech lies at the core of First Amendment concerns, it enjoys almost absolute protection. The Supreme Court took note of that fact in 1978 when it held, in *First National Bank of Boston* v. *Bellotti,* that corporations have a right to spend their stockholders' money to advertise a position on a public issue. In doing so, the Court struck down a Massachusetts law that made it a crime for a corporation to spend its funds to influence the outcome of a referendum unless the issue submitted to the voters would materially affect the corporation's business, property, or assets. In 1976, Massachusetts residents were asked to change the state constitution to permit a graduated income tax. As it stood, the constitution required that all persons be taxed at the same rate. Officers of many financial institutions, including First National Bank of Boston, believed the proposal mistaken and sought to use corporate funds to oppose it. But because the tax measure would not have a material effect on the institutions themselves, the law stood in their way. First National took the lead in asking state courts to declare the law unconstitutional, but they upheld it. The Supreme Court agreed to take the case.

First National Bank of Boston v. *Bellotti,* 435 U.S. 765, 98 S.Ct. 1407, 55 L.Ed.2d 707 (1978).

The Massachusetts courts had acted on the theory that the Supreme Court's commercial-speech cases gave the state the right to restrict corporate speech. They had held that there was an overriding public interest in preventing corporations from spending funds to influence the outcome of a referendum. The Supreme Court said that was a misreading of the commercial-speech doctrine. At the heart of the issue, the Court said, was the nature of the speech in question. Its subject, in this instance, was taxation, a central concern of every citizen. Corporations, like other citizens, have a right to speak on public issues, through advertising or by other means. They do not have to prove, any more than a real person would, that the issue in question would have a material effect on them.

Two years later, in *Consolidated Edison Co.* v. *Public Service Commission,*[70] the Supreme Court expanded on that holding. At issue were bill inserts used by Consolidated Edison to argue its case for nuclear power. The Natural Resources Defense Council argued that the company should be compelled to permit it to prepare inserts arguing against nuclear power. When that failed, the council succeeded in persuading the public service commission to ban all bill inserts of a political nature. The commission rationalized that utility customers hold widely divergent views and should not be made a captive audience for a company's opinions. The Court decided the case by direct application of the *First National Bank* precedent. It held that the state could regulate the time, place,

---

70. 447 U.S. 530, 100 S.Ct. 2326, 65 L.Ed.2d 319 (1980).

and manner of corporate speech, but it could not do so on the basis of the content of that speech. As long as Consolidated Edison did not lie to its customers, it could offer them its views on any subject.

In 1986, the Court carried the protection of corporate speech an additional step, nullifying a California rule requiring public utility companies to distribute bill inserts prepared by consumer groups.[71] In response to complaints about a newsletter mailed by Pacific Gas & Electric Co. with its bills, the state's Public Utilities Commission ordered the company to include four times a year messages prepared by an organization opposing its rate increase requests. Four of the five justices voting to strike down the order held that corporations, like individuals, can't be compelled to associate themselves with views with which they disagree. However, the fifth justice focused narrowly on the company's envelopes, seeing them as private property to which it could deny access by others. Similar regulations are in effect in New York, West Virginia, and Wisconsin.

The effect of the three decisions is to place corporate messages advocating a position on public issues at a higher level in the First Amendment hierarchy than messages designed to sell a product or service. The latter lie outside the realm of First Amendment protection if they promote an illegal product or promote a legal product in a deceptive way. Nondeceptive advertising for legal products is protected by the First Amendment, but still is subject to regulation if an overriding state interest requires it. But, in the three cases discussed in this section, the Supreme Court held that states cannot restrict a corporation's right to express a point of view on public issues, whether the corporation does so by placing advertisements in the media or by mailings to its customers. In the most recent case, the Court also held that states cannot compel corporations to become unwilling distributors of messages prepared by others.

In the Professional World

It would be misleading in the extreme to leave the impression that advertising claims are held in check only by the forces of law. This is no more true than the belief that the news staffs of the various media would engage in unbridled libel and invasion of privacy were it not for fear of lawsuits. Virtually all advertisers and media that accept advertising police themselves, applying professional standards of honesty and ethics that are products of experience and training. The several professional organizations representing people who prepare advertisements have codes of fair practices. As one example, the District Mail Marketing Association not only publishes a fourteen-page booklet, "Guidelines for Ethical Business Practices," but has a full-time director of ethical practices whose job is to investigate complaints.[72] Newspapers, magazines, and broadcasters have adopted standards designed to screen out ads that are deceptive, fraudulent, or considered to be in bad taste. Because of these checks, perhaps no more than 3 percent of the millions of advertisements published or broadcast in any year raise bona-fide legal questions.[73]

---

71. Pacific Gas and Electric Co. v. Public Utilities Commission of California, __U.S.__, 106 S.Ct. 903, 89 L.Ed.2d 1 (1986).
72. Direct Mail Marketing Association, Inc., 6 E. 43d St., New York, NY 10017.
73. S. Watson Dunn and Arnold M. Barban, *Advertising, Its Role in Modern Marketing*, 4th ed. (Hinsdale, Ill.: Dryden Press, 1978), p. 84.

To an extent unequaled by any other medium of expression, advertising operates in a fishbowl. The purpose of advertising is to call attention to a message designed to sell a product or service. Thus, advertising is likely to have more of an impact on more people than all but the most important news stories or commentary. If a reporter misstates a fact about an action taken by a city council, few aside from the persons immediately involved will know or care. If an advertiser makes overblown claims for a product, every dissatisfied user will know and care, and may take the further step of buying no more of that product or of any other products made by the same company. It is not surprising, then, that the guidelines adopted by the various advertising organizations focus on honesty and clarity. A typical code advises advertisers to be able to substantiate any claims made for a product, to avoid unfair disparagement of other products, and to give full price information. If gifts are offered as inducements, any conditions attached to the offer should be stated clearly. Because such codes are voluntary, they are not observed by all advertisers all of the time, but, measured strictly in terms of literal accuracy, the rate of compliance is high, as is indicated by the figure above.

Honesty is not solely a matter of ethics. There are good business reasons for it, as Eugene S. Pulliam, publisher of the *Indianapolis Star* and *News*, noted at the end of 1985. He quoted with approval a statement made by Leonard S. Matthews, president of the American Association of Advertising Agencies, in the organization's newsletter.[74] Matthews wrote: "We ought to examine every ad from the standpoint of 'Would my mother believe it?' or, 'Would I recommend this product to my friends?'" In Matthews's opinion, advertising "is much more honest than it has ever been." He gave four reasons for this, the first of which was that honesty is good business. He also took note of the role played by "a much brighter consumer of advertising," the higher ethical standards of the media, and advertising's own self-regulation program.

Even a superficial survey of the literature leaves little doubt that advertising professionals are committed, with Don Quixote, to the belief that honesty is the best policy. However, the same survey leaves no doubt that advertising, because of its pervasiveness and the role it therefore is believed to play in shaping society, remains controversial. Many of the questions raised probe at the professional's ethics. These questions lie in a realm where beliefs are strong, facts are evasive, and conclusions subject to heated debate. The major points at issue can only be noted, not resolved, in a text of this kind.

At what point does advertising become offensive? For years, television refused ads for vaginal deodorants, but had no qualms about underarm deodorants, or products designed to cope with digestive gases. Television and most newspapers will not advertise condoms. They do accept ads holding out the promise of intimate romance to the users of the right shaving lotion or shampoo. Each television network has a high-level executive with final authority to reject ads considered in bad taste. Other advertising media have someone who makes the same decisions. Obviously, there are few objective standards for determining what bad taste is. A bra advertisement may inform some segment of the audience, titillate another, and be condemned as salacious by still another.

Should children be protected from some kinds of advertising? Do ads for cereals

---

74. Eugene S. Pulliam, "Publisher's Memo: Advertising," *Indianapolis Star*, 29 December 1985.

in which sugar is first among the listed ingredients lure children into harmful eating habits? Do advertisements for expensive, but shoddy, toys lead them to pressure their parents into submission? Each Christmas season in recent years has seen demand for a particular brand-name toy reach near panic proportions. Cabbage Patch dolls is one instance. To what extent was that demand a product of television advertising? Wouldn't other kinds of dolls have served the same purpose at less cost? Obviously, many parents were unwilling to persuade their children to accept an alternative.

Does advertising reinforce stereotypes—about the young, the elderly, women, and others? When the women's movement came to the fore in the 1960s, the National Organization of Women listed ten advertisements it considered most insulting to women. These portrayed women as homebodies whose greatest fear was that their husbands might find their coffee bitter, whose greatest concern was avoiding ring around the collar, and who lived in the kitchen, preparing food and washing dishes. Such ads appear on television with lesser frequency, but might there also be a stereotype in the well-groomed, physically attractive young woman who is always on the go, always involved in making major business decisions? The American Association of Retired Persons has objected to commercials portraying the elderly as frail, somewhat befuddled people who putter around until someone offers them a glass of lemonade, or a powerful painkiller for their arthritis. Only recently have advertisers begun to discover that people over sixty do more traveling for pleasure than any other segment of the population.

Closely related to the above is the question as to whether advertising influences behavior. Its purpose, of course, is to influence buying decisions. But what else does it do? What, for instance, are the consequences of portraying young men as eager to get off work so they can troop to the nearest bar? If there are any women in those bars, they either are staring adoringly at the young men or are serving them beer by the pitcher. The men are laughing, chattering, clapping each other on the back in great camaraderie. Is there any connection with the fact that alcohol has become a major problem on college campuses or that driving under the influence has become a major cause of motor vehicle accidents?

Has advertising distorted the political process? Political campaigns have become advertising campaigns, with large sums poured into spot commercials on television and radio. Such campaigns put a premium on image and on simplification. For years after Senator Barry Goldwater ran for president in 1964, he had to contend with the belief that had he been elected he would have started a nuclear war. In part that belief was reinforced by a commercial used only a few times by his Democratic opponent, Lyndon B. Johnson. It showed a child picking petals off a daisy while a voice over counted down from ten. At zero, a nuclear mushroom cloud blotted out the scene. Such was the magnitude of Johnson's victory, that it is doubtful anything could have changed the result. Nor is there any way of measuring the one commercial's effect. Nevertheless, there are questions, even among advertising professionals, about the use of brief commercials as a campaign device. Some agencies refuse to prepare any political campaign advertisement that runs less than five minutes on the grounds that it is impossible to deal with any issue of substance in a shorter time.[75]

---

75. Dunn and Barban, *Advertising*, p. 93.

Other ethical questions deal with the propriety of direct comparisons with other products, with the manipulation of the fears and desires that we all share, with the selling of useless or even marginally harmful products, and with the influence of advertising on media content. In connection with the latter, one frequently asked question is whether magazines that rely heavily on cigarette advertising have downplayed the hazards of smoking. In another connection, there still are newspapers that report "grand reopenings" of advertisers who have done no more than remodel a store's front windows. There was a time when advertisers might also keep a story out of the paper by threatening to withdraw their ads. But today, when most communities are served by only one newspaper, and when shopping malls have made it difficult for one retailer to hold a dominant position, advertiser pressure on an editor is likely to be shrugged off.

Thus, while there is no reason to doubt the assertion that advertising "is much more honest than it has ever been," there also is no doubt that the questions do not end there. Advertising professionals, like their editorial counterparts, are aware that beyond the question "Is it legal?" lies the harder question "Is it right?"

FOR REVIEW

1. What is the meaning of "the doctrine of commercial speech?"

2. Explain the significance of the *Pittsburgh Press* case. On what rationale was it decided?

3. Compare and contrast the Supreme Court's decisions in *Bigelow* and *Virginia State Board*.

4. List each of the branches of the four-part test established by Justice Powell in the *Central Hudson Gas* case. Explain how each is applied.

5. What is meant by "deceptive advertising"? What standard is used in determining whether an advertisement is deceptive? Illustrate with examples.

6. Distinguish between "letter of compliance," "consent agreement," and "cease and desist order."

7. Define each of the following: "broadened cease and desist order," "affirmative disclosure," "affirmative acts," "corrective advertising," "advertising substantiation," "trade rules."

8. How can the Federal Trade Commission's power to order corrective advertising be harmonized with the *Central Hudson Gas* decision?

9. Explain the rationale that permits a news medium to refuse commercial advertising.

10. What is meant by the term "the right of access to the media"? Is there such a right with respect to newspapers or magazines?

11. What has the Supreme Court said about the argument that, in the interest of fairness, newspapers should be compelled to give reply space to persons who have been the subjects of critical stories or editorials?

12. Why and under what conditions can a state university newspaper be compelled to accept advertising? Under what conditions can it refuse to do so?

CHAPTER 12

COPYRIGHT LAW

The drafters of the Constitution recognized that persons who work with words—and with other means of expression—have a right to be paid for their efforts. They included this provision among the powers of Congress listed in Article I, section 8: "To promote the progress of science and useful arts, by securing for limited times to authors and inventors the exclusive right to their respective writings and discoveries."

Since 1790, that mandate has been carried into effect, in part, by a series of Copyright Acts, the last adopted in 1976 and amended in 1980 and 1984 to include computer programs and semiconductor chips, through which computers function. Copyright law sets the conditions under which those who have creative talent in any field of expression can protect their work from unauthorized copying. The purpose is to protect their right to profit from their talent and thus encourage its use. The law does so by granting them a monopoly for a fixed period over the uses that can be made of a protected work.

In a sense, then, copyright law complements the First Amendment. There might not be a vigorous marketplace of ideas if those with a talent for words, pictures, or other means of expression could not be sure of payment for their work. By protecting the right to profit from one's creative talents, the law encourages discussion in the public interest.

Looked at from another point of view, copyright law can be seen as placing limits on the free marketplace of ideas. Publishers, broadcasters, and film producers cannot freely use any work they please in preparing their own offerings. If they are going to make substantial use of copyrighted works produced by others, they must be prepared to pay a reasonable fee for such use.

Although copyright is grounded in the Constitution, it is defined by statute. Therefore, we will begin with an overview of the Copyright Act. Generally, the law protects any original work that can be fixed in some tangible means of expression. If the work is an article, a book, a poem, or some other form of written expression, the copyright covers the exact arrangement of words, phrases, sentences, and paragraphs. Courts have held that ideas, theories, historical incidents, and news cannot be copyrighted, but an author's account of them can be. However, copyright protection is not limited to words. Photographs, drawings, graphic devices, paintings, musical compositions, dance routines, and even pantomime can be protected from copying. The televised version of such major sports events as the Superbowl, the World Series, and the Masters Golf tournament is copyrighted by the originating network.

The Copyright Act gives the creators or owners of copyrighted works complete control over their use by others. Thus, a copyright is a form of property and can be sold, assigned, or inherited like any other kind of real property. However, the law also recognizes that in the everyday world, every author cannot research every work back to original sources. Some copying of someone else's work is inevitable, especially in such well-explored fields as history, biography, public affairs, and the various academic disciplines. If copying is minimal, and does not detract unduly from the commercial value of the original work, the law allows it as a "**fair use**." But if copying is substantial, or if it detracts from the commercial value of the original, it becomes an "**infringement**." This means that the copier can be required to pay damages to the owner of the original copyright. The law also authorizes prior restraint to keep the offending work off the market.

The First Amendment plays only a peripheral role in copyright law. Alleged infringers have argued in some instances that the work in question served a public interest of such importance that it was protected by the First Amendment. In 1985, in *Harper & Row, Publishers, Inc.* v. *Nation Enterprises*,[1] the Supreme Court of the United States rejected that argument. It held that whatever First Amendment interest there is in the copying of a protected work was taken into consideration by Congress when it defined "fair use."

This chapter also examines copyright questions raised by the new technology—copying machines, cable television, and video recorders. It ends with a topic not strictly a matter of copyright law: the systematic copying by one news outlet of news gathered by someone else. Courts have held that such taking, defined as "misappropriation," is a form of unfair competition.

---

1. __U.S.__, 105 S.Ct. 2218, 85 L.Ed.2d 588 (1985).

Major Cases

Harper & Row, Publishers, Inc. v. *Nation Enterprises,* __U.S., __, 105 S.Ct. 2218, 85 L.Ed.2d 588 (1985).

Hoehling v. *Universal City Studios, Inc.,* 618 F.2d 972 (2d Cir. 1980).

Iowa State University Research Foundation v. *American Broadcasting Companies, Inc.,* 621 F.2d 57 (2d Cir. 1980).

Jason v. *Fonda,* 526 F.Supp. 774 (C.D.Calif. 1981); aff., 698 F.2d 966 (9th Cir. 1982).

Pottstown Daily News v. *Pottstown Broadcasting,* 192 A.2d 657 (Pa. 1963).

Rosemont Enterprises, Inc., v. *Random House, Inc.,* 366 F.2d 203 (2d Cir. 1966); cert. den., 385 U.S. 1009 (1967).

Sid & Marty Krofft Television Productions, Inc. v. *McDonald's Corp.,* 562 F.2d 1157 (9th Cir. 1977).

Time Inc. v. *Bernard Geis Associates,* 293 F.Supp. 130 (S.D.N.Y. 1968).

Triangle Publications, Inc. v. *Knight-Ridder Newspapers,* 445 F. Supp. 875 (S.D.Fla. 1978); 626 F.2d 1171 (5th Cir. 1980).

Universal City Studios, Inc. v. *Sony Corporation of America,* 465 U.S. 1112, 104 S.Ct. 1619, 80 L.Ed.2d 1480 (1984).

The Copyright Act

So widespread is the knowledge that original compositions in any form may be protected that the Copyright Act is one of the few laws summarized in detail in the *World Almanac,* a popular reference work.

Since 1978, copyright has been governed only by federal law.[2] Under that law, the creator of any original work in any medium has a copyright on it from the moment it is put into tangible form. However, if the work is to be offered to the public, the originator needs to take two steps to protect his or her rights fully.

1. A notice of copyright should be placed on the work. The form of such notice is a C with a circle around it, followed by the date of first publication and the owner's name. The word "Copyright" or its abbreviation, "Cop.," may also be used.

2. The work should be registered with the Copyright Office at the Library of Congress. Forms may be obtained for the asking from the Office. To fully complete a copyright, a copy of the work, with or without registration, must be sent to the Library of Congress.

---

2. This section is based on Title 17, Copyrights, United States Code.

Registration need not be immediate. However, without registration, an owner's right to recover damages is limited if an infringement should occur.

A copyright is in effect for the life of the author and fifty years thereafter. If the work is done for hire, the copyright belongs to the employer, not the author, unless the terms of employment provide otherwise. If the copyright is owned by the employer, it is valid for one hundred years from the date of creation, or for seventy-five years from the date of publication, whichever is shorter. During the term of the copyright, the holder has the exclusive right to control the use of the composition by others. In the case of author-held copyrights, control passes to the author's heirs.

Because a copyright is a form of property, it may be bought and sold, and made the subject of a contract or passed on to an author's heirs through a will. Some examples will help clarify this point. A photographer who was hired to take pictures of a newsworthy boxer found that the promoter not only had the right to copyright his work but owned the negatives.[3] However, a photographer who arranged to take pictures of members of a high school graduating class in the hope that he could sell enough of them to make a profit held a valid copyright on the class photograph, which he also took.[4] Federal courts held that the first became an employee of the promoter, while the second was a free-lance entrepreneur.

Some newspapers are copyrighted. This means that the publisher controls the right to sell to others any staff-produced articles or photographs, unless the terms of employment state otherwise. The terms under which magazines buy articles from free-lance authors generally include the right to copyright the articles. However, an author of stature may be able to retain the copyright. An author who contracts with a publisher to write a book may find that under the terms of that contract the publisher owns the copyright. Federal employees who produce reports, or judges who write decisions, cannot copyright their work. Under terms of the law, what they write is in the **public domain** and can be used by anyone.[5] But professors at state universities, who are required to publish if they want to gain tenure or win promotions, are permitted by custom to copyright their writings. Theoretically, they are writing for themselves. The university hires them to teach.

Copyright, then, is a function of statute law. Because it is, a copyright is valid only if the procedures prescribed by the statute are followed. While all original works now are copyrighted when they are put in tangible form, the originator's rights can be protected fully only if at some time the work is registered with the Copyright Office and a copy filed with the Library of Congress.

What Copyright Protects

Section 102 of the Copyright Act describes the kinds of works that can be protected against copying. Because the section is written in legal language, it can be made more understandable by looking at each of its elements separately.

It is basic that the work in question must be original with the creator. If the work

---

3. Lumiere v. Robertson-Cole Distributing Corp., 280 F. 550 (2d Cir. 1922).
4. Altman v. New Haven Union Co., 254 F. 113 (D.Conn. 1918).
5. 17 U.S.C §105.

borrows from others, say by quoting extensively from the Bible or from Shakespeare, the copyright does not cover the borrowed quotations. Further, the original work must be expressed in some tangible form "now known or later developed." This means that a writer must put words on paper or onto a computer disk; a photographer must take a picture; a choreographer must diagram the positions of the dancers; a composer must take the notes pecked out on a piano and enter them onto a score. Whatever the form, it must make possible the communication of the work to others, because it is at that point that the work becomes vulnerable to copying. For illustratative purposes, §102 lists seven categories of "works of authorship." They are:

1. literary works

2. musical works, including any accompanying words

3. dramatic works, including any accompanying words

4. pantomimes and choreographic works

5. pictorial, graphic, and sculptural works

6. motion pictures and other audiovisual works

7. sound recordings

These categories apply to the completed form taken by the specific work or composition. The ideas, discoveries, or processes embodied in that completed form are not covered by copyright. However, thanks to the words "now known or later developed" found in §102, the forms of expression protected by copyright are almost infinitely variable. For instance, a federal court held in 1981 that a tiny silicon chip used to translate an operator's commands into computer language is a form of expression protected by copyright.[6] Printed on the chip was a minute replica of the computer program that made the translation possible. That, the court held, made the chip "a tangible medium of expression" within the meaning of the copyright statute.

The news of the day cannot be copyrighted. Neither can the notable events of an individual's life, or the facts of history. No news medium can gain the sole right to exploit a given news event by copyrighting its presentation of it. But a newspaper can copyright its particular account of a news event. Television networks can, and do, copyright their news programs. An author who conducts research into an individual's life can copyright his version of the events that made the individual of interest to the public. The *World Almanac* comprises facts, many of them taken from the public domain, but this does not prevent the Newspaper Enterprise Association from getting a copyright on each year's edition. It is entitled to protect the work it did in compiling those facts, and its particular presentation of them. But its copyright cannot prevent others from using the facts the Almanac contains.

Separating an idea from its expression frequently is difficult. Is a theory of history, for instance, an idea or a form of expression? The U.S. Court of Appeals for the Second Circuit had to grapple with that question in 1980. The explosion and fire that destroyed

---

6. Tandy Corp. v. Personal Micro Computers, Inc., 524 F.Supp. 171 (N.D.Calif. 1981).

the German dirigible *Hindenburg* at Lakehurst, New Jersey, in May 1937, with the loss of thirty-six lives, has been the subject of considerable speculation. The official verdict is that the fire probably was caused by static electricity that ignited the dirigible's highly flammable hydrogen. However, A. A. Hoehling spent years investigating the tragedy and came to a different conclusion. He concluded that a rigger, Eric Spehl, had planted a timed explosive device in one of the gas cells, intending to blow up the balloon after its passengers had disembarked. His purpose was to impress his girlfriend, an anti-Hitler Communist, in Germany. However, a thunderstorm delayed the ship's arrival, and Spehl was among those killed when his bomb went off. Hoehling described his theory in a book that had a limited market in 1962.

Hoehling v. *Universal City Studios, Inc.,* 618 F.2d 972 (2d Cir. 1980).

Ten years later, Michael Mooney took Hoehling's thesis and developed it into a fictionalized version entitled *The Hindenburg*. Universal City Studios bought the rights to Mooney's book and converted it into a motion picture released in 1975. Hoehling sued Universal for copyright infringement, and lost. In upholding the district court's summary dismissal of the suit, the court of appeals said:

> [T]he protection afforded the copyright holder has never extended to history, be it documented fact or explanatory hypothesis. The rationale for this doctrine is that the cause of knowledge is best served when history is the common property of all, and each generation remains free to draw upon the discoveries and insights of the past. Accordingly, the scope of copyright in historical accounts is narrow indeed, embracing no more than the author's original expression of particular facts and theories already in the public domain. As the case before us illustrates, absent wholesale usurpation of another's expression, claims of copyright infringement where works of history are at issue are rarely successful.

The court held that Hoehling's thesis was not subject to copyright. His conclusion that Spehl had planted a bomb was simply one of many possible interpretations of historical data. The court added:

> To avoid a chilling effect on authors who contemplate tackling an historical issue or event, broad latitude must be granted to subsequent authors who make use of historical subject matter, including theories or plots.

The court said its ruling would not excuse verbatim copying by one author of another's copyrighted work. But in this instance, it held, it was evident that each author had developed the material in an individual way.

In effect, the court sanctioned Mooney's and Universal's stealing of Hoehling's idea. The decision thus calls attention to the distinction between violation of copyright and plagiarism. Copyright treats creative works as property. Indeed, another term used for copyright law is "the law of literary property." In *Hoehling*, the court said it was all right for Mooney and Universal to take Hoehling's theory as to the cause of the *Hindenburg*'s explosion as long as they did not take the form in which he had expressed his theory. They would have violated his copyright on his book expounding the theory only had they quoted extensively enough from it without his permission to lower its market value.

Plagiarism can also be direct copying of another's work. But it also is plagiarism to take another's ideas and offer them as one's own. Thus, a student writing a term paper or a thesis about the *Hindenburg* could not properly present the idea that the dirigible was blown up by one of its riggers without attributing it to Hoehling. To put it another way, copyright is concerned with specific forms of expression and with payment for others' uses of those forms. Plagiarism is taking without acknowledgment not only the form of another's work but the ideas it presents.

Because today's news is tomorrow's history, the same principles applied in *Hoehling* also apply to the coverage of news events. A reporter who reads about a newsworthy disclosure in another publication, or sees an account of it on television, is not foreclosed from covering the same story. Reporters are free to go to sources mentioned in another's story and learn from them what they can. They also can seek out other sources who know something about the event. As long as the resulting story does not quote substantially from the original story, or paraphrase it without offering new information or insights, there is no risk of being penalized for copyright violation. However, if competing reporters either make no effort to find new information or are unable to find any, and simply rewrite the original without credit to the source, they are plagiarists, no matter how different the wording of the second story.

The importance of research, not only for journalists, but for all creators of copyrightable works, cannot be overemphasized. One who does research, or who possesses unique creative talent in any medium, has the capacity to produce original works. By definition, the purpose of copyright law is to protect original works. However, the law also recognizes that on occasion even the most creative persons cannot present something new without borrowing from an existing work. This recognition originally was established by the courts as the doctrine of fair use. Since 1978, that doctrine has been a part of the statute itself.

The Doctrine of Fair Use

Fair use, as defined in §107 of the Copyright Act, permits one author, composer, or artist to borrow limited amounts of material from another without seeking permission. It has nothing to do with the fact that honesty requires any taker, no matter how inconsequential his taking, to give credit to his sources.

Section 107 says that one author can quote another "for purposes such as criticism, comment, news reporting, teaching . . . , scholarship, or research" without infringing copyright. Teachers are permitted to reproduce copyrighted materials for classroom use if it is done spontaneously. This means that a teacher who finds an article in a magazine pertinent to the coursework can copy it without permission and distribute it to the students. However, if the article is of such value that the teacher plans to make it part of the course, the law requires that permission be obtained from the copyright owner.

In determining whether a use is fair or not, §107 requires courts to consider the following factors:

"(1) the purpose and character of the use, including whether such use is of a commercial nature or is for nonprofit educational purposes
"(2) the nature of the copyrighted work
"(3) the amount and substantiality of the portion used in relation to the copyrighted work as a whole
"(4) the effect of the use upon the potential market for or value of the copyrighted work."

Obviously, in writing the four factors into law, Congress did not set a mathematical formula that can be applied with precision to every instance of alleged copyright infringement. The standards must be applied to the facts of each case by a judge or jury. The verdict is a matter of judgment. However, some firm principles have emerged from the decisions, which are sampled below. People who understand those principles and apply them in their own work are not likely to infringe a copyright.

The classic case illustrating how courts separate a fair use from an infringement is *Rosemont Enterprises, Inc.* v. *Random House, Inc.* Although it was decided more than twenty years ago, it is still frequently applied by the courts. The work at issue in *Rosemont*

Rosemont Enterprises, Inc. v. Random House, Inc., 366 F.2d 203 (2d Cir. 1966); cert. den., 385 U.S. 1009 (1967).

was a mass-market biography of Howard Hughes. At one time, Hughes was a highly visible public figure. Born to wealth, he enlarged his inherited fortune by providing services to the oil industry, by producing movies, and by building aircraft during World War II. Physically attractive, he was the companion of the most beautiful movie stars of the era. But in his later years he retreated from public view, living in elaborately guarded hideouts, seeing no one except a few trusted associates. He protected his privacy with unmatched zeal, and

During World War II, Howard Hughes (wearing the hat) built what was then the world's largest airplane. His later attempt to prevent publication of an unauthorized biography led to a landmark decision expanding the meaning of "fair use" in copyright law. (UPI/Bettmann Newsphotos)

discouraged all attempts to pry into his life. This, of course, made him even more a subject of public curiosity.

Before Hughes became a complete recluse, *Look* magazine published a series of three articles on him in 1954. Nearly a decade later, Random House commissioned a *Life* magazine writer, Thomas Thompson, to prepare a biography of Hughes. Thompson worked from newspaper clippings and other articles, including the *Look* series. He supplemented this material by conducting at least fifteen interviews with persons who knew Hughes. When other commitments kept him from finishing the book, Random House hired John Keats to do so. He, too, did extensive checking on materials and he was listed as author of the completed work.

Hughes, of course, was aware of what was going on. At one point, his lawyer approached Bennett Cerf, then head of Random House, and offered to make it worth his while to stop work on the biography. Otherwise, Hughes would use his vast resources to make trouble. Cerf rejected the offer, and the book was published.

As part of its sales campaign for the biography, Random House sent galley proofs to a dozen leading magazines and newspapers for advance review purposes. Hughes somehow obtained one of these. There were two immediate consequences. Rosemont Enterprises, which had been organized by three of Hughes's associates not long before, bought the copyright to the *Look* articles. Then it asked the U.S. District Court in New York to prevent distribution of the Random House biography. Hughes's lawyers said Rosemont had been formed for the purpose of publishing an authorized biography of Hughes and had hired a writer to do so. The forthcoming Random House book, they said, infringed on the *Look* articles, which were to be used in preparing the authorized work, and thus would cause Rosemont great economic harm. There was no question that Thompson and Keats had drawn from the articles. This was acknowledged in the book. The district court judge reasoned that the doctrine of fair use applied only to scholarly works, not those designed for a popular market. He granted a temporary injunction pending trial. Random House appealed to the second circuit court of appeals, which reversed. Judge Leonard P. Moore wrote for the court.

He began with a physical comparison of the two works. The articles totaled 13,500 words, or 36 to 39 book-size pages. The biography ran to 116,000 words, or 304 pages. Naturally, many of the incidents in Hughes's life were described in both works, but actual duplication of language was limited to two direct quotations from the *Look* articles and one eight-line paraphrase, all of which were attributed to the articles. However, if general duplication of incidents was accepted as the test of infringement, the copying was more substantial. Up to 28 percent of the material in one article was duplicated in another form in the book.

But Judge Moore held that mere duplication of incidents taken from Hughes's life did not prove infringement. Any two accurate biographies of him obviously must include many of the same incidents. *Look*'s copyright, now owned by Rosemont, did not apply to the facts of Hughes's life. Copyright protection applied only to the precise mode of expression used by the author of the *Look* articles. Examining the articles in that light, Judge Moore found that direct copying of language made up only a small part of both works.

However, the district court had held that, given the popular nature of the Random House book, even minimal copying was an infringement. In its opinion, the doctrine of fair use was reserved for scholarly works. Judge Moore conceded that in previous cases fair use generally had been limited to works "in the fields of science, law, medicine, history and biography." Then he broke new ground by holding that books dealing with matters in the public interest are entitled to fair use of copyrighted materials even if the books are aimed at a mass audience. In this instance, the court held that a popular biography of Howard Hughes would serve an important public interest. If the district court's view was to prevail, the judge wrote, it would deny the public

> an opportunity to become acquainted with the life of a person endowed with extraordinary talents who, by exercising these talents, made substantial contributions in the fields to which he chose to devote his unique abilities. Inheriting a small fortune in early youth, Hughes can hardly qualify as a Horatio Alger hero in a "From Rags to Riches" story but a narration of his initiative, ingenuity, determination and tireless work to achieve his conception of perfection in whatever he did ought to be available to a reading public which, even in an affluent society, might well be reminded that affluence usually comes from the work of such entrepreneurs in business and industry.
>
> . . . Any biography of Hughes, of necessity, must recite the events of his life because biography in itself is largely a compilation of the past. Thus, in balancing the equities at this time in our opinion the public interest should prevail over the possible damage to the copyright holder.

That last sentence should be kept in mind in any approach to a fair use question. Courts deciding cases since *Rosemont* have looked at the public interest in resolving copyright infringement questions. In looking at the nature of the allegedly infringing work, courts have looked at its purpose. If the purpose is to serve some public interest in information, the courts are likely to hold that the use of material taken from another copyrighted work is fair, if the taking is not substantial and does not result in economic harm to the owner of the copyright on the original.

The appeals court completed its analysis by examining the claim that the publication of the book would cause Rosemont economic harm. It noted that the *Look* articles had not been republished in any form, nor had they earned any royalties. Therefore, there was no competition between them and the book. The claim that the book would detract from the market for Rosemont's planned authorized biography did not rise above speculation. No such work was in existence. Nor has it ever materialized.

The public interest rationale born in *Rosemont* proved crucial two years later in *Time Inc.* v. *Bernard Geis Associates*, a case growing out of the assassination of President John F. Kennedy. When he was shot to death on the streets of Dallas in 1963, Abraham Zapruder, a dress manufacturer, just happened to record the event with his eight-millimeter home movie camera. His film, in color, showed the president as the bullets struck him. *Life* magazine paid Zapruder $150,000 for exclusive rights to the film. Blown-up excerpts from it were used extensively by the magazine. Because there were no other photographs of the shooting itself, *Life* made copies of the Zapruder film for the commission named by President Lyndon B. Johnson to investigate the assassination. A number of still frames appeared in the final report with the notation that *Life* held exclusive rights to their use.

Time Inc. v. Bernard Geis Associates, 293 F.Supp. 130 (S.D.N.Y. 1968).

While the commission held that the evidence pointed conclusively to Lee Harvey Oswald as the lone assassin, others adopted the theory that the two bullets that struck the president had been fired from different locations. Among these theorists was Josiah Thompson, a professor of philosophy, who developed his belief into a book, *Six Seconds in Dallas*, published by Bernard Geis Associates, and distributed by Random House. As part of his research, Thompson studied the Zapruder film, a copy of which was in the National Archives. At one point, *Life* was interested enough in Thompson's work to hire him as a consultant in the preparation of its own articles questioning the conclusion of the commission. Through contacts made at the magazine, Thompson was able to see the Zapruder film and stills made from it. He tried and failed to get permission to use some of the stills in his book. Later, a *Life* editor was to testify that he had returned to his office unexpectedly one night and found Thompson using a camera, presumably to copy photographs made from the Zapruder film.

Thompson's finished book was illustrated with charcoal drawings that were identified as "exact copies" of frames taken from the Zapruder film. *Life*'s parent company, Time Inc., sued in federal district court in New York City for copyright infringement, arguing that there was no originality whatsoever in the artist's sketches. The court agreed on that point. Geis argued that the Zapruder film could not be copyrighted because it, too, involved no creativity. It was merely the accidental recording of an historical event. Here, the court disagreed. Zapruder had tried several locations before he found the one he thought would give him the best view of the president. Further, there is creativity in the way in which any photographer frames a particular shot. Therefore, photographs, even of news events, can be copyrighted.

Was Geis's use a fair use? The court's decision hinged on two points: the public's interest in the shooting of the president, and the degree of economic competition between the book and such use as *Life* might still make of the film. The court cited *Rosemont* in deciding for Geis. Thompson had done a great deal of original research in preparing a serious work expounding "a theory entitled to public consideration." Purchasers would not buy the book to get the Zapruder film. This already had been made available in several versions and could be studied at leisure and in its entirety by anyone willing to go to the National Archives. Thus it was perhaps more reasonable to speculate that the book might enhance rather than diminish *Life*'s market. The court held that the drawings in Thompson's book were a fair use of Zapruder's film.

The *Rosemont* and *Geis* decisions raise a question: In introducing the public interest element in copyright cases, was the second circuit recognizing a First Amendment defense for some kinds of infringement? A federal district court judge in Florida came to that conclusion in 1978 in ruling on *Triangle Publications, Inc. v. Knight-Ridder Newspapers*. Triangle publishes *TV Guide*, a localized weekly listing of television programs supplemented with news and comment on the medium. Editors of the *Miami Herald*, owned by Knight-Ridder, decided to publish a full-scale television magazine as part of the Sunday paper. The magazine would carry news and comment along with program listings and would be larger in size than *TV Guide*. To call attention to its new magazine, the

Triangle Publications, Inc. v. Knight-Ridder Newspapers, 445 F.Supp. 875 (S.D.Fla. 1978); 626 F.2d 1171 (5th Cir. 1980).

Herald ran a series of ads featuring side-by-side photographs of it and *TV Guide*. The purpose was to emphasize the new magazine's larger size.

Triangle filed suit, arguing that the photographs infringed its copyright. It asked for an order that would forbid further use of *TV Guide* in the *Herald*'s ads. The district court refused its request.

The court conceded that the cover, which was all the ads showed, was subject to copyright. It symbolized the essence of the magazine and might even be a work of art. The *Herald*'s use of the cover was the kind of "display" defined by the Copyright Act and was for a blatant commercial purpose. If the law was read strictly, *TV Guide* had a right to prevent such use.

If the court's analysis had ended there, the *Herald* would have been ruled an infringer. However, it proceeded to examine the Supreme Court's decisions holding that even purely commercial advertising is subject to First Amendment protection. It concluded that the commercial speech doctrine could be applied to this dispute. The *Herald*'s ads qualified for protection because they conveyed information. They told television viewers that by buying the Sunday *Herald* they could get all the program schedules that *TV Guide* had to offer along with a big package of general television news and features. Thus, because the advertisements represented "an important source of information for the education of the consumer in a free enterprise system," Triangle's suit must fail.

The district court's verdict was upheld on appeal to the U.S. Court of Appeals for the Fifth Circuit, but on different grounds. However, to the evident disgust of Judge John R. Brown, who wrote for the court, the other two members of the panel would not join him in condemning the lower court's First Amendment reasoning.

The fifth circuit court applied conventional fair use analysis in reaching its decision. It started by noting, as the lower court had, that the *Herald*'s use was commercial and that normally this would work against it. But *TV Guide* also was commercial in its nature. The nature of the use, then, was a neutral factor, neither supporting nor hurting the *Herald*'s case. The third and fourth factors in the analysis tipped the decision in the *Herald*'s favor. It had taken no more than *TV Guide*'s cover, an insubstantial part of the magazine. It had not copied any of the content—which is what people are looking for when they buy the magazine. Thus, the ads did not take content that would make it unnecessary for anyone to buy *TV Guide*. While it is true that the purpose of the ad was to persuade people to give up one magazine for another, this was legitimate business competition, not copyright infringement.

The meaning of the cases sampled above is clear. A use of copyrighted material in another work is fair if only a small part of the original work is taken and if it makes up only a small part of the second work. The court also must be able to conclude that the taking has little or no effect on the economic value of the original. Minimal taking, even for a work intended for the mass market, is most likely to be condoned if the work is in the public interest. In *Rosemont*, the court held there is a public interest in the biography of an unusual person. In *Geis*, there was a public interest in the author's belief that the assassination of President Kennedy could not have been the work of a lone gunman.

The idea that the First Amendment might excuse substantial taking of another's copyrighted work proved attractive—so much so that, as we will see later, the Supreme

Court came to grips with it in 1985 and did what Judge Brown wanted the fifth circuit to do in *Triangle*.

Copyright Infringement

The Question of Access

Courts considering copyright cases have recognized that it is possible for composers, authors, and artists working independently to come up with works presenting the same themes in roughly the same way. Thus, the threshold showing in an infringement action is *access*. The copyright owner who alleges harmful copying must show by the preponderance of the evidence that the alleged infringer saw his or her work. If that can't be done, the copyright owner must show that there is such an overwhelming similarity between the two works as to rise above the level of coincidence. Sonya Jason was not able to prove either point and therefore lost an infringement action against Jane Fonda and others in 1981.

In 1972, Jason had written and published at her own expense the book *Concomitant Soldier—Woman and War*. About half the press run of 1,100 copies was sold in New Jersey, where Jason lived. In 1977, some of the remainder were sold in Southern California. The general theme of the book dealt with the return of an injured soldier from war and the effect of his injury on the women in his life.

Jason v. Fonda, 526 F.Supp. 774 (C.D.Calif. 1981); aff., 698 F.2d 966 (9th Cir. 1982).

Jane Fonda toured military bases and hospitals during the Vietnam War and became active in the movement against the war. Those experiences gave her and Bruce Gilbert an idea for a movie, which they outlined to a writer, Nancy Dowd, in 1972. Dowd submitted a script to Fonda and Gilbert the next year. They submitted it to other writers for revision. The result was a movie, *Coming Home*, which was produced in 1977. Its theme, too, dealt with the return of an injured soldier and his effect on the women in his life. United Artists released the film in 1978, and it was used on the NBC television network the next year. Jason sued in the U.S. District Court in Los Angeles, alleging copyright infringement.

That court dismissed the action, holding that Jason could not prove that anyone connected with the film had seen her book. Further, the time sequence made it clear that most of the photography had been completed before Jason's book went on sale on the West Coast. Nor was there any substantial similarity between the book and the movie. While it was true that both dealt with the "effects of war on women, injured veterans and soldiers," these topics have been "the subject of countless works dating back for centuries." The book and the movie shared only themes, unprotectable ideas, and "commonly cited historical facts," none of which are subject to copyright. Aside from this, the movie was "substantially dissimilar to plaintiff's book," the court held.

Thus, if the author suing for infringement cannot prove that the other had access to her work, she must show that there is a substantial similarity between the two works. Such similarity must go beyond general themes or ideas into detailed plot development, situations, language, and characterization.

Fair Use or Infringement?

If a copyright owner can prove that an alleged infringer had access to his work, the next step is to determine whether the taking was a fair use or an infringement. Courts look first at the nature of the two works to determine whether they are commercial or scholarly, designed for the mass market to make a quick profit, or aimed at a limited audience with little thought of profit. If the alleged infringer is the author of a critical review or an article for a scholarly journal, courts are less likely to find an infringement. The next step is to determine how much of the original work was taken in relation to the whole. The same determination is made with respect to the alleged infringer's work. If the taking is substantial with regard to both works, the inquiry may end there. However, in most cases, the crucial question is whether the alleged infringement detracts from the commercial value of the original work. If the taking is of such a nature that there is no need to buy the original work, courts are likely to hold that there was an infringement. So important is this determination that courts have held there was an infringement even when a relatively small amount of the original was taken.

Such was the case in *Harper & Row, Publishers, Inc.* v. *Nation Enterprises*, decided by the Supreme Court in 1985. The problem began in April 1979 when *The Nation*, a magazine of political commentary, scored what its editors saw as a journalistic scoop.

Harper & Row, Publishers, Inc. v. *Nation Enterprises,* _U.S._, 105 S.Ct. 2218, 85 L.E.2d 588 (1985).

They did so by publishing excerpts from former President Gerald R. Ford's not yet released memoirs, *A Time to Heal*. The excerpts, including 300 to 400 words of direct quotation from Ford's book, gave new insights into former President Nixon's involvement in the Watergate burglary and into Ford's subsequent pardon of Nixon. The article also contained Ford's candid appraisal of some of the leading political figures of the day. Victor Navasky, the editor of *The Nation* and author of the article, was correct in his belief that he had a newsworthy scoop. The article became the subject of widespread news stories and commentary.

The publication also had two other effects. Harper & Row and The Reader's Digest Association, co-owners of the copyright on the book, had obtained Ford's permission to sell excerpts from the book to magazines and newspapers in advance of its publication. One of the purchasers was *Time* magazine, which agreed to pay $25,000 for the right to publish a 7,500-word excerpt dealing with the Nixon pardon. It had paid $12,500 in advance and had scheduled its article to appear in mid-April 1979. When *The Nation* article appeared, *Time* canceled the deal. Harper & Row reacted by suing *The Nation* for copyright infringement. After a six-day trial, the U.S. District Court for the Southern District of New York found that there was indeed an infringement and awarded Harper & Row $12,500 in actual damages.

The Nation appealed, arguing that the district court had not paid enough attention to the First Amendment value of its newsworthy scoop. The U.S. Court of Appeals for the Second Circuit agreed that the disclosures were "politically significant." It held that it is not "the purpose of the Copyright Act to impede the harvest of knowledge so necessary to a democratic state" or "chill the activities of the press by forbidding a circumscribed use of copyrighted words."[7] The court reversed the district court's decision,

---

7. 723 F.2d 195, at 197, 209 (2d Cir. 1982).

holding that when First Amendment interests were considered, *The Nation*'s article was a fair use, not an infringement.

The Supreme Court agreed to take the case and reversed the court of appeals, six-to-three. In doing so, it placed heavy emphasis on the fact that no part of Ford's book had been released officially for publication at the time the article appeared. The Court said the right to control release of one's work, and to prevent others from using it prior to release, is a key factor in fair use analysis. It noted that the timing of release not only is important to the value of a work, it also assures authors of the time "to develop their ideas free from fear of expropriation." The latter consideration alone, the Court said, "outweighs any short term 'news value' to be gained from premature publication of the author's expression."

However, the Court also dealt with the First Amendment question raised in the lower courts in this case, and by the federal district court in Florida in the *Triangle Publications* case discussed earlier. It noted that *The Nation* had sought to justify its copying of Ford's language "as essential to reporting the news story" embodied in his book. The magazine's lawyers argued in their brief that "the precise manner in which [Ford] expressed himself was as newsworthy as what he had to say." They argued further that the public's interest in getting that news as quickly as possible overrode the author's right to control the first publication of his autobiography.

Justice Sandra Day O'Connor, writing for a majority of the Court, rejected that argument. Adoption of *The Nation*'s theory of the law, she wrote, "would expand fair use to effectively destroy any expectation of copyright protection in the work of a public figure." Copyright would mean little, especially to public figures, if its protections "could be avoided merely by dubbing the infringement a fair use 'news report' of the book." The infraction is particularly grave, Justice O'Connor added, when, as in this instance, it preempts the author's right of first publication.

Turning directly to the First Amendment question, the justice noted that "the Framers intended copyright itself to be the engine of free expression." By protecting an author's right to profit from his work, "copyright supplies the economic incentive to create and disseminate ideas." At the same time, the law recognizes that First Amendment interests also are served by permitting some copying under limited circumstances. Justice O'Connor summed up the Court's position:

> In view of the First Amendment protections already embodied in the Copyright Act's distinction between copyrightable expression and uncopyrightable facts and ideas, and the latitude for scholarship and comment traditionally afforded by fair use, we see no warrant for expanding the doctrine of fair use to create what amounts to a public figure exception to copyright. Whether verbatim copying from a public figure's manuscript in a given case is or is not fair use must be judged according to the traditional equities of fair use.

With that said, the majority proceeded to apply the four-step analysis used to discriminate between a fair use and an infringement. It found that there was news in *The Nation*'s scoop, but that the magazine had exploited "the headline value of its infringement." Thus, the magazine's use of material from Ford's book was commercial. This weighed against its claim for fair use.

The Court viewed Ford's book as "unpublished historical narrative or autobiography." Copyright law recognizes a greater need to disseminate such works than works of fiction or fantasy. But the Court also found that the fact that the book was unpublished was "a critical element of its 'nature.' " The scope of fair use is narrower with respect to such works. Justice O'Connor clearly saw this as the crucial question. She wrote:

> In the case of Mr. Ford's manuscript, the copyrightholders' interest in confidentiality is irrefutable; the copyrightholders had entered into a contractual undertaking to "keep the manuscript confidential" and required that all those to whom the manuscript was shown also "sign an agreement to keep the manuscript confidential." . . . A use that so clearly infringes the copyrightholders' interests in confidentiality and creative control is difficult to characterize as "fair."

The Court went on to find that while only 13 percent of Navasky's article quoted directly from Ford's manuscript, he had extracted precisely those portions for which readers were most likely to buy the book. Further, his taking had led to direct economic loss through *Time*'s cancellation of its contract to publish an article based on the book. Therefore, *The Nation*'s use was an infringement for which it could be required to pay damages.

Justice William J. Brennan, Jr., writing for the Court's minority, protested that the decision resulted in "an exceedingly narrow definition of the scope of fair use." He predicted that it would "stifle the broad dissemination of ideas and information" and limit "the robust public debate essential to an enlightened citizenry." In the minority's view, Ford's book contained important historical information that neither he nor his publisher should be permitted to monopolize.

However, the decision stands as the Court's major pronouncement on the First Amendment aspects of the doctrine of fair use. In the majority's view, the Copyright Act furthers First Amendment interests by protecting the right of creators to profit from their work, and thus it encourages free expression. The law also recognizes, through the doctrine of fair use, that there are times when the public interest in ideas requires that creators share their work with others. In writing the doctrine, Congress and the courts have taken First Amendment interests into account. In *Harper & Row*, the court said that those who would copy from the newsworthy works of important public figures have no First Amendment right to do so beyond that already included in the definition of fair use. This is particularly true if the work has not yet been released to the public by the author or the owner of the copyright.

The Market Value Test

In most copyright infringement cases, the most important element in the four-part analysis is the last: "the effect of the use upon the potential market for or value of the copyrighted work." This is illustrated by two cases, in one of which the taking was minimal. In the other instance, there was no direct taking, but the overall pattern of similarities was held to exceed the limits of coincidence, especially when coupled with the originator's market loss.

The crucial factor in the first case, *Iowa State University Research Foundation* v. *American Broadcasting Companies, Inc.*, was the potential market value of a student-made film. Two students at Iowa State University made the film under supervision of a member of the faculty. Their subject was a fellow student, Dan Gable, an outstanding wrestler, who was destined to win a gold medal at the 1972 Olympics in Munich. The film was financed by the university's Research Foundation and Gable's parents. The foundation obtained a copyright on the film, reserving to one of the student producers the right to license its first television showing, but only with the knowledge and consent of the foundation.

Iowa State University Research Foundation v. *American Broadcasting Companies, Inc.*, 621 F.2d 57 (2d Cir. 1980).

The summer after the film was made, the student was employed by ABC Sports as a temporary videotape operator during the Olympic Games. When he heard producers Don Ohlmeyer and Doug Wilson talking about doing a biographical tape on Gable, he offered to show them the Iowa State film. They copied part of it. Three brief excerpts were used in the network's version of the Dan Gable story, which was aired three times.

When the Research Foundation asked the network to pay for its use of the excerpts, ABC denied taking any part of the film. But when a copyright infringement suit was filed, it admitted some copying, falling back on the defense of fair use. A federal district court held that there had been an infringement. When ABC appealed, the U.S. Court of Appeals for the Second Circuit affirmed. It focused on two elements in the four-part test: the commercial nature of ABC's taking—the network sold advertising spots at a premium during its coverage of the Olympics—and the potential harm to the market value of the student-made film. The court used strong language in condemning ABC's taking:

> The fair use doctrine is not a license for corporate theft, empowering a court to ignore a copyright whenever it determines the underlying work contains material of possible public importance. Indeed, we do not suppose that appellants would embrace their own defense theory if another litigant sought to apply it to the ABC evening news.
>
> Moreover, we must recognize that ABC's use of *Champion* was not motivated solely by its beneficence. While the fact that ABC sought to profit financially from the telecasts of the Olympics "does not, standing alone, deprive . . . [ABC] of the fair use defense, . . . it is relevant" that the film was used, at least in part, for "commercial exploitation." Thus, on balance, we cannot conclude that the purpose of ABC's use indicates the propriety of a finding of fair use.

ABC argued that the student film was designed for educational use and therefore had no significant television market. That was disproved, the court said, by the fact that Ohlmeyer and Wilson had found some of it good enough to use in their own filmed portrait of Gable. Furthermore, that and other filmed portraits ABC had used throughout its Olympic coverage were much like *Champion* in form and purpose. The court concluded that ABC had made its film on Gable to serve the same purpose as the Iowa State film. The taking of even a small portion of a copyrighted work under such circumstances was not a fair use.

Nor was it true that the Iowa State film was without value. Even before Gable had won his gold medal, the film had been widely circulated for a fee to civic groups and to schools. The court considered it quite possible that ABC's use of excerpts from it might have foreclosed wider use of it, perhaps even on television.

The court's award of damages was an arbitrary amount based solely on the trial judge's assessment of the case. He assessed ABC $250 for copying the film, a sum that had been mentioned by Ohlmeyer at the time as a possible fee. Additional assessments of $5,000 were made for each of the three showings of the film. The judge held that Iowa State's attorneys were reasonably entitled to $17,500, which ABC was required to pay. Thus ABC was required to pay $32,750 to the foundation.

A copyright can be infringed even when there is no overt, direct taking of the original.

Sid & Marty Krofft Television Productions, Inc. v. McDonald's Corp., 562 F.2d 1157 (9th Cir. 1977). If there is a great enough similarity in concept and execution to exceed the credible limits of coincidence, infringement is assumed. Two courts found that McDonald's Corporation and its advertising agency went beyond those limits in the hamburger chain's "McDonaldland" television commercials used during much of the 1970s.

The events leading up to the lawsuit began in 1969 when Sid and Marty Krofft created "H. R. Pufnstuf" for NBC television's Saturday morning lineup of children's shows. Peopled with puppets, moving trees, and talking books, it was an instant success, portraying the adventures of a small boy living in a fantasyland called "Living Island." Soon the Kroffts were marketing products and making endorsements based on their television series. An advertising agency, Needham, Harper & Steers, became interested. It was trying to win McDonald's advertising account and thought it might do so if it could offer the chain a "McDonaldland" theme based on "Living Island." But after seven or eight conversations between representatives of the two parties, a Needham officer telephoned Marty Krofft and said the advertising campaign had been rejected. In reality, Needham had won the McDonald's contract and was to prepare a series of television commercials depicting "McDonaldland." It hired away Krofft employees to make the costumes and the sets, and even to provide the voices for some of the McDonaldland puppets. These commercials appeared on television in 1971 and still were on the air seven years later.

The Kroffts sued for copyright infringement. They alleged that McDonaldland commercials had ruined their market for derivative toys and games and had cost them a contract with Kellogg's cereals. To cap it off, the "H. R. Pufnstuf" characters who had been cavorting through the Ice Capades, earning royalties for Krofft, had been replaced by similar characters from McDonaldland. McDonald's and the ad agency replied that they had taken nothing from the Kroffts except a general idea—that kids love fantasy— and therefore had not infringed. They pointed also to a considerable difference in detail between the puppet world of the commercials and that of "H. R. Pufnstuf."

The district judge told the jury that one work can infringe another even though there is no exact copying. It was for the jury to decide whether the similarities in concept and execution between "Living Island" and "McDonaldland" went beyond coincidence to leave the impression that one must have been copied from the other. At that point, differences in detail were to be ignored. The jurors were to focus on the similarities— in the basic ideas, in the sequencing of the ideas, in methods of expression. An appeals court was to say later that the jury acted correctly when it concluded that in creating McDonaldland the Needham agency had "captured the total concept and feel of the Pufnstuf show."

However, the jury's estimate of the value of the use to McDonald's pleased neither side. The Kroffts said the award of $50,000 was far too low. They figured they had lost at least $250,000 as a result of the infringement. McDonald's continued to insist there was no infringement. Both sides appealed.

In *Sid & Marty Krofft Television Productions, Inc.* v. *McDonald's Corp.*, the ninth circuit court of appeals held in 1977 that there had indeed been an illegal taking, but that the trial court had erred in refusing to require McDonald's to calculate the profits attributable to the commercials. If these could be calculated, the court held, the Kroffts were entitled to the larger of two sums—the profits made by McDonald's or their own losses, which they needed to prove. If neither figure could be calculated, they would be entitled to the damages fixed by the jury or to a discretionary sum fixed by the judge. The record does not show what happened on remand.

The point of this case cannot be overemphasized. While it is indeed true that copyright covers only a specific form of expression, and that ideas cannot be copyrighted, it also is true that a wholesale taking of another's creative concepts is an infringement. In this instance, the infringer was not saved by altering the identity of the imaginary characters and transporting them to another environment. In other instances—involving such things as movies, television skits, and even comic books—clever paraphrase, changes in sequence, and changes in the medium were not considered original enough to save the infringer.[8] If it can be shown that an alleged infringer had access to another's work, and that the two works are similar beyond the limits of coincidence, variations in details, no matter how ingenious, will not prevent a finding of infringement. Ideas can be borrowed, even theories of history, as *Hoehling* tells us, but not the pattern or concept of an entire work. Every historian writing about George Washington does not have to go back to the original documents for material. But a writer who simply prepares an article on Washington by paraphrasing and rearranging another's article, not only runs a risk of a copyright infringement action but is a plagiarist.

The Penalties for Copyright Infringement

The victim of a copyright infringement is entitled to an award of damages. Section 504 of the Copyright Act also authorizes the use of an injunction to prevent further distribution of the infringing work. Thus, copyright is another area in which prior restraints are permitted, notwithstanding the language of the First Amendment and the Supreme Court's reluctance to approve them generally. Restraint is justified in copyright cases on the theory that an infringer ought not be permitted to prosper by passing off another's creative work as his or her own. Nor should the piracy be permitted to rob the creator of the profit from the work.

The law permits courts to use two methods to calculate the damages an infringer must pay to the copyright owner. They are:

---

8. See Walt Disney Productions v. Air Pirates, 581 F.2d 751 (9th Cir. 1978); Sheldon v. Metro-Goldwyn Pictures Corp., 81 F.2d 49 (2d Cir. 1936); Marx v. United States, 96 F.2d 204 (9th Cir. 1938).

1. An award making good the copyright owner's losses from the infringement
    and taking the infringer's profits from it. The copyright owner has the
    burden of proof in calculating the infringer's gross revenue. The burden is
    then on the infringer to prove deductible expenses and other factors that
    might reduce the profit attributable to the infringement. Courts have held
    in cases involving movies that some part of the profit can be attributed to
    the box office appeal of the actors and actresses. A magazine publisher
    could show that a major part of its profits came from subscriptions and
    advertising contracts that were affected little, if any, by an infringing
    article. Calculations of profit and loss involve many such intangibles.
    Thus, it is seldom that a loss can be calculated with the precision of the
    Harper & Row case where the publisher could point to the $12,500 *Time*
    refused to pay for the canceled article after *The Nation* scored its scoop.

2. A statutory award fixed by the court. The copyright owner may elect this
    option at any time up to the point of final judgment. Such an award
    cannot be less than $250, unless the infringer was unaware of the taking,
    nor more than $10,000, unless the infringement is deemed willful, when
    the award can be raised to $50,000. If there are multiple infringements,
    the court may assess an award for each. This was illustrated in the *Iowa
    State* case where the court awarded the foundation $250 for ABC's copying
    of excerpts from the Gable film and $5,000 for each of the three subse-
    quent uses.

Whatever method is used to calculate the damages, the victim of the infringement
also is permitted to collect legal fees as part of the award.

Copying Machines, Jukeboxes, and Cable Television

Committees of Congress spent more than ten years in intermittent hearings before
members could reach agreement on the version of the copyright law now in effect. Four
areas generated considerable controversy, not all of which has been resolved. They are:

(1) codification of the definition of fair use

(2) the widespread use of photocopying machines, especially in schools and
     libraries

(3) jukeboxes

(4) cable television

Fair use has been dealt with in the preceding sections. This section deals with the
other three areas.

Educators and librarians went into the hearings essentially asking for a free hand to
use photocopying machines as needed for classroom and research purposes. Publishers,

NONCIRCULATING
BOOKS FOR USE
IN REFERENCE AREA
ONLY

The widespread use of copying machines, like this one in the University of Wisconsin Library, created special problems in copyright law. Libraries are not supposed to engage in copying that would take away the need to buy the publication involved. (Daniel S. Brody/Stock, Boston)

particularly of specialized scholarly journals, saw this as the road to their ruin.[9] Negotiations were shadowed by a decision of the U.S. Court of Claims that seemed to give public research libraries the right to copy journals on a wholesale basis. The four-to-three decision in *Williams & Wilkins Co.* v. *United States* in 1973[10] reversed a district court's finding that the National Institutes of Health and the National Library of Medicine had infringed the copyrights on four medical journals by making thousands of copies of articles from them. The claims court held that the interest in furthering medical research was important enough to override copyright law. How close the question was is indicated by the fact that the Supreme Court took the case and split four-four, thus upholding the lower court's decision.

Publishers asked for a provision that would require makers of photocopying machines to pay an annual license fee on each machine in use, with proceeds to be split among copyright holders. This proposal foundered on its own complexities. Had it been adopted, someone would have had to keep records showing whose copyrighted material had been copied by each machine. However, Congress did try to impose limits on copying by libraries and educators. These are found in §§107 and 108 of the Act and are explained

---

9. *Library Journal* followed the hearings on this point closely. See the issues of April through June 1976.
10. 487 F.2d 1345 (Ct.Cl. 1973); let stand by an equally divided Supreme Court, 420 U.S. 376 (1975).

in the House Judiciary Committee's *Notes* on the bill.[11] A teacher or student is permitted to make one copy of an article, a chapter from a book, or a sound recording for study purposes or for use in a classroom presentation. A teacher also can make multiple copies on a "spontaneous" basis for distribution to a class. But if such a copy is made a part of the syllabus and distribution becomes a planned part of the course, the use becomes an infringement. Libraries are not supposed to engage in copying that would substitute for buying the publication involved. Nebulous as these rules are, major publishers appear intent on trying to enforce them. In 1982, a group of publishers filed suit to restrain professors at New York University who allegedly were using a copying service to prepare collections of copyrighted works for student use.[12] The case resulted in an agreement by the professors to discontinue copying except on a limited basis without permission from the copyright owners.[13]

Jukeboxes did not come into existence until after the Copyright Act of 1909 became law. Therefore, there was nothing in the Act which pertained to their repeated use of recordings bearing copyrighted songs. When the law was revised in 1976, Congress sought to resolve the problem by imposing an annual license fee on each jukebox in operation. These fees are paid to a Copyright Royalty Tribunal to be divided among the copyright owners of the recorded music on an equitable basis.

Because cable television also had not been foreseen in 1909, it, too, presented unusual copyright problems when it came into existence in the 1950s. The first cable systems were called "community antenna television systems" because that is precisely what they were. People in towns at a distance from a television station, or in localities shielded by mountains, would erect a common antenna on some high point so that they might bring in programs more clearly. The Supreme Court recognized the nature of such systems in 1968 in its ruling in *Fortnightly Corp.* v. *United Artists Television, Inc.*[14] In its decision, the Court held that cable distribution of signals picked up from distant television stations was not a "performance" as defined by the Copyright Act. Therefore, cable operators could not be required to pay royalties to the owners of the copyrights on the programs they distributed. In 1974, in *Teleprompter Corp.* v. *Columbia Broadcasting System, Inc.*[15] the Court reiterated that reasoning, even though cable systems had become considerably more sophisticated and could offer their users various kinds of programing. When the present law was enacted in 1976, cable systems were using thousands of copyrighted programs and sharing them with millions of users. If the new law had required cable systems to obtain the right to use and pay royalties on each copyrighted program, it would have involved cable operators and their suppliers in endless negotiation.

Therefore, Congress authorized the Copyright Royalty Tribunal to establish a system for distributing licensing fees imposed on cable operators. The initial formula, adopted in 1980, gave the lion's share to movie producers and syndicators of television programs shown previously on the major networks. Major league baseball was among the winners of a minor share of the pool. The three major television networks, whose offerings made

---

11. House Report No. 94-1476.
12. "News Notes," *Media Law Reporter*, 4 January 1983.
13. David Margolick, "Publishers and N.Y.U. Settle Suit on College's Photocopying Rights," *New York Times*, 15 April 1983.
14. 392 U.S. 390, 88 S.Ct. 2084, 20 L.Ed.2d 190 (1968).
15. 415 U.S. 394, 94 S.Ct. 1129, 39 L.Ed.2d 415 (1974).

up most of the programing available on cable systems, were given nothing.[16] They challenged that decision in court, but the U.S. Court of Appeals for the District of Columbia upheld the royalty tribunal.[17]

In 1982, the Copyright Royalty Tribunal raised considerably the fee cable operators must pay to retransmit movie, sports, and entertainment programs brought in from distant "superstations." The principal targets of the increase were those cable systems using programs from WTBS-TV in Atlanta and WGN-TV in Chicago, which blanket the nation via satellite. The former carries all of the Atlanta Braves' baseball games and the latter, the Chicago Cubs'. At the time the increase was announced, owners of other major league baseball teams were asking for the right to black out cable offerings of competing games in each team's home territory. Congress temporarily deferred imposition of the fee increases in all but the top one hundred television markets.[18] The revised schedule took full effect in 1984.[19]

The Video Recorder and Copyright Law

When Congress revised the Copyright Act in 1976, effective in 1978, its members could not foresee an advance in technology that extended copying into a new dimension. This was Sony Corporation's development of Betamax, a video copying machine that sold for less than a thousand dollars and could be operated by almost anyone. Betamax took the copying of television programs out of the studio and brought it into the home.

Universal City Studios, Inc. v. Sony Corporation of America, 465 U.S. 1112, 104 S.Ct. 1619, 80 L.Ed.2d 1480 (1984).

This raised the fear among producers of movies and television programs that their works would be copied and sold in violation of copyright law. Their fears were heightened by Sony advertisements inviting television viewers to "record favorite shows" and "build a library" of "classic movies," sports events, and other entertainment. Fearing loss of revenue, Universal City Studios and Walt Disney Productions went to court, seeking an order that would bar further sales of Betamax. They argued that every buyer of a video recording device was a potential copyright infringer. Conceding the difficulty of going into the purchasers' homes to find out what was being done with copied programs, the plaintiffs asked the court to find that Sony was contributing to copyright infringement.

The district court rejected their plea, but in 1982, the U.S. Court of Appeals for the Ninth Circuit set Sony and other makers of home video recorders on their ears by holding that the devices did indeed contribute to copyright infringement. It passed the buck back to the district court to devise a suitable remedy. Sony reacted by asking the Supreme Court of the United States to intervene, which it did. In 1984, after hearing two rounds of oral argument in separate terms, the Court decided, five-to-four, that the

---

16. "Non-Network Firms Win Royalty Ruling on Cable-TV Shows," *Wall Street Journal*, 30 July 1980.
17. National Association of Broadcasters v. Copyright Royalty Tribunal, 675 F.2d 367 (D.C.Cir. 1982).
18. "Chances Dim for Bill on Copyright Issue of Cable Operators," *Wall Street Journal*, 6 December 1982; "Cable-TV Operators Get Temporary Break on Royalty Fee Rise," *Wall Street Journal*, 23 December 1982.
19. 49 F.R. No. 127, p. 26722, 29 June 1984.

copying of programs for one's personal use is a fair use, not an infringement. The majority decision, in *Universal City Studios, Inc.* v. *Sony Corporation of America*, was written by Justice John Paul Stevens. It concluded that most home copying is for convenience. Persons who cannot see a program when it is aired copy it so that they can see it at another time. This is called "time shifting." As long as the copies are not sold or used for other commercial purposes, there is no infringement of copyright law.

In reaching its decision, the Court rejected outright the argument that Sony was contributing to copyright infringement by selling its video recorders. Justice Stevens called this argument "an unprecedented attempt to impose copyright liability upon the distributors of copying equipment." He added:

> One may search the Copyright Act in vain for any sign that the elected representatives of the millions of people who watch television every day have made it unlawful to copy a program for later viewing at home, or have enacted a flat prohibition against the sale of machines that make such copying possible.

The dissenters, led by Justice Harry A. Blackmun, saw the decision as an erosion of the control that the Copyright Act gives to authors over the use of their works. They were not satisfied that most copying is authorized by implication because it does no more than change the time at which the program is viewed. They would have remanded for another trial at which the economic aspects of video recording could be explored more fully.

The decision shifted the fight to Congress where bills were introduced in behalf of both antagonists.[20] One side would require manufacturers of video recorders to pay a royalty to the movie industry for every device sold. The other would write the Supreme Court's decision into the Copyright Act. At the time of the decision, more than eight million video recorders were in use and sales were continuing at a rate in excess of five million a year. Such a tide seemed too strong to stem, as is evidenced by the fact that Congress has taken no action on any video recording bills.

Misappropriation

Every reporter borrows from the work of other reporters. Reporters working on newspapers in areas served by more than one paper are asked by their editors to follow up stories clipped from competing publications. Reporters from broadcasting stations find story ideas by reading the newspapers. A news feature may begin in one newspaper and then make its way, in altered form, of course, through several others and, perhaps, into the wire services, and end up as a special on the evening television news. It's part of the game, and as long as a reporter doesn't take too much, too often, all is well. But starting as far back as 1918 in *International News Service* v. *Associated Press*,[21] courts have penalized the systematic taking of news, even when it is not covered by copyright.

William Randolph Hearst established INS to offer his own newspapers and others an

20. Stephen Wermeil, "Home Taperecording of TV Shows is Approved 5-4 by Supreme Court," *Wall Street Journal*, 18 January 1984.
21. 248 U.S. 215, 29 S.Ct. 68, 63 L.Ed. 528 (1918).

alternative to AP as a source of news. AP alleged that many of the stories distributed by INS were thinly disguised rewrites of stories gathered by its own reporters. Evidence supported the charge, and the courts condemned INS's piracy as a form of unfair competition. In a nice turn of speech, the Supreme Court said the Hearst service was reaping where it had not sown—it was using the fruits of another's labor—which gave it an unfair advantage. Even though the AP news service was not copyrighted, and was widely used by its own members, the Court said INS could not take stories from that service and sell them as its own. Courts call such a systematic taking of another's work "**misappropriation**," a kind of distant cousin of copyright infringement. One case will suffice to illustrate how the news media have invoked the principles established in the *INS* case.

In the early 1960s, the newspapers in Pottstown, Pennsylvania, became convinced that radio station WPAZ was obtaining a goodly part of its local news by rewriting from them. The publisher asked a county court to issue an order preventing such taking.

Pottstown Daily News v. *Pottstown Broadcasting*, 192 A.2d 657 (Pa. 1963).
WPAZ resisted, arguing that the suit involved alleged copyright infringement and therefore could be acted on only by a federal court. The county court dismissed that argument and, on appeal, in *Pottstown Daily News* v. *Pottstown Broadcasting*, the Pennsylvania Supreme Court affirmed. It also held that the radio station was guilty of misappropriation. The grounds on which it did so may not please those journalists who believe newspapers exist solely to report the news, but the court did recognize the realities of the publishing business. It wrote:

> In this day and age, no court can fail to take note of the fact that newspapers, radio, and television stations compete with each other for advertising which has become a giant in our economy. In fact, the presentation of news by all three media is a service designed to attract advertisers.
>
> . . . The distinction we draw is fine; for the purpose of an action in unfair competition the specialized treatment of news items as a service the newspaper provides for advertisers gives to the New Company a limited property right which the law will guard and protect against wrongful invasion by a competitor. . . .
>
> . . . While a competitor may, subject to the patent, copyright, and trademark laws, imitate his rival's business practices, processes, and methods, yet the protection which the law affords to competition does not countenance the usurpation of a competitor's investment and toil.

So, news, then, is a form of property created out of work, time, and capital investment. Because it is a form of property, the creator can protect if from theft, especially when the thief wants to use it to lure advertising customers away from a competitor. The reasoning has nothing to do with the First Amendment, or with serving the public's interest in news. However, the reasoning has been applied by courts in other states to prevent the pirating of news, both by broadcasting stations and by "shoppers," newspapers published mainly for their value as an advertising medium. The usual remedy is an injunction preventing use of the complaining medium's news for six, twelve, or twenty-four hours. The decisions serve as a warning for all who would offer news to the public: Hire an adequate news staff, or be content with such news as the staff is able to get on its own.

To sum up, in its legal aspects the Copyright Act is concerned with the protection of creative works, whatever form they may take. It vests the creator of the work with a property right in it. That right may be bought and sold like any other form of property. The purpose is to encourage creativity by ensuring authors, artists, photographers, and other creative persons the right to profit from their work. The Act does so by giving copyright owners the right to prevent others from using their work without permission. Obtaining permission for a reuse usually involves payment of a fee.

The law has had to recognize, however, that a robust trade in ideas sometimes requires some taking of another's works. While ideas cannot be copyrighted, the form in which they are expressed can be. Episodes in the lives of noteworthy persons, history, and news events cannot be copyrighted, but biographies, histories, and news stories can be. In a highly competitive marketplace, where creative works are marketed and consumed like any other product, some taking of another's work is inevitable. Thus has evolved the doctrine of fair use. It originated in the decisions of courts interpreting the Copyright Act. Since 1978, it has been a part of the act itself. If a taking is minimal, if it serves a public interest, and if it does not detract unduly from the commercial value of the original, it can be justified as a fair use. But if a taking is so substantial that it takes away the incentive for buying the copied work, it is an infringement. If so, infringers can be required to give up their profits and make good the losses of the copyright owners from whom they copied. If those sums can't be calculated with precision, the court may award the victim of the infringement an arbitrary amount within limits fixed by the Act. It also is possible to get an injunction keeping the infringing work off the market.

In its only recent major cases interpreting the Copyright Act, the Supreme Court has held:

1. In *Harper & Row* that the First Amendment does not excuse a newsworthy infringement. The Court said that the First Amendment interest in a free marketplace of ideas is embodied in, and limited by, the doctrine of fair use.

2. In *Universal City Studios* that neither the sale of video recording devices nor their use to copy copyrighted programs for an individual's personal use is an infringement.

In the Professional World

Professional creators in any field are far more likely to benefit from the Copyright Act than they are to be restricted by it. Those who honestly attempt to do their own work, and they are in the majority, are highly unlikely to be infringers of copyright. A survey of copyright cases decided in 1985 found several instances in which plaintiffs alleged that successful movies infringed their copyrights, but none of the actions was successful. None of the reported cases involved the taking of news or commentary. Two of the actions involved magazines: *Hustler's* reproduction of two surrealistic fine arts photographs was held to be fair use,[22] but *High Society's*

---

22. Haberman v. Hustler Magazine, 626 F.Supp. 201 (D.Mass. 1986).

use of a retouched photograph of Raquel Welch in the nude was held to be an infringement.[23]

Other cases explored the limits of copying permitted by new forms of technology: computer software, data retrieval systems, and satellite dishes. Courts are holding that it is a violation of copyright to copy a computer program without authorization,[24] to key one firm's computerized legal research system to another firm's case reporting system,[25] or to use a satellite dish to bring professional football games to a bar's patrons.[26]

However, for most who work in the professional world, considerations of copyright law start with asking whether formalities of complying with the Act's registration terms should be observed. Since the law now assumes that works are copyrighted as soon as they take tangible form, why go to the bother and expense of registration with the Copyright Office? Not only does registration involve payment of a $10 fee, it also requires filling out a form and mailing it, along with two copies of the work, to Washington. The answer is that if a work has no market value, and the creator can be sure it is unlikely to have any, there isn't any point to registration. If a work does have value, however, and it is taken by someone else, the creator cannot pursue an infringement action unless the work is registered. Failure to place a copyright notice on the work may offer the infringer a defense, as an unknowing infringer is subject to minimum penalties.

The value of copyright protection for newspapers is debatable. Some publishers copyright each day's edition routinely. Others reserve copyright protection for exclusive investigatory stories. Some may even use the fact of copyright as a promotion device to sell readers on the story's importance. Many newspapers never copyright anything. However, if newspapers in the latter group buy syndicated materials, such as comic strips, crossword puzzles, advice columns, editorial commentary, or whatever, they contain material copyrighted by others.

Because most of the content in most daily newspapers is here today and forgotten tomorrow, it is not likely to have much market value beyond the price paid by the subscriber. However, publishers who do copyright their newspapers see two purposes in doing so. It gives the editors control over use of the occasional story that does have more than transient value and it serves notice on competitors, print or electronic, that they should research and prepare their own stories.

As noted earlier, copyright law condones the taking of one creator's work by another within limits. This can be done even without giving credit to the original creator as long as the taking is not such as to cause economic harm. Further, copyright offers no protection to creators of theories and the developers of ideas outside of that given to the form of the work embodying the theories and ideas. Thus, as *Hoehling* illustrates, there is nothing in the law to prevent writers from "borrowing" theories or ideas and crafting them into valuable commercial works. However, professionals in all fields recognize an obligation in such instances to give credit to the originator. A student who takes the outline for a term paper from

---

23. Sygma Photo News, Inc., v. High Society Magazine, Inc., 778 F.2d 89 (2d Cir. 1985).
24. E.F. Johnson Co. v. Uniden Corp. of America, 623 F.Supp. 1485 (D.Minn. 1985).
25. West Publishing Co. v. Mead Data Cent., Inc., 616 F.Supp. 1571) (D.Minn. 1985).
26. National Football League v. McBee & Bruno's, 621 F.Supp. 880 (E.D.Mo. 1985).

an encyclopedia article has an ethical duty to say so. To fail to do so, although not a violation of copyright, is plagiarism. In some instances, the penalties for the latter can be more severe. In rare instances, persons have been stripped of doctoral degrees because parts of their dissertations were taken without credit from other works. Newspaper reporters and columnists have lost their jobs because they tried to pass off another's work as their own.

The punishment need not always be overt. When this author became a Washington correspondent, he was welcomed by James Reston of the *New York Times,* who once had been employed by the author's publisher, James Cox. Reston offered advice on the rules of what was then a relatively small group of journalists. "You'll find you can't cover everything," Reston said. "None of us can. There'll be times when you may feel a need to copy a little from one of us. We all do it once in a while. But if you copy too much, too often, you'll soon be frozen out." It was sound advice then. It is sound advice yet.

FOR REVIEW

1. What is the purpose of copyright law? How is that purpose carried into effect? How does copyright law relate to the First Amendment?

2. What can be copyrighted? What cannot be? Illustrate with examples.

3. Explain the degree of protection provided by copyrighting a newspaper or a news story. What precautions should be taken by a reporter who is assigned to follow up another medium's copyrighted news story?

4. Define fair use. List and explain the elements that go into a determination of fair use. What is the significance of the *Rosemont Enterprises* decision with respect to the doctrine of fair use?

5. Compare and contrast the Supreme Court's decision in *Harper & Row* with the circuit court's decision in *Rosemont Enterprises* and the district court's decision in *Bernard Geis.* Collectively, what do they say about the First Amendment in copyright infringement cases?

6. On balance, does copyright law enhance or inhibit First Amendment interests? Justify your conclusions.

7. Define and illustrate with reference to cases an infringement of copyright. Which element of the test applied by the courts is most likely to prove decisive?

8. What rationale did the Supreme Court use in deciding the home video recorder case?

9. What is misappropriation? Of what significance is it to the news media?

CHAPTER 13

THE NEWS MEDIA AS BUSINESSES

Antitrust Law and the News Business

Some Disapproved Business Practices

Antitrust Law and the Marketplace of Ideas
Tucson: Joint Operating Agreements / Los Angeles: One Ownership in Adjacent Markets / Cincinnati: One Ownership in the Same City

The Marketplace of Ideas Today

Joint Operating Agreements

Joint Ownership of Newspapers and Broadcasting Stations

The Distribution of News and Opinion

Taxation of the Media

The First Amendment protects news, opinion, and advertising, as we have seen, but it does not grant the media immunity from laws regulating their business operations. At one time, some publishers attempted to argue that such things as minimum wage laws restricted freedom of the press, but the courts held otherwise. The general rule is that in their business operations, newspapers, magazines, book publishers, broadcasters, film makers, and cable operators must obey the same rules as nonmedia businesses. This means that they are subject to **antitrust laws** if they use predatory business practices to harm their competitors. They must comply with wages and hours laws, and they must pay normal taxes applying to other business entities. However, courts have held that the First Amendment protects the right to sell newspapers in public places and stands as a barrier against discriminatory taxation.

This chapter first examines antitrust law as it applies to the ownership of newspapers and broadcasting stations. In modern times, the law has been used primarily to challenge advertising rates and attempts by daily newspaper publishers to prevent the growth of free-circulation weeklies made up mostly of advertising. Despite an attempt by President

John F. Kennedy and his brother Robert to use antitrust law to encourage a competitive marketplace of ideas, the law has been ineffective in stemming the rapid growth of newspaper chains. However, regulations imposed by the Federal Communications Commission have limited newspaper ownership of broadcasting stations in the same city, and vice versa.

More than forty years ago, a persistent religious group, Jehovah's Witnesses, endured considerable persecution to establish that the First Amendment protects the right to disseminate ideas door to door or in public places. Today, the principles forged then protect the right of newspaper publishers to place coin-operated newspaper racks outside of supermarkets, or wherever else crowds are likely to pass by on foot in public places.

This book began with John Milton's argument against the licensing of printing in England. It will end by examining two decisions in which the Supreme Court held that discriminatory taxation aimed at newspapers, if unchecked, could do what the licensers of old sought to do—that is, suppress ideas considered harmful by government officials. The first of the two cases particularly serves as a reminder that the forces against which Milton argued so persuasively survive, even though, for the moment, they no longer prevail.

Major Cases

Associated Press v. *United States*, 326 U.S. 1, 65 S.Ct. 1416, 89 L.Ed. 2013 (1945).

Citizen Publishing Co. v. *United States*, 394 U.S. 131, 89 S.Ct. 927, 22 L.Ed.2d 148 (1969).

Federal Communications Commission v. *National Citizens Committee for Broadcasting*, 436 U.S. 775, 98 S.Ct. 2096, 56 L.Ed.2d 697 (1978).

Gannett Satellite Information Network, Inc. v. *Metropolitan Transportation Authority*, 745 F.2d 767 (2d Cir. 1984).

Grosjean v. *American Press Co.*, 297 U.S. 233, 56 S.Ct. 444, 80 L.Ed. 660 (1936).

Kansas City Star Co. v. *United States*, 240 F.2d 643 (8th Cir. 1957).

Minneapolis Star and Tribune Co. v. *Minnesota Commissioner of Revenue*, 460 U.S. 575, 103 S.Ct. 1365, 75 L.Ed.2d 295 (1983).

Syracuse Broadcasting Corp. v. *Newhouse,* 319 F.2d 683 (2d Cir. 1963).

United States v. *Times-Mirror Co.,* 274 F.Supp. 606 (C.D.Calif. 1967).

Antitrust Law and the News Business

When Congress adopted the Sherman Antitrust Act in 1890, its main targets were John D. Rockefeller's Standard Oil Company and Andrew Carnegie's United States Steel Company. These entrepreneurs had cut prices on a selective basis to freeze out competitors. They had made exclusive deals with favored customers. Their purpose was to establish monopolies that would let them charge what they pleased. Other targets of the Act were burgeoning monopolies in whiskey distilling, in the making of white lead for paints, and in sugar refining. Cartoons of the era picture such businesses as giant octopuses with tentacles reaching out across the nation. The original Act was strengthened by the Clayton Act of 1914, and the Robinson-Patman Act of 1936, which forbids discriminatory pricing.

It is doubtful, even when the Clayton Act was adopted, that anyone thought of antitrust law as applying to newspapers or magazines. First, there were no national newspapers in 1914, nor was there any dominant magazine. Second, publishing was a highly competitive business. As late as 1923, nearly half the cities with daily newspapers had two or more.[1] Finally, it was generally believed that newspapers, like other small businesses, were not engaged in interstate commerce. Therefore, they were presumed to be beyond the reach of federal law.

The Supreme Court demolished that assumption in 1934 with its decision in *Indiana Farmer's Guide Publishing Co.* v. *Prairie Farmer Publishing Co.*[2] It held that any publication that uses advertising or other content created in another state, or that sells copies by mail to residents of another state, is engaged in interstate commerce and therefore subject to federal laws. The Court also held that to become a monopoly, a business firm need not be a giant seeking to control a national market. A publisher is to be judged by the extent to which his or her magazine or newspaper dominates its market area. Because circulation of most newspapers is concentrated in what is called a retail trading zone defined by the shopping practices of their subscribers, the *Indiana Farmer's Guide* decision brought even the smallest newspapers within the reach of antitrust law.

The Court expanded the scope of its decision in 1945, when it rejected the argument that the First Amendment gives the news media immunity from antitrust laws. In this instance, the owner of the *Chicago Tribune,* the legendary Colonel Robert R. McCormick,

Associated Press v. United States, 326 U.S. 1, 65 S.Ct. 1416, 89 L.Ed. 2013 (1945).

had used his veto power as a director of the Associated Press to deny that agency's news service to Marshall Field's newly established morning *Sun.* The AP bylaws then in effect made it difficult and expensive for owners of a new newspaper to obtain the service if they were in direct competition with an existing

---

1. Of the 1,297 cities with daily newspapers, there were competing ownerships in 502. In the Matter of the Cincinnati Joint Operating Agreement, Docket No. 44-03-24-4; Recommended Decision, 1 May 1979, p. 12.
2. 293 U.S. 268, 55 S.Ct. 182, 79 L.Ed.2d 356 (1934).

member. This did not mean that they would be left without a wire service. At least two others, United Press and the International News Service, were then in competition with AP. However, Field took the position that AP was the best of the three, and that his newspaper would not be competitive without it.

The Department of Justice took up Field's cause and charged the Associated Press with violating antitrust laws. The government asked that AP's restrictive membership rules be declared illegal. The news agency offered two arguments in its defense, both grounded in the freedom of press clause of the First Amendment:

1. Because AP was engaged in the business of gathering and disseminating news, it should be granted immunity from antitrust law unless the government could show that its actions represented a clear and present danger to a vital government interest.

2. Because AP considered itself a cooperative news gathering agency, any government interference with its method of choosing members violated its First Amendment freedoms.

A United States district court in New York City rejected both arguments and ruled in the government's favor. AP took its case to the Supreme Court which, in *Associated Press* v. *United States*, upheld the district court's ruling five-to-three. Writing for the majority, Justice Hugo L. Black used reasoning that continues to be applied to the news media, not only in antitrust cases, but in other cases dealing with their business aspects. With respect to the first argument, he wrote:

> Member publishers of AP are engaged in business for profit exactly as are other business men who sell food, steel, aluminum, or anything else people need or want. . . . All are alike covered by the Sherman Act. The fact that the publisher handles news while others handle food does not, as we shall later point out, afford the publisher a peculiar constitutional sanctuary in which he can with impunity violate laws regulating his business practices.
>
> Nor is a publisher who engaged in business practices made unlawful by the Sherman Act entitled to a partial immunity by reason of the "clear and present danger" doctrine which courts have used to protect freedom to speak, to print, and to worship. . . . Formulated as it was to protect liberty of thought and of expression, it would degrade the clear and present danger doctrine to fashion from it a shield for publishers who engage in business practices condemned by the Sherman Act.

Justice Black was equally blunt in dismissing AP's second argument. He noted that the news agency was founded as a cooperative; that is, it was formed by newspapers who did no more than share local news of regional or national interest with one another. This sharing of news remained a principle of AP's operation in the 1940s and continues today. At the time of this case, AP's membership rules made it difficult and expensive for a direct competitor of an established member to enter the cooperative. The reasoning was simple: Why should an established newspaper be required to share its news with an upstart competing medium? In defending its rules, AP argued that if anyone who wanted the service had to be admitted to membership, the flow of news would be diminished. Where competition existed, no one would share news with the wire service until it no longer was news. Otherwise, the medium that got the news first would only be giving away its own scoop. Thus, as AP saw it, any change in the membership rules would restrict First Amendment freedoms. Justice Black disagreed:

It would be strange indeed . . . if the grave concern for freedom of the press which prompted adoption of the First Amendment should be read as a command that government was without power to protect that freedom. The First Amendment, far from providing an argument against application of the Sherman Act, here provides powerful reasons to the contrary. That amendment rests on the assumption that the widest possible dissemination of information from diverse and antagonistic sources is essential to the welfare of the public, that a free press is a condition of a free society. Surely, a command that the government itself shall not impede the free flow of ideas does not afford non-governmental combinations a refuge if they impose restraints upon that constitutionally guaranteed freedom. Freedom to publish means freedom for all and not for some. Freedom to publish is guaranteed by the Constitution, but freedom to combine to keep others from publishing is not. Freedom of the press from governmental interference under the First Amendment does not sanction repression of that freedom by private interests. The First Amendment affords not the slightest support for the contention that a combination to restrain trade in news and views has any constitutional immunity.

This decision has helped make an important point: The main concern of the First Amendment is the protection of the dissemination of news and opinion. It cannot be stretched to give those in the business of disseminating news and opinion an exemption from laws generally regulating business activities.

Some Disapproved Business Practices

The Court's decisions in *Indiana Farmer's Guide* and *Associated Press* have opened the way for a variety of antitrust actions against the news media since World War II.

One of the few cases to reach the Supreme Court, *Lorain Journal Co.* v. *United States*,[3] was noted in Chapter 11. By systematically refusing to sell advertising to merchants and others who bought time on a competing radio station, the publisher of the *Journal* engaged in "bold, relentless, and predatory commercial behavior" clearly designed to harm the station. All of this took place in a limited marketing area served both by the newspaper and the broadcaster. There was little question that the publisher was engaged in a scheme tending to promote monopoly, thus violating the Sherman Act. Lower courts have cited the case as a precedent in condemning similar refusals to accept advertising in Las Vegas, Nevada,[4] where the target was a competing newspaper; in Haverhill, Massachusetts,[5] where a competing newspaper also was involved, and in Providence, Rhode Island,[6] where a rental information service was the victim.

Taken together, the cases suggest care in exercising the right to refuse advertising. If refusals are based on established standards of acceptance, and those standards are applied with an even hand, legal problems are unlikely. But if the pattern of refusals points to a conspiracy to harm a competing medium, or a firm in competition with a favored advertiser, it may be possible to prove a violation of antitrust law. The most recent of the three preceding cases, *Home Placement Service* v. *Providence Journal*, raises a special

---

3. 342 U.S. 193, 72 S.Ct. 181, 96 L.Ed. 162 (1951).
4. Greenspun v. McCarran, 105 F.Supp. 662 (D.Nev. 1952).
5. Union Leader Corp. v. Newspapers of New England, 284 F.2d 586 (1st Cir. 1960).
6. Home Placement Service, Inc., v. Providence Journal Co., 682 F.2d 274 (1st Cir. 1982).

note of caution with respect to advertising offered by an arguably competing medium. Home Placement charged its customers a fee for providing them with a listing of available rental housing. This put it in competition with the *Providence Journal*, which sold classified advertising to owners of rental property seeking tenants. When Home Placement sought to advertise its service in the *Journal*, it was told it could not do so unless it agreed not to charge a fee for its service. Home Placement complied with the condition, but the U.S. Court of Appeals for the Second Circuit held that the newspaper's act violated antitrust law. This suggests that if a medium is offered an ad by a competing medium, it may neither refuse the ad nor insist that the ad be altered, unless it is demonstrably false or misleading.

Media owners who have achieved dominant positions in their markets must take particular care in setting advertising and circulation rates and in other actions that may affect competing media. If that dominance results in abuse, it may result in an antitrust action. For instance, in 1957, the U.S. Court of Appeals for the Eighth Circuit held that the Kansas City Star Company's advertising and circulation policies tended to create a monopoly. In an action brought by the United States government, the court struck down a series of all-or-nothing package deals, coupled with a diligently enforced advertising policy that helped the Star Company dominate Kansas City's advertising market in the early 1950s. It published three newspapers, the morning *Times*, the afternoon *Star*, and the *Sunday Star*, and owned radio station *WDAF* and the city's first television station, WDAF-TV. People who wanted to subscribe to one of the newspapers were required to buy all three. Advertisers likewise had to buy space in all three papers in order to get space in one. Star executives rationalized the arrangement by contending that they published only one newspaper with thirteen issues a week. There also were advertising tying arrangements between the newspaper and the television station. In some instances, advertisers seeking to buy time on WDAF-TV were told they could do so only if they bought space in the newspapers.

Kansas City Star Co. v. United States, 240 F. 2d 643 (8th Cir. 1957).

It was a profitable arrangement. It also was alleged to have a devastating effect on competing media. A publisher of a competing newspaper in Kansas City, Missouri, had gone out of business during World War II, leaving the *Times* and *Star* alone. Seven other dailies continued to publish in the metropolitan area, but the largest of these, the *Kansas City Kansan*, had a circulation of only 27,873 in 1951. In contrast, circulation of the three Star Company newspapers exceeded 350,000 a day. In 1952, those newspapers received 94 percent of the money spent on newspaper advertising in the Kansas City area. With broadcasting revenues included, the company accounted for 85 percent of the total advertising revenue billed by all media.

In a criminal proceeding, the Department of Justice charged the Star Company with unfair competitive practices in violation of the Sherman Act. Witnesses told a district court jury that the newspaper's advertising executives had used threats and intimidation to discourage advertisers from using competing media, to the latter's harm. Star advertisers who ignored the warnings found their ads placed in poor positions. A major league baseball player, who also owned a flower shop in Kansas City, was the target of another kind of threat. When he placed an ad in a competing newspaper, an advertising solicitor told him that even if he hit a hundred home runs a year, his name would never appear in the newspapers' sports page except in the box scores.

A jury found in 1957 that the unit advertising system "was used . . . with the intent and effect of excluding competition." It also held that an effect of the unit circulation policy was to discourage subscribers from taking any other newspaper. Therefore, the Star Company was guilty of violating the Sherman Act. The court ordered the newspaper to pay a fine of $5,000 and the advertising director, $2,500. In addition, the company was ordered to stop its unit sales of advertising and subscriptions, to stop tie-in sales between the broadcasting stations and the newspaper, and to stop threatening advertisers who did business with competing media. The company appealed.

The newspapers had argued that the government's action was an attempt to intimidate a free press and therefore violated the First Amendment. The appeals court disposed of that argument as follows:

> Publishers of newspapers must answer for their actions in the same manner as anyone else. A monopolistic press could attain in tremendous measure the evils sought to be prevented by the Sherman Antitrust Act. Freedom to print does not mean freedom to destroy. To use the freedom of the press guaranteed by the First Amendment to destroy competition would defeat its own ends, for freedom to print news and express opinions as one chooses is not tantamount to having freedom to monopolize. To monopolize freedom destroys it.

The decision came at a time when many cities of a hundred thousand population and up had become one-owner towns, with formerly independent morning and evening newspapers coming under the same ownership. The decision sent them a message: They must not force advertisers or subscribers to take both or none. If they offered a unit advertising rate, they must leave the way open for an advertiser to choose one newspaper or the other. And they must not use their dominant position to try to squeeze out suburban newspapers, or other kinds of advertising media, which were beginning to emerge in response to changing patterns of urban living.

In the aftermath of the court action described above, the Star Company and the Justice Department entered into a consent agreement that is still looked to for guidance in setting advertising rates in cities where one owner owns two newspapers, two broadcasting stations, or any combination thereof. The agreement forbade compulsory combinations of the kind condemned by the court. But it permitted the publisher to offer substantial discounts to firms that were willing to place ads in more than one newspaper.[7] As long as such combination rates are not set unreasonably low, so as it make it impossible for other media to compete economically, and as long as they are not manipulated with intent to harm a media competitor, they do not violate antitrust law.

The principles established in the *Kansas City* case were reinforced in 1963 by the U.S. Court of Appeals for the Second Circuit. In its decision, in *Syracuse Broadcasting Corp.* v. *Newhouse*, the court said Newhouse was simply using good business practices to buttress its position as the dominant advertising medium in Syracuse, New York. The company owned both newspapers in the city along with WSYR-TV and its companion radio station, WSYR.

Syracuse Broadcasting Corp. v. Newhouse, 319 F.2d 683 (2d Cir. 1963).

---

7. United States v. Kansas City Star Co., 1957 Trade Cas. (CCH) §68,857 (W.D.Mo. 1957).

Syracuse Broadcasting Corporation, owner of WNDR radio, suffered financial problems in the early 1960s that it blamed on the Newhouse combination. It filed a civil antitrust suit alleging:

1. That WSYR stations got a better break in the newspapers, in both the news columns and in advertising, than it did. One of these breaks, it said, was free advertising space.

2. That the newspapers had established a joint advertising rate so low that it was particularly attractive to national advertisers who might otherwise buy radio time.

3. That the newspapers were picking on WNDR by publishing unfavorable news stories about its financial problems.

A federal district court held that Syracuse Broadcasting did not prove its case, and, on appeal, the circuit court agreed, holding that "inequality of treatment [in news and advertising] is not sufficient to prove a violation of antitrust laws." It was reasonable to believe that the newspaper's editors might pay more attention to their publisher's broadcasting stations than to others. Syracuse Broadcasting would have to show that it had been frozen out of the news columns altogether or that the publisher had told the editors to suppress news about its station. Nor could the plaintiff prove that WSYR stations were getting free advertising. More likely, the court concluded, there was a trade-off between the newspapers and the Newhouse stations that ended up as a bookkeeping transaction. Nor did the complainant prove there was anything unreasonable about the joint advertising rate. As for the news stories, they merely reflected a truth— WNDR was having newsworthy financial problems. Therefore, Newhouse was acting reasonably and was not in violation of antitrust law.

Obviously, what is reasonable is a matter of opinion. The advertising market in any community has become extremely complex and highly competitive. All but a few cities in the United States are served by only one daily newspaper owner, which leads to talk of a monopoly press. However, few publishers are without competition even from print media. The spread of population from core cities into the suburbs has led to a proliferation of weeklies and even dailies that cater to the news and advertising needs of specific neighborhoods. Some publishers have found it highly profitable to compile publications devoted almost completely to advertising that are distributed free of charge to every household in a specified area. Newspapers have also become distributors of glossy, full-color advertising supplements prepared by others. When they do so, they are, in effect, charging the advertiser to use their carrier distribution system. The purpose is to forestall the advertiser's resort to direct mail or some other methods of distribution that would shut out the newspaper altogether. Competition for the advertiser's dollar and for the consumer's attention also comes from billboards, the infinite variety of point-of-sale advertisements encountered in any retail store, locally published magazines, and zoned editions of national magazines, which carry advertising aimed at particular areas.

All of this says nothing of the electronic delivery of advertising. A city with one newspaper may have three or more television stations, several times that many AM and FM stations, and a cable system, all vigorously seeking to sell time to advertisers. Because television stations particularly can point to research findings that the average person spends more time watching or listening to electronic media than reading newspapers, competition from this quarter is formidable.

For any of these media, the setting of advertising rates is a delicate matter. The rates must be competitive, or the media will be bypassed by advertisers seeking maximum results for each dollar spent. But the rates must be high enough to cover expenses and return a profit, or the advertising medium eventually will fail. In addition, the owner of any medium that has achieved a substantial share of the market must be aware of possible antitrust action. A recent survey of antitrust actions involving the communications media showed that every aspect of advertising rate-setting, including the placing of newspaper ads in favored positions on the front or back of separate sections, is subject to challenge.[8] Most complaints founder on the rule of reason, but the possibility of antitrust action, civil, or criminal, is a factor to be considered in any rate decision.

Antitrust Law and the Marketplace of Ideas

"To monopolize freedom destroys it," wrote the U.S. court of appeals in the *Kansas City Star* case in 1957. Five years later President John F. Kennedy picked up on that idea and set in motion a series of actions that carried antitrust law onto new ground. His purpose was to preserve what he saw as a diminishing marketplace of ideas. He sought to promote competition for news, and a diversity of opinion, by attacking the economic forces and business practices that were creating one-newspaper towns.[9]

Kennedy's policy had its origins in several currents then running strongly through the media and society. Some were political, others economic. The principal motivating factors were:

1. Most newspapers that took positions during the Kennedy-Nixon campaign of 1960 backed the Republican candidate—as they had in every presidential campaign in the previous forty years. Adlai Stevenson, who had few newspaper backers in his two runs for the presidency, may have been the first to use the phrase "a one-party press," but he was not the only Democrat to complain about the phenomenon. When Franklin D. Roosevelt ran for a fourth term in the midst of World War II, he had the editorial backing of only 22 percent of the dailies with 17.7 percent of the national circulation. In no campaign from 1940 through 1956 did any Republican candidate for president have the support of less than 60 percent of the daily newspapers backing one candidate or the other. In 1960,

8. Conrad M. Shumadine, Michael S. Ives, Walter D. Kelley, Jr., and William H. Shewmak, "Antitrust and the Media," *Communications Law 1985*, vol. 1 (New York: Practising Law Institute, 1985), pp. 729–991.

9. In this section, the author relies in part on conversations with attorneys who were with the Antitrust Division of the Department of Justice in that era, and on other sources in politics and in the newspaper business. The author was managing editor of the *Cincinnati Enquirer* and was to have been an expert witness in the divestment lawsuit directed at Scripps-Howard. The case was settled before it came to trial.

Kennedy was supported by only 16.4 percent of the dailies, representing 15.8 percent of the circulation.[10]

2. At an accelerating rate, most cities in the United States were becoming one-newspaper, or one newspaper-owner, towns. In 1923, 39 percent of the cities with daily newspapers had competing ownerships. By 1930, it was 20.6 percent. Thirty years later, when Kennedy was running for office, only 61 cities, or 4.2 percent of the 1,461 with daily newspapers, had competing ownerships.[11]

3. Newspaper chains were growing at an accelerating rate. In 1960, more than half the nation's daily newspapers were independently owned. The long-established chains—Hearst, Scripps-Howard, Knight-Ridder, Newhouse, Cox—seemed to have stabilized. But a new phenomenon had begun to emerge: chain ownership of smaller newspapers in one-newspaper towns. The leaders in such acquisitions were Gannett, headquartered in Rochester, New York, and Thomson, owned by Lord Thomson of Fleet, a Canadian, with world headquarters in London. In part, the rapid growth of newspaper chains was a factor of heredity. The children and grandchildren of patriarchs who had founded newspapers early in the century lost interest in journalism. Another contributing factor in the trend toward chain ownership was the inheritance tax, which made it difficult to keep a small newspaper in the family. The estate had more to gain by selling the newspaper and using part of the proceeds to pay the taxes on the estate.

In the mid-1980s, the problems with third- and fourth-generation family ownerships resulted in several noteworthy newspaper sales, all of them to chains. The biggest winner was the Gannett Company. Within a matter of months in 1985 and 1986, it bought the *Des Moines Register* from the Cowles family, the *Detroit News* from the Scripps family, and the *Courier-Journal* and *Louisville Times* from the Bingham family. The latter purchase was made possible when Barry Bingham, Sr., became convinced that his three children could not resolve their differences over control of the company. Gannett paid $300 million for the papers, outbidding several other prospective buyers.[12] The Bingham family had owned the Louisville newspapers for more than sixty years. Under the leadership of Bingham, and his son, Barry, Jr., the newspapers not only had won Pulitzer prizes but, through involvement of their editors in the Associated Press Managing Editors Association and the American Society of Newspaper Editors, had become a force in raising the ethical standards of newspapers. With these acquisitions, and its earlier

---

10. *Editor & Publisher* has surveyed daily newspaper endorsements of presidential candidates in every campaign, starting in 1932. Not until 1964, when President Lyndon B. Johnson ran against Barry Goldwater, did a majority of the editors making endorsements support a Democratic candidate. In each election since, a majority has endorsed the Republican candidate. In an editorial on 8 November 1980, the magazine noted, "The startling trend of these polls . . . has been the steady increase in the number of newspapers preferring not to take a stand with an editorial endorsement." In that year, nearly half the newspapers took no editorial position on the presidential election. That also was true in 1984.

11. Raymond B. Nixon, "Half of Nation's Dailies Now in Group Ownerships," *Editor & Publisher*, 17 July 1971, p. 7.

12. "Gannett Bids High—Again," *Newsweek*, 2 June 1986, p. 67.

Coin-operated newspaper vending machines, like these in Santa Monica, California, have proliferated. Attempts to regulate them have raised questions of First Amendment law for the courts to resolve. (Ken Robert Buck/The Picture Cube)

purchase of the *Cincinnati Enquirer*, Gannett shed its smalltown image and became not only the owner of the most daily newspapers, ninety-three, but the publisher controlling the largest daily circulation, more than a million of it attributable to *USA Today*.

As early as 1960, the trend toward chain ownership and one-newspaper towns was enough to convince the Kennedy administration that something needed to be done. As the president and his advisers saw it, people in too many cities were becoming a captive audience for one newspaper owner. Increasingly, that owner was not an individual who lived in the community, but a faceless corporation, with headquarters elsewhere, that was interested in only one thing: profit. Thus, the marketplace of ideas was becoming not a robust exchange for all kinds of political news and views, but a flabby monopoly offering one point of view, or, even worse, none at all. The president ordered the Antitrust Division of the Department of Justice to take action to preserve as much of the marketplace of ideas as still existed, and to try to restore what already had been lost.

Kennedy was assassinated before his order could be converted into action. However, his brother Robert carried on as attorney general under President Lyndon B. Johnson, who endorsed the program. Three antitrust suits filed in the mid-1960s against newspaper owners in as many cities were designed to send the news media a message. Each city was chosen to make a specific point. They were Tucson, Arizona, where two owners who long had shared common advertising, circulation, and printing operations, were about to become one; Los Angeles, where the Chandler family, owner of the *Times*, had bought the San Bernardino papers; and Cincinnati, where Scripps-Howard owned the *Post* and held 58 percent of the stock in the *Enquirer*.

Tucson: Joint Operating Agreements

The **joint operating agreement** in Tucson was one of the earliest, dating to 1940, and was typical of the way such arrangements operate. At the time it was formed, two owners were in head-to-head competition. The *Star* was making a modest profit, but the *Citizen* had dropped into the red. The two owners

Citizen Publishing Co. v. *United States,* 394 U.S. 131, 89 S.Ct. 927, 22 L.Ed.2d 148 (1969).

reached an agreement and organized a third company, Tucson Newspapers, Inc., which, in effect, would become the city's only newspaper publisher. It sold advertising for, and distributed, both newspapers. It operated the printing plant. As publisher, it decided what to charge for advertising and set subscription rates. Profit was pooled and distributed to the two owners according to a formula on which they had agreed at the time the joint operation began. Executives of the two papers were bound by an agreement not to take part in a competing newspaper in the Tucson area, even if they lost their present jobs.

The arrangement worked well for more than twenty years. Then the family that owned the *Star* lost interest and the paper was offered for sale. The small Brush-Moore chain, centered in Canton, Ohio, offered to buy. William A. Small, Jr., owner of the *Citizen*, exercised his option to buy under the operating agreement. The Justice Department filed suit to prevent that sale and to require that the *Star* be sold to anyone but Small. The resulting legal battle went to the Supreme Court, which not only upheld the department, but held in *Citizen Publishing Co.* v. *United States* that the joint operating agreement violated antitrust law. The decision raised doubt about the legality of each of the twenty-two other agreements then in existence, and sent shock waves through the newspaper business.

Justice William O. Douglas, writing for the Court, found three fatal flaws in the Tucson agreement. Tucson Newspapers' control of advertising and circulation rates amounted to illegal price fixing. Profit pooling, with distribution by formula, also violated antitrust law. So did the restrictions on participation in competing newspapers. That was market control. The Citizen Publishing Co. could defend the arrangement only if it could prove that the *Citizen* not only had been failing at the time of the original agreement in 1940, but that there was no other buyer who might have saved it. Douglas held that the evidence did not support such a conclusion. If the *Citizen* was indeed failing in 1940, why would the publishers of the *Star* be willing to enter into an agreement giving it a fixed share of the profit?

The joint operating agreement could survive, the Court held, only if it was rewritten to permit each newspaper to set its own advertising and circulation rates, to distribute profit in a manner that reflected performance, and to eliminate the restrictions on future employment.

The message in this instance may have been stronger than the Department of Justice intended. The original purpose of the suit had been to make certain that competing editorial operations were preserved in joint ownership cities. The agreements were not to be used as easy vehicles to one ownership. But the effect of the Supreme Court's decision was to make each party to a joint agreement sink or swim on the basis of individual performance. Both could still operate out of the same printing plant, but if advertising and circulation rates were to be set independently, the owners almost certainly would have to separate those vital operations.

Congress, under prodding from some publishers, had anticipated the Supreme Court's decision, and in July 1970, sixteen months after the Tucson decision, President Richard M. Nixon signed the Newspaper Preservation Act into law. [13]

Briefly, that law wiped out the effect of the Supreme Court's decision. With it, Congress gave its approval to the agreements then in existence. It also restored the Tucson agreement, except for the section on market control. Future joint operating agreements elsewhere could be entered into only with the approval of the attorney general. In any such proposal, one of the newspapers clearly would have to be failing.

The Newspaper Preservation Act has withstood challenge in the courts. [14] The *Bay Guardian*, a monthly newspaper in San Francisco, attacked the constitutionality of the Act in a suit asking that the joint operating agreement between the *Chronicle* and the *Examiner* be dissolved. Judge Oliver J. Carter of the federal district court in San Francisco held that no constitutional issue was involved. The antitrust laws are an act of Congress, and what Congress does in one era it can modify in another to meet changing conditions. The Newspaper Preservation Act merely grants newspapers an exception from antitrust law under certain narrowly drawn conditions. The agreement in San Francisco met those conditions, Carter held.

However, that did not end the matter. Judge Carter held that the suit could continue on its merits to determine whether the newspapers' advertising and circulation practices violated the Sherman Act. The *Guardian* and its publisher, Bruce Brugmann, were joined by a department store that claimed that the papers' joint advertising rate was so high that it had been forced out of business because it couldn't afford to use the newspapers. In May 1975 the suit was settled out of court with the newspapers' agreement to pay the seventeen plaintiffs $1.35 million. [15]

Thus, while the court held that joint operating agreements do not in themselves violate the antitrust act, the case stands as a reminder that the Newspaper Preservation Act does not immunize the participating newspapers from the workings of antitrust law. If they take advantage of the Act to set rates that harm a competitor, or freeze out potential advertisers, they are vulnerable to an antitrust action.

Los Angeles: One Ownership in Adjacent Markets

Los Angeles has the distinction of pioneering three post–World War II phenomena: the freeway, urban sprawl, and smog. The three are interrelated products of America's

13. Joe Lewels, Jr., "The Newspaper Preservation Act," *Freedom of Information Center Report No. 254*, School of Journalism, University of Missouri at Columbia, January 1971.
14. Bay Guardian Co. v. Chronicle Publishing Co., 344 F.Supp. 1155 (N.D.Calif. 1972).
15. Earl W. Wilken, "S.F. Printing Co. Settles Monopoly Suits Out-of-Court," *Editor & Publisher*, 31 May 1975, p. 7.

love affair with the automobile. Not only has the automobile been an influence on urban patterns, it has had an effect on the daily newspaper.

As the 1960s began, editors and publishers in the nation's major metropolitan areas became aware of a trend with disturbing implications. The population of most central cities was declining, and changing in nature. The population of suburban communities was skyrocketing, sometimes by as much as 100 percent in a decade. Metropolitan areas became decaying cores populated by minorities and the poor, surrounded by affluent suburbs comprised of the mainly white middle and upper classes. Central cities became centers of commerce during the day, but were nearly deserted at night.

These changes proved to be especially troubling for afternoon newspapers published in the larger cities. Their old audience—working-class people who lived in neat rows of well-kept dwellings near the city's center—had been dispersed in the suburbs. Delivery trucks had to fight traffic to reach the new suburban communities, many of whose residents no longer had much interest in the news of the central city. They felt themselves part of new communities. Further, publishers of afternoon newspapers found themselves in competition both with fringe-area publications and with the evening news and entertainment on television.

Morning newspapers had fewer distribution problems. Their trucks could move over deserted streets in the early hours of the morning. But they, too, had problems finding the best mix of local, suburban, and regional news to meet the needs of their dispersed audience.

In the early 1960s, some publishers sought to solve their problems by buying newspapers, dailies or weeklies, on the fringes of their circulation areas. They reasoned that by doing so they could offer readers a package: the central-city paper for the big picture, including heavy doses of business and sports news, and the neighborhood daily or weekly for intense coverage of local news. One of the pioneers in this movement was the *Los Angeles Times*.

By 1962, it had become the largest daily newspaper in Southern California, and one of the largest in the nation. It had competition from a Hearst-owned daily in Los Angeles, and from newspapers published in the rapidly growing suburbs, many of which had become cities in their own right. One of the latter is San Bernardino, a city of nearly a million population at the foot of the mountains sixty-five miles east of Los Angeles. For years prior to 1964, James Guthrie owned and published morning and afternoon papers there. In that year, he sold the papers to Norman Chandler, owner of the *Times*, to

United States v. Times-Mirror Co., 274 F.Supp. 606 (C.D. Calif. 1967).

forestall sale to the Pulitzer family whose liberal political views were objectionable to Guthrie. To Chandler, the purchase made sense. He saw the *Times* as a metropolitan newspaper. It covered Los Angeles, to be sure, but its focus was on the larger picture, starting with California, and going on to include the West as a region, the nation, and the world. The *Times* had a large Washington bureau and, in cooperation with the *Washington Post*, was in the process of establishing more bureaus in foreign countries than any other paper except the *New York Times*. However, it could not begin to cover in detail the many communities in the Los Angeles basin. One of the functions of the San Bernardino papers would be to fill some of the gaps by covering that city and its neighbors. Thus, the three papers would serve complementary functions.

The Justice Department didn't see it that way. What it saw was a first step along the road that would take the *Los Angeles Times* to an even more dominant position than it already held. It filed suit in federal district court in Los Angeles asking that Chandler be ordered to sell the San Bernardino papers. Again, as in Tucson, the government was attacking a publisher's business practices under antitrust law in an effort to preserve competing editorial operations.

The *Times* brought in expert witnesses from universities who supported its view of the complementary nature of the publications. These witnesses argued that not only do newspapers function differently as to the extent of their news coverage, but that in doing so they serve different advertising markets as well. Thus, in the experts' view, the purchase would lead to no diminution in competition and therefore did not violate antitrust law.

The court did not accept that argument. In *United States* v. *Times-Mirror Co.*, Judge Warren J. Ferguson said the antitrust act "directed that the courts must look to the effect and impact of the merger. If its effect is anti-competitive, then there is an violation." The fact was that the merger wiped out a thriving small business and made it a part of the largest newspaper business in the area. As a result of that merger, the *Times*'s share of the weekday circulation in the relevant marketing area rose from 10.6 percent to 54.8. And on Sundays, the rise was from 20.3 percent to 64.3. This, he held, showed a prima facie violation of the Clayton Act.

Judge Ferguson also looked at daily newspaper publication in the entire Los Angeles metropolitan area. In a decade, the number of dailies had risen from fifty-two to sixty-four, but the number of independent ownerships had declined from thirty-three to fourteen. Additionally, one newspaper, the West Coast edition of the *New York Times*, had recently failed.

The divestiture order did not lead to an increase in the number of independent publishers. The San Bernardino papers were bought by the Gannett chain. However, the message was clear: The Justice Department would oppose an attempt by a major metropolitan newspaper to hedge its position by buying newspapers in its own circulation zone, or even on its far reaches. Each metro daily would have to make it on its own. Events were to prove that some, even in such cities as Washington, Philadelphia, Minneapolis, and Cleveland, could not.

Cincinnati: One Ownership in the Same City

Until the middle 1950s, Cincinnati was a three-newspaper city. Scripps-Howard owned the afternoon *Post*. Members of the Scripps family lived in the city. The Taft family, which had produced a president of the United States and a prominent U.S. senator, owned the afternoon *Times-Star*. The morning and Sunday field was the sole province of the *Enquirer*, owned by the McLean estate and administered by a court in Washington, D.C. Because of that, it seemed ripe for buying by one of the two afternoon owners. To forestall that, employees of the *Enquirer* tried to buy it, but succeeded only in part. Scripps-Howard was able to buy 58 percent of the stock, but was content to operate the paper as a separate entity. When the Tafts lost the bidding battle, they sold the *Times-Star* to Scripps, which merged it with the *Post*. In 1960, when Kennedy was elected, Cincinnati was a one-owner city, although Scripps-Howard chose to exercise no direct control over the *Enquirer* management.

Both papers prospered under the arrangement. Looking to a time when both papers would need new presses, management began secret talks to explore the possibilities of a jointly owned printing plant. The Justice Department intervened in 1964 by filing an antitrust complaint. It asked a federal district court to order Scripps-Howard to sell one of the newspapers.

The government based its lawsuit on the premise that both newspapers were highly profitable, which was indeed true. Justice Department attorneys reasoned that there would be a more vigorous marketplace of ideas in Cincinnati if both newspapers were truly independent in all aspects of their operations. As evidence of the possibility of a monopoly in the field of news and opinion, as well as in the advertising market, the government pointed to the fact that Scripps also owned one of the three commercial television stations in Cincinnati and an associated radio station.

After several years of legal sparring, Scripps chose not to fight the suit. In 1968, it accepted a consent decree and put the *Enquirer* on the market. It was bought by American Financial Corporation, a locally owned holding company with interests in dairy stores, supermarkets, and banking, including ownership of one of the city's major banks. To comply with banking regulations, the new owner was also required to sell. The purchaser was Combined Communications, with headquarters in Phoenix. In 1979, Combined merged with Gannett.

The Marketplace of Ideas Today

With the benefit of more than twenty years of hindsight, it is evident that the plan conceived by John F. Kennedy and carried forward after his death has largely failed. The trend toward one-ownership cities and newspaper chains, which he perceived and sought to forestall, has intensified. Whether the marketplace of ideas has been diminished by that trend is subject to debate. A great deal depends upon how one defines the market and identifies the sources of ideas competing for attention.

If one focuses only on daily newspapers, there is no doubt about two facts. The number of cities of any size with truly competing daily newspapers is approaching the vanishing point, and newspaper groups, as they prefer to be called, now own more than two-thirds of the nation's 1,700 dailies, controlling about 80 percent of the total daily newspaper circulation.[16]

A review of the present status of the newspapers involved in the cases examined in the preceding section is suggestive of the larger picture. Today both newspapers in Tucson are owned by groups, the *Star* by the Pulitzer family, whose primary newspaper property is the *St. Louis Post-Dispatch*. The *Citizen* is one of Gannett's ninety-three dailies, including *USA Today*. The joint operating agreement condemned by the Supreme Court but restored by Congress through the Newspaper Preservation Act continues in effect. The *Los Angeles Times*, frustrated in its attempt to buy the San Bernardino papers, became owner of a substantial chain. Its holdings included the *Denver Post*, the *Dallas Times Herald*, the *Hartford Courant*, the *Baltimore Sun*, and *Newsday*, published in New York City's Long Island suburbs. Gannett owns the San

---

16. "Groups Still Own Most U.S. Dailies," *Editor & Publisher*, 28 April 1984, p. 76.

Bernardino papers. Other thriving papers in the Los Angeles area are owned by the Tribune company of Chicago, and Knight-Ridder, which is based in Miami. Scripps-Howard continues to own the *Cincinnati Post*, and, as noted, the *Enquirer* is a Gannett property. However, as we will see, there has been a marked change in the relation between the two papers.

In recent years, Gannett has been the most noteworthy of the newspaper groups, not only because of *USA Today*, but because of its expansion into major markets, making it the largest chain with ninety-three daily newspapers. Not far behind is Thomson, which is owned by Canadian and British interests. It had eighty-four United States dailies, all in smaller cities. No other of the 149 groups counted by *Editor & Publisher* in 1984 owned more than fifty papers.[17]

As group-owned newspapers have increased in number, cities with competing separate ownerships have decreased. The sixty-one such cities when Kennedy was elected president in 1960 have declined to fewer than fifty today, and in half of them the competing owners survive only because of joint operating agreements. The major cities served by only one newspaper owner include Philadelphia, Phoenix, Indianapolis, Memphis, Milwaukee, New Orleans, Cleveland, Jacksonville, St. Louis, San Diego, and Atlanta. In some of these, the single owner publishes newspapers with separate news staffs. In others, the two newspapers have combined their news staffs. In still others, there is only one newspaper. The trend reflects economic realities. Newsprint costs exceed $500 a ton. Reporters and editors are enjoying the highest salaries ever, which may still not be high enough, in light of newsroom turnover.[18] Competition for advertising has limited the extent to which newspapers can increase their rates and hence their revenue. Further, in cities with competing newspapers, advertisers tend to buy space in the paper that reaches the most potential customers. To be No. 2 can mean being left with too little advertising to support a newspaper.

The reality of today is clear. Most cities in the United States have only one daily newspaper. There is only one chance in three that that newspaper will not be part of a chain.

Joint Operating Agreements Today

When the Newspaper Preservation Act became law in 1970, it gave government approval not only to the joint operating agreement in Tucson, but to others in effect in twenty-one cities. Competing newspapers in the same city would be permitted to enter into such agreements in the future only if one of them was failing, and then only with the approval of the attorney general. The Act's avowed purpose was to preserve competing news and editorial operations in cities then served by two newspaper owners. The Act has not been altogether successful in serving that purpose. Since 1974, when competing publishers in Anchorage, Alaska, became the first to take advantage of the Act, the number of new agreements has been offset by instances in which papers failed despite being parties to such agreements.

---

17. 28 April 1984, p. 80.
18. David H. Weaver and G. Cleveland Wilhoit, *The American Journalist* (Bloomington: Indiana University Press, 1986), pp. 99–100.

The experience in Cincinnati illustrates the forces that can lead to creation of a joint operating agreement. When the Justice Department brought suit against Scripps-Howard in 1964, the *Post* had a circulation of 252,000 to the *Enquirer*'s 190,000 daily and 300,000 on Sunday.[19] By 1978, the *Post* had slipped to 184,000 while the *Enquirer* remained steady. Because of its decline in circulation, the *Post*, once the leader in weekday advertising, had slipped behind the *Enquirer* in ad linage in 1973. The gap widened each year thereafter. The *Post* began to lose money in 1970. By 1974, the losses had reached nearly $4 million a year. Only through drastic cost-cutting was the loss narrowed to about $1 million a year.

In 1977, Scripps-Howard decided it had had enough. After negotiations with Combined Communications, the then owner of the *Enquirer*, the two publishers asked the attorney general to approve a joint operating agreement. Unions representing the newspapers' employees filed objections, but after hearings that produced more than 6,000 pages of testimony, the request was approved. Shortly before it took effect, Combined Communications merged with Gannett. Today the *Post* and the *Enquirer* share a modern printing plant several blocks from their still-separate downtown editorial offices. It is near the site executives of the two newspapers envisaged in the 1960s.

Of the several newspapers that have failed despite joint operating agreements, the most notable is the *St. Louis Globe-Democrat*. The operating agreement between its owner, the Newhouse group, and the Pulitzer family, owner of the *Post-Dispatch*, was one of those in effect when the Newspaper Preservation Act became law. In 1983, Newhouse announced it was losing money and would cease publication of the *Globe-Democrat* at the end of that year.[20] Another owner took it over and tried to keep it going, but in 1986 the paper ceased publication, ending 133 years of operation.

As this episode suggests, joint operating agreements are not a guarantee of profitable operation. At the best, they give two owners who are willing to work at it an opportunity to coexist as competing news operations and survive as business entities. Their continued existence in about twenty-five cities serves as evidence that some publishers are willing to give it a try.

Because the material in this chapter thus far has dealt with the problem areas of the business of journalism, it may contribute to an overly gloomy assessment of the future of newspapers. The problems are a product of dramatic changes in the nature of newspaper journalism. Despite the notable failures of some once-powerful dailies in the nation's major cities, the number of daily newspapers remained constant over several decades at about 1,750, before dropping to 1,701 in 1983.[21] Deaths have been balanced by births of suburban dailies. In those same areas, weeklies, many of them devoted almost entirely to advertising, are thriving as never before. Publicly held newspaper companies, notably Gannett, New York Times, Knight-Ridder, Dow Jones, and the Tribune Company are reporting record earnings, despite costly investment in new ways

---

19. *Recommended Decision* in the matter of the Application by the Cincinnati Enquirer, Inc., and the E. W. Scripps Co. for Approval of a Joint Operating Agreement Pursuant to the Newspaper Preservation Act, 15 U.S.C. §1801 *et seq.*, 1 May 1979, pp. 28–31.
20. "St. Louis Daily in JOA Announces It Will Shut Down," *Editor & Publisher*, 12 November 1983, p. 10.
21. "Facts About Newspapers, 1985," American Newspaper Publishers Association, p. 4.

of delivering news and advertising. Electronic composition has greatly reduced composing room costs. New presses have given newspapers the capability to offer color rivaling that found in magazines. Computer-generated graphic devices give editors a new dimension in which to present information. Condensation, sparked on one side by higher paper costs and on the other by the example offered by *USA Today,* is offering readers more news more concisely than in earlier years. There is evidence that people are noticing the changes. Daily newspaper circulation, long flat, rose by more than a million copies a day, on the average, in 1982.[22] And in 1984, an investment banking firm in New York studied the financial performance of communications companies and reported that over a five-year period newspapers were among the leaders. During that period, newspapers reported an average profit margin of 15 percent, compared with a communications industry average of 14 percent.[23]

Joint Ownership of Newspaper and Broadcasting Stations

In the early days of broadcasting, many newspapers established radio stations and used them for promotion and as an additional outlet for news. In time, these stations became profitable in their own right, and many of the newspaper-owned broadcasters became pioneers in television. By the mid-1970s, there were 176 newspaper-radio combinations and eighty-three newspaper-television combinations.

In 1974, the Justice Department, again acting out of concern for the marketplace of ideas, asked the Federal Communications Commission to refuse to renew broadcasting licenses owned by newspapers in St. Louis and Des Moines.[24] Later, the request was expanded to include newspaper-broadcast combinations in Milwaukee and Salt Lake City. It chose to act through the FCC rather than go to court because Justice Department attorneys believed they would have an easier time proving that such combinations were not in the public interest than they would have proving violation of antitrust law. The FCC rejected Justice's request, but moved forward with its own study of the cross-ownership of newspapers and broadcasting stations in the same community.[25]

That study had begun in 1970,[26] and was to occupy the FCC and the courts for eight years, leading to a decision by the Supreme Court. By the mid-1970s, the FCC had agreed on the main thrust of a proposal: No newspaper would be permitted to start a new broadcasting station, or buy the license of an existing station, in its own community. All of the then existing cross-ownerships would have to be terminated within five years. This provoked a storm of protest that led to additional hearings. In the end, the FCC decided that diversity was not the only interest to be served. Some newspaper-broadcasting station combinations were doing a particularly good job of serving the public interest. In most instances the combinations had to meet vigorous competition from other

22. Jonathan Friendly, "On Eve of Convention, Newspaper Publishers Say Brighter Days Lie Ahead," *New York Times,* 24 April 1983.
23. Andrew Randolf, "Newspapers Are Good Investments," *Editor & Publisher,* 11 February 1984, p. 36.
24. "Justice Agency Urges FCC to Deny Licenses to 6 Stations It Says Are Newspaper Owned," *Wall Street Journal,* 4 January 1974.
25. "Broadcast Licenses Renewed in Rebuff to Justice Agency," *Wall Street Journal,* 25 October 1976.
26. Further Notice of Proposed Rule Making (Docket No. 18110), 22 F.C.C.2d 339 (1970).

broadcasting stations. When the proposal took final form in 1975, it still forbade future newspaper acquisitions in the same city. But the divestiture provision was limited to cities in which the only daily newspaper also owned the only broadcasting station delivering a clear signal to the community. The FCC identified only eighteen such communities, eight involving television stations. After further hearings, it ordered divestiture in sixteen.[27]

That order came under fire from two directions. The stations involved, backed by organizations of broadcasters and publishers, thought it went too far. A consumer advocate group, the National Citizens Committee for Broadcasting, didn't think it went

Federal Communications Commission v. National Citizens Committee for Broadcasting, 436 U.S. 775, 98 S.Ct. 2096, 56 L.Ed.2d 697 (1978).

far enough. Neither did the Justice Department, which also intervened. If diversity of ownership was essential to a robust marketplace of ideas, as the FCC recognized in principle, then that principle ought to be carried as far as practicable. Both sides went to the Court of Appeals for the District of Columbia Circuit, which found for the Citizens Committee. Under its ruling, no newspaper-broadcasting combination could stand unless the owner could prove that it qualified for exemption under rules laid down by the FCC. The FCC joined the losing owners in going to the Supreme Court. Ruling in *FCC* v. *National Citizens Committee for Broadcasting*, the Court upheld the rule against future acquisitions, but reversed the appeals court on divestiture.

Justice Thurgood Marshall, writing for the unanimous Court, held that the FCC had acted reasonably and within its powers in concluding that forced divestiture carried too far might actually result in a weakening of the marketplace of ideas. Surviving newspapers, or surviving broadcasting stations, might in some instances be too weak economically to provide truly independent voices. One or both might no longer be able to afford a vigorous news and public affairs staff. Given the realities of broadcast and newspaper ownership patterns, a strong independent local owner might be replaced by an outside chain owner. The Court, then, concluded that the FCC had acted rationally in limiting its divestiture order to sixteen cities.

A common theme runs through antitrust law as applied to the mass media: The First Amendment does not protect unfair competitive practices designed to create a monopoly. If media managers set advertising rates or buy other media enterprises so as to harm competitors, they risk an antitrust action. As the Supreme Court said in the *Associated Press* case in 1945, the First Amendment does not "afford the publisher a peculiar constitutional sanctuary in which he can with impunity violate laws regulating his business practices." However, as we will see, the First Amendment does protect the right to distribute news and opinion, and it also stands guard against attempts to tax the media in ways not applied to other forms of business.

The Distribution of News and Opinion

The Supreme Court has drawn a fine line between the door-to-door sales of goods or services, including magazine subscriptions, and the door-to-door dissemination of

---

27. Second Report and Order, as amended upon reconsideration, 53 F.C.C.2d 589 (1975), 47 CFR, §§73.35, 73.240, 73.636 (1976).

Concerned with lack of newspaper competition and the rise of chain ownership, President John F. Kennedy (right) ordered his attorney general, Robert Kennedy (center), to use antitrust laws to preserve a marketplace of ideas. The program was carried forward by Lyndon B. Johnson (left) after both Kennedys were assassinated. (UPI/Bettmann Newsphotos)

ideas. Local governments may regulate and even prohibit the former. They cannot restrict the latter, even when some people find the ideas obnoxious or when the ideas are printed in pamphlet form and sold. As a result of the Supreme Court decisions, newspapers are one of the few products that have a constitutional right to be sold in public places.

Ironically, this right was not won through the efforts of newspaper publishers. Rather, it was defined in a series of cases carried to the Supreme Court in the 1930s and 1940s by a small religious group, the Jehovah's Witnesses. Because of their beliefs and their methods of spreading them, the Witnesses were the subject of persecution and legal discrimination prior to and during World War II.[28] Witnesses sought converts by distributing pamphlets and other church publications on city streets and door to door. Because the Witnesses' message angered some people, and others considered their methods of solicitation a nuisance, many communities adopted ordinances prohibiting distribution of handbills or licensing door-to-door solicitors. The Witnesses attacked these ordinances in the courts, eventually winning a remarkable series of Supreme Court decisions. Rights won by the Witnesses in those cases are enjoyed today by every person or group seeking support for a cause and by publishers seeking to distribute newspapers.

One of the more notable Jehovah's Witnesses cases, *Lovell* v. *City of Griffith, Georgia*,[29] is described in chapter 2, where it illustrates a form of prior restraint. In that

---

28. David R. Manwaring, *Render Unto Caesar* (Chicago: University of Chicago Press, 1962), pp. 163–86.
29. 305 U.S. 444, 58 S.Ct. 666, 82 L.Ed. 949 (1938).

decision, the Court also dealt with the right to disseminate ideas, holding: "Liberty of circulating is as essential to that freedom as liberty of publishing; indeed, without the circulation, the publication would have little value."

Later decisions involving Jehovah's Witnesses, labor unions, civil rights advocates, and political demonstrators have established a firm principle of First Amendment law: Government may impose reasonable restrictions of time, place, and manner on the dissemination of ideas on the streets and sidewalks, in public parks, and in other public places, but it cannot forbid such use. To do so is an unacceptable prior restraint.

In recent years that principle has been tested anew by attempts to regulate and license the placement of coin-operated newspaper vending machines. Such machines, commonly called newsracks, have been in use for many years, but they did not attract much attention until the advent of Gannett's *USA Today* in 1982. Planned from the start as a national newspaper designed for people on the go, it was distributed through vending machines placed in airports, commuter bus and train stops, and other public places. Publishers of other newspapers reacted by placing their own vending machines in the same places, if they were not there already. In some instances, local governments removed the machines or attempted to regulate or tax them. This has led to several court decisions, including two by United States circuit courts of appeal, holding that the right to distribute newspapers through vending machines is protected by the First Amendment. However, once past that point, the decisions vary as to the regulations that may be imposed on placement of the racks and on whether governments can require publishers to pay a license fee. Two of the decisions, both by United States circuit courts of appeal, illustrate these variations.

Gannett Satellite Information Network, Inc. v. Metropolitan Transportation Authority, 745 F.2d 767 (2d Cir. 1984).

When Gannett began distribution of *USA Today* in New York City, it placed newsracks in the Metropolitan Transportation Authority's commuter railroad stations. MTA removed them because Gannett had not obtained the required license. The MTA permitted newsracks in its stations, but it charged a license fee of $75 per rack or $150 per station, whichever was greater. Other publishers had paid the fee.

When Gannett protested the MTA's removal of its racks, MTA replaced them and agreed to negotiate the amount of the fee. No agreement was reached, and Gannett asked a federal district court to declare the fee unconstitutional. It did so, but on appeal the U.S. Court of Appeals for the Second Circuit affirmed in part and reversed in part. In doing so, it held that newsracks are protected by the First Amendment because they are used to distribute news and opinion. It also held that although the MTA's stations are not public forums to the same degree as streets, sidewalks, and public parks, they are appropriate places for the sale of newspapers. Therefore, Gannett and other publishers have a right to place their racks in the stations, subject only to time, place, and manner regulations designed to prevent their becoming a hazard or a nuisance.

With respect to the license fee, the court reached a conclusion that has been criticized by some First Amendment lawyers.[30] It held that if the MTA was acting solely as an

---

30. Richard J. Ovelman, Samuel A. Terilli, Dan Paul, "Newsracks: Permits, Taxes, Regulations and the First Amendment," *Communications Law 1985,* Vol. 2 (New York: Practising Law Institute, 1985), pp. 783, 784.

arm of government, it could not impose a license fee on newsracks beyond what was needed to cover the incidental expenses associated with its regulatory activity. However, the court noted that the legislature had established the MTA with the expectation that it would be self-sustaining. Therefore, in operating the transit system and the stations, it was acting in a proprietary capacity. This meant that it could charge for the use of its property just like any private landowner. In this instance, the court held, the MTA's interest in earning revenue outweighed Gannett's First Amendment interest, especially since the publisher could place its racks elsewhere. If the decision is followed in other circuits, it means that public transportation authorities, airports, and other self-sustaining agencies of government can charge what the traffic will bear for the placement of newsracks on their property.

A decision of the U.S. Court of Appeals for the Eleventh Circuit in the same year also left the waters muddied. In *Miami Herald Publishing Co.* v. *City of Hallandale*,[31] the newsracks at issue were placed on public sidewalks. Hallandale is on Florida's east coast between Miami and Fort Lauderdale, in an area of intense newspaper competition. To cope with a proliferation of newsracks, the city enacted a series of ordinances regulating placement of the racks and requiring payment of license fees. The license could be revoked if a city official decided that racks were in violation of the regulations.

The *Miami Herald* asked a federal district court to declare the ordinances unconstitutional. That court held that the licensing scheme acted as a prior restraint and that the fee was an unconstitutional tax on the dissemination of ideas. The city appealed, arguing in part that under Florida law federal courts did not have primary jurisdiction to rule on the validity of a local tax. The *Herald* argued that because the fee was part of a licensing scheme designed to regulate the dissemination of ideas, it was subject to attack in federal courts.

The circuit court held that the fee was indeed a tax and would have to be attacked in the state courts. However, it said the remainder of the ordinance imposed regulatory provisions of the kind condemned in *Lovell*. Because the license could be revoked by decision of a city official, and because the regulations enforced by that official were not precise, the ordinance raised "the spectre of prior restraint."

The *Herald* followed up by asking a state court to invalidate the license fee. At this writing, the matter has not been resolved.

A survey of other recent cases decided by federal district courts and by state courts shows universal agreement on one point: Newsracks carry First Amendment protection. This means that local governments cannot forbid their placement on public property. However, governments can regulate their placement to prevent interference with vehicle or pedestrian traffic or even to protect aesthetic values. For instance, a California court upheld an ordinance prohibiting newsracks within three feet of "an area improved with lawns, flowers and trees."[32] Courts have upheld the assessment of fees reasonably calculated to cover the cost of administering such regulations as are imposed.

Taxation of the Media

As the above cases illustrate, one of the critical issues in newsrack regulation is the point at which a fee imposed to cover the cost of regulating a business becomes a tax

---

31. 734 F.2d 666 (11th Cir. 1984).
32. Kash Enterprises, Inc., v. City of Los Angeles, 562 P.2d 1302 (Calif. 1977).

on the distribution of ideas. Because the courts repeatedly have held that in its business aspects the news and opinion business is like any other, the former are acceptable. Therefore, any media organization must pay property, income, franchise, and excise taxes that are generally levied on business firms. However, the Supreme Court has held in two instances that any special tax levied on the news media is in violation of the First Amendment.

The first of these cases, *Grosjean* v. *American Press Co.*, struck down a tax that was clearly designed to punish daily newspapers whose editorials opposed a state governor's rise to power. The governor, Huey P. Long, was one of the most flamboyant political figures of this century. In the 1920's, he established a political machine in Louisiana that permitted members of his family to rule that state for more than forty years. Long went on to become a U. S. senator and an aspirant for the presidency. His career was cut short by an assassin in 1935.

Grosjean v. American Press Co., 297 U.S. 233, 56 S.Ct. 444, 80 L.Ed. 660 (1936).

In 1934, at Long's request, the Louisiana legislature enacted what appeared to be a general tax law. It imposed a 2 percent levy on the gross receipts of newspapers, magazines, periodicals, or books having a circulation within the state of more than 20,000 copies a week. In actuality, the tax applied to only nine publishers of thirteen daily newspapers, all of whom had editorialized against Long's regime. The publishers promptly asked a federal district court to declare the tax void as a violation of the First Amendment. When it did so, the state appealed to the U. S. Supreme Court, which affirmed unanimously.

Justice George Sutherland, whose writing style usually could be described as dull, wrote an eloquent essay on the meaning of freedom of the press. He went back to Milton and examined the history of attempts to control the press. One such method was through taxation. In some instances, the British sovereign used the threat of taxation to bring publishers into line. If that failed, taxes could be imposed at such a level as to drive them out of business. The American Revolution, Sutherland recalled, was in part a protest against the Stamp Tax, which had newspapers and pamphlets among its targets. Such taxes, he wrote, properly were called "taxes on knowledge," explaining:

> That the taxes had, and were intended to have, the effect of curtailing the circulation of newspapers, and particularly the cheaper ones whose readers were generally found among the masses of the people, went almost without question, even on the part of those who defended the act.
> . . . [T]he dominant and controlling aim was to prevent, or curtail the opportunity for, the acquisition of knowledge by the people in respect of their governmental affairs.

This tax was no different. Its purpose clearly was not to raise revenue as much as it was to punish Long's political opponents. It could be as vicious as direct censorship in diminishing the flow of vital information to the people. Therefore, the Court held, it was unconstitutional. But that did not end the matter:

> It is not intended by anything we have said to suggest that the owners of newspapers are immune from any of the ordinary forms of taxation for support of the government. But this is not an ordinary form of tax, but one single in kind, with a long history of hostile misuse against the freedom of the press.

. . . The newspapers, magazines, and other journals of the country, it is safe to say, have shed, and continue to shed, more light on the public and business affairs of the nation than any other instrumentality of publicity; and since informed public opinion is the most potent of all restraints upon misgovernment, the suppression or abridgment of the publicity afforded by a free press cannot be regarded otherwise than with grave concern. The tax here is bad not because it takes money from the pockets of appellees. If that were all, a wholly different question would be presented. It is bad because, in the light of its history and of its present setting, it is seen as a deliberate and calculated device in the guise of a tax to limit the circulation of information to which the public is entitled. . . . A free press stands as one of the great interpreters between the government and the people. To allow it to be fettered is to fetter ourselves.

Those last two sentences should be engraved in the minds of every American. The First Amendment, Sutherland was saying, is not a special privilege for those whom fortune has placed in journalism. Journalists are protected because they are the only independent interpreters of what those in government do for us or to us.

Nearly fifty years after the *Grosjean* decision, the Supreme Court again rejected an attempt to impose a special tax on publications. This tax was not prompted by political vindictiveness, but by the state of Minnesota's need for revenue, tempered by special treatment for newspapers. In 1967, it adopted a retail sales tax on most items, but excluded newspapers. To protect the sales tax, it imposed a use tax on items bought outside the state, but consumed in Minnesota. In 1971, the legislature amended the use tax to include the cost of paper and ink used in publication. No other items used in the manufacture of a retail product were subject to the tax. In 1974, the law was further amended to exclude the first $100,000 worth of paper and ink consumed by a publication in any calendar year. The effect was to exclude all but eleven publishers who produced 14 of the 388 paid-circulation newspapers in the state. Two-thirds of the revenue produced by the tax was paid by the Minneapolis Star and Tribune Co.

The newspaper company challenged the tax in the state courts and lost. Arguing that it was the victim of a special tax much like that in *Grosjean*, it carried an appeal to the Supreme Court. In *Minneapolis Star and Tribune Co.* v. *Minnesota Commissioner of Revenue*, the Court held in 1983 that although the comparison was not controlling, the use tax nevertheless violated the First Amendment. Justice Sandra Day O'Connor, writing for seven members of the Court, said the tax would have been proper had it been applied evenly to all kinds of business firms. But this one was not, failing the test of even-handedness in two important respects:

Minneapolis Star and Tribune Co. v. *Minnesota Commissioner of Revenue,* 460 U.S. 575, 103 S.Ct. 1365, 75 L.Ed.2d 295, (1983).

1. "It imposes a use tax that does not serve the function of protecting the sales tax."

2. "It taxes an intermediate transaction rather than the ultimate retail sale."

When the press is singled out for special taxation, Justice O'Connor continued, the state must prove that it has an overriding governmental interest for doing so. The power to tax is a "powerful weapon" that can weaken or cripple a target that stands by itself.

But when all are treated equally, the realities of politics serve to restrain the hand of the tax collector.

Minnesota said it had imposed the tax not to harm the press but to raise needed revenue. But that reason, standing alone, was not enough, O'Connor said. The same amount of revenue could have been raised by a slight increase in a levy applying to all business firms. Or, she suggested, the revenue could have been raised by applying the sales tax to the price of newspapers. The state further argued that the use tax gave the press favored treatment, imposing levies on it at a lower rate than those paid by other businesses. That made no difference, the Court held. The point was that the press was given differential treatment. This point was highlighted by the fact that even within the press, most publishers paid no tax, while a few carried most of the burden. O'Connor concluded:

> Whatever the motive of the legislature in this case, we think that recognizing a power in the State not only to single out the press but also to tailor the tax so that it singles out a few members of the press presents such a potential for abuse that no interest suggested by Minnesota can justify the scheme.

The decision thus reaffirmed the principle that the news media cannot be singled out for special tax treatment, even when that special treatment works to their advantage.

This chapter has reminded us that news and opinion media are like people with split personalities. In one part of their being, they are privileged vehicles for the dissemination of news and opinion, protected by the First Amendment. We have seen earlier that that protection is quite strong. The media are free to criticize government and government officials in the strongest terms, even to the point of calling for their overthrow. Nor is the First Amendment's protection limited to publications that are true, fair, or dedicated to a noble purpose. Freedom of the press protects some falsehoods lest strict insistence on truth dampen debate on public issues. The Supreme Court has said repeatedly that the First Amendment protects both fair and unfair opinion. Only radio and television have an obligation to try to treat all sides of issues with an even hand, and that is because they operate under license from the government. Otherwise, the broadcast media, like all other media, are protected even though they choose to deal in what many members of society consider trash. This includes portrayals of sexual activity up to the point at which the portrayal is found obscene, of violence, and of ideas many members of society consider to be repugnant. Even advertising, long considered beyond the reach of the First Amendment, now is protected unless it is false or seeks buyers for an illegal product. In short, because of the First Amendment, the content of the media is almost beyond regulation except by the forces of the marketplace.

But in the other part of their being, media are subject to regulation, not only by the marketplace but by government. Whatever product they offer the public, the media are business organizations. They must take in enough money from customers and advertisers to cover their costs or go out of business. Obviously, many media organizations not only cover their costs but make a comfortable margin of profit. Some media organizations have become giant conglomerates with revenues from circulation, advertising, and the sale of products running into billions of dollars a year. Annual profits of 15 to 20 percent on investment are not uncommon.

Therefore it is not surprising that courts have held that in their business operations the media are to be treated like anyone else. More than forty years ago, in the *Associated Press* case, the Supreme Court held that the First Amendment does not protect the news media from laws regulating their business aspects. In that instance, the Court held that member publishers could not treat the Associated Press news service like a private club. Their attempt to deny the service's news report to publishers who were in competition with them violated antitrust law. In the *Lorain Journal* case, the Court expanded on that principle, holding that a newspaper violated the law when it used its power as a dominant medium to discourage advertisers from buying time on a competing radio station. More recently, the Supreme Court held in the *Tucson* case that it also violates antitrust law if one publisher buys a competing newspaper, unless one or the other is clearly failing. However, passage of the Newspaper Preservation Act now makes it possible for competing publishers to combine some of their operations if that is required to ensure continued publication of two newspapers. Such arrangements, called joint operating agreements, are in effect in about twenty-five cities.

However, even in their business aspects, the media are not without First Amendment protection. In two sensitive areas, circulation and taxation, the Supreme Court has limited the power of government. Through the efforts of a religious group, Jehovah's Witnesses, the Supreme Court has said that people have a right to disseminate ideas in public places. In modern times, this has led to decisions holding that the First Amendment protects the right to place newsracks in public places. These may be subjected to reasonable regulations designed to protect the rights of others to use the streets and sidewalks safely, but they may not be banned altogether. The degree to which a fee may be imposed on newsracks is an open question, with most courts holding that it can be no higher than what is needed to cover the incidental costs ensuring that the regulations are complied with.

Twice, in *Grosjean* and in *Minneapolis Star*, the Supreme Court has held that a discriminatory tax imposed on media of news and opinion violates the First Amendment. In the latter case, it made no difference that the tax could be construed as treating newspapers more leniently than other kinds of business. The Court said that if it were to recognize a right to tax the media in ways not applied to other kinds of business, it would open the door for government to use the power to tax to influence or destroy its media critics. That, said Justice Sutherland in *Grosjean*, would restore the licensing power condemned by John Milton in *Areopagitica*.

In the Professional World

In the 1960s, President John F. Kennedy became concerned about what he saw as the disappearance of the marketplace of ideas. In part, his concern was political. Few newspapers had supported him editorially in his campaign for the presidency in 1960. He also knew that no Democratic presidential candidate, not even Franklin D. Roosevelt in the midst of World War II, had ever won much backing from newspaper publishers. But Kennedy also noted a steady decline in the number of cities with two truly competing daily newspapers and a growth in newspaper chains. And so he embarked on what has proved to be a losing battle to encourage competing, independent newspapers. Today, only a handful of cities support two newspapers, and two-thirds of all newspapers are part of a chain.

With the benefit of hindsight, it can be seen that President Kennedy's view of the marketplace of ideas was too narrow. The approximately 1,700 daily newspapers are only a small part of the marketplace in which media, print and electronic, scramble for an audience and for advertising revenue. Daily newspapers are outnumbered by far by the nearly 10,000 radio and television stations on the air. Further, studies consistently show that more people say they depend on television than on newspapers for news. Dailies also are outnumbered three-to-one by weekly newspapers, which have enjoyed their greatest growth in the suburbs around major cities. However, the belief on which Kennedy acted in planning a series of antitrust actions aimed at newspapers—that the publisher in a one-newspaper town is a monopolist—persists.

It is for that reason that publishers of daily newspapers, no matter what the size of their market, operate with constant awareness of antitrust implications flowing from their decisions. Failure to do so can lead to the expense of fighting an antitrust action. In recent years, publishers have come under attack because competitors concluded that their advertising rates were too low. Advertisers have attacked others for rates they believed to be too high. Publishers must take care if they decide to publish a weekly advertising supplement to be circulated free to some segment of their audience, or even if they establish zoned editions in which advertising is offered at a discount.[33] Publishers also have encountered antitrust problems when they attempted to change from juvenile to adult carriers and vice versa, or to insist that carriers sell the paper for the price set by the publisher.

Nor is entanglement in the antitrust thicket confined to newspaper publishers. Cable television franchising arrangements and decisions by cable operators to carry some stations, but not others, have led to antitrust actions.

Thus, in the professional world there is a vigorous marketplace—for ideas and entertainment, to be sure, but especially for advertising. And, judging from a survey of the cases, that marketplace contains many operators who are on the alert for practices that seem to give others an unfair competitive advantage.

The competition for advertising is linked to equally intense competition for the audience. All media use market surveys to determine not only the nature of their particular audience, but to probe the likes and dislikes, the varied interests, and the spending habits of the audience as a whole. Television programs literally live or die by the Nielsen Ratings. Newspapers are moving toward shorter stories, and more of them, and to greater use of graphics and color in response to marketing surveys. Some have developed whole sections—on recreation, dining out, places to go, sports, and business—to meet the needs of particular segments of the audience. Some editors feel uncomfortable with the marketing approach to news content, arguing that it is a form of pandering. Most have accepted it, concluding that if some adjustments in content can ensure a financially secure newspaper they can afford to give the audience what they think it needs along with what the audience says it wants.

---

33. Shumadine et al., "Antitrust and the Media," pp. 729–991.

With newspapers, the competition for an audience has affected circulation methods, too. Traditionally, most dailies, particularly those outside the major metropolitan areas, have sold 95 percent of their copies by subscription. Newspaper readers were believed to be daily readers. However, the same marketing surveys that probed reader interest in content also led to the discovery that a considerable part of the potential audience neither reads nor wants to read a newspaper every day. Many people want to be able to buy a newspaper whenever they feel like it. That discovery, coupled with the rise of national and regional newspapers, has led to the proliferation of newsracks. In many cities with only one daily newspaper it is not unusual for shoppers to confront batteries of racks offering the local paper, *USA Today*, the national edition of the *New York Times*, the *Wall Street Journal*, and three or four regional newspapers. This is evidence that single-copy sales have become important to all publishers. It is for that reason that publishers challenge attempts to license racks or unduly restrict their placement. However, litigation usually is a last resort. Negotiation, coupled with a reminder that newspaper distribution is a protected First Amendment activity, is the preferred course. Lawyers advise publishers to cooperate with any reasonable regulations and to respond quickly and positively to complaints about service or potential hazards.

FOR REVIEW

1. Three principles applied by the Supreme Court in the *Indiana Farmer's Guide* and *Associated Press* cases have made virtually all media subject to antitrust law. What are those principles and what is their meaning?

2. Is it true to say that a commercial newspaper can refuse advertising in all circumstances? Why or why not?

3. What rule of law is applied by the courts to determine whether advertising rates or other business practices are in compliance with antitrust law?

4. What factors seem to have motivated President Kennedy's attempt to use antitrust law to preserve a marketplace of ideas? Was his view of that marketplace a valid one? What is the nature of the marketplace today?

5. Define a joint operating agreement. What is the purpose of such an agreement?

6. What did the Supreme Court say about such agreements in the *Citizen Publishing Co.* case? With the benefit of hindsight, what has been the long-range effect of that decision?

7. What message to publishers is implicit in the antitrust actions brought against the *Los Angeles Times* and Scripps-Howard in Cincinnati?

8. What is the law with respect to joint ownership of newspapers and broadcasting stations in the same city?

9.   What is the connection between Jehovah's Witnesses and the newsracks that appear in many areas of heavy pedestrian traffic? What is the connection both have with Milton's *Areopagitica?*

10.   What principles with respect to the taxation of the media were established by the Supreme Court in the *Grosjean* and *Minneapolis Star* cases?

Appendix: *The Legal System*

As used in this text, "law" has two general meanings, each quite different, but nevertheless closely interrelated. The primary meaning refers to law as the legal rules by which we live. These include statutes enacted by Congress and state legislatures, ordinances adopted by local governing bodies, the rules adopted by administrative bodies at all levels; they also include the decisions of courts interpreting all of the above or applying rules based on custom, which is known as the common law. In this sense, put in basic terms, laws are the words that define conduct required of us, or forbidden to us, for the common good.

In its secondary meaning, law is the system of courts, judicial processes, and legal officers through which the rules are applied. In this sense, it is a means of resolving disputes to reach an end loosely described as justice.

In the first meaning of the term, laws usually are classified as to their origin. The major sources of such law are described below.

Statute Law

Statute law is the great body of law that is a product of legislative action: by Congress at the national level, by legislatures at the state level, and by city and county councils at the local level. In theory, statute law is drafted to reflect the people's will, as perceived by their elected representatives acting in their behalf. Such law provides for punishment of wrongdoing, but it also defines and makes provisions for benefits. The Social Security system, for instance, is the product of a large body of statute law. Such law is said to be prospective in that we are supposed to know what it is and guide our conduct accordingly. In reality, none of us can know, except in general terms, what is in the thousands of statutes under which we live. Federal law alone fills twenty-four volumes of the United States Code, and every session of Congress adds more.

Common Law

Voluminous as the body of statute law is, it cannot anticipate, and thus forestall, every kind of dispute that is apt to arise between individuals. And yet there must be some orderly means of resolving disputes because the alternative may be a resort to violence. Indeed, at one time dueling was an accepted means of settling differences. Ten centuries ago, courts in Medieval England began to recognize that a duel did not determine who was right, but only who was stronger. Thus courts began to apply common-sense principles to the resolution of disputes to which no statute applied. Some of these involved property rights. As early as the thirteenth century, courts began to deal with harm to reputation, which was seen as a form of property for which the victim of a damaging lie could be compensated. Over the centuries, a huge body of law, based on nothing more tangible than a court's sense of what justice required, has been established. This is known as common law. It is a product of cases, decided at a particular time on a specific set of facts. However, embedded in these cases are principles that editors of legal encyclopedias and digests have done their best to analyze and present in orderly form for the guidance of lawyers, judges, and students.

Because common law is a product of specific cases, it is more flexible than statute law. This is one of its strengths. It has survived and grown because it is adaptable to changing conditions. Some legal scholars hold that despite its flexibility it is, at bottom, based solidly on eternal principles, on verities, and on a sound sense of what the community will or will not stand for.

498

Administrative Law

In the last fifty years, Congress, to an increasing extent, has enacted laws stating broad objectives, leaving the details of reaching those objectives to administrative agencies. Under such laws, Congress sets goals and creates an agency charged with seeing that they are reached. The Environmental Protection Agency, for instance, was given the duty of holding air and water pollution to specified minimums. It is up to the agency to devise specific regulations and impose them on polluters so as to meet those minimums.

When regulations are drafted and adopted in accordance with procedures prescribed by Congress and the courts, they have the effect of law. They may be enforced through the agency's own hearing system, subject to an appeal to the courts. Because of the number of agencies empowered to regulate various aspects of society, and the complexity of the problems with which they try to cope, the body of administrative law surpasses in volume the statutes enacted by Congress. Administrative law is of special concern to broadcasters and advertisers.

Constitutional Law

Constitutions, federal and state, are not dead collections of words. They have been kept alive by courts' interpretations of what the words mean when applied to a specific set of facts. The body of these interpretations is called constitutional law. Because the federal Constitution lies at the very base of the hierarchy of laws, constitutional questions permeate all other kinds of law. Much of this text deals with the large body of constitutional law generated by the courts' interpretation of the speech and press clauses of the First Amendment.

No one can say with certainty what any part of the Constitution means until the Supreme Court has decided what it means in a particular case. This does not mean that lower courts can't interpret the Constitution. The judge of even a lowest-level state court has the authority to do so. But such decisions are subject to appeal and review by courts at a higher level. The higher the court in the hierarchy, the greater is the weight carried by its decisions. But the Supreme Court of the United States is the final authority on all federal constitutional questions. Even its decisions are not carved in stone. On occasion, the Court has changed its mind.

This does not exhaust the kinds of law with which lawyers and courts deal. But it does attempt to define those kinds of law with which the journalist is apt to work.

With respect to the systems or processes applied to the law, three are of interest to communicators. These are described below.

Criminal Law

Society so abhors some conduct—such as murder, robbery, and drug abuse—that it provides for its punishment. The rules defining such infractions make up the body of criminal law. With rare exceptions, criminal law is statute law. The purpose of the legislature in defining a crime and its punishment is to deter lawbreaking. All of us stand on notice that if we persist in writing checks when our bank account is empty, or take a bottle of expensive perfume without pausing to pay at the checkout counter, we run a risk of being arrested. If the victim persists in pressing charges and the prosecutor is agreeable, we may find ourselves in court, facing a judge.

If so, our fate will be determined by application of the processes of criminal law. Our offense no longer will be treated as a private matter but as an offense against society as a whole. Thus, in criminal cases, the state is the plaintiff and the prosecutor acts as its agent. However, the defendant is not helpless. The Constitution requires the court to assume that the accused is not guilty. The defendant may be tried by a jury if he or she so desires. In any event, the Constitution also requires the prosecutor to prove guilt beyond a reasonable doubt.

Criminal courts stand at the foundation of the legal system. In any jurisdiction, criminal cases, starting with traffic offenses and moving up the scale of the gravity of the infraction to murder, make up the bulk of the work of the courts. An earmark of criminal law is the nature of the penalty. Defendants can be deprived of property, by being required to pay a fine; of their liberty, by being sentenced to prison; or of their life, if the crime is serious enough.

Civil Law

When individuals disagree—over whether a physician's carelessness resulted in injury, whether a journalist's story defamed someone, or who was at fault in an automobile accident—they may ask a court to resolve their differences. Such disputes, and many others, become grist for the civil law system. While the state is not an essential party to a civil proceeding, it can be. If the state wants part of your land for a new highway, and you don't like what it offers to pay, the state may ask a court to decide on a fair price. The state also is involved in civil actions to the extent that it provides the forum—a court—and the rules for resolving the dispute.

The purpose of a civil action is to decide whether one party or the other has been wronged, and, if so, make good the victim's loss. If a precise dollar value can be placed on the loss, the award is for actual damages. If the claimed harm can't be measured precisely because it is attributed to such intangibles as mental anguish, humiliation, pain, and suffering, the award is for compensatory damages, sometimes called general damages. If the offending party's actions are considered particularly outrageous, the court may order an award of an additional sum designed to punish the offender and deter others. Such an award is for punitive damages. Some such awards can be quite large. They differ from the fines imposed in criminal cases in that fines are paid to the state. Awards of damages are paid to the victim.

Equity Law

One type of civil law, known as equity law, has assumed an identity of its own. It traces its origins to medieval England and to the belief that the king was the ultimate source of justice. When persons became embroiled in disputes that could not be resolved by reference to the common law, they looked to the king for relief. Originally, the monarch himself listened to the competing claims and made a decision based on the equities—that is, on a balancing of the rights of the one against those of the other in the search for a solution that would be fair to both.

In the United States, equity cases are heard by a judge. Usually, all that the disputing parties want is an order directing one or the other to perform a duty, or to refrain from performing an act considered harmful. If the duty is one required by law, the court may resolve the matter by issuing an order called a writ of mandamus. The latter is a Latin word meaning "We command." Such a writ also can be issued to prevent one of the parties from committing an act forbidden by law.

If one party to the equity action is seeking a remedy not required by law, the court may resolve the dispute by issuing an injunction. A farmer who believes that a storm sewer designed to serve a proposed subdivision would pour water on his land could ask a court to halt work on the sewer. A judge would hear arguments from both sides, and might even join in the discussion. The court's purpose would be to resolve the dispute with the least harm to both parties. This might be done by ordering the developers of the subdivision to revise their plan for the sewer. Or it could result in an injunction forbidding further work on it.

THE JUDICIAL SYSTEM

The courts, which make up the judicial system and bring law to life, are in all respects a separate and equal branch of government. They work with, but are independent of, the legislative branch, which writes statute law, and the executive branch, which sees that the statutes are carried into effect.

In a sense, however, the judicial system is superior to both, because it alone can decide what the state and federal constitutions mean. Thus, if a legislative body enacts a law in violation of some provision of the constitution, the courts have the authority, if asked, to nullify it. Likewise, if a president or governor acts in a manner not authorized by the constitution, the courts, if asked, can nullify the action. The proviso, "if asked," is important because courts cannot reach out and act on their own initiative. A case must be brought to them by someone who alleges harm. The courts, then, are the ultimate guardians of our constitutional rights. They stand as bulwarks against repressive acts of government, even those that may reflect the will of the people.

The United States has a dual system of courts, a fact that sometimes confuses the unknowing. Each state has its own courts, which deal with violations of that state's laws and constitution, and with civil actions involving its own residents. The federal government is served by a system of United States courts, which deal with violations of federal statutes, and with civil actions brought by residents of one state against residents of another. They also hear cases raising federal constitutional issues, although such cases may begin in state courts, too. The two systems are discussed separately below.

State Courts

At the lowest level, state courts dealing with minor offenses and small claims may be quite informal, not even taking a record of their proceedings. Names of such courts vary from state to state. Some may be called municipal courts; others, police courts, county courts, or small-claims courts.

The lowest-level trial courts of record also vary in what they are called. In most states, such courts operate at the county or parish level. (In Louisiana, a unit of government corresponding to the county is called a "parish." The name harks back to the time when Louisiana was owned by the French and governed with the help of the Roman Catholic Church. As another aspect of that heritage, Louisiana is the only state that has not adopted the English common law as the foundation for its legal system.) In some states, sparsely populated counties may be grouped together and served by one court called a district or circuit court. In a few states, lowest-level trial courts of record are called courts of common pleas. New York confuses the out-of-state beginning legal scholar by calling its basic trial courts "supreme" courts. Whatever the name, in these courts the great bulk of the legal work is done. Here individuals are tried on murder and other criminal charges, libel and other suits for damages are heard, and injunctions are sought.

Each state also has its system of appeals courts. In the more populous states, there are two layers of them, an intermediate appellate court, and a court of last resort. The intermediate courts in some states hear appeals from county courts in specified districts. In others, there may be two or more such courts, but they take appeals in rotation, no matter where they come from. Several states have specialized appeals courts, one branch hearing criminal appeals and another, civil.

However they are named or organized, appeals courts ordinarily don't conduct trials. Witnesses are heard and evidence is collected only in the lower trial courts. There a jury, or the judge, decides whose version of the facts to believe. Appeals courts are concerned with questions of law, which come to them through documents supported by legal citations called "briefs." Appeals courts permit lawyers representing the two sides to make limited oral arguments supporting their cases. Appeals are based on the contention that the trial judge erred in interpreting one or more points of law. Typical questions raised on appeal include: Did the judge improperly admit the defendant's confession as evidence? Were the instructions to the jury in accord with established principles of law?

Each state has a court of final appeal which usually also oversees the functioning of the entire judicial system. The name of this court also varies. Some are called supreme courts; others, the court of appeals. Massachusetts calls its highest court the Supreme Judicial Court. Whatever its name, a state's highest court has the final word on any case that deals exclusively with interpretation of that state's constitution or statutes. If no federal question has been raised in the courts below, a litigant who is displeased with the verdict of a state's highest court has no further appeal. Thus it is in no sense correct to view state courts as somehow inferior to those in the federal system. They are co-equal. It is a rule of judicial construction that in a case involving both state and federal questions, a federal court must honor a state supreme court's interpretation of the meaning of that state's constitution or statutes.

Federal Courts

Federal courts operate at three levels. At the trial level are the ninety-four United States District Courts, which may be found in the major cities of every state. Some districts are divided into divisions, and a judge may hold court in two or more cities on a rotating basis to serve the convenience of the litigants. Districts are given straightforward geographical names. Thus, the cluster of federal trial courts in New York City is identified collectively as the United States District Court, Southern District, New York. The Northern District is headquartered in Albany; the Eastern, in Brooklyn; and the Western, in Buffalo.

The district courts in New York, Connecticut, and Vermont make up the Second Circuit for appeal purposes. Their decisions are subject to review by the United States Court of Appeals, Second Circuit, which has its headquarters in New York City. There are eleven such circuits made up of as few as three states and as many as nine. There is a separate United States Circuit Court for the District of Columbia, which hears many appeals from the decisions of federal administrative agencies as well as from the District Court for the District of Columbia. As of the time of this writing, a thirteenth circuit court, called the Temporary Emergency Court of Appeals, also exists. It was formed to cope with backlogs of cases in some of the regular circuits.

At the apex of the federal judicial pyramid is the Supreme Court of the United States, the only court established by the Constitution. Each of its nine justices supervises in a loose way one or more of the circuits. In practice, that means little more than that the justice has the power to hear and act on emergency appeals from his or her assigned circuit, while the Court is in recess.

Federal judges are appointed for life by the president, subject to approval by the Senate. Historically, federal judgeships have been used to reward faithful members of the president's political party. However, some recent presidents have made a show of consulting the bar association and others in seeking judges of merit. This is especially true at the Supreme Court level, although even there presidents have sought to influence history by choosing justices who are considered likely to interpret the Constitution to their liking. This has resulted in some surprises. Earl Warren, for instance, whom Dwight Eisenhower named chief justice in the belief that he was a conservative, led the Court through one of its most liberal eras in protecting the rights of individuals.

Federal district courts are trial courts. They hear cases involving violations of federal statutes. They are also the starting point for any civil suit to which the federal government is a party, or which involves residents of different states, provided the amount at issue is more than $10,000, or provided that a fundamental right is at stake.

A litigant who is dissatisfied with the verdict of a district court can appeal to the appropriate circuit court of appeals for a review of disputed points of law. A circuit court's decisions are binding as precedents only within its own circuit. Thus it sometimes happens that one circuit may rule one way on a disputed point of law, and another will rule just the opposite. If the subject matter is of any consequence, it is likely that the Supreme Court will take one or both cases in order to resolve the difference.

GETTING A CASE TO THE SUPREME COURT

In our litigation-minded age, the Supreme Court of the United States is asked to resolve many kinds of questions. It is besieged with applications for review, which come to it in three ways:

1. by appeal
2. by application for a writ of certiorari
3. by certification

In theory, the Supreme Court must accept appeals from certain kinds of decisions by the lower courts, state or federal. Generally, these involve instances in which the lower courts have held that a state law or an act of Congress is invalid because it violates the federal Constitution. The Department of Justice also has a right to appeal an adverse decision of a district court in a criminal case. However, even in such cases there is no guarantee that the Supreme Court will review the decisions of the lower courts. The justices avoid taking cases on appeal by blandly asserting that they found "no substantial federal question" in them.

Most cases come to the Supreme Court through a petition for a writ of certiorari. The writ, if issued, is an order to the court below to deliver its file on the case to the Supreme Court for review. If petitioners are to have any chance of success, they must assert that the court below erred in applying a federal constitutional principle or a point of federal law to the decision of the case. Four of the nine justices must agree to take a case before a writ can be issued. In the overwhelming majority of cases, the Court refuses certiorari. Usually, no reason is given.

Certification seldom happens. The Court's procedures permit the circuit courts of appeal to ask it to clarify points of law essential to the decision of a pending case. The Supreme Court may choose to answer such questions, or it may ask that the case be sent up to it for decision.

By these three methods, the Court is asked to review about 5,000 cases each term, which runs from the first week of October until about the first week of July. Obviously such a tide of paper is enough to inundate the nine members of the Court who must, by necessity, assign most of the screening to their clerks. Because there is a limit to how much work the justices can do, they have become quite ruthless in rejecting cases. In recent years, their formal written decisions have been limited to about 140 cases a year.

HOW THE SUPREME COURT DECIDES A CASE

Cases submitted to the Supreme Court for review must be accompanied by briefs. Under the rules, these must state the issues presented by the case, and the questions of law it raises. The brief must contain a summary of the action taken in the lower courts, the arguments supporting the outcome sought by the litigant, and citations to cases, statutes or administrative rules believed to support the sought-after verdict. These briefs are of the utmost importance, for they frequently shape the Court's decision.

After the justices and their clerks have studied the briefs, a decision is reached on whether to schedule oral argument. If so, the maximum time permitted each side usually does not exceed an hour. Lawyers arguing their cases to the Court can never be sure that they will get to use all of their time as they had planned. One or more of the justices may choose to question a lawyer, or even to argue a point of law.

Each Friday morning, the justices meet in private to discuss cases awaiting decision. The chief justice presides. When a given case is under discussion, he asks each justice in turn, starting with the oldest in terms of years on the Court, to present his views. If the case is important, or deals with a topic on which the justices have strongly conflicting views, the discussion can get animated.

When the time comes to vote, the oldest justice in terms of service votes first, and the balloting continues in order of seniority.

The next step, and it can be an important one, is the assignment of the justice who is to write the decision of the Court. If the chief justice is a part of the majority, he makes the assignment and can give the task to himself or another justice. If the chief justice is not a part of the majority, the assignment is made by the senior justice voting with the majority. The justice charged with the writing usually circulates preliminary drafts among his colleagues for their comments. Other justices may feel moved to write concurring or dissenting opinions. In a concurring opinion, the justice agrees with the Court's decision, but does not fully agree with the legal reasoning used by the writer of the leading opinion. When all of the opinions on a given case reach final form, the decision is announced in open court, usually on Monday of each week. Late in the term, decisions are announced more frequently.

The decisions and opinions of the Court take several forms. If the Court decides that a case does not raise new points of law but can be used as a vehicle for reiterating a point the justices thought they had decided previously, the decision may take the form of a *per curiam* opinion. The Latin words simply mean "for the court." Such opinions are never signed by an individual justice, although one or more may choose to write a supplementary opinion. *Per curiam* opinions are not looked to as strong precedents, although they can serve to clarify a confusing point of law.

If five or more justices agree with the legal reasoning used by one of their number in writing an opinion, that opinion becomes a majority decision of the Court. Such decisions express the opinion of the Court on legal questions raised by the case and thus establish precedents that all lower courts are supposed to follow in deciding similar cases. It makes no difference whether such decisions are joined by only five of the justices or all nine. A majority always speaks for the Court.

Some justices may agree with the outcome of the case, but disagree with the legal reasoning used by the author of the leading opinion. As a result, only four, or even fewer, justices may find themselves in agreement with any one version of the verdict. Such minority opinions are called "plurality judgments" of the Court. Lower courts may and do look to them for guidance in deciding similar cases, but they are not required to follow them. Obscenity law was thrown into confusion for more than a decade because no more than four members of the Court could agree on how far the First Amendment goes in protecting portrayals of sexual activity.

Decisions of the Court are not always models of precision. In theory, the Court deals in a decision only with specific points of law raised in the proceedings of lower courts. But, now and then, the justice writing for the Court will comment on points of law that are not at issue, and have no bearing on the decision. Such references are known as *dicta*. In theory, these do not carry the force of law, but lawyers and lower-court judges may nevertheless be guided by them.

CONSTITUTIONAL LAW

Courts are required by their nature to interpret or construe the meaning of the law, whatever its source, and of the constitutions, state and federal. In doing so, they are supposed to be bound by rules that are embedded deeply in custom and are designed to make the law reasonably predictable. Under these rules, courts are supposed to construe statutes strictly and literally. A law written by a legislative body represents the will of the people and means what the plain meaning of its wording says it means, no more and no less. If the words are not clear on their face, courts go to legislative committee reports and the record of the debate to discern the intent of the legislators, and are guided accordingly.

Constitutions are viewed more broadly as statements of principle. If the language is so clear as to admit no doubt as to its meaning, it is followed. But if there is room for a difference of opinion, courts look first to the decisions of other courts and then to the intent of the drafters, if that can be discerned. If all else fails, courts fall back on their understanding of the general purpose of the questioned passage and of the constitution as a whole.

In all such matters of construction, a court is supposed to be bound by the decisions of higher courts to which it is subject. Such decisions are looked to as precedents. As a general rule courts follow precedents rigidly. They act on the principle of *stare decisis*—that is, of taking at face value a decision on a specific point of law previously made by a higher court with jurisdiction over them. However, if the facts of a present case at issue are not exactly like those of the ruling case, or if the question of law involved can be stated in somewhat different terms, precedent can be ignored or modified. If a lower court's decision based on what it sees as a somewhat different case is upheld on appeal, then there is a new precedent. It is this process that keeps the law flexible— too flexible, its critics say. Thus, the meaning of the law can be stated with certainty only in terms of the latest appeals court cases.

However, at any given moment, a state's supreme court decisions offer the last word on the meaning of that state's statutes and constitution. The same is true of the Supreme Court of the United States with respect to the federal statutes and Constitution.

Very early in the nation's history, under the leadership of one of our most brilliant chief justices, John Marshall, the Supreme Court staked out ground it holds to this day:

1. When a federal question is raised during the trial of a state case in a state court, it creates a right to take the case to the Supreme Court of the United States. *Cohens v. Virginia*, 6 Wheat. 264, 5 L.Ed. 257 (1821)

2. When the Supreme Court concludes that an act of Congress, or an action of the executive, violates the Constitution, the Court can declare either null and void. *Marbury v. Madison*, 1 Cranch 137, 2 L.Ed. 60 (1803)

3. The Court also can declare null and void a state statute, or even a section of a state constitution, that violates the federal Constitution. *McCulloch v. Maryland*, 4 Wheat. 316, 4 L.Ed. 579 (1819)

4. While state courts are free to interpret and apply the federal Constitution, if the state court's decision is overruled by the Supreme Court of the United States, the latter decision prevails. *Martin v. Hunter's Lessee*, 1 Wheat. 304, 4 L.Ed. 97 (1816)

These remarkable decisions converted the government of the United States from what the founders intended—a divided depository of only such powers as the states had delegated to it— into a strong central government. Through those decisions the Supreme Court took unto itself the authority to determine how far the Constitution permits that government's power to reach. Marshall found his authority in Article VI of the Constitution:

This Constitution, and the laws of the United States which shall be made in pursuance thereof; and all treaties made, or which shall be made, under the authority of the United States, shall be the supreme law of the land; and the judges in every state shall be bound thereby, any thing in the Constitution or laws of any State to the contrary notwithstanding.

In that paragraph, the Marshall Court found the barrier against the tyranny of the majority that Locke and his disciples were seeking when they spoke of the "Law of Nature." That paragraph, buttressed by the Marshall decisions, gives the courts authority to protect our rights as citizens against oppressive acts of Congress. Because the Supreme Court's decisions on the meaning of the Constitution and of statute law become a part of the law, those decisions, too, are "the supreme law of the land."

Such power is not supposed to be used lightly. Courts are to assume that legislators do not willfully violate the Constitution. They, like judges, take an oath to uphold it. Therefore, if courts can avoid deciding a case on constitutional grounds, they usually will do so. If a law or executive order does not affect fundamental rights, courts assume it is constitutional until the weight of evidence proves otherwise. If fundamental rights are at stake, the burden of proof is turned around. The state must prove that its attempts to restrict them are constitutional. The power to declare a law unconstitutional has been used sparingly by the courts. Up to 1982, the Supreme Court of the United States had found that only 118 acts of Congress violated the Constitution.

Glossary

acquit   to release from guilt

actual damages; actual injury   see compensatory damages

actual malice   The publication of defamatory material with reckless disregard for the truth or knowledge of its falsity

adversary hearing   legal procedure in which evidence is heard from opposing parties

adversary proceeding   a legal action taken by opposing parties

affadavit   a written account of facts, sworn to as true

agency record   documents in physical possession of a federal agency and subject to the Freedom of Information Act

appellate court   see court of appeals

antitrust laws   laws designed to prevent businesses from forming monopolies and interfering with free trade among competitors

bail   money or a bond posted to release someone from legal custody

blasphemy   spoken or written words that insult a divine power

burden of proof   the duty to prove a claim in an adversary proceeding

censor   to forbid the public dissemination of written, printed, filmed, or other material considered offensive, immoral, or dangerous to the public welfare

censorship   the prohibition of public distribution of written, printed, filmed, spoken, or other material considered offensive, immoral, or dangerous to the public welfare

circuit court   a court with jurisdiction over several judicial districts

class action suit   a legal action brought by some injured parties on behalf of themselves and all others similarly injured

classified materials   information restricted in access to a particular group of people. Usually applied by government to documents considered vital to national security

commercial speech   advertisements that are entitled to limited protection under the First Amendment

common law   law that develops not from written statutes but from custom and usage

common pleas court   a trial court with jurisdiction over civil and criminal cases

commute   to change; to reduce a prison sentence

compensatory (actual) damages   the actual loss suffered by a complainant

common carrier   a bus line, telephone company, ferry, or other organization without competition in a particular region that must do business with all would-be customers

constitutional law   the area of law focused on the interpretation, violation, and enforcement of the United States Constitution

constitutional right   a provision guaranteed by the United States Constitution, such as the right to freedom of speech or assembly

constitutional privilege   see constitutional right

contempt   behavior that interferes with court proceedings, impugns a court's dignity, or violates an order of a court

contract   agreement in which one party assumes the obligation to perform certain acts, and the other party agrees to give consideration for that performance

507

copyright the legal protection of original work that can be fixed in some tangible medium of expression

court of appeals a court that reviews lower courts' decisions

Criminal Syndicalism Act a law forbidding individuals to associate for the purpose of advocating violent changes in the form of government

cross-examination the questioning of a witness by the opposing party

declassification the process by which previously restricted information is made more widely available

defendants parties against whom lawsuits are brought by plaintiffs or who are accused of crime

dicta written opinions from judges that are not about issues essential to a case; dicta are not necessarily considered precedents for later court actions

discovery the pretrial process in an adversary proceeding by which participants must answer all questions and produce all documents concerning the facts of the case

due process the ordinary sequence of events in the provision of justice, to which everyone is entitled

entrapment acts by police, government agents, or other public officials to induce suspects into committing crimes

equal opportunity the legal requirement that everyone has the same rights to benefits such as jobs and, in the case of political candidates, to reach the public by radio or television

espionage spying

fairness doctrine a section of broadcast law requiring broadcasters to identify controversial public issues and to present competing points of view on them

fair use the doctrine in copyright law holding that minimal copying of another's original material is permissible if it does not detract unduly from the commercial value of the original

felony a serious crime

grand jury a body of citizens who evaluates information about a crime with the aim of determining whether a suspect may be charged with having committed it

hearing a legal proceeding during which evidence is heard so that the facts of a case may be established

hearsay information not personally seen or heard but based on something heard or seen by someone else

impeach to accuse or charge a public official with wrongdoing or to raise questions about the truth of a witness's testimony

indict to charge a suspect with a crime

infringement in copyright law, the substantial copying of another's original work or copying that detracts unduly from the original's commercial value

injunction a court order that requires a party to stop committing some act

intrusion behavior that violates a person's right to privacy, for which a plaintiff may win damages

invasion of privacy the violation of a person's right to be free from outside interference or publicity

joint operating agreement in antitrust law, an agreement between newspaper owners to conduct the business of two newspapers in concert; considered legal unless the agreement harms a competitor or freezes out potential advertisers

landmark case a case often quoted by lower courts; a court case that acts as a turning point in the law

law of contracts and commercial transactions laws governing agreements in which one party assumes the obligation to perform certain acts, and the other party agrees to give consideration for that performance

legal petition   a document that requests a certain act be undertaken

libel   the unjustified exposure of someone to public ridicule or hatred

matter of law   a case that raises a question that can be resolved if the law is applied to the facts

misappropriation   in copyright law, the systematic taking of another's original work

misdemeanor   a crime considered less serious than a felony and punishable by prison, fine, or both

mistrial   a trial canceled by a judge while it is going on and then followed by a new trial

motion to quash   to request a court make void a subpoena, indictment, or other order

natural rights   according to Locke, the personal rights that were people's in the free state of nature

negligence   failure to exercise the care justly expected of a reasonable and cautious person

neutral reportage   the privilege of news media to report evenhandedly the claims and counterclaims in highly charged controversies without the need to investigate each accusation; the privilege exists even when an organization doubts the truth of the claims it reports

obscenity   material that appeals to a prurient interest in sex or material that a jury finds arouses an obsessive or morbid interest in sex

ordinances   city or municipal laws

pardon   release a party from guilt for an offense

***per curiam* decision**   a decision from a court composed of more than one judge

permanent injunction   a court order that permanently restrains a party from committing some act

plaintiffs   parties who bring lawsuits against defendants

pleadings   defendants' answers to questions

plurality opinion   a judicial opinion offered by the greatest number of judges, but by less than a majority of the panel

police power   the inherent authority of the state to protect the health, safety, morals, and general welfare of its residents

precedent   a judicial decision that is later referred to as authority on a similar point of law

preferred position   the status imputed by court decisions to First Amendment rights and certain others guaranteed by the Bill of Rights to protect against government attempts to prevent "harmful" speech; a doctrine used as a weapon against censorship

preliminary hearings   legal proceedings preliminary to a trial during which evidence is heard so that the facts of a case may be established; see pretrial proceedings

preponderance of the evidence   the weight or credibility of evidence; a test required in some civil actions that the weight of evidence clearly support a claim

pretrial proceedings   hearings held before the beginning of a trial, during which evidence that might not be admissible at a formal trial may be offered; see preliminary hearings

previous restraint   see prior restraint

prior restraint   any attempt by government or courts to mandate the content of printed matter; a form of censorship that violates the First Amendment guarantee of freedom of speech and press

privilege   a right, benefit, or immunity

probation the court-ordered requirements of behavior and period of time for which a party convicted of a crime may stay out of jail

public domain in copyright law, material that cannot be copyrighted and that can be used by anyone

public file information about their operations that broadcasters must keep for public access, required by the Federal Communications Commission

punitive damages an award made by a court to a complainant that exceeds his or her actual loss; the purpose is to punish the offender

restraining order a court order that temporarily forbids a party from committing some act; a form of injunction (see injunction)

retraction a statement confessing to a mistake in an earlier statement

right of publicity the right of people, particularly celebrities, to control how others use their names

right to know the right, imputed to the public, of access to all information about what their various governments are doing

search warrant a court order authorized for good cause by a magistrate, allowing a search of private property

sedition the crime of acting to overthrow a government

seditious libel the crime of questioning the wisdom of a ruler's policies

separation of powers the doctrine under which Congress makes the law, the executive branch puts it into effect, and the judiciary settles disputes that arise from this process

sequester to isolate (a jury)

shield law statute under which journalists are entitled to protect the confidentiality of their sources

slander spoken words that falsely defame a person so that his or her reputation is harmed or others are deterred from dealing with him or her

statute a law passed by a legislature

subpoena a court order requiring someone to appear in court to testify

summary judgment a court decision by a judge, which circumvents a full jury trial, usually sought when the adversary parties agree on the facts of a case

superior court a court midway in authority between a lower, or inferior court, and a higher, or court of appeals; a trial court

temporary restraining order see restraining order

tort a private or civil wrong or injury, other than a breach of contract, for which one may recover damages

trade rules regulations governing certain industries that are proposed and published by the Federal Trade Commission after administrative hearings

trier of fact the person or people, usually a jury but sometimes judges, appointed to hear evidence and determine the truth from it

unconstitutional forbidden by the Constitution of the United States

United States district court a federal or state court with jurisdiction over a certain region

warrant a court order empowering a police officer, sheriff, or someone else to arrest someone, search a house, or the like

INDEX OF CASES